PRINCIPLES OF MICRO-CONOMICS
AND THE CANADIAN ECONOMY

SECOND EDITION

JOSEPH E. STIGLITZ
STANFORD UNIVERSITY

ROBIN W. BOADWAY
QUEEN'S UNIVERSITY

W · W · NORTON & COMPANY · NEW YORK · LONDON

The text of this book is composed in Zapf Book
with the display set in Kabel
Composition by TSI Graphics
Manufacturing by Rand McNally
Book design by Antonina Krass
Cover painting: Laszlo Moholy-Nagy, *LIS*, 1922
Oil on canvas, 131 × 100 centimeters
Courtesy of the Kunsthaus, Zurich
Special thanks to Hattula Moholy-Nagy

Library of Congress Cataloging-in-Publication Data

Stiglitz, Joseph E.
     Principles of microeconomics and the Canadian economy / Joseph E. Stiglitz,
Robin W. Boadway.—2nd ed.
          p.   cm.
     Includes bibliographical references and index.
     ISBN 0-393-97053-1 (pbk.)
     1. Microeconomics.   I. Boadway, Robin W., 1943–   .   II. Title.
     HB172.S863   1997
     338.5—dc20   96-9691

W. W. Norton & Company, Inc., 500 Fifth Avenue, New York, N.Y. 10110
     http://www.wwnorton.com

W. W. Norton & Company Ltd., 10 Coptic Street, London WCIA 1PU

2 3 4 5 6 7 8 9 0

To Andrew

CONTENTS IN BRIEF

Contents

PART TWO

PERFECT MARKETS

CHAPTER 6 THE CONSUMPTION DECISION • 105

CHAPTER 7 LABOUR SUPPLY • 132

CHAPTER 8 SAVING AND INVESTING • 155

CHAPTER 9 THE FIRM'S COSTS • 184

CHAPTER 10 PRODUCTION IN A COMPETITIVE INDUSTRY • 214

CHAPTER **11** | C O M P E T I T I V E
E Q U I L I B R I U M • 239

PART THREE

IMPERFECT MARKETS

CHAPTER **12** | M O N O P O L I E S   A N D   I M P E R F E C T
C O M P E T I T I O N • 259

CHAPTER 13 OLIGOPOLIES • 284

CHAPTER 14 GOVERNMENT POLICIES TOWARDS COMPETITION • 303

Chapter 15 TECHNOLOGICAL CHANGE • 323

Chapter 16 IMPERFECT INFORMATION • 341

Chapter 17 FINANCING, CONTROLLING, AND MANAGING THE FIRM • 362

PART FOUR

THE PUBLIC SECTOR

CHAPTER 18 GOVERNMENT AND PUBLIC DECISION MAKING • 387

CHAPTER 19 EXTERNALITIES AND THE ENVIRONMENT • 411

CHAPTER **20** TAXATION, REDISTRIBUTION, AND SOCIAL INSURANCE • 425

PREFACE

Beginning students should know the vitality of modern economics, and this book is intended to show them. When we wrote the First Edition, we felt that none of the available texts provided an adequate understanding of the principles of *modern* economics—both those that are necessary to understand how modern economists think about the world around them and those that are required to understand current economic issues. Apparently, our feelings were shared by many others, as reflected by the success the First Edition has enjoyed, by the feedback we have received from the market, and especially by the responses our own students have had to the book. With the benefit of this feedback, we have made a painstaking effort to improve the book from cover to cover, focusing both on clarity and on conciseness. We believe both students and their instructors will be pleased with the result.

As with the First Edition, this edition closely parallels the Second Edition prepared for the American market by Joseph Stiglitz alone. Both versions have benefited from his role in U.S. policy making as chairman of President Clinton's Council of Economic Advisers and as a member of the Cabinet. His experience has confirmed the view that the traditional principles course is far removed from economic policy concerns and the modern economic advances that can illuminate them.

The need to confront modern economic policy problems with modern economic analysis is no less true in Canada. Indeed, many of the problems are essentially the same. Through our collaboration we have been able to combine Stiglitz's policy experience with Boadway's intimate knowledge of the Canadian economy and the policy problems it faces.

Economics is the science of choice, and writing a textbook involves many choices. As we began working on the Second Edition, we were convinced that the choices made in the First Edition—for instance, the attention to new topics, such as technological change and finance, and the increased emphasis on information—moved the book in the right direction. But we were even more convinced that an understanding of these new topics had to be based on a solid foundation in established fundamentals, such as the law of supply and demand, the theory of household and firm decision making, and traditional perspectives on unemployment, inflation, and economic growth. Thus, the revision faced several seemingly conflicting challenges, not the least of which was the need to reinforce the exposition of the fundamentals while at the same time strengthening the discussion of new topics.

Several of the dramatic changes that loomed large in the early 1990s while the First Edition was being prepared still occupy centre stage, and new issues and perspectives have also emerged. The economic systems of formerly communist countries are still in collapse, with Eastern Europe and the former Soviet Union making slow and painful transitions to market economies. International investors, losing confidence in Mexico in 1995, precipitated a financial crisis that threatened to spread quickly and was only arrested through international cooperation. The countries of Africa have seen their desperate economic conditions worsen. The countries of East Asia, a bright spot in a world facing disappointment, have experienced unprecedented growth, in some cases at rates in excess of 10 percent year after year. Japan remains an economic powerhouse, while South Korea, Taiwan, and the other Asian "tigers" went from being poor backward countries to being major players by taking advantage of opportunities in international markets.

Beginning around 1973, growth in the industrialized countries, including Canada, slowed markedly. Here and in Europe, unemployment rates that in the 1960s had remained extremely low, often soared into double digits and stubbornly remained there. Economic inequality increased, with those at the bottom actually seeing their living standards deteriorate. The mid-1990s brought Canada signs of the reversal of some of these trends. Inflation fell to levels that had not been seen for a quarter of a century, and productivity began to pick up. The poverty rate began to decline, and incomes of all groups, especially those at the bottom, began to rise. But among many workers, anxiety remained high; while their real wages and incomes had begun to rise, they still had not recovered to their earlier peaks, and no one was sure these increases would continue. And unemployment remained stubbornly high, especially for new entrants into the labour force. Moreover, the enormous government debt that had built up over the past 15 years dramatically reduced the government's options: with a high proportion of the budget needed simply to pay interest on the debt, governments were hard pressed to maintain public services and to provide assistance to those in need. Moreover, another time bomb was on the horizon: aging baby boomers would soon put an unprecedented strain on the public pension and health care systems.

As the world has changed, expectations have changed as well. While there has been enormous improvement in the quality of air in our major cities and while Lake Erie has been rescued from becoming polluted to the point where life could not survive, our expectations about the environment have grown even faster; we have become increasingly aware of environmental costs. Longevity has increased, but our knowledge of how to prolong life has outstripped it, and rising health care costs have become a major political issue. The economic role of women has changed: not only have they taken a more active part in the labour force, but there has also been a revolution in expectations concerning the kinds of jobs women can hold.

And in virtually every one of the major issues facing the economy, there is a debate about the role of government. Government at all levels in Canada has grown enormously, largely due to the rapid growth of social programmes and of cash transfers to various groups in the economy. Before World War II, government took about one out of every six dollars of wages in taxes; today it takes more than one out of every three. There are differing views of government responsibility. For instance, people expect, even demand, that government do something about unemployment and provide free health care and education to all. But at the same time, there is a wider understanding of the limitations of government in an increasingly globalized economy. The increasing government deficits over the past decade, the largest in Canada's peacetime history, have meant that one of the wealthiest countries in the world seems short of money to maintain basic public programmes. Issues concerning the responsibilities, capabilities, and strategies of government in the economy have come to the centre of political debates.

These are exciting issues and events, and they fill the front pages of our newspapers and the evening television news shows. Yet in the recent past, teachers of the introductory course in economics have felt frustrated: none of the textbooks really conveyed this sense of excitement. Try as they might, none seemed to prepare the student adequately for interpreting and understanding these important economic events.

On reflection, one of the reasons for this becomes clear: the principles expounded in Alfred Marshall's classic textbook of a hundred years ago, or Paul Samuelson's now almost fifty years old, are not the principles for today. The way we economists understand our discipline has changed to reflect the changing world, but textbooks have not kept pace. Our professional discourse is built on a *modern* economics, but these new developments are simply not adequately reflected in any of the vast array of textbooks available to us as teachers.

Indeed, changes in economics over the past half century have been as significant as the changes in world events. The basic competitive model of the economy was perfected in the 1950s. Since then, economists have gone beyond that model in several directions as they have come to understand its limitations better. Earlier researchers paid lip service to the importance of incentives and to problems posed by limited information. However, it was only in the last two decades that real progress was made in understanding these issues. The 1996 Nobel Prize in economics was awarded to two economists who pioneered our understanding of the role of information and incentives in the economy. Their work, and the work of others in this field, have found immediate applications. The collapse of the Soviet bloc economies, the debt crisis facing many less developed countries, the rush of major bankruptcies in the financial sector, and the escalating costs of health and unemployment insurance programmes can all be viewed as consequences of the failure to provide appropriate incentives. Thus, a central question in the debate over growth and productivity should be: How can an economy provide stronger incentives for innovation? The debate over pollution and the environment centres around the relative merits of regulation and providing incentives not to pollute and to conserve resources.

The past fifty years have also seen a reexamination of the boundary between economics and business. Subjects like finance and management used to be relegated to business schools, where they were taught without reference to economic principles. Today we know that to understand how market economies actually work, we have to understand how firms finance and manage themselves. Tremendous insights can be gleaned through the application of basic economic principles, particularly those grounded in an understanding of incentives. Stories of corporate takeovers have been replaced on the front page by stories of bankruptcies as acquiring corporations have found themselves overextended. The 1990 Nobel Prize was awarded to three economists who made the greatest contribution to the integration of finance and economics. Yet introductory textbooks had not yet built in the basic economics of finance and management.

We have also come to appreciate better the virtues of competition. We now understand, for instance, how the benefits of competition extend beyond price to competition for technological innovation. At the same time, we have come to see better why, in so many circumstances, competition appears limited. Again, none of the available textbooks seemed to provide students with a sense of this new understanding.

Samuelson's path-breaking textbook is credited with being the first to integrate successfully the (then) new insights of Keynesian economics with traditional microeconomics. Samuelson employed the concept of the neoclassical synthesis—the view that once the economy was restored to full employment, the old classical principles applied. In effect, there were two distinct regimes to the economy. In one, when the economy's resources were underemployed, macroeconomic principles applied; in the other, when the economy's resources were fully employed, microeconomic principles were relevant. The belief that these were distinct regimes was reflected in how texts were written and courses were taught; it made no difference whether micro was taught before macro, or vice versa. In the last decades, economists came to question the split that had developed between microeconomics and macroeconomics. The profession as a whole came to believe that macroeconomic behaviour had to be related to underlying microeconomic principles; there was one set of economic principles, not two. But this view simply was not reflected in any of the available texts.

This book differs from most other texts in several ways. Let us highlight some of the most prominent distinctions.

- Reflecting the role of economics in policy making, we have introduced examples throughout the text to relate economic theory to recent policy discussions. In each chapter, a Policy Perspective box provides a vignette on a particular issue—such as the Goods and Services Tax, the reform of health care, environmental regulation, and patent protection for prescription drugs—both to enliven the course and to enrich the student's command over the basic material.
- Economists are a contentious lot, yet on most issues differences among economists pale in comparison to differences among noneconomists. Indeed, there is a high degree of consensus among economists, and we have drawn attention to this throughout the book with ten points of consensus in economics, among them scarcity, incentives, the benefits of trade, the role of prices, and competition.
- Rather than the traditional approach of stretching the competitive model out over the entire course, we cover it in a compact format in the first two parts of the book. This allows students to develop a complete picture of the basic model, before looking systematically at the role of imperfect markets. So when we turn to the discussion of the latter in Parts Three and Four, a better foundation has been laid for an understanding of such issues as technological change (Chapter 15), information problems and other imperfections in the product, capital, and labour markets (Chapter 16), and decision making within the firm (Chapter 17)—all subjects that get short shrift in other texts.
- Finance is recognized as an important part of economics. Chapter 8 introduces the basic ideas of time and risk, and presents a brief student's guide to investing. Chapter 16 shows how risk is traded on capital markets, and Chapter 17 discusses how firms raise the funds they need for investment and relates finance to struggles for corporate control.
- Throughout, issues of incentives and the problems posed by incomplete information are given prominence. To take but two of many examples, Chapter 16 discusses the role that reputation plays in providing firms with an incentive to maintain the quality of their products, and Chapter 17 discusses how firms try to motivate their managers and how managers try to motivate their workers—and the problems they encounter in doing so.
- As our understanding of the limitations of markets has increased, so has our understanding of the limitations of government, and the age-old question of the appropriate balance between government and the private sector has to be reexamined. This book looks at a wide range of policy issues, including how government can respond to the inefficiencies that arise from limited competition (Chapter 14) and what the government should do to preserve the environment (Chapter 19) and to promote greater equality (Chapter 20). The related issues of how and why government takes the decisions it does are considered in Chapter 18.

ACKNOWLEDGMENTS

It has been an honour and a delight to have the privilege of working with Joe Stiglitz in the preparation of this book. As most economists know, he is a remarkable person. Over the years, his writings in many fields have taught my cohort of teachers much. By the clarity and breadth of his work, Joe has served not only to define individual fields of economics (including risk and uncertainty, asymmetric information, tax and public expenditure theory, technological innovation, product diversity and market structure, capital theory, the operation of labour markets in both industrialized and developing countries, and decision making within institutions and bureaucracies, to name a few) but in many cases also to point out the common features of these various fields and the important role that incentives and information play in determining economic outcomes in each of them.

In particular, his application of economic analysis has always been motivated by a wish to explain important real-world phenomena. Writing technical articles for other teachers obviously did not go far enough. So he worked to create the *Journal of Economic Perspectives*, which has succeeded in making available the most abstract of advances in our discipline to a very wide audience of economists. His recent experience with President Clinton's Council of Economic Advisers allowed him to hone his skills at policy analysis further to the benefit of the country as well as economics. That he found time to work on a major revision of this text is testimony to his dedication to economics education.

My role in this venture has been to adapt the textbook to the special features of the Canadian economy and to the particular policy problems it faces. I am fortunate to have been given a free hand to do so and have tried to take advantage of the opportunity. This was not a difficult task. The principles of analysis are universal and apply to any market economy. It was simply a matter of showing their relevance to various issues of Canadian interest. These include our special industrial structure, which results from the combination of a relatively small population for our size, a rich endowment of natural resources, and a historic reliance on inflows of capital from abroad for our development; the importance of trade and financial flows with the rest of the world; the special relationship we have with our giant neighbour to the south, a relationship that has resulted in a sequence of negotiated trading arrangements; the role our government has assumed in providing an array of social programmes and programmes for regional development; and the importance of our relatively decentralized federal system of government. Not surprisingly, many of the current policy problems facing Canada are similar to those facing the United States as well as other developed economies, including lagging productivity growth, difficulties in balancing our trade in the face of increased international competition, and concerns about the way our governments go about their business, both in terms of the services they provide and the difficulty of covering their costs. These issues are all reflected in the Canadian Edition of this book.

Previous users of the book will recognize a considerable shortening of the text and a corresponding reduction in the number of chapters. This is in direct response to the advice of the several reviewers of the First Edition who recognized better than I that students need to do more than devote their attention to economics during their first year of study. The ideas have not changed, only the economy and efficiency with which they have been presented.

In addition to my deep debt to Joe Stiglitz for giving me the opportunity to participate in this venture, I have also received some exceptional help in preparing the Second Canadian Edition. I am particularly indebted to my colleague Ian Cromb, whose assistance and advice was invaluable in preparing the various Close-up, Policy Perspective, and Using Economics boxes in the text and in helping compile the data for the many tables and graphs. He brought to the collaboration not only his good judgment and good humour but also his wide experience as a principles instructor at Queen's and elsewhere in Canada. Alan Harrison of McMaster University also provided very helpful advice on how to approach various topics in student-friendly ways. My wife, Bernie, helped on this edition, as on the first one, with many of the editorial matters. I also benefited greatly from the reactions of my students in the introductory course at Queen's.

This edition and the previous one have benefited from numerous reviewers. The book has been improved immeasurably by their advice—some of which, quite naturally, was conflicting. In particular, I would like to thank: Douglas W. Allen, Simon Fraser University; James Feehan, Memorial University of Newfoundland; Hugh Grant, University of Winnipeg; Geoffrey B. Hainsworth, University of British Columbia; Michael J. Hare, University of Toronto; Ian J. Irvine, Concordia University; David Johnson, Wilfrid Laurier University; Rashid Khan, University of New Brunswick; Robert R. Kerton, University of Waterloo; R. F. Lucas, University of Saskatchewan; Henry Rempel, University of Manitoba; Ian Rongve, University of Regina; Peter Sinclair, Wilfrid Laurier University; and Leon P. Sydor, University of Windsor.

This book bears more than the logo of W. W. Norton, a company that reflects many of the aspects of organizational design that I discuss in the text. The book would not be nearly the one it is without the care, attention, and most important, the deep thought devoted to it by so many there. I cannot sufficiently acknowledge my indebtedness to Drake McFeely, who served as my editor on the First Edition (and succeeded Don Lamm as president of Norton), and Ed Parsons, who served as my editor on the Second Edition. Both have been concerned about the ideas *and* their presentation and both have been tough, but constructive, critics. Kate Scott, the manuscript editor, and Kelly Nusser, the project editor, contributed to the book with uncompromising care and precision. And Rosanne Fox showed that the practice of proofreading is indeed an art and that she is a wonderfully accomplished artist. All five made our work harder, so that readers of this book would have an easier time. Three others at Norton also deserve mention: Claire Acher, for outstanding editorial assistance, and Roy Tedoff and Jane Carter for coordinating the production of the book.

Three other people have worked closely with Joe Stiglitz on the two American Editions, and many of their contributions carry over to the Canadian Edition: Timothy Taylor on the First Edition and Felicity Skidmore and John Williams on the Second. All gave their energy and creativity to the enterprise, applying their deep understanding of economics with a commitment to the notion that it is important for modern economic ideas to be communicated widely. The book is immeasurably better as a result.

Necessary and valuable adjuncts to the book are the *Study Guide* for students and the *Instructor's Manual* and test bank for teachers. The *Study Guide* was very capably revised for the Second Canadian Edition by Alan Harrison of McMaster University. It was based on the U.S. Edition prepared by Lawrence Martin of Michigan State University. I took on the *Instructor's Manual* with the careful and helpful assistance of Travis Armour. Alan Harrison also prepared the test bank, and Stephen R. King and Rick M. McConnell are responsible for the unusual and effective computer tutorials.

Finally, though I tried to complete this task with minimal disruption to my family, I am sure that is not the way it seemed to them. At least they know that if it were not this, it would have been something else. In any case, they showed characteristic patience with my preoccupations. My only defence is to suggest that a good understanding of the principles of economics by whomever should study it at colleges and universities in Canada can only help to serve the interests of my sons' generation.

I especially dedicate this book to Andrew, who has struggled with a disease that few can understand. The plight of those like him should remind us that the study of economics serves a broader social purpose than just the self-interest of market participants.

OUTLINE FOR A SHORT COURSE IN MICROECONOMICS

This book is suitable for short courses offered under a semester system or other abbreviated schedules. Below we offer a provisional outline for such a short course, omitting several chapters. Naturally, to a large extent *which* topics get omitted is a matter of taste. The following is our selection for a short course using fifteen chapters.

Chapter Number	Chapter Title
1	The Automobile and Economics
2	Thinking Like an Economist
3	Trade
4	Demand, Supply, and Price
5	Using Demand and Supply
6	The Consumption Decision
7	Labour Supply
8	Saving and Investing
9	The Firm's Costs
10	Production in a Competitive Industry
12	Monopolies and Imperfect Competition
14	Government Policies towards Competition
16	Imperfect Information
18	Government and Public Decision Making
20	Taxation, Redistribution, and Social Insurance

OUTLINE FOR A ONE-SEMESTER FULL COURSE

This book may be used with its companion volume, *Principles of Macro-economics and the Canadian Economy* (Second Edition), in either a one- or two-semester course covering both microeconomics and macroeconomics. Below is our suggested outline for a one-semester course, including chapters from both books. Chapters from the macroeconomics volume are indicated with asterisks. The outline includes most of the fundamentals, but of necessity it must leave out some of the exciting new topics. Naturally, *which* topics get omitted is a matter of taste. The following is our selection for a short course using twenty chapters.

Chapter Number	Chapter Title
2	Thinking Like an Economist
3	Trade
4	Demand, Supply, and Price
5	Using Demand and Supply
6	The Consumption Decision
8	Saving and Investing
9	The Firm's Costs
10	Production in a Competitive Industry
12	Monopolies and Imperfect Competition
16	Imperfect Information
18	Government and Public Sector Decision Making
6*	Macroeconomic Goals and Measures
8*	The Full-Employment Model
10*	Overview of Unemployment Macroeconomics
11*	Aggregate Demand
13*	Money, Banking, and Credit
14*	Monetary Theory
16*	Inflation: Wage and Price Dynamics
20*	Intergenerational Transfers: Deficits and Public Pensions
21*	Trade Policy

Introduction

These days economics is big news. If we pick up a newspaper or turn on the television for the prime-time news report, we are likely to be bombarded with statistics on unemployment rates, inflation rates, exports, and imports. How well are we doing in competition with other countries, such as Japan? Everyone seems to want to know. Political fortunes as well as the fortunes of countries, firms, and individuals depend on how well the economy does.

What is economics all about? That is the subject of Part One. Chapter 1 uses the story of the automobile industry to illustrate many of the fundamental issues with which economics is concerned. The chapter describes the four basic questions at the heart of economics and how economists attempt to answer these questions.

Chapter 2 introduces the economists' basic model and explains why notions of property rights, profits, prices, and cost play such a central role in economists' thinking.

A fact of life in the modern world is that individuals and countries are interdependent. Even a wealthy country like Canada is dependent on foreign countries for vital imports. Chapter 3 discusses the gains that result from trade—why trade, for instance, allows greater specialization and why greater specialization results in increased productivity. It also explains the patterns of trade—why each country imports and exports the particular goods it does.

Prices play a central role in enabling economies to function. Chapters 4 and 5 take up the question of what determines prices. What causes prices to change over time? Why is water, without which we cannot live, normally so inexpensive, while diamonds, which we surely can do without, are very expensive? What happens to the prices of beer and cigarettes if the government imposes a tax on these goods? What happens if the government restricts the quantities that can be produced and sold, as in the case of some agricultural products? Sometimes the government passes laws requiring firms to pay wages of at least so much or forbidding landlords to charge rents that exceed a certain level; what are the consequences of these government interventions?

THE AUTOMOBILE AND ECONOMICS

Imagine the world a hundred years ago: no cars, airplanes, computers (and computer games!), movies—to say nothing of atomic energy, lasers, and transistors. The list of inventions since then seems almost endless.

Of all the inventions that have shaped the world during the past century, perhaps none has had so profound an effect as the automobile. It has changed how and where people work, live, and play. But like any major innovation, it has been a mixed blessing: traffic jams on the one hand, access to wilderness on the other. And the new opportunities it created for some were accompanied by havoc for others. Some occupations—such as blacksmiths—virtually disappeared. Others—such as carriage makers—had to transform themselves (into car body manufacturers) or go out of business. But the gains of the many who benefited from the new industry far outweighed the losses of those who were hurt.

The story of the automobile is familiar. But looking at it from the perspective of economics can teach us a great deal about the economic way of thinking.

1 What *is* economics? What are the basic questions it addresses?

2 In economies such as that of Canada, what are the respective roles of government and the private, or "market," sector?

3 What are markets, and what are the principal markets that make up the economy?

4 Why is economics called a social science?

5 Why, if economics is a science, do economists so often seem to disagree?

THE AUTOMOBILE: A BRIEF HISTORY

The idea of a motorized carriage occurred to many in North America and Europe at roughly the same time. An automobile was actually built in Canada as early as 1867, well before cars were first imported from the United States. But ideas alone are not enough. Translating ideas into marketable products requires solving technical problems and persuading investors to finance the venture.

If you visit a museum of early cars, you will see that the technical problems were resolved in a variety of ways, by many people working independently. At the turn of the century, the area around Detroit was full of innovators developing cars—Ransom E. Olds, the Dodge brothers, and Henry Ford. The spirit must have been much like that of "Silicon Valley" (the area in California between San Francisco and San Jose) in the past quarter century, which has been at the center of computer technology development: a spirit of excitement, breakthroughs made, and new milestones reached. The various automobile innovators could draw upon a stock of ideas "in the air." They also had the help of specialized firms that had developed a variety of new technologies and skills: new alloys that enabled lighter motors to be constructed and new techniques for machining that allowed for greater power, precision, and durability.

Henry Ford is generally given credit for having recognized the potential value of a vehicle that could be made and sold at a reasonable price. Before Ford, automobiles were luxuries, affordable only by the very rich. He saw the potential benefit of providing inexpensive transportation. After he introduced the Model T in 1909 at a "bargain" price of U.S.$900, he continued to cut the price—to U.S.$440 in 1914 and U.S.$360 in 1916. Sales skyrocketed from 58,000 in 1909 to 730,000 in 1916. Ford's prediction of a mass market for inexpensive cars had proved correct.

But success was not sudden or easy. To translate his idea into action Ford had to put together a company to produce cars, figure out how to produce them cheaply, and raise the capital required to make all this possible.

Raising capital was particularly difficult, since the venture was extremely risky. Would Ford be successful in developing his automobile? Would someone else beat him to it? Would the price of a car be low enough for many people to buy it? If he was successful, would imitators copy his invention, robbing him of the mass market he needed to make money?

Ford formed a partnership to develop his first car. He was to supply the ideas and the work, while his partners supplied the funds. It took three partnerships before Ford produced a single car. The first two went bankrupt, with the financial partners in each case accusing Ford of spending all of his time developing ideas instead of acting on them.

But were the first two sets of partners treated unfairly? After all, they knew the risks. Ford could have entered each partnership in good faith and simply been unable to deliver. Even in the third case his partners were unhappy, claiming that he managed to get the lion's share of the profits for himself.

Whatever the truth in Ford's case, the general problem of who contributes more in a partnership and who should get what share of any profits occurs often. Ford may have argued that his ideas were far more important than the mere dollars that the financiers provided to carry them out.

Ford's success was due as much to his ability to come up with innovative ways of providing incentives and organizing production as to his skill in solving technical problems. He demonstrated this ability with his original labour policies. He offered more than double the going wage and paid his workers the then princely sum of U.S.$5 a day. In exchange, Ford worked his employees hard; the moving assembly line he invented enabled him to set his workers a fast pace and push them to keep up. The amount produced per worker increased enormously. Still, it was clear that the high wages were ample compensation for the extra effort. Riots almost broke out as workers clamoured for the jobs he offered. Ford had rediscovered an old truth: in some cases, higher wages for employees can repay the employer in higher productivity, through greater loyalty, harder work, and less absenteeism.

Ford's success in increasing productivity meant that he could sell his cars far more cheaply than his rivals could. The lower prices and the high level of sales that accompanied them made it possible for him to take full advantage of the mass production techniques he had developed. At one point, however, Ford's plans were almost thwarted when a lawyer-inventor named George Baldwin Selden claimed that Ford had infringed on his patent.

Governments grant patents to enable inventors to reap the rewards of their innovative activity. These are generally for specific inventions, like a new type of braking system or transmission mechanism, not for general ideas. Ford's idea of an assembly line, for example, was not an invention that could be patented, and it was imitated by other car manufacturers. A patent gives the inventor the exclusive right to produce his invention for a limited time, thus helping to assure that inventors will be able to make some money from their successful inventions. Patents may lead to higher prices for these new products, since there is no competition from others making the same product. But the presumption is that the gains to society from the innovative activity more than compensate for the losses to consumers from the temporarily higher prices.

Selden had applied for, and been granted, a patent for a horseless, self-propelled carriage. He demanded that other car manufacturers pay him a royalty, which is a payment for the right to use a patented innovation. Ford challenged Selden's patent in court on the grounds that the concept of a "horseless, self-propelled carriage" was too vague to be patentable. Ford won. Providing cars to the masses at low prices made Ford millions of dollars and many millions of North Americans better off, by enabling them to go where they wanted to go more easily, cheaply, and speedily.

Automobile production quickly spread to Canada, largely through foreign investment in and around the Windsor, Ontario, area. The founding of Ford Motor Company of Canada in 1904 marked the beginning of the Canadian automobile industry. It became the heart of the manufacturing industry in central Canada, providing thousands of high-paying jobs both directly and indirectly to Canadian workers.

CRISIS IN THE NORTH AMERICAN AUTOMOBILE INDUSTRY

Today people think of computers and gene-splicing, not automobiles, as the new technologies. The story of the automobile is no longer emblematic of the latest technological breakthroughs. The changing fortunes of the automobile industry during the past two decades reflect a redefinition of North American industry.

There were more than a hundred automobile manufacturers in the fall of 1903, twenty-seven of which accounted for more than 70 percent of the total sales of the industry. By the early 1960s, however, only three companies were responsible for 88 percent of North American auto sales. Of the car manufacturers that existed at the beginning of the century, many had gone bankrupt or had given up on the automobile business, and the remainder had been consolidated into or taken over by the dominant firms.

The most serious problems faced by the auto industry in the 1960s involved air pollution and automobile safety. To reduce pollution, the Canadian and U.S. governments regulated the kind of exhaust fumes a car could produce, and design changes

Figure 1.1 CANADIAN AUTOMOBILE IMPORTS FROM THE UNITED STATES, JAPAN, AND GERMANY

Imports from Germany and, especially, Japan rose from the 1960s until 1990. Imports from the United States fell in the late 1980s but have surged in the 1990s. *Source:* Statistics Canada (65-006, 65007), CANSIM Database, 1996.

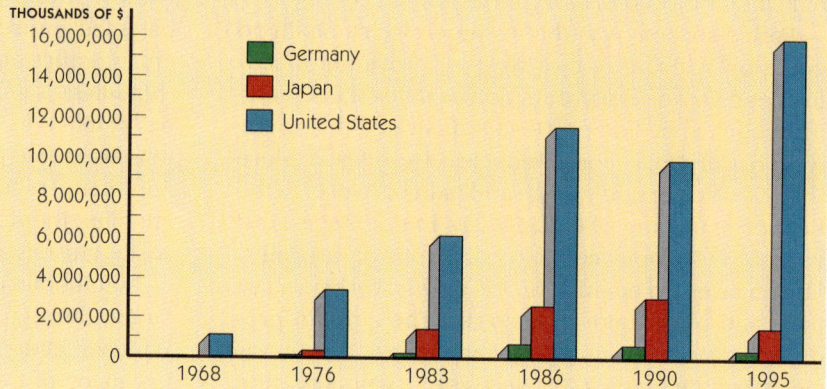

THOUSANDS OF $

Legend: Germany, Japan, United States

Years: 1968, 1976, 1983, 1986, 1990, 1995

followed. On the safety front, automobile companies quickly responded to demands for increased safety by providing seat belts.

This relatively rosy picture changed dramatically in 1973. That year, the Organization of Petroleum Exporting Countries (OPEC)—mainly countries in the Middle East—combined forces to hold down the supply of oil, create a scarcity, and thus push up its price. OPEC actually cut off all oil exports for a few tense weeks late in 1973. Its power was a surprise to many, including the automobile industry. North American cars then tended to be bigger and heavier than those in Japan and Europe. This was easily explained: incomes in the United States and Canada were higher; consumers could afford larger cars and the gasoline they guzzled. Also, Japan and Europe imposed much heavier taxes on gasoline, encouraging consumers in those countries to buy smaller, more fuel-efficient cars.

The North American auto industry thus was ill-prepared for the higher gas prices caused by OPEC's move. But other countries, especially Japan, stood ready to gain, with smaller, cheaper, and more fuel-efficient cars. Figure 1.1 shows the rapid growth of imports of new passenger cars into Canada between 1968 and 1994 from the United States, Japan, and Germany. The figures tell a story: car imports, which account for over a quarter of sales in Canada, rose rapidly over the period. However, those from outside

North America initially garnered a larger and larger share, rising from about 7 percent in 1968 to over 22 percent by the end of the 1980s before falling off to 13 percent by 1994.

It was clear that the Japanese firms were supplying what Canadian consumers wanted, but the effect on the domestic automobile industry was devastating. Profits fell and many workers, those whose high wages could not be justified by the level of productivity, were laid off.

PROTECTION FROM FOREIGN COMPETITION

In the early 1980s, the Big Three—Canadian subsidiaries of Chrysler, General Motors, and Ford—began to make a recovery from the hard times of the 1970s, for several reasons. Unions dramatically reduced their wage demands. Smaller and more fuel-efficient cars were developed. And the government stepped in to help protect the industry from foreign competition. Rather than imposing a tariff (tax) on car imports, the Canadian and U.S. governments negotiated with the Japanese government to restrain Japan's automobile exports. Although the export limits were called voluntary, they were actually negotiated under pressure. If the Japanese had not taken the "voluntary" step of limiting exports, Parliament and Congress probably would have passed laws forcing them to do so.

The reduced supply of Japanese cars led not only to increased sales of North American cars, but also to higher prices, for both Japanese and domestic cars. The domestic industry was subsidized not by the taxpayers in general but by those who bought cars, through these higher prices. The Japanese car manufacturers had little to complain about, since they too benefited from the higher prices. Had Japanese manufacturers gotten together and agreed to reduce their sales and raise prices, the action would have been viewed as a violation of Canadian anti-combines laws, which were designed to enforce competition. But here the government itself was encouraging less competition!

The Japanese responded in still another way to these restrictions. They decided to circumvent the limitations imposed on their exports by manufacturing cars here in Canada and the United States. Figure 1.2 shows the fraction of total Canadian production accounted for by General Motors, Ford, Chrysler, Honda, and "other" firms in 1971, 1991, and 1994. This picture reflects three phenomena. First, production in Canada is highly concentrated in a few firms. Thus, GM, with about 44 percent of total production, is shown as having close to one half of the pie. Second, whereas in 1971 Honda was not producing cars in Canada, by 1991 its production rose to over 11 percent of total Canadian production and was larger than that of the smallest American-owned producer, Chrysler. Third, by 1994 Chrysler had

Figure 1.2 SHARES OF AUTOMOBILE PRODUCTION IN CANADA

These pie charts show some of the changes in Canadian automobile production in recent decades. They show that production has remained concentrated, but that the shares of various companies have changed. Honda's production in Canada grew from zero to over 10 percent in the 1990s. Although Chrysler's production initially fell dramatically, it has since recovered its market share. *Source:* Statistics Canada, CANSIM Database 1995.

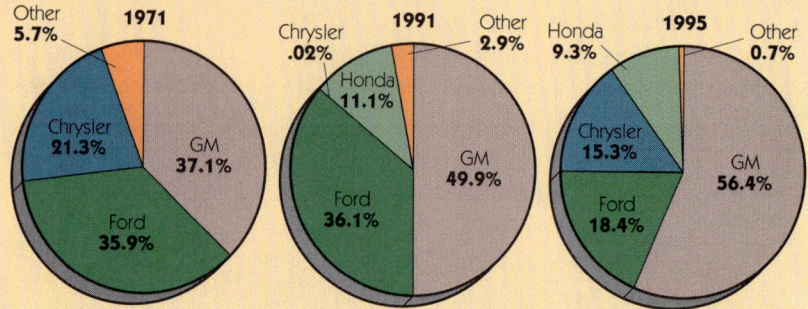

1971
Other 5.7%
Chrysler 21.3%
GM 37.1%
Ford 35.9%

1991
Chrysler .02%
Honda 11.1%
Other 2.9%
GM 49.9%
Ford 36.1%

1995
Honda 9.3%
Other 0.7%
Chrysler 15.3%
GM 56.4%
Ford 18.4%

rebounded dramatically, overtaking not only Honda but also Ford. Honda roughly held its own.

What would have happened had the automobile industry not been given the breather that the Japanese export restraints provided? We cannot tell. Perhaps it would have been forced to transform itself more quickly. Perhaps one or more firms would have gone out of business. What we do know is that during the 1980s, the industry worked hard to compete effectively with its Japanese rivals.

CANADA'S PLACE IN THE AUTOMOBILE INDUSTRY

More than any other industry, the automobile industry typifies the "openness" of the Canadian economy—its reliance on foreign investment and technology and its interrelationship with its American counterpart. The same companies that came to dominate the American industry also dominated the Canadian one, largely through branch plants or subsidiaries. Automobiles and parts produced in each country served the entire North American market. The fortunes of the Canadian automobile industry were interwoven with those of the U.S. automobile industry; these were formalized with the signing of the so-called Auto Pact in 1965 (technically called the Canada-U.S. Automotive Products Trade Agreement).

By the early 1990s, Canadian vehicle production was over two million units, employing more than 45,000 workers. Under the Auto Pact, as discussed below, the allocation of production was rationalized between Canada and the United States, with each country specializing in certain vehicle lines. In Canada, most activity is in light vehicle production (automobiles, minivans, and light trucks) and is dominated by the Big Three. But as a result of the relative ease of entry, efficient and competitive foreign automobile producers have been able to set up production facilities and gain a substantial share of the North American market. Asian-owned production from companies such as Toyota, Hyundai, and Suzuki has been growing rapidly and now accounts for over 30 percent of industry output. Part of the reason for setting up plants in Canada is to avoid the tariff levied on imported vehicles coming into Canada and the United States. In Canada, the tariff ranges from 6.0 to 9.2 percent of the value of vehicles, while the U.S. tariff rates are slightly lower.

Foreign producers have put considerable pressure on the Canadian industry, and are likely to continue to do so. For example, Japanese corporations are moving towards the production of more specialized and expensive midrange automobiles from the traditional smaller ones. As well, Japanese parts manufacturers are poised to begin making parts in Canada. The Big Three are responding partly by adopting Japanese methods, such as building stronger ties to component manufacturers, and partly by closing down existing plants and investing in modernization.

The development of the Canadian automobile industry has been heavily influenced by the Canada-U.S. Auto Pact, whose provisions remained the same under both the 1988 Canada-U.S. Free Trade Agreement and the subsequent North American Free Trade Agreement (NAFTA). The Auto Pact essentially stipulates that there be limited duty-free movement of automobile products across the Canada-U.S. border. This is **sectoral free trade,** or free trade in the products of a particular industry. Its two main goals are to integrate the North American auto industry to bring about more efficient patterns of investment, production, and trade, and to strengthen trade relations between the two countries. The main provision of the Auto Pact concerns the circumstances under which products can be imported duty-free. A manufacturer may import vehicles and original parts into Canada free of duty, provided the manufacturer maintains a ratio of production to sales in Canada at least as great as its 1964 production-to-sales ratio and at least 3 to 4.

The Auto Pact has apparently served Canada well, as attested by the relative success of the automotive industry. The Canadian automobile industry attracted over $12 billion of investment during the 1980s. The industry now faces the challenges of the 1990s, including continued competition from Asian automobile producers as well as the prospects for increased competition from Mexico as a result of the North American Free Trade Agreement.

Although the Canadian industry has been dominated by foreign-owned companies, there have been attempts in the past to produce a made-in-Canada car. Back in the 1950s, the Studebaker was produced in Walkerville, Ontario, largely to serve the British market. The company produced up to 15,000 cars per year but was unable to compete against the larger U.S.-based companies. A more spectacular case was that of the Bricklin car, a dream car intended to capture some of the upper end of the luxury market. It was to be produced in New Brunswick, though with franchises in the United States. The New Brunswick government agreed to provide financial support for the enterprise in the hope of creating permanent jobs in the province. As it turned out, the corporation declared bankruptcy in 1975 after two

years in operation and after producing 2,800 cars. The New Brunswick government lost a total of $23 million in the venture.

More recently, some independence was achieved on the labour side of the industry. In 1985 the Canadian Autoworkers Union (CAW) split from the International Union of United Automobile Workers of America (UAW), and now represents most automobile workers in Canada. At the time of the split, the CAW had about 140,000 workers, making it the sixth largest union in Canada.

WHAT IS ECONOMICS?

This narrative illustrates many facets of economics, but now a definition of our subject is in order. **Economics** is the study of how individuals, firms, governments, and other organizations within our society make **choices,** and how those choices determine the way the resources of society are used. **Scarcity** figures prominently in economics: choices matter because resources are scarce. Imagine an enormously wealthy individual who can have everything he wants. We might think that scarcity is not in his vocabulary—until we consider that time is a resource, and he must decide what expensive toy to devote his time to each day. When one takes time into account, scarcity is a fact in everyone's life.

To produce a single product, like an automobile, thousands of decisions and choices have to be made. Since any economy is made up not only of automobiles but of millions of products, it is a marvel that the economy functions at all, let alone as well as it does most of the time. This marvel is particularly clear if you consider instances when things do not work so well: the worldwide Great Depression in the 1930s, when almost 20 percent of the Canadian work force could not find a job; the countries of the former Soviet Union today, where ordinary consumer goods like carrots or toilet paper are often simply unavailable; the less developed economies of many countries in Africa, Asia, and Latin America, where standards of living have remained stubbornly low, and in some places have even been declining.

The fact that choices must be made applies to the economy as a whole as much as it does to each individual. Somehow, decisions are taken—by individuals, households, firms, and government—that together determine how the economy's limited resources, including its land, labour, machines, oil, and other natural resources, are used. Why is it that land used at one time for growing crops may, at another time, be used for an automobile plant? How was it that over the space of a couple of decades, resources were transferred from making horse carriages to making automobile bodies? that blacksmiths were replaced by auto mechanics? How do the decisions of millions of consumers, workers, investors, managers, and government officials all interact to determine the use of the scarce resources available to society? Economists reduce such matters to four basic questions concerning how economies function:

1. What is produced, and in what quantities? There have been important changes in consumption over the past fifty years. Spending for medical care, for example, was only 2 percent of total personal consumption in 1950. By 1990, more than one out of every ten dollars was spent on medical care, most of it by the government. What can account for changes like these? The economy seems to spew out new products like videocassette recorders and new services like automated bank tellers. What causes this process of innovation? The overall level of production has also shifted from year to year, often accompanied by large changes in the levels of employment and unemployment. How can economists explain these changes?

In Canada, the question of what is produced, and in what quantities, is answered largely by the private interaction of firms and consumers, but government also plays a role. Prices are critical in determining what goods and services are produced. When the price of some good rises, firms are induced to produce more of that good, to increase their profits. Thus, a central question for economists is, why are some goods or services more expensive than others? And why has the price of some goods increased or decreased?

2. How are these goods and services produced? There are often many ways of making something.

Textiles can be made with hand looms. Modern machines enable fewer workers to produce more cloth. Very modern machines may be highly computerized, allowing one worker to monitor many more machines than was possible earlier. The better machines generally cost more, but they require less labour. Which technique will be used, the advanced technology or the labour-intensive one? Henry Ford introduced the assembly line. More recently, car manufacturers have begun using robots, and automated machines have replaced tellers in providing banking services. What determines how rapidly technology changes?

In the Canadian economy, firms answer the question of how goods and services are produced, again with help from the government, which sets regulations and enacts laws that affect everything from the overall organization of firms to the ways they interact with their employees and customers.

3. For whom are these goods and services produced? Individuals who have higher incomes can consume more goods and services. But that answer only pushes the question back one step: What determines the differences in income and wages? What is the role of luck? of education? of inheritance? of savings? of experience and hard work? These questions are difficult to answer. For now, suffice it to say that while incomes are primarily determined by the private interaction of firms and households, government also plays a strong role, with taxes that redistribute income as well as programs like education and health care that enhance the ability of persons to earn incomes.

Figure 1.3 shows the relative pay in a variety of different occupations. To judge by income, each computer specialist receives almost twice as much of the economy's output as the average worker, and over four times as much as a bank teller.

4. Who takes economic decisions, and by what processes? In a **centrally planned economy,** as the Soviet Union used to be, the government takes responsibility for virtually every aspect of economic activity. The government provides the answers to the first three questions. A central economic planning agency works through a bureaucracy to say what will be produced and by what method, and who

Figure 1.3 WHO TAKES HOME CANADA'S OUTPUT?

This chart, using data for 1990, compares the earnings of workers in various occupations to the earnings of the unskilled worker. The average worker makes 3.0 times as much as the unskilled worker, and computer specialists make 5.6 times as much. *Source:* Statistics Canada, *Employment Earnings and Hours* (1993).

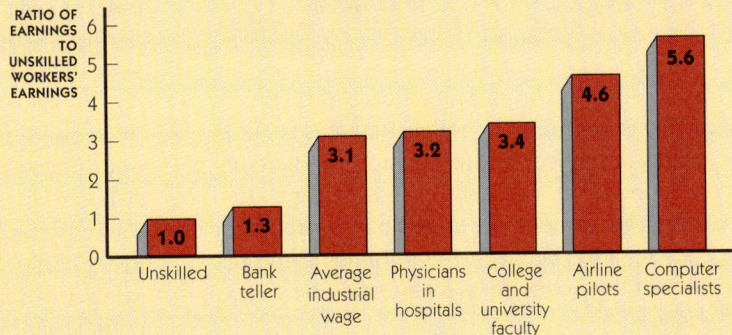

RATIO OF EARNINGS TO UNSKILLED WORKERS' EARNINGS

Occupation	Ratio
Unskilled	1.0
Bank teller	1.3
Average industrial wage	3.1
Physicians in hospitals	3.2
College and university faculty	3.4
Airline pilots	4.6
Computer specialists	5.6

shall consume it. At the other end of the spectrum are economies that rely primarily on the free interchange of producers and their customers to determine what, how, and for whom. Canada, which lies towards this latter end, has a **mixed economy;** that is, there is a mix between public (governmental) and private decision making. Within limits, producers make what they want to make; they use whatever method of production seems appropriate to them; and the output is distributed to consumers according to their income.

When economists examine an economy, they want to know to what extent economic decisions are taken by the government, and to what extent they are taken by private individuals. In Canada, while individuals for the most part take their own decisions about what kind of car to purchase, the government has inserted itself in a number of ways: it has taken actions that affect the imports of Japanese cars, that restrict the amount of pollutants a car can produce, and that promote fuel efficiency and automobile safety.

A related question is whether economic decisions are taken by individuals for their own interests or for the interest of an employer such as a business firm or government agency. This is an important distinction. We can expect people acting on their own behalf to take decisions that benefit themselves. When they act on behalf of organizations, however, a conflict of interest may arise. Observers often refer to corporations and governments as if they were a single individual. Economists point out that organizations consist, by definition, of a multitude of individuals and that the interests of these individuals do not necessarily coincide with one another or, for that matter, with the interests of the organization itself. Organizations bring a number of distinctive problems to the analysis of choice.

As you can see by their concern with decision making, economists are concerned not only with *how* the economy answers the four basic questions, but also *how well.* They ask, is the economy efficient? Could it produce more of some goods without producing fewer of others? Could it make some individuals better off without making some other individuals worse off?

BASIC QUESTIONS OF ECONOMICS

1 What is produced, and in what quantities?

2 How are these goods and services produced?

3 For whom are these goods and services produced?

4 Who takes economic decisions, and by what processes?

MARKETS AND GOVERNMENT IN THE MIXED ECONOMY

The primary reliance on private decision making in Canada reflects economists' beliefs that this reliance is appropriate and necessary for economic efficiency; however, economists also believe that certain interventions by government are desirable. Finding the appropriate balance between the public and the private sectors of the economy is a central issue of economic analysis.

MARKETS

The economic concept of markets is used to include any situation where exchange takes place, though this exchange may not necessarily resemble what takes place in traditional village markets. In department stores and shopping malls, customers rarely haggle over the price. When manufacturers purchase the materials they need for production, they exchange money for them, not other goods. Most goods, from cameras to clothes, are not sold directly from producers to consumers. They are sold from producers to distributors, from distributors to retailers, from retailers to consumers. All of these transactions are embraced by the concepts of **market** and **market economy.**

In market economies with competition, individuals make choices that reflect their own desires, and firms make choices that maximize their profits; to do so, they must produce the goods and services that consumers want, and they must produce them at lower cost than other firms. As firms compete in the quest for profits, consumers are benefited, both in the kinds of goods and services produced and the prices at which they are supplied. The market economy thus provides answers to the four basic economic questions—what is produced, how it is produced, for whom it is produced, and how these decisions are taken. And on the whole, the answers the market gives ensure the efficiency of the economy.

The market provides answers to the question of whom goods are produced for that not everyone finds acceptable. As with bidders at an auction, what market participants are willing and able to pay depends on their income. Some groups of individuals—including those without skills that are valued by the market—may receive such a low income that they could not feed and educate their children without outside assistance. Government provides the assistance by taking steps to increase income equality. These steps, however, often blunt economic incentives. While welfare payments provide an important safety net for the poor, the taxation required to finance them may discourage work and savings. If the government takes one out of three or even two dollars that an individual earns, that individual may not be inclined to work so much, whatever her income level. And if the government takes one out of two or three dollars a person earns from interest on savings, the person may decide to spend more and save less. Like the appropriate balance between the public and private sectors, the appropriate balance between concerns about equality (often referred to as **equity concerns**) and efficiency is a central issue of modern economics.

THE ROLE OF GOVERNMENT

The market provides answers to the basic economic questions *that on the whole* ensure efficiency. But in certain areas the solutions appear inadequate to many. There may be too much pollution, too much inequality, and too little concern about education, health, and safety. When the market is not perceived to be working well, people often turn to government.

Government plays a major role in modern economies. We need to understand both what that role is and why governments undertake the activities they do. Historically, governments in Canada have always taken an active role in economic affairs. The construction of the trans-Canadian railroad in the 1880s, which was instrumental in unifying the country, was only accomplished with the active financial support of the government. The system of tariff protection for manufacturing under the National Policy implemented by the 1889 Conservative government of Sir

CLOSE-UP: A FAILED ALTERNATIVE TO THE MIXED ECONOMY

While the mixed economy now is the dominant form of economic organization, it is not the only possible way of answering the basic economic questions. Beginning in 1917, an experiment in almost complete government control was begun in what became the Soviet Union.

What was produced in such an economy, and in what quantities? Government planners set the targets, which workers and firms then struggled to meet.

How were these goods produced? Again, since government planners decided what supplies would be delivered to each factory, they effectively chose how production occurred.

For whom were these goods produced? The government took decisions about what each job was paid, which affected how much people could consume. In principle, individuals could choose what to buy at government-operated stores, at prices set by the government. But in practice, many goods were unavailable at these stores.

Who took economic decisions, and by what process? The government planners decided, basing the decisions on their view of national economic goals.

At one time, all this planning sounded very sensible, but as former Soviet premier Nikita Khrushchev once said, "Economics is a subject that does not greatly respect one's wishes." Many examples of Soviet economic woes could be cited, but two will suffice. In the shoe market, the Soviet Union was the largest national producer in the world. However, the average shoe was of such low quality that it fell apart in a few weeks, and inventories of unwanted shoes rotted in warehouses. In agriculture, the Soviet government had traditionally allowed small private plots. Although the government limited the time farmers could spend on these plots, publicly run farming was so unproductive that the 3 percent of Soviet land that was privately run produced about 25 percent of the total farm output.

Today the standard of living in the former Soviet Union is not only below that in industrialized nations like those of North America, Japan, and Western Europe, but it is barely ahead of developing nations like Brazil and Mexico. Workers in the Soviet Union shared a grim one-liner: "We pretend to work and they pretend to pay us."

The collapse of the former Soviet Union was to a large extent the result of the failure of its economic system. Much of this text is concerned with explaining why mixed economies work as well as they do.

John A. Macdonald formed the basis of industrial policy for most of the twentieth century. The encouragement of high levels of immigration in the early 1900s was undertaken to develop the agricultural economy of the Prairie provinces. Government-owned corporations have been important in such industries as transportation, communications, and energy. Government has virtually taken over the provision of services in the areas of health, education, and welfare, services that were originally offered either by the private sector or by charitable organizations such as the churches. By tax and subsidy policies, governments have changed the fortunes of entire industries or segments of the nation. The National Energy Policy of the 1970s had an enormous impact on the oil and gas industry. Federal transportation policies have helped to economize on the costs of getting grain to foreign markets. And an active program of regional development subsidies has attempted to encourage industry to locate in high-unemployment regions of the Atlantic provinces and parts of Quebec. Many observers have noted the seemingly greater tendency to resort to government intervention in the Canadian economy than in the American.

The government sets the legal structure under which private firms and individuals operate. It regulates businesses to ensure that they do not discriminate by race or gender, do not mislead customers, are careful about the safety of their employees, and do not pollute the air and water. In some cases, such as telecommunications, even the prices that firms can charge are regulated. In many industries, government firms, called **Crown corporations,** operate as private businesses, sometimes in competition with private firms: examples have included PETRO Canada in the oil industry, Air Canada and Canadian National in transportation, the Canadian Broadcasting Corporation in entertainment, Canada Post, several provincial electrical utilities, as well as telephone companies and even automobile insurance plans in some provinces. Most schools as well as virtually all universities and hospitals are government-owned. In other cases, the government supplies goods and services that the private sector does not, such as providing for the national defence, building roads, and printing money. Government programmes provide for the elderly through Old Age Security, which pays income to retired individuals, and health care, which is fully funded by the government. The government helps those who have suffered economic dislocation, through unemployment insurance for those temporarily unemployed and disability insurance for those who are no longer able to work. The government also provides a "safety net" of support for the poor through various welfare programs.

One can easily imagine a government controlling the economy more directly. In countries where decision-making authority is centralized and con-centrated in the government, government bureaucrats might decide what and how much a factory should produce and set the level of wages that should be paid. At least until recently, governments in countries like the former Soviet Union and China attempted to control practically all major decisions regarding resource allocation.

THE THREE MAJOR MARKETS

The market economy revolves around exchange between individuals (or households), who buy goods and services (products) from firms, and firms, which take **inputs,** the various materials of production, and produce **outputs,** the goods and services that they sell. In thinking about a market economy, economists focus their attention on three broad categories of markets in which individuals and firms interact. The markets in which firms sell their outputs to households are referred to collectively as the **product market.** Many firms also sell goods and services to other firms; the outputs of the first firm become the inputs of the second. These transactions too are said to occur in the product market.

On the input side, firms need (besides the materials that they buy in the product market) some combination of labour and machinery with which their goods can be produced. They purchase the services of workers in the **labour market.** They raise funds with which to buy inputs in the **capital market.** Traditionally, economists have also highlighted the importance of a third input, land, but in modern industrial economies, land is of secondary importance. For most purposes, it suffices to focus attention on the three major markets listed here, and this text will follow this pattern.

As Figure 1.4 shows, individuals participate in all three markets. When individuals buy goods or services, they act as **consumers** in the product market. When people act as **workers,** economists say they "sell their labour services" in the labour market. When individuals buy shares of stock in a firm or lend money to a business, economists note that they are participating in the capital market, and refer to them as **investors.**

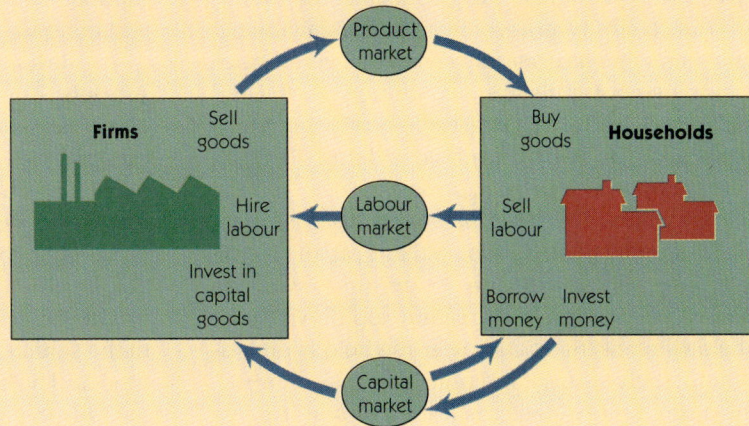

Figure 1.4 THE THREE MARKETS

To economists, people wear different hats: they are usually consumers in the product market, workers in the labour market, and borrowers and lenders in the capital market.

TWO CAVEATS

Terms in economics often are similar to terms in ordinary usage, but they can take on special meanings. The terms "market" and "capital" illustrate the problem.

Though the term "market" is used to conjure an image of a busy **marketplace,** there is no formal marketplace for most goods and services. There are buyers and sellers, and economists analyze the outcome *as if* there were a single marketplace in which all the transactions occurred.

Moreover, economists often talk about the "market for labour" as if all workers were identical. But workers obviously differ in countless ways. In some cases, these differences are important. We might then talk about the "market for skilled workers," or "the market for plumbers." But in other cases—such as when we are talking about the overall state of the economy and are focusing on the unemployment rate (the fraction of workers who would like jobs but cannot get them)—these differences can be ignored.

When newspapers refer to the **capital market,** they mean the bond traders and stockbrokers and the companies they work for on Bay Street in Toronto and other financial districts. When economists use the term "capital market" they have in mind a broader concept. It includes all the institutions concerned with raising funds (and, as we will see later, sharing and insuring risks), including banks and insurance companies.

The term "capital" is used in still another way—to refer to the machines and buildings used in production. To distinguish this particular usage, in this book we refer to machines and buildings as **capital goods.** "Capital markets" thus refers to the markets in which funds are raised, borrowed, and lent. **Capital goods markets** refers to the markets in which capital goods are bought and sold.

MICROECONOMICS AND MACROECONOMICS: THE TWO BRANCHES OF ECONOMICS

The detailed study of product, labour, and capital markets is called **microeconomics.** Microeconomics (*micro* is derived from the Greek word meaning "small") focuses on the behaviour of the units—the firms, households, and individuals—that make up the economy. It is concerned with how the individual units take decisions and what affects those decisions. By contrast, **macroeconomics** (*macro* comes from the Greek word meaning "large") looks at the behaviour of the economy as a whole, in particular the behaviour of such aggregate measures as overall rates of unemployment, inflation, economic growth, and the balance of trade. The aggregate numbers do not tell us what any firm or household is doing. They tell us what is happening in total, or on average.

It is important to remember that these perspectives are simply two ways of looking at the same thing. Microeconomics is the bottom-up view of the economy; macroeconomics is the top-down view. The behaviour of the economy as a whole is dependent on the behaviour of the units that make it up.

The automobile industry is a story of both micro- and macroeconomics. It is a story of microeconomic interactions of individual companies, investors, and labour unions. It is also a story of global macroeconomic forces like oil shortages and economic fluctuations. When auto companies laid off workers in the late 1970s, their problems boosted the overall unemployment rate. The recession of the early 1990s brought heavy reductions in car sales.

THE SCIENCE OF ECONOMICS

Economics is a **social science.** It studies the social problem of choice from a scientific viewpoint, which means that it is built on a systematic exploration of the problem of choice. This systematic exploration involves both the formulation of theories and the examination of data.

A **theory** consists of a set of assumptions (or hypotheses) and conclusions derived from those assumptions. Theories are exercises in logic: *if* the assumptions are correct, *then* the results follow. If all university graduates have a better chance of getting jobs and Ellen is a university graduate, then Ellen has a better chance of getting a job than a nongraduate. Economists make predictions with their theories. They might use a theory to predict what will happen if a tax is increased or if imports of for-

eign cars are limited. The predictions of a theory are of the form "If a tax is increased and if the market is competitive, then output will decrease and prices will increase."

In developing their theories, economists use **models.** To understand how economists use models, consider a modern car manufacturer trying to design a new automobile. It is extremely expensive to construct a new car. Rather than creating a separate, fully developed car for every engineer's or designer's conception of what she would like to see the new car be, the company uses models. The designers might use a plastic model to study the general shape of the vehicle and to assess reactions to the car's aesthetics. The engineers might use a computer model to study the air resistance, from which they can calculate fuel consumption, and a separate model for judging the car's comfort.

Just as the engineers construct different models to study a particular feature of a car, so too economists construct models of the economy—in words or equations—to depict particular features of the economy. An economic model might describe a general relationship ("When incomes rise, the number of cars purchased increases") or a quantitative relationship ("When incomes rise by 10 percent, the number of cars purchased rises, on average, by 12 percent") or make a general prediction ("An increase in the tax on gasoline will decrease the demand for cars").

DISCOVERING AND INTERPRETING RELATIONSHIPS

A **variable** is any item that can be measured and that changes. Prices, wages, interest rates, quantities bought and sold, are all variables. What interests economists is the connection among variables. When economists see what appears to be a systematic relationship among variables, they ask, could it have arisen by chance, or is there indeed a relationship? This is the question of **correlation.**

Economists use statistical tests to measure and test correlations. Consider the problem of deciding whether a coin is biased. If you flip a coin 10 times and get 6 heads and 4 tails, is the coin a fair one? Or is it weighted to heads? Statistical tests will say that the result of 6 heads and 4 tails could easily happen by chance, so the evidence does not prove that the coin is weighted. This does not prove that it is *not* slightly weighted. The evidence is just not strong enough for either conclusion. But if you flip a coin 100 times and get 80 heads, statistical tests will tell you that the possibility of this happening by blind chance with a fair coin is extremely small. The evidence supports the assertion that the coin is weighted.

A similar logic can be used on correlations in economic data. People with more education tend to earn higher wages. Is the connection merely chance? Statistical tests show whether the evidence is too weak for a conclusion, or whether it supports a particular answer.

CAUSATION VERSUS CORRELATION

Economists would like to accomplish more than just assert that different variables are indeed correlated. They would like to conclude that changes in one variable *cause* the changes in the other variable. The distinction between correlation and **causation** is important. If one variable "causes" the other, then changing one variable necessarily will change the other. If the relationship is just a correlation, this may not be true.

For instance, Figure 1.5 shows the relationship between level of schooling completed and annual income. There is no doubt that those with more years of schooling receive a higher income. But there are at least two possible explanations. One is that firms are willing to pay more for workers who are more productive and that education increases individuals' productivity. In this explanation, there is causation. More education "causes" greater productivity, which "causes" higher wages. The other explanation is that firms are willing to pay higher wages to those who are smarter even though they may not yet have many productive skills (and what skills they possess may have little to do with what they have learned in school), and those who are smarter survive longer in school. In this view, more able individuals stay in school longer and receive higher wages, but the schools do not "cause" increased productivity. There is a correlation, but no causation.

Sometimes there are systematic relationships between variables in which it is difficult to tell which variable is the cause, which the effect. For example, there is a systematic relationship between the number of children a woman has and the wages she earns. But the explanation for this relationship is not clear. Low wages mean that the income the woman must give up when she takes off work to have a child is less since less money is lost as a result of not working. Do low wages, then, induce women to have more children? Or does having more children

Figure 1.5 EDUCATION AND ANNUAL INCOME

A person's income grows with her level of education, as measured by years of schooling completed. However, this correlation does not prove that one factor causes the other. *Source:* 1986 Census.

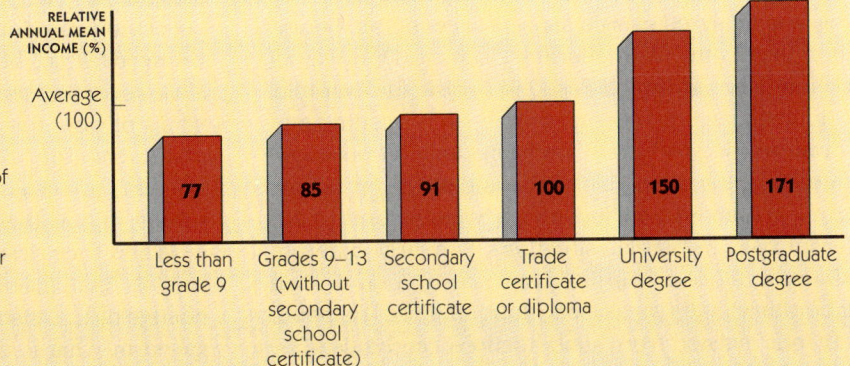

RELATIVE ANNUAL MEAN INCOME (%)

Average (100)

Less than grade 9	Grades 9–13 (without secondary school certificate)	Secondary school certificate	Trade certificate or diploma	University degree	Postgraduate degree
77	85	91	100	150	171

distract a woman from pursuing her career as avidly, and thus lead to low wages? Or is there a third factor, accounting for both the level of wages and the number of children?

EXPERIMENTS IN ECONOMICS

Many sciences use laboratory experiments to test alternative explanations, since experiments allow the scientist to change one factor at a time and see what happens. But the economy is not a chemistry lab. Instead, economics is like astronomy, in that both sciences must use the experiments that the natural world provides. Economists look for situations in which only one factor changes, and study the consequences of changing that factor. A change in the income tax system is an example of a natural experiment. But nature is usually not kind to economists; the world does not hold still. As the tax system changes, so do other features of the economy, and economists often have a difficult time deciding whether changes are the result of the new tax system or of some other economic change. Sometimes they can use what is called **econometrics,** the branch of statistics developed to analyze the particular measurement problems that arise in economics.

In a few cases, economists have engaged in social experiments. For example, they have given a selected group of individuals a different income tax schedule or welfare program from that given to another, otherwise similar, group. In recent years, a major new branch of economics, called **experimental economics,** has analyzed certain aspects of economic behaviour in a controlled laboratory setting. One way of seeing how individuals respond to risk, for example, is to construct a risky situation in such a setting and force individuals to take decisions and act on them. By varying the nature of the risk and the rewards, one can learn about how individuals will respond to different risks in real-life situations. Similarly, different kinds of auctions can be simulated in a controlled laboratory setting to see how bidders respond. Lessons learned from such auctions can be used by government in designing some of the auctions it conducts. Both social and laboratory experiments have

provided economists with valuable insights concerning economic behaviour.

But even with all available tools, the problem of finding a variety of correlations between several different types of data and having to discern which connections are real and which are only apparent is a difficult one. Economists' interest in these questions is motivated by more than just curiosity. Often, important policy questions depend on what one believes is really going on. Whether a country thinks it worthwhile to pour more resources into higher education may depend on whether it believes that the differences in wages observed between those with and without a postsecondary education are largely due to the skills and knowledge acquired during college or university, or whether they are mainly related to differences in ability between those who make it through college or university and those who do not.

The important lessons to remember here are (1) the fact of a correlation does not prove a causation; (2) the way to test different explanations of causation is to hold all of the factors constant except for one, and then allow that one to vary; (3) data do not always speak clearly, and sometimes do not allow any conclusions to be drawn.

WHY ECONOMISTS DISAGREE

Economists are frequently called upon to make judgments on matters of public policy. Should the government reduce the deficit? Should inflation be reduced? If so, how? In these public-policy discussions, economists often disagree. They differ in their views of how the world works, in their *description* of the economy, in their predictions of the consequences of certain actions. And they differ in their values, in how they evaluate these consequences.

When they describe the economy, and construct models that predict either how the economy will change or the effects of different policies, they are engaged in what is called **positive economics.** When they evaluate alternative policies, weighing up the various benefits and costs, they are engaged

CLOSE-UP: ECONOMISTS AGREE!

Try the following six statements out on your classmates or your family to see whether they, like the economists surveyed, disagree, agree with provisos, or agree:

| | Percentage of economists who | | |
	Disagree	Agree with provisos	Agree
1. Tariffs and import quotas usually reduce general economic welfare.	6.5	21.3	71.3
2. A minimum wage increases unemployment among young and unskilled workers.	20.5	22.4	56.5
3. A ceiling on rents reduces the quantity and quality of housing available.	6.5	16.6	76.3
4. The cause of the rise in gasoline prices that occurred in the wake of the Iraqi invasion of Kuwait is the monopoly power of large oil companies.	67.5	20.3	11.4
5. The trade deficit is primarily a consequence of the inability of domestic firms to compete.	51.5	29.7	18.1
6. Cash payments increase the welfare of recipients to a greater degree than do transfers-in-kind of equal cash value.	15.1	25.9	58.0

Among the general population, these are controversial questions. You will find many people who believe that restricting foreign imports is a good thing; that government regulation of wages and rents has few ill effects; that the trade deficit is mainly caused by the inability of domestic companies to compete; that government should avoid giving cash to poor people (because they are likely to waste it); and that oil companies are the cause of higher oil prices.

But when professional economists are surveyed, there is a broad agreement that many of those popular answers are misguided. The percentages listed above are from a survey carried out in the United States in 1990. Notice that healthy percentages of economists apparently believe that most import quotas are economically harmful; that government control of wages and rents does lead to adverse consequences; that oil companies are not to blame for higher oil prices; that the trade deficit is not caused by the competitive problems of individual companies; that cash payments benefit the poor more than direct (in-kind) transfers of food, shelter, and medical care.

Sources: Richard M. Alston, J. R. Kearl, and Michael B. Vaughan, "Is There a Consensus Among Economists in the 1990s?" *American Economic Review* (May 1992); J. R. Kearl, Clayne L. Pope, Gordon C. Whiting, and Larry T. Wimmer, "A Confusion of Economists?" *American Economic Review* (May 1979), pp. 28–37.

in what is called **normative economics.** Positive economics is concerned with what "is," with describing how the economy functions. Normative economics deals with what "should be," with making judgments about the desirability of various courses of action. Normative economics makes use of positive economics. We cannot make judgments about whether a policy is desirable unless we have a clear picture of its consequences. Good normative economics also tries to be explicit about precisely what values or objectives it is incorporating. It tries to couch its statements in the form "If these are your objectives . . . , then this is the best possible policy."

Consider the normative and positive aspects of the proposal to restrict imports of Japanese cars. Positive economics would describe the consequences: the increased prices consumers have to pay; the increased sales of domestic cars; the increased employment and increased profits; the increased pollution and oil imports, because domestic cars on average are less fuel-efficient than Japanese cars. In the end, the question is, *should there be restraints on imports of Japanese cars?* This is a normative question: normative economics would weigh these various effects—the losses of the consumers, the gains to workers, the increased profits, the increased pollution, the increased oil imports—to reach an overall judgment. Normative economics develops systematic frameworks within which these complicated judgments can be conducted in a systematic way.

DISAGREEMENTS WITHIN POSITIVE ECONOMICS

Even when they describe how the economy works, economists may differ for two main reasons. First, economists differ over what is the appropriate model of the economy. They may disagree about how well people and firms are able to perceive and calculate their self-interest, and whether their interactions take place in a competitive or a noncompetitive market. Different models will produce different results. Often the data do not allow us to say which of two competing models provides a better description of some market.

Second, even when they agree about the appropriate theoretical model, economists may disagree about quantitative magnitudes, which will cause their predictions to differ. They may agree, for instance, that reducing the tax on interest income will encourage individuals to save more, but they may produce different estimates about the amount of the savings increase. Again, many of these disagreements arise because of inadequate data. We may have considerable data concerning savings in Canada over the past century. But institutions and economic conditions today are markedly different from those of fifty or even ten years ago.

DISAGREEMENTS WITHIN NORMATIVE ECONOMICS

There are generally many consequences of any policy, some beneficial, some harmful. In comparing two policies, one may benefit some people more, another may benefit others. One policy is not unambiguously better than another. It depends on what you care more about. A cut in the tax on the profits from the sale of shares might encourage savings, but at the same time, most of the benefits accrue to the very wealthy; hence, it increases inequality. A reduction in taxes to stimulate the economy may reduce unemployment, but it may also increase inflation. Even though two economists agree about the model, they may make different recommendations. In assessing the effect of a tax cut on unemployment and inflation, for instance, an economist who is worried more about unemployment may recommend in favour of the tax cut, while the other, concerned about inflation, may recommend against it. In this case, the source of the disagreement is a difference in values.

But while economists may often seem to differ greatly among themselves, in fact they agree more than they disagree: their disagreements get more attention than their agreements. (See box, page 17.) Most important, when they do disagree, they seek to be clear about the source of their disagreement: 1) to what extent does it arise out of differences in models, 2) to what extent does it arise out of differences in estimates of quantitative relations, and 3) to what extent does it arise out of differences in values? Clarifying the sources of and reasons for disagreement can be a very productive way of learning more.

CONSENSUS ON THE IMPORTANCE OF SCARCITY

Most of what we have discussed in this chapter fits within the areas on which there is broad consensus among economists. This includes the observation that the Canadian economy is a mixed economy and that there are certain basic questions that all economic systems must address. We highlight the most important points of consensus throughout the book, beginning here, with our first. The most important point of consensus in this chapter concerns scarcity:

1   Scarcity

There is no free lunch. Having more of one thing requires giving up something else. Scarcity is a basic fact of life.

REVIEW AND PRACTICE

SUMMARY

1 Economics is the study of how individuals, firms, and governments within our society make choices. Choices are unavoidable because desired goods, services, and resources are inevitably scarce.

2 There are four basic questions that economists ask about any economy. (1) What is produced, and in what quantities? (2) How are these goods and services produced? (3) For whom are these goods and services produced? (4) Who takes economic decisions, and by what processes?

3 Canada has a mixed economy; there is a mix between public and private decision making. The economy relies primarily on the private interaction of individuals and firms to answer the four basic questions, but government plays a large role as well. A central question for any mixed economy is the balance between the public and private sectors.

4 The term "market" is used to describe any situation where exchange takes place. In Canada's market economy, individuals, firms, and government interact in product markets, labour markets, and capital markets.

5 Economists use models to study how the economy works and to make predictions about what will happen if something is changed. A model can be expressed in words or equations, and is designed to mirror the essential characteristics of the particular phenomena under study.

6 A correlation exists when a change in one variable is associated with a predictable change in another variable. However, the simple existence of a correlation does not prove that one factor causes the other to change. Additional outside factors may be influencing both.

7 Positive economics is the study of how the economy works. Disagreements within positive economics centre on the appropriate model of the economy or market and on the value of different empirical estimates of the consequences of change. Normative economics deals with the desirability of various actions. Disagreements within normative economics centre on differences in the values placed on the various costs and benefits resulting from change.

KEY TERMS

sectoral free trade	Crown corporations	capital goods	model
scarcity	inputs	microeconomics	correlation
centrally planned economy	outputs	macroeconomics	causation
mixed economy	product market	social science	positive economics
market economy	labour market	theory	normative economics
	capital market		

REVIEW QUESTIONS

1 Why are choices unavoidable?

2 How are the four basic economic questions answered in the Canadian economy?

3 What is a mixed economy? Describe some of the roles government might play, or not play, in a mixed economy.

4 Name the three main economic markets, and describe how an individual might participate in each one as a buyer and seller.

5 Give two examples of economic issues that are primarily microeconomic, and two that are primarily macroeconomic. What is the general difference between microeconomics and macroeconomics?

6 What is a model? Why do economists use models?

7 When causation exists, would you also expect a correlation to exist? When a correlation exists, would you also expect causation to exist? Explain.

8 "All disagreements between economists are purely subjective." Comment.

PROBLEMS

1 Characterize the following events as microeconomic, macroeconomic, or both.
(a) Unemployment increases this month.
(b) A drug company invents and begins to market a new medicine.
(c) A bank lends money to a large company but turns down a small business.
(d) Interest rates decline for all borrowers.
(e) A union negotiates for higher pay.
(f) The price of oil increases.

2 Characterize the following events as part of the labour market, the capital market, or the product market.
(a) An investor tries to decide which company to invest in.
(b) With practice, the workers on an assembly line become more efficient.
(c) The opening up of the economies in Eastern Europe offers new markets for Canadian products.
(d) A big company that is losing money decides to offer its workers a special set of incentives to retire early, hoping to reduce its costs.
(e) A consumer roams around a shopping mall, looking for birthday gifts.
(f) The federal government needs to borrow more money to finance its level of spending.

3 Discuss the incentive issues that might arise in each of the following situations. (Hint: Remember the history of the automobile industry at the start of this chapter.)
(a) You have some money to invest, and your financial adviser introduces you to a couple of software executives who want to start their own company. What should you worry about as you decide whether to invest?

(b) You are running a small company, and your workers promise that if you increase their pay, they will work harder.

(c) A large industry is going bankrupt and appeals for government assistance.

4 Name ways in which government intervention has helped the automobile industry in the last two decades, and ways in which it has injured the industry.

5 On the back of a bag of cat litter it is claimed, "Cats that use cat litter live three years longer than cats that don't." Do you think that cat litter actually causes an increased life expectancy of cats, or can you think of some other factors to explain this correlation? What evidence might you try to collect to test your explanation?

6 Life expectancy in Sweden is 78 years; life expectancy in India is 57 years. Does this prove that if an Indian moved to Sweden he would live longer? That is, does this prove that living in Sweden causes an increase in life expectancy, or can you think of some other factors to explain these facts? What evidence might you try to collect to test your explanation?

2

THINKING LIKE
AN ECONOMIST

Everyone thinks about economics, at least some of the time. We think about money (we wish we had more of it) and about work (we wish we had less of it). But there is a distinctive way that economists approach economic issues, and one of the purposes of this course is to introduce you to that way of thinking. This chapter begins with a basic model of the economy. We follow this with a closer look at how the basic units that the economy comprises—individuals, firms, and governments—take choices in situations where they are faced with scarcity. In Chapters 3 through 5, we study ways in which these units interact with one another, and how those interactions "add up" to determine how society's resources are allocated.

KEY QUESTIONS

1 What is the basic competitive model of the economy?

2 What are incentives, property rights, prices, and the profit motive, and what roles do these essential ingredients of a market economy play?

3 What alternatives to the market system are there for allocating resources, and why do economists tend not to favour these alternatives?

4 What are some of the basic techniques economists use in their study of how people make choices? What are the various concepts of costs that economists use?

THE BASIC COMPETITIVE MODEL

Though different economists employ different models of the economy, they all use a basic set of assumptions as a point of departure. The economist's basic model has three components: assumptions about how consumers behave, assumptions about how firms behave, and assumptions about the markets in which these consumers and firms interact. The model ignores government, not because government is not important, but because before we can understand the role of government we need to see how an economy without a government might function.

RATIONAL CONSUMERS AND PROFIT-MAXIMIZING FIRMS

The fact of scarcity, which we encountered in Chapter 1, implies that individuals and firms must make choices. Underlying much of economic analysis is the basic assumption of **rational choice,** that people weigh the costs and benefits of each possibility. This assumption is based on the expectation that individuals and firms will act in a consistent manner, with a reasonably well-defined notion of what they like and what their objectives are, and with a reasonable understanding of how to attain those objectives.

In the case of an individual, the rationality assumption is taken to mean that he makes choices and decisions in pursuit of his own self-interest. Different people will, of course, have different goals and desires. Sally may want to drive a Porsche, own a yacht, and have a large house; to attain those objectives, she knows she needs to work long hours and sacrifice time with her family. Andrew is willing to accept a lower income to get longer vacations and more leisure throughout the year.

Economists make no judgments about whether Sally's preferences are "better" or "worse" than Andrew's. They do not even spend much time asking why different individuals have different views on these matters, or why tastes change over time. These are important questions, but they belong more to the province of psychology and sociology. What economists are concerned about are the consequences of these different preferences. What decisions can they expect Sally and Andrew, rationally pursuing their respective interests, to take?

In the case of firms, they are in the business of making profits for their owners. The rationality assumption is taken to mean that they choose their inputs and outputs to maximize profits.

COMPETITIVE MARKETS

To complete the model, economists make assumptions about the places where self-interested consumers and profit-maximizing firms meet: markets. Economists begin by focusing on the case where there are many buyers and sellers, all buying and selling the same thing. You might picture a crowded farmers' market to get a sense of the number of buyers and sellers—except that you have to picture everyone buying and selling just one good. Let's say we are in Ontario in the autumn, and the booths are all full of peaches.

Each of the farmers would like to raise his prices.

INGREDIENTS IN THE BASIC COMPETITIVE MODEL

1 Rational, self-interested consumers

2 Rational, profit-maximizing firms

3 Competitive markets with price-taking behaviour

That way, if he can still sell his peaches, his profits go up. Yet with a large number of sellers, each is forced to charge close to the same price, since if any farmer charged much more, he would lose business to the farmer next door. Profit-maximizing firms are in the same position. In an extreme case, if a firm charged any more than the going price, it would lose *all* its sales. Economists label this case **perfect competition.** In perfect competition, each firm is a **price taker,** which simply means that because it cannot influence the market price, it must accept that price. The firm takes the market price as given because it cannot raise its price without losing all sales, and at the market price it can sell as much as it wishes. Even if it sold ten times as much, this would have a negligible effect on the total quantity marketed or the price prevailing in the market. Perhaps the best example of real markets that in the absence of government intervention would probably be perfectly competitive is the markets for agricultural goods. There are so many wheat farmers, for instance, that each farmer believes he can grow and sell as much wheat as he wishes and have no effect on the price of wheat. (Later in the book, we will encounter markets with limited or no competition, like monopolies, where firms can raise prices without losing all their sales.)

On the other side of our farmers' market are rational individuals, each of whom would like to pay as little as possible for her peaches. Why can't she pay less than the going price? Because the seller sees another buyer in the crowd who will pay the going price. Thus, the consumers also take the market price as given, and focus their attention on other factors—their taste for peaches, primarily—in deciding how many to buy.

This model of consumers, firms, and markets—rational, self-interested consumers interacting with rational, profit-maximizing firms, in competitive markets where firms and consumers are both price takers—is the **basic competitive model.** The model has one very strong implication: if actual markets are well described by the competitive market, then the economy will be efficient: resources are not wasted, it is not possible to produce more of one good without producing less of another, and it is not even possible to make anyone better off without making someone else worse off. These results are obtained without government.

Virtually all economists recognize that actual economies are not *perfectly* described by the competitive model, but most still use it as a convenient benchmark—as we will throughout this book. We will also point out important differences between the predictions of the competitive model and observed outcomes, which will guide us to other models which may provide a better description of particular markets and situations. Economists recognize too that while the competitive market may not provide a *perfect* description of some markets, it may provide a good description—with its predictions matching actual outcomes well, though not perfectly. As we shall see, economists differ in their views about how many such markets there are, how good the "match" is, and how well alternative models do in rectifying the deficiency of the competitive model in any particular case.

PRICES, PROPERTY RIGHTS, AND PROFITS: INCENTIVES AND INFORMATION

For market economies to work efficiently, firms and individuals must be informed and have incentives to act on available information. Indeed, incentives can be viewed as at the heart of economics. Without incentives, why would individuals go to work in the morning? Who would undertake the risks of bringing out new products? Who would put aside savings for a rainy day? There is an old expression about the importance of having someone "mind the store." But without incentives, why would anyone bother?

Market economies provide information and incentives through *prices, profits, and property rights.* Prices provide information about the relative scarcity of different goods and services. The **price system** ensures that goods and services go to those individuals who are most willing and able to pay for them, and are supplied by the firms that can provide them at least cost. Prices convey information to firms about how individuals value different goods.

The desire for profits motivates firms to respond to the information provided by prices. By producing what consumers want in the most efficient way, in ways that use the least scarce resources, they increase their profits. Similarly, rational individuals' pursuit of self-interest induces them to respond to prices: they buy goods and services that are more expensive—in a sense relatively more scarce—only if the goods and services provide commensurately greater benefits.

For the profit motive to be effective, firms need to be able to keep at least some of their profits. Households, in turn, need to be able to keep at least some of what they earn or receive as a return on their investments. (The return on their investments is simply what they receive back in excess of what they invested. If they receive back less than they invested, the return is negative.) There must, in short, be **private property,** with its attendant **rights.** Property rights include both the right of the owner to use the property as she sees fit and the right to sell it.

These two attributes of property rights give individuals the incentive to use property under their control efficiently. The owner of a piece of land tries to figure out the most profitable use of the land, for example, whether to build a store or a restaurant. If he makes a mistake and opens a restaurant when he should have opened a store, he bears the consequences: the loss in income. The profits he earns if he takes the right decisions—and the losses he bears if he takes the wrong ones—give him an incentive to think carefully about the decision and do the requisite research. The owner of a store tries to make sure that her customers get the kind of merchandise and the quality of service they want. She has an incentive to establish a good reputation, because if she does so, she will do more business and earn more profits.

The store owner will also want to maintain her property—which is not just the land anymore, but includes the store as well—because she will get more for it when the time comes to sell her business to someone else. Similarly, the owner of a house has an incentive to maintain *his* property, so that he can sell it for more when he wishes to move. Again, the profit motive combines with private property to provide incentives.

INCENTIVES VERSUS EQUALITY

While incentives are at the heart of market economies, they come with a cost: inequality. Any system of incentives must tie compensation with performance. Whether through differences in luck or ability, performance of different individuals will differ. In many cases it will not be possible to identify why performance is high. The salesperson may claim that the reason his sales are high is superior skill and effort, while his colleague may argue that it is dumb luck.

If pay is tied to performance, there will inevitably be

HOW THE PROFIT MOTIVE DRIVES THE MARKET SYSTEM

In market economies, incentives are supplied to individuals and firms by the chance to own property and to retain some of the profits of working and producing.

some inequality. And the more closely tied compensation is to performance the greater the inequality. The fact that the greater the incentives, the greater the resulting inequality is called the **incentive-equality trade-off.** If society provides greater incentives, total output is likely to be higher, but there will also probably be greater inequality.

One of the basic questions facing society in the choice of tax rates and welfare systems concerns how much incentives would be diminished by an increase in tax rates to finance a better welfare system and thus reduce inequality? What would be the results of those reduced incentives?

WHEN PROPERTY RIGHTS FAIL

Prices, profits, and property rights are the three essential ingredients of market economies. We can learn a lot about why they are so important by examining a few cases where property rights and prices are interfered with. Each example highlights a general point. Whenever society fails to define the owner of its resources and does not allow the highest bidder to use them, inefficiencies result. Resources will be wasted or not used in the most productive way.

Ill-Defined Property Rights Fish are a valuable resource. Not long ago, the area southeast of Newfoundland, called the Grand Banks, was teeming with fish, especially cod. Not surprisingly, it was also teeming with fishermen, who saw an easy livelihood scooping out the fish from the sea. Since there were no property rights, everyone tried to catch as many fish as he could. A self-interested fisherman would rationally reason that if he did not catch the fish, someone else would. The result was a tragedy: the Grand Banks was overfished, to the point where not only was it not teeming with fish, but commercial fishing became unprofitable. Beginning in 1977, foreign fishing was reduced by the extension of Canada's offshore jurisdiction to include most of the Grand Banks. Canada and the United States agreed to a treaty limiting the amount of fish that each country's fishermen could take. More recently, fishing for some species, such as the northern cod, has

been stopped altogether. Only by limiting the quantity taken can the fish stocks be restored.

Similar problems arise in the use of freshwater bodies of water. For many years, industrial firms flushed waste containing harmful chemicals into the lakes, rivers, and streams of the country, essentially treating water as a free resource. The result was a deterioration of the quality of water to an extent that was harmful to other users. Again, the problem arose because of a lack of definition of property rights. Governments have gradually intervened with a variety of regulatory measures to attempt to redress the costs that had been imposed by pollution.

The problem of ill-defined property rights is more general than the situation of fishermen and freshwater users. *Any* time society fails to define the owners of its resources and does not allow the highest bidder to use them, we can expect inefficiencies to result. Resources will be wasted or will not be used in the most productive way.

Restricted Property Rights In some instances, those who have property rights are not allowed the full freedom to use the property as they wish for as long as they wish, or to buy and sell it. In Canada, much of the timberland is provincial Crown land that is leased to firms wishing to cut trees for profit. The sale of licences combined with taxes imposed on the basis of the number of trees cut (stumpage fees) was a valuable and seemingly inexhaustible source of revenue to provincial governments. However, leases were only temporary, thus conferring only partial property rights to the leaseholders. The value of timber as a resource depends upon the extent to which reforestation is undertaken. However, the benefit of reforestation accrues sometime in the future, perhaps many years later. Since leasehold only confers temporary property rights on the logging industry, the incentive does not exist to engage in reforestation practices that will generate the largest long-term benefit from the forests, and the forests may be inefficiently used. When forest resources seemed endless, insufficient reforestation may not have been perceived as a great problem. However, recent concern has led governments to attempt to regulate reforestation practices on Crown lands held in leasehold by timber firms.

Entitlements as Property Rights Property rights do not always mean that you have full ownership or control. A **legal entitlement,** such as the right to occupy an apartment for life at a rent that is controlled, common in some large cities, is viewed by economists as a property right. Individuals do not own the apartment and thus cannot sell it, but they cannot be thrown out, either. Because the individual in a rent-controlled apartment cannot (legally) sell the right to live in her apartment, as she gets older she may have limited incentives to maintain its condition, let alone improve it.

A similar situation exists with the use of frequencies on the airwaves. They are allocated by a federal regulatory agency, the Canadian Radio-television and Telecommunications Commission (C.R.T.C.). The result is that those who value the slots most are not necessarily those to whom they are allocated. Thus, for example, a large commercial station would be willing to pay a great deal of money for the frequency held by a nonprofit organization, such as a university. But the nonprofit organization is not allowed to sell its entitlement to the frequency. The result is that frequencies are allocated differently from how a market would allocate them.

CONSENSUS ON INCENTIVES

Incentives, prices, profits, and property rights are central features of any economy. Our second consensus point concerns incentives:

2 Incentives

> *Providing appropriate incentives is a fundamental economic problem. In modern market economies, profits provide incentives for firms to produce the goods individuals want, and wages provide incentives for individuals to work. Property rights also provide people with important incentives, not only to invest and to save, but to put their assets to the best possible use.*

RATIONING

The price system is only one way of allocating resources, and a comparison with other systems will help to clarify the advantages of markets. When individuals get less of a good than they would like at the terms being offered, the good is said to be **rationed.** Different rationing schemes are different ways of deciding who gets society's scarce resources.

Rationing by Queues Rather than supplying goods to those willing and able to pay the most for them, a society could give them instead to those most willing to wait in line. This system is called **rationing by queues.** Tickets are often allocated by queues, whether they are for movies, sporting events, or rock concerts. A price is set, and it will not change no matter how many people line up to buy at that price. (The high price that scalpers can get for "hot" tickets is a good indication of how much more than the ticket price people would be willing to pay.)

Rationing by queues is thought by many to be a more desirable way of supplying medical services than the price system. Why, it is argued, should the rich—who are most able to pay for medical services—be the ones to get better or more medical care? Using this reasoning, Canada provides free medical care to everyone. To see a doctor, all you have to do is wait in line. Rationing medicine by queues turns the allocation problem around: since the value of time for low-wage workers is lower, they are more willing to wait, and therefore they get a disproportionate share of (government-supplied) medical services.

In general, rationing by queues is an inefficient way of distributing resources because the time spent in line is a wasted resource. There are usually ways of achieving the same goal within a price system that can make everyone better off. Returning to the medical example, if some individuals were allowed to pay for doctors' services instead of waiting in line, more doctors could be hired with the proceeds, and the lines for those unable or unwilling to pay could actually be reduced.

Rationing by Lotteries **Lotteries** allocate goods by a random process, like picking a name from a hat. University dormitory rooms are usually assigned by lottery. So are seats in popular courses; when more students want to enroll in a section of a principles of economics course than the size of the section allows, there may be a lottery to determine who gets to enroll. In another example of distribution by lottery, the Ontario Ministry of Natural Resources conducted public meetings to determine how to rehabilitate the moose population by controlling the annual moose harvest. The results of the meetings showed that the public preferred the lottery draw to the first-come, first-served technique on the grounds that it would provide an equal chance for all residents. However, lotteries are also inefficient because the scarce resources do not go to the individual or firm that values them the most and is willing and able to pay the most.

Rationing by Coupons Most governments in wartime use **coupon rationing.** People are allowed so many litres of gasoline, so many kilograms of sugar, and so much flour each month. To get the good, you have to pay the market price *and* produce a coupon. The reason for coupon rationing is that without coupons prices might soar, inflicting a hardship on poorer members of society.

Coupon systems take two forms, depending on whether coupons are tradable or not. Coupons that are not tradable give rise to the same inefficiency that occurs with most of the other nonprice systems—goods do not in general go to the individuals who are willing and able to pay the most. There is generally room for a trade that will make all parties better off. For instance, I might be willing to trade some of my flour ration for some of your sugar ration. But in a nontradable coupon system, the law prohibits such transactions. When coupons cannot be legally traded, there are strong incentives for the establishment of a **black market,** an illegal market in which the goods or the coupons for goods are traded.

Rationing by Government Regulation Sometimes direct **government regulation** is used to ration the amounts that can be bought or sold. There are numerous examples of this. Many countries have oper-

ated capital controls that restrict the amount of foreign currency that can be purchased. The amount of game that can be taken by recreational hunters is often subject to regulation. Some communities limit the number of bags of garbage that can be left out by households for collection. Quantity controls are often used to restrict the amounts of pollutants emitted by firms. In each of these cases, the quantity restriction typically bears no direct relation to the value put on the item by the various users of it. As a result, the item is likely to be inefficiently allocated among users.

In some cases this inefficiency is overcome by allowing persons to trade their quotas. This is typically the case with agricultural and fishing quotas, and has been suggested by economists for pollution controls. Being able to buy and sell quotas will ensure that those who value the restricted item most will have the opportunity to use it.

OPPORTUNITY SETS

We have covered a lot of ground so far in this chapter. We have seen the economist's basic model, which relies on competitive markets. We have seen how the profit motive and private property supply the incentives that drive a market economy. And we have gotten our first glimpse at why economists believe that market systems, which supply goods to those who are willing and able to pay the most, provide the most efficient means of allocating what the economy produces. They are far better than the nonprice rationing schemes that have been employed. It is time now to return to the question of choice. Market systems leave to individuals and firms the question of what to consume. How are these decisions taken?

For a rational individual or firm, the first step in the economic analysis of any choice is to identify what is possible—what economists call the **opportunity set,** which is simply the group of available options. If you want a sandwich and you have only roast beef and tuna fish in the refrigerator, then your op-

The spectrum of radio frequencies is a scarce resource and therefore has economic value. As with other scarce resources, society is best served if it is used in the most efficient way. In Canada, as in most countries, government is the steward of the use of these frequencies. The Canadian government has exercised this prerogative by assigning frequencies on the basis of applications by potential users. Thus, radio stations must be granted a licence to use a particular frequency by the Canadian Radio-television and Telecommunications Commission on the basis of a written submission. There is no reason to believe that such licences will go to those who are able to use them most efficiently, or to those who will best satisfy consumer preferences.

Now, a new use for part of the radio frequency spectrum has been developed, and that is to transmit signals over long distances for the next generation of cellular telephones. This will free cellular telephone companies from the need to use the transmission systems of standard telephone companies, and would immediately increase the convenience and flexibility of cellular phone use. The government must decide how to allocate the scarce frequency spectrum among alternative cellular telephone companies. Two alternatives are possible. One is to adopt the procedure of allocating them on the basis of bureaucratic discretion as to which companies

will best serve Canada's interest, as outlined above. As with any rationing system, there is no guarantee that the allocations will go to the firms that can use them most efficiently and produce the best service for potential consumers.

The alternative is to use the price system. One way to do this is for the government to sell the rights to use the frequencies by auction. As Professor Daniel Vincent of the University of Western Ontario has argued, auctioning the rights to the highest bidders will have two advantages. First, it will ensure that some of the value of the property rights to the frequencies accrues to the public rather than ending up as profits in the hands of the companies. And second, it will ensure that the companies that can use the frequencies most efficiently and at least cost are the ones that obtain the licences. They are the ones that will earn the most profits, and so can make the highest bids for the licences.

There is a lot at stake. On the basis of experience in the United States, where such licences have been allocated by auction, Professor Vincent estimates that up to $3 billion would be bid for the rights to use these frequencies in Canada.

Source: Daniel R. Vincent, "Industry Canada Is Taking Itself to the Cleaner's," *The Globe and Mail,* December 7, 1995.

portunity set consists of a roast beef sandwich, a tuna fish sandwich, a strange sandwich combining roast beef and tuna fish, or no sandwich. A ham sandwich is out of the question. Defining the limitations facing an individual or firm is a critical step in economic analysis. One can spend time yearning after the ham sandwich, or anything else outside the opportunity set, but when it comes to making choices and facing decisions, only what is within the opportunity set is relevant.

BUDGET AND TIME CONSTRAINTS

Constraints limit choices and define the opportunity set. In most economic situations, the constraints that limit a person's choices—that is, those constraints that actually are relevant—are not sandwich fixings, but time and money. Opportunity sets whose constraints are imposed by money are referred to as **budget constraints;** opportunity sets whose constraints are prescribed by time are called **time constraints.** A billionaire may feel that his choices are limited not by money but by time; while for an unemployed worker, time hangs heavy—lack of money rather than time limits his choices.

The budget constraint defines a typical opportunity set. Consider the budget constraint of Alfred, who has decided to spend $100 on either cassette recordings or compact discs. A CD costs $10, a cassette $5. So Alfred can buy 10 CDs or 20 cassettes; or 9 CDs and 2 cassettes; or 8 CDs and 4 cassettes. The various possibilities are set forth in Table 2.1. And they are depicted graphically in Figure 2.1:[1] Along the vertical axis we measure the number of cassettes purchased, and along the horizontal axis we measure the number of CDs. The line marked B_1B_2 is Alfred's budget constraint. The extreme cases,

[1] See the Chapter Appendix for help in reading graphs.

Table 2.1 ALFRED'S OPPORTUNITY SET

Cassettes	CDs
0	10
2	9
4	8
6	7
8	6
10	5
12	4
14	3
16	2
18	1
20	0

where Alfred buys only CDs or cassettes, are represented by the points B_1 and B_2 in the figure. The dots between these two points, along the budget constraint, represent the other possible combinations. The cost of each combination of CDs and cassettes must add up to $100. The point actually chosen by

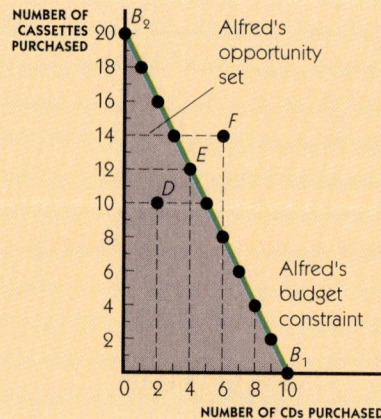

Figure 2.1 ALFRED'S BUDGET CONSTRAINT

The budget constraint identifies the limits of an individual's opportunity set between CDs and cassettes. Points B_1 and B_2 are the extreme options, where he chooses all of one and none of the other. His actual choice is point E. Choices from the shaded area are possible, but less attractive than choices actually on the budget constraint.

Figure 2.2 AN OPPORTU-NITY SET FOR WATCHING TV AND OTHER ACTIVITIES

This opportunity set is limited by a time constraint, which shows the trade-off a person faces between spending time watching television and spending it on other activities. At 5 hours of TV time per day, point D represents a typical choice for a Canadian.

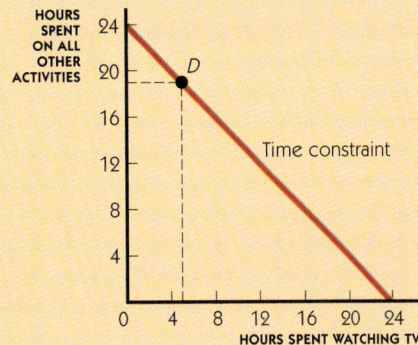

Alfred is labeled E, where he purchases 4 CDs (for $40) and 12 cassettes (for $60).

Alfred's budget constraint is the line that defines the outer limits of his opportunity set. But the whole opportunity set is larger. It also includes all points below the budget constraint. This is the shaded area in the figure. The budget constraint shows the maximum number of cassettes Alfred can buy for each number of CDs purchased, and vice versa. Alfred is always happiest when he chooses a point on his budget constraint rather than below it. To see why, compare the points E and D. At point E, he has more of both goods than at point D. He would be even happier at point F, where he has still more cassettes and CDs, but that point, by definition, is unattainable.

Figure 2.2 depicts a time constraint. The most common time constraint simply is that the sum of what an individual spends her time on each day—including sleeping—must add up to 24 hours. The figure plots the hours spent watching television on the horizontal axis and the hours spent on all other activities on the vertical axis. People—no matter how rich or how poor—have only 24 hours a day to spend on different activities. The time constraint is quite like the budget constraint. A person cannot spend more than 24 hours or fewer than zero hours a day watching TV. The more time she spends watching television the less time she has available for all other activities. Point D (for "dazed") has been added to the diagram at 5 hours a day—this is the amount of time the typical Canadian chooses to spend watching TV.

THE PRODUCTION POSSIBILITIES CURVE

Business firms and whole societies face constraints. They too must make choices limited to opportunity sets. The amounts of goods a firm or society could produce, given a fixed amount of land, labour, and other inputs, are referred to as its **production possibilities.**

As one commonly discussed example, consider a simple description of a society in which all economic production is divided into two categories, military spending and civilian spending. Of course, each of these two kinds of spending has many different elements, but for the moment, let's discuss the choice between the two broad categories. For simplicity, Figure 2.3 refers to military spending as "guns" and civilian spending as "butter." The production of guns is given along the vertical axis, the production of butter along the horizontal. The possible combinations of military and civilian spending—of guns and butter—is the opportunity set. Table 2.2 sets out some of the possible combinations: 90 million guns and 40 million tonnes of butter, or 40 million guns and 90 million tonnes of butter. These possibilities are depicted in the figure. In the case of a choice involving production decisions, the boundary of the opportunity set—giving the maximum amount of guns that can be produced for each amount of butter and vice versa—is called the **production possibilities curve.**

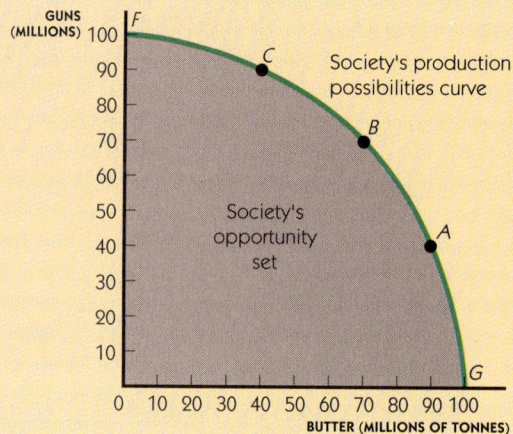

Figure 2.3 THE GUNS AND BUTTER TRADE-OFF

A production possibilities curve can show society's opportunity set. This one describes the trade-off between military spending ("guns") and civilian spending ("butter"). Points *F* and *G* show the extreme choices, where the economy produces all guns or all butter. Notice that unlike the budget and time constraints, the production possibilities line curves, reflecting diminishing returns.

Table 2.2 PRODUCTION POSSIBILITIES FOR THE ECONOMY

Guns (millions)	Butter (millions of tonnes)
100	0
90	40
70	70
40	90
0	100

When we compare the individual's opportunity set and that of society, reflected in its production possibilities curve, we notice one major difference. The individual's budget constraint is a straight line, while the production possibilities curve bows outwards. There is a good reason for this. An individual typically faces fixed **trade-offs:** if Alfred spends $10 more on CDs (that is, he buys one more CD), he has $10 less to spend on cassettes (he can buy two fewer cassettes).

On the other hand, the trade-offs faced by society are not fixed. If a society produces only a few guns, it will use those resources—the men and machines—that are best equipped for gun making. But as society tries to produce more and more guns, doing so becomes more difficult; it will increasingly have to rely on those who are less and less good at producing guns. It will be drawing these resources out of the production of other goods—in this case, butter. Thus, when the economy increases its production of guns from 40 million a year (point *A*) to 70 million (*B*), butter production falls by 20 million tonnes, from 90 million to 70 million tonnes. But if production of guns is increased further, to 90 million (*C*), an increase of only 20 million, butter production has to decrease by 30 million tonnes, to only 40 million tonnes. For each increase in the number of guns, the reduction in the number of tonnes of butter produced gets larger. That is why the production possibilities curve is curved.

The importance of the guns-butter trade-off was seen dramatically during World War II, when car production plummeted almost to zero as the automobile factories' production was diverted to tanks and other military vehicles.

In another example, assume that a firm owns land that can be used for growing wheat but not corn, and land that can grow corn but not wheat. In this case,

Table 2.3 DIMINISHING RETURNS

Labour in cornfield (no. of workers)	Corn output (bushels)	Labour in wheat field (no. of workers)	Wheat output (bushels)
1,000	60,000	5,000	200,000
2,000	110,000	4,000	180,000
3,000	150,000	3,000	150,000
4,000	180,000	2,000	110,000
5,000	200,000	1,000	60,000

the only way to increase wheat production is to move workers from the cornfields to the wheat fields. As more and more workers are put into the wheat fields, production of wheat goes up, but each successive worker increases production less. The first workers might pick the largest and most destructive weeds. Additional workers lead to better weeding, and better weeding leads to higher output. But the additional weeds rooted up are smaller and less destructive, so output is increased by a correspondingly smaller amount. This is an example of the general principle of **diminishing returns.** Adding successive units of any input such as fertilizer, labour, or ma-

chines to a fixed amount of other inputs—seeds or land—increases the output, or amount produced, but by less and less.

Table 2.3 shows the output of the corn and wheat fields as labour is increased in each field. Assume the firm has 6,000 workers to divide between wheat production and corn production. Thus, the second and fourth columns together give the firm's production possibilities, which are depicted in Figure 2.4.

INEFFICIENCIES: BEING OFF THE PRODUCTION POSSIBILITIES CURVE

There is no reason to assume that a firm or an economy will always be on its production possibilities curve. Any inefficiency in the economy will result in a point such as A in Figure 2.4, below the production possibilities curve. One of the major quests of economists is to look for instances in which the economy is inefficient in this way.

Whenever the economy is operating below the production possibilities curve, it is possible for us to have more of every good—more wheat and more corn, more guns and more butter. No matter what goods we like, we can have more of them. That is why we can unambiguously say that points below the production possibilities curve are undesirable. But this does not mean that every point on the production possibilities curve is better than any point below it. Compare points A and C in Figure 2.4. Corn

Figure 2.4 THE WHEAT AND CORN TRADE-OFF

This production possibilities curve shows that as wheat production increases, it becomes necessary to give up larger and larger amounts of corn. Or to put the same point a different way, as corn production falls, the resulting increase in wheat production gets smaller and smaller. Point A illustrates an inefficient outcome in this opportunity set.

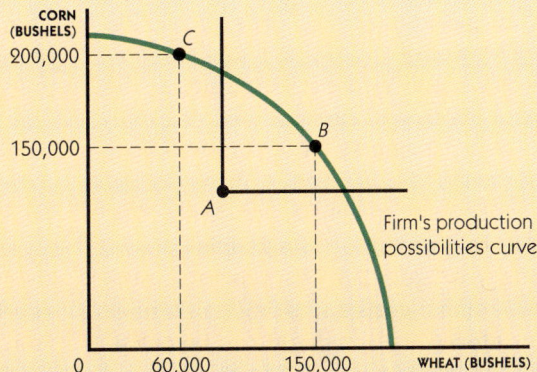

production is higher at *C*, but wheat production is lower. If people do not like corn very much, the increased corn production may not adequately compensate them for the decreased wheat production.

There are many reasons why the economy may be below the production possibilities curve. If land better suited for the production of corn is mistakenly devoted to the production of wheat, the economy will operate below its production possibilities curve. If some of society's resources—its land, labour, and capital goods—are simply left idle, as happens when there is a depression, the economy operates below the production possibilities curve. The kinds of inefficiencies discussed earlier in the chapter with inadequately or improperly defined property rights also result in operating below the production possibilities curve.

COST

The beauty of an opportunity set like the budget constraint, the time constraint, or the production possibilities curve is that it specifies the cost of one option in terms of another. If the individual, the firm, or the society is operating on the constraint or curve, then it is possible to get more of one thing only by sacrificing some of another. The "cost" of one more unit of one good is how much you have to give up of the other.

Economists thus think about cost in terms of trade-offs within opportunity sets. Let's go back to Alfred choosing between CDs and cassettes in Figure 2.1. The trade-off is given by the **relative price,** the ratio of the prices of CDs and cassettes. In our example, a CD cost $10, a cassette $5. The relative price is $10 ÷ $5 = 2; for every CD Alfred gives up, he can get two cassettes. Likewise, societies and firms face trade-offs along the production possibilities curve, like the one shown in Figure 2.3. There, point A is the choice where 40 million guns and 90 million tonnes of butter are produced. The trade-off can be calculated by comparing points *A* and *B*. Society can have 30 million more guns by giving up 20 million tonnes of butter.

Trade-offs are necessary because resources are scarce. If you want something, you have to pay for it; you have to give up something. If you want to go to the library tomorrow night, you have to give up going to the movies. If a sawmill wants to make more two-by-four beams from its stock of wood, it will not be able to make as many one-by-four boards.

OPPORTUNITY COSTS

If someone were to ask you right now what it costs to go to a movie, you would probably answer, "Eight dollars," or whatever you paid the last time you went to the movies. But with the concept of trade-offs, you can see that a *full* answer is not that simple. To begin with, the cost is not the $8 but what that $8 could otherwise buy. Furthermore, your time is a scarce resource that must be figured into the calculation. Both the money and the time represent opportunities forgone in favour of going to the movie, or what economists refer to as the **opportunity cost** of the movie. To apply a resource to one use means that it cannot be put to any other use. Thus, we should consider the next-best, alternative use of any resource when we think about putting it to any particular use. This next-best use is the formal measurement of opportunity cost.

Some examples will help to clarify the idea of opportunity cost. Consider a student, Sarah, who enrolls in university. She thinks that the cheque for tuition and room and board represents the costs of her education. But the economist's mind immediately turns to the job she might have had if she had not enrolled at university. If Sarah could have earned $15,000 from September to June, this is the opportunity cost of her time, and this forgone income must be added to the university bills in calculating the total economic cost of the school year.

Now consider a business firm that has bought a building for its headquarters that is bigger than necessary. If the firm could receive $20 per month in rent for each square metre of space that is not needed, then this is the opportunity cost of leaving the space idle.

The analysis can be applied to the government as well. The British Columbia government owns a vast amount of wilderness. In deciding whether it is

CLOSE-UP: OPPORTUNITY COSTS AND SMOKING

Since the 1970s when evidence began to accumulate that smoking is potentially harmful to one's health, governments have used regulations and tax policy both to discourage smoking and to raise revenues to cover the costs imposed on society by smokers. Not surprisingly, this has given rise to a battle of rights between smokers and nonsmokers. Nonsmokers claim that smokers impose large external costs on the rest of society which are not reflected in the price paid for cigarettes. On the other hand, smokers argue that the price and taxes they pay are more than enough compensation for any costs they impose on society, and that these policies unnecessarily interfere with their freedom to choose the amount of perfectly legal products they should consume.

The concept of opportunity cost can help us evaluate the net costs imposed on society by smokers. The question is whether the price paid by smokers covers all the costs to society of the activity. In the case of cigarettes, in addition to the production costs and the costs voluntarily assumed by smokers in deciding to smoke, there are certain external costs imposed on society at large. These include especially the health services provided to smokers and nonsmokers alike for smoking-related diseases. In addition, some economists count as part of social costs the opportunity cost of potential output lost due to the premature death of some smokers. On the other hand, smokers compensate society over and above the costs of producing cigarettes. This compensation takes two forms. One is the substantial government revenues from taxes on tobacco products. The other is the reduction in transfer payments that results from the fact that early death results in a reduction in public pension benefits that would otherwise accrue to elderly persons. In addition, premature death also economizes on certain types of public services used by the elderly, especially health services and residential care facilities.

A recent study by economists André Raynauld and Jean-Pierre Vidal of the University of Montreal attempted to place dollar values on these various amounts. They estimated that, using 1986 data, the social costs attributable to smoking were $669 million for all of Canada. These include both the total hospitalization and medical services costs and the cost to properties of accidental fires blamed on smokers' negligence. Against this, however, reductions in future hospital, medical, and residential care costs amounted to $462 million, leaving a net cost of $207 million. Note that the authors assume that smokers know that smoking is bad for their health and that they internalize the risk of premature death in their decision to smoke. Therefore, loss of years of a smokers' life is not an extra cost. The authors also state that there is no evidence that smoking is a cause of death for nonsmokers.

These costs are more than made up for by the taxes paid by smokers, estimated to be $3.17 billion and the savings in pension plan payments of $1.42 billion. When set against the net external costs imposed on nonsmokers, this leads Raynauld and Vidal to conclude that it is a myth that smokers impose a cost on society. Of course, many persons will dispute the choice of items to include in the costs of smoking and the way in which they are measured. Because of the difficulty of computing some costs, other economists may differ in their conclusions about the net costs of smoking.

Source: André Raynauld and Jean-Pierre Vidal, "Smokers' Burden on Society: Myth and Reality In Canada," *Canadian Public Policy* 18 (September 1992): 300–317.

worthwhile to convert some of that land into a provincial park, the government needs to take into account the opportunity cost of the land. The land might be used for growing timber or for grazing sheep. Whatever the value of the land in its next-best use, this is the economic cost of the provincial park. The fact that the government does not have to buy the land does not mean that the land should be treated as a free good.

Thus, in the economist's view, when rational firms and individuals take decisions—whether to undertake one investment project rather than another, whether to buy one product rather than another—they take into account *all* of the costs, the full opportunity costs, not just the direct expenditures.

SUNK COSTS

Economic cost includes costs, as we have just seen, that noneconomists often exclude, but it also ignores costs that noneconomists include. If an expenditure has already been made and cannot be recovered no matter what choice is made, a rational person would ignore it. Such expenditures are called **sunk costs.**

To understand sunk costs, let's go back to the movies, assuming now that you have spent $8 to buy a movie ticket. You were skeptical about whether the movie was worth $8. Half an hour into the movie, your worst suspicions are realized: the movie is a disaster. Should you leave the movie theatre? In making that decision, the $8 should be ignored. It is a sunk cost; your money is gone whether you stay or leave. The only relevant choice now is how to spend the next 90 minutes of your time: watch a terrible movie or go do something else.

Or assume you have just purchased a fancy laptop computer for $2,000. But the next week, the manufacturer announces a new computer with twice the power for $1,000; you can trade in your old computer for the new one by paying an additional $400. You are angry. You feel you have just paid $2,000 for a computer that is now almost worthless, and you have gotten hardly any use out of it. You decide not to buy the new computer for another year, until you have gotten at least some return for your investment. Again, an economist would say that you are not ap-

proaching the question rationally. The past decision is a sunk cost. The only question you should ask yourself is whether the extra power of the fancier computer is worth the additional $400. If it is, buy it. If not, don't.

MARGINAL COSTS

The third aspect of cost that economists emphasize is the extra costs of doing a little more of something, what economists call the **marginal costs.** These are weighed against the (additional) **marginal benefits** of doing it. The most difficult decisions we take are not whether to do something or not. They are whether to do a little more or a little less of something. Few of us waste much time deciding whether or not to work. We have to work; the decision is whether to work a few more or a few less hours. A country does not consider whether or not to have an army; it decides whether to have a larger or smaller army.

Jim has just obtained a job for which he needs a car. He must decide how much to spend on the car. By spending more, he can get a bigger and more luxurious car. But he has to decide whether it is worth a few hundred (or thousand) marginal dollars for a larger car or for extra items like cute hubcaps, power windows, and so on.

Polly is thinking about flying to Banff for a ski weekend. She has three days off from work. The air fare is $200, the hotel room costs $100 a night, and the ski ticket costs $35 a day. Food costs the same as at home. She is trying to decide whether to go for two or three days. The *marginal* cost of the third day is $135, the hotel cost plus the cost of the ski ticket. There are no additional transportation costs involved in staying the third day. She needs to compare the marginal cost with the additional enjoyment she will have from the third day.

People, consciously or not, think about the trade-offs at the margin in most of their decisions. Economists, however, bring them into the foreground. Like opportunity costs and sunk costs, marginal analysis is one of the critical concepts that enable economists to think systematically about the costs of alternative choices.

BASIC STEPS OF RATIONAL CHOICE

Identify the opportunity sets.

Define the trade-offs.

Calculate the costs correctly, taking into account opportunity costs, sunk costs, and marginal costs.

REVIEW AND PRACTICE

SUMMARY

1 The economists' basic model consists of rational, self-interested individuals and profit-maximizing firms, interacting in competitive markets.

2 The profit motive and private property provide incentives for rational individuals and firms to work hard and efficiently. Ill-defined or restricted property rights can lead to inefficient or counterproductive behaviour.

3 Society often faces choices between equality, which means allowing people more or less equal amounts of consumption, and efficiency, which requires incentives that enable people or firms to receive different benefits depending on their performance.

4 The price system in a market economy is one way of allocating goods and services. Other methods include rationing by queues, by lottery, by coupon, and by government regulation.

5 An opportunity set illustrates what choices are possible. Budget constraints and time constraints define individuals' opportunity sets. Both show the trade-offs of how much of one thing a person must give up to get more of another.

6 A production possibilities curve defines a firm's or society's opportunity set, representing the possible combinations of goods that the firm or society can produce. If a firm or society is producing below its production possibilities curve, it is said to be inefficient, since it could produce more of either good (or both goods) without producing less of the other.

7 The opportunity cost is the cost of using any resource. It is measured by looking at the next-best, alternative use to which that resource could be put.

8 A sunk cost is a past expenditure that cannot be recovered, no matter what choice is made in the present. Thus, rational decision makers ignore them.

9 Most economic decisions concentrate on choices at the margin, where the marginal (or extra) cost of a course of action is compared with its extra benefits.

KEY TERMS

perfect competition

price taker

basic competitive model

property rights

incentive-equality trade-off

rationing systems

opportunity sets

budget constraints

time constraints

production possibilities curve

diminishing returns

opportunity cost

sunk costs

marginal costs and benefits

REVIEW QUESTIONS

1 What are the essential elements of economists' basic competitive model?

2 Consider a lake in a provincial park where everyone is allowed to fish as much as he wants. What outcome do you predict? Might this problem be averted if the lake were privately owned, or fishing licences were sold?

3 Why might government policy to make the distribution of income more equitable lead to less efficiency?

4 List advantages and disadvantages of rationing by queues, by lottery, by coupon, and by government regulation. If the government permitted a black market to develop, might some of the disadvantages of these systems be reduced?

5 What are some of the opportunity costs of going to university? What are some of the opportunity costs a province should consider when deciding whether to widen a highway?

6 Give two examples of a sunk cost, and explain why they should be irrelevant to current decisions.

7 How is marginal analysis relevant in the decision about which car or which house to purchase? After you have decided which car to purchase, how is marginal analysis relevant?

PROBLEMS

1 Imagine that many businesses are located beside a river into which they discharge industrial waste. There is a city downstream that uses the river as a water supply and for recreation. If property rights to the river are ill defined, what problems may occur?

2 Suppose an underground reservoir of oil resides under properties owned by several different individuals. As each well is drilled, it reduces the amount of oil that others can take out. Compare how quickly the oil is likely to be extracted in this situation with how quickly it would be extracted if one person owned the property rights to drill for the entire pool of oil.

3 In some provinces, hunting licences are allocated by lottery; if you want a licence, you send in your name to enter the lottery. If the purpose of the system is to ensure that those who want to hunt the most get a chance to do so, what are the flaws of this system? How would the situation improve if people who won licences were allowed to sell them to others?

4 Imagine that during time of war, the government imposes coupon rationing. What are the advantages of allowing people to buy and sell their coupons? What are the disadvantages?

5 Kathy, a university student, has $20 a week to spend; she spends it either on junk food at $2.50 a snack, or on gasoline at $.50 per litre. Draw Kathy's opportunity set. What is the trade-off between junk food and gasoline? Now draw each new budget constraint she would face if

(a) a kind relative started sending her an additional $10 per week

(b) the price of a junk food snack fell to $2

(c) the price of gasoline rose to $.60 per litre.

In each case, how does the trade-off between junk food and gasoline change?

6 Why is the opportunity cost of going to medical school likely to be greater than the opportunity cost of going to university? Why is the opportunity cost of a woman with a university education having a child greater than the opportunity cost of a woman with just a secondary education having a child?

7 Bob likes to divide his recreational time between going to movies and listening to compact discs. He has twenty hours a week available for recreation; a movie takes two hours, and a CD takes one hour to listen to. Draw his "time budget constraint." Bob also has a limited amount of income to spend on recreation. He has $60 a week to spend on recreational activities; a movie costs $5, and a CD costs $12. (He never likes to listen to the same CD twice.) Draw his budget constraint. What is his opportunity set?

Whether the old saying that a picture is worth a thousand words under- or overestimates the value of a picture, economists find graphs extremely useful.

For instance, look at Figure 2.5; it is a redrawn version of Figure 2.1, showing the budget constraint—the various combinations of CDs and cassettes an individual, Alfred, can purchase. More generally, a graph shows the relationship between two variables—here, the number of CDs and the number of cassettes that can be purchased. The budget constraint gives the maximum number of cassettes that can be purchased, given the number of CDs that have been bought.

In a graph, one variable (here, CDs) is put on the horizontal axis and the other variable on the vertical axis. We read a point such as E by looking down to the horizontal axis and seeing that it corresponds to 4 CDs, and by looking across to the vertical axis and seeing that it corresponds to 12 cassettes. Similarly, we read point A by looking down to the horizontal axis and seeing that it corresponds to 5 CDs, and by looking across to the vertical axis and seeing that it corresponds to 10 cassettes.

In the figure, each of the points from the table has been plotted, and then a curve has been drawn through those points. The "curve" turns out to be a straight line in this case, but we still use the more general term. The advantage of the curve over the individual points is that with it, we can read off from the graph points on the budget constraint that are not in the table.

Sometimes, of course, not every point on the graph is economically meaningful. You cannot buy half a cassette or half a CD. For the most part, we ignore these considerations when drawing our graphs; we simply pretend that any point on the budget constraint is actually possible.

SLOPE

In any diagram, the amount by which the value along the vertical axis increases from a change in a unit along the horizontal axis is called the **slope,** just like the slope of a mountain. Slope is sometimes described as "rise over run," meaning that the slope of a line can be calculated by dividing the change on the vertical axis (the "rise") by the change on the horizontal axis (the "run").

Look at Figure 2.5. As we move from E to A, increasing the number of CDs by 1, the number of cassettes purchased falls from 12 to 10. For each

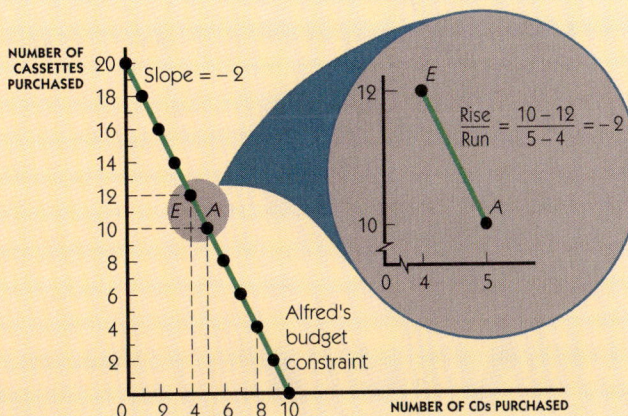

Figure 2.5 READING A GRAPH: THE BUDGET CONSTRAINT

Graphs can be used to show the relationship between two variables. This one shows the relationship between the variable on the vertical axis (the number of cassettes Alfred can buy) and the variable on the horizontal axis (the number of CDs).

The slope of a curve like the budget constraint gives the change in the number of cassettes that can be purchased as Alfred buys one more CD. The slope of the budget constraint is negative.

Slope = −2

$$\frac{\text{Rise}}{\text{Run}} = \frac{10 - 12}{5 - 4} = -2$$

Alfred's budget constraint

NUMBER OF CASSETTES PURCHASED

NUMBER OF CDs PURCHASED

Figure 2.6 **POSITIVELY SLOPED CURVE**

Income increases with the number of years of schooling.

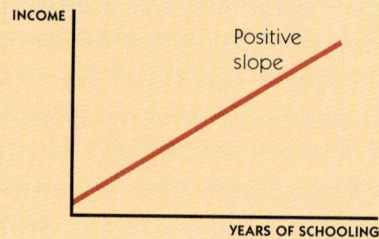

additional CD bought, the feasible number of cassettes that can be purchased falls by 2. So the slope of the line is

$$\frac{\text{rise}}{\text{run}} = \frac{10 - 12}{5 - 4} = \frac{-2}{1} = -2.$$

When, as in Figure 2.5, the variable on the vertical axis falls when the variable on the horizontal axis increases, the curve, or line, is said to be **negatively sloped.** A budget constraint is always negatively sloped. But when we describe the slope of a budget constraint, we frequently omit the term "negative." We say the slope is 2, knowing that since we are de-

scribing the slope of a budget constraint, we should more formally say that the slope is negative 2. Alternatively, we sometimes say that the slope has an absolute value of 2.

Figure 2.6 shows the case of a curve that is **positively sloped.** The variable along the vertical axis, income, increases as schooling increases, giving the line its upward tilt from left to right.

In later discussions, we will encounter two special cases. A line that is very steep has a very large slope; that is, the increase in the vertical axis for every unit increase in the horizontal axis is very large. The extreme case is a perfectly vertical line, and we say then that the slope is infinite (Figure 2.7, panel A). At the

Figure 2.7 **LIMITING CASES**

In panel A, the slope of a vertical straight line is infinite. In panel B, the slope of a horizontal straight line is zero.

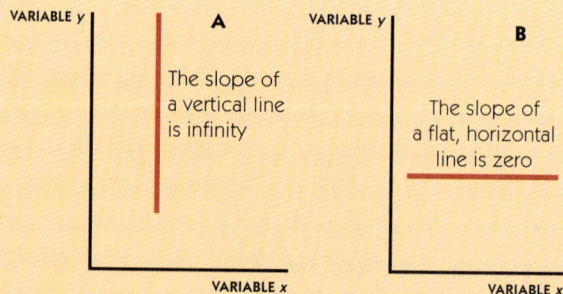

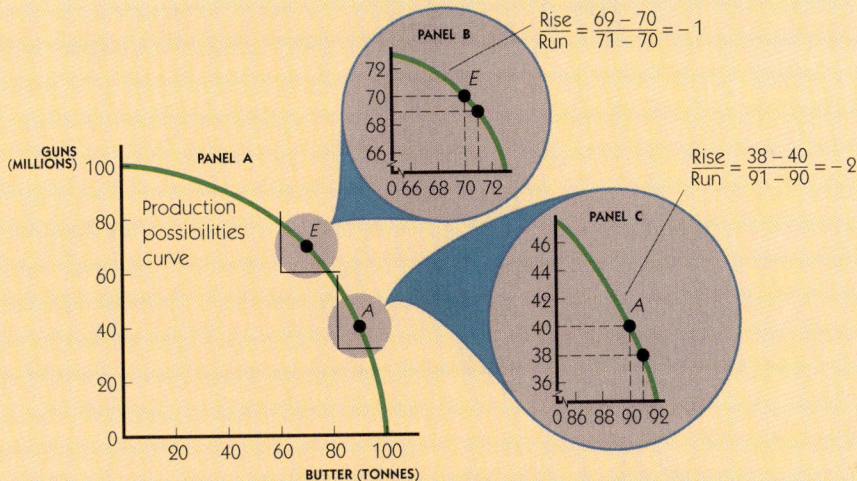

Figure 2.8 THE GUNS AND BUTTER TRADE-OFF

Panel A shows a trade-off between military spending ("guns") and civilian spending ("butter"), where society chooses point E. Panel B is an enlargement of the area around E, which focuses on the slope there, which also measures the marginal trade-offs society faces near that point. Similarly, panel C is an enlargement of the area around A and shows the marginal trade-offs society faces near that point.

other extreme is a flat, horizontal line; since there is no increase in the vertical axis no matter how large the change along the horizontal, we say that the slope of such a curve is zero (panel B).

Figures 2.5 and 2.6 both show straight lines. Everywhere along the straight line, the slope is the same. This is not true in Figure 2.8, which repeats the production possibilities curve shown originally in Figure 2.3. Look first at point E. Panel B of the figure blows up the area around E, so that we can see what happens to the output of guns when we increase the output of butter by 1. From the figure, you can see that the output of guns decreases by 1. Thus, the slope is

$$\frac{\text{rise}}{\text{run}} = \frac{69 - 70}{71 - 70} = -1.$$

Now look at point A, where the economy is producing more butter. The area around A has been blown up

in panel C. Here, we see that when we increase butter by 1 more unit, the reduction in guns is greater than before. The slope at A is

$$\frac{\text{rise}}{\text{run}} = \frac{38 - 40}{91 - 90} = -2.$$

With curves such as the production possibilities curve, the slope differs as we move along the curve.

INTERPRETING CURVES

Look at Figure 2.9. Which of the two curves has a larger slope? The one on the left appears to have a slope that has a larger absolute value. But look carefully at the axes. Notice that in panel A, the vertical axis is stretched relative to panel B. The same distance that represents 20 cassettes in panel B represents only 10 cassettes in panel A. In fact, both panels

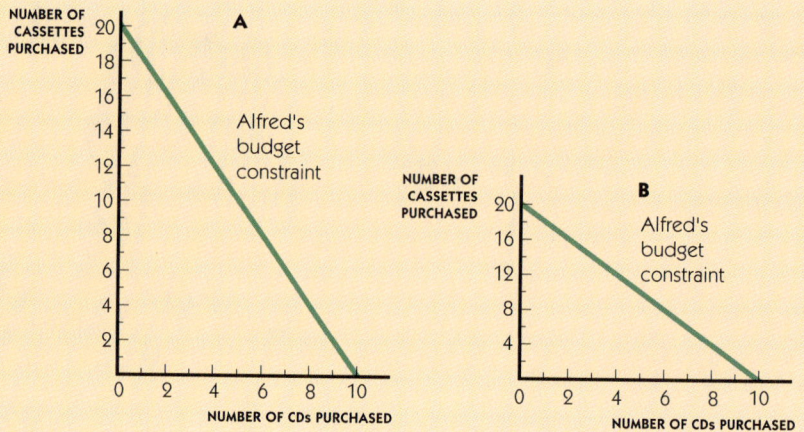

Figure 2.9 **SCALING AND SLOPE**

Which of these two lines has the steeper slope? The units along the vertical axis have changed. The two curves have exactly the same slope.

represent the same budget constraint. They have exactly the same slope.

This kind of cautionary tale is as important in looking at the graphs of data that were common in Chapter 1 as it is in looking at the relationships presented in this chapter that produce smooth curves. Compare, for instance, panels A and B of Figure 2.10.

Which of the two curves exhibits more variability? Which looks more stable? Panel B appears to show that car production does not change much over time. But again, a closer look reveals that the axes have been stretched in panel A. The two curves are based on exactly the same data, and there is really no difference between them.

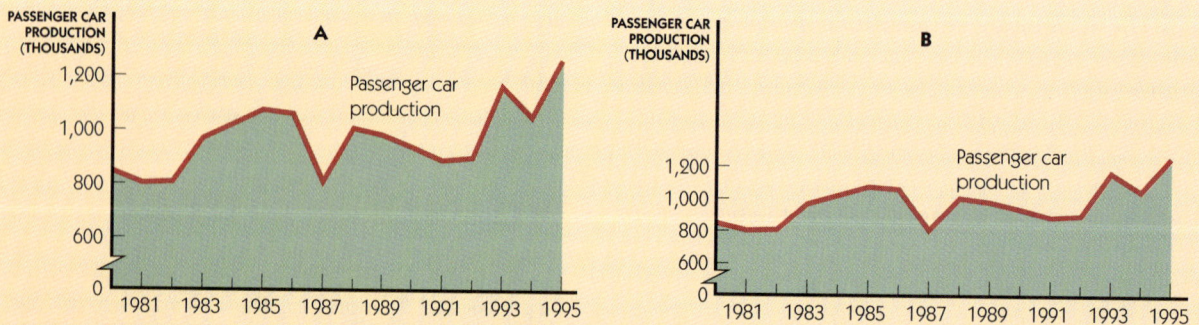

Figure 2.10 **SCALING AND GRAPHS OF DATA**

Which of these two curves shows greater variability in the output of cars over time? The two curves plot the same data.

The vertical scale has again been changed. *Source:* Motor Vehicle Manufacturers Association of Canada, 1995.

CHAPTER 3

TRADE

A creature on another planet looking down at a developed modern economy on earth might compare human activity to an enormous ant colony. Each ant seemingly has an assigned task. Some stand guard. Some feed the young. Some harvest food and others distribute it. Some shuffle paper, scribble notes in books, and keyboard at computer consoles. Others work in factories, tightening screws, running machines, and so on. How is all of this activity coordinated? No dictator or superintelligent computer is giving instructions. Yet somehow an immense amount is accomplished in a reasonably coordinated way. Understanding how a complex economy operates—how it is that certain individuals do one task, others do another, how information is communicated and decisions taken—is a central objective of economics.

This chapter discusses the problem of economic interdependence at two levels: individuals and firms within a country, and countries within the world economic community. Many of the same principles apply at both levels.

KEY QUESTIONS

1 Why is trade (exchange) mutually beneficial?

2 What are the similarities and differences between trade (exchange) between individuals within a country and trade between countries?

3 What determines what any particular country produces and sells on the international market? What is meant by comparative advantage, and why does it play such an important role?

4 What are the gains from specialization?

5 How valid is the argument, so often heard in political circles, that trade should be restricted?

THE BENEFITS OF ECONOMIC INTERDEPENDENCE

We begin by considering the benefits of trade, specifically the exchange of goods that are already available in the economy.

THE GAINS FROM TRADE

When individuals own different goods or have different desires, or both, there is an opportunity for trades that benefit all parties to the trade. Kids trading hockey cards learn the basic principles of exchange. One has two Mario Lemieux cards, the other has two Eric Lindros cards. A trade will benefit both of them. The same principle applies to countries. Canada has more natural gas than it can use, but it does not produce enough fruit to feed its populace. The United States has more fruit than Americans can consume, but needs natural gas. Trade can benefit both countries.

Voluntary trade involves only winners. If a trade would make a loser of any party, that party would choose not to trade. Thus, a fundamental consequence of voluntary exchange is that it benefits everyone involved.

FEELING "JILTED" IN TRADE

In spite of the seemingly persuasive argument that individuals engage in trade voluntarily only if they think they will be better off as a result, people often walk away from a deal believing they have been hurt.

It is important to understand that when economists say that a voluntary trade makes the two traders better off, they do not mean that it makes them both happy.

Imagine, for example, that Frank brings an antique rocking chair to a flea market to sell. He is willing to sell it for $100 but hopes to sell it for $200. Helen comes to the flea market planning to buy such a chair, hoping to spend only $100, but willing to pay as much as $200. They argue and negotiate, eventually settle on a price of $125, and make the deal. But when they go home, they both complain. Frank complains the price was too low, and Helen that it was too high.

From an economist's point of view, such complaints are self-contradictory. If Frank *really* thought $125 was too low, he would not have sold at that price. If Helen *really* thought $125 was too high, she would not have paid the price. Economists argue that people reveal their preferences not by what they say, but by what they do. If one voluntarily agrees to make a deal, one also agrees that the deal is, if not perfect, at least better than the alternative of not making it.

Two common objections are made to this line of reasoning. Both involve Frank's or Helen's "taking advantage" of the other. The implication is that if a buyer or a seller can take advantage, then the other party may be a loser rather than a winner.

The first objection is that either Frank or Helen may not really know what is being agreed to. Perhaps Frank doesn't realize that the chair is an antique; Helen does, and by neglecting to tell Frank, manages to buy it for only $125. Perhaps Frank knows the rockers fall off but sells the chair without telling this to Helen, thus keeping the price high. In either case, lack of relevant information makes someone a loser after the trade.

The second objection concerns equitable division of the **gains from trade.** Since Helen would have been willing to pay as much as $200, anything she pays less than that is **surplus,** the term economists use for a gain from trade. Similarly, since Frank would have been willing to sell the chair for as little as $100, anything he receives more than that is also surplus. The total dollar value of the gain from trade is $100—the difference between the maximum price Helen was willing to pay and the minimum price at which Frank was willing to sell. At a price of $125, $25 of the gain went to Frank, $75 to Helen. The second objection is that such a split is not fair.

Economists do not have much patience with these objections. Like most people, they favour making as much information public as possible, and they think vendors and customers should be made to stand behind their promises. But economists also point out that second thoughts and "If only I had known" are not relevant. If Frank sells his antique at a flea market instead of having it evaluated by reputable antique dealers, he has made a voluntary decision to save his time and energy. If Helen buys an antique at a flea market instead of going to a reputable dealer, she knows she is taking a risk.

The logic of free exchange, however, does not say that everyone must express happiness with the result. It simply says that when people choose to make a deal, they prefer making it to not making it. And if they prefer the deal, they are by definition better off *in their own minds* at the time the transaction takes place.

The objections to trade nonetheless carry an important message: most exchanges that happen in the real world are considerably more complicated than the Frank-Helen chair trade. They involve problems of information, estimating risks, and expectations about the future. These complications will be discussed throughout the book. So without going into too much detail at the moment, let's just say that if you are worried that you do not have the proper information to make a trade, shop around, get a guarantee or expert opinion, or buy insurance. If you choose to plunge ahead without these precautions, don't pretend you didn't have other choices. Like those who buy a ticket in a lottery, you know you are taking chances.

ECONOMIC RELATIONS AS EXCHANGES

Individuals in our economy are involved in masses of voluntary trades. They "trade" their labour services (time and skills) to their employer for dollars. They then trade dollars with a multitude of merchants for goods (like gasoline and groceries) and services (like plumbing and hair styling). The employer trades the goods it produces for dollars, and trades those dollars for labour services. Even your savings account can be viewed as a trade: you give the bank $100 today in exchange for the bank's promise to give you $105 at the end of the year, your original deposit plus 5 percent interest.

Unlike Frank's sale of the rocking chair to Helen, most trades take place anonymously at prices that are posted beforehand rather than decided by one-on-one bargaining. But even though neither party has any influence over the market price, there are still gains from trade associated with market transactions. When the price of a loaf of bread is $1.50, consumers will purchase it if the value they place on a loaf is at least $1.50. That goes not only for the first loaf they purchase but for the second, third, and so on. The excess of the value they place on all loaves of bread they purchase above what they actually pay for them is referred to as their **consumer surplus**—simply, their individual gain from trade. Similarly, producers will supply the bread as long as the cost of supplying the bread is no more than $1.50. The excess of the price of bread over the cost of producing it is called **producer surplus.** The total gain from trade in the bread market is the sum of consumer and producer surpluses of all buyers and sellers. The notions of consumer and producer surplus are important in understanding the benefits of the market system of allocating resources and will be returned to in later chapters.

TRADE BETWEEN COUNTRIES

Why is it that people engage in this complex set of economic relations with others? The answer is that people are better off as a result of trading. Just as individuals *within* a country find it advantageous to trade with one another, so too do countries find trade advantageous. Just as it is impossible for any individual to be self-sufficient, it is impossible for a country to be self-reliant without sacrificing its standard of living. Canada has long been part of an international economic community, and this participation has grown in recent decades. How has this affected the three main markets in the Canadian economy?

Interdependence in the Product Market   In 1994, close to a third of the good and services sold in Canada were **imports,** goods produced abroad but sold domestically. Roughly two thirds of motor vehicles sold in Canada were imported, along with a third of the oil, virtually all of the CDs and VCRs, and some basic foodstuffs like bananas, coffee, and tea. Not surprisingly, two thirds of the imports into Canada came from the United States, and that proportion may even rise as the Canada-U.S. Free Trade Agreement negotiated by the two countries in 1987 continues to work its way through. At the same time, Canadian producers sell a third of everything they produce as **exports,** goods produced domestically but sold abroad; almost three quarters of Canada's exports go to the United States. Fully 70 percent of motor vehicles produced in Canada are exported, as are 30 percent of oil and gas produced, and even higher proportions of wheat and forest products.

The Canadian economy has always been heavily dependent on trade, though the extent of dependency has changed over time. The share of both exports and imports plummeted dramatically during the Great Depression and rose rapidly in World War II. Figure 3.1 shows how exports and imports have varied as a proportion of national income, known as gross domestic product (GDP), over the postwar period. The proportions initially declined from the immediate postwar levels of just over one quarter of GDP to less than one fifth in the mid-1950s. They have been increasing for much of the postwar period, reaching almost one third, with temporary declines during major recessions. Canadian trade as a share of GDP is comparable to that of Britain and France, and over twice as high as that of the United States. This reflects the fact that smaller countries tend to be more dependent than larger ones on international trade.

Earnings from exports constitute a major source of income for some of our largest corporations, accounting for 85 percent of sales for Chrysler Canada, 84 percent for Pratt & Whitney Canada, and 60 percent for IBM Canada. Table 3.1 gives some other examples of large companies that rely heavily on exports. It is interesting to note that over half of these companies are foreign-owned, which is another feature of a highly open economy like Canada's.

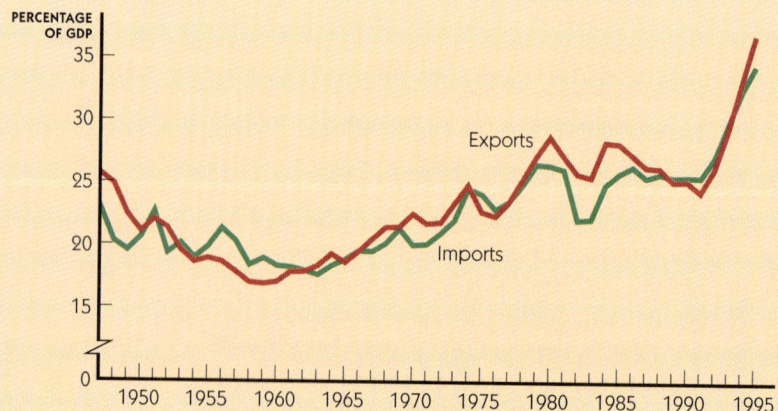

Figure 3.1 INTERNATIONAL TRADE

Here, Canadian imports and exports are both expressed as a percentage of the gross domestic product (GDP). Notice that trade has increased in the last thirty years and that imports have grown relative to exports in recent years. *Source:* Statistics Canada, CANSIM Database 1996.

Table 3.1 EXPORT-DEPENDENT BIG COMPANIES

Company and product	Rank by export sales	Exports as percentage of sales
Chrysler Canada (automobiles)	2	85
Pratt & Whitney Canada (aerospace)	14	84
Canfor (forest products)	18	81
Stone Consolidated (forest products)	23	73
Canadian Reynolds (metals)	26	73
General Motors Canada (automobiles)	1	67
Falconbridge (mining)	17	67
IBM Canada (computers)	4	60
Abitibi-Price (forest products)	16	55
Fletcher Challenge Canada (forest products)	19	53
Ford Canada (automobiles)	3	52
Bombardier (engineering)	7	47
Inco (nickel)	13	41
MacMillan Bloedel (forest products)	11	36
Amoco Canada (energy)	9	35
Noranda (resources)	8	34

Source: The Globe and Mail Report on Business Magazine, July 1995, p. 89.

Interdependence in the Labour Market International interdependence extends beyond the mere shipping of goods between countries. More than 98 percent of Canadian citizens either immigrated here from abroad or are descended from people who did so. The flow of immigrants has varied considerably over time. The numbers increased rapidly from the 1850s until World War I. In the period 1910–14, about three million settlers arrived from Europe and Britain, mainly to the Prairie provinces. Immigration fell dramatically during the war and did not pick up again until the mid-1920s, again largely from the British Isles and Europe. It fell off considerably after the Crash of 1929 and was virtually nonexistent until after World War II. In the late 1940s and early 1950s, the numbers of immigrants started to increase rapidly; again they were mainly Europeans, many of them having been displaced by the war. By the end of the 1950s, the immigrant profile started to change considerably: from rural to urban workers, and from European to other nationalities. The annual number of immigrants tripled between 1961 and 1967, when it reached 220,000. It then fell off and averaged about 140,000 per year until the early 1980s. With the recession of 1981–82, immigration began to fall to less than 100,000, but since then it has gradually recovered to 200,000. By 1989, almost one half of all immigrants came from Asia, about one quarter from Europe, one eighth from North and Central America, and the remainder mostly from Africa and South America. These proportions have held steady in the 1990s.

The nations of Europe have increasingly recognized the benefits that result from this international movement of workers. One of the important provisions of the treaty establishing the European Union (EU), an agreement among most countries within Western Europe, allows for the free flow of workers between member nations of the EU.

Interdependence in the Capital Market Canada has always borrowed heavily from abroad, but the country also invests heavily overseas. In 1994, Canadians invested approximately $13 billion in foreign countries (factories, businesses, buildings, loans, etc.), while foreign investors invested over $30 billion in Canada. Canadian companies have sought out profitable opportunities abroad, where they can use their special skills and knowledge to earn high returns. They have established branches and built factories in the United States, Europe, Latin America, and elsewhere in the world.

Just as the nations of Western Europe have recognized the advantages that follow from the free flow of goods and labour among their countries, so too have they recognized the gains from the free flow of capital. Funds can be invested where they yield the highest returns. Knowledge and skills from one country can be combined with capital from another to produce goods that will be enjoyed by citizens of all countries. Though the process of liberalizing the flow of goods, labour, and capital among countries of the European Union has been going on for more than twenty years, 1992 marks the crucial date at which all remaining barriers were officially removed.

MULTILATERAL TRADE

Many of the examples to this point have emphasized two-way trade. Trade between two individuals or countries is called **bilateral trade.** But exchanges between two parties is often less advantageous than trade between several parties, called **multilateral trade.** Such trades are observed between sports teams. The Toronto Blue Jays send a catcher to the St. Louis Cardinals, the Cardinals send a pitcher to the Montreal Expos, and the Expos send an out-fielder to the Blue Jays (see Figure 3.2A). No two of the teams was willing to make a two-way trade, but all can benefit from the three-way swap.

Countries function in a similar way. Japan has no domestic oil; it imports oil from Arabian countries. The Arabian countries want to sell their oil, but they want wheat and food, not the cars and television sets that Japan can provide. Canada can provide the missing link by buying cars and televisions from Japan and selling food to the Arab nations. Again, this three-way trade, shown in Figure 3.2B, offers gains that two-way trade cannot. The scores of na-tions active in the world economy create patterns far more complex than these simplified examples.

Figure 3.3 illustrates the construction of a Ford Escort in Europe, and dramatizes the importance of multilateral and interconnected trade relations. The parts that go into an Escort come from all over the world. Similar diagrams could be constructed for many of the components in the diagram; the alu-minum alloys may contain bauxite from Jamaica, the chrome plate may use chromium from South Africa, the copper for wiring may come from Chile.

Multilateral trade means that trade between any two participants may not balance. In Figure 3.2B, the Arab countries send oil to Japan but get no goods (only yen) in return. No one would say that the Arab countries have an unfair trade policy with Japan. Yet some politicians, newspaper columnists, and busi-ness executives complain that since Canada imports more from a particular country (often Japan) than it exports to that country, the trade balance is "unfair." There is a popular saying, "Trade is a two-way street." But trade in the world market involves hundreds of possible streets between nations. While there are legitimate reasons to be concerned with the overall

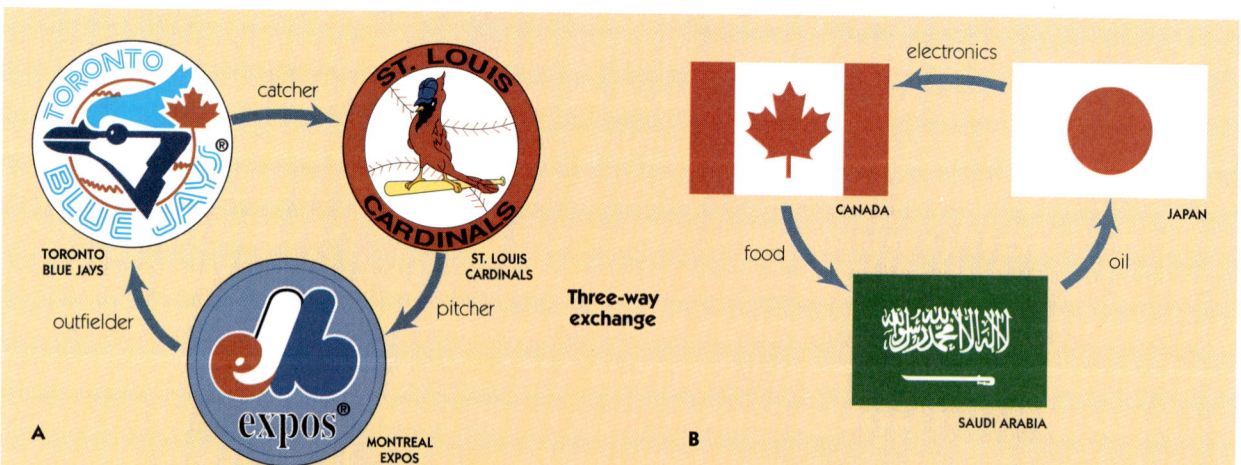

Figure 3.2 MULTILATERAL EXCHANGE

Panel A shows a multilateral, three-way trade among baseball teams. Notice that no two of the teams have all the ingredients for a mutually beneficial exchange. Panel B illustrates a multilateral exchange in international trade.

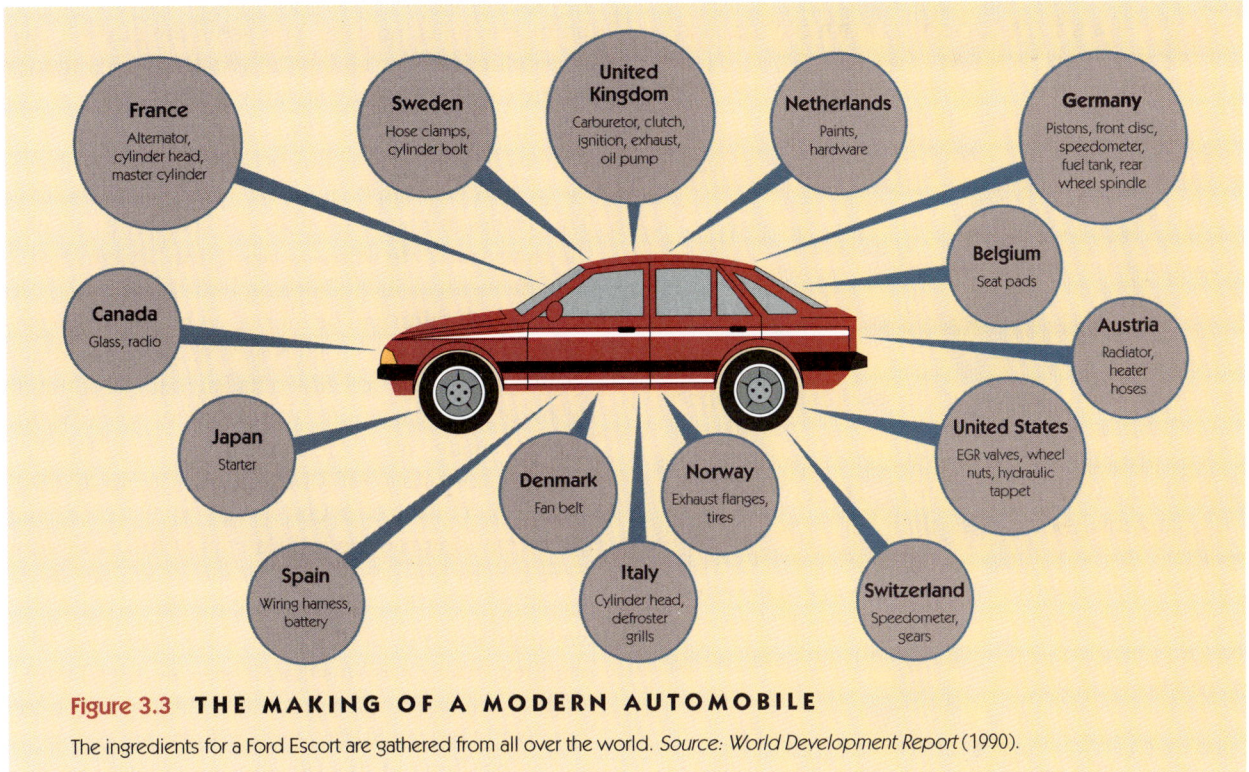

Figure 3.3 THE MAKING OF A MODERN AUTOMOBILE

The ingredients for a Ford Escort are gathered from all over the world. *Source: World Development Report* (1990).

Canadian trade deficit, there is no reason why Canadian exports and imports with any particular country should be balanced.

COMPARATIVE ADVANTAGE

We have so far focused on exchanges of existing goods. But clearly, most of what is exchanged must first be produced. Trade allows individuals and countries to concentrate on what they produce best.

Some countries are more efficient at producing almost all types of goods and services than other countries. The possession of superior production skills is called having an **absolute advantage,** and these advanced countries are said to have an absolute advantage over the others. How can the countries with disadvantages successfully engage in trade? The answer lies in the principle of **comparative ad-** **vantage,** which states that individuals and countries specialize in producing those goods in which they are *relatively,* not absolutely, more efficient.

To see what comparative advantage means, let's say that both Canada and Japan produce two goods, TV sets and wheat. The amount of labour needed to produce these goods is shown in Table 3.2. (These numbers are all hypothetical.) Canada is more efficient (spends fewer worker hours) at making both products. Canada can rightfully claim to have the more efficient TV industry, and yet it imports TV sets from Japan. Why? The opportunity cost, or *relative* cost, of making a TV set (in terms of labour used) in Japan relative to the cost of producing a tonne of wheat is low compared with Canada. That is, in Japan, it takes 15 times as many hours (120/8) to produce a TV set as a tonne of wheat; in Canada, it takes 20 times as many hours (100/5) to produce a TV set as a tonne of wheat. While Japan has an absolute

Table 3.2 LABOUR COST OF PRODUCING TV SETS AND WHEAT (worker hours)

	Canada	Japan
Labour required to make a TV set	100	120
Labour required to make a tonne of wheat	5	8

*dis*advantage in producing TV sets, it has a *comparative* advantage.

The principle of comparative advantage applies to individuals as well as countries. The president of a company might type faster than her secretary, but it still pays to have the secretary type her letters, because the president may have a comparative advantage at bringing in new clients, while the secretary has a comparative (though not absolute) advantage at typing.

PRODUCTION POSSIBILITIES SCHEDULES AND COMPARATIVE ADVANTAGE

The easiest way to understand the comparative advantage of different countries is to use the production possibilities schedule first introduced in Chapter 2. Figure 3.4 depicts hypothetical production possibili-

ties schedules for two countries, China and Canada, producing two commodities, textiles and buses. In both schedules, point E represents the current level of production. Let us look at what happens if each country changes its production by 100 buses.

China has a comparative advantage in producing textiles. If it reduces its bus production by 100, its textile production can be increased by 10,000 garments. This trade-off between buses and garments is called the **marginal rate of transformation.** By contrast, if Canada reduces its bus production by 100 buses, its textile production can be increased by only 1,000 garments. Conversely, if it increases its bus production by 100, it will have to reduce its garment production by only 1,000 garments. We can now see why the world is better off if each country exploits its comparative advantage. If China moves from E to E' (decreasing bus production by 100), 10,000 more garments can be produced. If Canada at the same time increases its bus production by 100, only 1,000 fewer garments will be produced. In the new situation, the world production of buses is unchanged, but world production of garments has increased by 9,000. So long as the production trade-offs differ—that is, so long as the marginal rates of transformation differ—it pays for China to specialize increasingly in textiles, and for Canada to specialize increasingly in buses. Notice that the analysis only requires knowledge about the production trade-offs. We do not need to know how much labour or capital is required in either country to produce either buses or garments.

Figure 3.4 EXPLOITING COMPARATIVE ADVANTAGE

The production possibilities schedules for China and Canada, each manufacturing two commodities, garments and buses, illustrate the trade-offs at different levels of production. Point E shows the current level of production for each country; E' illustrates a production decision that better exploits each country's comparative advantage.

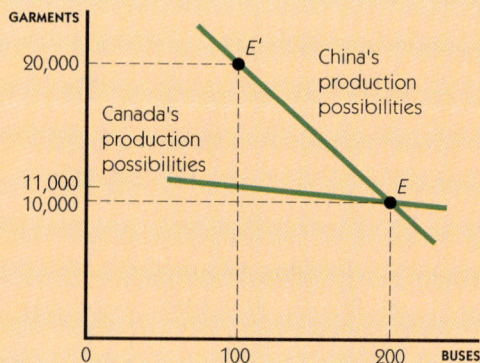

USING ECONOMICS: COMPARATIVE ADVANTAGE AND THE GAINS FROM TRADE

Problem: Using the earlier example of Japan and Canada, producing wheat and TV sets, calculate the trade-offs and show the gains from specialization.

Assume that both countries have 240,000 worker hours, initially divided equally between producing wheat and TV sets.

Solution: First, draw the production possibilities curves, as in the figure below. Since the costs (in worker hours) of producing each unit of each commodity are fixed, the production possibilities schedule is a straight line. If Canada used all its labour to produce TV sets, it would produce 2,400 TV sets; if it used all its labour to produce wheat, it would produce 48,000 tonnes of wheat. If Japan used all its labour to produce TV

sets, it would produce 2,000 TV sets; if it used all its labour to produce wheat, it would produce 30,000 tonnes of wheat.

In both curves, use point A to mark the current point of production, at which labour is equally divided between TV sets and wheat.

Next, calculate the slope of the production possibilities curve, giving the trade-offs: in Canada, increasing wheat output by 1,000 tonnes leads to a reduction of TV sets by 50, while reducing wheat output by 1,000 tonnes in Japan leads to an increase in TV sets of 66⅔. Thus, each shift of wheat production by 1,000 tonnes from Japan to Canada increases world TV set production by 16⅔.

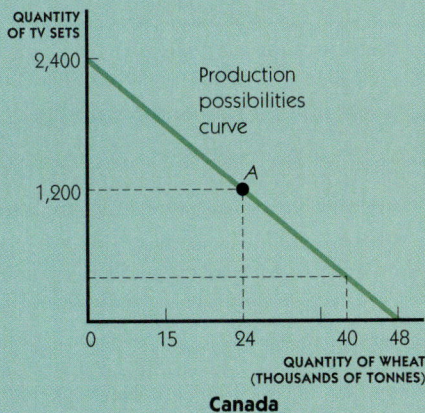

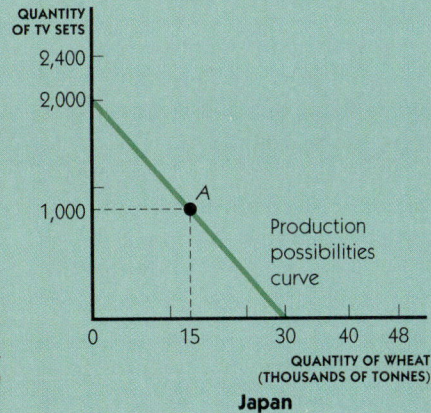

Canada

Japan

Though it pays countries to increase production and export of goods in which they have a comparative advantage and to import goods in which they have a comparative disadvantage, this may not lead to complete specialization. Thus, Canada continues to be a producer of textiles in spite of heavy imports from the Far East. This does not violate the principle

of comparative advantage: not all textiles require the same skill and expertise in manufacturing. Thus, while China may have a comparative advantage in inexpensive textiles, Canada may have a comparative advantage in higher-quality textiles. At the same time, the comparative advantage of other countries is so extreme in producing some goods that it does not pay for Canada to produce them at all: TVs, VCRs, and a host of other electronic gadgets, for example.

COMPARATIVE ADVANTAGE AND SPECIALIZATION

To see the benefits of specialization, consider the pencil. A tree containing the right kind of wood must be felled; it must be transported to a sawmill and cut into pieces that can be further processed into pencil casings. Then the graphite that runs through the pencil's center, the eraser at its tip, and the metal that holds the two together must each be produced by specially trained people. The pencil is a simple tool. But to produce it by oneself would cost a fortune in money and an eternity in time.

Why Specialization Increases Productivity Specialization increases productivity, thus enhancing the benefits of trade, for three reasons. First, specializing avoids the time it takes a worker to switch from one production task to another. Second, by repeating the same task, the worker becomes more skilled at it. And third, specialization creates a fertile environment for invention.

Workers may possess roughly equal skills before they begin specializing. But after workers have begun specializing, switching them back and forth between jobs will make production less efficient.

Dividing jobs so that each worker can practice a particular skill, called the **division of labour,** may increase productivity hundreds or thousands of times. Almost anyone who practices simple activities—like sewing on a button, shooting a basketball, or adding a column of numbers—will be quite a lot better at them than someone who has not practiced. Similarly, a country that specializes in producing sports cars may develop a comparative advantage. With its relatively large scale of production, it can divide tasks into separate assignments for different people; as they become better at their own tasks, productivity is increased.

At the same time, the division of labour often leads to invention. As someone learns a particular job extremely well, she might figure out ways of doing it better—including inventing a machine to do it. Specialization and invention reinforce each other. A slight initial advantage in some good leads to greater production of that good, thence to more in-vention, and thence to even greater production and further specialization.

Limits of Specialization The extent of division of labour, or specialization, is limited by the size of the market. There is greater scope for specialization in mass-produced manufactured goods like picture frames than in custom-made items like the artwork that gets framed. That is one reason why the costs of production of mass-produced goods have declined so much. Similarly, there is greater scope for specialization in a big city than a small town. That is why small stores specializing in a particular food or type of clothing thrive in cities but are rarer in smaller places.

The very nature of specialization limits gains. Repetitive jobs can lead to bored and unproductive workers. And single-track specialization inhibits the new insights and ideas that can come from engaging in a variety of work activities.

WHAT DETERMINES COMPARATIVE ADVANTAGE?

Earlier we learned that comparative advantage determines the pattern of trade. But what determines comparative advantage? In the modern world, this turns out to be a complex matter.

Natural Endowments In first laying down the principle of comparative advantage in the early 1800s, the great British economist David Ricardo used the example of Portugal's trade with Britain. In Ricardo's example, Portugal had an absolute advantage in producing both wool and wine. But it had a comparative advantage in producing wine, because compared with Britain it could produce wine better than it could produce wool. Thus, Britain had a comparative advantage in producing wool. In this and other early examples, economists tended to assume that a nation's comparative advantage was determined largely by its **natural endowments.** Countries with soil and climate that are *relatively* better for grapes than for pasture will produce wine; countries with soil and climate that are relatively better for pasture than for grapes will produce sheep and hence wool. Canada's abundance of arable land gives us a comparative advantage in agriculture.

Natural endowments still count in the modern

CLOSE-UP: THE COMPARATIVE ADVANTAGE OF CANADA

Three lists of goods define Canada's comparative advantage today. The first are those of which Canada exports a great deal and imports little—presumably the goods in which we have a strong comparative advantage. The second consists of goods of which Canada imports a great deal and exports little in which we have a strong comparative disadvantage. The third are goods of which Canada is both a high importer and high exporter in which we have neither a comparative advantage nor disadvantage and in which trade is presumably based on the gains from specialization.

Category 1: High Exports, Low Imports   Pulp and paper, lumber, wheat and other grains, fish and fish products, ores and concentrates, precious metals, aluminum, copper, nickel and other metals, nonmetallic minerals, fertilizers, coal, electricity. Notice that most of these goods are based on natural resources, as might be expected.

Category 2: High Imports, Low Exports Communications and electronics equipment, fruit and vegetables, cotton, wool and textiles, chemicals, consumer goods. In contrast with category 1, these goods tend either to be manufactured goods or agricultural goods for which the Canadian climate is unsuited.

Category 3: High Imports and Exports   Vehicles and parts, aircraft and parts, other transport equipment, oil and natural gas, industrial machinery, agricultural machinery, iron and steel, plastics, food products. Some of these goods are exported from one area of the country and imported into another, so transport costs play an important role. Others are manufactured goods that represent global industries in which products are shipped around the world.

economy: countries that have an abundance of low-skilled labour relative to other resources, such as South Korea and Hong Kong, have a comparative advantage in producing goods like textiles, which require a lot of handwork. But in today's technological age nations can also act to *acquire* a comparative advantage.

Acquired Endowments   The Japanese have little in the way of natural resources, yet they are a major player in international trade, in part because they have **acquired endowments.** Their case underscores the principle that by saving and accumulating capital and building large factories, a nation can acquire a comparative advantage in goods that, like steel, require large amounts of capital in their production. And by devoting resources to education, a nation can develop a comparative advantage in goods whose production requires a skilled labour force. Thus, the resources—human and physical—that a country has managed to acquire for itself can also give rise to comparative advantage.

Superior Knowledge   In the modern economy, comparative advantage may come simply from expertise in using resources productively. Switzerland has a comparative advantage in watches because over the years the country has accumulated superior knowledge and expertise in watchmaking. Belgium has a comparative advantage in fine lace; its workers have developed the requisite skills. A quirk of fate might have led Belgium to acquire a comparative advantage in watches and Switzerland one in lace.

Although sometimes patterns of specialization occur as an accident of history, in modern economies they are more likely to be a consequence of deliberate decisions. The U.S. semiconductor industry is a case in point. This industry manufactures the tiny silicon chips that control computers. Semiconductors were invented by an American, Robert Noyce,

THE FOUR BASES OF COMPARATIVE ADVANTAGE

1 Natural endowments, which consist of geographical determinants such as land, natural resources, and climate

2 Acquired endowments, which are the physical capital and human skills a nation has developed

3 Superior knowledge, including technological advantages, which may be acquired either as an accident of history or through deliberate policies

4 Specialization, which may create comparative advantages between countries that are similar in all other respects

and in the 1970s the United States had a powerful comparative advantage in manufacturing semiconductors; Japan managed to become a close competitor in the 1980s, but in the 1990s the United States has regained its leadership. The rise of the U.S. semiconductor industry was built in part on decisions by the federal government to fund the necessary research—primarily so the semiconductors could be used in guided missiles and other weapons. The rise of the Japanese industry was similarly based on decisions by that government to support its semiconductor industry.

Stories like that of the semiconductor industry have led some economists to argue that a government that wants to gain a technological advantage in a certain industry should encourage that industry by, for instance, supporting research relevant to that industry. In Canada, government support for the nuclear energy and aerospace industries have resulted in the country's occupying a niche in world markets for nuclear reactors and commuter airplanes.

Specialization   Earlier we saw how comparative advantage leads to specialization. Specialization may also lead to comparative advantage. The Swiss make fine watches and have a comparative advantage in that market based on years of unique experience. Such superior knowledge, however, does not explain why Britain, Germany, and the United States, which are at roughly the same level of technological expertise in building cars, all trade cars with one another. How can each country have a comparative advantage in making cars? The answer lies in specialization.

Both Britain and Germany may be better off if Britain specializes in producing sports cars and Germany in producing luxury cars, because specialization increases productivity. Countries enhance, or simply develop, a comparative advantage by spe-

cializing, just as individuals do. As a result, similar countries enjoy the advantages of specialization even when they specialize in different variations of basically similar products.

THE PERCEIVED COSTS OF INTERNATIONAL INTERDEPENDENCE

If the argument that voluntary trade must be mutually beneficial is so compelling, why has there been from time to time such strong antitrade sentiment in Canada and many other countries? This antitrade feeling is often labelled **protectionism,** because it calls for protecting the economy from the effects of trade. Those who favour protectionism raise a number of concerns. Some of the objections to international trade parallel the objections to trade among individuals noted earlier. Did they get a fair deal? Was the seller in a stronger bargaining position? For individuals and countries, such concerns revolve around how the *surplus* associated with the gains from trade is divided. Weak countries may feel that they are being taken advantage of by stronger countries. Their weaker bargaining position may mean that the stronger countries get *more* of the gains from trade. But this does not contradict the basic premise: both parties gain from voluntary exchange. All countries—weak as well as strong—are better off as a result of voluntary exchange.

But an important difference exists between trade among individuals and trade among countries. Some individuals within a country benefit from trade and

Despite the fact that the Canadian Constitution gives the federal government jurisdiction over international and interprovincial trade, the provinces have effectively been able to undertake policies that protect their own producers of some products within provincial borders. Beer is a case in point. Until recently, Ontario residents were unable to purchase Moosehead beer in Ontario, despite the fact that this Maritime brand is the most popular Canadian beer sold in the United States. The Ontario government did this by restricting distribution of beer to government-regulated outlets operated by the Ontario breweries, and these outlets only sold beer brewed in Ontario plants. Other provinces with breweries accomplished the same thing by other means, such as by selling the beer in provincially owned retail stores. The effect of this was not only to restrict the number of brands available but also to increase the cost of beer to the consumer and to induce inefficient methods of production. Thus, the major breweries were forced to operate small-scale plants in many provinces rather than concentrating their efforts in larger plants that could produce at lower costs.

The signing of the Canada–U.S. Free Trade Agreement in 1988 signalled the beginning of the end of this form of protection of the Canadian breweries. The practice has also been found to be in contravention of the General Agreement on Tariffs and Trade (GATT), which establishes rules of conduct for international trade with most other countries in the world. Provinces such as Ontario were forced to admit imported beer for sale in order to comply with these rules. They have begun to do so only gradually, recognizing that large-scale producers in the United States could underprice inefficient Canadian producers by a considerable margin, at least until the latter have a chance to rationalize their operations.

In fact, the provinces have found other ways to provide implicit protection to domestic breweries. In Ontario, a significant "handling" charge was imposed on imported beers. As well, a large "environmental tax" was imposed on beer cans and not on beer bottles or soft-drink cans. Since beer imported from the United States tends to be canned rather than bottled, this effectively imposed a differential cost on imported beer. (It also incidentally hurt Ontario can producers.) More recently, the Ontario government has imposed a "minimum price" on beer, allegedly for social reasons. This also tends to eliminate the cost advantage of imported beer.

As is often the case, entrepreneurs will find ways to skirt regulations that artificially keep prices high. In Ontario, firms have sprung up in most cities that specialize in assisting consumers to brew their own beer. Not only can this be done at relatively low cost, it can also avoid the punitive taxes imposed on alcoholic beverages by the federal and provincial governments.

some lose. Since the trade as a whole is beneficial to the country, the gains to the winners exceed the losses to the losers. Thus, in principle, those who benefit within the country could more than compensate those who lose. In practice, however, those who lose remain losers and obviously oppose opening up trade, using the argument that trade results in lost jobs and reduced wages. These concerns have become particularly acute as unskilled workers see themselves competing against the low-wage unskilled workers in Asia and Latin America: How can they compete without lowering their wages?

These concerns played a prominent role first in the debate in the late 1980s over the signing of the Canada-U.S. Free Trade Agreement, which allows American goods and services into Canada with no duties at all, and then in the early 1990s with the prospect of the North American Free Trade Agreement (NAFTA), which extends the privilege to Mexico. Advocates of freer trade pointed out that (1) more jobs would be created by the new export opportunities than would be lost through competition from American and Mexican firms, and (2) the jobs created pay higher wages, reflecting the benefits from specialization in comparative advantage.

Textile workers in Quebec who lose their jobs as a result of imports of inexpensive clothing from China cannot instantly convert themselves into forest workers in New Brunswick or engineers working for Bombardier. But the fact is that jobs are being destroyed and created all the time, irrespective of trade. Over the long run, the economic incentive of the new jobs at Bombardier may induce some in Manitoba to leave their semiskilled jobs and get the training that makes them eligible for the skilled jobs at Bombardier. The vacancy that that creates may be filled by someone who moves in from Ontario, leaving a vacancy there for the laid-off textile worker in Quebec.

Because of the practical complications and the very real costs of retraining and relocation, there is increasing recognition that government may need to play a role in facilitating job movements. To the extent that such assistance increases the number of winners from trade, it should reduce opposition to trade.

CONSENSUS ON BENEFITS OF TRADE

While the perceived costs of economic interdependence cannot be ignored—especially when they become the subject of heated political debate—the fact that the country as a whole benefits from freer trade is one of the central tenets on which there is a consensus among the vast majority of economists. Trade is our third consensus point:

3 Trade

There are gains from voluntary exchanges. Whether between individuals or across national borders, all can gain from voluntary exchange. Trade allows parties to specialize in those activities in which they have a comparative advantage.

REVIEW AND PRACTICE

SUMMARY

1 The benefits and costs of economic interdependence apply to individuals and firms within a country as well as to countries within the world. No individual and no country is self-sufficient.

2 Both individuals and countries gain from voluntary trade. There may be cases when there are only limited possibilities for bilateral trade (exchange between two parties), but the gains from multilateral trade (exchange among several parties) may be great.

3 The principle of comparative advantage asserts that countries should export the goods in which their production costs are *relatively* low.

4 Specialization tends to increase productivity for three reasons: specializing avoids the time it takes a worker to switch from one production task to another; workers who repeat a task become more skilled at it; specialization creates a fertile environment for invention.

5 A country's comparative advantage can arise from natural endowments or can result from acquired endowments, superior knowledge, or specialization.

6 There is a basic difference between trade among individuals and trade among countries: with trade among countries, some individuals within the country may actually be worse off. Though in principle, those who gain could more than compensate those who lose, such compensation is seldom provided. Though free trade enhances national income, fears about job loss and wage reductions among low-skilled workers have led to demands for protection. Government assistance to facilitate the required adjustments may be desirable.

KEY TERMS

gains from trade	imports
surplus consumer	exports
producer surplus	bilateral trade
	multilateral trade

absolute advantage	specialization
comparative advantage	natural endowments
division of labour	acquired endowments
marginal rate of transformation	protectionism

REVIEW QUESTIONS

1 Why are all voluntary trades mutually beneficial?

2 Describe a situation (hypothetical, if need be) where bilateral trade does not work, but multilateral trade is possible.

3 What are some of the similarities of trade between individuals and trade between countries? What is a key way in which they differ?

4 Does a country with an absolute advantage in a product necessarily have a comparative advantage in that product? Does a country with an absolute disadvantage in a product necessarily not have a comparative advantage in that product? Explain.

5 Why does specialization tend to increase productivity?

6 "A country's comparative advantage is dictated by its natural endowments." Discuss.

7 "If trade with a foreign country injures anyone in this country, the government should react by passing protectionist laws to limit or stop that particular trade." Comment.

PROBLEMS

1 Four players on a bantam hockey team discover that they have each been collecting hockey cards, and they agree to get together and trade. Is it possible for everyone to benefit from this agreement? Does the fact that one player starts off with many more cards than any of the others affect your answer?

2 Leaders in many less developed countries of Latin America and Africa have often argued that because they are so much poorer than the wealthy nations of the world, trade with the more developed economies of North America and Europe will injure them. They maintain that they must first become self-sufficient before than can benefit from trade. How might an economist respond to these claims?

3 If Canada changes its immigration quotas to allow many more unskilled workers into the country, who is likely to gain? Who is likely to lose? Consider the impact on consumers, on businesses that hire low-skilled labour, and on low-skilled labour in both Canada and the workers' countries of origin.

4 David Ricardo illustrated the principle of comparative advantage in terms of the trade between England and Portugal in port wine and wool. Suppose that in

England it takes 120 labourers to produce a certain quantity of wine, while in Portugal it takes only 80 labourers to produce that same quantity. Similarly, in England it takes 100 labourers to produce a certain quantity of wool, while in Portugal it takes only 90. Draw the opportunity set for each country, assuming that each has 72,000 labourers. Assume that each country commits half its labour to each product in the absence of trade, and designate that point on your graph. Now describe a new production plan, with trade, that can benefit both countries.

5 In 1981, the Canadian government prodded Japanese automakers to limit the number of cars they would export to Canada. Who benefited from this protectionism in Canada and in Japan? Who was injured in Canada and in Japan? Consider companies that produce cars, their workers, and consumers who buy cars.

6 For many years an international agreement called the Multifiber Agreement has limited the amount of textiles that the developed economies of North America and Europe can buy from poor countries in Latin America and Asia. Textiles can be produced by relatively unskilled labour with a reasonably small amount of capital. Who benefits from the protectionism of the Multifiber Agreement, and who suffers?

CHAPTER 4

DEMAND, SUPPLY, AND PRICE

C hoice in the face of scarcity, as we have seen, is the fundamental concern of economics. **Price,** to an economist, is what is given in exchange for a good or service and is a signal of choice. When the forces of supply and demand operate freely, price measures scarcity. As such, prices convey critical economic information. When the price of a resource used by a firm is high, the company has a greater incentive to economize on its use. When the price of a good that the firm produces is high, the company has a greater incentive to produce more of that good, and its customers have an incentive to economize on its use. In these ways and others, prices provide our economy with incentives to use scarce resources efficiently.

KEY QUESTIONS

1 What is meant by demand? Why do demand curves normally slope downwards? On what variables, other than price, does the quantity demanded depend?

2 What is meant by supply? Why do supply curves normally slope upwards? On what variables other than price does the quantity supplied depend?

3 Why do economists say that the equilibrium price occurs at the intersection of the demand and supply curves?

4 How do shifts in the demand and supply curves affect the equilibrium price?

THE ROLE OF PRICES

Prices are the way participants in the economy communicate with one another. Assume a drought hits the country, reducing drastically the supply of corn. Households will need to reduce their consumption of corn or there will not be enough to go around. But how will they know this? Suppose newspapers across the country ran an article informing people they would have to eat less corn because of a drought. What incentive would they have to pay attention to it? How would each family know how much it ought to reduce its consumption? As an alternative to the newspaper as a means of communication, consider the effect of an increase in the price of corn. The higher price conveys all the relevant information. It tells families corn is scarce at the same time as it provides incentives for them to consume less of it. Consumers do not need to know anything about why corn is scarce.

Price changes and differences present interesting problems and puzzles. In the late 1980s, while the price of an average house in Toronto went up by 20 percent, the price of a house in Regina increased by only 2 percent. Why? During the same period, the price of computers fell dramatically, while the price of bread rose, but at a much slower rate than the price of housing in Toronto. Why? The "price" of labour is just the wage or salary that is paid. Why does a physician earn twice as much as a university professor, though the university professor may have

performed better in the university courses they took together? Why did average wage rates rise in Canada in the postwar period? Why is the price of water, without which we cannot live, very low in most cases, but the price of diamonds, which we can surely live without, very high? The simple answer to all these questions is that in market economies like that of Canada, price is determined by supply and demand. Changes in prices are determined by changes in supply and demand.

Understanding the causes of changes in prices and being able to predict their occurrence is not merely of academic interest. One of the events that precipitated the French Revolution was the rise in the price of bread, for which the people blamed the government. Large price changes have also given rise to recent political turmoil in several countries, including Morocco, the Dominican Republic, Russia, and Poland.

The public sees much more in prices than the impersonal forces of supply and demand: the landlord raised the rent on the apartment; the oil company or the gas station owner raised the price of gasoline. These people and companies *chose* to raise their prices, says the average citizen, in moral indignation. True, replies the economist, but there must be some factor that made these people and companies believe that a higher price was not a good idea yesterday, but is today. And economists point out that at a different time, these same impersonal forces can force the same landlords and oil companies to cut their prices. Economists see prices, then, as symptoms of underlying causes, and focus on the forces of demand and supply behind price changes.

DEMAND

Economists use the concept of **demand** to describe the quantity of a good or service that a household or firm chooses to buy at a given price. It is important to understand that economists are concerned not just with what people desire, but with what they choose to buy given the spending limits of their budget constraint and the prices of various goods and services. In analyzing demand, the first question they ask is how the quantity of a good or service purchased by an individual changes as the price changes, keeping all other determinants of demand constant.

THE INDIVIDUAL DEMAND CURVE

Think about what happens as the price of chocolate bars changes. At a price of $5.00 you might never buy one. At $3.00 you might buy one as a special treat. At $1.25 you might buy a few, and if the price declined to $.50, you might buy a lot. The table in Figure 4.1 summarizes the weekly demand of one individual, Roger, for chocolate bars at these different prices. We can see that the lower the price, the larger the quantity demanded. We can also draw a graph that shows the quantity Roger demands at each price. The quantity demanded per week is measured along the horizontal axis, and the price is measured along the vertical axis. Figure 4.1 plots the points.

A smooth curve can be drawn to connect the points. This curve is called the **demand curve.** The demand curve gives the quantity demanded at each price. Thus, if we want to know how many chocolate bars a week Roger will demand at a price of $1.00, we simply look along the vertical axis at the price $1.00, find the corresponding point A along the demand curve, and then read down to the horizontal axis. At a price of $1.00, Roger buys 6 chocolate bars each week. Alternatively, if we want to know at what price he will buy just 3 chocolate bars, we look along the horizontal axis at the quantity 3, find the corresponding point B along the demand curve, and then

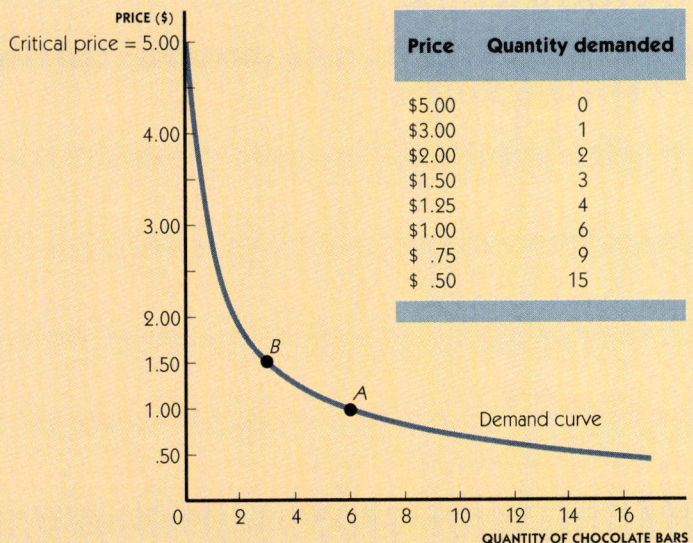

Figure 4.1 AN INDIVIDUAL'S DEMAND CURVE

This demand curve shows the quantity of chocolate bars that Roger consumes at each price. Notice that quantity demanded falls as the price increases, and the demand curve slopes down.

Price	Quantity demanded
$5.00	0
$3.00	1
$2.00	2
$1.50	3
$1.25	4
$1.00	6
$ .75	9
$ .50	15

read across to the vertical axis. Roger will buy 3 chocolate bars at a price of $1.50.

As the price of chocolate bars increases, the quantity demanded decreases. This can be seen from the numbers in Figure 4.1, and in the shape of its demand curve, which slopes downward from left to right. This relationship is typical of demand curves and makes common sense: the cheaper a good or service is (the lower down we look on the vertical axis), the more of it a person will buy (the farther right on the horizontal axis); the more expensive, the less a person will buy.

THE MARKET DEMAND CURVE

Suppose there were a simple economy made up of two people, Roger and Jane. Figure 4.2 illustrates how to add up the demand curves of these two individuals to obtain a demand curve for the market as a whole. We "add" the demand curves horizontally by taking at each price the quantities demanded by Roger and by Jane and adding the two together. Thus, in the figure, at the price of $.75 Roger demands 9 chocolate bars and Jane demands 11 per week, so that the total market demand is 20 chocolate bars per week. The same principles apply no

matter how many people there are in the economy. The **market demand curve** gives the total quantity of the good that will be demanded per period at each price. The table in Figure 4.3 summarizes the information for our example of chocolate bars; it gives the total quantity of chocolate bars demanded by everybody in the economy at various prices. If we had a figure like Figure 4.1 for each person in the economy, we would construct the table in Figure 4.3 by adding up, at each price, the total quantity of chocolate bars purchased per week. Figure 4.3 tells us, for instance, that at a price of $3.00 per chocolate bar, the total market demand for chocolate bars is 1 million per week, and that lowering the price to $2.00 increases market demand to 3 million.

Figure 4.3 also depicts the same information in a graph. As with Figure 4.1, price lies along the vertical axis, but now the horizontal axis measures the quantity demanded each week by everyone in the economy. Joining the points in the figure together, we get the market demand curve. If we want to know what the total demand for chocolate bars will be when the price is $1.50 per chocolate bar, we look on the vertical axis at the price $1.50, find the corresponding point A along the demand curve, and read down to the horizontal axis; at that price, total demand is 4 million chocolate bars. If we want to know what the

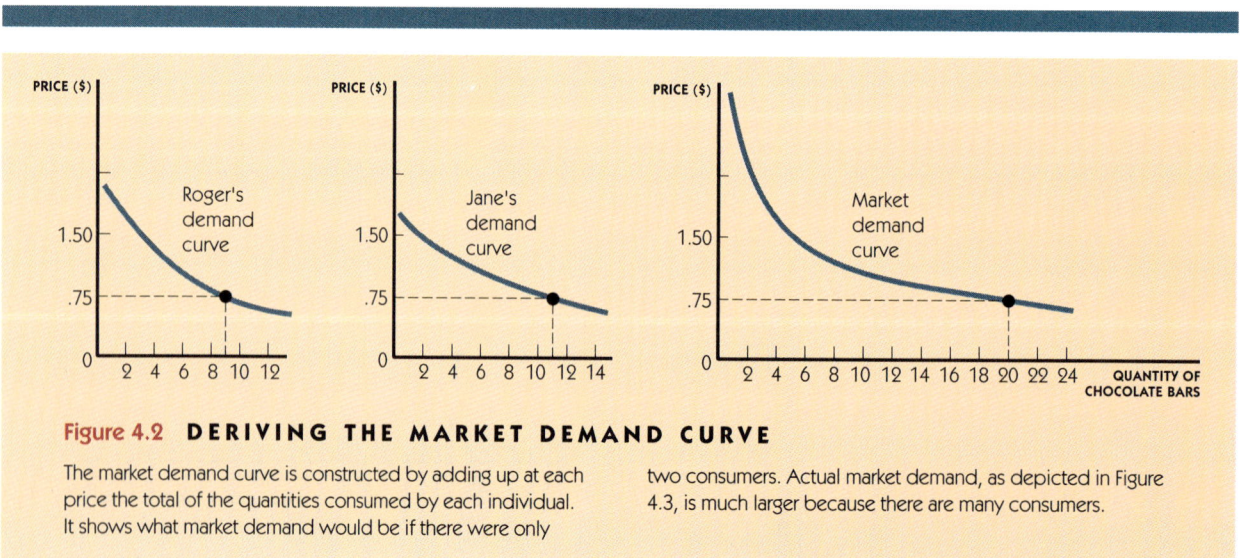

Figure 4.2 **DERIVING THE MARKET DEMAND CURVE**

The market demand curve is constructed by adding up at each price the total of the quantities consumed by each individual. It shows what market demand would be if there were only two consumers. Actual market demand, as depicted in Figure 4.3, is much larger because there are many consumers.

Figure 4.3 THE MARKET DEMAND CURVE

The market demand curve shows the quantity of the good or service demanded by all consumers in the market at each price. The market demand curve is downward-sloping, for two reasons: at a higher price each consumer buys less, and at high enough prices some consumers decide not to buy at all—they exit the market.

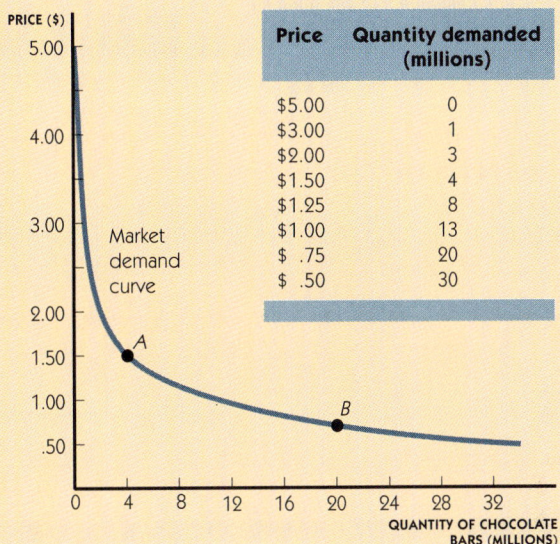

Price	Quantity demanded (millions)
$5.00	0
$3.00	1
$2.00	3
$1.50	4
$1.25	8
$1.00	13
$ .75	20
$ .50	30

price of chocolate bars will be when the demand equals 20 million, we find 20 million along the horizontal axis, look up to find the corresponding point B along the market demand curve, and read across to the vertical axis; the price at which 20 million chocolate bars are demanded is $.75.

Notice that just as the individual's demand decreases when the price of chocolate bars increases, so too when the price of chocolate bars increases, market demand decreases. Thus, the market demand curve also slopes downward from left to right. This general rule holds both because each individual's demand curve is downward-sloping and because as the price is increased, some individuals will decide to stop buying altogether. We have already examined the first of these reasons, but the second

deserves a closer look. In Figure 4.1, for example, Roger **exits the market**—consumes a quantity of zero—at the price of $5.00, at which his demand curve hits the vertical axis.

SHIFTS IN DEMAND CURVES

A demand curve depicts the quantity demanded at various prices, when all other factors are held constant. When the price of a good increases, the quantity demanded of that good decreases, when everything else is held constant. But in the real world, everything is not held constant. Any changes other than the price of the good in question shift the whole demand curve—change the amount that will be demanded at

DEMAND CURVE

The demand curve gives the quantity of the good demanded per stated time period at each price, holding all other determinants of demand constant.

Figure 4.4 SHIFTS IN THE DEMAND CURVE

A leftwards shift in the demand curve means that a lesser amount will be demanded at every given market price.

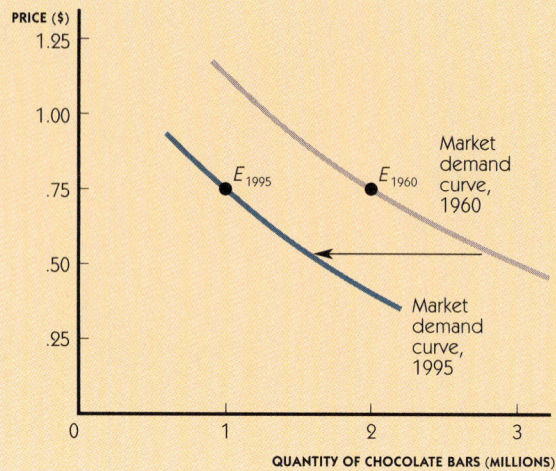

each price. The shift in the demand curve for chocolate bars as Canadians have become more weight-conscious provides a good example. Figure 4.4 shows hypothetical demand curves for chocolate bars in 1960 and in 1995. We can see from the figure, for instance, that the demand for chocolate bars at a price of $.75 has decreased from 2 million chocolate bars per week (point E_{1960}, the original equilibrium) to 1 million (point E_{1995}), as people have reduced their purchase of chocolate bars.

SOURCES OF SHIFTS IN DEMAND CURVES

Two of the factors that shift the demand curve—changes in income and in the price of other goods—are specifically economic factors. As an individual's income increases, she normally purchases more of any good or service. Thus, rising incomes shift the demand curve to the right, as illustrated in Figure 4.5. At each price, she consumes more of the good.

Figure 4.5 A RIGHTWARDS SHIFT IN THE DEMAND CURVE

If at each price there is an increase in the quantity demanded, then the demand curve will have shifted to the right, as depicted. An increase in income, an increase in the price of a substitute, or a decrease in the price of a complement can cause a rightwards shift in the demand curve.

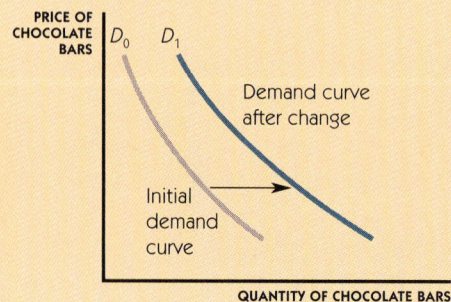

Changes in the price of other goods, particularly closely related goods, will also shift the demand curve for a good. For example, when the price of margarine increases, some individuals will substitute butter. Butter and margarine are thus **substitutes.** When people choose between butter and margarine, one important factor is the relative price, that is, the ratio of the price of butter to the price of margarine. An increase in the price of butter and a decrease in the price of margarine both increase the relative price of butter. Thus, both induce individuals to substitute margarine for butter.

Chocolate bars and granola bars can also be considered substitutes, as the two goods satisfy a similar need. Thus, an increase in the price of granola bars makes chocolate bars relatively more attractive, and hence leads to a rightwards shift in the demand curve for chocolate bars. At each price, the demand for chocolate bars is greater. Two goods are substitutes if an increase in the price of one *increases* the demand for the other.

Sometimes, however, an increase in a price of other goods has just the opposite effect. Consider an individual who takes sugar in her coffee. In deciding on how much coffee to demand, she is concerned with the price of a cup of coffee *with* sugar. If sugar becomes more expensive, she will demand less coffee. For this person, sugar and coffee are **complements;** that is, an increase in the price of one *decreases* the demand for the other. A price increase of sugar shifts the demand curve of coffee to the left. At each price, the demand for coffee is less. Similarly a *decrease* in the price of sugar shifts the demand curve for coffee to the right.

Noneconomic factors can also shift market demand curves. The major ones are changes in tastes and in the composition of the population. The chocolate bar example is a change in taste. Other taste changes over the past decade in Canada include a shift from hard liquor to wine and from fatty meats to low-cholesterol foods. Each of these taste changes has shifted the whole demand curve of the goods in question.

Population changes that shift demand curves are often related to age. Young families with babies purchase disposable diapers. The demand for new houses and apartments is closely related to the number of new households, which in turn depends on the number of individuals of marriageable age. The Canadian population has been growing older, on average, both because life expectancies are increasing and because birthrates fell somewhat after the baby boom that followed World War II. So there has been a shift in demand away from diapers and new houses. Economists working for particular firms and industries spend considerable energy ascertaining population effects, called **demographic effects,** on the demand for the goods their firms sell.

Sometimes demand curves shift as the result of new information. The shifts in demand for alcohol and meat—and even more so for cigarettes—are related to improved consumer information about health risks.

Changes in the availability of credit also can shift demand curves for goods like cars and houses, which people typically buy with the help of loans. When banks reduce the money available for consumer loans, the demand curves for cars and houses shift.

Finally, what people think will happen in the future can shift demand curves. If people think they may become unemployed, they will reduce their spending. In this case, economists say that their demand curve depends on expectations.

SHIFTS IN A DEMAND CURVE VERSUS MOVEMENTS ALONG A DEMAND CURVE

The distinction between changes that result from a *shift* in the demand curve and changes that result from a *movement along* the demand curve is crucial to understanding economics. A movement along a demand curve is simply the change in the quantity demanded as the price changes. Figure 4.6A illustrates a movement along the demand curve from point A to point B; *given a demand curve*, at lower prices, more is consumed. Figure 4.6B illustrates a shift in the demand curve to the right; *at a given price*, more is consumed. Quantity again increases from Q_0 to Q_1, but now the price stays the same.

In practice, both effects are often present. Thus, in panel C of Figure 4.6, the movement from point A to point C—where the quantity demanded has been reduced from Q_0 to Q_2—consists of two parts: a change in quantity demanded, resulting from a shift in the de-

SOURCES OF SHIFTS IN MARKET DEMAND CURVES

A change in income

A change in the price of a substitute

A change in the price of a complement

A change in the composition of the population

A change in tastes

A change in information

A change in the availability of credit

A change in expectations

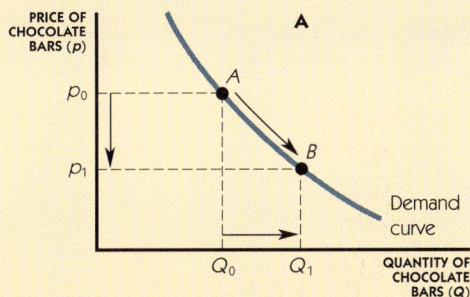

Figure 4.6 MOVEMENT ALONG THE DEMAND CURVE VERSUS SHIFT IN THE DEMAND CURVE

Panel A shows an increase in quantity demanded caused by a lower price—a movement along a given demand curve. Panel B illustrates an increase in quantity demanded caused by a shift in the entire demand curve, so that a greater quantity is demanded at every market price. Panel C shows a combination of a shift in the demand curve (the movement from point A to B) and a movement along the demand curve (the movement from point B to point C).

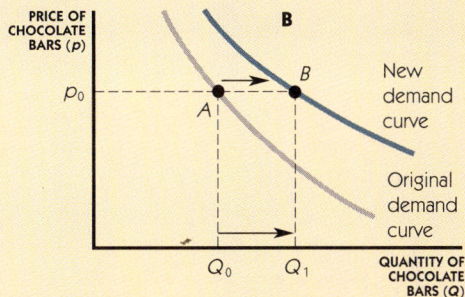

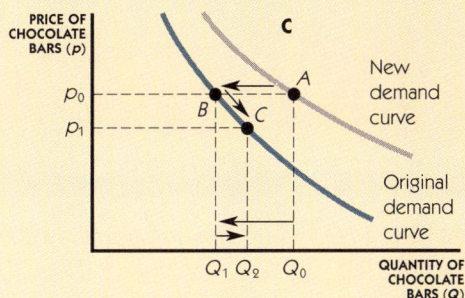

mand curve (the reduction in quantity from Q_0 to Q_1), and a movement along the demand curve as price changes (the increase in quantity from Q_1 to Q_2).

SUPPLY

Economists use the concept of **supply** to describe the quantity of a good or service that a household or firm would like to sell at a particular price. "Supply" in economics refers to such seemingly disparate choices as the number of chocolate bars a firm wants to sell and the number of hours a worker is willing to work. As with demand, the first question

economists ask is, how does the quantity supplied change when price changes, keeping all other determinants of supply constant?

The table in Figure 4.7 shows the number of chocolate bars that the Melt-in-the-Mouth Chocolate Company would like to supply to the market at each price, per week. As the price rises, so does the quantity supplied. Below $1.00, the firm finds it unprofitable to produce. At $2.00 it would like to sell 85,000 chocolate bars per week. At $5.00 it would like to sell 100,000.

Figure 4.7 also depicts these points on a graph. The curve drawn by connecting the points is called the **supply curve.** It shows the quantity that Melt-in-the-Mouth will supply per week at each price, holding all other factors constant. As with the demand curve, we put the price on the vertical axis and the quantity supplied on the horizontal axis. Thus, we can read point A on the curve as indicating that at a

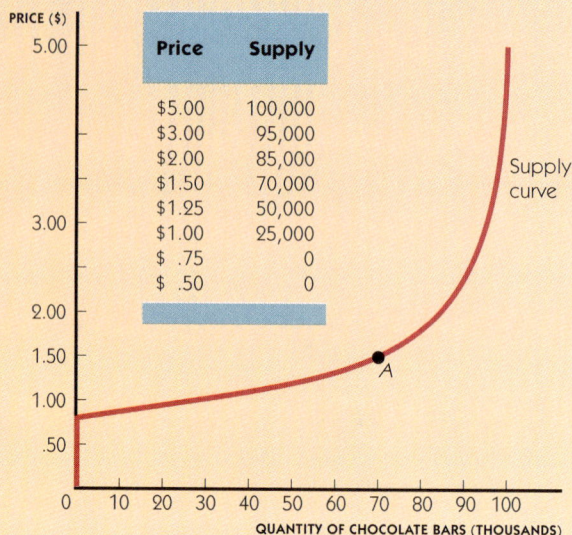

Price	Supply
$5.00	100,000
$3.00	95,000
$2.00	85,000
$1.50	70,000
$1.25	50,000
$1.00	25,000
$ .75	0
$ .50	0

Figure 4.7 ONE FIRM'S SUPPLY CURVE

The supply curve shows the quantity of a good a firm is willing to produce at each price. Normally a firm is willing to produce more as the price increases, which is why the supply curve slopes upwards.

price of $1.50 the firm would like to supply 70,000 chocolate bars.

In direct contrast to the demand curve, the typical supply curve slopes upward from left to right; at higher prices firms will supply more. This is because higher prices yield suppliers higher profits—giving them an incentive to produce more.

MARKET SUPPLY

The **market supply** of a good or service is simply the total quantity that all the firms in the economy are willing to supply per time period at a given price. Similarly, the market supply of labour is simply the total quantity of labour that all the households in the economy are willing to supply at a given wage. The table in Figure 4.8 tells us, for instance, that at a

price of $2.00, firms will supply 7 million chocolate bars per week, while at a price of $.50, they will supply only 0.5 million.

Figure 4.8 also shows the same information graphically. The curve joining the points in the figure is the **market supply curve.** The market supply curve gives the total quantity of a good that firms are willing to produce at each price. Thus, we read point *A* on the market supply curve as showing that at a price of $.75, the firms in the economy would like to sell 2 million chocolate bars per week.

As the price of chocolate bars increases, the quantity supplied increases, other things remaining equal. The market supply curve slopes upwards from left to right for two reasons: at higher prices each firm in the market is willing to produce more, and at higher prices more firms are willing to enter the market to produce the good.

The market supply curve is calculated from the

SUPPLY CURVE

The supply curve gives the quantity of the good or service supplied at each price all other factors remaining constant.

Figure 4.8 THE MARKET SUPPLY CURVE

The market supply curve shows the quantity of a good or service all firms in the market are willing to supply at each price. The market supply curve is normally upward-sloping, both because each firm is willing to supply more of the good or service at a higher price and because higher prices entice new firms to produce.

Price	Total market supply (millions)
$5.00	8.2
$3.00	8.0
$2.00	7.0
$1.50	5.9
$1.25	4.7
$1.00	3.4
$ .75	2.0
$ .50	0.5

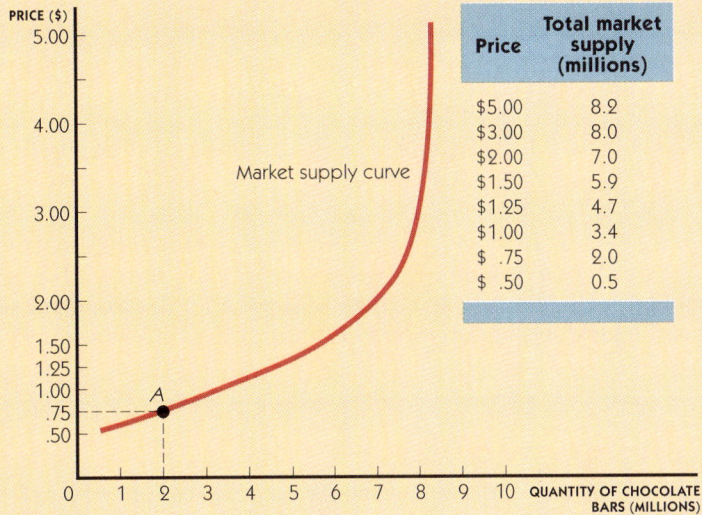

supply curves of the different firms in the same way that the market demand curve is calculated from the demand curves of the different households: at each price we add horizontally the quantities that each firm is willing to produce.

Figure 4.9 shows how this is done in a market with only two producers. At a price of $1.25, Melt-in-the-Mouth Chocolate produces 50,000 chocolate bars, while the Chocolates of Choice Company produces 40,000. So the market supply is 90,000 bars.

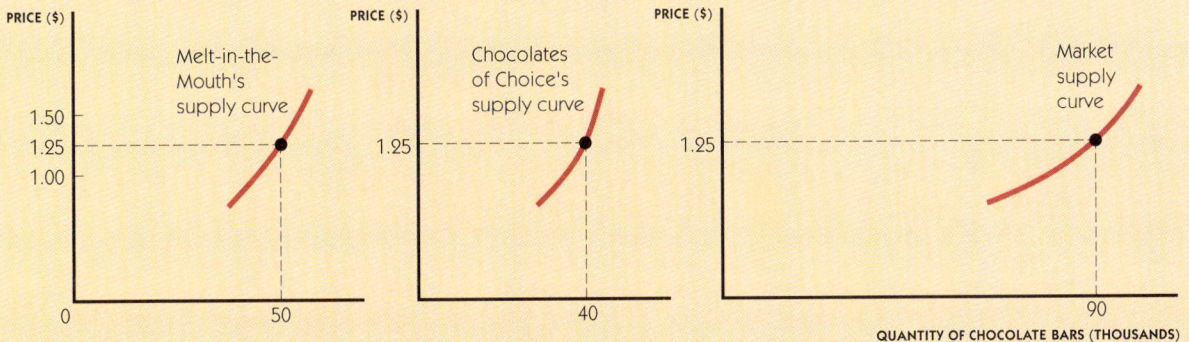

Figure 4.9 DERIVING THE MARKET SUPPLY CURVE

The market supply curve is constructed by adding up the quantity that each of the firms in the economy is willing to supply at each price. It shows what market supply would be if there were only two producers. Actual market supply, as depicted in Figure 4.8, is much larger because there are many producers.

SHIFTS IN SUPPLY CURVES

Just as demand curves can shift, supply curves too can shift when other determinants of supply change, so that the quantity supplied at each price increases or decreases. Suppose a drought hits the Prairie provinces. Figure 4.10 illustrates the situation. The supply curve for wheat shifts to the left, which means that at each price of wheat, the quantity farmers are willing to supply per period is smaller.

SOURCES OF SHIFTS IN SUPPLY CURVES

There are several sources of shifts in market supply curves, just as in the case of the market demand curves already discussed. One is changing prices of the inputs used to produce a good. Figure 4.11 shows that as corn becomes less expensive, the supply curve for cornflakes shifts to the right. Producing cornflakes costs less, so at every price firms are willing to supply a greater quantity. That is why the quantity supplied along the curve S_1 is greater than the quantity supplied, at the same price, along the curve S_0.

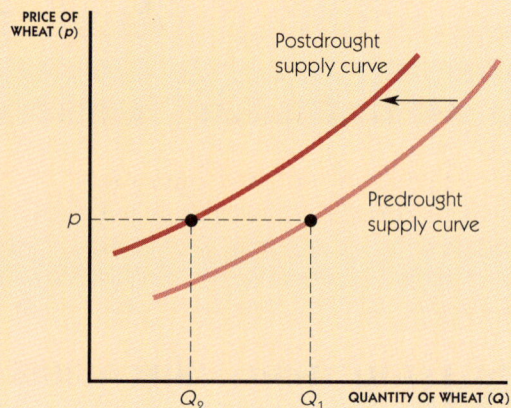

Figure 4.10 SHIFTING THE SUPPLY CURVE TO THE LEFT

A drought or other disaster (among other possible factors) will cause the supply curve to shift to the left, so that, at each price, a smaller quantity is supplied.

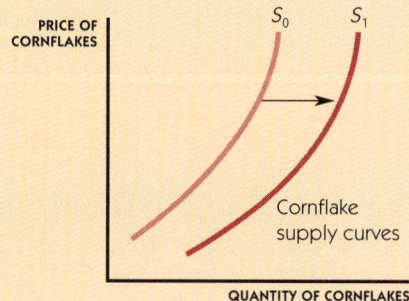

Figure 4.11 SHIFTING THE SUPPLY CURVE TO THE RIGHT

An improvement in technology or a reduction in input prices (among other possible factors) will cause the supply curve to shift to the right, so that, at each price, a larger quantity is supplied.

For the Canadian prairies and the midwestern United States, 1988 brought one of the worst droughts ever recorded. Wheat production was down 40 percent in Canada and 10 percent in the United States; corn production fell by 24 percent in Canada and 35 percent in the United States; soybean production was down 9 percent in Canada and 20 percent in the United States; and oats and barley were down 13 percent in Canada and 40 percent in the United States.

From an economist's perspective, an unpredictable event like a severe drought is a good example of a shift in the supply curve. The drought reduced the amount of any crop that could be supplied at any given price, which means that the supply curve itself shifted to the left.

As an economist would predict, this shift in the supply curve led to higher prices for these farm products. To cite some examples from the Winnipeg Commodity Exchange, feed-wheat prices rose by almost 50 percent between 1987 and 1988, corn prices by 43 percent, and soybeans by 50 percent. Overall, crop prices rose by about 12 percent.

The drought also had a number of predictable side effects on substitute and complement goods. For example, higher prices in North America stimulated foreign agricultural production. Canadian farmers planted many more hectares in 1989, to make up for some of their lost production the previous year. Since much grain is fed to cattle, the higher price of grain led many farmers to slaughter their cattle sooner than they had originally planned. As a result, meat production rose slightly in 1988, and meat prices (adjusted for inflation) dropped slightly. Supermarket prices increased sharply for consumers in the middle of the summer; fruit and vegetable prices were up 5 percent in July 1988.

Despite these many side effects, the drought of 1988 had only a temporary effect on prices and quantities. Because of stockpiles of goods and the possibility of buying farm products from other nations, the agricultural system has enough flexibility to live through a bad year.

Another source of shifts is changes in technology. The technological improvements in the computer industry over the past two decades have led to a rightwards shift in the market supply curve. Yet another source of shifts is nature. The supply curve for agricultural goods may shift to the right or left depending on weather conditions, insect infestations, or animal diseases.

Reduction in the availability of credit may curtail firms' ability to borrow to obtain inputs needed for

SOURCES OF SHIFTS IN MARKET SUPPLY CURVES

A change in the prices of inputs

A change in technology

A change in the natural environment

A change in the availability of credit

A change in expectations

production, and this too will induce a leftwards shift in the supply curve. Finally, changed expectations can also lead to a shift in the supply curve. If firms believe that a new technology for making cars will become available in two years' time, this belief will discourage investment today and will lead to a temporary leftwards shift in the supply curve.

SHIFTS IN A SUPPLY CURVE VERSUS MOVEMENTS ALONG A SUPPLY CURVE

Distinguishing between a movement *along* a curve and a *shift* in the curve itself is just as important for supply curves as it is for demand curves. In Figure 4.12A, the price of chocolate bars has gone up, with a corresponding increase in quantity supplied. Thus, there has been a movement along the supply curve.

By contrast, in Figure 4.12B, the supply curve has shifted to the right, perhaps because a new production technique has made it cheaper to produce chocolate bars. Now, even though the price does not change, the quantity supplied increases. The quantity supplied in the market can increase either because the price of the good has increased, so that for a *given supply curve* the quantity produced is higher, or because the supply curve has shifted, so that at a *given price* the quantity supplied has increased.

LAW OF SUPPLY AND DEMAND

This chapter began with the assertion that supply and demand work together to determine the market price in competitive markets. Figure 4.13 puts a market supply curve and a market demand curve on the same graph to show how this happens. The price actually paid and received in the market will be determined by the intersection of the two curves. This point is labeled E_0, for equilibrium, and the corresponding price ($.75) and quantity (20 million) are called, respectively, the **equilibrium price** and the **equilibrium quantity.**

Since the term "equilibrium" recurs throughout the book, it is important to understand the concept clearly. Equilibrium describes a situation where there are no forces (reasons) for change. No one has an incentive to change the result—the price or quantity in the case of supply and demand.

Physicists also speak of equilibrium in describing a weight hanging from a spring. Two forces are working on the weight. Gravity is pulling it down; the spring is pulling it up. When the weight is at rest, it is in equilibrium, with the two forces just offsetting each other. If one pulls the weight down a little bit, the force of the spring will be greater than the force of gravity, and the weight will spring up. In the absence of any further intrusions, the weight will bob

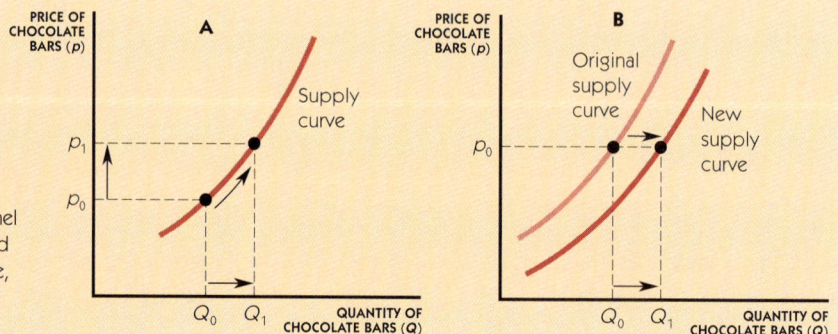

Figure 4.12 MOVEMENT ALONG THE SUPPLY CURVE VERSUS SHIFT IN THE SUPPLY CURVE

Panel A shows an increase in quantity supplied caused by a higher price—a movement along a given supply curve. Panel B illustrates an increase in quantity supplied caused by a shift in the entire supply curve, so that a greater quantity is supplied at every market price.

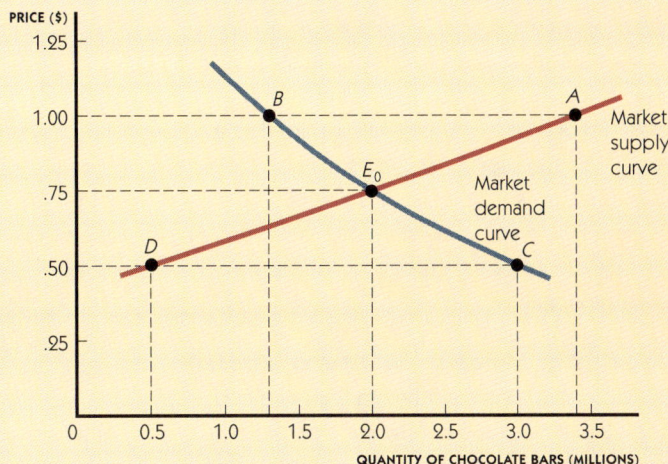

Figure 4.13 SUPPLY AND DEMAND EQUILIBRIUM

Equilibrium occurs at the intersection of the demand and supply curves, at point E_0. At any price above E_0, the quantity supplied will exceed the quantity demanded, the market will be out of equilibrium, and there will be excess supply. At any price below E_0, the quantity demanded will exceed the quantity supplied, the market will be out of equilibrium, and there will be excess demand.

back and forth and eventually reach its equilibrium position.

An economic equilibrium is established in the same way. At the equilibrium price, consumers get precisely the quantity of the good they are willing to buy at that price, and producers sell precisely the quantity they are willing to sell at that price. Neither producers nor consumers have any incentive to change.

But consider the price of $1.00 in Figure 4.13. There is no equilibrium quantity here. First find $1.00 on the vertical axis. Now look across to find point A on the supply curve, and read down to the horizontal axis; point A tells you that at a price of $1.00, firms want to supply 3.4 million chocolate bars. Now look at point B on the demand curve. Point B shows that at a price of $1.00, consumers only want to buy 1.3 million chocolate bars. Like the weight bobbing on a spring, however, this market will work its way back to equilibrium in the following way. At a price of $1.00 there is **excess supply** of 2.1 million chocolate bars. As producers discover that they cannot sell as much as they would like at this price, some of them will lower their prices slightly, hoping to take business from other producers. When one producer lowers prices, his competitors will have to respond, for fear that they will end up unable to sell their goods. As prices come down,

consumers will also buy more, and so on until the market reaches the equilibrium price and quantity.

Similarly, assume that the price is lower than $.75, say $.50. At the lower price, there is **excess demand:** individuals want to buy 3 million chocolate bars (point C), while firms only want to produce 0.5 million (point D). Consumers unable to purchase all they want will offer to pay a bit more; other consumers, afraid of having to do without, will match these higher bids or raise them. As prices start to increase, suppliers will also have a greater incentive to produce more. Again the market will tend toward the equilibrium point.

To repeat for emphasis: at equilibrium, no purchaser and no supplier has an incentive to change the price or quantity. In competitive market economies actual prices tend to be the equilibrium prices, at which demand equals supply. This is called the **law of supply and demand.** Note: this law does not mean that at every moment of time the price is precisely at the intersection of the demand and supply curves. As with the example of the weight and the spring, the market may bounce around a little bit when it is in the process of adjusting. What the law of supply and demand does say is that when a market is out of equilibrium, there are predictable forces for change.

Every economic model, including the model of how supply and demand determine the equilibrium price and quantity in a market, is constructed of three kinds of relationships: behavioural relationships, identities, and equilibrium relationships. Recognizing these component parts will help you understand how economists think and understand the source of many of their disagreements.

As described in the text, the demand curve represents a relationship between the price and the quantity demanded. The statement that normally as prices rise the quantity of a good demanded decreases is a description of how individuals behave. It is called a behavioural relationship. The supply curve for each firm is also a behavioural relationship.

Economists disagree over behavioural relationships in at least two ways. First, they may differ over the strength of the connection. For any given product, does a change in price lead to a large change in the quantity demanded or a small one? Second, economists may sometimes even disagree over the direction of the effect. There are some special cases where a higher price may actually lead to a *lower* quantity supplied.

The statement that the market demand is equal to the sum of the individual demands is an identity. An identity is a statement that is true according to the definition of the terms; in other words, market demand is *defined* to be the sum of the demands of all individuals. Similarly, it is an identity that market supply is equal to the sum of the supplies of all firms; the terms are defined in that way. Economists rarely disagree over identities, since disagreements over definitions are pointless.

Finally, an equilibrium relationship exists when there are no forces for change. In the supply-and-demand model, the equilibrium occurs when the quantity demanded is equal to the quantity supplied. An equilibrium relationship is not the same as an identity. It is possible for the economy to be out of equilibrium, at least for a time. Of course, being out of equilibrium implies that there are forces for change pushing towards equilibrium. But an identity must always hold true at all times, as a matter of definition.

Economists usually agree about what an equilibrium would look like, but they often differ on whether the forces pushing the markets towards equilibrium are strong or weak, and thus on whether the economy is fairly close to equilibrium or sometimes rather far from it.

USING DEMAND AND SUPPLY CURVES

The concepts of demand and supply curves—and market equilibrium as the intersection of demand and supply curves—constitute the economist's basic model of demand and supply. This model has proved to be extremely useful. It helps explain why the price of one commodity is high and that of another is low. It also helps *predict* the consequences of certain changes. Its predictions can then be tested against

what actually happens. One of the reasons that the model is so useful is that it gives reasonably accurate predictions.

Figure 4.14 repeats the demand and supply curve for chocolate bars discussed earlier in the chapter. Now, however, assume that sugar becomes more expensive. As a result, at each price the amount firms are willing to supply is reduced. The supply curve shifts to the left, as in panel A. There will be a new equilibrium, at a higher price and a lower quantity of chocolate consumed.

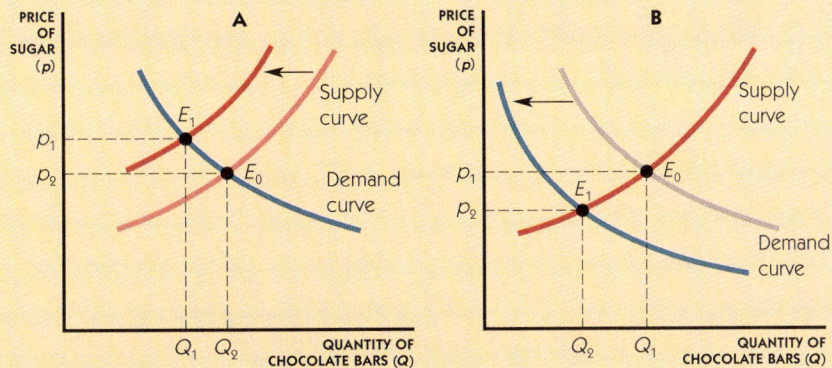

Figure 4.14 **EFFECTS OF SHIFTS IN THE SUPPLY AND DEMAND CURVES FOR CHOCOLATE BARS**

An increase in the price of sugar results in firms supplying fewer chocolate bars at each price; the supply curve for chocolate bars shifts to the left, as in panel A. At the new equilibrium, E_1, there is a higher price and a lower quantity. If consumers become more health conscious, they may demand fewer chocolate bars at each price; the demand curve for chocolate bars shifts to the left, as in panel B. There will be a new equilibrium, E_1, at a lower price and a lower quantity of chocolate bars consumed.

Alternatively, assume that Canadians become more health-conscious, and as a result at each price fewer chocolate bars are consumed: the demand curve shifts to the left. Again, there will be a new equilibrium at a lower price and a lower quantity of chocolate bars consumed.

This illustrates how changes in observed prices can be related to shifts in either the demand or the supply curve. When the war in Kuwait interrupted the supply of oil from the Middle East in 1990, it caused a shift in the supply curve. The model predicted the result: an increase in the price of oil. This increase was the natural process of the law of supply and demand.

ing it to say, "Supply and demand." That prices are determined by the law of supply and demand is one of the most long-standing and widely held ideas of economists. It provides our fourth consensus point:

4 Prices

In competitive markets, prices are determined by the law of supply and demand. Shifts in the demand and supply curves lead to changes in the equilibrium price. Similar principles apply to the labour and capital markets. The price for labour is the wage, and the price for capital is the interest rate.

CONSENSUS ON THE DETERMINATION OF PRICES

The law of supply and demand plays such a prominent role in economics that there is a joke about teaching a parrot to be an economist simply by teach-

PRICE, VALUE, AND COST

To an economist, price is the amount given in exchange for a good or service. In this sense, price is determined by the forces of supply and demand. Adam Smith, often thought of as the founder of

Figure 4.15 SUPPLY AND DEMAND FOR WATER

Point *A* shows that people are willing to pay a relatively high price for the first few units of water. But to the right of *B*, people have plenty of water already and are not willing to pay much for an additional amount. The price of water will be determined at the point where the supply curve crosses the demand curve. In most cases, the resulting price is extremely low.

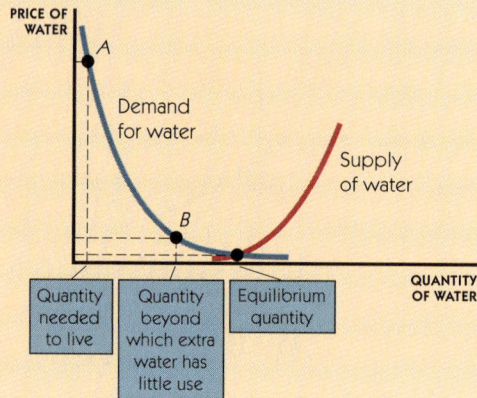

PRICE OF WATER

A

Demand for water

Supply of water

B

QUANTITY OF WATER

Quantity needed to live

Quantity beyond which extra water has little use

Equilibrium quantity

modern economics, called our notion of price "value in exchange" and contrasted it to the notion of "value in use":

The things which have the greatest value in use have frequently little or no value in exchange; and, on the contrary, those which have the greatest value in exchange have frequently little or no value in use. Nothing is more useful than water, but it will purchase scarce any thing; scarce any thing can be had in exchange for it. A diamond, on the contrary, has scarce any value in use; but a very great quantity of other goods may frequently be had in exchange for it.[1]

The law of supply and demand can help to explain the diamond-water paradox and many similar examples where "value in use" is very different from "value in exchange." Figure 4.15 presents a demand and a supply curve for water. Individuals are willing to pay a high price for the water they need to live, as illustrated by point *A*, on the demand curve. But above some quantity, *B*, people will pay almost nothing more for additional water. In most of the inhabited parts of the world water is readily available, so it gets supplied in plentiful quantities at low prices. Thus, the supply curve of water intersects the demand curve to the right of *B*, as in the figure; hence

[1] *The Wealth of Nations* (1776), Book I, Chapter IV.

the low equilibrium price. Of course, in the desert the water supply may be very limited and as a result the price will be very high.

To an economist the statements that the price of diamonds is high and the price of water is low are statements about supply-and-demand conditions. They say nothing about whether diamonds are "more important" or "better" than water. In Adam Smith's terms, they are not statements about value in use.

One way to think of the difference between the value in exchange versus the value in use is to distinguish between the *marginal* value of an object and its *total* value. The marginal value is the value of an additional unit of an object. An individual's demand curve can be thought of as a schedule of his marginal values, or marginal benefits. Thus, in Figure 4.1 Roger was willing to pay $3.00 for the first chocolate bar. That was the marginal value he attached to it. He was only willing to pay $2.00 for the second bar; it had a lower value to him. As the number of chocolate bars increased, the marginal value of each additional bar declined. His total value can be thought of as the sum of the values of all chocolate bars purchased. Thus, if he bought four chocolate bars, the total value he attached to them could be thought of as the sum of the marginal values of each ($3.00 + $2.00 + $1.50 + $1.25). Geometrically, the total value is like the area under his demand curve, while the marginal value is what he is willing to pay for the last unit. Goods like water can have a high value in use but a low value in exchange if they are plentiful enough to more than satisfy basic requirements, so that their marginal value has become quite small even though their total value is large.

Just as economists take care to distinguish the words "price" and "value," they also distinguish the *price* of an object (what it sells for) from its *cost* (the expense of making the object). This is another crucial distinction in economics. The costs of producing a good affect the price at which firms are willing to supply that good. An increase in the costs of production will normally cause prices to rise. And in the competitive model, *in equilibrium,* the price of an ob-

ject will equal its cost of production (including the amount needed to pay a firm's owner to stay in business rather than seek some other form of employment). But there are important cases—as we shall see in later chapters—where price does not equal cost.

When we think of the competitive model, it is interesting to consider the case of a good in fixed supply, such as land. Normally, land is something that cannot be produced, so its cost of production can be considered infinite (though there are situations where land can be produced, as when the Netherlands filled in part of the sea to expand its usable land). Yet there is still an equilibrium price of land—where the demand for land is equal to its (fixed) supply.

REVIEW AND PRACTICE

SUMMARY

1 An individual's demand curve gives the quantity demanded of a good or service per time period at each possible price. It normally slopes down, which means that the person demands a greater quantity of the good at lower prices and a lesser quantity at higher prices.

2 The market demand curve gives the total quantity of a good or service demanded per time period by all individuals in an economy at each price. As the price rises the quantity demanded falls, both because each person demands less of the good and because some people exit the market.

3 A firm's supply curve gives the amount of a good or service the firm is willing to supply per time period at each price. It is normally upward-sloping, which means that firms supply a greater quantity of the good at higher prices and a lesser quantity at lower prices.

4 The market supply curve gives the total quantity of a good that all firms in the economy are willing to produce per time period at each price. As the price rises, the quantity supplied rises, both because each

firm supplies more of the good and because some additional firms enter the market.

5 The law of supply and demand says that in competitive markets, the equilibrium price is that price at which quantity demanded equals quantity supplied. It is represented on a graph by the intersection of the demand and supply curves.

6 A demand curve shows *only* the relationship between quantity demanded and price. Changes in tastes, in demographic factors, in income, in the prices of other goods, information, the availability of credit, or expectations are reflected in a shift of the entire demand curve.

7 A supply curve shows *only* the relationship between quantity supplied and price. Changes in factors such as technology, the prices of inputs, the natural environment, expectations, or the availability of credit are reflected in a shift of the entire supply curve.

8 It is important to distinguish movements along a demand curve from shifts in the demand curve, and movements along a supply curve from shifts in the supply curve.

KEY TERMS

demand curve	complement	market supply curve	excess demand
market demand curve	demographic effects	equilibrium price	law of supply and demand
substitute	supply curve	excess supply	

REVIEW QUESTIONS

1 Why does an individual's demand curve normally slope down? Why does a market demand curve normally slope down?

2 Why does a firm's supply curve normally slope up? Why does a market supply curve normally slope up?

3 What is the significance of the point where supply and demand curves intersect?

4 Explain why, if the price of a good is above the equilibrium price, the forces of supply and demand will tend to push the price towards equilibrium. Explain why, if the price of the good is below the equilibrium price, the market will tend to adjust towards equilibrium.

5 Name some factors that could shift the demand curve out to the right.

6 Name some factors that could shift the supply curve in to the left.

PROBLEMS

1 Imagine a company lunchroom that sells pizza by the slice. Using the following data, plot the points and graph the demand and supply curves. What is the equilibrium price and quantity? Find a price at which excess demand would exist and a price at which excess supply would exist, and plot them on your diagram.

Price per Slice	Demand (Number of Slices per Week)	Supply (Number of Slices per Week)
$1	420	0
$2	210	100
$3	140	140
$4	105	160
$5	84	170

2 Suppose a severe drought hit the sugarcane crop. Predict how this would affect the equilibrium price and quantity in the market for sugar and the market for honey. Draw supply and demand diagrams to illustrate your answers.

3 Imagine that a new invention allows each mine worker to mine twice as much coal. Predict how this will affect the equilibrium price and quantity in the market for coal and the market for heating oil. Draw supply and demand diagrams to illustrate your answer.

4 Canadians' tastes have shifted away from beef, towards chicken. Predict how this change affects the equilibrium price and quantity in the market for beef, the market for chicken, and the market for roadside hamburger stands. Draw supply and demand diagrams to illustrate your answer.

5 During the 1970s the postwar baby boomers reached working age, and it became more acceptable for married women with children to work. Predict how this increase in the number of workers is likely to affect the equilibrium wage and quantity of employment. Draw supply and demand curves to illustrate your answer.

CHAPTER 5

USING DEMAND AND SUPPLY

The concepts of demand and supply are among the most useful in economics. The demand and supply framework explains why dentists are paid more than lawyers, or why the income of unskilled workers has increased less than that of skilled workers. It can also be used to predict what the demand for condominiums or disposable diapers will be fifteen years from now, or what will happen if the government increases the tax on cigarettes. Not only can we predict that prices will change, we can predict by how much they will change.

This chapter has two purposes. The first is to develop some of the concepts required to make these kinds of predictions, and to illustrate how the demand and supply framework can be used in a variety of contexts.

The second is to look at what happens when governments interfere with the workings of competitive markets. Rents may seem too high for poor people to afford adequate housing. The price of wheat may seem unfairly low, not adequate to compensate farmers for their work. Political pressure constantly develops for government to intervene on behalf of the group that has been disadvantaged by the market—whether it be poor people, farmers, or oil companies, which ask for government help when the price of oil falls. The second part of this chapter traces the consequences of political interventions into the workings of some markets.

KEY QUESTIONS

1 What is meant by the concept of elasticity? Why does it play such an important role in predicting market outcomes?

2 What happens when market outcomes are interfered with, as when the government imposes price floors and ceilings? Why do such interferences give rise to shortages and surpluses?

SENSITIVITY TO PRICE CHANGES: THE PRICE ELASTICITY OF DEMAND

If tomorrow supermarkets across the country were to cut the price of bread or milk by 50 percent, the quantity demanded of these items would not change much. If stores offered the same reduction on premium ice cream, however, demand would increase

substantially. Why do price changes sometimes have small effects and at other times large ones? The answer lies in the shape of the demand and supply curves.

The demand for ice cream is more sensitive to price changes than is the demand for milk, and this is reflected in the shape of the demand curves, as illustrated in Figure 5.1. The demand curve for ice cream (panel A) is much flatter than the one for milk (panel B). When the demand curve is somewhat flat, a change in price, say from $2.00 a litre to $2.10, has

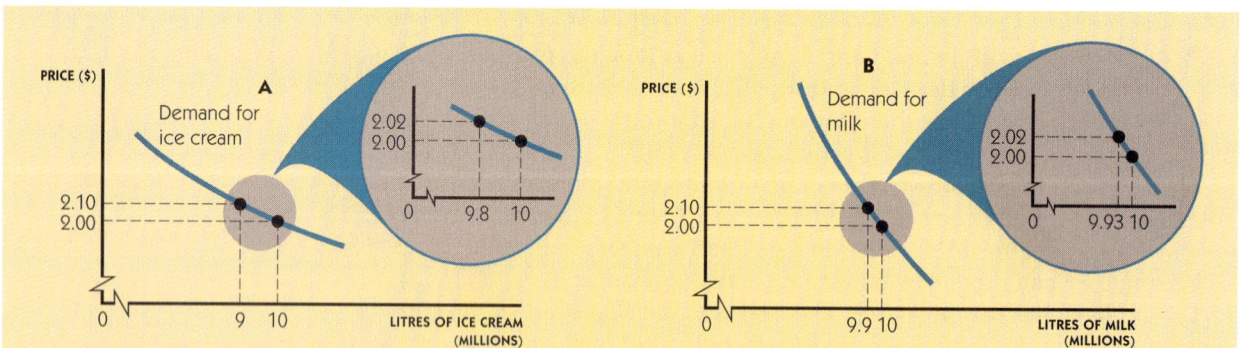

Figure 5.1 ELASTIC VERSUS INELASTIC DEMAND CURVES

Panel A shows a hypothetical demand curve for ice cream. Note that quantity demanded changes rapidly with fairly small price changes, indicating that demand for ice cream is elastic. The telescoped portion of the demand curve shows that a 1 percent rise in price leads to a 2 percent fall in quantity demanded. Panel B shows a hypothetical demand curve for milk. Note that quantity demanded changes very little, regardless of changes in price, meaning that demand for milk is inelastic. The telescoped portion of the demand curve shows that a 1 percent rise in price leads to a .7 percent fall in quantity demanded.

a large effect on the quantity consumed. In panel A, the demand for ice cream decreases from 10 million litres at a price of $2.00 a litre to 9 million litres at a price of $2.10 per litre.

By contrast, when the demand curve is steep it means that a change in price has little effect on quantity. In panel B, the demand for milk decreases from 10 million litres at $2.00 per litre to 9.9 million litres at $2.10 per litre. But saying that the demand curve is steep or flat just pushes the question back a step: why are some demand curves steeper than others?

The answer is that though substitutes exist for almost every good or service, substitution will be more difficult for some goods and services than for others. When substitution is difficult, if the price of a good increases the quantity demanded will not decrease by much, and if the price falls the quantity demanded will not increase much. The typical consumer does not substitute milk for beer—or anything else—even if milk becomes a good deal cheaper.

On the other hand, when substitution is easy a fall in price may lead to a large increase in quantity demanded. For instance, there are many good substitutes for ice cream, including sherbets and frozen yogurts. The price decrease for ice cream means that these close substitutes have become relatively more expensive, and the demand for ice cream would thus increase significantly.

For many purposes, economists need to be precise about how steep or how flat the demand curve is. For precision they use the concept of the **price elasticity of demand**—the "price elasticity" or the "elasticity of demand," for short. The price elasticity of demand is defined as the absolute value of the percentage change in the quantity demanded divided by the percentage change in price. That is,

$$\text{elasticity of demand} = -\frac{\text{percent change in quantity demanded}}{\text{percent change in price}}.$$

The minus sign is included because when the price increases, quantities demanded are reduced, and vice versa. The minus sign makes the elasticity of demand a positive number. Thus, if the quantity demanded falls by 8 percent in response to a 2 percent increase in price, the elasticity of demand is 4.

It is easiest to calculate the elasticity of demand when there is just a 1 percent change in price. Then the elasticity of demand is just the percent change in the quantity demanded. In the telescoped portion of Figure 5.1A, we see that increasing the price of ice cream from $2.00 a litre to $2.02—a 1 percent increase in price—reduces the demand from 10 million litres to 9.8 million, a 2 percent decline. So the price elasticity of demand for ice cream is 2.

By contrast, assume that the price of milk increases from $2.00 a litre to $2.02 (again a 1 percent increase in price), as shown in the telescoped portion of Figure 5.1B. This reduces demand from 10 million litres per year to 9.93 million. Demand has gone down by .7 percent, so the price elasticity of demand is .7. Larger values for price elasticity indicate that demand is more sensitive to changes in price. Smaller values indicate that demand is less sensitive to price changes.

Why is elasticity defined in terms of percentage changes rather than in terms of the actual change in quantity demanded divided by a change in price (or the inverse of the slope of the demand curve)? The reason is that a percentage change is a unitless number, whereas the size of an actual change depends on the units in which quantities are measured. Thus, the change in quantity of milk demanded from a $1 change in price will depend upon whether quantities are measured in litres or millilitres, whereas the percentage change in quantity demanded will be independent of units of measurement.

PRICE ELASTICITY AND REVENUES

The revenue received by a firm from selling a good is price times quantity. We write this in a simple equation. Letting R denote revenues, p price, and Q quantity:

$$R = pQ.$$

This means that when price goes up by 1 percent, whether revenues go up or down depends on the magnitude of the decrease in quantity. If quantity

PRICE ELASTICITY OF DEMAND

Elasticity	Description	Effect on Quantity Demanded of 1% Increase in Price	Effect on Revenues of 1% Increase in Price
Zero	Perfectly inelastic (vertical demand curve)	Zero	Increased by 1%
Between 0 and 1	Inelastic	Reduced by less than 1%	Increased by less than 1%
One	Unitary elasticity	Reduced by 1%	Unchanged
Greater than 1	Elastic	Reduced by more than 1%	Reduced; the greater the elasticity, the more revenue is reduced
Infinite	Perfectly elastic (horizontal demand curve)	Reduced to zero	Reduced to zero

decreases by more than 1 percent, then total revenues decrease; by less than 1 percent, they increase. We can express this result in terms of the concept of price elasticity.

Business firms must pay attention to the price elasticity of demand for their products. Suppose a cement producer, the only one in town, is considering a 1 percent increase. The firm hires an economist to estimate the elasticity of demand, so that the firm will know what will happen to sales when it raises its price. The economist tells the firm that its demand elasticity is 2. This means that if the price of cement rises by 1 percent, the quantity sold will decline by 2 percent.

The firm's executives will not be pleased by the findings. To see why, assume that initially the price of cement was $1,000 per tonne, and 100,000 tonnes were sold. To calculate revenues, you multiply the price times the quantity sold. So initially revenues were $1,000 × 100,000 = $100 million. With a 1 percent increase, the price will be $1,010. If the elasticity of demand is 2, then a 1 percent price increase results in a 2 percent decrease in the quantity sold. With a 2 percent quantity decrease, sales are now 98,000 tonnes. Revenues are down to $98.98 million ($1,010 × 98,000), just slightly over 1 percent. Because of the high elasticity, this cement firm's price *increase* leads to a *decrease* in revenues.

The price elasticity of demand works the same way for price decreases. Suppose the cement producer

decided to decrease the price of cement 1 percent, to $990. With an elasticity of demand of 2, sales would then increase 2 percent, to 102,000 tonnes. Thus, revenues would *increase* to $100,980,000 ($990 × 102,000), that is, by a bit less than 1 percent. When the change in revenues more than offsets the change in prices, we say that the demand for that good is **relatively elastic,** or *sensitive* to price changes.

In the case where the price elasticity is **unity,** or 1, the decrease in the quantity demanded just offsets the increase in the price, so price increases have no effect on revenues. If the price elasticity is less than unity, then when the price of a good increases by 1 percent, the quantity demanded is reduced by less than 1 percent. Since there is not much reduction in demand, elasticities in the range between 0 and 1 mean that price increases will increase revenues. And price decreases will decrease revenues. We say the demand for that good is **relatively inelastic,** or *insensitive* to price changes.

EXTREME CASES

There are two extreme cases that deserve attention. One is that of a flat demand curve, a curve that is perfectly horizontal. We say that such a demand curve is perfectly elastic, or has **infinite elasticity,** since even a slight increase in the price results in demand dropping to zero. The other case is that of a steep demand curve, a curve that is perfectly vertical. We say that such a demand curve is perfectly inelastic, or has **zero elasticity,** since no matter what the change in price, demand remains the same.

PRICE ELASTICITIES IN THE CANADIAN ECONOMY

The elasticity of demand for most foods is low (an increase in price will not affect demand much). The elasticity of demand for most luxuries, such as perfume, ski trips, and Mercedes cars, is high (an increase in price will lead to much less demand). Table 5.1 gives one set of estimates of the elasticities of demand for broad commodity groups in Canada. The price elasticity of demand for food is .47, in contrast to the price elasticity for transportation, which is 1.37. These are for broad commodity groups. One might expect that for specific goods within these broad categories, the price elasticity of demand would be much higher. For example, the price elasticity of purchased meals or snack foods would be higher than that for food broadly defined. More generally, goods for which it is easy to find substitutes will have high price elasticities; goods for which substitutes cannot easily be found will have low price elasticities.

Table 5.1 SOME PRICE ELASTICITIES IN THE CANADIAN ECONOMY

Commodity Group	Elasticity
Elastic demands	
Household expenses	1.28
Transportation	1.37
Inelastic demands	
Tobacco and alcohol	.54
Clothing	.52
Food	.47
Shelter	.38
Miscellaneous	.67

Source: Alan Powell, "Post-War Consumption in Canada: A First Look at the Aggregates," *Canadian Journal of Economic and Political Science* 31 (November 1965): 559–65.

CALCULATING PRICE ELASTICITIES

In practice, the data economists have for calculating elasticity seldom represent very small changes in prices. Rather, economists observe, say, an 8 percent change in quantity resulting from a 4 percent change in price. They calculate what is sometimes called the **arc elasticity** (to distinguish it from the **point elasticity,** referring to a *small* change) by the earlier formula:

$$\text{elasticity} = -\frac{\text{percentage change in quantity}}{\text{percentage change in price}}$$

which in this case is 2.

The percentage change in quantity is

$$\text{percentage change in quantity} = \frac{\text{change in quantity}}{\text{quantity}} \times 100 = \frac{\Delta Q}{Q} \times 100$$

where the symbol Δ, the Greek letter delta, means "change in." Thus, ΔQ means "change in quantity." Similarly, if Δp means change in price,

$$\text{percentage change in price} = \frac{\text{change in price}}{\text{price}} \times 100 = \frac{\Delta p}{p} \times 100.$$

Thus, the elasticity can be written

$$\text{elasticity} = -\frac{\Delta Q/Q \times 100}{\Delta p/p \times 100} = -\frac{\Delta Q}{\Delta p} \times \frac{p}{Q}.$$

This raises a slight technical problem. What values of p and Q do we use in calculating elasticities—the initial ones, the final ones, or values somewhere in between? If the change is small enough, it makes little difference. For large changes, however, it does make a difference. A common procedure is to use values of p and Q that are midway between the initial and final points.

ELASTICITY AND SLOPE

The elasticity of a curve is often confused with its slope. The best way to see the distinction is to look at the **linear demand curve.** The linear demand curve is a straight line, depicted in Figure 5.2. Recall that when we draw the demand curve, we put price on the vertical axis and output on the horizontal axis. Thus, the quantity demanded is related to the price by the equation

$$Q = a - bp.$$

If $a = 100$ and $b = 2$, at a price of 1, $Q = 98$; at a price of 2, $Q = 96$; at a price of 3, $Q = 94$, and so forth.

The demand curve also gives the price at which a particular quantity of the good will be demanded. Thus, we can rewrite the equation to read

$$p = \frac{a}{b} - \frac{Q}{b},$$

so that (with $a = 100$, $b = 2$ as before), at $Q = 100$, $p = 0$; at $Q = 99$, $p = 0.5$; at $Q = 98$, $p = 1$.

Slope gives the change along the vertical axis per unit change along the horizontal axis:

$$\text{slope} = \frac{\text{change in price}}{\text{change in quantity}} = \frac{\Delta p}{\Delta Q}.$$

Equivalently, slope is the change in price for a unit change in quantity. In our example, as we change quantity by 1, price changes by $-\frac{1}{2}$. More generally, the slope of the linear demand equation above is $-\frac{1}{b}$.[1]

We can now rewrite the expression for elasticity as

$$\text{elasticity} = -\frac{\Delta Q/Q}{\Delta p/p} = -\frac{\Delta Q}{\Delta p} \times \frac{p}{Q}$$

$$= b \times \frac{p}{Q}$$

$$= -\frac{1}{\text{slope}} \times \frac{p}{Q}.$$

Everywhere along a linear demand curve the slope

[1]To see this, observe that at $Q + 1$, the price is

$$\frac{a}{b} - \frac{Q+1}{b}.$$

The change in price is

$$\frac{a}{b} - \frac{Q}{b} - \left(\frac{a}{b} - \frac{Q+1}{b} \right) = \frac{a}{b} - \frac{Q}{b} - \frac{a}{b} + \frac{Q+1}{b} = \frac{1}{b}.$$

is the same, but the elasticity is very high at low levels of output and very low at high levels of output.

The formula for elasticity has one other important implication, illustrated in Figure 5.3. Of two demand curves going through the same point, the flatter demand curve has the higher elasticity. At the point where they intersect, p and Q (and therefore p/Q) are the same. Only the slopes differ. The one with the smaller slope has the greater elasticity.

SMALL VERSUS LARGE PRICE CHANGES

Often, economists are interested in what would happen if there were a large price change. For instance, if a 50 percent tax were imposed on cigarettes, what would happen to demand?

When price changes are small or moderate, we can *extrapolate*. That is, we can extend what we know to make conclusions beyond the range of what we know. For example, if a 1 percent change in price results in a 2 percent change in quantity, then a 3 percent change in price will probably result in an approximately 6 percent change in quantity.

With large price changes, however, such extrapolation becomes riskier. The reason is that *price elasticity is typically different at different points along the demand curve*. Thus, in the linear case considered above, the slope of the demand curve $(-\frac{1}{b})$ is constant. The elasticity (bp/Q) will fall as one moves down the demand curve, since p is falling while Q is rising.

THE DETERMINANTS OF THE ELASTICITY OF DEMAND

In our earlier discussion we noted one of the important determinants of the elasticity of demand: the availability of substitutes. There are two important determinants of the degree of substitutability: the quantity of the good consumed and the length of time it takes to make an adjustment.

When the price of a commodity is low and the consumption is high, a variety of substitutes exist. Figure 5.4 illustrates the case of aluminum. When the price of aluminum is low, it is used as a food wrap (aluminum foil), as containers for canned goods, and in airplane frames because it is lightweight. As the

Figure 5.2 LINEAR DEMAND CURVE

The linear demand curve is a straight line; it is represented algebraically by the equation $Q = a - bp$. The slope of the demand curve is a constant. However, the elasticity varies with output. At low outputs (high prices) it is very high. At high outputs (low prices) it is very low.

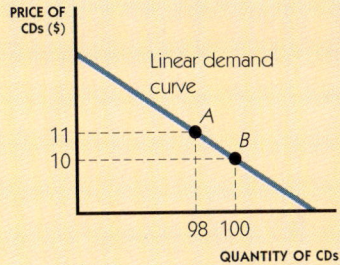

PRICE OF CDs ($)

Linear demand curve

A

B

11

10

98 100

QUANTITY OF CDs

Figure 5.3 COMPARING ELASTICITIES

If two demand curves intersect, at the point of intersection, the flatter demand curve has the greater price elasticity.

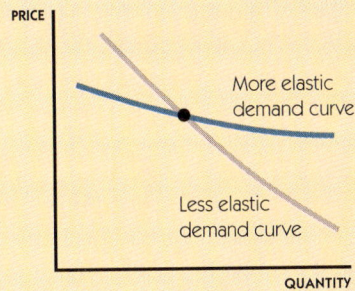

PRICE

More elastic demand curve

Less elastic demand curve

QUANTITY

Figure 5.4 CHANGING ELASTICITY ALONG A DEMAND CURVE

Near point *A*, where the price is high, the demand curve is quite steep and inelastic. In the area of the demand curve near *B*, the demand curve is very flat and elastic.

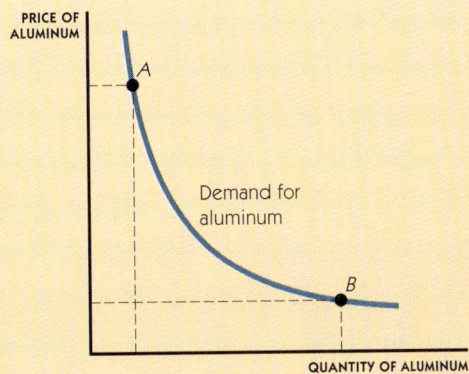

PRICE OF ALUMINUM

A

Demand for aluminum

B

QUANTITY OF ALUMINUM

Figure 5.5 **ELASTICITY OF DEMAND OVER TIME**

Demand curves tend to be inelastic in the short run, when there is little time to adapt to price changes, but more elastic in the long run.

PRICE OF GASOLINE

Short-run demand for gasoline

Long-run demand for gasoline

QUANTITY OF GASOLINE

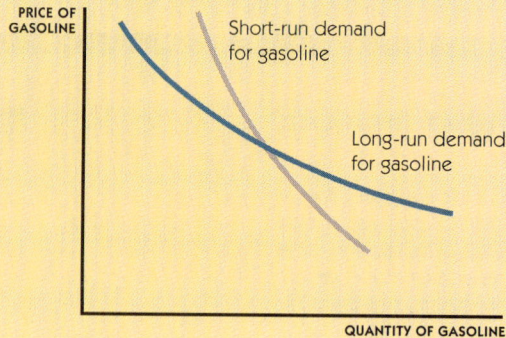

price increases, customers seek out substitutes. At first, substitutes are easy to find, and the demand for the product is greatly reduced. For example, plastic wrap can be used instead of aluminum foil. As the price rises still further, tin is used instead of aluminum for cans. At very high prices, say near point A, aluminum is used only where its lightweight properties are essential, such as in airplane frames. At this point it may take a *huge* price increase before some other material becomes an economical substitute.

A second important determinant of the elasticity of demand is the length of the time period over which responses are measured. Because it is always easier to find substitutes and to make other adjustments when you have a longer time to make them, the elasticity of demand is normally larger in the **long run**—in the period in which all adjustments can be made—than it is in the **short run,** when at least some adjustments cannot be made. Figure 5.5 illustrates the difference in shape between short-run and long-run demand curves for gasoline.

The sharp increase in oil prices in the 1970s provides an outstanding example. The short-run price elasticity of gasoline was .2 (a 1 percent increase in price led to only a .2 percent decrease in quantity demanded), while the long-run elasticity was .7 or more; the short-run elasticity of fuel oil was .2, and the long-run elasticity was 1.2. In the short run, consumers were stuck with their old gas-guzzling cars, their draughty houses, and their old fuel-wasting habits. In the long run, however, consumers bought smaller cars, became used to houses with slightly lower temperatures, installed better insulation in their homes, and turned to alternative energy

sources. The long-run demand curve was therefore much more elastic (flatter) than the short-run curve. Indeed, the long-run elasticity turned out to be much larger than anticipated.

How long is the long run? There is no simple answer. It will vary from product to product. In some cases adjustments can occur rapidly; in other cases they are very gradual. As old gas guzzlers wore out, they were replaced with fuel-efficient compact cars. As furnaces wore out, they were replaced with more efficient ones. New homes are now constructed with more insulation, so that gradually, over time, the fraction of houses that are well insulated is increasing.

THE PRICE ELASTICITY OF SUPPLY

Supply curves normally slope upwards. As with demand curves, they are steep in some cases and flat in others. The degree of steepness reflects sensitivity to price changes. A steep supply curve, like the one for oil in Figure 5.6A, means that a large change in price generates only a small change in the quantity firms want to supply. A flatter curve, like the one for chicken in Figure 5.6B, means that a small change in price generates a large change in supply. Just as with demand, economists have developed a precise way of representing the sensitivity of supply to prices in a way that parallels the one already introduced. The **price elasticity of supply** is defined as the percentage change in quantity supplied divided by the percentage change in price (or the percentage change in

Figure 5.6 DIFFERING ELASTICITIES OF SUPPLY

Panel A shows a supply curve for oil. It is inelastic: quantity supplied increases only a small amount with a rise in price. Panel B shows a supply curve for chicken. It is elastic: quantity supplied increases substantially with a rise in price.

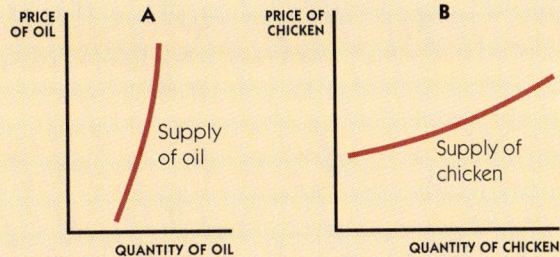

quantity supplied corresponding to a price change of 1 percent).

$$\text{Elasticity of supply} = \frac{\text{percentage change in quantity supplied}}{\text{percentage change in price}}.$$

The elasticity of supply of oil is low: an increase in the price of oil will not have a significant effect on the total supply. The amount of oil that has been discovered and can be extracted is relatively fixed. Though some wells can be exploited more intensively and some new wells can be brought into production, an increase in price will have proportionately little effect on the available supply. The supply of chicken, on the other hand, is much more responsive to price. Existing producers can increase their output readily, and new producers can easily enter the market.

As is the case with demand, if a 1 percent increase in price results in more than a 1 percent increase in supply, we say the supply curve is elastic. If a 1 percent increase in price results in less than a 1 percent increase in supply, the supply curve is inelastic. In the extreme case of a vertical supply curve—where the amount supplied does not depend at all on price—the curve is said to be perfectly inelastic, or to have *zero* elasticity, and in the extreme case of a horizontal supply curve, the curve is said to be perfectly elastic, or to have *infinite* elasticity.

Just as the demand elasticity differs at different points of the demand curve, so too does the supply elasticity differ at different points of the supply curve. Figure 5.7 shows a typical supply curve in manufacturing. An example might be ball bearings. At very low prices, plants are just covering their operating

Figure 5.7 CHANGING ELASTICITY ALONG A SUPPLY CURVE

When output is low and many machines are idle, a small change in price can lead to a large increase in quantity produced, so the supply curve is flat and elastic. When output is high and all machines are working close to their limit, it takes a very large price change to induce even a small change in output; the supply curve is steep and inelastic.

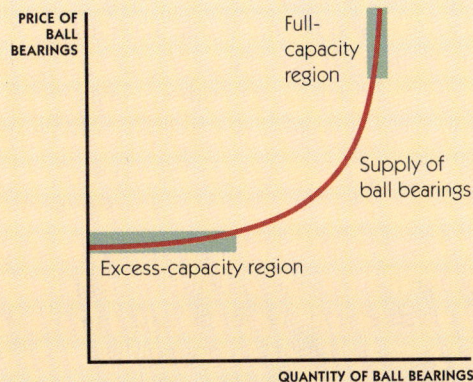

costs. Some plants are shut down; there is excess capacity in the industry. In this situation, a small increase in price elicits a large increase in supply. The supply curve is relatively flat (elastic). But eventually, all machines are being worked to full capacity throughout the day. In this situation, it may be hard to increase supply further, so that the supply curve becomes close to vertical (inelastic). In other words, however much the price increases, the supply will not change very much.

SHORT RUN VERSUS LONG RUN

Economists distinguish between the responsiveness of supply to price in the short run and in the long run, just as they do with demand. The long-run supply elasticity is greater than the short-run. We define the short-run supply curve as the supply response *given the current stock of machines, buildings, and land devoted to production.* The long-run supply curve assumes that firms can adjust the stock of machines, buildings, and land.

Farm crops are a typical example of a good whose supply in the short run is not very sensitive to changes in price; that is, the supply curve is steep (inelastic). After farmers have done their spring planting, they are committed to a certain level of production. If the price of their crop goes up, they cannot go back and plant more. If the price falls, they are stuck with the crop they have. In this case, the supply curve is relatively close to vertical, as illustrated by the steeper curve in Figure 5.8.

The long-run supply curve for many crops, in contrast, is very flat (elastic). A relatively small change in price can lead to a large change in the quantity supplied. A small increase in the price of soybeans relative to the price of wheat may induce many farmers to shift their planting from wheat and other crops to

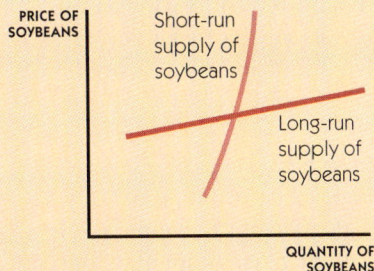

Figure 5.8 ELASTICITY OF SUPPLY OVER TIME

Supply curves may be inelastic in the short run and very elastic in the long run, as in the case of agricultural crops like soybeans.

soybeans, generating a large increase in the quantity of soybeans. This is illustrated in Figure 5.8 by the flatter curve.

Earlier, we noted the response of consumers to the marked increase in the price of oil in the 1970s. The long-run demand elasticity was much higher than the short-run. So too for supply. The higher prices drove firms, both in Canada and abroad in places like the United States, Mexico, and the North Sea off the coast of Great Britain, to explore for more oil. Though the alternative supplies could not be increased much in the short run (the short-run supply curve was inelastic, or steep), in the long run new supplies were found. Thus, the long-run supply elas-

ticity was much higher (the supply curve was flatter) than the short-run supply elasticity.

IDENTIFYING PRICE AND QUANTITY ADJUSTMENTS

When the demand curve for a good such as wine shifts to the right—when, for instance, wine becomes more popular, so that at each price the demand is greater—there is an increase in both the equilibrium price of wine and the quantity demanded, or consumed. Similarly, when the supply curve for a good such as corn shifts to the left—say, because of a drought that hurt the year's crop, so that at each price farmers supply less—there is an increase in the equilibrium price of corn and a decrease in quantity. Knowing that the shifts in the demand or supply curve will lead to an adjustment in both price *and* quantity is helpful, but it is even more useful to know whether most of the impact of a change will be on price or on quantity. It is the price elasticity of both the demand and supply curves that determine how much adjustment occurs in the price relative to the quantity in response to shifts in demand or supply.

USING DEMAND AND SUPPLY ELASTICITIES

In Chapter 4 we saw how the law of supply and demand can be used to help explain changes in prices and to understand the consequences of, say, bad weather. The law of supply and demand, together

PRICE ELASTICITY OF SUPPLY

Elasticity	Description	Effect on Quantity Supplied of 1% Increase in Price
Zero	Perfectly inelastic (vertical supply curve)	Zero
Between 0 and 1	Inelastic	Increased by less than 1%
One	Unitary elasticity	Increased by 1%
Greater than 1	Elastic	Increased by more than 1%
Infinite	Perfectly elastic (horizontal supply curve)	Infinite increase

with the concepts of demand and supply elasticity, help us be more precise in our predictions. They help us *quantify* the magnitudes of price and quantity changes as a result of, say, bad weather, which shifts the supply curve, or of increased consumer awareness of the health hazards of alcohol, which shifts the demand curve.

Figure 5.9 shows the typical range of outcomes. If the supply curve is highly elastic (approaching the horizontal, as in panel A), shifts in the demand curve will be reflected more in changes in quantity than in price. If the supply curve is *relatively* inelastic (approaching the vertical, as in panel B), shifts in the demand curve will be reflected more in changes in price than in quantity. If the demand curve is highly elastic (approaching the horizontal as in panel C), shifts in the supply curve will be reflected more in quantity than in price. Finally, if the demand curve is *relatively* inelastic (approaching the vertical as in

panel D), shifts in the supply curve will be reflected more in changes in price than in quantity.

The extreme cases can be easily seen by extending the graphs in Figure 5.9. If one tilts the supply curve in panel A to be completely flat (perfectly elastic), a shift in the demand curve will have no effect on price. If one tilts the supply curve in panel B to be vertical (perfectly inelastic), a shift in the demand curve will have no effect on quantity.

Because demand and supply curves are likely to be less elastic (more vertical) in the short run than in the long run, shifts in the demand and supply curves are more likely to be reflected in price changes in the short run, but in quantity changes in the long run. In fact, price increases in the short run provide the signals to firms to increase their production. Therefore, short-run price increases can be thought of as responsible for the output increases that occur in the long run.

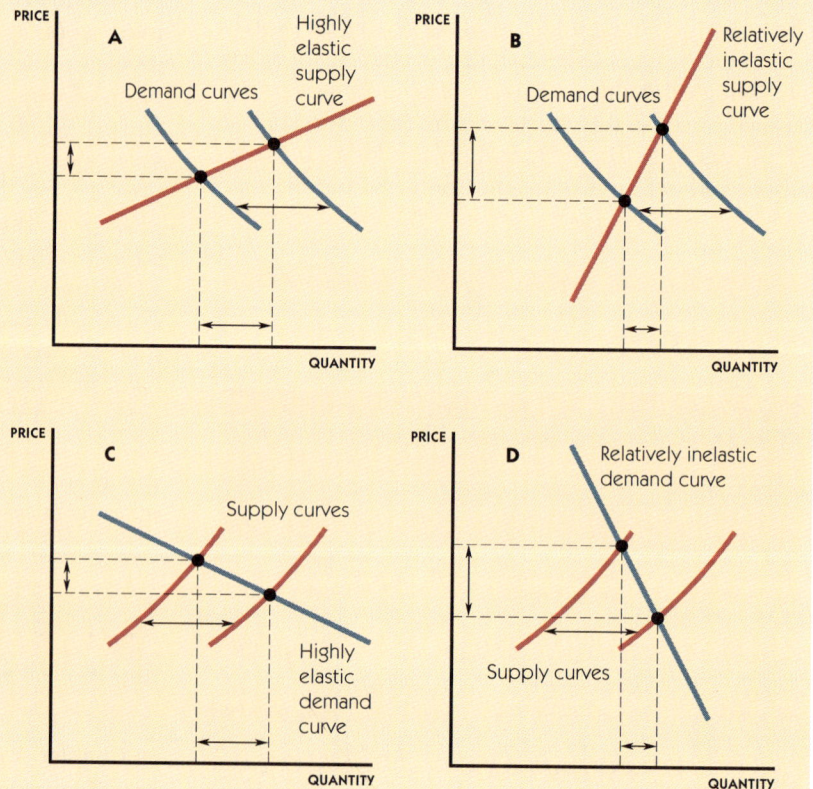

Figure 5.9 ELASTICITY OF DEMAND AND SUPPLY CURVES: THE NORMAL CASES

Normally, shifts in the demand curve will be reflected in changes in both price and quantity, as seen in panels A and B. When the supply curve is highly elastic, shifts in the demand curve will result mainly in changes in quantities; if it is relatively inelastic, shifts in the demand curve will result mainly in price changes. Likewise, shifts in the supply curve will be reflected in changes in both price and quantity, as seen in panels C and D. If the demand curve is highly elastic, shifts in the supply curve will result mainly in changes in quantities; if it is relatively inelastic, shifts in the supply curve will result mainly in price changes.

PRICE OF CIGARETTES

A: A TAX ON CIGARETTES

Supply curve after tax

Supply curve before tax

Price paid by consumers

10¢

Price without tax
Price received by producers

Demand curve

Q_1 Q_0

QUANTITY OF CIGARETTES (Q)

PRICE OF CHEDDAR CHEESE

B: A TAX ON CHEDDAR CHEESE

Supply curve after tax

Supply curve before tax

Price paid by consumers

Price without tax

10¢ Demand curve

Price received by producers

Q_1 Q_0

QUANTITY OF CHEDDAR CHEESE (Q)

Figure 5.10 **PASSING ALONG A TAX TO CONSUMERS**

A tax on the output of an industry shifts the supply curve up by the amount of the tax. Panel A shows that if the demand curve is relatively inelastic, as it is for cigarettes, then most of the tax will be passed on to consumers in higher prices. Panel B shows that if the demand curve is relatively elastic, as it is for cheddar cheese, then the tax cannot be passed along to consumers in higher prices, and must instead be absorbed by producers.

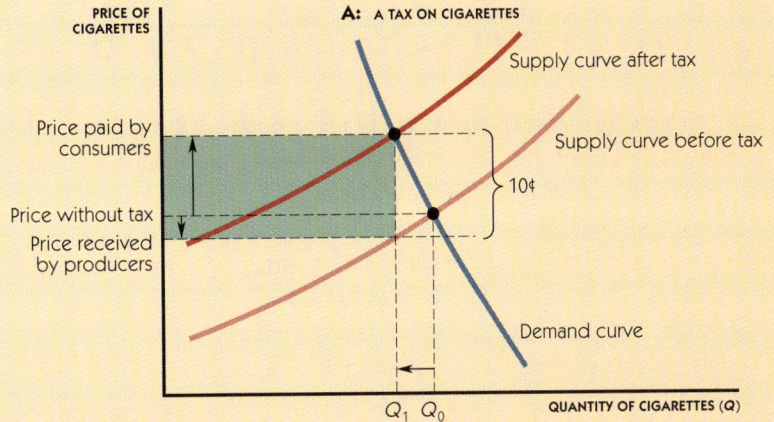

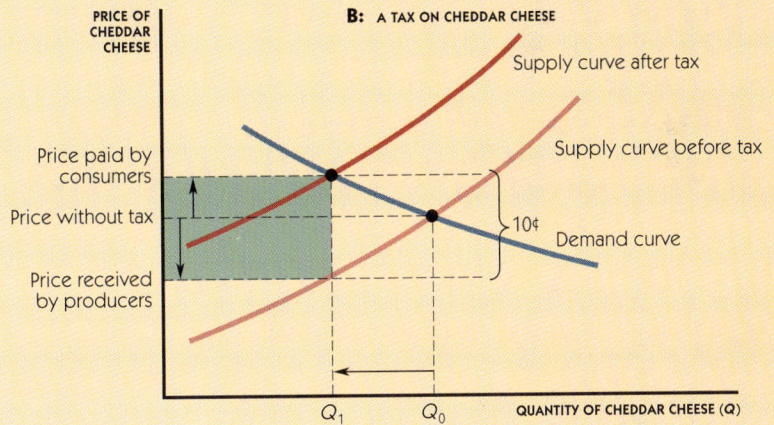

TAX POLICY AND THE LAW OF SUPPLY AND DEMAND

Understanding the law of supply and demand is vital for many questions of public policy. One of the important ways economists use this law is in projecting the effect of taxes. Assume that the tax on a pack of cigarettes is increased by 10 cents, that the tax is imposed on cigarette retailers, and that all the companies try to pass on the cost increase to consumers by raising the price of a pack by 10 cents. At the higher price fewer cigarettes will be consumed, with the decrease in demand depending on the price elasticity of demand. With lower demand firms may reduce

their price; by how much depends on the price elasticity of supply. The new equilibrium is depicted in Figure 5.10A.

For firms to produce the same amount as before, they must receive 10 cents more per pack (which they pass on to the government). Thus, the supply curve is shifted up by 10 cents. Since the demand for cigarettes is relatively inelastic, this shift will result in a large increase in price and a relatively small decrease in quantity demanded.

When a tax on producers results in consumers paying a higher price, economists say the tax is "passed on" or "shifted" to consumers. The fact that the consumer bears the tax (even though it is collected from the producers) does not mean that the producers are "powerful" or have conspired together. It simply

CLOSE-UP: ARE PAYROLL TAXES JOB KILLERS?

An increasingly important source of tax revenue for governments is the system of payroll taxes, that is, taxes that apply on the wages and salaries of employees. Payroll taxes include unemployment insurance premiums and Canada Pension Plan contributions paid to the federal government, as well as provincial taxes levied on wages and salaries and used to finance workers' compensation programs and, in some provinces, to contribute to health and/or postsecondary education spending. According to Statistics Canada, employers paid an average of 7.8 percent of wages and salaries to federal and provincial governments in 1993 compared with 6.7 percent in 1990 and only 2.3 percent in 1970. (This does not include the amount that the employees themselves contributed, which is a significant proportion of employer contributions.) However, the rates vary considerably across provinces, ranging from 10.0 percent in Quebec to about 8.0 percent in Ontario, Manitoba, and Newfoundland to about 5.8 percent in Alberta, British Columbia, and Saskatchewan.

Not surprisingly, business organizations such as the Canadian Chamber of Commerce view the increase in payroll taxes with some alarm. They argue that a payroll tax is a "tax on jobs" and as such discourages firms from hiring workers. Is that a justifiable concern? There are a number of reasons why we might be cautious in supposing that payroll taxes have killed jobs.

For one thing, the standard supply and demand analysis tells us that when a tax is imposed on a market, the market will respond by some combination of price increase and quantity reduction.

Imagine Figure 5.10 applying to the market for labour with the wage rate on the vertical axis and the quantity of labour on the horizontal axis. The more inelastic the demand and supply curves for labour, the less will be the reduction in quantity of labour as a result of the tax, and vice versa.

In the case of labour markets, we might expect that the demand is highly elastic, given that Canadian firms must compete in international markets and so cannot afford to let their labour costs increase. However, although Canadian payroll taxes are increasing, they still remain well below those of other industrialized nations, including the United States and Western European countries. This makes it easier for firms to absorb the tax without losing their ability to compete. At the same time, the supply of labour may be quite inelastic. In these circumstances, a good part of the payroll tax might be absorbed in the form of lower after-tax wages for workers, and relatively little in the form of reduced employment.

In the end, the effect of payroll taxes on employment is an empirical question, one that economists are only now beginning to grapple with. A recent study by two economists from Lakehead University, Livio Di Matteo and Michael Shannon, estimated that a 1 percent increase in the payroll tax would cause employment to fall by .32 percent, resulting in over 40,000 lost jobs.

Sources: Bruce Little, "Quebec Payroll Taxes Highest," *The Globe and Mail,* September 22, 1995; Livio Di Matteo and Michael Shannon, "Payroll Taxation in Canada: An Overview," *Canadian Business Economics* (Summer 1995): 5–22.

reflects the system of supply and demand. Note, however, that the price did not rise the full 10 cents. Producers receive slightly lower after-tax prices and therefore bear a small fraction of the tax burden.

A tax imposed on a good or service for which the demand is very elastic leads to a different result. Assume, for instance, that the government decides to tax cheddar cheese (but no other cheeses). Since many cheeses are almost like cheddar, the demand curve for cheddar cheese is very elastic. In this case, as Figure 5.10B makes clear, most of the tax is absorbed by the producer, who receives (net of tax) a lower price. Production of cheddar cheese is reduced drastically as a consequence.

Which of these two cases applies can be important for tax policy. If the government is primarily interested in a tax as a source of revenue, it would prefer to apply the tax to goods that have inelastic demands. In Figure 5.10, tax revenues are indicated by the shaded areas. The less elastic the demand for the good being taxed, the larger the shaded area. But if the purpose of the tax is to discourage consumption of the good, the more elastic the demand, the more successful the measure will be, even though less tax revenue will be raised. Finally, if the government is concerned about the fairness of the tax, it may prefer not to tax heavily goods whose demands are inelastic because goods that are consumed proportionately more by low-income persons will have lower income elasticities of demand, and these are typically also goods with low price elasticities of demand.

SHORTAGES AND SURPLUSES

The law of supply and demand works so well most of the time in a developed modern economy that everyone can take it for granted. If you are willing to pay the "market price"—the prevailing price of the good or service as determined by the intersection of demand and supply—you can obtain almost anything. Similarly, if a seller of a good or service is willing to charge no more than the market price, he can always sell what he wants to.

When the price is set so that demand equals supply—so that any individual can get as much as she wants at that price, and any supplier can sell the amount he wants at that price—economists say that the market **clears,** or is in equilibrium. But when the market does not clear, there are dramatic shortages or surpluses. To an economist, a **shortage** means that people would like to buy something, but they simply cannot find it for sale at the going price. A **surplus** means that sellers would like to sell their product, but they cannot sell as much of it as they would like at the going price. These cases where the market does not seem to be working are often the most forceful reminders of the importance of the law of supply and demand. The problem is that the "going price" is not the market equilibrium price.

Shortages and surpluses can be seen in Figure 5.11, the standard supply and demand diagram. In both

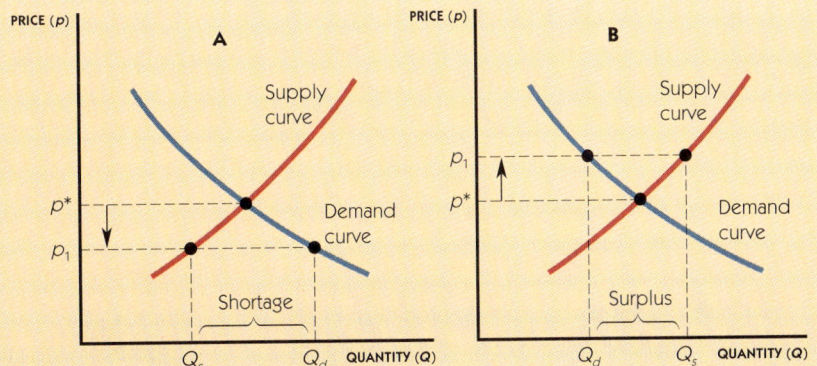

Figure 5.11 SHORTAGES AND SURPLUSES

In panel A, the actual price p_1 is below the market-clearing price p^*. At a price of p_1, quantity demanded exceeds quantity supplied, and a shortage exists. In panel B, the actual price p_1 is above the equilibrium price p^*. In this case, quantity supplied exceeds quantity demanded, and there is a surplus, or glut, in the market.

For the past dozen years or so, Canadian smokers have faced skyrocketing prices for cigarettes and other tobacco products as a direct consequence of government tax policies. Cigarettes are subject to an impressive array of taxes at both the federal and provincial levels of government. At the federal level, these include a specific excise tax, an excise duty on domestically manufactured tobacco, and a customs duty on imports. As well, cigarettes are subject to the Goods and Services Tax (GST) applicable to all consumer products. The provinces collect a specific excise tax on cigarettes, and most of them include cigarettes in the provincial retail sales tax base. The combined efforts of provincial and federal governments have led to an increase in cigarette taxes of 250 percent in the past fifteen years.

Why do governments find tobacco taxes an attractive instrument of policy? Two reasons are usually given. One is that the demand for cigarettes is relatively inelastic, which makes the tax a reliable source of revenue. If the demand for a product is inelastic, the attempt by producers to pass the tax on to consumers will not cause much decline in demand, and the government will collect a great deal of additional revenue. The second reason is to discourage the purchase of cigarettes by Canadians, since smoking is viewed as being an activity with adverse health effects, at least some of which are borne by nonsmokers.

The relative effectiveness of the policy in meeting these two objectives clearly depends upon the elasticity of demand. If the demand is very inelastic, the tax is a good source of revenue but an ineffective instrument for discouraging smoking. On the other hand, if it is more elastic, it will succeed in discouraging demand but will raise relatively little revenue. The evidence is somewhat mixed. Empirical studies have shown that in the short run the elasticity of demand for cigarettes is around -0.3 (so a 10 percent increase in price would lead to a 3 percent decline in demand), while in the long run it is closer to -1.2. The higher elasticity in the long run suggests that it takes some time before smokers adjust to a price increase and reduce smoking, presumably owing to the addictive nature of the product. It has also been found that the elasticity is higher among the young than among the old. These results would suggest that cigarette taxes are more of an instrument for discouraging smoking than for raising revenues, at least in the long run. In fact, since the long-run elasticity is greater than unity, an increase in cigarette taxes should lead to a decline in tax revenues in the long run: a 10 percent increase in prices leads to a greater than 10 percent decline in sales.

Pushing cigarette taxes ever higher to restrict consumption, however, has led to an unforeseen problem, which detracts considerably from its perceived success and frustrates both objectives of cigarette tax policy. Since Canadian cigarette taxes have increased much more than those in the United States, the incentive to smuggle cigarettes into Canada from the United States for personal consumption or for resale has correspondingly increased.

Moreover, most Canadian cigarettes that have been exported to the United States free of tax are smuggled back in. Over the period 1985–91, exports of cigarettes to the United States

panels A and B, the market equilibrium price is p^*. In panel A, the going price, p_1, is below p^*. At this price demand exceeds supply; you can see this by reading down to the horizontal axis. Demand is Q_d; supply is Q_s. The gap between the two points is the "shortage." With the shortage, consumers scramble to get the limited supply available at the going price.

In panel B, the going price, p_1, is above p^*. At this price demand is less than supply. Again we denote the demand by Q_d and the supply by Q_s. There is a surplus in the market of $Q_s - Q_d$. Now sellers are scrambling to find buyers.

At various times and for various goods, markets have not cleared. There have been shortages of apartments in Toronto; farm surpluses have plagued both Western Europe and North America; in 1973 there was a shortage of gasoline, with cars lined up in long lines outside of gasoline stations. Unemployment is a type of surplus, when people who want to work find that they cannot sell their labour services at the going wage.

In some markets, like the stock market, the adjustment of prices to shifts in the demand and supply curves tends to be very rapid. In other cases, such as in the housing market, the adjustments tend to be sluggish. When price adjustments are sluggish, shortages or surpluses persist as prices adjust. For instance, houses tend not to sell quickly during periods of decreased demand, which translate only slowly into lower housing prices.

When the market is not adjusting quickly toward equilibrium, economists say that prices are **sticky.** Even in these cases, the analysis of market equilibrium is useful. It indicates the direction of the changes—if the equilibrium price exceeds the current price, prices will tend to rise. Moreover, the rate at which prices fall or rise is often related to the gap, at the going price, between the quantity demanded and the quantity supplied.

INTERFERING WITH THE LAW OF SUPPLY AND DEMAND

The law of supply and demand, which governs how prices are set, can produce results that some individuals or groups do not like. For example, a reduced supply of oil may lead to a higher equilibrium price for oil. The higher price is not a malfunction of the law of supply and demand, but this is little comfort to those who use gasoline to power their cars and oil to heat their homes. Low demand for unskilled labour may lead to very low wages for unskilled workers. An increase in the demand for apartments in Vancouver leads, in the short run (with an inelastic supply), to an increase in rents—to the delight of landlords and the dismay of renters.

In each of these cases, pressure from those who did not like the outcome of market processes has led governments to act. The price of oil and natural gas was at one time regulated; minimum wage laws set a minimum limit on what employers can pay, even if the workers are willing to work for less; and rent control laws limit what landlords can charge. The concerns behind these interferences with the market are understandable, but the agitation for government action is based on two errors.

First, someone (or some group) was assigned blame for the change: the oil price rises were blamed on the oil companies, low wages on the employer, and rent increases on the landlord. As already explained, economists emphasize the role of anonymous market forces in determining these prices. After all, if landlords or oil companies are basically the same people today as they were last week, there must be some reason that they started charging different prices this week. Sometimes the price increase is the result of producers colluding to raise prices. This was the case in 1973, when the oil-exporting countries got together to raise the price of oil. The more common situation, however, is illustrated by the increase in the price of oil in August 1990, after Iraq's invasion of Kuwait. There was no collusion this time. The higher price simply reflected the anticipated reduction in the supply of oil. People rushed to buy, increasing short-term demand and pushing up the equilibrium price.

The second error was to forget that as powerful as governments may be, they can no more repeal the law of supply and demand than they can repeal the law of gravity. When they interfere with its working, the forces of supply and demand will not be balanced. There will either be excess supply or excess demand. Shortages and surpluses create problems of their own, often worse than the original problem the government was supposed to resolve.

Two straightforward examples of governments' overruling the law of supply and demand are **price ceilings,** which impose a maximum price that can be charged for a product, and **price floors,** which impose a minimum price. Rent control laws are price ceilings, and minimum wage laws are price floors. A closer look at each will help highlight the perils of interfering with the law of supply and demand.

PRICE CEILINGS: THE CASE OF RENT CONTROL

Price ceilings—setting a maximum charge—are always tempting to governments because they seem an easy way to assure that everyone will be able to afford a particular product. Thus, in the last couple of decades in Canada, price ceilings have been set for a wide range of goods, from natural gas to oil to rental accommodation. In each case the result has been to create shortages at the controlled price. More people want to buy the product than there are products, because producers have no incentive to produce more of the good. Those who can buy at the cheaper price benefit; producers and those unable to buy suffer.

The effect of **rent control** laws—setting the maximum rent that a landlord can charge for a one-bedroom apartment, for example—is illustrated by Figure 5.12. In panel A, R^* is the market equilibrium rental rate, at which the demand for housing equals the supply. However, the local government is concerned that at R^*, many poor people cannot afford housing in the city, so it imposes a law that says that rents may be no higher than R_1. At R_1, there is an excess demand for apartments. While the motives behind the government action may well have been praiseworthy, the government has created an artificial scarcity.

As with many government policies, there are some gainers and some losers. The gainers will be the households that happen to be lucky enough to have an apartment. Their rent will be lower than it otherwise would have been. Among the losers will be the owners of rental accommodation, who will receive lower rents and incomes than in the absence of rent controls. There are also the potential landlords who would otherwise have supplied rental accommodation at the market price, but are unable to cover costs at the controlled rent. Perhaps the most important losers are the households that are unable to find rental accommodation, given the limited supply. Among these will be low-income households, who are presumably the ones that the policy was meant to benefit.

The extent of the shortage created and the number of low-income households unable to find rental accommodation will depend upon the extent to which quantities demanded and supplied respond to the artificially lowered price. As we have seen, the less elastic the demands and supplies, the less will be the response of quantities to price changes. Thus, if demands and supplies were very inelastic, the amount of excess demand created will be small, and

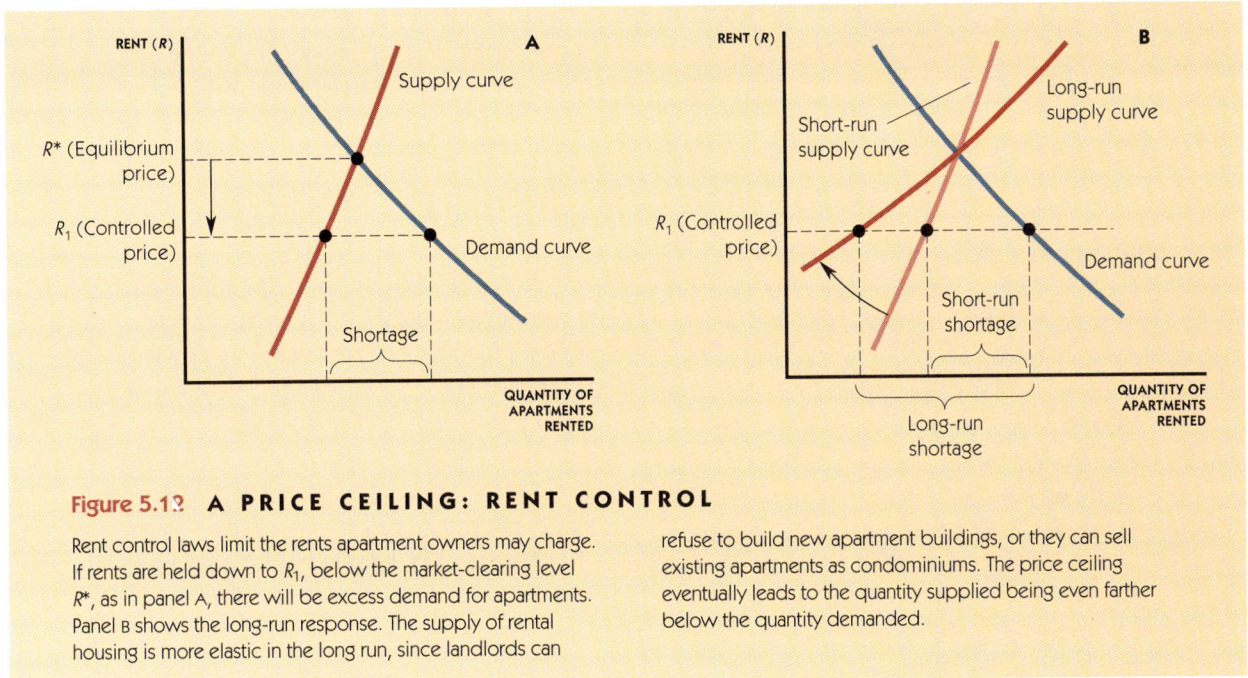

Figure 5.12 A PRICE CEILING: RENT CONTROL

Rent control laws limit the rents apartment owners may charge. If rents are held down to R_1, below the market-clearing level R^*, as in panel A, there will be excess demand for apartments. Panel B shows the long-run response. The supply of rental housing is more elastic in the long run, since landlords can refuse to build new apartment buildings, or they can sell existing apartments as condominiums. The price ceiling eventually leads to the quantity supplied being even farther below the quantity demanded.

the government may have accomplished what they set out to do with limited disruption to the market. In the short run, both demands and supplies are likely to be quite inelastic, so rent controls might be temporarily beneficial.

However, the problems caused by rent control are likely to be worse in the long run than in the short run, because long-run supply curves are more elastic than short-run supply curves. In the short run, the quantity of apartments does not change much. But in the long run, the quantity of apartments can decline for several reasons, as landlords try to minimize the losses from rent control. Apartments may be abandoned as they deteriorate; they can be converted to condominiums and sold instead of rented; and apartment owners may not wish to construct new ones if they cannot charge enough in rent to cover their costs. Figure 5.12B illustrates how the housing shortages under rent control will increase over time. As time goes by, more and more would-be residents will be unable to find rental housing in the market. Since renters tend to be poorer than those who can buy a home, a shortage of rental housing will tend to hurt the poor most.

PRICE FLOORS: THE CASE OF THE MINIMUM WAGE

To many Canadians, it has long seemed fair that if you work full time fifty-two weeks a year at some job, you ought to earn enough to support yourself and a family. Yet there are some jobs, especially those demanding low skill levels, for which this may not be the case. In the absence of government intervention, the wage rates on such jobs might be so low as to leave the worker and the worker's family below the poverty line. The result is either that other members of the family are forced to go to work or all are forced to live in poverty. Given this possibility it is easy to see the source of the sentiment for

CLOSE-UP: RENT CONTROL IN ONTARIO

Rent control was implemented by most provinces in Canada as part of the general policy of wage and price controls to fight inflation in 1974 and 1975. When inflation subsided, so did wage and price controls. In some places, however, rent control remained in effect. In Ontario the immediate impact of rent control was a decline in rental housing starts from 26,000 in 1973 to 15,000 in 1974 to 3,800 in 1975. The response to this decline in supply has been for governments to become increasingly involved as suppliers or subsidizers in the rental market. Given this subsidization and the social and political opposition to rent decontrol, rent control has become entrenched since 1974 in Ontario.

Although the rationale behind rent control is to give lower-income persons access to affordable housing, other economic classes often benefit most from the system. The decreased supply of rental units reduces the turnover rate and thus the availability of rental housing. The original occupiers of the regulated housing are the initial winners.

Contributing to this allocation problem is the existence of "key money." In 1985 in Toronto, a tenant occupying a one-bedroom apartment in a prime downtown location might be offered a $2,000 cash inducement to vacate ($5,000 for a two-bedroom apartment). In this manner, cheap rent-controlled housing was transferred to those who could afford to make key-money payments. The government's rent-control objectives were undermined, and a black market for rental housing was established.

Until 1986, rental units constructed after 1975 were not subject to rent control. Since middle- to upper-income persons could more easily gain access to the limited number of regulated units becoming available (through the black market), lower-income persons were left either to scramble for a place in the newer, uncontrolled, and more expensive units, or were forced into run-down areas or even onto the street.

In 1986 several changes to the Ontario system of rent control were enacted in order to enhance equity and efficiency. Landlords were allowed to cover maintenance costs in their yearly rent increases, thereby reducing the incentive to allow rent-controlled units to become run down. And, post-1975 construction was included in the rent-control scheme. Still, in 1987, the vacancy rate of rental units in Toronto was only 0.1 percent. In the early 1980s, the four western provinces and New Brunswick all removed the rent controls that had been in existence since the 1970s. Vacancy rates in 1987 for Vancouver, Edmonton, and St. John were 2.3 percent, 5.5 percent, and 5.4 percent, respectively.

It appears that rent controls have not been effective in providing low-cost housing to the poor. In addition to the effects on the rental market itself, there have also been effects on the owner-occupied housing market and on labour mobility. The severe shortage of rental housing is seen by some economists as a problem that only decontrol and a freely functioning market can solve.

Sources: Lawrence B. Smith, "An Economic Assessment of Rent Controls: The Ontario Experience," In Richard J. Arnott and Jack M. Mintz, eds., *Rent Control: The International Experience* (Kingston, Ontario: The John Deutsch Institute for the Study of Economic Policy, 1987), pp. 57–72; R. Andrew Muller, "Ontario's Options in the Light of the Canadian Experience with Decontrol," In Richard J. Arnott and Jack M. Mintz, eds., *Policy Forum on Rent Controls in Ontario* (Kingston, Ontario: The John Deutsch Institute for the Study of Economic Policy, 1987), pp. 21–38.

governments to interfere with the market and attempt to force firms to pay a decent wage. In Canada, all provinces and territories have enacted **minimum wages** at rates ranging from $4.75 in Newfoundland and Prince Edward Island to $6.85 in Ontario and $7.00 in British Columbia. Rates have tended to be raised periodically to keep pace with the cost of living, and have tended to be about half the average wage for all workers.

The minimum wage is an example of a price floor. While price ceilings are meant to help demanders (buyers), price floors are meant to help suppliers (sellers). With a price floor such as the minimum wage, buyers (employers) cannot pay less than the government-set minimum wage.

Price floors have predictable effects, too. The reasoning is simply the reverse of that for price ceilings. If the government attempts to raise the minimum wage higher than the equilibrium wage, the demand for workers will be reduced and the supply increased. There will be an excess supply of labour. Of course, those who are lucky enough to get a job will be better off at the higher wage than at the market equilibrium wage; but there are others who might have been employed at the lower market equilibrium wage who cannot find work and are worse off. These tend to be among the least skilled workers.

How much unemployment does the minimum wage create? That depends on the level at which the minimum wage is set and on the elasticity of demand and supply for labour. If the minimum wage is set low enough, then it has little effect, either on wages or on employment. Panel A of Figure 5.13 shows a market in which an equilibrium wage is above the minimum wage. A small increase in the minimum wage has no effect on either the wage rate or the employment level. With the current level of minimum wages, only very unskilled individuals are affected. Most other workers, even the unskilled, get paid more than the minimum wage.

Panel B of Figure 5.13 shows the case where the demand and supply for unskilled labour are very inelastic, so that wages can be increased significantly with little increase in unemployment. In Panel C, demand and supply for unskilled labour are both very elastic, and the minimum wage has been set

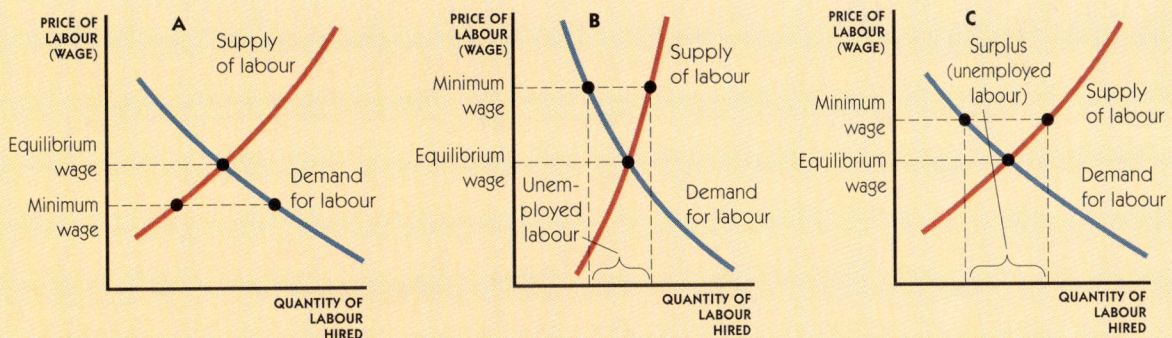

Figure 5.13 EFFECTS OF MINIMUM WAGES

In panel A, the minimum wage is below the equilibrium wage. However, since the minimum wage is a price floor, there is nothing to stop the market from paying the higher equilibrium wage, and any increase in the minimum wage will have no effect so long as the minimum wage remains below the equilibrium wage. In panel B; an increase in the minimum wage will result in very little increase in unemployment, as the demand and supply curves for labour are inelastic. In panel C, the demand and supply curves are more elastic; the minimum wage is above the equilibrium wage, creating a large surplus of workers who would like to work but cannot find jobs. Increases in the minimum wage in this case will increase unemployment significantly.

significantly above the market equilibrium wage. As a result, substantial unemployment is generated by the minimum wage.

QUANTITY CONTROLS: SUPPLY MANAGEMENT IN AGRICULTURE

Price ceilings and floors represent direct interference with market prices. Alternatively, governments can regulate quantities traded on markets, and thereby indirectly determine market prices. For example, if governments can restrict the quantity of a product supplied, this will artificially increase the market price. As with minimum prices, they may be tempted to do this to make suppliers better off.

An example of quantity controls is the system of **supply management** that has been used in some sectors of Canadian agriculture, such as the markets for milk, turkeys, chickens, and eggs. Under this system the government's regulatory agency controls the aggregate supply of all producers through the issuing of **quotas** denominated in units of the product. In order to produce, say, 1,000 turkeys, a producer must be allocated a quota of 1,000. Producers without a quota cannot produce. The quotas might initially have been allocated to producers in accordance with their actual production. However, once issued, the quotas can be traded and have a market price.

The effect of quotas on the market for turkeys can be illustrated in Figure 5.14. The equilibrium price would have been p_e and the equilibrium quantity Q_e. Suppose the government now sets the total number of quotas at Q. At this quantity, the price that consumers would pay would be p. If quotas could be freely sold and bought, they would naturally end up going to the producers who would value them most; those with the lowest costs of production. In terms of the supply curve, producers whose costs are c or below would be the lowest-cost ones. They would be willing to pay at least $p-c$ for a quota to produce each turkey, since this is the difference between the selling price they would receive and the costs to the marginal producer. Producers whose costs were higher than c would not pay $p-c$ for a quota, since that would entail their making a loss. Thus, the equilibrium price for the quota would be $p-c$, and the total value of quotas to produce turkeys in a given period would be given by the shaded area.

The use of quotas has some advantages over price floors as a way of assisting producers. For one thing, quotas avoid the excess supply induced by price floors. In the case of agricultural products, this excess supply is pure waste. For another, the fact that quotas are tradable implies that the most efficient producers

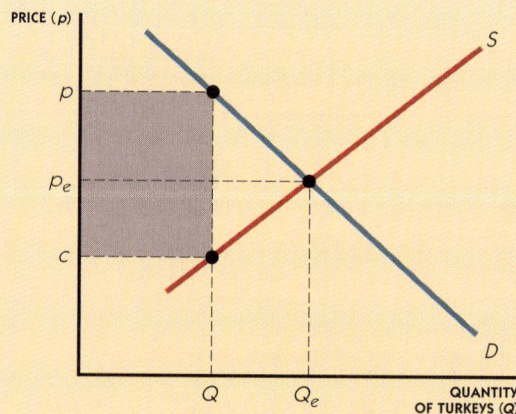

Figure 5.14 QUOTAS IN AGRICULTURE

If the government establishes a quota of Q units of turkeys, the market price of turkeys will be p, and the value of the quota per period will be given by the shaded area between p and c.

should be the ones who end up supplying the product, since the price of quotas will be bid up to force the higher-cost producers out of the market.

On the other hand, there are disadvantages of quotas. For one, since quotas involve artificially restricting the quantity and increasing the price, consumers are among the losers. For another, the output of the market is not allowed to settle at its most efficient level, that is, the level where the marginal benefit to consumers (i.e., the price) is equal to the marginal cost of supplying the product. Finally, since quotas are typically applicable not just to this year's production but to production in future years as well, the full benefit of a quota is much larger than that illustrated in the diagram. The latter only shows the value of the quota in one production period. If the quota lasts indefinitely, its value must include that of all future years as well. This can make the dollar value of a quota immense. Much of this value accrues to the producers lucky enough to be allocated a quota when the quota is first established. It does nothing to improve the incomes of new producers wishing to enter the industry in the future. They end up having to pay an enormous price for a quota to the existing owners. To that extent, it does nothing to assist those whom it was intended to benefit.

ALTERNATIVE SOLUTIONS

Large changes in prices cause distress. It is natural to try to find scapegoats and to look to the government for a solution. Such situations call for compassion, and the economists' caution can seem coldhearted. But the fact remains that in competitive markets, the price changes are simply the impersonal workings of the law of supply and demand; without the price changes there will be shortages and surpluses. The examples of government attempts to interfere with the workings of supply and demand provide an important cautionary tale: one ignores the workings of the law of supply and demand only at one's peril. This does not mean, however, that the government should simply ignore the distress caused by large price and wage changes. It only means that government must take care in addressing the problems; price controls, including price ceilings and floors, are unlikely to be effective instruments.

Later chapters will discuss ways in which the government can address dissatisfaction with the consequences of the law of supply and demand—by making use of the power of the market rather than trying to fight against it. For example, if the government is concerned with low wages paid to unskilled workers, it can try to increase the demand for these workers. A shift to the right in the demand curve will increase the wages these workers receive. The government can do this either by subsidizing firms that hire unskilled workers or by providing more training to these workers and thus increasing their productivity.

If the government wants to increase the supply of housing to the poor, it can provide housing subsidies for the poor, which will elicit a greater supply. If government wants to conserve on the use of gasoline, it can impose a tax on gasoline. Noneconomists often object that these sorts of economic incentives have other distasteful consequences, and sometimes they do. But government policies that take account of the law of supply and demand will tend to be more effective, with fewer unfortunate side effects, than policies that ignore the predictable economic consequences that follow from disregarding the law of supply and demand.

SUMMARY

1 The price elasticity of demand describes how sensitive the quantity demanded of a good is to changes in the price of the good. When demand is inelastic, an increase in the price has little effect on quantity demanded; when demand is elastic, an increase in the price has a large effect on quantity demanded.

2 If price changes do not induce much change in demand, the demand curve is steep and is said to be inelastic, or insensitive to price changes. If the demand curve is rather flat, indicating that price changes induce large changes in demand, demand is said to be elastic, or sensitive to price changes. Demand for necessities is usually quite inelastic; demand for luxuries is elastic.

3 The price elasticity of supply describes how sensitive the quantity supplied of a good is to changes in the price of the good.

4 If price changes do not induce much change in supply, the supply curve is very steep and is said to be inelastic. If the supply curve is very flat, indicating that price changes cause large changes in supply, supply is said to be elastic.

5 The extent to which a shift in the supply curve is reflected in price or quantity depends on the shape of the demand curve. The more elastic the demand, the more a given shift in the supply curve will be reflected in changes in equilibrium quantities and the less it will be reflected in changes in equilibrium prices. The more inelastic the demand, the more a given shift in the supply curve will be reflected in changes in equilibrium prices and the less it will be reflected in changes in equilibrium quantities.

6 Likewise, the extent to which a shift in the demand curve is reflected in price or quantity depends on the shape of the supply curve.

7 Demand and supply curves are likely to be more elastic in the long run than in the short run. Therefore a shift in the demand or supply curve is likely to have a larger price effect in the short run and a larger quantity effect in the long run.

8 Elasticities can be used to predict to what extent consumer prices rise when a tax is imposed on a good. If the demand curve for a good is very inelastic, consumers in effect have to pay the tax. If the demand curve is very elastic, the quantities produced and the price received by producers are likely to decline considerably.

9 Government regulations may prevent a market from moving toward its equilibrium price, leading to shortages or surpluses. Price ceilings lead to excess demand. Price floors lead to excess supply.

10 Surpluses from price floors can be avoided by a system of quotas, but quotas benefit the select group of producers who are initially allocated the quotas.

KEY TERMS

price elasticity of demand	infinite elasticity of supply	market clearing	short-run elasticity
price elasticity of supply	zero elasticity of demand	sticky prices	long-run elasticity
infinite elasticity of demand	zero elasticity of supply	price ceiling	quotas
		price floor	

REVIEW QUESTIONS

1 What is meant by the elasticity of demand and the elasticity of supply? Why do economists find these concepts useful?

2 Is the slope of a perfectly elastic demand or supply curve horizontal or vertical? Is the slope of a perfectly inelastic demand or supply curve horizontal or vertical? Explain.

3 If the elasticity of demand is unity, what happens to total revenue as the price increases? What if the demand for a product is very inelastic? What if it is very elastic?

4 Under what condition will a shift in the demand curve result mainly in a change in quantity? in price?

5 Under what condition will a shift in the supply curve result mainly in a change in price? in quantity?

6 Why do the elasticities of demand and supply tend to change from the short run to the long run?

7 Under what circumstances will a tax on a product be passed along to consumers?

8 Why do price ceilings tend to lead to shortages? Why do price floors tend to lead to surpluses?

9 What determines the market price of a quota?

PROBLEMS

1 Suppose the price elasticity of demand for gasoline is .2 in the short run and .7 in the long run. If the price of gasoline rises 28 percent, what effect on quantity demanded will this have in the short run? in the long run?

2 Imagine that the short-run price elasticity of supply for a farmer's wheat is .3, while the long-run price elasticity is 2. If prices for wheat fall 30 percent, what are the short-run and long-run changes in quantity supplied? What are the short- and long-run changes in quantity supplied if prices rise by 15 percent? What happens to the farmer's revenues in each of these situations?

3 Assume that the demand curve for hard liquor is highly inelastic and the supply curve for hard liquor is highly elastic. If the tastes of the drinking public shift away from hard liquor, will the effect be larger on price or on quantity? If the federal government decides to impose a tax on manufacturers of hard liquor, will the effects be larger on price or on quantity? What is the effect of an advertising program that succeeds in discouraging people from drinking? Draw diagrams to illustrate each of your answers.

4 Imagine that wages (the price of labour) are sticky in the labour market, and that a supply of new workers enters that market. Will the market be in equilibrium in the short run? Why or why not? If not, explain the relationship you would expect to see between the quantity demanded and supplied, and draw a diagram to illustrate. Explain how sticky wages in the labour market affect unemployment.

5 For each of the following markets, explain whether you would expect prices in that market to be relatively sticky or not:
  (a) the stock market
  (b) the market for autoworkers
  (c) the housing market
  (d) the market for cut flowers
  (e) the market for pizza-delivery people

6 Suppose a government wishes to ensure that its citizens can afford adequate housing. Consider three ways of pursuing that goal. One method is to pass a law requiring that all rents be cut by one quarter. A second method offers a subsidy to all builders of homes. A third provides a subsidy directly to renters equal to one quarter of the rent they pay. Predict what effect each of these proposals would have on the price and quantity of rental housing in the short run and the long run.

PART TWO

PERFECT MARKETS

Microeconomics and macroeconomics provide two perspectives from which we can view the economy. One focuses on the behaviour of the parts, the other on the behaviour of the whole; one focuses on the choices of households and the production decisions of firms, the other on the aggregate consequences of those individual decisions and actions for the nation's output, employment levels, productivity growth, balance of payments, and inflation rates.

This book focuses on microeconomics. Part Two explores in depth the basic microeconomic assumptions of rational, well-informed consumers interacting with profit-maximizing firms in competitive markets. This set of assumptions, as we learned in Chapter 2, constitutes economists' basic model. Here we study the implications of this model and examine the powerful insights it affords. It turns out that, while this basic model is a good starting point, consumers are often not as well-informed, and markets are often not as competitive, as the model assumes them to be. Part Three expands on and enriches the basic model in ways that make it more realistic.

The economy consists of three groups of participants—individuals or households, firms, and government—interacting in three markets—the labour, capital, and product markets. Part Two follows those divisions, with one important exception: the detailed discussion of government is postponed to Part Four. The objective in Part Two is to understand how a purely private market economy might operate. Chapters 6 and 7 discuss how individuals and households decide what goods and services to consume and how much labour to supply. Chapter 8 considers how much of a household's income is consumed and how much is set aside as savings, and discusses how the household invests its savings in different types of assets. Chapters 9 and 10 analyze how firms take their decisions concerning how much to produce and how to produce it.

Finally, Chapter 11 brings households and firms together in the three markets. Households supply labour, and firms demand labour. The interaction of this supply and demand for labour determines the wage rate and the level of employment. Households supply savings or capital, and firms demand capital so that they can build factories and buy new machines. Their interaction in the capital market determines the interest rate and the equilibrium level of savings and investment in the economy. Households take their income, both what they earn as workers and the return on their savings, and use it to buy goods. With the workers they have hired, machines they have purchased, and factories they have built, firms produce goods. Firms' supply of goods and households' demand for goods interact in the product market, and this interaction determines the prices of the myriad of goods we consume. When all three markets clear simultaneously, the economy is in general equilibrium. One of the key features of a perfectly competitive economy in general equilibrium is that resources are allocated efficiently, as shown in this chapter.

CHAPTER 6

THE CONSUMPTION DECISION

lose to 10 million Canadian households taken together make an astounding number of spending choices every day. These decisions contribute to the overall demand for cars and bicycles, clothes and housing, and masses of other products available on the market. The members of each household also take decisions that affect how much income they will have to spend, like whether to work overtime or whether both partners in a marriage should work. They decide how much of their income to save. And they decide where to put the nest eggs they do save.

These four sets of decisions—about spending, working, saving, and investing—represent the basic economic choices facing the household. This chapter focuses on spending decisions and how these decisions are affected by taxes and other government policies. Chapter 7 discusses work-related decisions. Chapter 8 deals with household decisions concerning how much to save and how to invest those savings.

These microeconomic decisions have macroeconomic consequences. Household decisions about whether to buy a car that is imported from Japan or one that is Canadian-made will affect our trade deficit. Choices about how much one should work will affect overall levels of unemployment and production. Household decisions about savings and investment will affect the future growth of the economy.

KEY QUESTIONS

1 Where does the demand curve come from? Why is it normally downward sloping?

2 How does an increase in income shift the demand curve? How do changes in the prices of other goods shift the curve?

THE BASIC PROBLEM OF CONSUMER CHOICE

The first basic problem facing a consumer, though easy to state, is hard to resolve: What should he do with whatever income he has to spend? He must allocate his available income among alternative goods. Should he buy CDs, go to the movies, eat chocolate bars, or purchase sweaters? In the absence of scarcity the answer would be easy: have it all!

Chapter 2 provided the basic framework for economic decision making. The consumer defines his opportunity set, what is *possible* given the constraints he faces, and then chooses the most preferred point within this set. This chapter begins by reviewing how we define the opportunity set, and then asks how it changes—and how what the individual chooses changes—when incomes and prices change.

THE BUDGET CONSTRAINT

The individual's opportunity set is defined by the budget constraint. If a person's weekly after-tax paycheque comes to $300 and he has no other income, this is his budget constraint. Total expenditures on food, clothing, rent, entertainment, travel, and all other categories cannot exceed $300 per week. (For now we ignore the possibilities that individuals may borrow money, or save money, or change their budget constraints by working longer or shorter hours.)

The line *BC* in Figure 6.1A shows a simplified individual budget constraint. A student, Fran, has a total of $300 each semester to spend on "fun" items. Figure 6.1 assumes that there are two goods, chocolate bars and compact discs (CDs). The simplified assumption of only two goods is an abstraction that highlights the main points of the analysis.

Let's say that a chocolate bar costs $1, while a CD costs $15. If Fran spent all her income on chocolate bars, she could purchase 300 chocolate bars (point *B* on the budget constraint). If she spent all her income on CDs, she could buy 20 CDs (point *C* on the budget constraint). Fran can also choose any of the intermediate choices on line *BC*. For example, she could buy 10 CDs (for $150) and 150 chocolate bars (for $150), or 15 CDs ($225) and 75 chocolate bars ($75). Each combination of purchases along the budget constraint totals $300.

As we learned in Chapter 2, a budget constraint diagram has two important features. First, although any point in the shaded area of Figure 6.1A is feasible, only the points on the line *BC* are really relevant. This is because Fran is not consuming her entire budget if she is inside her budget constraint. Second, by looking along the budget constraint, we can see the trade-offs she faces—how many chocolate bars she has to give up to get 1 more CD, and vice versa. Look at points *F* and *A*. This part of the budget constraint is blown up in panel B. At point *A*, Fran has 10 CDs; at *F*, she has 11. At *F*, she has 135 chocolate bars; at *A*, 150. To get 1 more CD, she has to give up 15 chocolate bars.

These are her trade-offs, and they are determined by the relative prices of the two goods. If one good costs twice as much as another, to get 1 more unit of the costly good we have to give up 2 units of the cheaper good. If, as here, one good costs fifteen times as much as another, to get 1 more unit of the

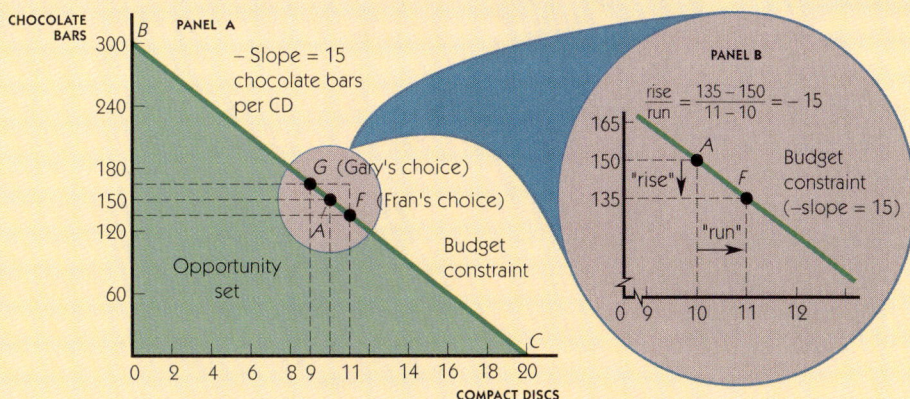

Figure 6.1 AN INDIVIDUAL'S BUDGET CONSTRAINT

Panel A is a budget constraint that shows the combinations of compact discs (at $15) and chocolate bars (at $1) that an individual could buy with $300. Fran chooses point F, with a relatively large number of CDs; Gary chooses point G, with a relatively large number of chocolate bars. Panel B shows that the trade-off of moving from 10 CDs to 11 (point A to F) is 15 chocolate bars.

costly good we have to give up 15 units of the less costly good.

The **slope** of the budget constraint also tells us what the trade-off is. The slope of a line measures how steep it is. As we move 1 unit along the horizontal axis (from 10 to 11 CDs), the slope measures the size of the change along the vertical axis. The slope is the rise (the movement up or down on the vertical axis) divided by the run (the corresponding horizontal movement). The slope of this budget constraint is thus 15.[1] It tells us how much of one good, at a given price, we need to give up if we want 1 more unit of the other good; it tells us, in other words, what the trade-off is.

Notice that the relative price of CDs to chocolate bars is 15; that is, a CD costs fifteen times as much as a chocolate bar. But we have just seen that the slope

of the budget constraint is 15, and that the trade-off (the number of chocolate bars Fran has to give up to get 1 more CD) is 15. It is no accident that these three numbers—relative price, slope, and trade-off—are the same.

This two-product example was chosen because it is easy to illustrate with a graph. But this logic can cover any number of products. Income can be spent on one item or a combination of items. The budget constraint defines what a certain amount of income can buy, which depends on the prices of the items. Giving up some of one item would allow the purchase of more of another item or items.

Economists represent these choices by putting the purchases of the good upon which they are focusing attention, say CDs, on the horizontal axis and "all other goods" on the vertical axis. By definition, what is not spent on CDs is available to be spent on all other goods. Fran has $300 to spend altogether. A more realistic budget constraint for her is shown in Figure

[1] We ignore the negative sign. See the appendix to Chapter 2 for a more detailed explanation of the slope of a line.

CLOSE-UP: CHANGING RELATIVE PRICES

Everyone notices how prices change over time. A favourite complaint is that things seem to be more expensive than they used to be. That prices in general have risen continuously over time is undoubtedly true, as a glance at Statistics Canada's monthly reports of the inflation rate—the change in the consumer price index—will confirm. However, what affects consumption decisions is the change in prices for various commodities relative to incomes, and relative to each other. A recent issue of *The Globe and Mail* allows us to infer how relative prices have changed over the last 20 years.

The table below compares the opportunity costs of quantities of goods in terms of the amount of time worked by the average worker for a representative sample of goods between 1974 and 1994. We have learned that opportunity costs and relative prices are one and the same. Thus one way to interpret the above data

is as an indication of how the prices of each commodity have changed relative to the price of labour, or the average wage rate. The fact that in order to buy a litre of Fleecy the average worker had to work 5.33 minutes in 1974 and 6.22 minutes in 1994 means that between 1974 and 1994 the price of Fleecy rose relative to the average wage. On the other hand, since the amount of work needed to buy a Timex watch fell from 3.13 hours in 1974 to 1.76 hours in 1994 the price of a watch fell relative to the average wage.

The data can also be used to compare how the relative price of two of the commodities has changed over time. For example, in 1974 ground beef cost 23.13 minutes of work while chicken legs cost 11.46 minutes of work. Thus, in 1974 the relative price of ground beef to chicken legs was approximately 2. In 1994 both cost 13.88 minutes of work, so the relative price was 1. This

Minutes of Work Required to Pay for				Hours of Work Required to Pay for		
	1974	1994			1974	1994
Fleecy (litre)	5.33	6.22	Men's dress shirt		2.70	3.17
Pork chops (kg)	23.42	38.93	Men's slacks		2.02	4.23
Kraft Dinner (box)	2.70	4.19	Timex watch		3.13	1.76
Ground beef (kg)	23.13	13.88	Vacuum cleaner		39.95	28.21
Nectarines (kg)	9.78	8.29	18″ electric mower		20.22	12.69
Shredded Wheat (box)	7.95	18.15	26″ colour TV		19.10	49.36
Chicken legs (kg)	11.46	13.88	Kenmore washer		65.16	38.72
Movie ticket	24.26	33.86	Kenmore dryer		42.69	26.73

NOTE: The above figures are based on the average weekly salary in 1974 ($178.09) and 1994 ($567.02).
Source: The Globe and Mail, December 16, 1995, p. D5.

means that the slope of the budget line between ground beef and chicken legs fell from 2 in 1974 to 1 in 1994. Similarly, in 1974 the price of a 26-inch colour TV set relative to a vacuum cleaner was .48 (19.10/39.95) while in 1994 it was 1.75 (49.36/28.21). Thus, the budget line between these two goods too became steeper over the 20 years.

It is important to note that these data can be used to determine only changes in the slopes of budget lines, not changes in their positions. That is, they can be used to show the incentive that consumers have to substitute one good for another. If consumers' real incomes were unchanged, only substitution effects would apply; changes in demand would be determined by these relative price changes. In fact, real incomes have risen at the same time and that will also affect demands for each of the commodities.

6.2. The intersection of the budget constraint with the vertical axis, point *B*—where purchases of CDs are zero—is $300. If Fran spends nothing on CDs, she has $300 to spend on other goods. The budget constraint intersects the horizontal axis at 20 CDs (point *C*); if she spends all her income on CDs and CDs cost $15 each, she can buy 20. If Fran chooses a point such as *F*, she will buy 11 CDs, costing $165, and she will have $135 to spend on other goods ($300 − $165). The distance 0*D* on the vertical axis measures what she spends on other goods; the distance *BD* measures what she spends on CDs.

CHOOSING A POINT ON THE BUDGET CONSTRAINT: INDIVIDUAL PREFERENCES

The budget constraint and a recognition of possible trade-offs is the starting point for the study of consumer behaviour. The process of identifying the budget constraints and the trade-offs is the same for *any* two people. If a person walks into a store that only accepts cash with $300, any economist can tell you his budget constraint and the trade-offs he faces by looking at the money in his pocket and the prices on the

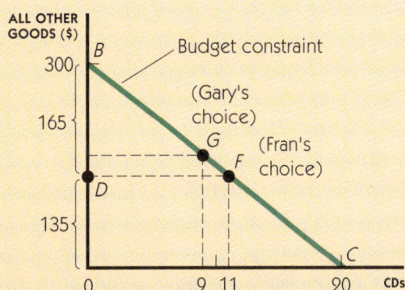

Figure 6.2 ALLOCATING A BUDGET BETWEEN A SINGLE GOOD AND ALL OTHERS

Some budget constraints show the choice between a particular good, in this case CDs, and all other goods. The other goods that might be purchased are collectively measured in money terms, as shown on the vertical axis.

shelves. What choice will he make? Economists narrow their predictions to points on his budget constraint; any individual will choose *some* point along the budget constraint. But the point actually chosen depends on the individual's preferences: Fran, who likes to listen to music, might choose point *F* in Figure 6.1, while Gary, who loves chocolate, might choose *G*.

Few people will choose either of the extreme points on the budget constraint, *B* or *C* in Figure 6.1, where only one of the goods is consumed. The reason for this is that the more you have of a good—say, the more CDs you have relative to another good such as chocolate bars—the less valuable is an additional unit of that good relative to additional units of another good. At points near *C*, it seems safe to assume that to most individuals, an extra CD does not look as attractive as some chocolate bars. Certainly, at *B* most people would be so full of chocolate bars that an extra CD would look preferable.

Where the individual's choice lies depends on how she values the two goods. Chapter 2 emphasized the idea that in taking decisions, people look at the *margin;* they look at the extra costs and benefits. In this case, the choice at each point along the budget constraint is between 1 more CD and 15 more chocolate bars. If Gary and Fran choose different points along the budget constraint, it is because they value the marginal benefits (how much better off they feel with an *extra* CD) and the marginal costs (how much it hurts to give up 15 chocolate bars) differently. Gary chooses point *G* in Figure 6.1 because that is the point where, for him, the marginal benefit of an extra CD is just offset by what he has to give up to get the extra CD, which is 15 chocolate bars. When Fran, who loves listening to music, considers point *G*, she realizes that for her, at that point CDs are more important and chocolate bars less important than they are for Gary. So she trades along the line until she has enough CDs and few enough chocolate bars that, for her, the marginal benefits of an extra CD and the marginal costs of 15 fewer chocolate bars are equal. This point, as we have supposed, is *F*.

The same reasoning holds for a budget constraint like the one shown in Figure 6.2. Here, Gary and Fran are choosing between CDs and all other goods, measured in dollar terms. Now in deciding to buy an extra CD, each one compares the marginal benefit of an extra CD with the marginal cost, what has to be given up in other goods. With CDs priced at $15, choosing to buy a CD means giving up $15 of other goods. For Gary, the marginal benefit of an extra CD equals the cost, $15, when he has only 9 CDs and can therefore spend $165 on other goods. For Fran, who has more of a taste for CDs, the marginal benefit of an extra CD does not equal this marginal cost until she reaches 11 CDs, with $135 to spend elsewhere. Thus, the price is a quantitative measure of the marginal benefit.

WHAT HAPPENS TO CONSUMPTION WHEN INCOME CHANGES

When an individual's income increases, he has more to spend on consumption. Normally, he will buy a little more of many goods, although his consumption of some goods will increase more than that of others, and different individuals will spend their extra income in different ways. Jim may spend much of his extra income going out to eat in restaurants more often, while Bill may spend much of his extra income buying a more expensive car.

The **income elasticity of demand** (which parallels the *price elasticity of demand* presented in Chapter 5) measures how much the consumption of a particular good increases with income:

$$\text{income elasticity of demand} = \frac{\text{percentage change in consumption}}{\text{percentage change in income}}.$$

The income elasticity of demand, in other words, is the percentage change in consumption that would result from a 1 percent increase in income. If the income elasticity of demand of a certain good is greater than 1, a 1 percent increase in an individual's income results in a more than 1 percent increase in expenditures on that good. The amount he spends on that good increases more than proportionally with income; that is, the share of income spent on that good rises as income rises. Economists refer to goods whose income

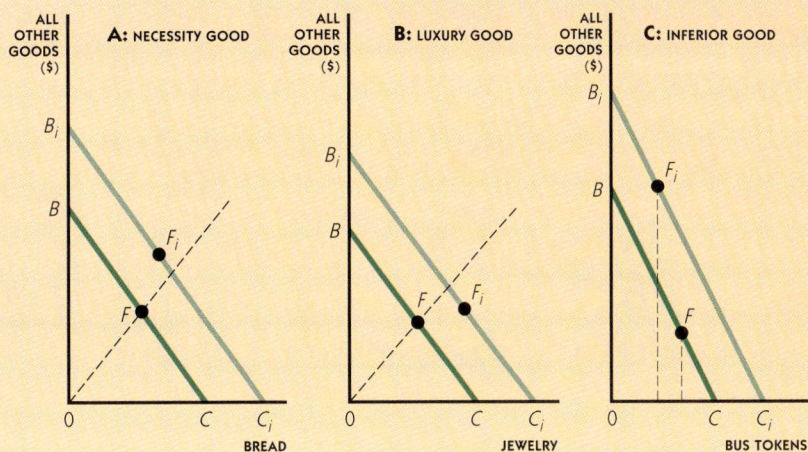

Figure 6.3 NORMAL VERSUS INFERIOR GOODS

The effect on consumption of a change in income depends on the nature of the good. For necessities, higher income leads to less then proportionate increases in consumption, as in panel A. For luxuries, higher income leads to more than proportionate increases in consumption, as in panel B. For inferior goods, higher income leads to lower consumption, as in panel C.

elasticity exceeds 1 as **luxuries.** Luxuries might include movies, expensive automobiles, restaurant dining, and vacations. Alternatively, if the income elasticity of demand is less than 1, then a 1 percent increase in income results in a less than 1 percent increase in expenditures. Such a good is referred to as a **necessity.** In this case, the share of income a consumer spends on that good decreases with a rise in income. Typical necessities include food, clothing, and shelter.

The consumption of some goods actually decreases as income increases and increases as income decreases. These goods are called **inferior** goods. They are in sharp contrast to **normal** goods, the consumption of which increases with income. In other words, goods for which the income elasticity is *negative* are, by definition, inferior, while all other goods are called normal. For instance, if Fran, who has been riding the bus to work, gets a large raise, she may find that she can afford a car. After buying the car, she will spend less on bus tokens. Thus, in this particular sense, bus rides represent an inferior good.

Figure 6.3 depicts the effect of income changes on Fran's demand for normal and inferior goods. Panel A shows the case of a normal good, bread, whose income elasticity is less than unity: it is a necessity. An increase in income shifts the budget line outward from BC to B_iC_i. Fran's consumption point changes

from F to F_i. The consumption of bread rises less than proportionately with income. Panel B shows the case of another normal good, jewelry, a luxury good whose income elasticity is greater than unity. In this case, the new consumption point F_i reflects a more than proportionate increase in the demand for jewelry. Finally, panel C shows the case of an inferior good, bus tokens. As Fran's income rises, her purchases of bus tokens actually fall.

Figure 6.4 shows how families at different income levels spend some of their income. The population is divided into five equal-sized groups, or quintiles, according to income. We see that *on average*, the lowest quintile of the population (the poorest 20 percent) spend over 30 percent of their income on housing. This should be contrasted with the richest 20 percent, who spend only a seventh of their income on housing. Similarly, the poorest 20 percent spend about a fifth of their income on food, while the richest 20 percent spend only a tenth.

Information like that contained in Figure 6.4 is of great practical importance. For example, it helps determine how a tax will affect different groups. Anybody who consumes alcohol will be hurt by a tax on alcohol. But if the poor spend a larger fraction of their income on alcohol, as the figure suggests, they will bear a disproportionately large share of the tax.

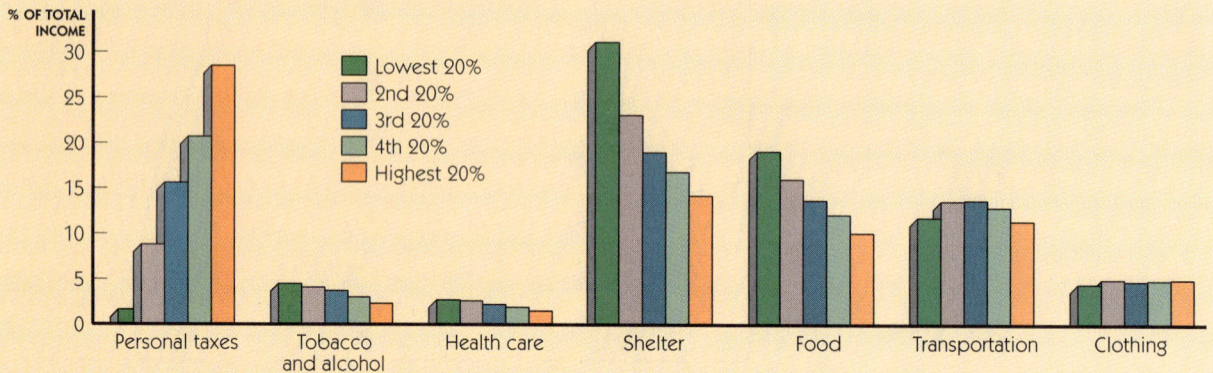

Figure 6.4 HOW HOUSEHOLDS OF DIFFERENT INCOMES SPEND THEIR MONEY

The poor spend far higher proportions of their income on basic necessities like food and housing than do the rich. *Source*: Statistics Canada, *Family Expenditure in Canada 1992*, Catalogue No. 62-555.

A CLOSER LOOK AT THE DEMAND CURVE

In Chapter 4 we saw the principal characteristic of the demand curve: when prices rise, the quantity of a good demanded normally falls. Here, we take a closer look at why. This will help us understand why some goods respond more strongly to price changes, that is, have a greater price elasticity.

Let us return to our earlier example of Fran buying CDs in Figure 6.2. If the price of CDs rises from $15 to $20, Fran cannot continue to buy the same number of CDs and the same amount of other goods as she did before. Earlier, Fran bought 11 CDs. If she bought the same number of CDs, it would cost her $55 more, and she would have $55 less to spend on other goods. No matter what she does, Fran is worse off as a result of the price increase. It is *as if* she had less income to spend. When she has less income to spend, she reduces her expenditure on each good,

including CDs. This part of the response to the higher price is called the **income effect.** An increase in income of about $55, or 18 percent ($55 ÷ 300 × 100), would offset the price increase.[2] Assume the income elasticity is approximately 1; that is, with income reduced by 18 percent, she would reduce purchases of CDs by 18 percent, which is about 2 CDs. This part of the reduction of the demand of CDs, from 11 to 9, is the income effect.

The magnitude of the income effect depends on two factors: how important the commodity is to the individual—how large a fraction of the individual's income is spent on the good—and how large the income elasticity is. Since in most cases individuals spend a relatively small fraction of their income on any particular good, the income effect is relatively

[2] Actually, it would slightly overcompensate. With the $55 increase, Fran could buy exactly the same bundle of goods as before, but as we shall shortly see, she will *choose* to reallocate her spending. The reallocation will make her better off.

After the huge increase in the price of oil in the late 1970s, the government wanted to conserve energy by discouraging the use of oil. One plan, proposed in the ill-fated Clark Conservative government budget of 1979, entailed the federal government raising the price of gasoline by imposing an excise tax but refunding it by providing a credit against income tax. Some critics ridiculed the idea. What's the point of collecting a tax and then refunding it? The answer is simple: the substitution effect.

Imagine that Lucy has an income of $20,000. She spends $500 a year, 2.5 percent of her income, on gasoline; at a price of $.50 a litre she can buy 1,000 litres. Assume first that the tax on a litre of gasoline is raised by $.10, increasing the price Lucy pays to $.60 a litre. If the price elasticity of demand for gasoline is .5, then this price increase will lead to a fall in the quantity demanded of 10 percent (20 percent × .5 = 10 percent). Now Lucy is buying 900 litres (90 percent of 1,000) at a price of $.60 a litre—and spending a total of $540. Government revenue is $.10 × 900 = $90. Assume the government refunds Lucy the $90. (The refund depends not on the actual amount of the gasoline tax paid by Lucy but on the average amount paid by all taxpayers. In this example, Lucy is an average person, so her refund is just equal to the gasoline tax she paid.) Is the government undoing the income effect of the higher gasoline price by giving consumers income? Not entirely. If Lucy continues to spend about 2.5 percent of her additional income on gasoline, her expenditure on gasoline goes up by just over $2 (2.5 percent × $90 refund). Her consumption of gasoline is still lower than it would have been without the tax combined with the rebate.

small. But in the case of housing, on which individuals spend on average between a quarter and a third of their income, the income effect of an increase in the price of housing is significant.

Let us go back to Fran and the CDs. At the higher price, giving up one CD gets her more of other goods—more chocolate bars, more movies, more tapes, more sweaters. The relative price of CDs, or the trade-off between CDs and other goods, has changed. At the higher price she *substitutes* goods that are less expensive for the more expensive CDs. Not surprisingly, this effect is called the **substitution effect.** The magnitude of the substitution effect depends on how easily Fran can substitute other goods. If Fran still owns her tape player, and if the price of tapes remains unchanged, then the substitution effect might be large. She may drop the number of CDs she purchases to 2. But if Fran has no tape player, if the only entertainment she likes is listening to music, and if she dislikes all the music played by the local radio stations, then the substitution effect may be small. She may drop the number of CDs she purchases only to 8.

The income and the substitution effect can be depicted graphically using what economists call **the theory of revealed preference.** Figure 6.5 depicts Fran's choice of CDs. Initially, when the budget line is BC, Fran chooses the point F. In choosing point F, she reveals that she prefers that point to all other points on the budget line BC. Suppose now the price of CDs falls, causing the budget line to rotate to BC_i. Fran chooses a point F_i on her new budget line. To

Figure 6.5 INCOME AND SUBSTITUTION EFFECTS

When the price of CDs falls but the consumer's income changes so that the original bundle of goods F could be bought, the consumer will likely substitute CDs for other goods, moving from F to F_c (the substitution effect). When the income is then returned to its original level, more CDs will be bought as the income effect takes the consumer from F_c to F_i.

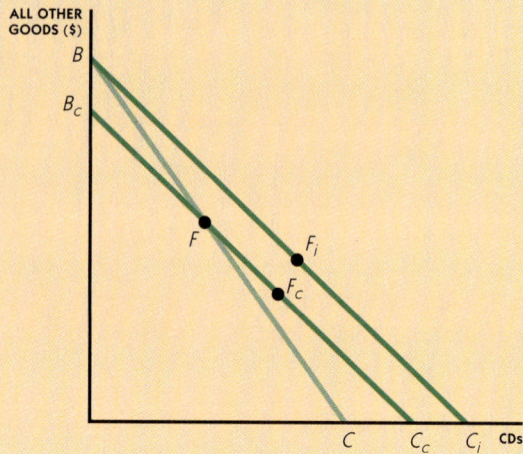

determine how much Fran's demand for CDs rises when the price of CDs falls, it is useful to divide the move from F to F_i into two steps.

In the first step the price of CDs is reduced but Fran's income is also reduced, so that at the new price she could just buy the combination of CDs and other goods that she did before. That is, the budget line is rotated around the initial point F to B_cC_c as shown in the figure. This pure price change will allow Fran to buy the same combination of CDs and other goods F that she could buy before, but it will also make available to her combinations that she could not previously afford (all those along the segment FC_c). We would expect that she would move to a point such as F_c, where she has substituted CDs for other goods. (She would definitely not move along the segment B_cF, since F has already been revealed to be preferred to any point along that segment.) This is the substitution effect corresponding to a pure price change that enables her to buy the original combination of CDs and other goods.

However, she can do better than that. Her real income will have risen because of the fall in price of CDs. The second part of the change consists of the movement of her budget line parallel outwards to its final position BC_i. This movement is the income ef-

fect; it causes her to increase her consumption of CDs even further, moving from the point F_c to F_i. The overall effect of the fall in the price of CDs is the sum of the substitution effect ($F - F_c$) and the income effect ($F_c - F_i$).

The demand curve traces out how the quantity demanded of a good changes as its price changes. The shape reflects the combination of income and substitution effects. Figure 6.6 depicts how Fran's demand curve for CDs is constructed. Panel A shows how Fran's budget line changes as the price of CDs changes. A fall in the price of CDs causes the budget line to rotate from BC to BC_d. Fran increases her demand for CDs from 11 to 15. By the same token, when the price of CDs rises, Fran's budget line rotates from BC to BC_i. Fran's demand for CDs falls from 11 to 6.

Panel B plots, for each price of CDs, the quantity consumed. This is the demand curve. Note that the vertical axis now represents the price of CDs. The points F_i, F, and F_d correspond to the prices and quantities given in panel A, and the smooth line connecting the points is based on the assumption that the analysis of the previous paragraph could be applied to smaller price changes, and that it would produce all the points shown as the demand curve.

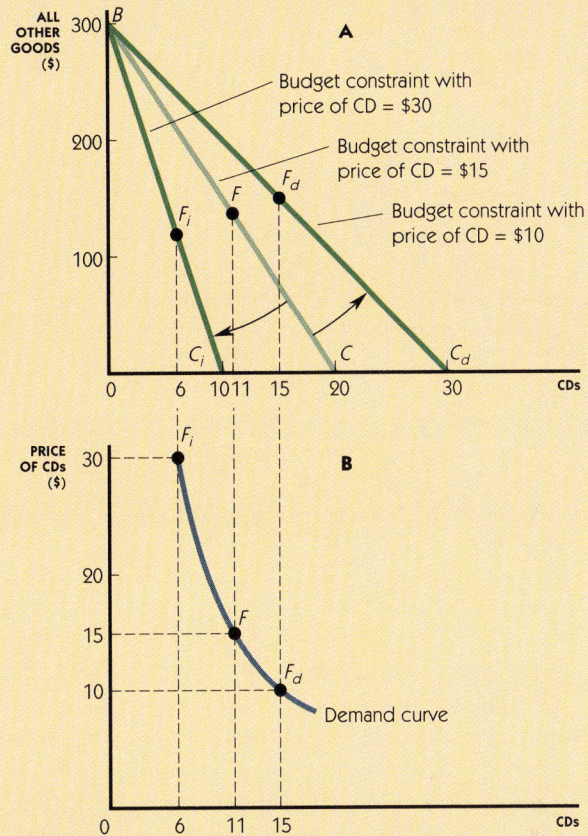

Figure 6.6 DERIVING DEMAND CURVES FROM SHIFTING BUDGET CONSTRAINTS

In panel A, the budget constraint rotates down to the left as the price of CDs increases, leading Fran to change consumption from F to F_i. The budget constraint rotates to the right when the price of CDs decreases, and Fran moves from F to F_d. Panel B shows the corresponding demand curve for CDs, illustrating how the rising prices lead to a declining quantity consumed.

THE IMPORTANCE OF DISTINGUISHING BETWEEN INCOME AND SUBSTITUTION EFFECTS

Distinguishing between the income and substitution effects of a change in price is important for two reasons.

Understanding Responses to Price Changes First, the distinction improves our understanding of consumption responses to price changes. Thinking about the substitution effect helps us understand why some demand curves have a low price elasticity and others a high price elasticity. It also helps us understand why the price elasticity may well differ at different points along the demand curve. Assume Bob is purchasing steaks 25 times a month, because the price is so low— a point such as B in Figure 6.7. As the price rises, Bob purchases fewer steaks. It is easy to cut back on eating steaks. He simply substitutes hamburger, ham, lamb chops, or chicken. But at a very high price, point A, Bob is consuming only 3 steaks a month. Now he really relishes each of his steaks. He is less willing to substitute. A further increase in price will still lead to a decline in quantity demanded, but not a large one. Generally, when an individual is consuming lots of

Figure 6.7 THE CHANGING ELASTICITY OF A SINGLE DEMAND CURVE

At point *B* a lot of steak is being consumed, and the benefit derived from an extra steak is relatively low. As the price of steak rises from point *B*, many substitutes are available, and the demand curve is elastic. But by the time point *A* is reached and little steak is being consumed, the benefit of an extra steak is relatively high, most of the readily available substitutes have been tried, and the demand curve is relatively inelastic.

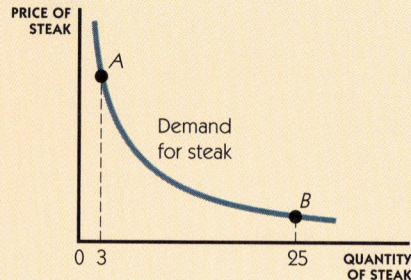

some good or service, substitutes are easy to find and a small increase in price leads to a large reduction in the quantity demanded; but as consumption gets lower, it becomes increasingly difficult to find good substitutes.

Or consider the effect of an increase in the price of one good on the demand for *other* goods. There is always an income effect; the income effect, by itself, would lead to a reduced consumption of all commodities. But the substitution effect leads to *increased* consumption of substitute commodities. Thus, an increase in the price of Coke will lead to increased demand for Pepsi at each price; the demand curve for Pepsi shifts to the right, because the substitution effect outweighs the slight income effect.

Understanding Inefficiencies Associated with Taxes

A second reason to focus on income and substitution effects is to identify some of the inefficiencies associated with taxation. The purpose of a tax is to raise revenue so that the government can purchase goods; it represents a transfer of purchasing power from the household to the government. If the government is to obtain more resources, individuals have to consume less. Thus, any tax must have an income effect.

But beyond that, taxes often **distort** economic activity. The distortion caused by taxation is associated with the substitution effect. Take the window tax imposed in medieval England. It was intended to raise revenue. It led, instead, to the construction of windowless houses—a major distortion of the tax. Most of the distortions associated with modern taxes are somewhat more subtle. Consider a tax on airline tickets or on telephone calls. Reducing consumption of things that are against society's interest can be a legitimate goal of taxation. But the government does not think flying or making telephone calls is a bad thing. The tax is levied to raise revenues. But it results in fewer air flights and telephone calls anyway—an unintentional consequence. Any tax leads to *some* reduction in consumption, through the income effect. But most taxes also change relative prices, so they have a substitution effect. It is the substitution effect that gives rise to the distortion. If the substitution effect is small, the distortion is small; if the substitution effect is large, the distortion is large.

UTILITY AND THE DESCRIPTION OF PREFERENCES

We have seen that people choose a point along their budget constraint by weighing the benefits of consuming more of one good against the costs—what they have to forgo of other goods. Economists refer to the benefits of consumption as the **utility** that individuals get from the combination of goods they consume. Presumably a person can tell you whether or not he prefers a certain combination of goods to another. Economists say that the preferred bundle of goods gives that individual a higher level of utility than the other bundle of goods he could have chosen. Similarly, economists say that the individual will choose the bundle of goods—within the budget constraint—that maximizes his utility.

In the nineteenth century, social scientists, including the British philosopher Jeremy Bentham, hoped that science would someday develop a machine that could actually measure utility. A scientist could simply hook up some electrodes to an individual's head and read off how "happy" she was. Most modern economists believe that there is no *unique* way to measure utility, but that there are useful ways of measuring changes in how well off a person is.

For our purposes, a simple way to measure utility will suffice: we ask how much an individual would be willing to pay to be in one situation rather than another. For example, if Joe likes chocolate ice cream

more than vanilla, it stands to reason that he would be willing to pay more for a scoop of chocolate ice cream than for a scoop of vanilla. Or if Diane would rather live in British Columbia than Ontario, it stands to reason that she would be willing to pay more for the West Coast location.

Notice that how much a person is willing to pay is different from how much he *has* to pay. Just because Joe is willing to pay more for chocolate ice cream than for vanilla does not mean he will have to pay more. What he has to pay depends on market prices; what he is willing to pay reflects his preferences. Willingness to pay is an acceptable measure of utility, which is useful for purposes such as thinking about how an individual allocates his income along his budget constraint. But the hopes of nineteenth-century economists, that we could find some way of measuring utility that would allow us to compare how much utility Fran got from a bundle of goods with how much utility Gary obtained, are now viewed as pipe dreams.

Using willingness to pay as our measure of utility, we can construct a diagram like Figure 6.8A, which shows the level of utility Mary receives from

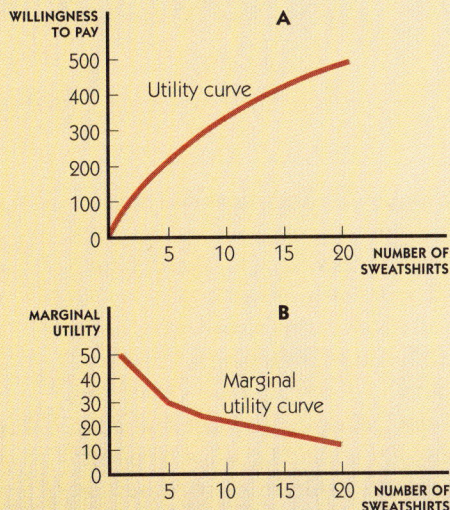

Figure 6.8 UTILITY AND MARGINAL UTILITY

Panel A shows that utility increases continually with consumption, but tends to level off as consumption climbs higher. Panel B explicitly shows marginal utility; notice that it declines as consumption increases.

Table 6.1 UTILITY AND MARGINAL UTILITY

Number of Sweatshirts	Mary's Willingness to Pay (Utility)	Marginal Utility	Number of Pizzas	Mary's Willingness to Pay (Utility)	Marginal Utility
0	0		0	0	
		50			18
1	50		1	18	
		45			16
2	95		2	34	
		40			15
3	135		3	49	
		35			14
4	170		4	63	
		30			13
5	200		5	76	
		28			12
6	228		6	88	
		26			11
7	254		7	99	
		24			10
8	278		8	109	
		23			9
9	301		9	118	
		22			8
10	323		10	126	
		21			7
11	344		11	133	
		20			6
12	364		12	139	
		19			5
13	383		13	144	
		18			4
14	401		14	148	
		17			
15	418				
		16			
16	434				
		15			
17	449				
		14			
18	463				
		13			
19	476				
		12			
20	488				

sweatshirts as the number of sweatshirts she buys increases. This information is also given in Table 6.1. Here we assume that Mary is willing to pay $200 for 5 sweatshirts, $228 for 6 sweatshirts, $254 for 7 sweatshirts, and so on. Thus, 5 sweatshirts give her a utility of 200, 6 a utility of 228, and 7 sweatshirts a utility of 254. Mary's willingness to pay increases with the number of sweatshirts, reflecting the fact that additional sweatshirts give her additional utility. The extra utility of an additional sweatshirt, measured here by the additional amount she is willing to pay, is the **marginal utility.** The numbers in the third column of Table 6.1 give the marginal (or extra) utility she received from her last sweatshirt. When Mary owns 5

sweatshirts, an additional sweatshirt yields her an additional or marginal utility of 28 (228 − 200); when she owns 6 sweatshirts, an additional one gives her a marginal utility of only 26 (254 − 228). Panel B traces the marginal utilities of each of these increments.[3]

As an individual's bundle of goods includes more and more of a good, each successive increment increases her utility less. This is the law of **diminishing marginal utility.** The first sweatshirt is very desirable, and additional ones are attractive as well. But each sweatshirt does not increase utility by as

[3] Since marginal utility is the extra utility from an extra unit of consumption, it is measured by the slope of the utility curve in panel B.

much as the one before, and at some point, Mary may get almost no additional pleasure from adding to her sweatshirt wardrobe.

When Mary has a given budget and must choose between two goods that cost the same, say sweatshirts and pizza, each of which costs $15, she will make her choice so that the marginal utility of each good is the same. Table 6.1 shows Mary's willingness to pay (utility) for both sweatshirts and pizza. Look at what happens if Mary buys 20 sweatshirts with her $300 and no pizza. The marginal utility of the last sweatshirt is 12, and that of the first pizza is 18. If she switches $15 from sweatshirts to pizza, she loses a utility of 12 from the decreased sweatshirts, but gains 18 from her first pizza. It obviously pays for her to switch.

Now look at the situation when she has decreased her purchases of sweatshirts to 17 and increased purchases of pizza to 3. The marginal utility of the last sweatshirt is 15, and that of the last pizza is also 15. At this point, she will not want to switch anymore. If she buys another sweatshirt, she gains 14, but the *last* pizza, her third, which she will have to give up, has a marginal utility of 15; she loses more than she gains. If she buys another pizza, she gains 14, but the last sweatshirt (her seventeenth) gave her 15; again, she loses in net. We can thus see that with her budget, she is best off when the marginal utility of the two goods is the same.

The same general principle applies when the prices of two goods differ. Assume that a sweatshirt costs twice as much as a pizza. So long as the marginal utility of sweatshirts is more than twice that of pizzas, it still pays for Mary to switch to sweatshirts. To get one more sweatshirt, she has to give up two pizzas, and we reason, as before, that she will adjust her consumption until she gets to the point where the marginal utilities of the two goods, *per dollar spent,* are equal. This is a general rule: in choosing between two goods, a consumer will adjust her choices to the point where the marginal utilities are proportional to the prices. Thus, the last unit purchased of a good that costs twice as much as another must generate twice the marginal utility as the last unit purchased of the other good; the last unit purchased of a good that costs three times as much must generate three times the marginal utility as the last unit purchased of the other good; and so on.

This general rule becomes even more powerful if we think about it in relation to a budget constraint diagram. We saw earlier that Fran chose the point along the budget constraint where the marginal *benefit* of an extra CD was equal to its price. The price measured what she had to give up in other goods to get one more CD. It was the marginal or opportunity cost of the extra CD. The reason Fran chose point *F* rather than *G* in Figure 6.1 is that *F* was the point where the marginal utilities of CDs and chocolate bars were proportional to their prices, or 15 to 1. For Fran, at *G* the marginal utility of an extra CD exceeded its price, while that of a chocolate bar was less than its price. As she moved down the budget constraint to *F*, the marginal utility of CDs decreased and that of chocolate bars increased, until the marginal utility of each equaled its price. We can express this in an equation

$$MU_x = p_x$$

which says that the marginal utility (*MU*) of any good (*x*) must equal its price (*p*).[4]

In the example we have just analyzed, we assumed Mary's willingness to pay for sweatshirts—her measure of utility—does not depend on how many pizzas, or other goods, she has. This is seldom the case. The utility, and hence marginal utility, of sweatshirts will depend on the number of pizzas, books, and other goods she has. Thus, even when the price of sweatshirts remains the same, if the price of other goods changes she will change her consumption of those other goods *and* sweatshirts. The same thing will happen if Mary's income changes. The number of sweatshirts at which her marginal utility of an extra sweatshirt equals 15 will change. What matters for choices is *relative* price, so Mary will also change her choices if the price of sweatshirts changes and other prices remain unchanged.

CONSUMER SURPLUS

Assume you go into a store to buy a can of soda. The store charges you $.50. You would have been willing to pay $1. The difference between what you paid and

---

[4] The result holds because we are measuring utility as willingness to pay. More generally, the result cited earlier, that the marginal utility per dollar spent must be the same for all goods, can be written $MU_x/p_x = MU_y/p_y$ for any two goods, *x* and *y*; or $MU_x/MU_y = p_x/p_y$, the ratio of marginal utilities must equal the price ratio.

CLOSE-UP: SALES OF FOREIGN AND NORTH AMERICAN CARS BY PROVINCE

When we focus on how price, income, and other explicitly economic variables affect demand, it is important not to lose sight of other factors that make a difference too, like geography, demographics, and taste.

In the mid-1990s, North American manufacturers accounted for almost 77 percent of the Canadian car market, Japanese manufacturers for 17 percent, and automakers from other countries for the remaining 6 percent. But the sales of cars by origin were not evenly distributed throughout the country. The table shows how the shares in each province varied from the average. Both Quebec and British Columbia were well below the average for sales of North American cars (and well above for foreign ones), while Newfoundland, Ontario, and the Prairie provinces were the opposite. Apparently, both geography and tastes matter. Sales of Japanese cars were higher, not only in the Far West, which is closer to Japan, but also in

Quebec. The provinces with lower population density tended to demand proportionately more North American cars.

Interestingly, these patterns tend to be fairly stable over time. In 1981, cars manufactured in North America accounted for a smaller proportion of sales nationwide than in 1994 (71.5 percent compared with 76.6 percent). However, the 1981 variations of the provinces from the average is remarkably similar to that of 1994. Sales of North American cars in Quebec and British Columbia were considerably below the average, while those in the rest of the country were above the national average. These differences cannot be explained on the basis of price and income differences alone. For example, the three higher-income provinces—Ontario, Alberta, and British Columbia—have very different patterns. Similarly, some of the lower-income provinces also have different patterns; compare Newfoundland with Quebec.

	North American		Japanese		Other Foreign	
	1981	1994	1981	1994	1981	1994
Newfoundland	80.0	79.8	16.1	15.1	3.9	5.1
Prince Edward Island	77.9	77.8	16.6	12.4	5.4	9.8
Nova Scotia	77.4	77.5	18.2	16.5	4.4	6.0
New Brunswick	78.0	84.1	17.7	12.7	4.3	3.2
Quebec	64.9	68.6	27.5	23.7	7.6	7.8
Ontario	75.4	80.9	19.7	13.9	4.9	5.3
Manitoba	81.5	83.3	15.3	13.4	3.2	3.3
Saskatchewan	83.3	84.9	14.4	11.2	2.3	3.9
Alberta	75.4	83.4	20.6	12.4	3.9	4.1
British Columbia	60.8	72.4	33.2	19.8	6.0	7.8
National Average	71.5	76.6	23.0	17.3	5.5	6.1

Source: Statistics Canada, CANSIM Database 1996, *New Motor Vehicle Sales,* Catalogue No. 63-007.

what you would have been willing to pay is called **consumer surplus.**

We can calculate the consumer surplus Mary gets from buying pizza from her demand curve. To see how we do this, use the marginal utility analysis of the previous section. We saw that at 11 pizzas, Mary is willing to pay $6 for one more; at 12, she is willing to pay $5.

Mary buys pizza up to the point where the price is equal to the marginal utility of the last pizza she chooses to buy. Of course, she pays the same price for each of the pizzas she purchases. Suppose pizzas cost $5 and Mary buys 13. The thirteenth pizza gives her a marginal utility of 5 and costs $5. Mary is getting a bargain: she would have been willing to pay more for the earlier pizzas. For her first pizza, she would have been willing to pay $18, for the second $16, and so forth. She would have been willing to pay a total of $144 ($18 + $16 + $15 + $14 + $13 + $12 + $11 + $10 + $9 + $8 + $7 + $6 + $5) for the 13 pizzas. The difference between what she *has* to pay for 13 pizzas—$5 × 13, or $65—and what she would have been willing to pay, $144, is her consumer surplus. In this case, her consumer surplus is $79.

There is always some consumer surplus, so long as a consumer has to pay only a fixed price for all the items she purchases. The fact that demand curves are downward-sloping means that the previous units the consumer purchases are more valuable than the marginal units. She would have been willing to pay more for these earlier units than for the last unit, but she does not have to.

In Figure 6.9, the total amount Mary would have been willing to pay for 13 pizzas is the total area under the demand curve between the vertical axis and 13, the combination of the lightly and heavily shaded areas. This area is the sum of the willingness to pay for the first, second, third, and so on, up to 13 pizzas. The amount Mary actually has to pay is the heavily shaded area—the price, $5, times the quantity, 13 pizzas. Her consumer surplus is the *difference*, the lightly shaded area above the price line and below the demand curve, over the range of the quantity of purchases.

LOOKING BEYOND THE BASIC MODEL:
HOW WELL DO THE UNDERLYING ASSUMPTIONS MATCH REALITY?

In the market economy, the question "For whom are goods produced?" has a simple answer: goods are produced for consumers. A theory of consumer

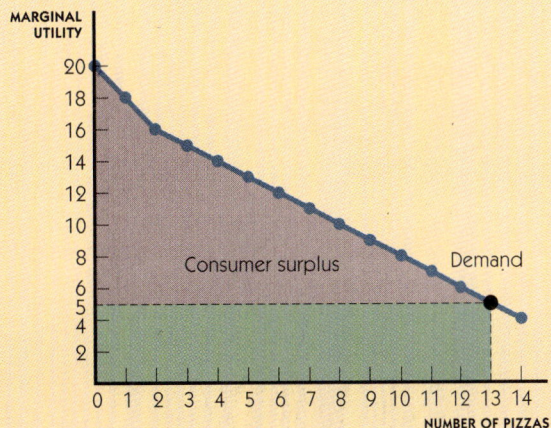

Figure 6.9 CONSUMER SURPLUS

The demand curve plots the amount Mary would be willing to pay for her first, second, third, and so on, pizza. The total amount she is willing to pay for 13 pizzas is the area under the demand curve up to the thirteenth pizza. The amount she actually has to pay is the heavily shaded area. The consumer surplus is the difference between the two, the lightly shaded area above the line and below the demand curve, over the range of the quantity purchased.

Taxes interfere with the allocation of an economy's resources and reduce the consumer surplus, or gains from trade, obtained by participating in the market economy. The higher the taxes, the greater the loss in consumer surplus. In evaluating the costs associated with the government's shifting scarce resources from the private sector to itself, economists include both the value of the resources and the loss in consumer surplus arising from the use of taxes. The latter is referred to as the *deadweight loss* of taxes; when added to the value of resources obtained for the public sector, the result is the *social cost* of taxation. It is relevant for policy purposes. For tax-financed government spending projects to be beneficial on economic grounds, they should yield benefits at least as large as the social cost of the taxes needed to finance them.

The figure below illustrates these concepts. All the goods and services that consumers buy are treated as an aggregate amount, simply referred to as consumption. The average price charged by the market for this consumption is called the price level. The demand curve D shows the quantity of aggregate consumption that consumers in the economy would purchase at various price levels. It is downward-sloping because if the price of consumer goods is lower, consumers will buy more goods, either because they spend money that they otherwise would have saved, or because they decide to work longer and harder to earn more income to buy more goods. If the average price level charged by producers is p, consumers buy q consumer goods. Consumer surplus is the area abc. (The supply curve is drawn as horizontal, reflecting the assumption that supply is perfectly elastic.)

Suppose the government imposes a tax on all consumer purchases at the rate of t. The price level faced by consumers rises to $p(1 + t)$, and demand falls to q_1. Consumer surplus falls to edc, a reduction of $abde$. But the government obtains tax revenue of $fbde$, which reflects the value of resources it can buy from the private sector. Thus, the *net* loss to the economy is the loss to consumers from the rise in price less the

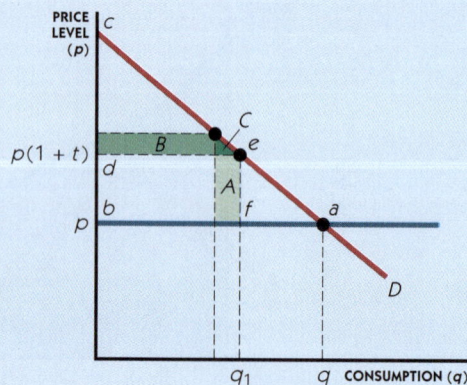

gain in resources to the government, *afe* (*abde − fbde*). This triangular area is the deadweight loss of taxes.

Now suppose the government is considering increasing its tax rate to obtain more revenues. The increase in tax revenues is the shaded area *B* less the shaded area *A*. To obtain this additional tax revenue, the deadweight loss rises by *A + C*. The deadweight loss per dollar of additional tax revenue raised is thus (*A + C*)/(*B − A*). Together with the dollar of tax revenues raised, the social cost of raising an additional dollar of tax revenue is 1 + (*A + C*)/(*B − A*). This is called the *marginal cost of public funds*. The amount by which the marginal cost of public funds exceeds unity depends upon the elasticity of the demand curve. The more elastic the demand curve, the larger will be the area (*A + C*) relative to (*B − A*), and the higher the marginal cost of public funds.

Various estimates have been made of the marginal cost of public funds for Canada. Various economists have found it to be as low as 1.2 and as high as 2. The implications of this are potentially profound. If the marginal cost of public funds is, say, 1.5, that suggests that the benefits of new public projects should be 50 percent higher than the costs to justify the social costs of financing them by taxes.

choice is, therefore, critical to understanding market economies. The model of budget constraints and individual preferences sketched in this chapter is the economist's basic model of consumer choice. It is a powerful one whose insights carry well beyond this course. Still, the model has been criticized. Four criticisms are summarized here. The first has no economic merit. The other three are somewhat relevant. The first criticism is that the model does not reflect the thought processes consumers really go through. This line of criticism is like criticizing the physicist's model of motion, which predicts with great precision how billiard balls will interact, simply because most pool players do not go through the equations before taking a shot. The appropriate question is whether the economic model of consumer choice can reliably be used to make predictions. By and large it can. Many businesses have found the model useful for predicting the demand for their products, and economists have used the model with remarkable success to predict consumer behaviour in a variety of circumstances.

The second criticism questions the model's assumption that individuals know what they like, which is to say that they have well-defined preferences. This criticism has merit. Having well-defined preferences means that if you gave someone a choice between two bundles of goods—one consisting of two apples, three oranges, and one pear and the other consisting of three apples, two oranges, and four pears—he could tell you quickly which he preferred. Furthermore, well-defined preferences imply that if you asked him tomorrow and the day after, he would give you the same answer. But in many cases, if you asked someone which of two things he preferred, he would say, "I don't know. Let me try them out." And what he likes may change from day to day. His preferences may, moreover, be affected by what others like. How else can we account for frequent fads in foods and fashions as well as other aspects of our lives?

The third criticism has to do with the model's assumption that individuals know the prices of each good in the market. People often do not know prices. They know that there are bargains to be found, but they know it is costly to search for them. While we can talk meaningfully about the price of a bushel of wheat, what do we mean by the "price" of a couch, or a house? If we are lucky and stumble onto a deal, we might find a leather couch for $1,000. If unlucky, even after searching all day, we may not find one for under $1,500. When we get the bargain leather couch home, if we are lucky we will find it is even better than we thought. If we are unlucky, the couch will fall apart.

The final criticism is that sometimes prices and

preferences interact in a more complicated way than this chapter has depicted. People's attitudes toward a good or service can depend on its price. More expensive goods may have snob appeal. And when the quality of certain goods cannot easily be checked, individuals may judge quality by price. Because better, more durable things are generally more costly, a cheap item is assumed to be of poor quality and an expensive item of good quality. In either case, demand curves will look quite different from those described in this chapter. Lowering the price for a good may actually lower the demand.

The fact that the basic economic model needs to be extended or modified for some goods in some instances does not deny its usefulness in the vast majority of situations, where it provides just the information that businesses and governments need for making important decisions. Even in those instances where the model does not work so well, it provides a basic framework that allows us to enhance our understanding of the behaviour of households. By asking which of the assumptions underlying the model seems inappropriate in that particular situation, we are guided in our search for a better model of consumption.

REVIEW AND PRACTICE

SUMMARY

1 The amount of one good a person must give up to purchase another good is determined by the relative prices of the two goods, and is illustrated by the slope of the budget constraint.

2 The demand curve for an individual is derived by tracing out the different quantities demanded of a good along a budget constraint as the price of the good changes and the budget constraint rotates.

3 Consumption of a normal good rises as income rises. Consumption of an inferior good falls as income rises.

4 As a good becomes more expensive relative to other goods, an individual will substitute other goods

for the higher-priced good. This is the substitution effect. In addition, as the price of a good rises, a person's buying power is reduced. This is the income effect. Normally, both the substitution effect and the income effect reduce the quantity demanded of a good as its price rises.

5 When substitution is easy, demand curves tend to be elastic, or flat. If substitution is difficult, demand curves tend to be inelastic, or steep.

6 Economists sometimes describe the benefits of consumption by referring to the utility that people get from a combination of goods. The extra utility of consuming one more unit of a good is referred to as the marginal utility of that good.

KEY TERMS

slope	inferior good	substitution effect	diminishing marginal utility
income elasticity of demand	normal good	utility	
theory of revealed preference	income effect	marginal utility	consumer surplus

REVIEW QUESTIONS

1 How is the slope of the budget constraint related to the relative prices of the goods on the horizontal and vertical axes?

2 How can the budget constraint appear the same even for individuals whose tastes and preferences differ dramatically?

3 Is the income elasticity of demand positive or negative for a normal good?

4 If the price of a normal good increases, how will the income effect cause the quantity demanded of that good to change?

5 If the price of a good increases, how will the substitution effect cause the quantity demanded of that good to change?

6 Does a greater availability of substitutes make a demand curve more or less elastic? Explain.

7 Why does marginal utility tend to diminish?

8 What is meant by consumer surplus?

PROBLEMS

1 Consider a student who has an entertainment budget of $120 per term and spends it on either concert tickets at $10 apiece or movie tickets at $6 apiece. Imagine that movie tickets start decreasing in price, first falling to $4, then $3, then $2. Graph the four budget constraints, with movies on the horizontal axis. If the student's demand curve for movies is represented by the function $D = 60 - 10p$, graph both her demand curve for movies and the point she will choose at each price on the budget line.

2 Choose two normal goods and draw a budget constraint illustrating the trade-off between them. Show how the budget line shifts if income increases. Arbitrarily choose a point on the first budget line as the point a particular consumer will select. Now find two points on the new budget line such that the new preferred choice of the consumer must fall between these points.

3 DINKs, households with "double income, no kids," are invading your neighbourhood. You decide to take advantage of this influx by starting a gourmet takeout food store. You know that the price elasticity of demand for your food from DINKs is .5 and the income elasticity of demand is 1.5. From the standpoint of the quantity that you sell, which of the following changes would concern you the most?

    (a) The number of DINKs in your neighbourhood falls by 10 percent.

    (b) The average income of DINKs falls by 5 percent.

4 Compare a relatively poor person, someone with an income of $10,000 per year, with a relatively wealthy person, someone who has an income of $60,000 per year. Imagine that the poor person drinks 15 bottles of wine per year at an average price of $10 per bottle, while the wealthy person drinks 50 bottles of wine per year at an average price of $20 per bottle. If a tax of $1 per bottle is imposed on wine, who pays the greater amount? Who pays the greater amount as a percentage of income? If a tax equal to 10 percent of the value of the wine is imposed, who pays the greater amount? Who pays the greater amount as a percentage of income?

Suppose the income elasticity of demand for alcoholic beverages is .6. Consider two people with incomes of $20,000 and $40,000. If all alcohol is taxed at the same rate, by what percentage more will the tax paid by the $40,000 earner be greater than that paid by the $20,000 earner? Why might some people think this unfair?

5 Consider two ways of encouraging local governments to build or expand public parks. One proposal is for the provincial government to provide grants for public parks. A second proposal is for the government to agree to pay 25 percent of any expenditures for building or expansion. If the same amount of money would be spent on each program, which do you predict would be most effective in encouraging the development of local parks? Explain your answer, using the ideas of income and substitution effects.

APPENDIX: INDIFFERENCE CURVES AND THE CONSUMPTION DECISION[5]

This chapter explained the consumption decision in terms of the budget constraint facing the individual and the individual's choice of her most preferred point on the budget constraint. Effects of changes in prices on the quantity demanded were analyzed in terms of income and substitution effects.

To facilitate a more rigourous analysis of choices and the consequences of changes in prices, economists have developed an extremely useful tool called **indifference curves.** Indifference curves give the combinations of goods among which an individual is indifferent or which yield the same level of utility. This appendix shows how indifference curves can be used to derive the demand curve and to separate more precisely changes in consumption into income and substitution effects.

USING INDIFFERENCE CURVES TO ILLUSTRATE CONSUMER CHOICES

In this chapter solutions to consumer choice problems were characterized as having two stages: first, identify the opportunity set, and second, find the most preferred point in the opportunity set. For a consumer with a given income to spend on goods, the budget constraint defines her opportunity set. Figure 6.10 repeats the budget constraint for Fran, who must divide her income between chocolate bars and CDs. In the chapter, we simply said that Fran chose the most preferred point along the budget constraint. If she likes CDs a lot, she might choose point B; if she has a stronger preference for chocolate, she might choose point A.

The concept of the indifference curve can help us see which of these points she chooses. The indifference curve shows the various combinations of goods

that make a person equally happy. For example, in Figure 6.11, the indifference curve I_0 gives all those combinations of chocolate bars and compact discs that Fran finds just as attractive as 150 chocolate bars and 10 CDs (point A on the curve). At B, for instance, she has 12 CDs but only 130 chocolate bars—not so much chocolate, but in her mind the extra CDs make up for the loss. The fact that B and A are on the same indifference curve means that Fran is indifferent. That is, if you asked her whether she preferred A to B or B to A, she would answer that she couldn't care less.

Indifference curves simply reflect preferences between pairs of goods. Unlike demand curves, they have nothing to do with budget constraints or prices. The different combinations of goods along the indifference curve cost different amounts of money. The indifference curves are drawn by asking an individual which he prefers: 10 chocolate bars and 2 CDs or 15 chocolate bars and 1 CD? or 11 chocolate bars and 2 CDs or 15 chocolate bars and 1 CD? or 12 chocolate bars and 2 CDs or 15 chocolate bars and 1 CD? When he answers, "I am indifferent between the two," the two points that represent those choices are on the same indifference curve.

Moving along the curve in one direction, Fran is willing to accept more CDs in exchange for fewer chocolate bars; moving in the other direction, she is willing to accept more chocolate bars in exchange for fewer CDs. Any point on the same indifference curve by definition makes her just as happy as any other—whether it is point A or C or an extreme point like D, where she has many chocolate bars and very few CDs, or F, where she has relatively few chocolate bars but more CDs.

However, if Fran were to receive the same number of chocolate bars but more CDs than at A—say 150 chocolate bars and 15 CDs (point E)—she would be better off on the principle that "more is better." The new indifference curve I_1 illustrates all those combinations of chocolate bars and CDs that make her just as well off as the combination of 150 chocolate bars and 15 CDs.

Figure 6.12 shows a variety of indifference curves for Fran. Because more is better, Fran (or any individual) will prefer a choice on an indifference curve that is higher than another. On the higher indifference curve, she can have more of both items. By def-

---

[5] This appendix may be skipped without loss of understanding of later chapters.

Figure 6.10 BUDGET CONSTRAINT

The budget constraint defines the opportunity set. Fran can choose any point on or below the budget constraint. If she has strong preferences for CDs, she might choose B; if she has strong preferences for chocolate bars, she might choose point A.

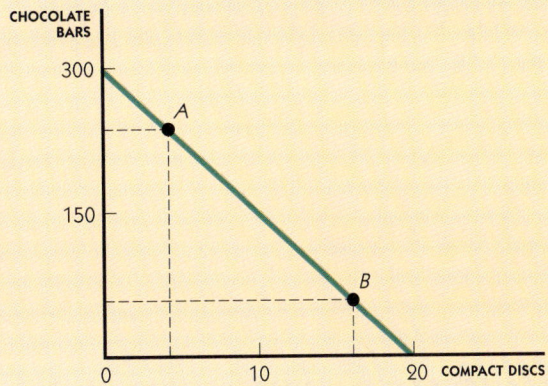

Figure 6.11 AN INDIFFERENCE CURVE

An indifference curve traces combinations of goods among which an individual is indifferent. This one reflects Fran's taste for CDs and for chocolate bars. She is just as well off (has an identical amount of utility) at all points on the indifference curve: A, B, C, D, or F.

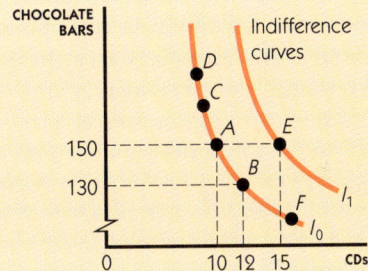

Figure 6.12 MULTIPLE IN-DIFFERENCE CURVES

By definition, an indifference curve describing Fran's tastes can be drawn through any point in the diagram. Four of the infinite number of possibilities are shown here. Because more is better, Fran will prefer indifference curves that are higher like I_3, to those that are lower, like I_0.

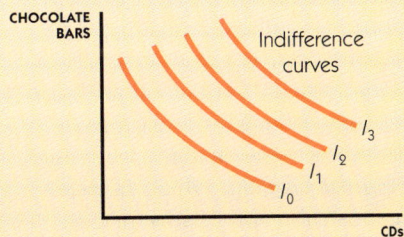

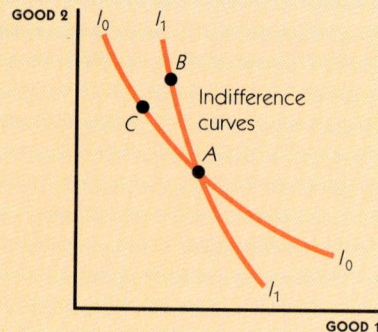

Figure 6.13 **WHY INDIFFERENCE CURVES CANNOT CROSS**

If two indifference curves crossed, a logical contradiction would occur. If curves crossed at point A, then Fran would be indifferent between A and B, between A and C, and therefore between B and C. But since B involves higher consumption of both goods than C, B is clearly preferred to C.

inition, we can draw an indifference curve for *any* point in the space of an indifference curve diagram. Also by definition, indifference curves cannot cross, as Figure 6.13 makes clear. Assume that the indifference curves I_0 and I_1 cross at point A. That would mean that Fran is indifferent between A and all points on I_0, and between A and all points on I_1. In particular, she would be indifferent between A and B, between A and C, and accordingly between B and C. But B is clearly preferred to C; therefore, indifference curves cannot cross.

INDIFFERENCE CURVES AND MARGINAL RATES OF SUBSTITUTION

The slope of the indifference curve measures the number of chocolate bars that the individual is willing to give up to get another compact disc. The technical term for the slope of an indifference curve is the **marginal rate of substitution.** The marginal rate of substitution tells us how much of one good an individual is *willing* to give up in return for one more unit of another. This concept is quite distinct from the amount a consumer *must* give up, which is determined by the budget constraint and relative prices.

If Fran's marginal rate of substitution of chocolate bars for CDs is 15 to 1, this means that if she is given 1 more CD, she is willing to give up 15 chocolate

bars. If she only had to give up 12 chocolate bars, she would be happier. If she had to give up 20, she would say, "That's too much—having one more CD isn't worth giving up twenty chocolate bars." Of course, Gary could have quite different attitudes toward CDs and chocolate bars. His marginal rate of substitution might be 25 to 1. He would be willing to give up 25 chocolate bars to get 1 more CD.

The marginal rate of substitution rises and falls according to how much of an item an individual already has. For example, consider point F back in Figure 6.11, where Fran has a lot of CDs and few chocolate bars. In this case Fran already has bought all her favourite CDs; the marginal CD she buys now will be something she likes, but not something she is wild over. In other words, because she already has a large number of CDs, having an additional one is less important. She would rather have some chocolate bars instead. Her marginal rate of substitution of chocolate bars for CDs at F is very low; for the sake of illustration, let's say that she would be willing to give up the marginal CD for only 10 chocolate bars. Her marginal rate of substitution is 10 to 1 (chocolate bars per CD).

The opposite situation prevails when Fran has lots of chocolate bars and few CDs. Since she is eating several chocolate bars almost every day, the chance to have more is just not worth much to her. But since she has few CDs, she does not yet own all of her favourites. The marginal value of another chocolate bar is relatively low, while the marginal value of another CD is relatively high. Accordingly, in this situation, Fran might insist on getting 30 extra chocolate bars before she gives up 1 CD. Her marginal rate of substitution is 30 to 1 (chocolate bars per CD).

As we move along an indifference curve, we increase the amount of one good (like CDs) that an individual has. In Fran's case, she requires less and less of the other good (chocolate bars) to compensate her for each one-unit decrease in the quantity of the first good (CDs). This principle is known as the **diminishing marginal rate of substitution.** As a result of the principle of diminishing marginal rate of substitution, the slope of the indifference curve becomes flatter as we move from left to right along the curve.

USING INDIFFERENCE CURVES TO ILLUSTRATE CHOICES

By definition, an individual does not care where he sits on any *given* indifference curve. But he would prefer to be on the highest indifference curve possible. What limits him is his budget constraint. As Figure 6.14 illustrates, the highest indifference curve that a person can attain is the one that just touches the budget constraint—that is, the indifference curve that is *tangent* to the budget constraint. The point of tangency (labelled E) is the point the individual will choose. Consider any other point on the budget constraint, say A. The indifference curve through A is below the curve through E; the individual is better off at E than at A. On the other hand, consider an indifference curve above I_0, for instance I_1. Since every point on I_1 lies above the budget constraint, there is no point on I_1 that the individual can purchase given his income.

When a curve is tangent to a line, the curve and line have the same slope at the point of tangency. Thus, the slope of the indifference curve equals the slope of the budget constraint at the point of tangency. The slope of the indifference curve is the marginal rate of substitution; the slope of the budget constraint is the relative price. This two-dimensional diagram therefore illustrates a basic principle of consumer choice: *individuals choose the point where the marginal rate of substitution equals the relative price.*

This principle makes sense. If the relative price of CDs and chocolate bars is 15 (CDs cost $15 and chocolate bars cost $1) and Fran's marginal rate of substitution is 20, Fran is willing to give up 20 chocolate bars to get 1 more CD, but only *has* to give up 15; it clearly pays her to buy more CDs and fewer chocolate bars. If her marginal rate of substitution is 10, she is willing to give up 1 CD for just 10 chocolate bars; but if she gives up 1 CD, she can get 15 chocolate bars. She will be better off buying more chocolate bars and fewer CDs. Thus, if the marginal rate of substitution exceeds the relative price, Fran is better off if she buys more CDs; if it is less, she is better off if she buys fewer CDs. When the marginal rate of substitution *equals* the relative price, it does not pay for her to either increase or decrease her purchases.

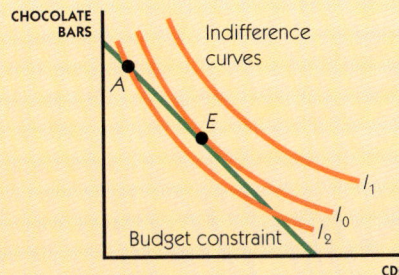

Figure 6.14 INDIFFERENCE CURVES AND THE BUDGET CONSTRAINT

The highest feasible indifference curve that can be reached is the one just tangent to the budget constraint, or indifference curve I_0 here. This individual's budget constraint does not permit her to reach I_1, nor would she want to choose point A, which would put her on I_2, since along I_2 she is worse off.

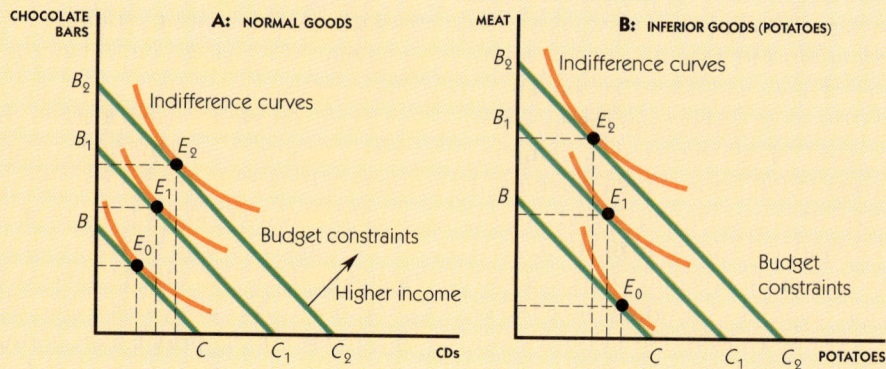

Figure 6.15 **NORMAL AND INFERIOR GOODS WITH INDIFFERENCE CURVES**

Panel A shows the case of two normal goods. An increase in income shifts the budget constraint out from BC to B_1C_1 to B_2C_2, and the consumption of both goods rises from E_0 to E_1 to E_2. Panel B shows the case of an inferior good. As the budget constraint shifts out, consumption of potatoes falls.

INCOME ELASTICITY

Budget constraints and indifference curves show why, while goods normally have a positive income elasticity, some goods may have a negative income elasticity. As incomes increase, the budget constraint shifts out to the right in a parallel line, say from BC in Figure 6.15 to B_1C_1 to B_2C_2. The choices—the points of tangency with the indifference curves—are represented by the points E_0, E_1, and E_2. In panel A, we see the normal case, where as the budget constraint shifts out, more of both chocolate bars and CDs are consumed. But panel B illustrates the case of inferior goods. Potatoes are on the horizontal axis, and meat is on the vertical. As incomes rise, the points of tangency E_1 and E_2 move to the left; potato consumption actually falls.

SUBSTITUTION AND INCOME EFFECTS

Indifference curves also permit a precise definition of the substitution and income effects. Figure 6.16 plots Jeremy's indifference curve between CDs and chocolate. Jeremy's original budget constraint is line BC and his indifference curve is I_0; the point of tangency, the point he chooses, is point E_0. Suppose the price of chocolate increases. Now he can buy fewer chocolate bars, but the number of CDs he can buy, were he to spend all of his income on CDs, is unchanged. Thus, his budget constraint becomes flatter; it is now line B_2C. While Jeremy originally chose point E_0 on the indifference curve I_0, now he chooses E_1 on the *lower* indifference curve I_1.

The price change has moved Jeremy's choice from E_0 to E_1 for two reasons: the substitution effect and the income effect. To see how this has happened, let's isolate the two effects. First, we focus on the substitution effect by asking what would happen to Jeremy's consumption if we changed relative prices, but did not change how well off he was. To keep him just as well off as before the price change, we must keep him on the same indifference curve, I_0. Thus, the substitution effect is a movement along an indifference curve. As the price of chocolate rises, Jeremy, moving down the indifference curve, buys more CDs and fewer chocolate bars. The movement from E_0 to

Figure 6.16 SUBSTITUTION AND INCOME EFFECTS WITH INDIFFERENCE CURVES

As the price of a good increases, the budget constraint rotates down. The change of Jeremy's choice from E_0 to E_1 can be broken down into an income and a substitution effect. The line B_1C_1 shows the substitution effect, the change that would occur if relative prices shifted but the level of utility remained the same. (Notice that Jeremy stays on the same indifference curve in this scenario.) The substitution effect alone causes a shift from E_0 to E_2. The movement between B_1C_1 and the new budget constraint B_2C shows the income effect, the change that results from changing the amount of income but leaving relative prices unchanged. The income effect alone causes a shift from E_2 to E_1.

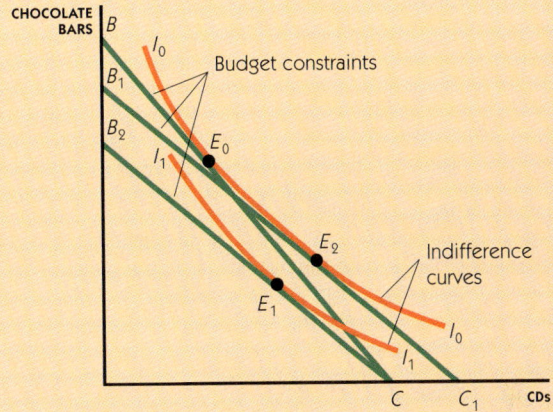

E_2 is the substitution effect. The budget constraint B_1C_1 represents the new prices, but by definition it does not account for the income effect since Jeremy is on the same indifference curve that he was on before.

To keep Jeremy on the same indifference curve when we increase the price of chocolate requires giving Jeremy more income. The line B_1C_1 is the budget constraint with the *new* prices that would leave Jeremy on the same indifference curve. Because prices are the same, the budget constraint B_1C_1 is par-allel to B_2C. We now need to take away the income that left Jeremy on the same indifference curve. We keep prices the same (at the new levels), and we take away income until we arrive at the new budget constraint B_2C, and the corresponding new equilibrium E_1. The movement from E_2 to E_1 is called the income effect, since only income is changed. We have thus broken down the movement from the old equilibrium, E_0, to the new one, E_1, into the movement from E_0 to E_2, the substitution effect, and the movement from E_2 to E_1, the income effect.

CHAPTER 7

LABOUR SUPPLY

The first of the four basic decisions of the household—how individuals choose to spend their money—was discussed in Chapter 6. How much money people have to spend depends in turn on two other basic decisions: how much they choose to work (and earn) and how much they save (or spend from savings). This chapter focuses on the first of these two decisions. We will see that consumer theory can be applied directly to analyzing how households divide their time between working and other activities. We will also see how the supply curve for labour can be derived and what shape it might have. Chapter 8 then focuses on the household's decision on how much of their income to save or how much to spend from their previous savings, and how to invest their savings.

KEY QUESTIONS

1 How can the basic tools introduced in Chapter 6 to analyze consumers' expenditure decisions be applied to such important aspects of life as work, education, and retirement?

2 What determines the number of hours an individual works, or whether she chooses to work or not? How do income and substitution effects help us to understand why labour supply may not be very responsive to changes in wages?

3 Why do economists think of education as an investment, and refer to the result as human capital? What role

does education play beyond the accumulation of human capital?

4 How do economic factors affect other aspects of family life, such as decisions concerning family size?

5 How do we explain the large differences in the amount of money paid to different groups of workers who appear to have similar abilities? What role does discrimination play?

6 How do unions affect the supply of workers and their working conditions?

THE LABOUR SUPPLY DECISION

Patterns of labour supply have changed greatly in the past three decades. The average work week for a production worker has declined from 40 hours in 1950 to fewer than 35 hours today. At the same time, the fraction of women in the labour force has increased enormously. As a result, the typical married household now devotes more hours to work outside the home than it did in 1900. The number of hours

worked in different jobs and industries also varies. As Figure 7.1 shows, miners work close to 40 hours per week on average, whereas those in the financial sector work fewer than 30 hours.

THE CHOICE BETWEEN LEISURE AND CONSUMPTION

Economists use the basic model of choice to help understand these patterns of labour supply. The decision about how much labour to supply is a choice

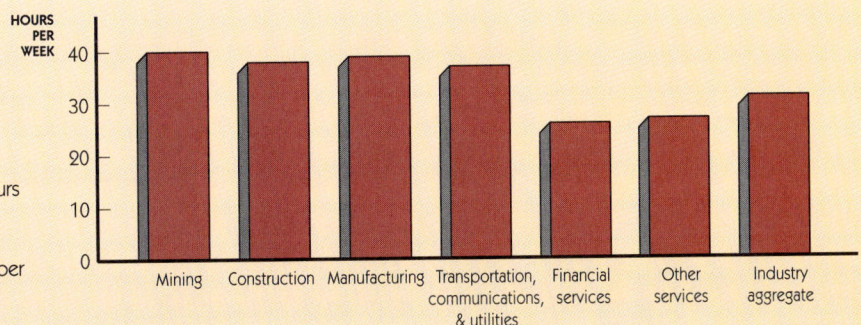

Figure 7.1 **AVERAGE WEEKLY HOURS OF WORK BY INDUSTRY, 1994**

The bars here compare the average hours worked per week in different jobs and industries. *Source:* Statistics Canada, *Canadian Economic Observer,* December 1995, Table 9.

between consumption, or income, and leisure. To an economist "leisure" means all the time an individual could potentially work for pay that he actually spends not working. The time parents spend caring for their children, for example, is leisure in this special sense. By giving up leisure a person receives additional income and therefore increases his consumption. By working less and giving up some consumption, a person obtains more leisure. An increase in income does not necessarily translate *immediately* into consumption; the individual has to decide whether to spend his extra income now or in the future. We tackle this in the next chapter. Here we assume that the person spends all his income.

Even though the typical job seems to represent a fixed time requirement, there are a variety of ways in which people can influence how much labour they will supply. Many workers may not have discretion as to whether they will work full time, but they have some choice as to whether or not they will work overtime. In addition, many individuals moonlight; they take up second jobs that provide them with additional income. Most of these jobs—like driving a taxi—provide considerable discretion in the number of hours

worked. Hence, even when people have no choice about how much they work at their primary job, they still have choices. Further, the fact that jobs differ in their normal work week means that a worker has some flexibility in choosing a job that allows her to work the amount of hours she wishes. Finally, economists believe that the social conventions concerning the "standard" work week—the 40-hour week that has become the 35-hour week—respond over time to the attitudes (preferences) of workers.

We now apply the analysis of Chapter 6 to an individual's choice between work and leisure. Figure 7.2 shows the budget constraint of Steve, who earns an hourly wage of $5. Accordingly, for each hour less of leisure Steve enjoys—for each extra hour he works—he earns $5 more: his consumption increases by $5. Underlying this budget constraint is his time constraint. He has only so many hours a day, say 16, to spend either working or at leisure. For each extra hour he works, he has 1 less hour of leisure. If he works 1 hour, his income is $5, if he works 2 hours, his income is $10, and so forth. If he works 16 hours—he has no leisure—his income is $5 × 16 = $80. The budget constraint trade-off is $5 per hour.

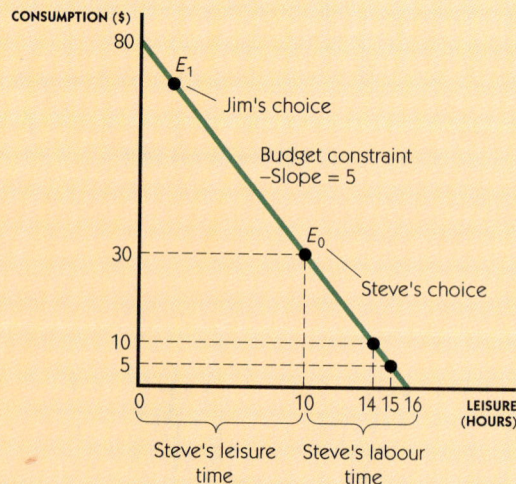

Figure 7.2 **A B U D G E T C O N S T R A I N T B E T W E E N L E I S U R E A N D I N C O M E**

Individuals are willing to trade leisure for an increase in income, and thus in consumption. The budget constraint shows Steve choosing E_0, with 10 hours of daily leisure, 6 hours of work, and $30 in daily wages.

Steve will choose a point on the budget constraint according to his own preferences. He must choose the appropriate trade-off between consumption and leisure. Let's suppose that he chooses point E_0. At E_0, he has 10 hours of leisure, which means that he works 6 hours out of a total available time of 16 hours and makes $30.

In deciding which of the points along the budget constraint to choose, Steve balances out the marginal benefits of what he can buy with an additional hour's wages with the marginal costs—the value of the hour's worth of leisure that he will have to forgo. Steve and his brother Jim assess the marginal benefits and marginal costs differently: Steve chooses point E_0, while his brother chooses point E_1. Jim values the material things in life more and leisure less.

For Steve, at E_0 the marginal benefit of the extra concert tickets or other goods and services he can buy with the money he earns from working an extra hour just offsets the marginal cost of that hour, the extra leisure he has to give up. At points to the right of E_0 Steve has less leisure (so the marginal value of leisure is greater) and he has more goods (so the marginal value of the extra goods he can get is lower). The marginal benefit of working more exceeds the marginal costs, and so he works more— he moves toward E_0. Converse arguments apply to Steve's thinking about points to the left of E_0.

We can use the same kind of reasoning to see why the workaholic Jim chooses a point to the left of E_0. At E_0 Jim values goods more and leisure less; the marginal benefit of working more exceeds the marginal cost. At E_1 the marginal benefit of working an extra hour (the extra consumption) just offsets the marginal cost.

This framework can be used to analyze the effect of changes in income and wages on the work–leisure decision in the same way that we discussed the effects of changes in income and prices on purchases of goods and services. For instance, an increase in income normally leads individuals to consume more of all "goods," including leisure: at fixed wages, as incomes rise, labour supply decreases. Figure 7.3 shows the effect on Steve's labour supply of having

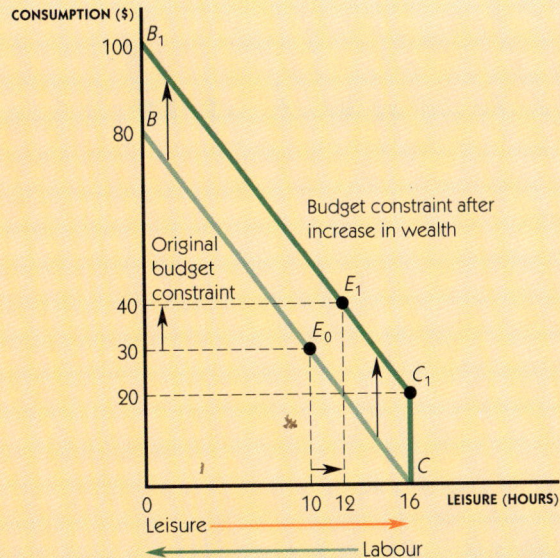

Figure 7.3 NONLABOUR INCOME AND LABOUR SUPPLY

When Steve obtains $20 per day of other income, his budget line shifts parallel outwards. Normally, this induces him to take more leisure (sell less labour) and more consumption.

WAGE CHANGES AND LABOUR SUPPLY

As wages rise, individuals become better off. This income effect induces them to work less. Offsetting this is the substitution effect—the greater return to working provides an incentive to work longer hours. Either effect may dominate. Thus, the quantity of labour supplied may increase or decrease with wage increases.

$20 per day of income from other sources, such as interest income from his investments. His new budget constraint will be B_1C_1. Steve will take two more hours of leisure per day, reducing his labour supply from six hours to four hours.

Changes in wages have both an income effect and a substitution effect. An increase in wages makes individuals better off. When individuals are better off they work less. This is the income effect. But an increase in wages also changes the trade-offs. By giving up one more hour of leisure, the individual can get more goods. Because of this, individuals are willing to work more. This is the substitution effect.

In the case of the typical good, we saw that the income and substitution effects reinforced each other. A higher price meant individuals were worse off, and this led to reduced consumption of the good; a higher price meant that individuals substituted away from the good whose price had increased. *With labour sup-*

ply, income and substitution effects work in the opposite direction, so the net effect of an increase in wages is ambiguous.

Figure 7.4A shows the normal case of an upward-sloping labour supply curve, where the substitution effect dominates. Panel B illustrates the case of a backward-bending labour supply curve. At high wages, the income effect of further increases in wages outweighs the substitution effect, so that labour supply decreases. Doctors, dentists, and other high-income professionals who work only a four-day week may be evidence of a labour supply curve that is backward-bending at high-income levels.

If income and substitution effects just outweigh each other, then labour supply will be relatively unaffected by wage changes. The evidence is that, at least for men, the labour supply elasticity—the percentage increase in hours worked as a result of a 1 percent increase in real wages—is positive but small.

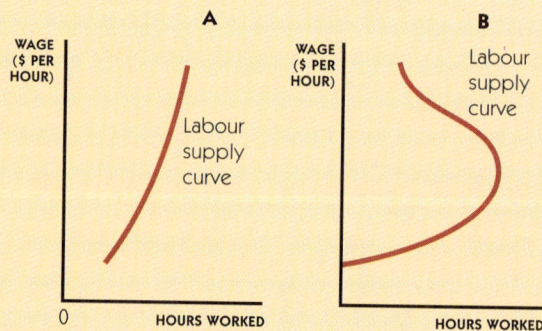

Figure 7.4 DERIVING THE LABOUR SUPPLY CURVE

Panel A shows the case where the substitution effect exceeds the income effect by just a bit, so increases in wages lead to only a small change in labour supply, and the labour supply curve is almost vertical. In panel B, the substitution effect dominates the income effect at low wages, so that the labour supply curve is upward-sloping; and the income effect dominates the substitution effect at high wages, so that the labour supply curve is downward-sloping over that range. Thus, the labour supply curve bends backward.

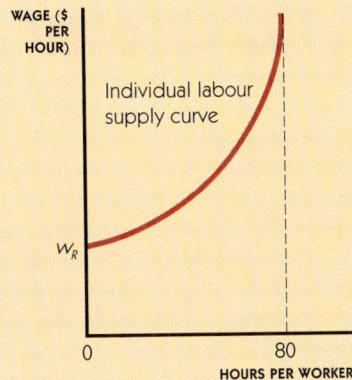

Figure 7.5 **THE INDIVIDUAL LABOUR SUPPLY CURVE**

The reservation wage W_R is the minimum wage at which an individual supplies labour.

That is why in spite of the huge increase in wages over the past fifty years, average hours worked by men has not changed much.

LABOUR FORCE PARTICIPATION

The decision as to how much labour to supply can be divided into two parts: whether to work, and if so, how much to work. The decision about *whether* to work is called the **labour force participation decision.** Figure 7.5 shows the labour supply curve for an individual, that is, how many hours he is willing to supply at each wage. The minimum wage at which the individual is willing to work, W_R, is called the **reservation wage.** Below the reservation wage, the individual does not participate in the labour force.

For men, the question of whether to work has traditionally had an obvious answer. Unless they were very wealthy, they have had to work to support themselves and their families. The wage at which they would decide to work rather than not work was, accordingly, very low. For most men, a change in the wage still does not affect their decision of whether to work. It affects only their decision about how many hours to work, and even this effect is small.

Most women now work for pay too. Women, however, have faced different social expectations from men. Only a few decades ago, not only was there some question as to whether women should work, the social presumption was that working women would drop out of the labour market when they had children. And many mothers did not reenter the market even after their children had grown. Whether by social convention or by choice, most women seemed almost indifferent about whether they worked. Small changes in the wage rate thus had the potential of causing large changes in the fraction of women who worked. The labour supply curve for women appeared to be very elastic (flat). Some economists have estimated a female labour supply elasticity as large as .9: a 1 percent increase in wages leads to a .9 percent increase in labour supply.

Today the traditional presumptions about the role of women have changed. Most women without small children participate in the labour market, and many with children leave for only relatively short periods of time. It is important to note here that the labour force, as economists define it, includes not only those who have jobs but also those who are looking for jobs. In 1901, only 13.5 percent of all women were in the labour force; by 1994 that figure had risen to 57.6 percent. Figure 7.6 shows the dramatic increase in female labour force participation during the past 40 years.

Figure 7.6 FEMALE LABOUR FORCE PARTICIPATION

While under one quarter of all women were in the labour force in 1951, more than half are in the labour force today. *Sources:* Statistics Canada, *Canadian Economic Observer*, December 1995, Table 8; M. C. Urquhart, ed., *Historical Statistics of Canada*, Series C56-69 (Toronto: Macmillan and Company of Canada, 1965).

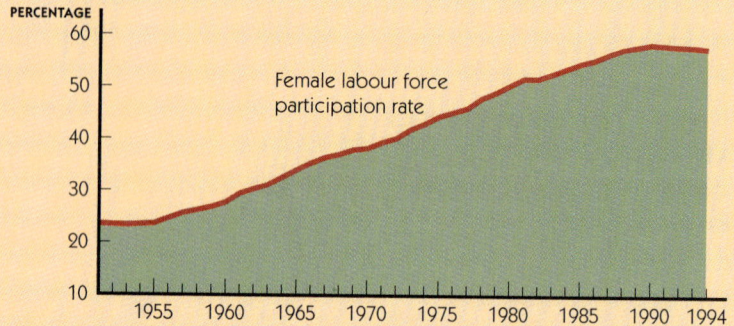

This change can be viewed partly as a *shift* in the labour supply curve for women and partly as a *movement* along it. In other words, because of social factors, there would have been a substantial increase in the number of women in the labour force regardless of what happened to the wage rate. Job opportunities for women have increased enormously in the past thirty years, and relative wages have risen. Thus, the return to working has increased and the opportunity cost of being out of the labour force has gone up. Even in the absence of social change, these factors would be expected to lead to increased labour force participation by women. The increased participation of women as a result of higher wages is a *movement* along the labour supply curve.

But two other changes have contributed to the trend as well. Beginning around 1973, real wages stopped growing at the rate they had been during the period following World War II. Individuals and families had come to expect regular increases in their income. When these increases stopped, they felt the loss. This development encouraged many married women to take part-time or full-time jobs as a way of keeping the family income increasing and, in some cases, to prevent it from decreasing.

There has also been a change in attitudes, on the part of both women and employers, leading to a *shift* in the labour supply curve for women to the right.

Enrollments of women in professional schools increased dramatically, reflecting changed attitudes among the women themselves. And outright discrimination against women was barred with the institution of the Charter of Rights and Freedoms in 1982. Large employers adopted affirmative action programmes whereby they made a commitment to increase the number of women employees, particularly in managerial and more highly skilled jobs.

TAX POLICY AND LABOUR SUPPLY

The effect of a change in wages on labour supply has important policy implications. For example, we often hear that an increase in taxes discourages people from working. An increase in tax rates is equivalent to a decrease in wages, since it decreases the after-tax wage received by the worker. But if the labour supply curve is backward-bending, then a tax increase and its accompanying reduction in the after-tax wage can actually increase the labour supply.

Differences in views about the relative magnitudes of the income and substitution effects on labour supply have played an important role in recent debates over tax policy. When asked how they would respond

USING ECONOMICS: TAX RATES, TAX REVENUES, AND LABOUR SUPPLY

The responsiveness of labour supply to changes in the after-tax wage rate is important for tax policy. To see why, consider Jill, who can choose to work as many hours as she wishes at the wage rate of $10 per hour. When the tax rate is 25 percent, she works 40 hours per week and earns $400. Of this, $100 is paid in taxes and $300 is left for her consumption. The government reduces the tax rate to 20 percent. Jill realizes that if she continues to work 40 hours, she will now pay only $80 in taxes and have $320 left for consumption. She could maintain her previous consumption level by working only 37.5 hours per week and would have more leisure time; this would be an extremely strong income effect. In this case, government revenues would fall to $75, three quarters of what they were before the tax was cut.

On the other hand, Jill might reason that each additional hour worked now yields $8 of after-tax income rather than $7.50. She can increase her consumption a lot by working more hours; this is the substitution effect. Whether the income effect, which encourages her to take more leisure, or the substitution effect, which encourages her to work more, dominates is a matter of preference.

But it is also a matter that affects government revenues dramatically. If the substitution effect is large enough relative to the income effect, the cut in tax rate can actually increase government revenues. For example, if Jill increases her working hours from 40 to 55 per week, her income will rise to $550 and her taxes paid will increase from $100 to $110.

---

to a tax increase, workers do not answer in terms of income and substitution effects. They say things like "I have to work longer hours to maintain my standard of living" or "I work less, because it doesn't pay to work so hard." But economists interpret these different responses in the analytical framework of income and substitution effects. In particular, economists are interested in what happens *on average,* and what happens to particular groups of people within the economy.

For men, the consensus is that the labour supply elasticity is relatively low, so that changing taxes has little effect on either labour force participation or hours worked. But some economists believe that men's labour supply elasticity is quite large, and that the high tax rate on high incomes that prevailed until 1988 had a strong adverse effect on labour supply. In

1988, marginal income tax rates were lowered, especially for higher-income taxpayers. A few economists and politicians argued that the substitution effect would be enormous, but their predictions were not borne out. The evidence by and large indicates that the labour supply response elasticity for men is actually low. Hours worked increased little if at all as a result of the tax cuts.

In contrast to the small labour supply response of men to tax rate changes, the labour supply response of women is large. Higher wages bring many more women into the labour force and higher taxes send many more women out of it. A look at the Canadian income tax makes it easy to see why taxes can have such a large effect on female labour force participation. Under the Canadian income tax system, the tax costs of a woman entering the labour force as a second family earner can be significant. For one thing, the spousal tax credit, which was $1,006 at the federal level in 1994 plus a lesser amount in each of the provinces, is no longer available to the husband if his spouse works. This will cause family taxes to rise by this amount. Furthermore, the woman's whole income becomes subject to income tax.

Not only does a household face high taxes on the additional income when both adults work, but these families have some additional costs, like child care or the higher food bills from eating out or buying frozen dinners. Because of the higher tax liabilities and the fact that much of the extra income may go to cover the extra expenses, the financial incentive for secondary earners to work may be low, and thus changes in the after-tax wage rate can have significant effects on the number of secondary earners who decide to work. A sobering fact of life is that the spouse looking for the household's second job is usually the wife.

For these reasons it is often stated that the tax system discriminates against working spouses relative to nonworking ones. As economists put it, nonworking spouses produce household services that are not taxed, while similar services that must be purchased by two-earner families are taxed. Partly in response to this, and partly simply as a result of the increase in female labour market participation, it has been argued that governments should assume some responsibility for the provision of day-care facilities for working parents, either through tax assistance or through direct provision. The federal government has stated this to be one of its long-run objectives.

Not only income taxes but also sales taxes affect the supply of labour. Since the ultimate objective of earning income is to be able to spend it eventually on consumer goods, the ability to obtain consumer goods by supplying more labour will be affected by the fact that not only the income but also the purchase of consumer goods bears some tax. In Canada, sales tax rates are significant. Ontario levies a retail sales tax of 8 percent; the tax is larger in some provinces and smaller in others. Since 1991 the federal government has levied an additional 7 percent Goods and Services Tax (GST) on most consumer purchases. The effect of the resulting 15 percent overall sales tax rate should be equivalent to a comparable income tax on labour supplies.

THE RETIREMENT DECISION

Retirement is another important aspect of the labour force participation decision. In 1900, a 40-year-old Canadian man could expect to live until age 68. At the same time, 68 percent of men over age 65 were in the labour force. Thus, the typical worker stayed on the job until he died, or until he was too sick to work. Today a 40-year-old man can expect to live to be over 74, but only 12 percent of men over 64 are working or looking for work. In addition, only 77 percent of men between the ages of 45 and 64 are in the labour force. Retirement after 65 has become the expectation, and the number of middle-aged retirees is expected to continue to grow.

These retirement decisions too can be understood in terms of a basic economic model. Increased lifetime wealth has led individuals to choose more leisure over their lifetime. The fact that when people are better off they wish to enjoy more leisure is, as we saw earlier, the income effect. The decision to retire earlier can be thought of as a decision to enjoy more leisure. Indeed, it makes sense for people to choose more leisure in their later years, when their productivity has reached its peak and their wages are not going to increase.

At the same time, wages today are much higher than they were fifty years ago. This means that it is more costly for people to retire early—the amount of consumption (income) they have to give up is larger. This is the substitution effect. Evidently, for many men the income effect dominates the substitution effect.

HUMAN CAPITAL AND EDUCATION

The nation's output depends not only on the number of hours people work but also on how productive those hours are. One of the important determinants of workers' productivity—and therefore wages—is education.

By staying in school longer, which usually means delaying entry into the labour force, people can

CLOSE-UP: ECONOMIC INCENTIVES FOR PARENTHOOD

Birthrates in Europe have fallen so low that the population of the European nations is likely to begin shrinking. It takes an average of 2.1 children per woman of childbearing age to keep the population at a steady level, and as the table here shows, only Ireland among European countries exceeds that rate. Meanwhile, birthrates in many African nations are three times as high. Of course, many cultural and historical factors go to make up these differences, but economists also argue that economic factors play a role.

In relatively poor countries, children are a source of labour for the family when they are young and a source of social security for aged parents. But as a society grows wealthier, moves away from a reliance on farming, and establishes systems of pensions and social security, the economic benefits of having children decrease while the opportunity costs rise. Around the world, birthrates tend to fall as people become wealthier.

Economists who study the labour market in Europe have pointed out that unless other factors intervene, the number of adult workers in Europe soon will not match the expected demand of business for labour at current wages. Employers in many European countries are already reporting that it is difficult to find workers for low-paid jobs like food servers and agricultural workers. If European wages rise sharply in all industries because of a lack of workers, it will push up costs for European companies and make it harder for them to compete in world markets.

One solution to the labour shortage problem would be immigration from African nations with higher birthrates. But while such immigration might be economically beneficial for all parties, it is often politically unpopular in Europe, usually from concerns over an influx of people from a different culture. France has attempted to implement a more direct solution, where mothers receive substantial welfare payments and tax breaks as an incentive to have more children. But so far, at least, the birthrate in France has remained low.

Source: Alan Riding, "Western Europe, Its Births Falling, Wonders Who'll Do All the Work," *New York Times,* July 22, 1990, p. A1.

European nations	Birthrate	African nations	Birthrate
Ireland	2.0	Ethiopia	7.5
United Kingdom	1.8	Chad	5.9
France	1.8	Zaïre	6.0
Denmark	1.8	Mali	7.1
Belgium	1.6	Burkina Faso	6.9
Netherlands	1.6	Nigeria	5.9
Greece	1.4	Niger	7.4
Portugal	1.5	Mozambique	6.5
Germany	1.3	Tanzania	6.3
Spain	1.2	Somalia	6.8
Italy	1.3	Sudan	6.1

Source: World Bank, *World Development Report* (1994), Table 26. Data are for 1992.

increase their expected annual income. In addition, working *harder* in school and giving up leisure may result in better grades and skills, which in turn will result in higher wages in the future. Thus, students face a trade-off between leisure today and consumption, or income, in the future.

Spending a year at university has its obvious costs—tuition, room, and board. But there are also opportunity costs, such as the income that would have been received from a job. These opportunity costs are costs of going to school just as much as are any direct tuition payments. Economists say that the investment in education produces **human capital,** making an analogy to the **physical capital** investments that businesses make in plant and equipment. Human capital is developed by formal schooling, on-the-job learning, and many other investments of time and money that parents make in their children.

Canada invests an enormous amount in human capital. In fact, human capital is more significant than physical capital. As much as two thirds to three fourths of all capital is human capital. This investment is financed both publicly and privately. Local, provincial, and federal governments spend about $40 billion a year on education. Government expenditures on primary and secondary education are the largest category of expenditure at the local and provincial levels, accounting for more than 20 percent of total expenditures.

The enormous increase in education levels in the past 50 years is illustrated in Table 7.1. Among those 65 and older, only about one fifth have at least one year of college or university; more than half those in the 35–44 age group do. More generally the table shows that the amount of education obtained falls systematically with age.

EDUCATION AND ECONOMIC TRADE-OFFS

The production possibilities curve introduced in Chapter 2 can illustrate how decisions concerning investments in human capital are taken. To do so, we divide an individual's life into two periods: "youth" and "later working years." Figure 7.7 depicts the relationship between consumption in youth and in later life. As the individual gives up consumption in his youth, staying in school longer increases his ex-

Table 7.1 HIGHEST LEVEL OF EDUCATION, BY AGE, IN 1991

Age group	Without high school or trade certificate	With high school or trade certificate only	Percentage of total age group With some nonuniversity postsecondary	With some university	With university degree
20–24	21.2	20.0	28.9	21.0	8.9
25–34	23.0	20.3	30.4	10.3	16.0
35–44	24.9	20.9	26.3	10.7	17.2
45–54	37.2	19.1	22.0	8.4	13.3
55–64	53.5	16.5	16.7	5.8	7.5
65 and older	64.4	13.5	12.3	4.8	5.1

Source: Census of Canada 1991, "The Nation," "Education," Table 2, Statistics Canada 1992, Catalogue No. 93-328.

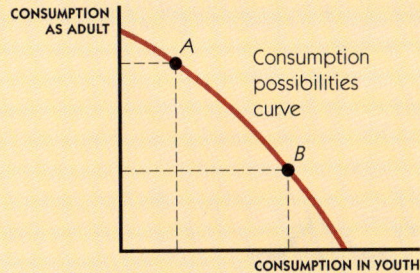

Figure 7.7 EDUCATION AND THE TRADE-OFF BETWEEN CURRENT AND FUTURE EARNINGS

Point *A* represents a choice of a reduced income and better education in the present, with a higher income in the future. Point *B* represents the choice of higher income and less education now, with a lower level of income in the future.

pected future consumption because he can expect his income to go up. The curve has been drawn to show diminishing returns: spending more on education today (reducing consumption) raises future income, but each additional investment in education provides a smaller and smaller return.

Point *A* represents the case where Everett is a full-time student through four years of college, with little income until graduation (his youth) but with a high income in later life. Point *B* represents the consequences of dropping out of school after high school. When he does this, Everett has a higher income in his youth but a lower income in later life. Other possible points between *A* and *B* represent cases where Everett drops out of college after one or two years.

THE WIDENING WAGE GAP

Those who have a university education are paid more on average than those who fail to complete high school. The average wage of workers with at least four years of university is two thirds greater than that of workers whose formal education ended with a high school diploma. Because unskilled workers generally cannot perform the same jobs as skilled workers, it is useful to think about the wages of the two groups as determined in separate labour markets, as illustrated in Figure 7.8. Panel A shows the demand and supply

curves of unskilled workers, panel B those of skilled workers. The equilibrium wage for skilled workers is higher than that for unskilled workers.

What happens if a change in technology shifts the demand curve for skilled labour to the right, to DS_1, and the demand curve for unskilled labour to the left, to DU_1? The wages of unskilled workers will decrease from wu_0 to wu_1, and those of skilled workers will increase from ws_0 to ws_1. In the long run, this increased wage gap induces more people to acquire skills, so the supply of unskilled workers shifts to the left, and that of skilled workers shifts to the right. As a result, the wage of unskilled workers rises from wu_1 to wu_2, and that of skilled workers falls from ws_1 to ws_2. These long-run supply responses thus dampen the short-run movements in wages.

Over the past two decades, the ratio of university graduates to high school graduates, and the ratio of wages of high school graduates to those of nongraduates has increased enormously. Indeed, the real wages (wages adjusted for changes in the cost of living) of unskilled workers has fallen dramatically—by as much as 30 percent. Though there have been shifts in both demand and supply curves, the primary explanation of these shifts is a change in the relative demand for skilled labour, probably attributable largely to changes in technology.

Will the predicted shifts in long-run labour supply that result from unskilled workers' acquiring more skills—thus reducing the current wage gap—in fact

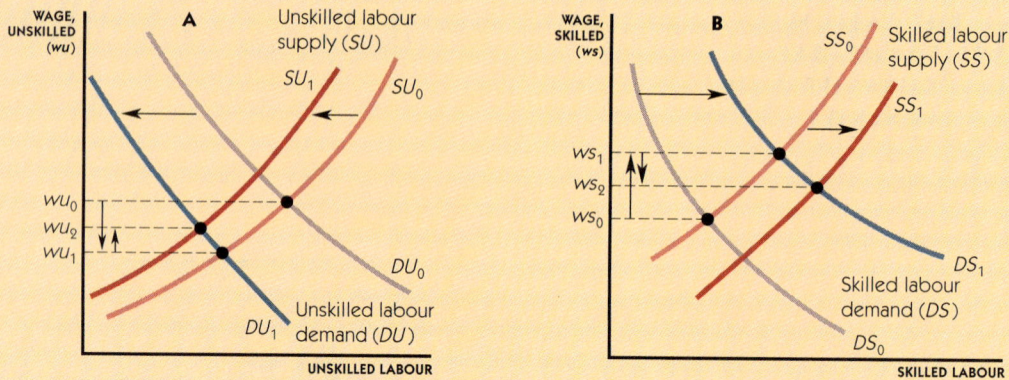

Figure 7.8 THE MARKET FOR SKILLED AND UNSKILLED LABOUR

In panel A, the invention of a new machine shifts the demand curve for unskilled labour to the left, and reduces wages from wu_0 to wu_1. In panel B, the new machine shifts the demand curve for skilled labour out to the right, and thus raises wages from ws_0 to ws_1. Over time, this increased difference in wages may lead the supply curve for unskilled labour to shift back to the left, raising wages for unskilled labour somewhat from wu_1 to wu_2, and the supply curve for skilled labour to shift out to the right, reducing wages for skilled labour from ws_1 to ws_2.

occur? We cannot be certain. If they do occur, how long will it take for the wage gap to be reduced to the levels that prevailed in the 1960s? In the meantime, many worry about the social consequences of steadily increasing wage and income inequality.

WAGE DIFFERENTIALS

The basic competitive model suggests that if the goods being sold are the same, prices will also be the same. Wages are the price in the labour market; but even in the absence of unions, similar types of workers performing similar types of jobs are sometimes paid quite different wages. For example, some secre-

taries are paid twice as much as others. How can economists explain differences like these?

They begin by pointing to **compensating wage differentials.** Understanding compensating wage differentials begins with the observation that although different jobs may have the same title, they can be quite different. Some jobs are less pleasant, require more overtime, and are in a less convenient location. These are **nonpecuniary** attributes of a job. Others include the degree of autonomy provided the worker, the closeness with which her actions are supervised, and the risk she must bear, whether in a physical sense or from the variability in income. Economists expect wages to adjust to reflect the attractiveness or unattractiveness of these nonpecuniary characteristics. Compensating wage differentials arise because firms have to compensate their workers for the negative aspects of a job.

Other differences are accounted for by differences

in the productivity of workers. These are **productivity wage differentials.** Some workers are much more productive than others, even with the same experience and education.

Compensating and productivity wage differentials fall within the realm of basic competitive market analysis. But other wage differentials are due to imperfect information. It takes time to search out different job opportunities. Just as one store may sell the same object for a higher price than another store, one firm may hire labour for a lower wage than another firm. The worker who accepts a lower-paying job simply because he did not know about the higher-paying one down the street faces an **information-based differential.**

Limited information has important implications for firms. First, in the standard competitive model, firms face a horizontal supply curve for labour. If they raise wages ever so little above the "market" wage, they can obtain as much labour as they want. In practice, mobility is more limited. Even if workers at other firms knew about the higher wage offer, they might be reluctant to switch. They may not be well matched for the job, or the employer may be offering high wages because the work is unattractive in one way or another.

Second, firms worry about the quality of their work force. If an employer offers a higher wage to someone working for another firm and the worker accepts, the employer might worry. Did the worker's current employer—who presumably knows a lot about the worker's productivity—fail to match the job offer because the worker's productivity does not warrant the higher wage? Does the worker's willingness to leave demonstrate "lack of loyalty," or "an unsettled nature"—in which case, he may not stick with the new firm long enough to make his training worthwhile? These concerns again impede labour mobility—as employers prefer to keep their existing labour force even when there are lower-paid workers with similar credentials whom they might recruit at a lower wage.

Different groups of individuals may differ in their mobility. For instance, older workers may be much more reluctant to move than younger workers. Sometimes firms take advantage of these differences to pay lower wages. Knowing that older workers will not leave even if wages fail to keep pace with inflation, employers may hold back raises from them, thus discriminating against their age and lower mobility.

DISCRIMINATION

Discrimination is said to occur if two workers of seemingly similar *work-related* characteristics are treated differently. Paying higher wages to more educated workers is not discrimination, as long as the higher level of education is related to higher productivity. If older workers are less productive, then paying them lower wages is not discrimination. But if older workers are just as productive as younger workers, then taking advantage of their lower mobility *is* discrimination.

Forty years ago there was open and outright discrimination in the labour market. Some employers simply refused to hire aboriginals. Today much of the discrimination is more subtle. Firms seek to hire the best workers they can for each job at the lowest cost possible, operating with imperfect information. Employers use whatever information they have available. On average, employers may have found that those holding a degree from a well-established university are more productive than those holding a degree from a less established one. Of those aboriginals who have managed to get a postsecondary education, more may have gone to the less established universities or colleges. Screening the applicant pool to pick those with degrees from well-established universities effectively screens out many aboriginals. This more subtle form of discrimination is called **statistical discrimination.**

Some discrimination is neither old-fashioned prejudice nor statistical discrimination. Employers may just feel more comfortable dealing with people with whom they have dealt in the past. In a world in which there is so much uncertainty about who is a good worker and in which a bad worker can do enormous damage, top management may rely on certain trusted employees for recommendations. Such judgments are inevitably affected by friendships and other ties. Many claim that if discrimination is to be eliminated, this form of discrimination, based on "old boy networks," has to be broken.

When firms pay lower wages to, say, women or minorities, it is called **wage discrimination.** Today, wage discrimination is perhaps less common than **job discrimination,** where disadvantaged groups have less access to better-paying jobs. Women are often said to face a "glass ceiling": they can climb up to middle management jobs, but can't get beyond that to top management.

Some market forces tend to limit the extent of discrimination. If a woman is paid less than a man of comparable productivity, it pays a firm to hire the woman. Not to hire her costs the firm profits. To put it another way, the firm pays a price for discriminating. If there are enough firms that put profits above prejudice, then the wages of women will be bid up towards the level of men of comparable productivity.

In fact, both federal and provincial governments have enacted legislation to encourage the fair treatment of women and potentially disadvantaged minorities in labour markets. The measures undertaken have been of two forms: those intended to preclude discrimination in pay **(pay equity)** and those intended to encourage equal employment opportunities **(employment equity).**

LOOKING BEYOND THE BASIC MODEL: LABOUR UNIONS

Labour unions are organizations of workers formed to obtain better working conditions and remuneration for their members. Given that they act collectively on behalf of their members, they are large enough to influence the wage rate at which labour is supplied; thus they are noncompetitive in nature. The main weapon they have is the threat of a collective withdrawal of labour, known as a **strike.**

THE RISE AND DECLINE OF LABOUR UNIONS

Labour unions are important institutions in our economy; in Canada they play a much more important role than in the United States, though a some-what less important one than in many European countries. The idea of the labour union was first introduced into Canada by European immigrants in the early nineteenth century, and the earliest recorded trade union was formed by printers in 1827 in Quebec City. But the main impetus did not occur until the second half of the nineteenth century with the coming of the industrial revolution to Canada. Unions in the United States developed first and then spread to Canada, initially in the crafts and skilled trades in cities such as Montreal, Toronto, and St. John. American unions encouraged the local unions in Canada to combine and become part of an international union structure, and many did. Thus, the National Typographical Union of the United States became the International Typographical Union, and so on.

The trade union movement grew rapidly but intermittently until after World War II, a period when both the nature of the work force and the industrial structure began to change noticeably. The work force was becoming much more educated, and the proportion of women in the work force was increasing rapidly. The service industries were growing relative to the traditional goods-producing sectors and would continue to grow. While the service sector made up 28 percent of unionized workers at the turn of the century, this had risen to 70 percent by 1981. Most important, the public sector was becoming larger and larger as governments implemented the welfare state. By 1986, the two largest unions in Canada were public-sector unions, the Canadian Union of Public Employees and the National Union of Public Employees.

These changes heavily influenced the trend in union membership. It continued to rise gradually from about 25 percent of nonagricultural employment in 1946 to about 30 percent in 1966 and about 36 percent in 1975. But the proportion has remained virtually unchanged since then. These aggregate numbers mask an important change in the composition of unionized workers. While the proportion of public employees who are unionized rose from 3 percent to 20 percent from 1961 to 1990, unionization in the private sector has actually fallen in the past twenty years. This reflects a trend that is also occurring in the United States and is even more marked there than in Canada. Why the recent and continuing decline?

POLICY PERSPECTIVE:
THE MIXED LEGACY OF COMPARABLE WORTH

The wage earned by an average female working full time in Canada is about 70 percent of the wage of the average male worker. Moreover, many women feel that they have been guided and pushed into a "pink-collar ghetto" of predominantly female jobs, like secretaries or receptionists, where wages are lower than in jobs held by men that require comparable skills and carry similar responsibilities. And a far higher proportion of women than of men are employed only part time (49 percent versus 32 percent). Should governments enact policies intended to redress this?

One way to address this complaint would be to raise wage levels in the jobs traditionally held by women. In 1978, the principle of equal pay for work of equal value was recognized in the Canadian Human Rights Act as applying to jobs in the public sector under federal jurisdiction. Provincial and territorial governments have also introduced such pay equity legislation, but Ontario is the only province to have extended the legislation to the private sector (1988) and to have implemented a proactive (investigations are initiated independently) as opposed to a complaints-based process. Some jurisdictions have contemplated "comparable worth" policies similar to those tried by some state governments in the United States, where jobs are compared through a points system on the basis of factors such as skill level required, responsibility, effort, and working conditions, and wages are adjusted accordingly.

Many economists argue that this kind of job evaluation is not acceptable since it is often logically inconsistent. They point out that the comparable worth study of the U.S. National Academy of Sciences somehow managed to award more points to truck drivers than to university professors. They also suggest that it may be inappropriate to award points and thus higher wages for "unpleasant" working conditions. For instance, although some of us find employment as a butcher or a plumber distasteful, others may enjoy it.

It is also important to determine the impact that pay equity or comparable worth policies have on other economic variables, such as the level of employment and wages in both targeted and nontargeted sectors. In comparable worth jobs, it has been found that wages for both women and men rise, but employment falls for both because of the higher wage costs. This employment effect moves workers, predominantly men, into the nontargeted sector, causing wages to fall there. The increased supply of men in the nontargeted sector tends to discourage women from finding employment in "nontraditional" jobs. Consequently, for women in the nontargeted sector, both wages and employment fall. Thus, the ultimate losers of comparable worth policies may be women themselves.

Moreover, comparable worth policies do not attempt to reduce the ratio of women working in the "pink-collar ghetto." Nor do they address what many women regard as one of the main difficulties faced by women in the labour market: the inability to find a full-time job.

Source: Mark Killingsworth, "Benefits and Costs of Comparable Worth," in M. G. Abbott, ed., *Pay Equity: Means and Ends* (Kingston, Ontario: The John Deutsch Institute for the Study of Economic Policy, June 1990), pp. 47–62.

One explanation is that, whether as a result of union pressure or technological progress, working conditions for workers have improved enormously. Workers see less need for unions.

A second reason is related to the changing nature of the Canadian economy. Unions have declined as the traditionally unionized sectors, like automobiles and steel, have weakened, and the service sector, in which unions have been weak, has grown.

Third, unions may be less effective in competitive markets. When competition is limited, there are monopoly (or imperfect competition) profits or rents. Unions may be successful in obtaining for their workers a share in those rents. But when markets are competitive, firms cannot charge more than the market price for their goods, and if they are to survive, they simply cannot pay their workers more than the competitive wage.

ECONOMIC EFFECTS OF UNIONS

The source of union power is collective action. When workers join together in a union, they no longer negotiate as isolated individuals. The threat of a strike or a work slowdown poses many more difficulties for an employer than does the threat of any single employee quitting.

In the perfectly competitive model of labour markets, workers are price takers, facing a given market wage. But in situations where there is a downward-sloping demand curve for labour, as in Figure 7.9, unions have some power to be price setters. As a result of this power, a worker at a given level of skill who works in a unionized establishment will be paid more than a comparable worker in a competitive industry. The firm would like to hire that lower-priced, nonunion worker, and the nonunionized worker could easily be induced to move, but the firm has a union contract that prevents it from doing so. But as the union raises the price of labour (the wage), firms will employ fewer workers. Higher wages are obtained at the expense of lower employment. In the figure, when wages rise from the competitive level w_c to w_m employment is reduced from L_c to L_m.

SHORT-RUN GAINS AT THE EXPENSE OF LONG-RUN LOSSES

Sometimes unions can increase both employment and wages. They present the employer with, in effect, two alternatives: either pay high wages *and* maintain the same employment level or go out of

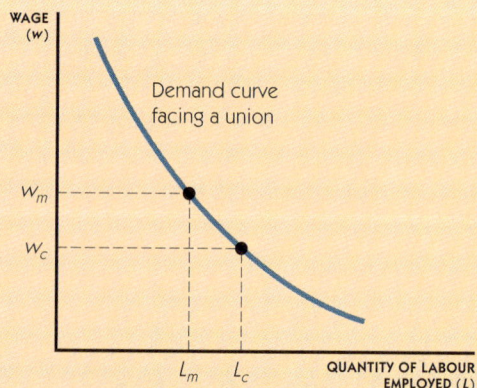

Figure 7.9 THE UNION AS A MONOPOLY SELLER OF LABOUR

Unions can be viewed as sellers of labour, with market power. When they increase their wage demands, they reduce the demand for their members' labour services.

business. If the employer already has sunk costs in machines and buildings, he may give in to the union demands. In effect, the union thus takes away some of the employer's profits. In competitive markets, where there are no monopoly profits, the higher wages can only come out of employers' return to capital. But these employers will lose interest in investing in more capital. As capital wears out, the employer has less and less to lose from the union threat. As he refuses to invest more, jobs decrease. Even if the union makes short-run gains, they come at the expense of a long-run loss in jobs.

EFFECTS ON NONUNION WORKERS

The gains of today's union members may not only cost future jobs but also be at the expense of those in other sectors of the economy, for two reasons. First, the higher wages may well be passed on to consumers in the form of higher prices, particularly if product markets are not perfectly competitive. Second, the increased wages and reduced employment in the union sector drive down wages in the nonunionized sector as the supply of nonunion labour increases. Some argue the opposite—that high union wages "pull up" wages in nonunion firms. The nonunion firms may, for instance, pay higher wages to reduce the likelihood of unionization. In particular sectors this effect is important, but most economists believe that the overall effect on nonunion workers is negative.

JOB SECURITY AND INNOVATION

The economy as a whole benefits from innovation, but particular groups are likely to suffer from innovation. In an innovative economy, workers who are dislocated by new inventions are expected to learn new skills and seek out new jobs. If labour doesn't shift in response to changes in demand (resulting from new technologies), the economy will be inefficient.

Technological changes may threaten the job security unions seek for their members. As a result, unions have attempted to retard innovations that might decrease the demand for their members' labour services. Job transitions are necessary for economic efficiency, but they are costly and the costs are borne largely by the workers. Before the advent of unions and laws providing unemployment compensation,

the human toll was considerable. Individuals could not buy insurance against these employment risks, but they could form unions, and union attempts to enhance job security were a response to this important problem. Today many countries are looking for ways of insulating workers against the risks of job transition without impeding the labour mobility that is so important for economic efficiency.

UNIONS AND POLITICS

Unions have learned that what they cannot get at the bargaining table they may be able to obtain through the political process. Thus, they have actively campaigned for higher minimum wages.

At the same time unions have shown in their political stances that they recognize the economic forces that determine both the strength of their bargaining positions and, more generally, the level of wages. Thus, they have been active supporters of policies of high employment. They have sought to restrict imports from abroad, believing that this will increase the demand for Canadian products and therefore the demand for labour. They have also been strongly opposed both to the Canada-U.S. Free Trade Agreement and to the North American Free Trade Agreement (NAFTA).

Finally, unions have been strong advocates through the political process of safer working conditions. Today, Part II of the Canadian Labour Code authorizes regulations to deal with safety and health problems and gives workers the right to refuse to work where their health or safety could be in danger. The kind of episodes such as occurred in the asbestos industry, where workers were exposed to life-threatening risks, probably could not occur today.

LIMITS ON UNION POWER

In Canada, no union has a monopoly on *all* workers. At most, a union has a monopoly on the workers currently working for a particular firm. Thus, the power of unions is partly attributable to the fact that a firm cannot easily replace its employees. When a union goes on strike, the firm may be able to hire some workers, but it is costly to bring in and train a whole new labour force. Indeed, most of the knowledge needed to train the new workers is in the hands of the union members. While one bushel of wheat may be very much like another, one worker is not very much like another. Workers outside the firm are not perfect substitutes for workers, particularly skilled ones, inside.

THE THREAT OF REPLACEMENT

In industries in which skills are easily transferable across firms, or where a union has not been successful in enlisting the support of most of the skilled workers, a firm can replace striking workers, and union power will be limited. The extent to which this is possible depends upon the province in which the firm is operating. For example, in Quebec and British Columbia, the hiring of replacement workers is not permitted. Even in cases where it is permitted, workers may be reluctant to cross union picket lines to do a striker's work. This can occasionally escalate to violent confrontations, as happened during the 1992 strike at the Giant Gold Mine in Yellowknife, resulting in the suspicious death of nine replacement workers in an underground explosion.

In many cases, however, workers' skills are firm-specific. Just as, from the employers' perspective, workers outside the firm are not perfect substitutes for workers within, from the workers' perspective one job is not a perfect substitute for another. Thus, there is often value to both workers and firms in preserving ongoing employment relationships. The two parties are tied to each other in what is referred to as a bargaining relationship. The bargaining strengths of the two sides are affected by the fact that a firm, at a cost, can obtain other employees, and employees, at a cost, can get other jobs. The total amount by which the two sides together are better off continuing their relationship than ending it is referred to as the "bargaining surplus." A large part of the negotiations between unions and management are about how to split this surplus.

THE THREAT OF UNEMPLOYMENT

Unions have come to understand that higher wages—other things being equal—mean lower levels of employment. This will be especially true for industries that face competition from abroad. If job opportunities in general are weak, workers laid off as a result of higher wages will have difficulty finding a job elsewhere. The level of unemployment will rise. This was evident in the early 1980s, as a deep recession threatened a number of union jobs, especially in the automobile industry, which faced the added threat of Japanese imports.

In the longer run, those laid off in the unionized sector as a result of higher negotiated wages will eventually relocate in the nonunionized sector. The increased supply of workers outside the unionized industries will introduce pressures to reduce wages there, leading to a reallocation of demand from the unionized to the nonunionized sector. In the end, the bargaining strength of the unions will have been weakened by the induced lowering of wages in the nonunion sector. Several European countries have

UNIONS AND IMPERFECT COMPETITION IN THE LABOUR MARKET

Economic effects

  Higher wages for union members, with fewer union jobs and lower wages for nonunion members

  Improved job security, sometimes at the expense of innovation and economic efficiency

  Minimum wages, restrictions on imports, improved working conditions, other gains achieved through the political process

Determinants of union power

  Political and legal environment

  Economic environment: threat of replacement and unemployment

national unions, which embrace a much larger proportion of the labour force. These unions may be successful at attaining wages that are above the market-clearing level. In these countries, unions are thought to contribute significantly to the overall unemployment level.

REVIEW AND PRACTICE

SUMMARY

1 The decision about how to allocate time between work and leisure can be analyzed using the basic ideas of budget constraints and preferences. Individuals face a trade-off along a budget constraint between leisure and income. The amount of income a person can obtain by giving up leisure is determined by the wage rate.

2 In labour markets, the substitution and income effects of a change in wages work in opposite directions. An increase in wages makes people feel better off, and they wish to enjoy more leisure now as well as more consumption; this is the income effect. But the substitution effect of an increase in wages raises the opportunity cost of leisure, and encourages more work. The overall effect of a rise in wages will depend on whether the substitution or income effect is actually larger.

3 An upward-sloping labour supply curve represents a case where the substitution effect of rising wages outweighs the income effect. A relatively vertical labour supply curve represents a case where the substitution and income effects of rising wages are nearly equal. A backward-bending labour supply curve represents a case where the substitution effect dominates at low wages (labour supply increases as the wage increases), but the income effect dominates at high wages (labour supply decreases as the wage increases).

4 The basic trade-off between leisure and income can also be used to analyze decisions such as when to enter the labour force (leave school) and when to retire (leave the labour force).

5 Human capital adds to economic productivity just as physical capital does. It is developed by education, on-the-job learning, and investments of time and money that parents make in their children.

6 Economic considerations have some impact on decisions about whether to have children and other seemingly noneconomic choices.

7 Explanations for wage differentials include compensating differentials (differences in the nature of jobs), productivity differentials (differences in productivity among workers), imperfect information (workers do not know all the job opportunities that are available), and discrimination.

8 The proportion of Canadian workers in private-sector unions has declined since the 1960s. Possible reasons include laws that have improved working conditions; the decline in manufacturing industries, where unions have traditionally been strong, relative to service industries; foreign competition; and a more anti-union atmosphere in the legal structure.

9 Union power is limited by the ability of companies to bring in new, nonunion workers and by the threat of unemployment to union members.

KEY TERMS

labour force participation	human capital	statistical discrimination	employment equity
reservation wage	compensating wage differentials	pay equity	

REVIEW QUESTIONS

1 How do people make choices about the amount of time to work, given their personal tastes and relative wages in the market?

2 How will the income effect of a fall in wages affect hours worked? How will the substitution effect of a fall in wages affect hours worked? What does the labour supply curve look like if the income effect dominates the substitution effect? if the substitution effect dominates the income effect?

3 Describe how students invest time and money to acquire human capital.

4 True or false: "If a person did not acquire any useful job skills when she got an educational degree, she would have no *economic* reason to get the education." Explain.

5 Would you expect an increase in women's wages to increase or decrease family size? What about an increase in men's wages?

6 What are the alternative explanations for wage differentials?

7 What effect will successful unions have on the level of wages paid by unionized companies? on the capital investment by those companies? What effect will they have on wages paid by nonunionized companies?

8 Does it make sense for a union to resist the introduction of an innovation in the short run? in the long run?

PROBLEMS

1 Imagine that a wealthy relative dies and leaves you an inheritance in a trust fund that will provide you with $20,000 per year for the rest of your life. Draw a diagram to illustrate this shift in your budget constraint between leisure and consumption. After considering the ideas of income and substitution effects, decide whether this inheritance will cause you to work more or less.

2 Most individuals do not take a second job (moonlight), even if they could get one, for instance as a taxi driver. This is in spite of the fact that their "basic job" may require them to work only 37 hours a week. Most moonlighting jobs pay less per hour than the basic job. Draw a typical worker's budget constraint. Discuss the consequences of the kink in the budget constraint.

3 Under current economic conditions, let's say that an unskilled worker will be able to get a job at a wage of $5 per hour. Now assume the government decides to assure that all people with a weekly income of less than $150 will be given a cheque to bring them up to the $150 level. Draw one such worker's original bud-

get constraint and the constraint with the welfare programme. Will this welfare programme be likely to cause a recipient who originally worked 30 hours to work less? How about a recipient who worked less than 30 hours? More than 30 hours? Explain how the government might reduce these negative effects by offering a wage subsidy that would increase the hourly wage to $6 per hour for each of the first 20 hours worked, and draw a revised budget constraint to illustrate.

4 "The fact that the average woman is paid less than the average man in the Canadian economy proves to most economists that discrimination against women is widespread." Discuss.

5 There is a negative correlation between a woman's real wage and her family size. This chapter mentioned two possible interpretations: women with higher real wages *choose* to have smaller families; or larger family sizes might cause women to receive lower wages. What evidence might help you choose between these two explanations?

6 Explain how both these points can be true simultaneously:

(a) Unions manage to raise wages paid to their members.

(b) Unions do not affect the average level of wages paid in the economy.

7 How might each of the following factors affect the power of unions?

(a) A province passes a right-to-work law.

(b) Foreign imports increase.

(c) The national unemployment rate falls.

(d) Corporate profits increase.

APPENDIX: INDIFFERENCE CURVES AND THE LABOUR SUPPLY DECISION

This appendix investigates the labour supply decision using the indifference curve approach applied to the consumption decision in the appendix to Chapter 6.

Figure 7.10 shows Tom's budget constraint between leisure and consumption. As we saw in this chapter, the trade-off along this budget constraint is between leisure and consumption: the less leisure, the more consumption, and vice versa. The slope of the budget constraint is the wage. The figure also shows two indifference curves; each gives the combinations of leisure and consumption among which Tom is indifferent. As usual, since people prefer more of both consumption and leisure if that is possible, Tom will move to the highest indifference curve he can attain. This will be the one that is just tangent to the budget constraint.

The slope of the indifference curve is the marginal rate of substitution between leisure and consumption. It measures the amount of extra consumption Tom requires to compensate him for forgoing one additional hour of leisure. At the point of tangency between the indifference curve and the budget constraint, point *E*, both have the same slope. That is, the marginal rate of substitution equals the wage at this point.

As in the earlier appendix, we can easily see why Tom chooses this point. Assume his marginal rate of substitution is $15 per hour, and his wage is $20 per hour. If he works an hour more—gives up an hour's worth of leisure—his consumption goes up by $20. But to compensate him for the forgone leisure, he only requires $15. Since he gets more than he requires by working, he clearly prefers to work more.

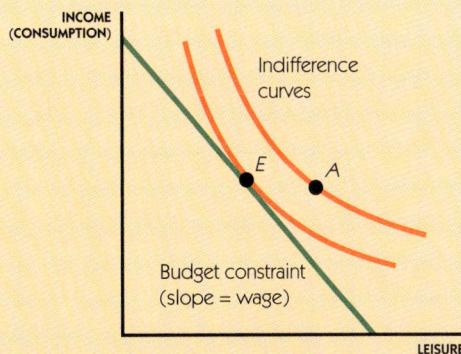

Figure 7.10 INDIFFERENCE CURVES AND LEISURE/INCOME CHOICES

An individual will choose the combination of leisure and income at *E*. Point *A* would be more desirable, but it is not feasible. Other points on the budget line or inside it are feasible, but they lie on lower indifference curves and are therefore not as desirable.

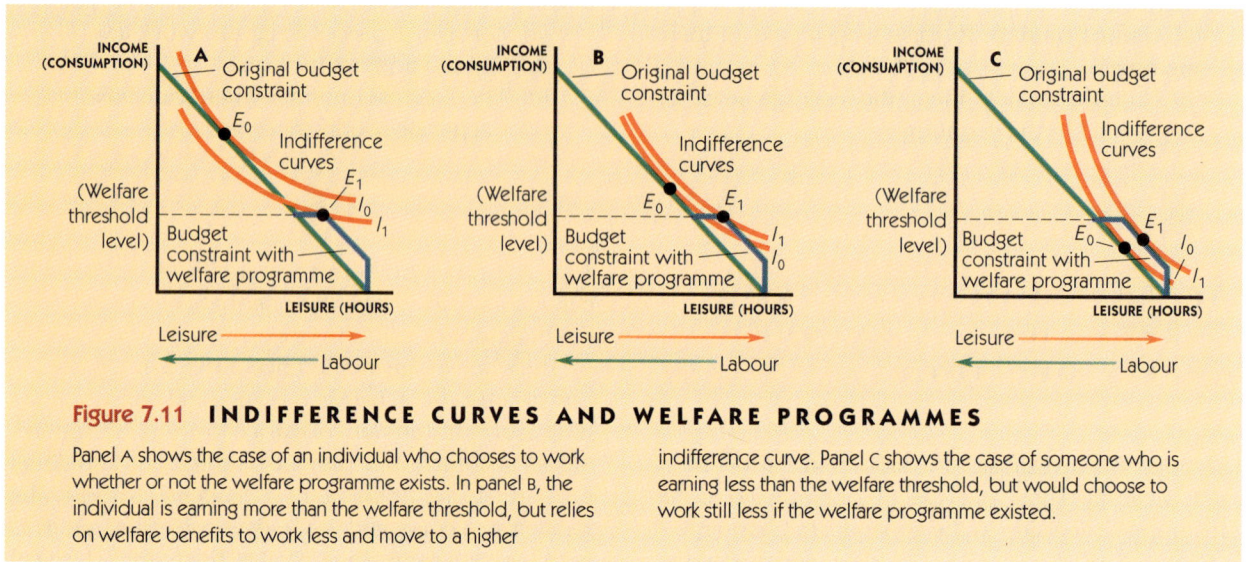

Figure 7.11 INDIFFERENCE CURVES AND WELFARE PROGRAMMES

Panel A shows the case of an individual who chooses to work whether or not the welfare programme exists. In panel B, the individual is earning more than the welfare threshold, but relies on welfare benefits to work less and move to a higher indifference curve. Panel C shows the case of someone who is earning less than the welfare threshold, but would choose to work still less if the welfare programme existed.

DECIDING WHETHER TO WORK

How to use indifference curves to analyze how people decide whether to work or not is shown in Figure 7.11. Consider a low-wage individual facing a welfare system in which there is a fixed level of benefits if one's income is below a threshold level. Benefits are cut off once income exceeds a certain level. The indifference curve I_0 is tangent to the budget constraint without welfare, and the point of tangency is E_0. The curve I_1 is the highest indifference curve consistent with the person receiving welfare.

The three possible cases are illustrated in panels A, B, and C. In panel A, the indifference curve through point E_0, I_0, is higher than the curve I_1. The individual chooses to work at E_0, and is unaffected by the welfare programme. In panels B and C, the person works sufficiently little to be eligible for welfare; that is, I_1 is higher than I_0, and so he chooses point E_1. In panel B, the individual realizes that if he works more, he will lose his welfare benefits. He earns just (little) enough to be eligible for welfare. In panel C, his marginal rate of substitution is equal to the wage rate; that is, the indifference curve I_1 is tangent to the budget constraint. The welfare system has only an income effect.

CHAPTER 8

SAVING AND INVESTING

A rallying cry for politicians is that we must invest more for our future: the choices we make today will affect living standards in the future. Much of economics is thus *future-oriented*. Though the basic principles of making choices apply here as well, there are some distinctive aspects of future-oriented choices that contrast with the static nature of the consumption and labour supply decisions discussed in the previous two chapters. The first part of this chapter focuses on those aspects. We then show how basic consumer theory can be used to analyze people's decisions as to how much of their incomes to consume now and how much to save for future consumption. Finally, we consider how people invest the funds they have set aside as savings—what assets they decide to acquire.

INTEREST

When you put money into a bank account you are involved in a future-oriented transaction. You have lent your money to the bank, and the bank has promised to pay you back. But banks offer more than security; they offer you a *return* on your savings. This return, like the return on any loan, is called **interest.** If you put $1,000 in the bank at the beginning of the year, and the interest rate is 10 percent per year, you will receive $1,100 at the end of the year. The $100 is the payment of interest, while the $1,000 is the repayment of the **principal,** the original amount lent to the bank.

To an economist the interest rate is a price. Normally we express prices in terms of dollars. If the price of an orange is $1.00, we must give up $1.00 to get one orange. Economists talk about the relative price of two goods as the amount of one good you have to give up to get one more unit of the other. The relative price is the ratio of the two "dollar" prices.

For example, if the price of an apple is $.50 and the price of an orange is $1.00, then the relative price (the ratio of the prices) is 2. If we wish to consume one more orange, we have to give up two apples. Thus, the relative price describes a trade-off. Similarly, if the interest rate is 10 percent, by giving up $1.00 worth of consumption today a saver can have $1.10 worth of

consumption next year. Thus, the rate of interest tells us how much future consumption we can get by giving up $1.00 worth of current consumption. One plus the interest is the relative price between present and future consumption.

THE TIME VALUE OF MONEY

Interest rates are normally positive. This means that *$1.00 today is worth more in the future.* If you have $1.00 today, you can put it into the bank and, if the interest rate is 5 percent, receive $1.05 at the end of next year. In short, in this example, $1.00 today is worth $1.05 next year.

Economists use the concept of **present discounted value** to calculate and express how much less $1.00 in the future is worth than $1.00 today. The present discounted value of $100 a year from now is what you would pay today in return for receiving $100 a year from now. Suppose the interest rate is 10 percent. If you put $90.91 in the bank today, at the end of the year you will receive $9.09 interest, which together with the original amount will total $100. Thus, $90.91 is the present discounted value of $100 a year from now, if the interest rate is 10 percent.

There is a simple formula for calculating the present discounted value (PDV) of any amount to be received a year from now. Suppose annual interest is calculated at the rate r; thus, the interest rate is r times

100 percent. If the interest rate is 10 percent, $r = .10$. Then \$1 today is worth $\$(1 + r)$ a year from now, since if it is saved it will earn interest at the rate r. Equivalently, dividing by $(1 + r)$, $\$1/(1 + r)$ today is worth \$1 next year. That is, the present discounted value of \$1 to be received next year is $\$1/(1 + r)$ today.

To check this formula, consider the present discounted value of \$100. According to the formula, it is $\$100/(1 + r)$. In other words, take the present discounted value, $\$100/(1 + r)$ and put it in the bank. At the end of the year you will have

$$\frac{\$100}{1 + r} \times (1 + r) = \$100,$$

confirming our conclusion that $\$100/(1 + r)$ today is the same as \$100 one year from now.

If the interest rate increases, the present discounted value of \$100 a year from now will decrease. For example, if the interest rate should rise to 20 percent, the present discounted value of \$100 a year from now becomes \$83.33 ($^{100}/_{1.2}$).

The present discounted value of \$100 received two years from now can be calculated in a similar way. If I were given \$100 today and I put it in the bank, at the end of the year I would have $\$100(1 + r)$. If I left it in the bank for another year, in the second year I would earn interest on the total amount in the bank at the end of the first year, $r \times 100(1 + r)$. Therefore, at the end of the two-year period I would have

$$100(1 + r) + [r \times 100 (1 + r)]$$
$$= 100(1 + r)(1 + r)$$
$$= 100(1 + r)^2.$$

In performing these calculations we have taken account of the interest on the interest, called **compound interest.** By contrast, **simple interest** does

Table 8.1 PRESENT DISCOUNTED VALUE OF \$100

Year received	Present discounted value
Next year	$\frac{1}{1+r} \times 100 = \frac{100}{1+r}$
Two years from now	$\frac{1}{1+r} \times \frac{100}{1+r} = \frac{100}{(1+r)^2}$
Three years from now	$\frac{1}{1+r} \times \frac{100}{(1+r)^2} = \frac{100}{(1+r)^3}$

not take into account the interest you earn on interest you have previously earned. If the rate of interest is 10 percent and is compounded annually, \$100 today is worth \$110 a year from now and \$121 (*not* \$120) in two years' time. Thus, the present discounted value today of \$121 two years from now is \$100. Table 8.1 shows how to calculate the present discounted value of \$100 received next year, two years from now, and three years from now.

We can now see how to calculate the value of an investment project that will yield a return over several years. We look at what the returns will be each year, adjust them to their present discounted values, and then add these values up. Table 8.2 shows how this is done for a project that yields \$10,000 next year and \$15,000 the year after, and that you plan to sell in the third year for \$50,000. The second column of the table shows the return in each year. The third column shows the discount factor—what we multiply the return by to obtain the present discounted value of that year's return. The calculations assume an

PRESENT DISCOUNTED VALUE

Present discounted value of \$1.00 next year =
$$\frac{\$1.00}{1 + \text{interest rate}}.$$

Often the annual interest rate is denoted by r, so the right-hand side of the equation becomes $\frac{\$1.00}{1 + r}$.

Table 8.2 CALCULATING PRESENT DISCOUNTED VALUE OF A THREE-YEAR PROJECT

Year	Return	Discount factor $(r = .10)$	Present discounted value $(r = .10)$	Present discounted value $(r = .20)$
1	$10,000	$\dfrac{1}{1.10}$	$ 9,091	$ 8,333
2	$15,000	$\dfrac{1}{(1.10)^2} = \dfrac{1}{1.21}$	$12,397	$10,417
3	$50,000	$\dfrac{1}{(1.10)^3} = \dfrac{1}{1.331}$	$37,566	$28,935
Total	$75,000	—	$59,054	$47,685

interest rate of 10 percent. The fourth column multiplies the return by the discount factor to obtain the present discounted value of that year's return. In the bottom row of the table, the present discounted values of each year's return have been added up to obtain the total present discounted value of the project. Notice that it is much smaller than the number we obtain simply by adding up the returns, which is the "undiscounted" yield of the project.

Suppose the cost of the project were $50,000 at time zero. Since the PDV of the project's returns is $59,054 when the rate of interest is 10 percent, the project is worth undertaking. That is, the investor would be better off putting her $50,000 into the project than investing it in the capital market and receiving an interest rate of 10 percent per year.

Now suppose that the interest rate rises to 20 percent so the discount factors become $1/1.20$ in year 1, $1/1.44$ in year 2, and $1/1.728$ in year 3. The last column of Table 8.2 shows the PDVs at this higher interest rate; the total PDV falls to $47,685. Given a project cost of $50,000, the project will no longer be worth undertaking. This illustrates the fact that as the interest rate rises, the number of projects that are worth undertaking falls; that is, the demand for investment funds falls.

The concept of present discounted value is important because so many decisions in economics are ori-

ented to the future. Whether a decision is taken by a person buying a house or saving money for retirement, or by a company building a factory or making an investment, the decision maker must be able to value money that will be received in one, two, five, or ten years in the future. Economists call this the **time value of money.** The concept of present discounted value tells us precisely how to measure the time value of money.

THE MARKET FOR LOANABLE FUNDS

The previous section explained how the interest rate is a price, the price of capital, similar to the price of any other good, like apples and oranges. The price of borrowing a dollar is the dollar plus the annual rate of interest. In calculating the present discounted values, firms or individuals take the interest rate as given. But obviously the interest rate changes over time. How is the interest rate determined? Like other prices, the interest rate is determined by the law of supply and demand.

At any given time there are some people and companies who would like to borrow so they can spend more than they currently have. Rachel has her first job and knows she needs a car for transportation; George needs kitchen equipment, tables, and chairs to open his sandwich shop. Others would like to save, or spend less than they currently have. John is putting aside money for his children's university education and for his retirement; Bill is putting aside money to make a down payment on a house.

Exchanges that occur over time are called **intertemporal trades.** The gains from trade discussed in Chapter 3 apply equally well here. When one individual lends money to another, both gain. John and Bill can lend money to Rachel and George. John and Bill will get paid interest in the future, to compensate them for letting Rachel and George use their funds now. Rachel and George are willing to pay the interest because to them, having the funds today is worth more to them than waiting. The borrower may be a business firm like the one owned by George, who believes that with these funds he will be able to make an investment that will yield a return far higher than the interest rate he is charged today. Or the borrower may be an individual facing some emergency, such as a medical crisis, that requires funds today. The borrower may simply be a free spirit who wishes to consume as much as he can (as much as lenders are willing to give him) and let the future take care of itself.

How is the supply of funds to be equated with the demand? As the interest rate rises, some borrowers will be discouraged from borrowing. Rachel may de-

cide to ride her bicycle to work and postpone buying a new car until she can save up the money herself or until interest rates come down. At the same time, as the interest rate rises some savers may be induced to save more. Their incentives for savings have increased. John realizes that every extra dollar he saves today will produce more money in the future, so he may put more aside. Figure 8.1 shows the supply-and-demand curves for loanable funds. Here the interest rate is the "price," and the amount of money lent and borrowed is the quantity. At r^*, the demand for funds equals the supply of funds.

Although we have spoken about the interest rate as the price of trading loanable funds, in fact the rate of return payable on funds traded on capital markets can take differing forms. For example, instead of lending money to a business firm in return for interest payments in the future, you might actually buy shares in the firm. In this case, the return you get from buying shares consists of future dividends paid out of the firm's profits. You might also get a capital gain if the value of your share rises and you sell the share for a profit. Presumably you will buy shares in a firm only if the rate of return you expect to get is comparable to what you would get from lending your money at the going interest rate. Thus, when we say that the interest rate is determined on the market for loanable funds, we recognize more generally that it is the rate of return on all forms of saving and investment that is being determined.

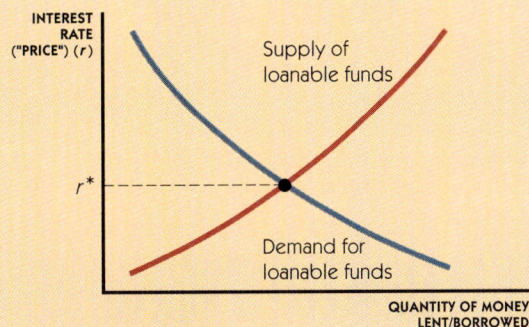

Figure 8.1 SUPPLY AND DEMAND FOR LOANABLE FUNDS

The amount of money lent and borrowed is the quantity, and the interest rate is the price. At the equilibrium interest rate r^*, the supply of loanable funds equals the demand.

INFLATION AND THE REAL RATE OF INTEREST

The interest rate, we have seen, is a price. It tells how much more than a dollar we can get next period if we give up one dollar today. But except for misers like Scrooge who store money for its own sake, dollars are of value only because of the goods that can be bought with them. Because of inflation—the increase in prices over time—dollars in the future buy fewer goods than dollars today. In deciding both whether to borrow and whether to lend, individuals want to know how much *consumption* they get tomorrow if they give up a dollar's worth of consumption today. The answer is given by the **real rate of interest.** This is distinguished from the **nominal rate of interest,** the rate one sees posted at one's bank and in the newspaper, which simply describes the number of dollars one gets next year in exchange for a dollar today. There is a simple relationship between the real interest rate and the nominal interest rate: the real interest rate equals the nominal interest rate minus the rate of inflation. If the nominal interest rate is 10 percent and the rate of inflation is 6 percent, then the real interest rate is 4 percent. By lending out (or saving) a dollar today, you can increase the amount of goods that you get in one year's time by 4 percent.

Consider an individual who decides to deposit $1,000 in a savings account. At a 10 percent interest rate, at the end of the year she will have $1,100. But prices meanwhile have risen by 6 percent. A good that cost $1,000 in the beginning of the year now costs $1,060. In terms of "purchasing power," she has only $40 extra to spend ($1,100 − $1,060)—4 percent more than she had at the beginning of the year. This is her real return. In an inflationary economy, a borrower is in a similar situation. He knows that if he borrows money, the dollars he gives back to repay the loan will be worth less than the dollars he receives today. Thus, what is relevant for individuals to know when deciding either how much to lend (save) or how much to borrow is the *real* interest rate, which takes account of inflation. The real interest rate is what should appear on the vertical axis of Figure 8.1.

BUDGET CONSTRAINTS AND SAVINGS

The assumption that individuals spend their money in a rational manner, thinking through the alternatives clearly, holds for the savings as well as the spending and working decisions. In taking their savings decisions, individuals are taking a decision about *when* to spend, or consume. If they consume less today—if they save more today—they can consume more tomorrow.

We use the budget constraint to analyze this choice. Instead of showing the choice between two goods, the budget constraint now shows, as in Figure 8.2, the choice between spending in two time periods. This is similar to our discussion of human capital investment decisions. The only difference is that instead of "youth" and "later working years," the two time periods here are "working years" and "retirement years." Consider the case of Joan. She faces the lifetime budget constraint depicted in the figure. The first period is represented on the horizontal axis, the second on the vertical. Her wages during her working life (the first period) are *w*. Thus, at one extreme, she could consume all of *w* the first period (point C) and have nothing for her retirement. At the other extreme, she could consume nothing in the first period, save all of her income, and consume her savings with accumulated interest in the second (point B). If we use *r* to denote the rate of interest, her con-

---

REAL INTEREST RATE
Real interest rate = nominal interest rate − rate of inflation

Figure 8.2 THE TWO-PERIOD BUDGET CONSTRAINT

The two-period budget constraint *BC* describes the possible combinations of current and future consumption available. Wages not spent in period 1 become savings, which earn interest. As a result, forgoing a dollar of consumption today increases future consumption by more than a dollar.

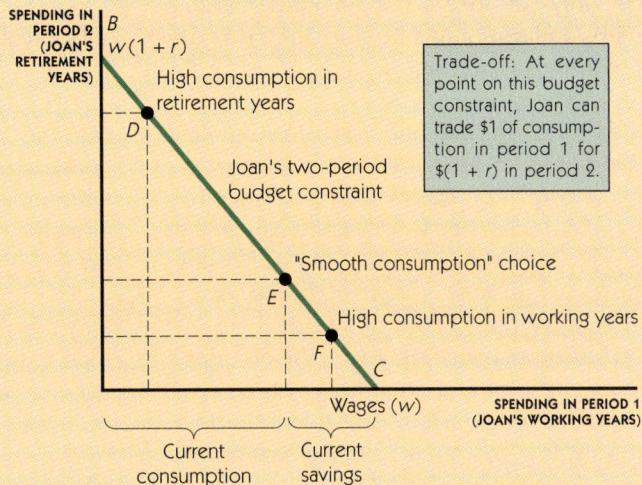

SPENDING IN PERIOD 2 (JOAN'S RETIREMENT YEARS)

$w(1 + r)$

High consumption in retirement years

Joan's two-period budget constraint

Trade-off: At every point on this budget constraint, Joan can trade $1 of consumption in period 1 for $(1 + r)$ in period 2.

"Smooth consumption" choice

High consumption in working years

Wages (*w*)

SPENDING IN PERIOD 1 (JOAN'S WORKING YEARS)

Current consumption

Current savings

sumption in the second period is $w(1 + r)$. In between these extremes lies a straight line that defines the rest of her choices. She can choose any combination of first- and second-period consumption on this line. This is Joan's two-period budget constraint.

By postponing consumption—that is, by saving—Joan can increase the total amount of goods that she can obtain because she is paid interest on her savings. The cost, however, is that she must wait to enjoy the goods. But what is the relative price, the amount of future consumption she has to trade off for one more unit of current consumption? To put it another way, how much extra future consumption can she get if she gives up one unit of current consumption?

If Joan decides not to consume one more dollar today, she can take that dollar, put it in the bank, and get back at the end of the year that dollar plus interest. If the interest rate is 10 percent, for every dollar of consumption that Joan gives up today she can get $1.10 of consumption next year. The relative price of consumption today relative to consumption tomorrow is thus 1 plus the interest rate. Because Joan must give up more than $1.00 of consumption in the second period to get an additional $1.00 worth of consumption today, current consumption is more expensive than future consumption. As was emphasized

above, what Joan cares about in evaluating the trade-offs between consumption during her working years versus consumption in retirement is the *real* rate of interest, taking into account inflation.

In this example, where Joan's life is divided into a working period and a retirement period, what is relevant is the average length of time between the time that money is earned and saved and the time that the savings are used in retirement. For an average person this is perhaps 35 years. In making her calculations, Joan will take into account the fact that if she leaves her money in the bank, it will earn compound interest, meaning that interest will be paid on interest already earned, not just on the amount of principal saved.

In recent years the real rate of interest has been around 4 percent a year. If interest were not compounded, earning 4 percent a year for 35 years would simply provide an overall return of 35×4 percent = 140 percent. If Joan puts $1.00 in the bank today, in 35 years she will get back—in real terms—$2.40. However, if interest is compounded annually, for each dollar deposited the calculation is $(1 + .04)^{35}$ = 3.946. So the total interest paid will be 294.6 percent. If she puts $1.00 in the bank today, in 35 years she will get back—in real terms—$3.94 (that is, her original dollar *plus* the interest). Compound interest makes a big difference.

Thus, the slope of Joan's budget constraint is 3.94—for every dollar of consumption she gives up during her working years, she gets $3.94 of additional consumption in retirement.

Joan chooses among the points on this budget constraint according to her personal preferences. Consider, for example, point *D*, where Joan is consuming very little during her working life. Since she is spending very little in the present, any additional consumption now will have a high marginal value. She will be relatively eager to substitute present consumption for future consumption. At the other extreme, if she is consuming a great deal in the present, say at point *F*, additional consumption today will have a relatively low marginal value, while future consumption will have a high marginal value. Hence, she will be relatively eager to save more for the future. She chooses a point in between, *E*, where consumption in the two periods is not too different. She has *smoothed* her consumption; that is, consumption in each of the two different periods is about the same. This kind of savings, motivated to smooth consumption over one's lifetime and to provide for retirement, is called **life-cycle savings.**

SAVINGS AND THE INTEREST RATE

What happens to Joan's savings if the interest rate increases? Her new budget constraint is shown in Figure 8.3 as *B'C*. If she does no saving, the interest rate has no effect on her consumption. She simply consumes her income during her working years, with nothing left over for retirement. But for all other choices, she gets more consumption during her retirement years.

The increased interest rate has both an income and a substitution effect. Because Joan is a saver, higher interest rates make her better off. Because she is better off, she consumes more today, that is, she reduces savings. This is the income effect. But her return to savings—to postponing consumption—is increased. For each dollar of consumption she postpones, she gets more consumption when she retires. This induces her to consume less—to save more. This is the substitution effect. Thus, the substitution and income effects work in opposite directions, and the *net* effect is ambiguous. Either may dominate. A higher interest rate may lead to more or less savings.

What happens on *average* is a difficult empirical question. Most estimates indicate that the substitu-

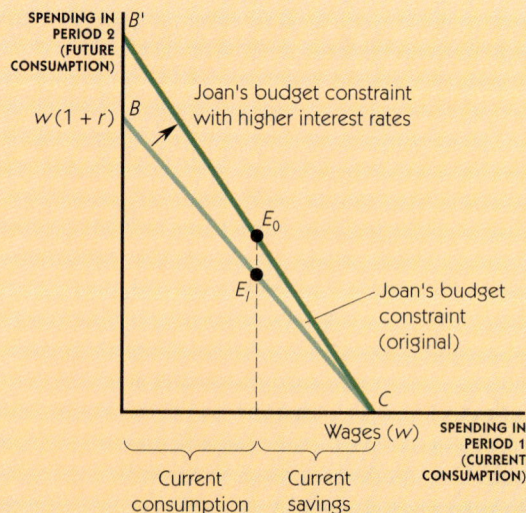

Figure 8.3 SAVINGS AND THE INTEREST RATE

An increase in interest rates rotates the budget constraint out from *BC* to *B'C*. The fact that the individual is better off means that there is an income effect, leading to greater consumption in the present (and the future). However, the higher interest rate makes future consumption cheaper; the substitution effect, associated with the changed slope, leads to greater savings now.

tion effect outweighs the income effect, so that an increase in real interest rates has a slightly positive effect on the rate of savings.

The magnitude of the response of savings to interest rates is an important question. Government policies aimed at increasing the interest rate individuals receive, such as exempting certain forms of savings from taxation, are based on the belief that an increase in the interest rate on savings will significantly increase total (aggregate) savings in the economy. Since wealthy people save more, reducing taxes on interest—which increases the effective interest rate to the saver—obviously benefits them more.

OTHER DETERMINANTS OF SAVINGS

We have now seen how individuals' decisions about savings can be looked at using the techniques of consumer choice analysis presented in Chapter 6. For savings, the two basic determinants are income and interest rates. As incomes rise, individuals want to consume more in their retirement, and hence must save more. As interest rates change, the income and substitution effects work in different directions, so the net effect is ambiguous.

The basic model provides great insight into the determinants of savings. But several motives for saving fall outside the basic model and have important implications for understanding the determinants of savings.

First, people typically want to leave something to their heirs. This is the **bequest motive.** Some economists argue that the few wealthy people save more in total over their lives than the much more numerous group that is the rest of society because of the bequest motive. Another motive for savings is the **precautionary motive.** This "saving for a rainy day" protects against emergencies for which one has no insurance coverage. Precautionary savings is particularly important for small businesses and farmers

THE SAVINGS DECISION

The savings decision is a decision of *when* to consume: today or tomorrow.

The slope of the budget constraint between consumption today and consumption tomorrow is determined by the rate of interest.

A principal motive of savings is to smooth consumption, so that consumption during working years and consumption during retirement years is about the same.

whose incomes can vary enormously from year to year. Still another, related, motive is to save for a particular purpose. **Target savings** is directed toward needs for which it may be hard to borrow sufficient funds, such as a down payment on a house or a university education.

AGGREGATE SAVINGS

The sum of the savings of all individuals and governments in society is called **aggregate savings.** At any one time, some individuals are saving and others are spending their savings, or **dissaving.** Aggregate private savings is the two activities taken together. Governments also contribute to the aggregate level of savings. Governments that spend more than they take in through taxation run **budget deficits** that must be financed by borrowing. This borrowing represents public dissaving and must be added to aggregate private savings to determine the aggregate savings rate of the economy.

CONCERN ABOUT THE LEVEL OF SAVINGS

The importance of the savings rate for economic growth has become increasingly recognized by economists. Growth rates depend upon the rate of investment, which in turn is partly determined by the amount that Canadians are willing to save to finance the investment. The alternative is to use foreign borrowing to pay for investment, but that creates indebtedness that must be repaid in the future. Though the Canadian savings rate exceeds that of the United States and is not low by the standards of the Organization for Economic Cooperation and Development (whose members are the highly industrialized countries of the world), it is considerably lower than that of the fastest-growing economies in the world, especially those in the Far East such as Japan, South Korea, Thailand, Malaysia, Taiwan, Indonesia, Singapore, and Hong Kong. The concern about the level of savings has led economists to ask why savings is lower in some countries than others and what sorts of incentives might be used to encourage savings.

DEMOGRAPHIC FACTORS

One possible factor contributing to low savings rates is the demographic structure of the population. Canada's population is aging. A more slowly growing population combined with increasing life expectancy results in a larger proportion of the population who are elderly. Working people typically save, whereas retirees dissave. Therefore, in a country with an aging population, the savings rate will be lower than that of faster-growing populations with higher birthrates.

GOVERNMENT DEBT

As mentioned earlier, aggregate savings includes both individual savings and government savings. In recent years, both federal and provincial governments in Canada have been running large and persistent deficits. This means that governments have been large dissavers and have reduced the aggregate savings rate significantly.

DIFFERENCES IN SPENDING PATTERNS: MORE VARIETY IN CONSUMER DURABLES

One reason why household savings may be lower today than in earlier times is that the demand for consumer durables (housing, cars, TV sets, VCRs, computers, etc.) have risen dramatically. The variety and quality of such goods has increased dramatically, and increasing affluence leads to devoting a higher proportion of one's budget to them. The purchase of consumer durables requires greater consumer spending up front, and that entails less income to set aside as savings for future consumption, or more dissaving early in life as consumers borrow to acquire these durables. The more income is spent on consumer durables, the less is available for financing private-sector investments.

PUBLIC PENSIONS

Some economists argue that the public provision of pensions and other benefits in retirement has con-

Figure 8.4 THE EFFECT OF PUBLIC PENSIONS ON SAVINGS

A public pension system that taxes workers an amount T and provides a retirement benefit of $T(1+r)$, comparable to what Joan would have obtained had she saved and invested the money, leaves the budget constraint unchanged. Accordingly, individuals will choose the same consumption as before. Because public pensions are operated on a pay-as-you-go system rather than being funded, savings are now reduced by the full magnitude of the tax T.

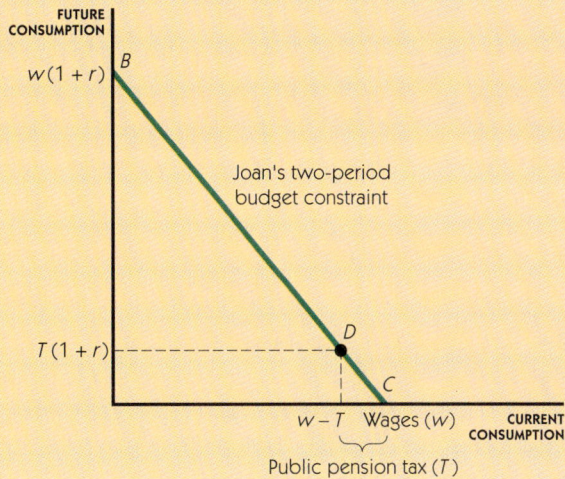

tributed to the decrease in savings rates. To understand their argument, we need to know how the public pension system is structured.

The public pension system in Canada consists of a number of components, including Old Age Security paid to all persons 65 years and older; the Guaranteed Income Supplement paid according to income; the Canada and Quebec Pension Plans, which are contributory plans available to all working persons; and various provincial supplements. As well, many **benefits in kind** (provision of goods or services rather than cash), such as free medical care, are provided to retired people, and these should have essentially the same effects as public pensions. The system is unlike a private pension plan in which people pay money into a fund while they work and get it back, with interest, when they retire. Instead, a good part of the pension payments to the currently retired are paid for out of tax revenues, most of which are levied on those currently working. This is called a **pay-as-you-go system,** to distinguish it from standard pensions, where accounts build up over time, to be paid out after individuals retire. The latter are **funded pensions,** while pay-as-you-go pensions are unfunded.

To see the argument that pay-as-you-go pensions may affect the savings rate, look at Figure 8.4, which shows Joan's budget constraint BC from Figure 8.2. Assume that in their working lives, invididuals pay an amount T in taxes to finance the benefits for those

who are retired. Assume further, for simplicity, that the public pension benefit they receive in retirement is $T(1 + r)$; that is, individuals get back what they contribute, with interest. Assume for the moment that Joan did no other saving and paid no other taxes. She would now consume $w - T$ (her wage minus her public pension tax payments) the first period, and $T(1 + r)$ the second period. Her consumption in the two periods is represented by the point D. The first period's consumption is reduced by T as a result of the public pension programme; the second period's consumption is increased by $T(1 + r)$. But this is a point on the original budget constraint—it is precisely what Joan would have had, had she saved T dollars herself.

Of course, if Joan decides to save still more, her consumption during her retirement will increase; again, for each dollar of reduced current consumption, her retirement consumption increases by $1 + r$. If she would like to save less than T, she could theoretically borrow money in the present and pay it back in the future. It is apparent that this hypothetical public pension programme has left Joan's budget constraint completely unaffected. Since the budget constraint is unaffected, her consumption is unaffected: she will choose to consume the same amount the first period (while she is working) and the same amount the second period (in retirement).

But the public pension programme nonetheless has some consequences. Individuals no longer need

In the last 25 years transfer payments to the elderly have increased dramatically, rising from about $1 billion in 1967 to over $35 billion in 1994. After adjusting for inflation, this represents a real increase of about 800 percent. These transfers take two main forms. The first are the Old Age Security and Guaranteed Income Supplements paid out to persons 65 and older. These payments are financed by current tax revenues paid largely by the current working population. They are referred to as "unfunded pension payments," reflecting the fact that, unlike with private savings, contributions are not put into a fund and invested to pay for future benefits. Federal government unfunded public pensions are often accompanied by provincial supplements, at least for the less well off pensioners. In addition, the elderly also receive various services from the public sector which they would otherwise have to provide for out of their retirement incomes.

The second form of payment to the elderly is the Canada Pension Plan (or Quebec Pension Plan in that province), which is a pension plan financed out of a fund made up of contributions based on earnings. Though the pensions are paid out of a fund, the Plan is not operated as a private pension plan would be. For one thing, the plan is not fully funded, since the size of the fund is not sufficient to cover the payments to future retirees who have contributed in the past. Thus the fund is gradually running out and is projected to be depleted by 2015, at which time the system will be equivalent to an unfunded one in which payments are just covered by current contributions. Also, while private pension funds are invested in the capital market and

help finance a significant chunk of the country's capital stock, the Canada Pension Plan funds are lent at favourable interest rates to the provinces in the proportions in which their residents have contributed to it. To the extent that these loans simply induce the provinces to spend more, no funds are freed up for financing investment in the private sector.

Economists have long pointed out the disadvantages of operating public pensions on an unfunded basis. As public pension payments rise, people feel less need to save for retirement. The taxes or contributions they pay during their working years to finance the pensions of the currently retired might otherwise have been saved for retirement and helped to finance additions to the capital stock. Instead they go to finance the consumption of the retired. The result is a reduced rate of investment and of economic growth.

There is some concern that as the proportion of the population over age 65 increases and as the Canada Pension Plan's funds run out, taxes on the current working population will have to increase dramatically to finance the current level of transfers to the elderly. This, along with the continuing need to finance government deficits, will keep the savings rate much lower than it would otherwise be. To counter this, the federal government has opted to encourage people to save more for their own retirement so that they will be less reliant on government transfers. Improving tax incentives for retirement savings is the main vehicle for doing this. The extent to which people can contribute to tax-deductible Registered Retirement Savings Plans has been increased significantly.

SOME EXPLANATIONS OF LOW SAVINGS RATES

Public sector dissaving: Governments have been running high budget deficits, using up savings that would otherwise go to finance investment.

Increased demand for consumer durables: Consumers who spend more on consumer durables have less left to save.

High public pension benefits: The recent growth in public pension benefits people receive when they retire has discouraged them from saving.

Improved capital markets: The market for borrowers is more perfect—the rate of interest paid by a borrower is closer to the rate paid to a saver; since it is cheaper to borrow, current consumption is increased and savings is reduced.

---

to save as much for retirement. The government is in effect providing for them. Before this programme went into effect, the amount of current public pension tax payments, *T*, was part of the nation's savings. Now national savings go down by *T*. (Of course, this would not be the case with a funded type of public pension. A funded programme would still have effects: "public" savings through the pension would supplant private savings, but total savings would be unaffected.)

IMPROVED CAPITAL MARKETS

Reduced savings rates can also be attributed to the improved functioning of capital markets in today's economy. Individuals usually must pay a higher interest rate when they borrow than the interest rate they receive from saving. The difference, often 3 or 4 percent more, is due to the administrative costs and profits for the lending institution and to the chance of default by the borrower. The effect of any innovation that lowers administrative costs reduces the difference between the rate at which people can borrow and the rate at which they can lend. Any change that lowers the interest rate charged to borrowers has both an income effect and a substitution effect on borrowers. The improved capital market makes the individual better off. His budget constraint has moved out—this means he would like to consume more both today and tomorrow. The fact that when individuals are better off they like to increase their consumption of most goods is, as we learned in Chapter 6, the income effect. The substitution effect arises from the fact that current consumption is now less

expensive relative to future consumption, which is just another way of saying that it is cheaper to borrow; the individual substitutes current consumption for future consumption. The substitution effect results from the change in the *slope* of the budget constraint. This too makes current consumption more desirable. The income and substitution effects of lowered interest rates facing borrowers reinforce each other; current consumption is increased, and savings is reduced. Changes that make it easier for people to borrow will always tend to reduce savings.

In recent decades it has become easier and easier for Canadians to borrow. The development of "home equity loans" in the 1980s allowed individuals who already owned houses to borrow up to 80 percent of the value of a house. Credit cards like Visa and Master-Card became much more popular in the 1980s, enabling consumers to obtain credit more easily than before. These kinds of improvements in the capital market make it easier for people to borrow and allow them to make choices that they would otherwise have been unable to make. However, by encouraging borrowing these steps also reduce savings.

INVESTMENT ALTERNATIVES

Every saver faces a myriad of possibilities when it comes to investing her savings. The choices she makes depend on the money she has to invest, what originally motivated her to save, her willingness to bear risk, and where she is in life. Of the seemingly endless array of places to put one's money, five are most important: bank deposits, including certificates of deposit (CDs); housing; bonds; stocks; and mutual funds. In making choices among them, investors focus on four characteristics: return, risk, liquidity, and tax liability.

BANK DEPOSITS

As a student, your major savings are likely to be earnings from a summer job that will be spent during the next school year. If so, the decision of where to invest is generally uncomplicated. A **savings account** or a similar account in a bank or trust company offers three advantages: it pays you interest, it allows easy access to your money, and it offers security, because even if the bank or trust company goes broke the federal government, through the Canadian Deposit Insurance Corporation, insures bank deposits of up to $60,000.

After leaving school, investment decisions become more difficult. You may want to put away some savings to make a down payment on a house. (With the average house selling for $150,000, a 20 percent down payment would be $30,000.) As savings increases, the value of a few extra percentage points of interest also increases. A **certificate of deposit (CD),** in which you deposit money in a bank for a preset length of time, is as safe as an ordinary bank account and yields a slightly higher return. The drawback of a CD is that if you withdraw the money before the preset time has expired, you pay a penalty. The ease with which an investment can be turned into cash is called its **liquidity.** Perfectly liquid investments can be converted into cash speedily and without any loss in value. CDs are less liquid than standard savings accounts.

HOUSING

Two thirds of Canadian households invest by owning their own homes. This investment is far riskier than putting money into a bank or a certificate of deposit. Home prices usually increase over time, but not always. In 1987, the price of housing in Victoria declined by 5 percent, and in 1991, the price of hous-

ing declined in many urban areas. In addition, when prices do rise, the rate of increase is uncertain. Prices may be almost level for a number of years and then shoot up by 20 percent in a single year. Note that while the bank or trust company may provide most of the funds for the purchase of a house, the owner bears the risk, since she is responsible for paying back the loan regardless of the market price of the house.

Housing as an investment has two other attributes—one attractive and one unattractive. On the positive side, unlike financial assets, the rate of return from owning a house is nontaxable, and the increased value of a house is not liable for capital gains tax either. On the negative side, housing is usually fairly illiquid. Houses differ one from another, and it often takes considerable time to find someone who really likes your house; if you try to sell your house quickly, on average you will receive less than you would if you had two or three months in which to sell it. Moreover, the costs of selling a house are substantial, often more than 5 percent of the value of the house—in any case more than the costs of selling stocks and bonds.

BONDS

Bonds are a way for corporations and government to borrow. The borrower—whether it is a company, province, municipality, or the Canadian government—promises to pay the lender (the purchaser of the bond, or investor) a fixed amount in a specified number of years. In addition, the borrower agrees to pay the lender each year a fixed return on the amount borrowed. Thus, if the interest rate is 10 percent, a $10,000 bond will pay the lender $1,000 every year, and $10,000 in the prearranged number of years. The period remaining until a loan or bond is to be paid in full is called its **maturity.** Bonds that mature within a few years are called **short-term bonds;** those that mature in more than 10 years are called **long-term bonds.** A long-term government bond may have a maturity of 20 or even 30 years.

Bonds may seem relatively safe, because the investor knows what amounts will be paid. But consider a corporate bond that promises to pay $10,000 in 10 years and pays $1,000 every year until then. Imagine that an investor buys the bond, collects interest for a couple of years, and then realizes that he needs cash and wants to sell the bond. There is no guarantee that he will get $10,000 for it. He may get more and he may get less. If the market interest rate has fallen to 5 percent since the original bond was issued, a new $10,000 bond now would pay only $500 a year. Clearly, the original bond, which pays $1,000 a year, is worth considerably more. Thus, a decline in the interest rate leads to a rise in the value of bonds; and by reverse logic, a rise in the interest rate leads to a decline in the value of bonds. This uncertainty about market value is what makes long-term bonds risky.[1]

Even if the investor holds the bond to maturity, that is, until the date at which it pays the promised $10,000, there is still a risk, since he cannot know for sure what $10,000 will purchase 10 years from now. If the general level of prices increases at a rate of 7 percent over these 10 years, the real value of the $10,000 will be just one-half what it would have been had prices remained stable during that decade.[2]

Because of the higher risk caused by these uncertainties, long-term bonds must compensate investors by paying higher returns, on average, than comparable short-term bonds. And because every corporation has at least a slight chance of going bankrupt, corporate bonds must compensate investors for the higher risk by paying higher returns than government bonds. The higher returns more than compensate for the additional bankruptcy risk, however, according to economic research. That is, if an investor purchases a very large number of good-quality corporate bonds, the likelihood that more than one or two will default is very small, and the overall return will be considerably higher than the return from

purchasing government bonds of the same maturity (the same number of years until they come due).

Some corporate bonds are riskier than others— that is, there is a higher probability of default. These bonds must pay extremely high returns to induce investors to take a chance on them. When Chrysler looked on the verge of bankruptcy in 1980, Chrysler bonds were yielding returns of 23 percent. Obviously, the more a firm borrows, the more likely it is to be unable to meet its commitments, and the riskier are its bonds. Especially risky bonds are called **junk bonds;** the yields on such bonds are much higher than those from a financially solid firm, but the investor must calculate in the probability of default.

SHARES OF STOCK

You might also choose to invest in shares of corporate stock. When a person buys shares in a firm, she literally owns a fraction (a share) of the total firm. Thus, if the firm issues 1 million shares, an individual who owns 100 shares owns .01 percent of the firm. Investors choose stocks as investments for two reasons.

First, firms pay some fraction of their earnings— all their receipts after paying workers, suppliers of materials, and all interest due on bank and other loans—directly to shareholders. These payments are called **dividends.** On average, firms distribute one third of earnings as dividends; the remainder, called **retained earnings,** is kept for investment in the company. The amount of a dividend, unlike the return on a bond, depends on a firm's earnings and on what proportion of those earnings it chooses to distribute to shareholders.

In addition to receiving dividends, those who invest in stocks hope to make money by choosing stocks that will appreciate in value, and then sell them at the higher price. What the shareholder invests when she buys her shares is called the **principal.** The increase in the realized price of a share (or any other asset) is called a **capital gain.** (If the asset is sold at a price below that at which it was purchased, the investor realizes a **capital loss.**)

Shares of stock are risky for a number of reasons. First, the earnings of firms vary greatly. Even if firms do not vary their dividends, differences in profits will

---

[1] The market price of the bond will equal the present discounted value of what it pays. For instance, a 3-year bond that pays $10 per year each of 2 years and $110 at the end of the 3rd year has a value of

$$\frac{10}{1+r} + \frac{10}{(1+r)^2} + \frac{110}{(1+r)^3},$$

where r is the market rate of interest. We can see that as r goes up, the value of the bond goes down, and vice versa.

[2] If prices rise at 7 percent a year, with compounding, the price level in 10 years is $(1.07)^{10}$ times the level it is today; $(1.07)^{10}$ is approximately equal to 2; prices have doubled.

lead to differences in retained earnings, and these will be reflected in the value of the shares. In addition, the stock price of a company depends on the beliefs of investors as to, for instance, the prospects of the economy, the industry, and that particular firm. Loss of faith in any one could lead to a drop in stock price. Thus, an individual who had to sell all his shares because of some medical emergency might find they had declined significantly in value. Even if the investor believes the shares will eventually return to a higher value, he may be unable to wait.

Shares of stock are riskier than bonds. This is because when a firm goes bankrupt and must pay off its investors, the law requires bondholders to be paid off as fully as possible before shareholders receive any money at all. As a result, a bondholder in a bankrupt company is likely to be paid some share of her original investment, while a shareholder may receive nothing. Over the long run, shares of stock have yielded very high returns. While corporate bonds yielded on average an annual real rate of return of 2 percent in the period from 1926 to 1994, shares of stock yielded a real return of nearly 7 percent in the same period.

MUTUAL FUNDS

A **mutual fund** gathers funds from many different investors into a single large pool of funds, with which it can then purchase a large number of assets. A *money market* mutual fund invests its funds in CDs and comparably safe assets.

The advantage of a money market mutual fund is that you get higher rates of interest than on bank accounts and still enjoy liquidity. The fund managers know that most individuals will leave their money in the account, and some will be adding money to the account as others pull money out. They are thus able to put a large proportion of the fund in certificates of deposit and still not have to pay the penalties for early withdrawal. In this way, money market mutual funds give investors the easy access to their funds associated with banks, while providing them the higher returns associated with CDs.

Money market mutual funds may also invest their customers' money in short-term government bonds, called **Treasury bills,** or **T-bills.** Treasury bills are available only in large denominations ($1,000 or more). They promise to repay a certain amount (their face value, say, $10,000) in a relatively short period, less than 90 or 180 days, and investors buy them at less than their face value. The difference between the amount paid and the face value becomes the return to the purchaser.

With most money market mutual funds, you can even write a limited number of cheques a month against your account. The major disadvantage of mutual funds is that unlike bank accounts, they are not guaranteed by the federal government. However, some money market funds invest only in government securities or government-insured securities, making them virtually as safe as bank accounts.

Other mutual funds invest in stocks and bonds. Typically, they buy stocks or bonds in dozens, sometimes hundreds, of different companies. Investors recognize the advantage of **diversification**—of not putting all their eggs in the same basket. If you put all your savings into a single stock and that firm has a bad year, you'll suffer a large loss. If you own stock in two companies, there is a chance that losses in one company will be offset by gains in the other. Mutual funds, in effect, allow much broader diversification. Of course, if the whole stock market does badly, a stock mutual fund will suffer too. When stocks go down, bonds typically go up, so some mutual funds invest in both stocks and bonds. Others invest in risky ventures which, if successful, promise high returns; these are sometimes referred to as "growth" funds. There are many other specially designed mutual funds, and together they are enormously popular. For most investors, the first foray into the bond or stock market is through the purchase of a mutual fund.

DESIRABLE ATTRIBUTES OF INVESTMENTS

Table 8.3 sets forth the various investment opportunities we have described, with a list of their most important attributes. We now take a closer look at these attributes. As investors survey the broad range of opportunities available to them, they balance their personal needs against what the different investment

Table 8.3 ALTERNATIVE INVESTMENTS AND HOW THEY FARE

Investment	Return	Risk	Tax advantages	Liquidity
Savings accounts	Low	Low	None	High
CDs (certificates of deposit)	Slightly higher than savings accounts	Low	None	Slightly less than savings accounts
T-bills	About same as CDs	Low	None	Small charge for selling before maturity
Canada Savings Bonds	Slightly higher than T-bills	Low	None	No charge for selling before maturity
Federal government long-term bonds	Normally slightly higher than T-bills	Uncertain market value next period; uncertain purchasing power in long run	None	Small charge for selling before maturity
Corporate bonds	Higher return than federal bonds	Risks of long-term federal bonds plus risk of default	None	Slightly less liquid than federal bonds (depends on corporation issuing bond)
Stocks	High	High	Capital gains receive slight tax preference	Those listed on major stock exchanges are highly liquid; others may be highly illiquid
Houses	High returns from mid-1970s to mid-1980s; in many areas, negative returns in late 1980s, early 1990s	Used to be thought safe; viewed to be somewhat riskier now	Some special tax advantages	Relatively illiquid; may take long time to find "good buyer"
Mutual funds	Reflect assets in which funds are invested	Reflect assets in which funds are invested; reduced risk from diversification	Reflect assets in which funds are invested	Highly liquid

options have to offer them. The ideal investment would have a high rate of return, be low risk, and be tax-exempt. But finding such an asset is about as likely as finding the fountain of eternal youth. You can only expect to get more of one desirable property—say, higher returns—at the expense of another desirable property, such as safety. To understand what is entailed in these trade-offs, we need to take a closer look at each of the principal attributes.

EXPECTED RETURNS

First on the list of desirable properties are high returns. Returns have two components: the interest or dividend payments and the capital gain. The capital gain is the difference between what you invest in an asset, the principal, and what you receive when you sell it. Thus, if you buy some stock for $1,000, receive $150 in dividends during the year, and at the end of the year sell the stock for $1,200, your total return is $150 + $200 = $350. If you sell the stock for $900, your total return is $150 − $100 = $50. If you sell it for $800, your total return is a *negative* $50.

Returns can take on a number of forms. In the case of a bond, the amount you get back in excess of the amount you invest is interest. Stocks may pay dividends. Real estate returns may come in the form of rent, or payment for the use of the real estate. Bonds, stocks, and real estate all produce returns in the form of capital gains (or losses) when they are sold. If you buy an apartment building for $150,000 and sell it for $160,000, you have made a capital gain of $10,000; note that this is in addition to any rent you may have collected while you owned the house.

In estimating the total return to an asset, the wise investor combines the asset's ongoing return (interest payments on a bank account or bond, dividends, rent, and so on) with its potential capital gain. But two problems still remain in comparing the returns to different assets. First, the returns may occur in different years. An asset that costs $1,000 and yields a $300 return next year is far preferable to one that costs the same amount and yields $300 in ten years' time. Dollars received at later dates are worth less than dollars today. To make adjustments for the difference in timing, we need to compare the present discounted value of the returns.

The second problem is that even if each of two assets will yield all of its returns next year, neither will have a guaranteed return, and the expected returns of the two assets may differ. To make the right comparison in this case, we apply the concept of **expected returns.** The expected return to an asset is a statistical summing up—a single number that combines the various possible returns per dollar invested with the chances that each of these returns will actually be paid. Average returns *expected* in the future are the relevant focus here. Past returns should only be considered to the extent they give us a clue about expected future performance.

For simplicity, suppose that one of the two assets is a stock costing $100 that has a long tradition of paying $4 each year in dividends. The dividend thus supplies a 4 percent return; but some estimate is needed of its potential capital gain. Figure 8.5 plots the probabilities of different expected returns for this stock and gives three possible outcomes for when the stock is sold a year from now. One possibility is that the stock will fetch only $97. The stock will nevertheless produce a 1 percent return ($97 + $4 = $101). Suppose, further, that experts give this outcome a 1 in 4 chance of occurring (a 25 percent probability). A second possibility is that the stock's price will be $104 and thus produce an 8 percent return ($104 + $4 = $108). This possibility is given a 2 in 4 chance of occurring (a 50 percent probability). The third possibility is that the stock will sell for $111, producing a return of 15 percent ($111 + $4 = $115). Like the first possibility, this is given a 1 in 4 chance of occurring (a 25 percent probability). The sum of the probabilities must by definition add up to 1.

The next step in calculating the expected return is to multiply each of the possible outcomes by the chance, or probability, that it will occur, as illustrated in Table 8.4. The sum of these products, 8 percent, is the expected return. We would then go through the same series of calculations with the other investment opportunity. If all other important characteristics of the two opportunities were the same, we would presumably choose the one with the higher expected return.

Different individuals will differ in their judgments concerning the likelihood of various returns. To some extent people's views are based on historical experience. When economists say that the average return to

Figure 8.5 A PROBABILITY DISTRIBUTION OF POSSIBLE RATES OF RETURN

There are three possible levels of return for this asset: a 1 in 4 chance of a 1 percent return, a 2 in 4 chance of an 8 percent return, and a 1 in 4 chance of a 15 percent return. The expected return is calculated by multiplying the possible returns times their probability of happening, and adding the results.

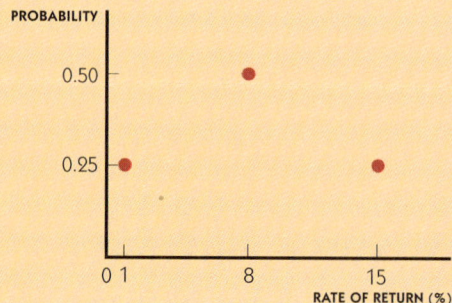

Table 8.4 CALCULATING EXPECTED RETURNS

Outcome (return)	Probability	Outcome x probability
1 percent	25 percent	.25 percent
8 percent	50 percent	4.00 percent
15 percent	25 percent	3.75 percent
		Sum = 8.00 percent

stocks is higher than the return to bonds, they mean that historically, on average, over the past century, the returns to stocks have been higher. This does not necessarily mean that the return to stocks next year will be higher than the return to bonds, or that the return to particular stocks will be higher than the return to particular bonds. An individual who believes that a major economic downturn is likely may believe that the expected return to stocks next year will be lower than the return to bonds, and will weight his expected return calculation accordingly.

An important first lesson in investment theory is: *If there were no differences between assets other than the ways in which they produce returns (interest, dividends, etc.), then the expected returns to all assets would be the same.* Why? Because investors seeing the return to an asset that yielded more than this average would bid more for the asset. If the 8 percent return given in the stock example above looked high relative to other options, investors desirous of that return would bid the stock price up above $100. As the price rose, the expected return would decline. The upward pressure would continue until the expected return declined to match the level of all other investments. The process by which expected returns to all assets that are identical in every essential respect approach equality is referred to as **arbitrage.**

In fact, the expected returns per dollar invested for different assets differ markedly from one another. The reason is that a number of other important attributes affect an asset's return. These include the risk that it will not pay the expected return; its treatment under tax law; and its liquidity, or the ease with which

it can be sold. An asset that is less risky or more liquid or receives favourable tax treatment will have higher demand. The higher demand will lead to higher prices and thus to lower returns. Therefore, the before-tax expected return will be lower on assets that are safer, more liquid, or tax-favoured. Economists say that such desirable assets sell at a **premium,** while assets that are riskier or more illiquid sell at a **discount.** Even in these circumstances a process of arbitrage is at work; assets of comparable risk and liquidity must yield the same expected returns.

The next three sections explore these additional attributes of investments—risk, tax considerations, and liquidity—and how they create premiums and discounts.

RISK

It has been said that financial markets are the places where risk is bought and sold. A full appreciation of this insight is beyond our scope here, but it does underline the important risks associated with most assets. The investor may receive a high or a low return. She may even get back less than she put in—a loss. Often this uncertainty concerns what the asset will be worth next week, next month, or next year. The price of a stock may go up or down. Long-term bonds are risky; even though the interest they pay is known, their market value may fluctuate. Moreover, because there is uncertainty about future inflation, there is uncertainty about the *real* return paid by a bond, even though the nominal return is fixed.

A prime consideration for any investor, therefore, is the riskiness of any investment alternative. Bank accounts, in this regard, are safe. Since the Canadian Deposit Insurance Corporation came into being in 1967, no one in Canada has lost her money in an insured bank account. But investments in housing, stocks, bonds, and most other investments all involve risk. The return may be substantially lower than what you expected, or you may lose some or all of your money.

Some assets are riskier than others; that is, they may have a greater chance of very low returns and a greater chance of very high returns. Figure 8.6 provides a slightly more complex version of Figure 8.5. This time, instead of describing only three possible payoffs, the diagram depicts all possible payoffs

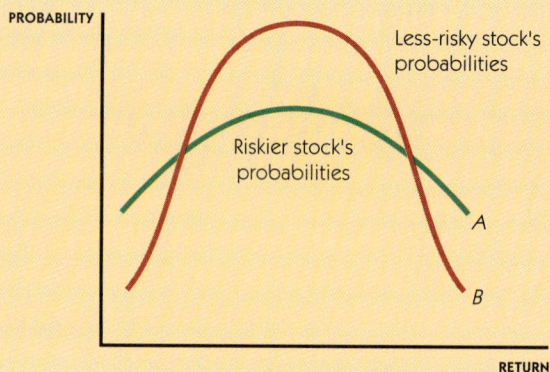

Figure 8.6 **ILLUSTRATING RISK WITH PROBABILITY DISTRIBUTIONS**

These two probability distributions are both symmetrical, around the same midpoint; thus, they both have the same expected return. However, the stock shown by curve A has a higher chance of very high or very low returns, and thus is riskier than the stock shown by curve B.

for each of two stocks. The two stocks represented here have the same average return, but the stock whose return is described by curve *A* is riskier than the stock whose return is described by curve *B*. There is a greater chance of both very low and very high returns.

TAX CONSIDERATIONS

The government is a silent partner in almost all investments. It is not the kind of partner you would ordinarily choose—it takes a fraction of the profits, but leaves you with almost all the losses. Still, investors must take into account the fact that a substantial fraction of the returns to a successful investment will go to the government as taxes. Since different assets are treated differently in the tax law, tax considerations are obviously important in choosing a portfolio. After all, individuals care about after-tax returns, not before-tax returns. Investments that face relatively low tax rates are sometimes said to be **tax-favoured.**

The types of assets that are tax-favoured vary from time to time. Resource industries have historically been treated generously by the tax system, mainly reflected in the amount of deductions and exemptions that the tax system has allowed. Small businesses receive special tax treatment, as do businesses in depressed regions. Investments in apartment units, in research and development, in exploration and devel-

opment, and in filmmaking have also been favourably treated. Assets that yield a substantial part of their return in the form of a capital gain are taxed less heavily, as are savings held in an insurance policy. Many of these assets yield returns lower than corporate bonds of comparable risk and liquidity, yet people buy them because the return is largely free from tax. The higher demand for these tax-favoured assets drives up their price, which drives down their rate of return. We can expect the interest rate to decline to the point where the after-tax return is at most only slightly higher than for an ordinary taxable bond of comparable risk.

Consider two assets, identical in all respects except their tax treatment. Both promise to pay $110 next year, $10 of which is interest. The price of the taxable asset is $100. The equilibrium price for a tax-favoured asset is greater than $100. This means that its average return before tax is less than 10 percent—less than the return on the taxable asset. If most investors have to pay 30 percent of any interest income in taxes, then the after-tax return is $7, not $10. They will be willing to buy the tax-favoured asset so long as its yield is at least 7 percent. Below that level, they will buy the taxable asset instead. Thus, the equilibrium price of the tax-favoured asset is $110 ÷ $1.07 = $102.80. That is, the tax-favoured asset yields the same return at a price of approximately $103 as the taxable asset does at $100.

Investing in housing, particularly a house to live

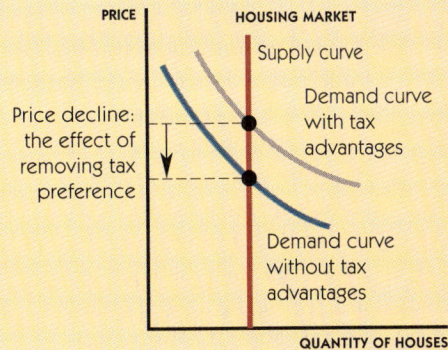

Figure 8.7 EFFECT OF REMOVING TAX PREFERENCES FOR HOUSING

Removing tax preferences for housing will shift the demand curve for housing down, and this will, in the short run (with an inelastic housing supply), cause marked decreases in the price of housing.

in, is another tax-favoured form of investment enjoyed by many Canadians. The implicit rate of return on owner-occupied housing is untaxed. In addition, the capital gain from a house that is used for your principal residence is untaxed. If the tax advantages of home ownership were ever withdrawn, we could expect housing prices to decline precipitously, as illustrated in Figure 8.7. It is not likely that tax preferences for housing will be suddenly removed, however, because so many voters own houses, and politicians are loath to anger such a large number of their constituents.

Finally, some tax advantages accrue to the individual investor rather than to the assets she chooses to hold. For example, individuals may invest in tax-sheltered Registered Retirement Savings Plans (RRSPs) up to an annual limit. Most types of financial assets can be held in this form. Although RRSPs are meant primarily to be a device for saving for retirement, there is nothing to preclude a person from putting funds into an RRSP for a time and then removing them before retirement. As long as they are in the fund, they can accumulate tax-free. Of course, it would be unwise not to use the limits to their fullest when deciding how to hold one's savings. Not to do so is to incur tax liabilities unnecessarily.

LIQUIDITY

The fourth important attribute to consider is liquidity. An asset is liquid if the costs of selling it are very low. A bank account is completely liquid (except when the bank goes bankrupt), because you can turn it into cash at virtually no charge by writing a cheque. Corporate stock in a major company is fairly liquid, because the costs of selling at a well-defined market price are relatively small.

In the basic competitive model, all assets are assumed to be perfectly liquid. There is a well-defined price at which anything can be bought and sold; any household or firm can buy or sell as much as it wants at that price; and the transaction is virtually without cost. But these assumptions are not always met. There are often significant costs of selling or buying an asset. The costs of selling a house, for instance, can run as high as 7 percent of the value of the house. At times, even corporate bonds have been fairly illiquid. The prices at which such bonds could be bought and sold have been known to differ by several percentage points.

EFFICIENT MARKET THEORY

The demand for any asset depends on all four of the attributes just discussed—average return, risk, tax treatment, and liquidity. In a well-functioning market there are no bargains to be had; you get what you pay for. If some asset yields a higher average return than most other investments, it is because that asset has a higher risk, is less liquid, or receives unfavourable tax treatment.

That there are no bargains does not mean the investor's life is easy. He still must decide what he wants, just as he does when he goes into a grocery store. Figure 8.8A shows the kind of choices he faces. For simplicity, we ignore liquidity and tax considerations and focus only on average returns and risk. The figure shows the opportunity set in the way that is usual for this case. Because "risk" is bad, to get less risk we have to give up some average returns. That is why the trade-off has its unusual positive slope. Panel B shows the more familiar version of an opportunity set, by putting a measure of "safety" on the horizontal axis. Greater safety can only be obtained at the expense of a lower average return. Reading from either panel, we can see that assets with greater risk have a higher average return. Point *A* represents a government T-bill—no risk but low return. Point *B* might represent a stock or mix of stocks of average riskiness, point *C* one of high risk. A very risk-averse person might choose *A*, a less risk-averse person *B*, a still less risk-averse person *C*.

The theory that prices perfectly reflect the characteristics of assets—there are no bargains—is called the **efficient market theory.** It can be readily explained with reference to the stock market.

When economists refer to an efficient stock market, they mean one in which relevant information is known to a sizable number of participants. If enough participants have quick and ready access to each stock's average return, its risk, its tax treatment, and

so on, stock prices will move as if the whole market had the information. All it takes is a few people knowledgeable enough to recognize a bargain, and prices will be quickly bid up or down to levels that reflect complete information. And if stock prices reflect complete information, even uninformed buyers, purchasing at current prices, will reap the benefit.

Because prices in an efficient market already reflect all available information, any price changes are a response to *unanticipated* news. If it was already known that something good was going to occur—for instance, that some new computer better than all previous computers was going to be unveiled—the price of its stock would reflect this (it would be high) before the computer actually hit the market. Since tomorrow's news is by definition unanticipated, no one can predict whether it will cause the stock price to rise or fall. In an efficient stock market, prices will move unpredictably, depending on unexpected news. When a stock has an equal chance of going up in value more or less than the market as a whole, economists say that its price moves like a **random walk.**

Although there is an upward drift in the level of all stock prices, whether any particular stock will do better or worse than that average is unpredictable. If the stock market is indeed a random walk, it is virtually impossible for investors to beat the market. You can do just as well by throwing darts at the newspaper financial page as you can by carefully studying the prospects of each firm. The only way to do better than the market, on average, is to take greater risks; but taking greater risks means that there is a larger chance of doing worse than the market too.

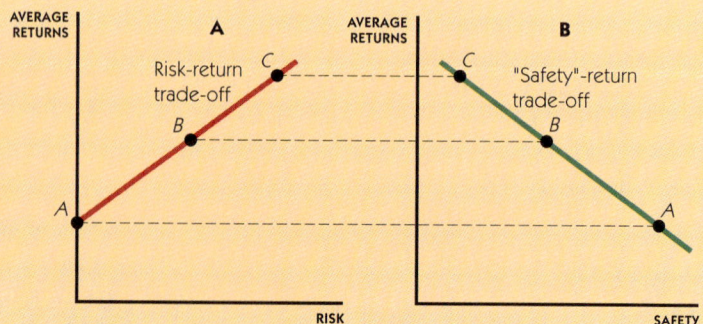

Figure 8.8 THE RISK-RETURN TRADE-OFF

To get more return, an investor must accept more risk, as is shown in panel A. Safety can be thought of as the inverse of risk. In panel B, the corresponding trade-off between safety and return is shown; to get more safety, an investor gives up some return.

STRATEGIES FOR INTELLIGENT INVESTING

So far, we have investigated major investment alternatives available to those who save, some of the important attributes of each, and the ways in which their prices reflect these attributes. If you are lucky enough—have enough money—to be considering some of these alternatives, keep in mind the following four simple rules. These rules will not tell you how to make a million by the time you are twenty-five, but they will enable you to avoid the worst pitfalls of investing.

1 *Know the attributes of each asset, and relate them to your personal situation.* Each asset has characteristic returns, risk, tax treatment, and liquidity. In making choices among different assets, your attitude toward each of these attributes should be *compared with the average attitudes reflected in the marketplace.*

Most individuals prefer safer, tax-favoured, more liquid assets. That is why those assets sell at a premium and produce a correspondingly lower average return. Are you willing to pay the amount required by the market for the extra safety or extra liquidity? If you are less risk-averse than average, you will find riskier assets attractive. You will not be willing to pay the higher price—and accept the lower return—for a safer asset. And if you are confident that you are not likely to need to sell an asset quickly, you will not be willing to pay the premium that more liquid assets require. If you are putting aside money for tuition next year, you probably will not want to buy common stocks.

2 *Give your financial portfolio a broad base.* In choosing among financial assets, you need to look not only at each asset separately, but at all of your assets together. A person's entire collection of assets is called her **portfolio.** (The portfolio also includes liabilities—what she owes—but they take us beyond the scope of this chapter.) This rule is seen most clearly in the case of risk. One of the ways you reduce risk is by diversifying your investment portfolio. With a well-diversified portfolio, it is extremely unlikely that something will go wrong with all the assets simultaneously. An investor with a diversified portfolio must still worry about events like recessions or changes in the interest rate, which will tend to make all stocks go up or down. But events that affect primarily one firm will have a small impact on the overall portfolio.

Many mutual funds claim more than just diversification: they claim that their research and insight into markets enable them to pick winners. Our discussion of efficient markets casts doubt on these claims. Many mutual funds do no research, claim no insights, and do nothing more than provide portfolio diversification. These are called **indexed funds.** The Toronto Stock Exchange (TSE) 35 Index reflects the average price of 35 stocks chosen to be representative of the market as a whole. TSE-indexed funds buy exactly the same mix of stocks that constitute the TSE 35 Index, so naturally these indexed funds do just as well as—no better and no worse than—the TSE 35 Index.

Because the index funds have low expenses, particularly in comparison with funds that are trying to outguess the market, they yield higher average returns to their investors than other funds with comparable risk.

3 *Look at all of the risks you face, not just those in your financial portfolio.* Many people may be far less diversified than they believe. For example, consider someone who works for the one big company in town. She owns a house, has a good job, has stock in the company, money in the bank, and a pension plan. But if that single company goes broke, she will lose her job, the value of her stock will fall, the price of her house is likely to decline as the local economy suffers, and even the pension plan may not pay as much as expected.

4 *Think twice before you think you can beat the market!* Efficient market theory delivers an important message to the personal investor. If an investment advisor tells you of an opportunity that beats the others on all counts, don't believe him. The bond that will produce a higher-than-average return carries with it more risk. The bank account that has a higher interest rate has less liquidity. The dream house at an unbelievable price probably has a leaky roof. The tax-favoured asset will have a lower return—and so on. Efficient market theory, as we have seen, says that information about these characteristics is built in to the price of assets, and hence built in to the returns. Basically, investors can adjust the return to their portfolio only by adjusting the risk they face.

CONSENSUS ON FINANCIAL MARKETS

Our economic system is often referred to as *capitalism*, reflecting the importance that capital markets—or, more generally, financial markets—play in our economy. The central role of these markets constitutes another major area of consensus among economists. Our fifth consensus point is:

5 **Financial Markets**

Financial markets are a central part of modern economies. They are essential for raising capital for new enterprises, expanding new businesses, and sharing risks.

REVIEW AND PRACTICE

SUMMARY

1 The interest rate is a price. It equates the supply of funds by savers and the demand by borrowers. Savers receive interest for deferring consumption, and borrowers pay interest so that they can consume or invest now and pay later.

2 The fact that the market interest rate is positive means that a dollar received today is worth more than a dollar received in the future. The present discounted value of a dollar in the future is the amount that, if received today, is equal to what a dollar will be worth in the future, given the prevailing rate of interest. This is the time value of money.

3 The real interest rate, which measures a person's actual increase in buying power when she saves money, is equal to the nominal interest rate (the amount paid in dollars) minus the inflation rate.

4 In deciding how much to save, people face a trade-off between current and future consumption. The amount of extra consumption an individual can obtain in the future by reducing present consumption is one plus the real rate of interest.

5 Life-cycle savings are what individuals save now so that they will be able to consume more after retirement. People also save to leave a bequest to children; as a precaution against unexpected illness, accident, or loss of income; and to meet a particular target, like a down payment on a house or university tuition.

6 An increase in the interest rate rotates the budget constraint and makes savers better off. The resulting income effect leads to an increase in current and future consumption and a decrease in savings. An increase in the real rate of interest makes it more attractive to save; this is the substitution effect and it leads to a decrease in current consumption (increase in savings). The net effect is ambiguous, though it appears in practice that an increase in the real interest rate has a slightly positive effect on savings.

7 Aggregate savings is the sum of the savings less dissavings of all individuals plus the net savings of governments. Higher levels of aggregate savings provide more finance for private-sector investment, which generates job creation and economic growth. Aggregate savings is lower in Canada than in some other countries because of an aging population, large government dissaving (budget deficits), pay-as-you-go public pensions, high levels of demand for consumer durables, and improvements in capital markets that make consumer borrowing easier.

8 Investment options for individuals' savings include bank accounts, real estate, bonds, or shares of stock. Returns on investment can be received in four main ways: interest, dividends, rent, and capital gains.

9 Assets can differ in four main ways: in their average returns, their riskiness, their treatment under tax law, and their liquidity.

10 The expected return on an asset is calculated by multiplying each of the possible outcomes by the probability of its occurring and adding the results.

11 By holding assets that are widely diversified, individuals can offset many of the risks associated with specific assets, but not the risks associated with the market as a whole.

12 There are four rules for intelligent investors: (1) evaluate the characteristics of each asset and relate them to your personal situation; (2) give your financial portfolio a broad base; (3) look at all the risks you face, not just those in your financial portfolio; (4) think twice before believing you can beat the market.

KEY TERMS

interest	life-cycle savings	liquidity	arbitrage
principal	bequest motive	dividends	efficient market theory
present discounted value	precautionary motive	retained earnings	indexed funds
real interest rate	pay-as-you-go system	diversification	
nominal interest rate	funded pensions	expected returns	

REVIEW QUESTIONS

1 Who is on the demand side and who is on the supply side in the market for loanable funds? What is the price in that market?

2 Would you prefer to receive $100 one year from now, or five years from now? Why? Does your answer change if the rate of inflation is zero?

3 What is the relationship between the nominal interest rate and the real interest rate?

4 How can a choice of consumption in the present determine the amount of consumption in the future?

5 How do you determine the price of future consumption in terms of present consumption?

6 For savers, how will the income effect of a higher interest rate affect current savings? How will the substitution effect of a higher interest rate affect current savings?

7 How will the income effect of lowered interest rates for borrowers affect current consumption? How will the substitution effect influence current consumption?

8 How does a government system of pay-as-you-go public pensions affect the level of savings?

9 Suppose an investor is considering two assets with identical expected rates of return. What three characteristics of the assets might help differentiate the choice between them?

10 True or false: "Two assets must have equal expected returns." If we modify the statement to read "Two assets that are equally risky must have equal expected returns," is the statement true? Explain your answer.

11 What is the efficient market theory? What implications does it have for whether you can beat the market? Does it imply that all stocks must yield the same expected return?

12 True or false: "A single mutual fund may be a more diversified investment than a portfolio of a dozen stocks." Explain.

PROBLEMS

1 Imagine that $1,000 is deposited in an account for five years; the account pays 10 percent interest per year, compounded annually. How much money will be in the account after five years? What if the rate of interest is 12 percent? What if the annual rate of interest is 12 percent, but the interest is compounded monthly?

2 Suppose you want to buy a car three years from now, and you know that the price of a car at that time will be $10,000. If the interest rate is 7 percent per year, how much would you have to set aside today to have the money ready when you need it? If the interest rate is 5 percent, how much would you have to set aside today?

3 This chapter analyzed the savings decision of an individual who worked for one period and was retired the next, and received no public pension in his retirement.
  (a) Show how the budget constraint changes if the individual receives a fixed public pension in retirement. Discuss what this does to savings.
  (b) Show how the budget constraint changes if the individual is taxed the first period of his life and receives a fixed public pension in retirement. Discuss what this does to savings.

4 This chapter focused on how interest rates affect savers. If an individual is a net debtor (he owes money), what is the income effect of an increase in interest rates. Will an increase in the interest rates that he has to pay induce him to borrow more or less?

5 In the context of the life-cycle model of savings, explain whether you would expect each of the following situations to increase or decrease household savings.
  (a) More people retire before age 65.
  (b) There is an increase in life expectancy.
  (c) The government passes a law requiring private businesses to provide more lucrative pensions.

6 Explain how each of the following changes might affect people's motivation for saving.
  (a) Inheritance taxes are introduced.
  (b) A government programme allows university students to obtain student loans more easily.
  (c) The government promises to assist anyone injured by natural disasters like hurricanes, tornadoes, and earthquakes.
  (d) More couples decide against having children.
  (e) The economy does far worse than anyone was expecting in a given year.

7 Imagine a lottery where 1 million tickets are sold at $1 apiece, and the winning ticket receives a prize of $700,000. What is the expected return to buying a ticket in this lottery? Will a risk-neutral person buy a ticket in this lottery? What about a risk-averse person?

8 Would you predict that
(a) the before-tax return on housing would be higher or lower than the before-tax return on other assets?
(b) investors would be willing to pay more or less for a stock with a high return when the economy is booming and a low return when the economy is in a slump than they would pay for a stock with just the opposite pattern of returns?
(c) an investment with low liquidity would sell at a premium or a discount compared with a similar investment with higher liquidity?

9 Each of two investments has a 1 in 10 chance of

paying a return of −10 percent; a 1 in 5 chance of paying 2 percent; a 1 in 3 chance of paying 6 percent; a 1 in 5 chance of paying 10 percent; and a 1 in 6 chance of paying 12 percent. Draw this probability distribution, and calculate the expected return for these two investments. If investment A is a house and investment B is a share of corporate stock, how might liquidity or tax considerations help you decide which of these investments you prefer?

10 Imagine a short-term corporate $1,000 bond that promises to pay 8 percent interest over three years. This bond will pay $80 at the end of the first year and the second year, and $1,080 at the end of the third year. After one year, however, the market interest rate has increased to 12 percent. What will the bond be worth to a risk-neutral investor at that time? If the firm appears likely to go bankrupt, how will the expected return on this bond change?

APPENDIX: INDIFFERENCE CURVES AND THE SAVINGS DECISION

The appendices to Chapters 6 and 7 explained how to use indifference curves to analyze how households decide what amounts to spend on different goods and how much labour to supply. The same analysis can be applied to the savings decision.

The decision of how much to save is viewed as a decision about how much of lifetime income to consume now and how much to consume in the future. This trade-off is summarized in the two-period budget constraint introduced in the chapter, with present consumption measured along the horizontal axis and future consumption along the vertical axis. The slope of the budget constraint is $1 + r$, where r is the rate of interest, the extra consumption we get in the future from forgoing a unit of consumption today.

Figure 8.9 shows three indifference curves. The

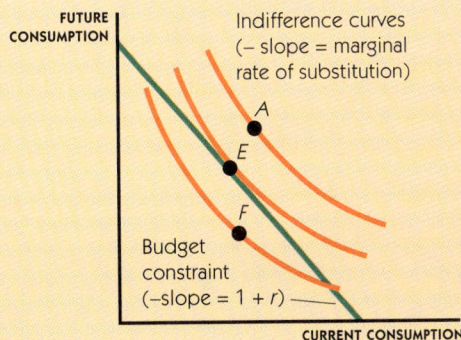

Figure 8.9 INDIFFERENCE CURVES AND SAVINGS BEHAVIOUR

An individual will choose the combination of present and future consumption at *E*. Point *A* would be more desirable, but it is not feasible. Point *F* is feasible, but it lies on a lower indifference curve and is therefore less desirable.

indifference curve through point *A* gives all the combinations of consumption today and consumption in the future among which the individual is indifferent (she would be just as well off, no better and no worse, at any point along the curve as at *A*). Since people generally prefer more consumption to less consumption, they would rather be on a higher than a lower indifference curve. The highest indifference curve a person can attain is one that just touches—that is, is tangent to—the budget constraint. The point of tangency we denote by *E*. The individual would clearly prefer the indifference curve through *A*, but no point on that curve is attainable; the indifference curve is everywhere above the budget constraint. She could consume at *F*, but the indifference curve through *F* lies below that through *E*.

As we learned in the appendix to Chapter 6, the slope of the indifference curve at a certain point is equal to the marginal rate of substitution at that point. In this case it tells us how much future consumption a person requires to compensate him for a decrease in current consumption by 1 unit, to leave him just as well off. At the point of tangency, the slope of the indifference curve is equal to the slope of the budget constraint. The marginal rate of substitution at that point, *E*, equals $1 + r$. If the individual forgoes a unit of consumption, he gets $1 + r$ more units of consumption in the future, and this is exactly the amount he requires to compensate him for giving up current consumption. On the other hand, if the marginal rate of substitution is less than $1 + r$, it pays the individual to save more. To see why, assume $1 + r = 1.5$, while the person's marginal rate of substitution is 1.2. By reducing his consumption by a unit, he gets 1.5 more units in the future, but he would have been content getting only 1.2 units. He is better off saving more.

EFFECT OF CHANGES IN THE INTEREST RATE

With indifference curves and budget constraints, we can see the effect of an increase in the interest rate. Figure 8.10 shows the case of an individual, Maggie, who works while she is young and saves for her re-

Figure 8.10 INCOME AND SUBSTITUTION EFFECTS OF A HIGHER INTEREST RATE

An increase in the interest rate rotates the budget constraint, moving it from *BC* to B_2C. The substitution effect describes what happens when relative prices are changed but Maggie remains on the same indifference curve; there is a shift in the budget line from *BC* to B_1C_1, and an increase in savings from E_0 to E_2. The income effect is the result of an outward shift of the budget line, keeping relative prices the same; the income effect is described by the shift from B_1C_1 to B_2C, and the increase in present consumption from E_2 to E_1.

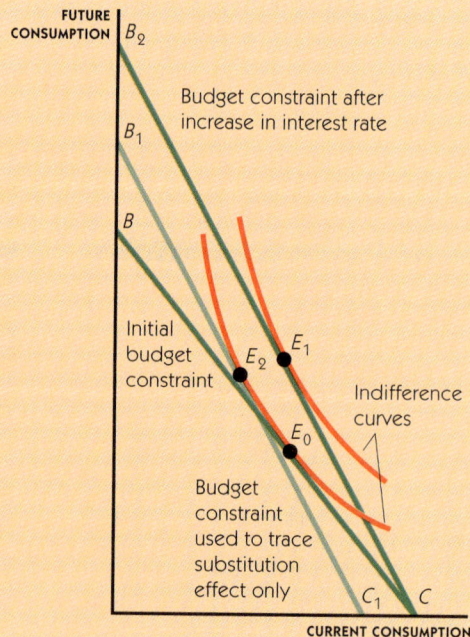

tirement. The vertical axis gives consumption during retirement years, the horizontal axis consumption during working years. An increase in the rate of interest rotates the budget constraint, moving it from BC to B_2C. It is useful to break the change down into two steps. In the first, we ask what would have happened if the interest rate had changed but Maggie remained on the same indifference curve. This is represented by the movement of the budget constraint from BC to B_1C_1. As a result of the increased interest rate, Maggie consumes less today—she saves more. This is the substitution effect, and it is seen in the movement from E_0 to E_2 in the figure.

Since Maggie is a saver, the increased interest rate makes her better off. To leave Maggie on the same indifference curve after the increase in the interest rate, we need to reduce her income. Her true budget constraint, after the interest rate increase, is B_2C, parallel to B_1C_1. The two budget constraints have the same slope because the after-tax interest rates are the same. The movement from B_1C_1 to B_2C is the second step. It induces Maggie to increase her consumption from E_2 to E_1. At higher incomes and the same relative prices (interest rates), people consume more every period, which implies that they save less. The movement from E_2 to E_1 is the income effect.

Thus, the substitution effect leads her to save more, the income effect to save less, and the net effect is ambiguous. In this case, there is a slight increase in savings.

THE FIRM'S COSTS

The previous three chapters focused on the decisions of households and individuals. In this chapter and the following one, the focus shifts to the decisions of firms. While households are assumed to take decisions in pursuit of satisfaction, we suppose that firms take decisions to maximize their profits. In their pursuit of profits, firms help to answer two of the four fundamental economic questions: "What goods should be produced, and in what quantities?" and "How should these goods be produced?"

Once again, the basic competitive model is our starting point. Many firms, all making the same product, compete with one another to sell that product to well-informed customers, who instantaneously recognize and act upon any price differences. Because customers are well informed about prices, all firms in a competitive market must accept the price set for their product by the forces of supply and demand in the market as a whole. Any firm trying to sell above that price will lose all its customers. Firms in competitive markets are, therefore, **price takers.** The classic example of competitive markets are agricultural markets—thousands of farmers producing,

1 What do cost curves—curves relating costs to the level of production—look like in an economy where output depends on a single input to production?

2 In the long run, firms can vary some inputs that they cannot vary in the short run. As a result, in the long run, cost curves may look different than they do in the short run. What is the relationship between long-run and short-run cost curves?

3 What additional issues are raised when there are several inputs?

say, wheat. A farmer does not waste time wondering what price to set for the wheat he has to sell. He knows he will get the "going price."

The competitive firm is also a price taker in the markets for its inputs. It faces a given wage rate for its labour and given prices for its machines and equipment and its other purchased inputs. Nonetheless, a firm does have some control over its costs because the quantity of the various inputs it purchases is related to its level of production. This chapter focuses on understanding the relationship between levels of production and cost for the competitive firm. Chapter 10 shows how a firm uses this relationship to maximize its profits by its choice of production level.

Even though we talk in terms of "production" and "goods," it is important to bear in mind that only one third of the Canadian economy consists of industries that produce goods in the conventional sense—manufacturing, mining, construction, and agriculture. The other two thirds of the economy—industries like transportation, education, health care, wholesale and retail trade, and finance—produces primarily services.

PROFITS, COSTS, AND FACTORS OF PRODUCTION

A business that fails to make a profit over time will cease to exist because it will not have enough money to pay its bills. If businesses are to continue, they are under pressure to make money. The motivation of making as much money as possible—maximizing profits—provides a useful starting point for discussing the behaviour of firms in competitive markets.

The definition of **profits** is simple:

profits = total revenues − total costs.

The **total revenues** a business receives from selling its products are calculated as the quantity it sells of the product times the price of the product. A firm's **total costs** are defined as the total expense of producing the good. What the firm uses to produce the goods are called inputs, or **factors of production:** labour, materials, and capital goods. Labour costs are what the company has to pay for the workers it hires and the managers it employs to supervise the workers. The costs of materials include raw materials and intermediate goods and services. Intermediate goods are whatever supplies the company purchases from other firms—seeds, fertilizer, and gasoline for a farm; iron ore, coal, coke, limestone, and electric power for a steel company. The costs of services include things like legal and accounting fees and payments to advertising and consulting firms.

All firms work to keep their costs as low as possible. Within limits they can vary the mix of labour, materials, capital goods, and production processes they use, and they will do so until they find the lowest-cost method of producing a given quantity of product. The simplest way of understanding how firms find the lowest-cost point is to look at a firm that has only one variable factor of production. All other factors of production are assumed to be fixed. Later we turn to the case where some of the fixed factors can also be varied.

PRODUCTION WITH A SINGLE VARIABLE FACTOR

A wheat farmer with a fixed amount of land who uses only labour to produce his crop is our example. The more labour he applies to the farm (his own time, plus the time of workers that he hires), the greater the output. Labour is the single variable factor, or input. The same principles would also apply to the case of a factory, a store, or a restaurant of a given size.

The relationship between the inputs used in production and the level of output is called the **production function.** Figure 9.1 shows the farmer's production function; the data supporting the figure are set forth in Table 9.1. The output produced per unit of labour input, or the ratio of output to labour employed at any level of production, is called the **average product** of labour. Thus, when the output is 120,000 bushels of wheat the average product is 20 bushels per hour worked; when the output rises to 170,000 bushels, the average product has fallen to 17 bushels per hour worked. The average products of labour are given by the last column in the table. Diagrammatically, the average product at a given point on the production function is given by the slope of a line from the origin to that point.

The increase in output corresponding to an increase in labour input is the **marginal product** of labour. For example, when the number of hours worked per year rises from 7,000 to 8,000, output increases by 15,000 bushels, from 140,000 to 155,000. When the farmer is employing 8,000 hours, the marginal product of 1,000 more hours is 10,000 bushels. The marginal product of an extra hour of labour will, accordingly, be 10 bushels. The marginal product is given in the third column of the table. Diagrammatically, it is given by the slope of the production function.

DIMINISHING RETURNS

In the case of the wheat farmer, as more and more labour is added to a fixed amount of land the marginal product of labour diminishes. This is another application of the concept of **diminishing returns,** which we originally encountered in Chapter 2. In the case of a firm's production function, diminishing returns implies that output increases less than proportionately with input. If labour is doubled, output is less than doubled. Increasing the number of hours worked from 7,000 to 8,000 raises output by 15,000 bushels, but increasing the hours worked from 8,000 to 9,000 raises output by only 10,000 bushels. Diminishing returns sets in with a vengeance at higher levels of input; mov-

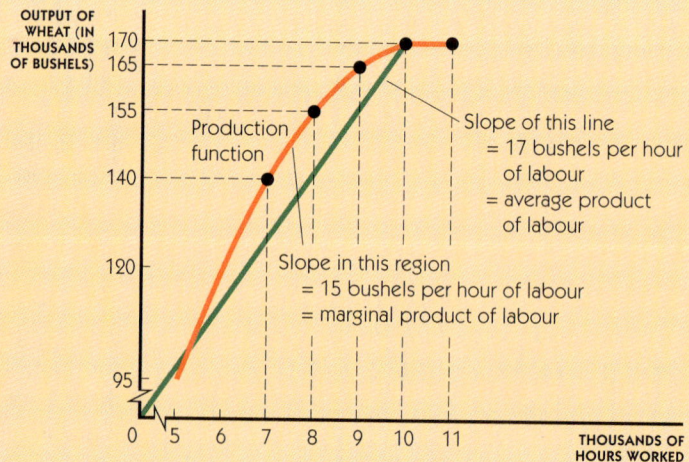

Figure 9.1 PRODUCTION FUNCTION WITH DIMINISHING RETURNS TO AN INPUT

As the amount of the input (labour) increases, so does the output (wheat). But there are diminishing returns to labour; increases in labour result in successively smaller increases in wheat output on the margin. Since the slope of the curve is the marginal product of labour, on the graph, this means the slope flattens out as the amount of labour increases. The average product of labour is the slope of a line from the origin to a point on the production function.

OUTPUT OF WHEAT (IN THOUSANDS OF BUSHELS)

Production function

Slope of this line
= 17 bushels per hour of labour
= average product of labour

Slope in this region
= 15 bushels per hour of labour
= marginal product of labour

THOUSANDS OF HOURS WORKED

Table 9.1 LEVEL OF OUTPUT WITH DIFFERENT AMOUNTS OF LABOUR

Number of hours worked	Amount of wheat produced (bushels)	Marginal product (additional bushels produced by 1,000 additional hours of labour)	Average product (bushels produced per hours worked)
5,000	95,000	25,000	19.0
6,000	120,000	20,000	20.0
7,000	140,000	15,000	20.0
8,000	155,000	10,000	19.4
9,000	165,000	5,000	18.3
10,000	170,000	0	17.0
11,000	170,000		15.5

ing from 10,000 to 11,000 hours worked adds nothing. This point occurs when the output of the firm has reached its maximum, or **full capacity,** level.

INCREASING RETURNS

Although a production function with diminishing returns is an important case, other cases do occur. Figure 9.2A shows a production function where increasing an input (here, labour) raises output more than proportionately. A firm with this kind of production function has **increasing returns.** In the single-input case depicted, it is clear that the marginal product of the input increases with the amount produced; that is, when the firm is producing a lot, adding one more worker increases output by more than it does when the firm is producing little. In Figure 9.2A, this is reflected in the fact that the slope of the production function rises as output rises. Note as well that the average product of labour will also be increasing as output increases, since the slope of a line from the origin to the production function increases as one moves up the production function.

Imagine a business that picks up garbage. If this business counts only one out of every five houses as customers, it will have a certain cost of production. But if the company can expand to picking up the garbage from two out of every five houses, although it will need more workers, the workers will be able to drive a shorter distance and pick up more garbage faster. Thus, a doubling of output can result from a less than doubling of labour. Many examples of increasing returns, like garbage collection, involve providing service to more people in a given area. Telephone companies and electric utilities are two other familiar instances.

DIMINISHING RETURNS

As more and more of one input is added, *while other inputs remain unchanged,* the marginal product of the added input diminishes.

Figure 9.2 **PRODUCTION FUNCTIONS WITH INCREASING, CONSTANT, AND CHANGING RETURNS TO AN INPUT**

In panel A, the returns to labour are increasing. Successive increases in labour will result in successively larger increases in output; both the marginal and the average products of labour will increase. In panel B, the returns to labour are constant; a given increase in labour input always results in the same increase in output. The marginal and average products of labour are constant. In panel C, the returns to labour (and the marginal product of labour) are initially increasing up to point A and then decreasing after that. The average product of labour increases up to point E^* and decreases after that. The point E^* is the point of maximum productivity for the plant.

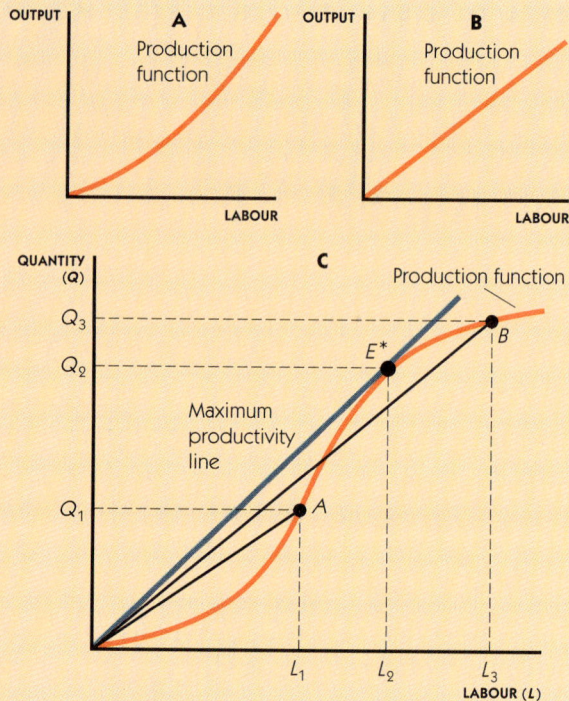

CONSTANT RETURNS

In the case of increasing returns, output grows faster than the input, while with diminishing returns, the input grows faster than output. The intermediate case is one where if the input changes, the output changes at the same rate. This is the case of **constant returns.** Figure 9.2B shows constant returns, when the relationship between input and output is a straight line. Both the marginal and the average products of labour will be constant here.

MIXED CASES

The production function may exhibit decreasing returns throughout part of its range and increasing returns elsewhere. Panel C of Figure 9.2 shows a typical example of this. When output is small, increasing returns apply. Workers are able to take on more specialized tasks and become more productive. Eventually, the benefits of specialization are exhausted, and because the capacity of the plant is fixed, diminishing

returns set in. In this case, the marginal product of labour (slope of the production function) will initially rise and then fall. Similarly the average product of labour (the slope of a line from the origin to the production function) will initially rise and then fall. The average product will be highest at the point E^* where the line from the origin is the steepest. At this point, the average product and the marginal product are the same, since both are equal to the slope of the production function. At outputs below E^*, such as A, the average product will be lower than the marginal product, while the opposite will apply at outputs above E^*, such as B. This relationship will be of use to us later in this chapter.

FIXED VERSUS VARIABLE INPUTS

Firms typically require a certain level of input just to start production. Before it can open its doors, for instance, a firm may need land (or space) and some machines. It will have to hire someone to run the per-

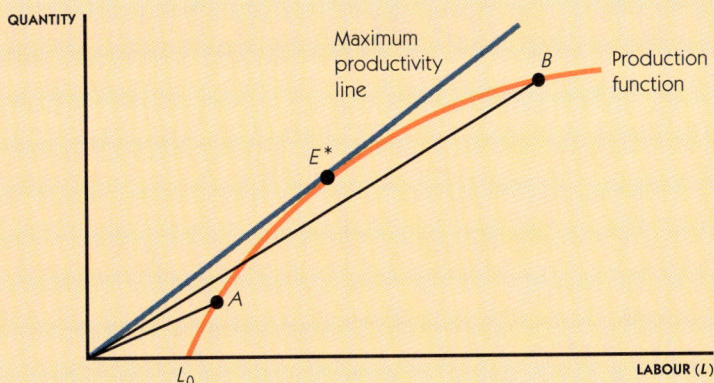

Figure 9.3 PRODUCTION FUNCTION WITH FIXED AND VARIABLE LABOUR INPUTS

An amount of labour L_0 is fixed. Output is produced by workers hired in excess of L_0. If the production function for production workers has decreasing returns, the marginal product declines as output increases. However, the average product initially increases, reaches a maximum at E^*, and then declines.

sonnel office and someone to supervise the workers. These are called **fixed inputs,** because they do not depend on the level of output. The quantities of **variable inputs,** in contrast, rise and fall with the level of production. For instance, the firm can work its space and machines for one shift a day, or it can run them for all twenty-four hours. It simply hires more workers and uses more materials. These workers and materials are variable inputs.

Figure 9.3 shows a production function when there are both fixed and variable inputs. An amount of labour L_0 is fixed. Workers hired over and above that represent the production workers. The production function drawn for them is assumed to be one with diminishing returns throughout. The marginal product of labour falls as output increases. However, as shown by the points A, B, and E^*, the average product (output per worker) for the firm as a whole initially increases, reaches a maximum at E^*, and then declines.

COST CURVES

The production function is important to the firm because the inputs it depicts determine the costs of production. The case of a production function with fixed inputs is the most common production function in the economy, and a look at the kinds of costs it generates will give us an overview of the major categories of cost upon which economists concentrate.

FIXED AND VARIABLE COSTS

The costs associated with fixed inputs are called **fixed costs.** They include the costs of the inputs simply required to set the firm up and run its administrative services, referred to as **overhead costs.** They also include the costs of the factors of production, such as the amount of machinery and equipment currently available to the firm, which we are holding fixed for the present analysis, but which we allow to vary later in this chapter. Whether the firm produces nothing or produces at full capacity, it antes up the same fixed cost to pay for its overhead costs and other fixed factors of production. Figure 9.4 shows how costs depend on output. Panel A depicts fixed costs as a horizontal line—by definition, they do not depend on the level of output. As an example, consider a would-be wheat farmer who has the opportunity to buy a farm and its equipment for $25,000. His fixed costs are $25,000.

Variable costs correspond to variable inputs. These costs rise or fall with the level of production. Any cost that the firm can change during the time period under study is a variable cost. To the extent that such items as labour costs or costs of materials can go up or down as output does, these are variable costs. If we give our farmer only one variable input, labour, then his variable costs would be, say, $15 per hour for each worker times the number of hours worked by all workers. The variable costs corresponding to levels of

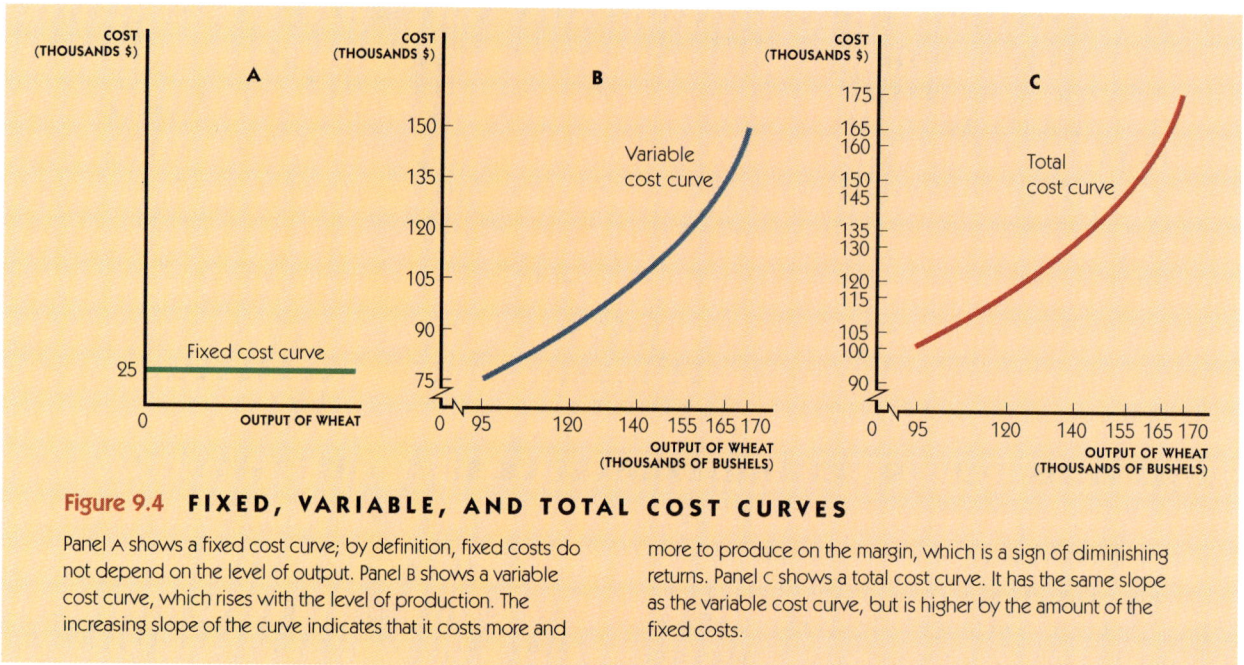

Figure 9.4 **FIXED, VARIABLE, AND TOTAL COST CURVES**

Panel A shows a fixed cost curve; by definition, fixed costs do not depend on the level of output. Panel B shows a variable cost curve, which rises with the level of production. The increasing slope of the curve indicates that it costs more and more to produce on the margin, which is a sign of diminishing returns. Panel C shows a total cost curve. It has the same slope as the variable cost curve, but is higher by the amount of the fixed costs.

output listed in Table 9.1 are shown in Table 9.2 and plotted in Figure 9.4B. As output increases, so do variable costs, so the curve slopes upward. However, because of the principle of diminishing returns, labour inputs and thus costs rise more than proportionately with output, so the slope of the variable cost curve increases with output.

TOTAL COSTS

Table 9.2 also includes a column labelled "Total cost." **Total costs** are defined as the sum of variable and fixed costs, so this column differs from the variable costs column by $25,000, the amount of the firm's fixed cost. The total cost curve, summarizing these points, is shown in Figure 9.4C.

MARGINAL COST AND MARGINAL PRODUCT

As with the economic decisions we have discussed earlier in this book, the most important cost for the firm's decision makers is the **marginal cost.** This is

the extra cost corresponding to each additional unit produced.[1] In the case of the wheat farmer's costs (Table 9.2), as he increases labour input from 7,000 hours to 8,000 hours, output increases by 15,000 bushels. Thus, to produce 1,000 extra bushels requires $1,000/15 = 66^2/_3$ extra hours. The cost of producing an extra 1,000 bushels is $66^2/_3$ hours × wage per hour. If the wage is $15 per hour, the marginal cost of 1,000 bushels is $1,000.

More generally, the marginal cost is the change in total cost for a change in output, or $\Delta TC/\Delta Q$ in obvious notation. Since the change in total cost is just the wage rate w times the additional workers required, $\Delta TC = w\Delta L$. Therefore, the marginal cost is $w\Delta L/\Delta Q$, or $w/(\Delta Q/\Delta L)$. Thus, if MPL is the marginal product of labour (15 bushels per hour) and w is the wage

[1] There is a simple relationship between the marginal cost curve and the total cost curve. The marginal cost is just the slope of the total cost—the change in total costs (movement along the vertical axis, in Figure 9.4C) resulting from a unit change in output (movement along the horizontal axis).

Table 9.2 COST OF PRODUCING WHEAT

Output (bushels)	Labour required (hours)	Total variable cost (at a wage of $15 per hour)	Total cost ($)	Marginal cost ($ per bushel)	Average cost ($ per bushel)	Average variable cost ($ per bushel)
95,000	5,000	75,000	100,000	—	1.05	.79
120,000	6,000	90,000	115,000	.60	.96	.75
140,000	7,000	105,000	130,000	.75	.93	.75
155,000	8,000	120,000	145,000	1.00	.94	.77
165,000	9,000	135,000	160,000	1.50	.97	.82
170,000	10,000	150,000	175,000	3.00	1.03	.88

rate ($15 per hour), the marginal cost of producing an extra unit of output is just w/MPL ($1 per bushel).

The marginal cost curve depicted in Figure 9.5 is upward sloping. This is the typical case. It reflects the fact that as more is produced, it becomes harder and harder to increase output further—an example of the familiar principle of diminishing marginal returns. (Marginal cost curves reflecting increasing or constant returns to scale have different shapes. These are discussed later in the chapter.)

AVERAGE COST

The final set of costs that concern the business firm are its **average costs.** These are simply total costs divided by output. The average cost curve gives average costs corresponding to different levels of output. Figure 9.5 also shows the average cost curve corresponding to the total cost curve depicted in Figure 9.4C. To find the average cost for any level of output, we draw a line from the origin to the point on the

Figure 9.5 MARGINAL AND AVERAGE COST CURVES

The marginal cost is the extra cost of producing one more unit of output. With diminishing returns, marginal costs increase with the level of output. Average costs, also shown here, are total costs divided by output.

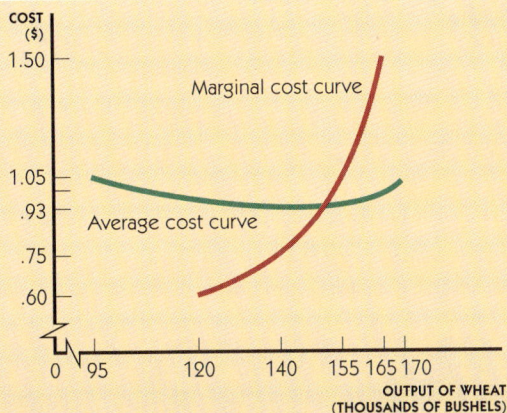

total cost curve for that level of output. The slope of that line is

$$\frac{\text{total costs}}{\text{output}} = \text{average costs.}$$

AVERAGE FIXED COSTS AND AVERAGE VARIABLE COSTS

Average fixed costs are simple fixed costs divided by output. Since fixed costs do not change with output, average fixed costs must fall as output rises. This is referred to as the phenomenon of spreading overhead costs. The concept of **average variable costs** will be useful in the next chapter when we discuss the production decision. These are total variable costs divided by output.

THE U-SHAPED AVERAGE COST CURVE

The typical average cost curve is taken to be U-shaped. To see why, we examine the typical production function in more detail. Shown in Figure 9.6A, it is the same production function with a fixed input we saw

earlier (Figure 9.3). Recall the following three properties of that production function:

1 A certain amount of labour, labelled L_0, is required before any output can be produced.

2 Because of diminishing returns, more and more labour is required to produce each additional unit of output; that is, the marginal product of labour, given by the slope of the production function, declines as output rises. It eventually becomes 0 once the full capacity of the firm is reached.

3 There is a level of output at which the output per unit of input—the average product of labour—is maximized, Q^*.

Panel B shows what these three properties imply for the total cost curve. First, there are fixed costs c_0 corresponding to the costs of overhead labour L_0 plus those of any other fixed factors. Second, diminishing returns mean that not only do total costs rise as output increases, but the total cost curve becomes steeper and steeper.

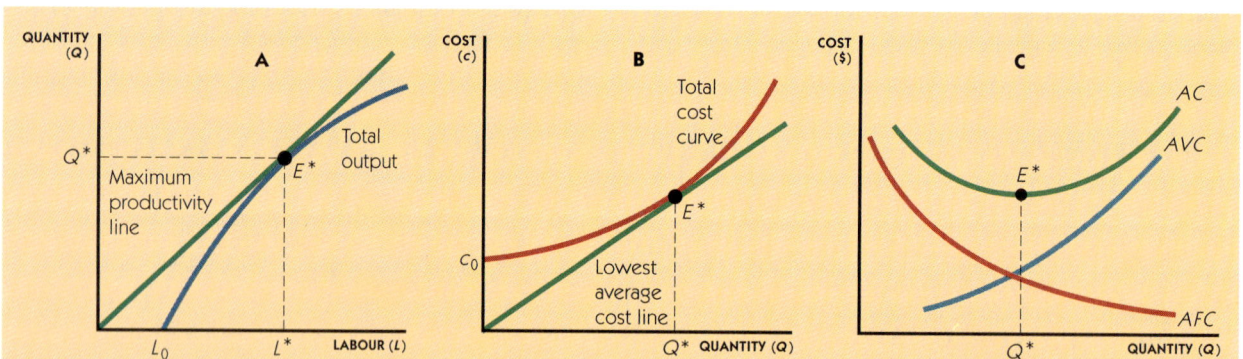

Figure 9.6 RELATING THE TYPICAL PRODUCTION FUNCTION TO THE TOTAL COST CURVE

Panel A shows a typical production function. Average productivity is maximized at E^*. Panel B shows the usual shape of a total cost curve that corresponds to this typical production function. Diminishing returns cause the slope of the curve to become steeper; the point of lowest average cost—given by the slope of a line through the origin—corresponds to the

point of highest average productivity. Panel C converts the total cost curve into average curves: average fixed costs, which is fixed costs c_0 divided by output; average variable costs, which is variable costs (total costs less c_0) divided by output; and average costs, which is total cost divided by output (or average fixed costs plus average variable costs).

Panel C depicts the various average cost curves associated with this total cost curve. The curve labelled *AFC* is the average fixed cost curve, obtained by dividing fixed costs c_0 by output. Naturally it declines as output rises. The curve *AVC* represents average variable costs, which is just variable costs divided by output. Since variable costs rise more than proportionately with output as a result of diminishing returns, the *AVC* curve rises at an increasing rate. Average costs are then the sum of average fixed costs and average variable costs. The average cost curve is the curve *AC* found by adding *AFC* and *AVC* vertically. It can also be obtained by taking the slopes of lines from the origin to each point along the total cost curve of panel B.

That output per unit input is maximized at Q^* has one important implication. Average costs, total costs divided by output, are minimized at the output level Q^*. This is shown in Figure 9.6C. With small outputs, average costs decline as output increases. If the *only*

Figure 9.7 RELATING THE MARGINAL COST CURVE TO THE AVERAGE COST CURVE

The average cost curve is usually U-shaped. It initially declines as the fixed costs are spread over a larger amount of output, and then rises as diminishing returns to the variable input become important. With a U-shaped average cost curve, the marginal cost curve will cross the average cost curve at its minimum.

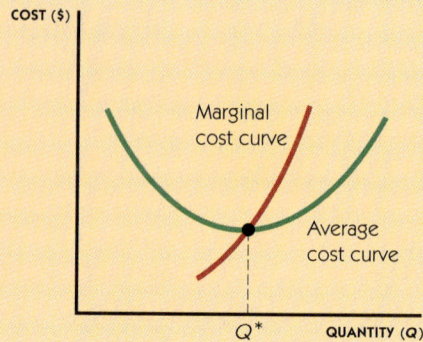

costs were fixed costs, then average costs (which would then equal the fixed costs divided by the output) would decrease in proportion to the increase in output. This same principle holds even if not all costs are fixed. Average costs still decline because there are more units of production by which to divide fixed costs. With large outputs, average costs increase, as the law of diminishing returns sets in with strength. Output increases less than proportionately with input; equivalently, to get a 1 percent increase in output, one needs much more than a 1 percent increase in input.

Even if the average cost curve is U-shaped, the output at which average costs are minimized may be very great, so high that there is not enough demand to justify producing that much. Thus, when economists refer to declining average costs, they mean that those costs are declining over the level of output that is likely to prevail in the market.

Relationship between Average and Marginal Cost Curves The relationship between average costs and marginal costs is reflected in Figure 9.7. The marginal cost curve intersects the average cost curve at the bottom of the U—the *minimum* average cost. To understand why the marginal cost curve will *always* intersect the average cost curve at its lowest point, consider the relationship between average and marginal costs. As long as the marginal cost is below the average cost, producing an additional unit will pull down the average. Thus, everywhere that the marginal cost is below average cost, the average

cost curve is declining. If marginal cost is above average cost, then producing an additional unit will raise the average. So everywhere that the marginal cost is above average cost, the average cost curve must be rising. The point between where the U-shaped average cost curve is falling and where it is rising is the minimum point.[2]

ALTERNATIVE SHAPES OF COST CURVES

Earlier, we saw that production functions may exhibit increasing or constant returns. If there are increasing returns, output increases more than proportionately with the input and total costs increase more slowly than output, as seen in panel A of Figure 9.8. In this case average and marginal costs decline, as illustrated in panel B.

If there are constant returns, doubling inputs doubles output, which will cost twice as much. In this case, total costs are simply proportional to output (panel C), and average and marginal costs are constant (panel D).

Panels E and F show the case where there is a fixed cost, but beyond that, marginal costs are constant. In this case, average costs are declining.

---

[2] This relationship between average and marginal cost can be seen geometrically using panel B of Figure 9.6. The marginal cost is the slope of the total cost curve. The average cost is the slope of a line from the origin to a point on the total cost curve. At outputs below Q^*, the average cost exceeds the marginal cost, while above Q^*, the opposite is true.

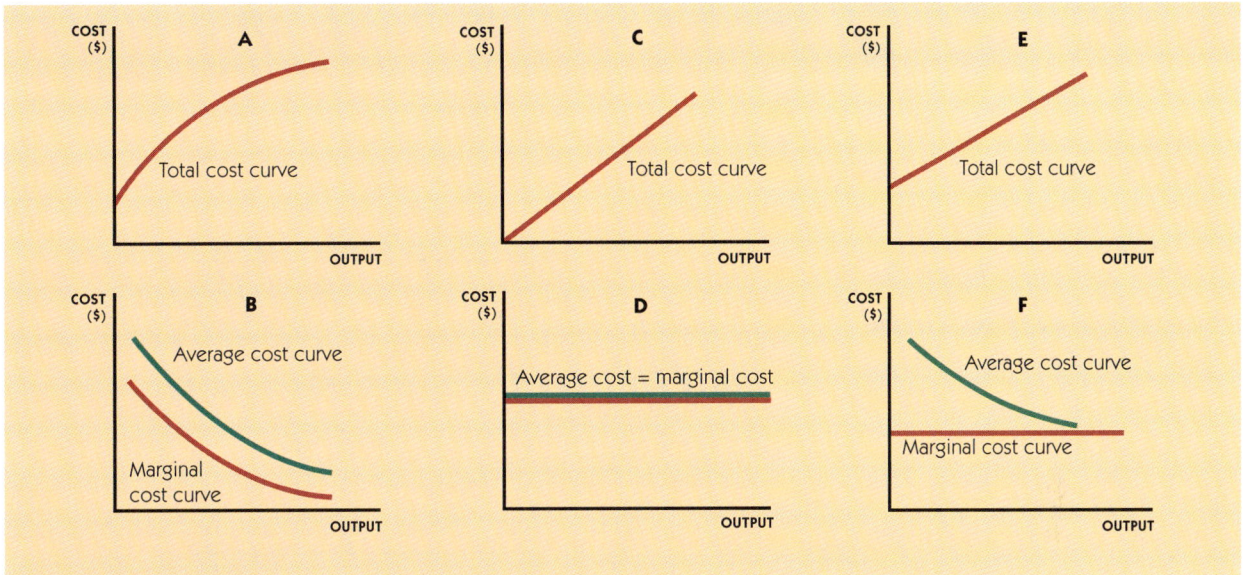

Figure 9.8 **COST CURVES WITH INCREASING OR CONSTANT RETURNS**

Panels A and B show total, marginal, and average cost curves with increasing returns. Since the cost of producing an additional unit of output is falling, average costs decline as production increases. Panel C shows a total cost curve with constant returns; since returns to the variable factor are constant and fixed costs are zero, the total cost curve begins at the origin and its slope does not change. Panel D shows marginal and average costs with constant returns; marginal cost does not change, and so the average cost does not change either. Panels E and F show total, average, and marginal costs for the case where there is a fixed cost, but the costs of producing each unit are constant.

CHANGING FACTOR PRICES AND COST CURVES

The cost curves shown thus far are based on the fixed prices of each of the inputs firms purchase. An increase in the price of a variable factor will shift up all of the cost curves—total, average, and marginal. Panel A of Figure 9.9 shows this for the average and marginal cost curves. However, if the price of a fixed factor increases, only the average cost curve will shift up. The marginal cost curve will remain unchanged since it includes only variable costs. Panel B shows the effect of an increase in the price of a fixed factor.

COST CONCEPTS

Total costs: Total costs of producing output = fixed costs + variable costs

Fixed costs: Costs that do not depend on output

Variable costs: Costs that do depend on output

Marginal costs: Extra cost of producing an extra unit = total cost of $(Q + 1)$ units minus total cost of Q units of output

Average costs: Total costs divided by output

Average fixed costs: Fixed costs divided by output

Average variable costs: Variable costs divided by output

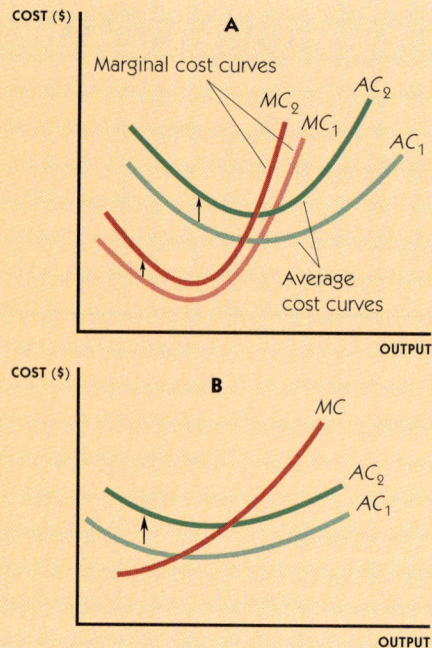

Figure 9.9 HOW CHANGES IN INPUT PRICES AFFECT COST CURVES

An increase in the price of a variable input will shift the average and marginal cost curves upward as in panel A. An increase in the price of a fixed factor will shift the average, but not the marginal, cost curve upward as in panel B.

PRODUCTION WITH MANY FACTORS

The basic principles of the case with only two factors—one fixed, one variable—apply also to firms producing many products with many different inputs. The only fundamental difference is that with many factors it becomes possible to produce the same output in several different ways. Cost minimization, therefore, involves weighing the costs of different mixes of inputs.

Up to this point, we have referred to the distinction between inputs that are fixed (their cost does not vary with quantity produced) and inputs that are variable (their cost does depend on quantity produced). We have sidestepped the fact that inputs and costs may be fixed for some period of time, but if the time period is long enough, they can vary with production. Take the inputs of labour and machines. In the short run, the supply of machines may be fixed. Output is then increased only by increasing labour. In the longer run, both machines and workers can

be adjusted. The short-run cost curve, then, is the cost of production with a *given* stock of machines. The long-run cost curve is the cost of production when all factors are adjusted.[3]

We begin by analyzing the firm's short-run and long-run cost curves, given the prices of its inputs. The long-run cost curve will reflect the mix of labour and capital inputs that the firm should use to produce any given quantity of output. Following that, we consider what happens when factor prices change and the firm is induced to change its mix of inputs. How the firm reacts to a change in input prices is referred to as the principle of substitution. The analysis of it is somewhat complicated, and is considered in more detail in the appendix to this chapter.

[3] The distinction between short-run and long-run costs corresponds to the distinction between short-run and long-run supply curves introduced in Chapter 4. Chapter 10 will make clear the relationship. It is an exaggeration to think that only capital goods are fixed in the short run while all of labour is variable. In some cases capital goods may easily be varied; a firm can, for instance, rent cars. And in some cases, as when a company has long-term contracts with its workers, it may be very difficult to vary labour in the short run.

SHORT-RUN COST CURVES

If we think of the number of machines as being fixed in the short run, and labour as the principal input that can be varied, our preceding analysis of production with a single variable factor provides a good description of short-run cost curves. Thus, short-run *average* cost curves are normally U-shaped.

The short-run *marginal* cost curve in Figure 9.10 presents a pattern often seen in manufacturing. Marginal costs are approximately constant over a wide range. As long as their newest machines are not being fully used, firms find that increasing production by 10 percent requires increasing the number of production workers by 10 percent and the inputs of other materials (raw materials, intermediate goods) by 10 percent. Idle machines are simply put to work. Eventually, however, the cost of producing extra units goes up. Workers have to work more hours (and often they get paid more—time and a half or double time—for these extra hours). Overworked machines break down more frequently. Older, poorer machines have to be put to use. At the full-capacity level of output, it is impossible to push a factory to a higher level of production in the short run.

We have thus identified two key properties of the short-run marginal cost curve. (1) When there is excess capacity, the marginal cost of producing each extra unit does not increase much; the marginal cost curve is relatively flat. (2) But eventually the marginal cost curve becomes steeply upward-sloping. (Remember, we are focusing here on the short run, so we assume the number of machines is fixed; there is a particular capacity for which the plant was designed.)

Before we turn to the long run, it is useful to recall the meaning of fixed versus overhead costs. So far, both of these terms simply referred to costs that do not depend on the level of output. This in fact confuses two related but distinct concepts. Even if a firm could adjust all factors of production, some overhead costs would still be required for the company to exist at all. For a firm to be in business at all, it probably needs telephone service. **Fixed costs** are costs that are fixed in the short run, whether or not they represent overhead costs. For example, if a firm has a long-term lease on its buildings, its rental costs are fixed in the short run.

In the long run, some of the fixed costs of the firm become variable costs as now the firm can adjust the size of the buildings it occupies and the machinery and equipment it invests in. However, its overhead costs remain fixed, independent of the level of output.

LONG-RUN COST CURVES

Even if the short-run average cost curves for a given manufacturing facility are U-shaped, the long-run average cost curve may not have the same shape. As production grows, it will pay at some point to build a second plant, and then a third, a fourth, and so on. Panel A of Figure 9.11 shows the total costs of produc-

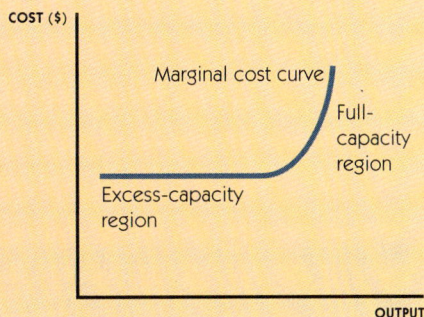

Figure 9.10 SHORT-RUN MARGINAL COSTS

When there is excess capacity, the marginal cost of producing an extra unit may not increase much, and so the marginal cost curve is flat. But when capacity is approached, marginal costs may rise rapidly.

ing different levels of output, assuming that the firm builds one plant. This curve is marked TC_1. It also shows the total costs of producing different levels of output, assuming the firm builds two plants (TC_2) and three plants (TC_3). In going from TC_1 to TC_2, the fixed costs have risen (the intercept on the vertical axis), but so has the full-capacity output that the firm can produce. How many plants will the company build? Clearly, the firm wishes to minimize the (total) costs of producing at any level of output. Thus, the *relevant* total cost curve is the lower boundary of the three curves, which is heavily shaded. Between 0 and Q_1, the firm produces using one plant; between Q_1 and Q_2, it uses two plants; and for outputs larger than Q_2, it uses three plants.

We can see the same results in panel B, using average cost curves. Obviously, if the firm minimizes the total costs of producing any particular output, it minimizes the average cost of producing that output. The figure shows the average cost curves corresponding to the firm's producing with one, two, and three plants. The company chooses the number of plants that minimizes its average costs, given the level of output it plans to produce. Thus, if the firm plans to

produce less than Q_1 it builds only one plant; AC_1 is less than AC_2 for all outputs less than Q_1. If the firm plans to produce between Q_1 and Q_2 it builds two plants, because AC_2 is, in this interval, less than either AC_1 or AC_3. Similarly, for outputs greater than Q_2 the firm builds three plants.

In this case, the long-run average cost curve is the heavily shaded bumpy curve in Figure 9.11B. For large outputs, the bumps look very small. In drawing long-run average cost curves, therefore, we typically ignore the bumps and draw smooth curves. The distinction between the long-run and the short-run average cost curve is that along the former both labour and capital inputs are changing, while along the latter only labour is changing, since capital is a fixed factor.

We now need to ask whether long-run average cost curves are normally flat or slope upwards or downwards. To answer this question, remember how we analyzed the shape of the short-run average cost curve, or the average cost curve with a single variable input. We first described the production function, relating the level of input to the level of output. If output increases less than proportionately with the input,

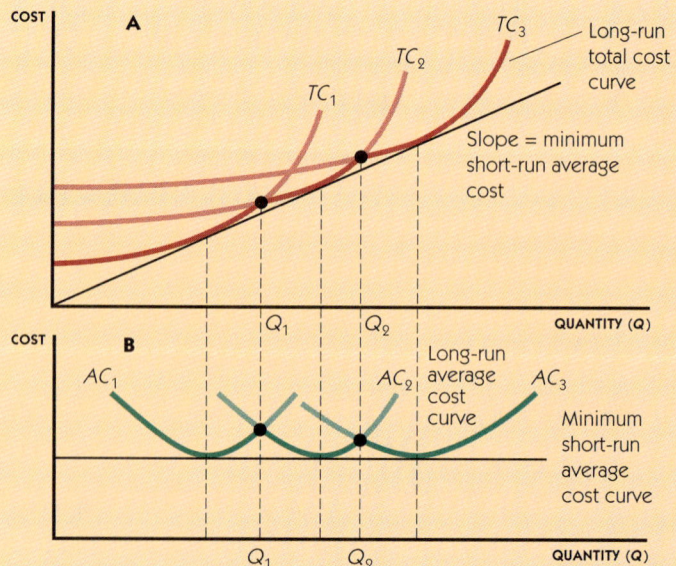

Figure 9.11 SHORT-RUN AND LONG-RUN COST CURVES

Panel A shows a series of short-run total cost curves, TC_1, TC_2, and TC_3, each representing a different level of fixed capital input. In the long run, a cost-minimizing firm can choose any of these, so the long-run total cost curve will be the lowest cost of producing any level of output, as shown by the heavily shaded lower boundary of the curves. Panel B shows a series of short-run average cost curves, AC_1, AC_2, and AC_3, each representing a different level of fixed capital input. In the long run, a cost-minimizing firm can choose any of these, so the long-run average cost curve will be the heavily shaded lower boundary of the curves.

Figure 9.12 THE SHAPE OF THE LONG-RUN AVERAGE COST CURVE

If there are many possibilities for varying the scale of the firm, and thus many short-run average cost curves, the long-run average cost curve defined by their joint boundary can be thought of as very flat, or smooth. In this case, the long-run average cost curve is drawn as horizontal. The firm can increase output simply by replicating identical plants, and there are constant returns to scale.

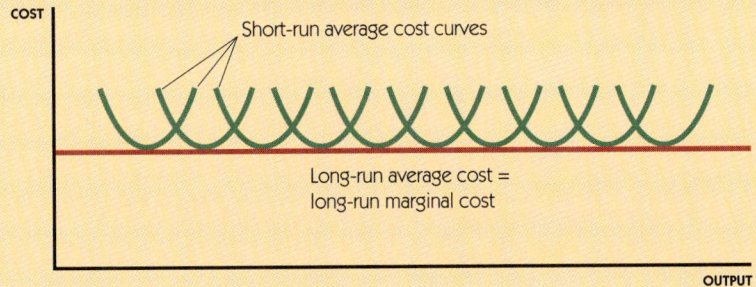

COST

Short-run average cost curves

Long-run average cost = long-run marginal cost

OUTPUT

there are diminishing returns, and the average cost curve is rising. If output increases more than proportionately with the input, there are increasing returns, and the average cost curve is falling.

Exactly the same kind of analysis applies when there are many inputs. We ask, what happens when all of the inputs increase together? If, when all of the inputs increase together and in proportion, output increases just in proportion, there are **constant returns to scale;** if output increases less than proportionately, there are **diminishing returns to scale;** and if output increases more than proportionately, there are **increasing returns to scale,** or **economies of scale.**

Many economists argue that constant returns to scale are prevalent in manufacturing; a firm can increase its production simply by replicating its plants. Then the long-run average and marginal costs equal minimum short-run average costs. The average and marginal cost curves for such a case are depicted in Figure 9.12, where there are many, many plants, and the long-run average cost curve is flat. (The small "bumps" are caused by the fact that output may not be a simple multiple of the output at which a plant attains its minimum average costs; but, as the figure shows, these bumps become relatively insignificant if output is very large.)

There are, however, also costs to establishing a firm—the overhead costs. The firm must bear these costs whether it operates one, two, or a hundred plants. These overhead costs include not only the

costs of the corporate headquarters, but also the basic costs of designing the original plant. Thus, we more commonly think of the long-run average cost curve as slightly downward-sloping, as in Figure 9.13A.

But sometimes small is beautiful and big is bad. In these cases there are diminishing returns to scale. As the firm tries to grow, adding additional plants, it faces increasing managerial problems; it may have to add layer upon layer of management, and each of these layers increases its cost. When the firm is very small, the owner can watch all his workers. When the firm has grown to 10 employees, the owner can no longer supervise his workers effectively; a new supervisor may be needed every time his firm hires 10 more workers. By the time the firm has grown to 100 workers, he has 10 supervisors. Now the owner spends most of his time looking after the supervisors, not the workers directly.

Eventually the owner finds it difficult to keep tabs on the supervisors, so it becomes necessary to hire a manager for them. Notice that in this pattern, the number of supervisors and managers is a growing proportion of the workers in the firm. An organization with 10 workers requires only 1 supervisor; with 100 workers, it requires 10 supervisors and a manager; with 1,000 workers, 100 supervisors, 10 managers, and 1 supermanager. Besides the raw numbers of administrative people, decisions now must pass through a number of layers of bureaucracy, and communication will often be slower. Thus, marginal costs—the additional costs incurred for an increase in output—will

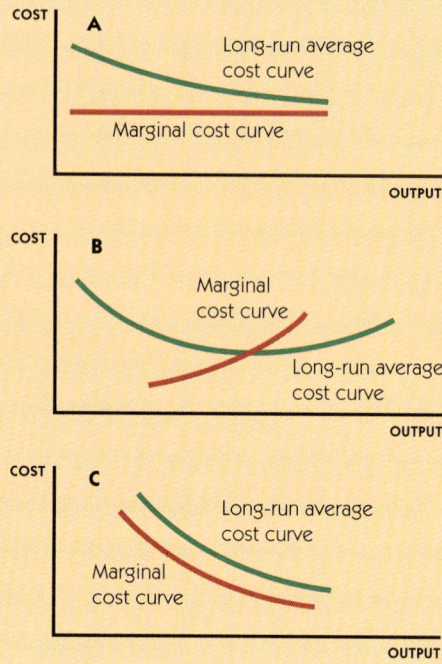

Figure 9.13 LONG-RUN AVERAGE COSTS

Panel A shows that with overhead costs, long-run average costs may be declining, but they flatten out as output increases. In panel B, with managerial costs increasing with the scale of the firm, eventually average and marginal costs may start to rise. Panel C shows that if there are increasing returns to scale, long-run costs may be continuously falling.

rise with output. Eventually, average costs will rise, and we will have a U-shaped long-run average cost curve as illustrated in Figure 9.13B.

Increasing returns to scale are also possible in some industries, even for very large outputs. As the firm produces a higher output, it can take advantage of larger and more efficient machines that it would not pay a small firm to purchase. If there are increasing returns to scale over the relevant range of output, then the long-run average cost curve and the marginal cost curve will be downward-sloping, as in Figure 9.13C.

Whether a particular industry is better described by Figure 9.12, 9.13A, 9.13B, or 9.13C depends upon the importance of overhead costs and returns to scale, and on the extent to which managerial problems grow with size. Economists typically think of the U-shaped long-run average cost curve of Figure 9.13B as the norm, since it encompasses both the scale economies associated with overhead costs and the disadvantages that size eventually implies for the firm. The only issue becomes at what level of output decreasing returns to scale set in. We return to this important question below.

THE PRINCIPLE OF SUBSTITUTION

The analysis of long-run cost curves assumed that the prices of the various factors (e.g., labour and capital) were a given for the firm. What happens if these prices were to change? Two effects of changing factor prices can be identified. The first is that an increase in the price of one or more factors will cause the various cost curves to shift up, both the short-run and long-run curves. This is analogous to what was illustrated in Figure 9.9 earlier.

The second effect applies when the *relative* price of factors of production changes. There are usually several ways a good can be produced in the long run, using different combinations of various inputs.

CLOSE-UP: MINIMUM EFFICIENT SCALE IN CANADIAN MANUFACTURING

How many firms will an industry support? This is an important question to answer because the more firms there are, the more competitive the industry will be. The answer is in part determined by the *minimum efficient scale* (MES) of the typical firm in the industry: the level of output at which the average cost of production is at its minimum. In other words, the MES is the output corresponding to the lowest point on a U-shaped long-run average cost curve, which is the type that economists typically assume applies in competitive industries. Competition forces firms to operate at the MES, assuming the MES is small enough relative to total industry output so that competition actually prevails.

Melvyn Fuss of the University of Toronto and the Indian economist Vinod Gupta have estimated the long-run average cost curves in several Canadian manufacturing industries. As the ac-

companying table shows, the estimates of MES relative to the size of the market differ significantly across industries, from a high of 13.13 percent in the cigarette industry to a low of 1.09 percent in petroleum refining. Also reported are the percentage cost increases of operating a plant that is one half the size of MES. This can be interpreted as a measure of the "steepness" of the shape of the U, reflecting how much of a cost disadvantage firms would face that did not operate at their MES. Again, there is significant variation across industries.

These results would indicate that one might expect different levels of competition across industries. Industries like shoes, petroleum refining, and storage batteries would appear to be able to support significantly more firms than the cigarette and brewery industries.

Industry	MES as a percentage of industry size	Cost disadvantage at one half of MES (%)
Breweries	8.85	4.80
Cigarettes	13.13	2.35
Nonrubber shoes	.07	.01
Steel	7.34	1.62
Storage batteries	3.32	2.46
Cement	4.19	36.60
Glass bottles	6.84	4.53
Petroleum refining	1.09	1.65

Source: M. A. Fuss and V. K. Gupta, "A Cost Function Approach to the Estimation of Minimum Efficient Scale, Returns to Scale, and Suboptimal Capacity: With an Application to Canadian Manufacturing," *European Economic Review* 25 (1981): 123–35.

Which way the firm chooses will depend upon the prices of the factors of production. Figure 9.14 shows the combinations of labour and capital that can be used to produce a given level of output. The point labelled *A* is the least capital-intensive (most labour-

intensive), while *B* is the most capital-intensive (least labour-intensive). Given the prices of labour and capital, the firm will choose the least-cost combination of labour and capital to produce the output. Suppose the firm is currently producing at point *A*, using

USING ECONOMICS: THE PRINCIPLE OF SUBSTITUTION

The table below illustrates two alternative ways of making car frames, one a highly automated process requiring little labour, and the other a less-automated process that uses more assembly-line workers. Each method produces the same quantity of output (say, 10,000 car frames per day). In this simple example, we assume all workers are identical (of equal skill) and hence get paid the same wage whichever process is used. Similarly, we assume all machines cost the same. The table shows the daily wage and capital costs for each process for two situations which differ only in the hourly wage rate.

In the top part of the table, when the wage rate is $5 per worker per hour and the rental cost of machines is $1,000 per day, the less-automated process clearly produces the output at the lower costs. Thus, the firm would choose to use 500 man-hours of labour and only one machine. However, as the bottom part shows, it the wage rate rose to $20 per worker per hour, the firm would find it less costly to produce its output using the more-automated process. The firm would substitute machines for man-hours and use 4 machines along with only 50 man-hours.

COSTS OF PRODUCTION

	Inputs	More-automated process	Less-automated process
Low-wage	Labour	50 man-hours @ $5 = $ 250	500 man-hours @ $5 = $ 2,500
situation	Machines	4 machines @ $1,000 = $4,000	1 machine @ $1,000 = $ 1,000
	Total	$4,250	$ 3,500
High-wage	Labour	50 man-hours @ $20 = $1,000	500 man-hours @ $20 = $10,000
situation	Machines	4 machines @ $1,000 = $4,000	1 machine @ $1,000 = $ 1,000
	Total	$5,000	$11,000

relatively large amounts of labour relative to capital. If the price of labour rises relative to the price of capital, it may pay the firm to switch to point B, substituting machines for men. The firm simply compares the additional cost of purchasing $K_2 - K_1$ more machines against the savings from having $L_1 - L_2$ less labour employed. If the relative price of labour rises by enough, it might pay the firm to become even more capital-intensive by substituting more machines for labour, thus moving to point C.

Although Figure 9.14 provides only three stark alternatives, it should be clear that in some cases the alternative possibilities for production will form a continuum, where the cost of one input increases a bit, the cost of another falls a bit, and output remains the same. In other words, the firm can smoothly

Figure 9.14 THE PRINCIPLE OF SUBSTITUTION

A firm can produce a given level of output using various combinations of inputs, such as those given by points A, B, and C. If the price of labour rises relative to the price of capital, and if the cost of the additional capital is less than the saving in cost of hiring less labour, then it will pay the firm to substitute capital for labour.

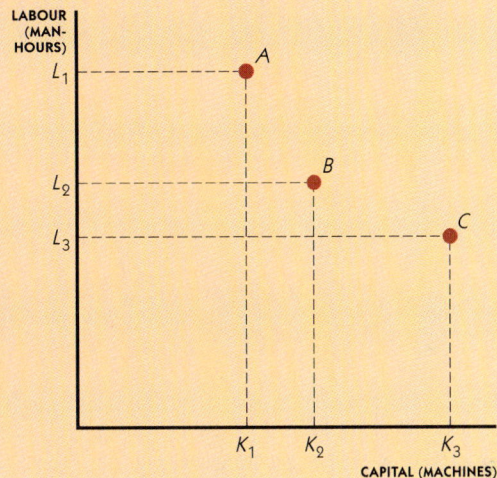

substitute one input for another. For instance, in producing cars, different machines vary slightly in the degree of automation. Machines requiring less and less labour to run them cost more. When firms take their decisions about investment, they thus have a wide range of intermediate choices between those described in the figure.

One of the most important consequences of the principle of cost minimization in the case of multiple factors of production is that when the price of one input (say, oil) increases relative to that of other factors of production, the change in relative prices causes firms to substitute cheaper inputs for the more costly factor. This is an illustration of the general **principle of substitution** we encountered in Chapter 4.

In some cases, substitution is quick and easy; in other cases, it may take time and be difficult. When the price of oil increased fourfold in 1973 and doubled

again in 1979, firms found many ways to economize on the use of oil. For instance, companies switched from oil to gas (and in the case of electric power companies, often to coal) as a source of energy. More energy-efficient cars and trucks were constructed, often using lighter materials like ceramics and plastics. These substitutions took time, but they did eventually occur.

The principle of substitution should serve as a warning to those who think they can raise prices without bearing any consequences. Argentina has almost a world monopoly on linseed oil. At one time, linseed oil was universally used for making high-quality paints. Since there was no competition, Argentina decided that it would raise the price of linseed oil and assumed everyone would have to pay it. But as the price increased, paint manufacturers learned to substitute other natural oils that could do almost as well.

Raising the price of labour (wages) provides

THE PRINCIPLE OF SUBSTITUTION

An increase in the price of an input will lead the firm to substitute other inputs.

CLOSE-UP: ROBOTS IN NORTH AMERICA AND JAPAN

When workers feel threatened by robots, it is the principle of substitution that underlies their fear. Their concern is that the increased productivity of industrial robots will encourage industry to use more of them. They further believe that the declining price of computerized brainpower will hold down the price of robots, reinforcing the shift from human labour to robots. But this fear has not been realized, not even in Japan, where robots have been widely used.

By the end of the 1980s, about two thirds of the world's robots were employed in Japan. The total number of robots in the United States, about 37,000, was roughly equal to the additional number of new robots in Japan in a single year.

A number of possibilities have been cited for why the United States and Canada might lag behind Japan in robot use. Interest rates have tended to be lower in Japan, which means that Japanese businesses are more willing to make investments in robots that may take a decade or more to pan out. North America has been more open to low-skilled immigrant labour than has Japan, which has forced Japanese companies to focus more heavily than their U.S. and Canadian counterparts on ways of conserving human labour.

Many North American companies seem to have started out with very complex robots, which promptly broke down, while Japanese companies began with simple robots and worked towards greater complexity. Businesses found that sophisticated robots were not easy to pro-gramme and keep running. Businesses that redesigned their assembly lines to make it easy for the robots often found that the redesign had made it easier for human workers too. Keith McKee, director of the Manufacturing Productivity Center at the Illinois Institute of Technology, described the overall reaction to robots: "A lot of companies will buy a robot or two and then find that its care and feeding is more difficult than the care and feeding of a man."

Instead of substituting for jobs that people can do, robots have proved to be best of all at jobs that people *cannot* do, for reasons of size or safety. Such jobs include handling radioactive waste in nuclear reactors; mass spray-painting in a closed room where paint is thick in the air; welding with 200-pound machines; handling jobs of infinite repetition, like wrapping or screwing in bolts; or doing tasks that involve very small-scale work, perhaps even microscopic. These are jobs that most people do not mind giving up.

In North America, robots have yet to arrive in a way that could even threaten to displace human labour. In Japan, robots are allowing people to move on to more high paid and flexible tasks. Robots (like many other new inventions) may add to the marginal product of labour, rather than subtracting from it.

Sources: Andrew Tanzer and Ruth Simon, "Why Japan Loves Robots and We Don't," *Forbes,* April 16, 1990, pp. 148–53; Peter T. Kilborn, "Brave New World Seen for Robots Appears Stalled by Quirks and Costs," *New York Times,* July 1, 1990, sec. 1, p. 14.

another example. Unions in the auto and steel industries successfully demanded higher wages for their members during the boom periods of the 1960s and 1970s, and firms paid the higher wages. But at the same time, the firms redoubled their efforts to mechanize their production and to become less dependent on their labour force. Over time, these efforts were successful and led to a decline in employment in those industries.

The overall effect of changes in factor prices on a firm's cost curves depends both on the changes in the average level of factor prices and on changes in relative prices. If all factor prices rise by 5 percent, cost curves will also rise by 5 percent. However, if the average rise in factor prices is 5 percent as a result of the price of labour rising by 8 percent while all other factor prices remain constant, cost curves will rise by less than 5 percent. This is because firms can avoid bearing the full impact of the rise in labour costs by substituting capital for labour.

LOOKING BEYOND THE BASIC MODEL:
COST CURVES AND THE COMPETITIVENESS OF MARKETS

The degree of competition in an industry depends to a considerable degree on the structure of costs in that industry. This leads us to several insights that take us beyond the basic model. Consider the case of one company that is producing all the market wants in an industry with declining long-run average costs. If any new company wishes to enter this market and produce less than the incumbent firm, its average costs will be higher than that of the incumbent company. So long as the original firm produces more than the entrant, its costs will be lower, so it can undercut the newcomer—and in fact charge a price so low that the new firm suffers a loss while the incumbent firm still makes a profit. Indeed, if the original merchant charges a price just equal to his average costs (or threatens to do so if an entrant tries to crash into his market), there is no way that a rival can profitably enter.

If, in contrast, the incumbent firm is the only firm producing for the entire market but is on the upward-sloping portion of a long-run average cost curve, a new company might aim at producing less with a lower average cost. Now, at least one new company will be able to undersell the original firm, and competitive forces will have some power.

The magnitude of the output at which average costs are minimized depends largely on the size of fixed costs relative to the costs that vary with the level of output. In industries in which fixed costs are low there will normally be many firms, since average costs will reach their minimum value at a relatively low level of output. Since the average cost curve may begin to rise quite rapidly beyond a relatively small output, small firms have the power to undersell larger firms, and there will be many firms in the market. Businesses with low fixed costs include real estate and travel agencies. In these industries, the typical firm is small, and there are thousands of them.

In industries in which fixed costs are high, however, the minimum average costs will be attained at a very high output, so there will be relatively few firms. Low-cost producers in these industries tend to be large firms, and relatively few fill the market demand. Makers of automobiles and household appliances are examples. Fixed costs loom large in the chemical industry too, so it is not surprising that many major chemicals are produced by only a few firms. In some industries, fixed costs are so large that average costs are declining throughout the output levels demanded in the market. In these cases, at least within any locality, there will be only one firm. Examples include electricity and other utility companies and transportation facilities. A main cost for most utilities is the cost of the wires for electricity and telephone or pipes for water and sewage.

Expenditures to develop a new product are like high fixed costs in their effect on entry into a market. Of course firms can choose to spend more or less on research or on developing new products, but these costs do not increase with the firm's level of output. It is not surprising, then, that in many of the sectors of the economy in which research and development expenditures are important, there are relatively few firms. For example, the chemical industry is controlled by a small number of firms.

ECONOMIES OF SCOPE

Most firms produce more than one good. Deciding which goods to produce and in what quantities and how to produce them (the first and second basic economic questions) are central problems facing firm managers. The problems would be fairly straightforward, were it not for some important interrelations among the products. The production of one product may affect the costs of producing another.

In some cases, products are produced naturally together; we say they are **joint products.** Thus, a sheep farm naturally produces wool, lamb meat, and mutton. If more lambs are slaughtered for meat, there will be less wool and less mutton.

If it is less expensive to produce a set of goods together than separately, economists say that there are

economies of scope. The concept of economies of scope helps us understand why certain sets of activities are often undertaken by the same firms. Issues of economies of scope have also played an important role in discussions of regulation over the past two decades. For example, Canada Post has a monopoly over first-class mail service, which includes both urban and rural delivery. Some persons have advocated allowing other firms to compete for the delivery of first-class mail. This might result in a selective creaming off of the lower-overhead, large-scale urban market, leaving Canada Post to service the higher-cost routes. Critics argue that this might reduce efficiency by reducing the ability of Canada Post to exploit economies of scope in the provision of both urban and rural mail services. Similar arguments apply to the provision of long distance as opposed to local telephone services by Bell Canada, and to high-volume versus low-volume air and rail transportation services by Air Canada and VIA Rail, respectively.

REVIEW AND PRACTICE

SUMMARY

1 A firm's production function specifies the level of output resulting from any combination of inputs. The increase in output corresponding to an increase in any input is the marginal product of that input.

2 Short-run marginal cost curves are generally upward-sloping, because diminishing returns to a single variable factor of production imply that it will take ever increasing amounts of the input to produce a marginal unit of output.

3 The typical short-run average cost curve is U-shaped. With U-shaped average cost curves, the marginal and average cost curves will intersect at the minimum point of the average cost curve.

4 All profit-maximizing firms choose the method of production that will minimize costs for the level of output they wish to produce, because the lowest costs will allow the highest amount of profit.

5 Economists often distinguish between short-run and long-run cost curves. In the short run, a firm is generally assumed not to be able to change its capital stock. In the long run, it can. Even if short-run average cost curves are U-shaped, long-run average cost curves can take on a variety of shapes. They can, for instance, be flat, continuously declining, or U-shaped.

6 When a number of different inputs can be varied, and the price of one input increases, the change in relative prices of inputs will encourage a firm to substitute relatively less expensive inputs; this is an application of the principle of substitution.

7 Economies of scope exist when it is less expensive to produce two products together than it would be to produce each one separately.

KEY TERMS

profits

total revenues

production function

average product

marginal product

fixed inputs

variable inputs

average productivity

fixed or overhead costs

variable costs

total costs

marginal cost

average costs

average variable costs

constant, diminishing, or increasing returns to scale (economies of scale)

economies of scope

REVIEW QUESTIONS

1 What is a production function? When there is a single (variable) input, why does output normally increase less than in proportion to input? What are the alternative shapes that the relationship between input and output takes? What is the relationship between these shapes and the shape of the cost function?

2 What is meant by these various concepts of cost: total, average, average variable, marginal, and fixed? What are the relationships between these costs? What are short-run and long-run costs? What is the relationship between them?

3 Why are short-run average cost curves frequently U-shaped? With U-shaped average cost curves, what is the relationship between average and marginal costs? If the average cost curve is U-shaped, what does the total cost curve look like?

4 What happens to average, marginal, and total costs when the price of an input rises?

5 What are diminishing, constant, and increasing returns to scale? When might you expect each to occur? What is the relationship between these properties of the production function and the shape of the long-run average and total cost curves?

6 If a firm has a number of variable inputs and the price of one of them rises, will the firm use more or less of this input? Why?

7 What are economies of scope, and how do they affect what a firm chooses to produce?

PROBLEMS

1 Tom and Dick, who own the Tom, Dick, and Hairy Barbershop, need to decide how many barbers to hire. The production function for their barbershop looks like this:

Number of barbers	Haircuts provided per day	Marginal product
0	0	
1	12	
2	36	
3	60	
4	72	
5	80	
6	84	

Calculate the marginal product of hiring additional barbers, and fill in the last column of the table. Over what range is the marginal product of labour increasing? constant? diminishing? Graph the production function. By looking at the graph, you should be able to tell at what point the average productivity of labour is highest. Calculate average productivity at each point to illustrate your answer.

2 The overhead costs of the Tom, Dick, and Hairy Barbershop are $160 per day, and the cost of paying a barber for a day is $80. With this information, and the information in problem #1, make up a table with column headings in this order: Output, Labour required, Total variable cost, Total cost, Marginal cost, Average variable cost, and Average cost. If the price of a haircut is $10 and the shop sells 80 per day, what is the daily profit?

3 Using the information in problems #1 and #2, draw the total cost curve for the Tom, Dick, and Hairy Barbershop on one graph. On a second graph, draw the marginal cost curve, the average cost curve, and the average variable cost curve. Do these curves have the shape you would expect? Do the minimum and average cost curves intersect at the point you expect?

4 Suppose a firm has the choice of two methods of producing: one method entails a fixed cost of $10 and a marginal cost of $2; the other entails a fixed

cost of $20 and a marginal cost of $1. Draw the total and average cost curves for both methods. At what levels of output will the firm use the low fixed cost technology? At what levels of output will it use the high fixed cost technology?

5 A firm produces cars using labour and capital. Assume that the average product of labour—total output divided by the number of workers—has increased in the last few months. Does that mean that workers are working harder? Or that the firm has become more efficient? Explain.

APPENDIX: COST MINIMIZATION WITH MANY INPUTS

This appendix shows how the basic principles of cost minimization can be applied to a firm's choice of the mix of inputs to use in production. To do this, we make use of a set of concepts and tools similar to those presented in the appendix to Chapter 6, in the analysis of how households take decisions about what mix of goods to purchase.

ISOQUANTS

The alternative ways of producing a particular quantity of output can be graphically represented by **isoquants.** The first part of the term comes from the Greek word *iso*, meaning "same," while "quant" is just shorthand for "quantity." Thus, isoquants illustrate the different combinations of inputs that produce the same quantity.

Consider this simple extension of the Using Economics example on page 202. A firm can buy three different kinds of machines, each of which produces car frames. One is a highly mechanized machine that requires very little labour. Another is much less automated and requires considerably more labour. In between is another technique. These represent three different ways of producing the same quantity.

Assume the firm wishes to produce 10,000 car

frames a day. It could do this by using four highly mechanized machines or two of the moderately mechanized machines or one of the nonmechanized machines. The total capital and labour requirements for each of these possibilities are represented in Figure 9.15. The horizontal axis shows the capital requirements, while the vertical axis shows the labour requirements. The labour and capital associated with the highly mechanized production process is shown by point *A*, the moderately mechanized by point *B*, and the unmechanized by point *C*.

If the firm wishes, it can produce half of its output on the highly mechanized machines and half on the moderately mechanized machines. If it chooses this option, its capital requirements will be halfway between the capital that would be required if it used only *A* or only *B*, and its labour requirements will also be halfway between. This halfway-between choice is illustrated by point *X*. By similar logic, the firm can achieve any combination of capital and labour requirements on the straight line joining *A* and *B* by changing the proportion of highly mechanized and moderately mechanized machines. And by changing the proportion of moderately mechanized and low-mechanized machines, it can achieve any combination of capital and labour requirements on the straight line joining *B* and *C*. The curve *ABC* is the isoquant. It gives all those combinations of capital and labour requirements that can produce 10,000 automobile frames per day. All of these input combinations give the same output.

Consider now what happens if many techniques are available instead of only three. The isoquant con-

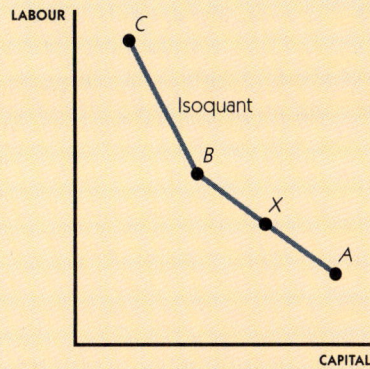

sists of points designating each of the techniques, and the short line segments connecting these points that represent combinations of two techniques, as shown in Figure 9.16A. When many, many production techniques are available, the isoquant looks much like a

smooth curve, and economists often draw it that way, as in panel B.

Many different isoquants can be drawn, each representing one particular level of output, as in panel B. Higher isoquants represent higher levels of produc-

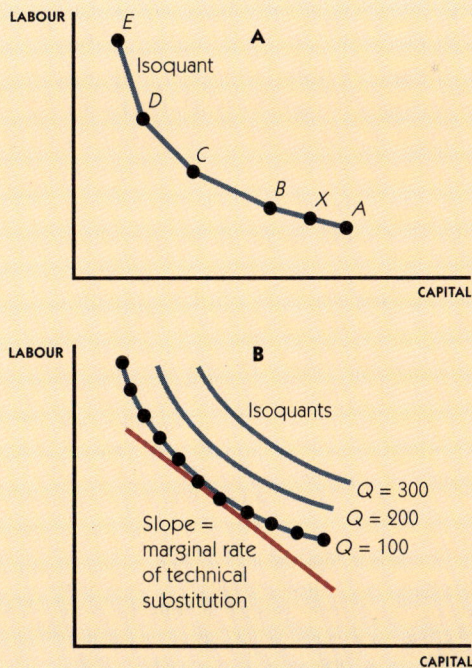

tion; lower isoquants represent lower levels.[4] There is also a simple relationship between the production functions discussed above and isoquants. The production function gives the output corresponding to each level of inputs. The isoquant tells what are the levels of inputs that can yield a given level of output.

MARGINAL RATE OF TECHNICAL SUBSTITUTION

The idea of marginal rate of substitution was introduced in the appendix to Chapter 6 to describe how individuals are willing to trade off less of one good for more of another. The concept is also useful in analyzing what technology firms will choose. In the case of firms, the marginal rate of substitution is defined not by individual preferences but by actual physical facts. If a firm reduces one input by a unit and then raises another input enough so that the final output remains the same, the amount of extra input required is called the **marginal rate of technical substitution.**

An example should help to clarify this idea. If a firm can reduce the amount of capital it uses by one machine, hire two more workers, and produce the same quantity, then it is possible for two workers to replace one machine. In this case, the marginal rate of technical substitution between workers and machines is 2/1. The marginal rate of technical substitution is just the slope of the isoquant, as Figure 9.16B shows diagrammatically: the slope simply tells how much of an increase in labour is needed to offset a one-unit decrease in capital to produce the same amount of output.[5]

Notice that the marginal rate of technical substitu-

tion and the slope of the isoquant change with the quantities of labour and capital involved. With fewer and fewer machines it becomes increasingly difficult to substitute workers for machines. The marginal rate of technical substitution rises, and the slope of the isoquant becomes steeper and steeper. At the other end of the isoquant, with more and more machines it becomes easier and easier to replace one of them. The marginal rate of technical substitution diminishes as the number of workers increases, and the slope of the isoquant becomes flatter. There is a **diminishing marginal rate of technical substitution** in production, just as there was a diminishing marginal rate of substitution in consumption.

The marginal rate of technical substitution can be calculated from the marginal products of labour and capital. If adding one more worker increases the output of automobile frames by one, the marginal product of an extra worker in this industrial process is one. Let us also imagine that adding one machine leads to an increase in car output of, say, two a day. So in this industrial process, the marginal product of a machine is two. In this example, adding two workers and reducing machine input by one leaves output unchanged. Thus, the marginal rate of technical substitution is 2/1. In general, the marginal rate of technical substitution is equal to the ratio of the marginal products.

The principle of diminishing returns explains why the marginal rate of technical substitution diminishes as a firm adds more and more workers. As it adds more workers, the marginal product of an additional worker diminishes. As the number of machines is reduced, the marginal product of an additional machine is increased. When a firm considers the choices along an isoquant where machines are becoming more productive at the margin and workers are becoming less productive at the margin, it becomes increasingly costly to replace machines with additional workers.

Notice that calculating the marginal rate of substitution does not tell the firm whether it *should* substitute workers for machines, or machines for workers. The number itself only provides factual information about what the trade-off would be, based on the technology available to the firm. To decide which combination of inputs should be chosen, the firm must also know the market prices of the various inputs.

---

[4] Readers who have read the Chapter 6 appendix on indifference curves should recognize the similarities between isoquants and indifference curves: while indifference curves give those combinations of goods that yield the individual the same level of utility, the isoquant gives those combinations of goods (inputs) that yield the firm the same level of output.

[5] Again, readers who earlier studied indifference curves will recall that the slope of the indifference curve is also called the marginal rate of substitution; it tells us how much extra of one good is required when consumption of another good is reduced by one unit, if we wish to leave the individual at the same level of welfare—on his indifference curve.

COST MINIMIZATION

Minimizing costs will require marginal decision making. Firms know the technology they are currently using and can consider changing it by trading off some inputs against others. To decide whether such a trade-off will reduce costs, they can simply compare the market price of the input they are reducing with the price of the input they are increasing. If a firm can replace one machine with two workers and maintain the same output, and if a worker costs $12,000 a year and a machine costs $25,000 a year to rent, then by reducing machines by one and hiring two workers, the firm can reduce total costs. On the other hand, if a worker costs $13,000, it would pay to use two fewer workers (for a saving of $26,000) and rent one machine (for a cost of $25,000).

The only time that it would not pay the firm either to increase labour and reduce the number of machines or to decrease labour and increase the number of machines is when the marginal rate of technical substitution is equal to the relative price of the two factors. The reason for this is similar to the reason why individuals set their personal marginal rates of substitution equal to the ratio of market prices. The difference is that the individual's marginal rate of substitution is determined by individual preferences, while the firm's marginal rate of technical substitution is determined by technology.

ISOCOST CURVES

The **isocost** curve gives the combinations of inputs that cost the same amount. The isocost curve is analogous to an individual's budget constraint, which gives the combinations of goods that cost the same amount. If a firm faces fixed prices for its inputs, the isocost curve is a straight line whose slope indicates the relative prices; that is, if each worker costs, say, $50 per day, then if the firm reduces the labour used by one, it could spend $50 per day on renting more machines. If renting a machine for a day costs $100, then the firm can rent one more machine with the amount it would save by reducing the input of labour by two. There are, of course, many isocost lines, one for each level of expenditure. Lower isocost lines represent lower expenditures on inputs. Costs along line $C_1 C_1$ in Figure 9.17 are lower than costs along CC. The different isocost lines are parallel to one another, just as different household budget constraints representing different income levels are parallel.

Notice that all firms facing the same prices for inputs will have the same isocost lines. Similarly, different individuals with the same income face the same budget constraint, even when their preferences differ. However, the isoquant curves that describe each firm are based on the product the firm is making and the technology and knowledge available to the firm. Thus, isoquant curves will differ from firm to firm.

Isoquant curves and isocost lines can illuminate

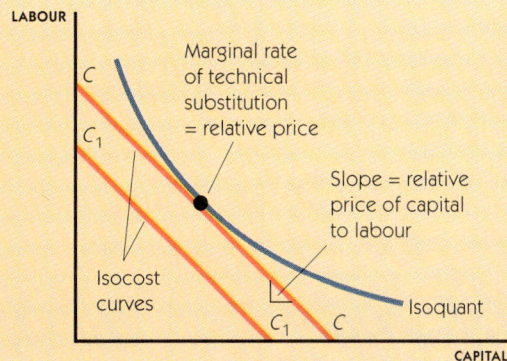

Figure 9.17 COST MINIMIZATION

Cost-minimizing firms will wish to produce as much output as they can given a particular level of expenditure, so they will choose the highest isoquant they can reach with a given isocost curve, which will be the isoquant tangent to the isocost curve.

the behaviour of a cost-minimizing firm. For example, any efficient profit-maximizing firm will wish to maximize the output it obtains from any given expenditure. Or to rephrase the same point, the firm must reach the highest possible isoquant, given a particular level of expenditure on inputs, represented by a particular isocost line. The highest possible isoquant will touch the isocost line at a single point; the two curves will be tangent.

The problem of cost minimization can be described in a different way. Consider a firm that has a desired level of output and wishes to minimize its cost. The firm chooses an isoquant, and then tries to find the point on the isoquant that is on the lowest possible isocost line. Again, the cost-minimizing firm will choose the point of tangency between the isocost line and the isoquant.

At the point of tangency, the slopes of the two curves are the same. The slope of the isoquant is the marginal rate of substitution. The slope of the isocost line is the relative price. Thus, *the marginal rate of technical substitution must equal the relative price.*

APPLYING THE DIAGRAMMATIC ANALYSIS

The isoquant/isocost diagram can be used to show how a change in relative prices affects the optimal mix of inputs. A change in relative prices changes the isocost line. In Figure 9.18, an increase in the wage makes the isocost curves flatter. CC is the original isocost curve that minimizes the costs of producing output Q_0 (that is, CC is tangent to the isoquant Q_0).

C_1C_1 is the isocost line with the new higher wages that is tangent to the original isoquant. Obviously, to produce the same level of output will cost more if wages are increased. The figure also shows what this change in relative prices in the form of higher wages does to the cost-minimizing combination of inputs: as one would expect, the firm substitutes away from labour towards capital, from point E_0 to E_1.

Of course, the magnitude of the substitution will differ from industry to industry, depending on an industry's isoquant. In addition, substitution is likely to be much greater in the long run than in the short run, as machines wear out, firms look for ways to conserve on the more expensive inputs, and so on. The figure represents these different possibilities for substitution. In panel A, the possibilities for substitution are very limited. The isoquant is quite "curved." This figure might illustrate a case where it is very difficult to substitute (at least in the short run) machines for labour—illustrated, perhaps, by the use of blast furnaces in producing steel. In panel B, substitution is very easy; the isoquant is quite flat. This would illustrate an opposite case; for example, given the increased possibilities for automation afforded by modern technology, substituting machines for labour is often relatively easy for a firm.

DERIVING COST CURVES

The cost curves in this chapter represent the minimum cost of producing each level of output, at a particular level of input prices. Figure 9.19A shows the

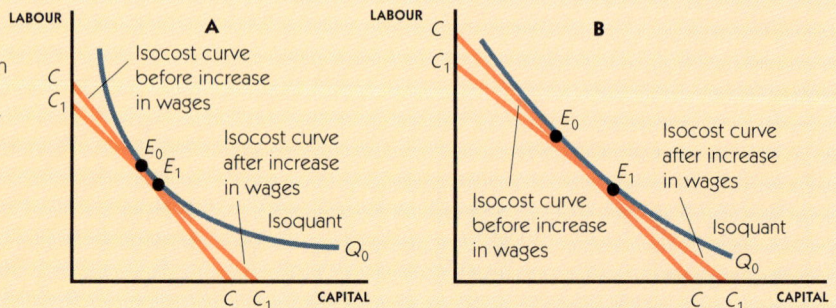

Figure 9.18 CHANGING FACTOR PRICES

This firm has chosen the level of production associated with the isoquant shown, and the cost-minimizing combination of labour and capital for producing that amount is originally at E_0. But as wages rise, relative prices shift, and the cost-minimizing method of producing the given amount becomes E_1. In panel A, an increase in wages leads to little substitution. But in panel B, an increase in wages leads to a much larger amount of substitution.

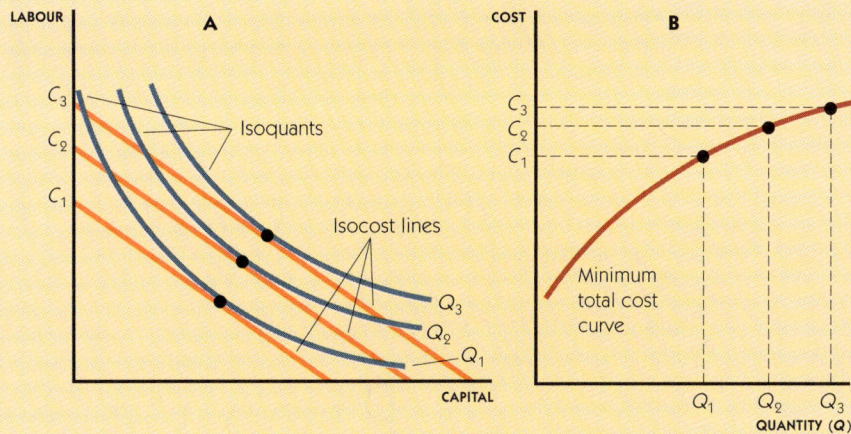

Figure 9.19 **DERIVING THE TOTAL COST CURVE**

The total cost curve describes how total cost changes at different levels of output. Panel A shows three isoquants representing different levels of output, and three isocost curves tangent to those isoquants, representing the least-cost way of producing each of these amounts. Panel B plots the actual level of costs for each of these levels of output, producing the familiar total cost curve.

cost-minimizing way of producing three different levels of output, Q_1, Q_2, and Q_3. Panel B then plots the actual level of costs associated with each of these levels of output. That is, the isocost curves tangent to the isoquants in panel A show the minimum level of costs associated with each output. Tracing out the costs associated with each level of output provides the total cost curve. And once we have the total cost curve, we know how to derive the marginal cost curve (the slope of the total cost curve) and the average cost curve (the slope of a line from the origin to the total cost curve).

10

PRODUCTION IN A COMPETITIVE INDUSTRY

C hapter 9 defined profits as the difference between revenues and costs. In this chapter we consider how firms maximize their profits by balancing the extra benefit from producing one more unit, hiring one more worker, or buying one more machine with the extra costs. We have already learned the basic tools for assessing the extra costs. In this chapter we learn how to calculate the extra benefits and examine how firms weigh extra costs against these extra benefits. This balancing process dictates the profit-maximizing firm's production decision.

This chapter rounds out the discussion of markets because, in taking their production decisions, firms provide the final ingredients for a complete model of the economy. With all the ingredients in hand—the basic economic decisions of individuals and households to maximize satisfaction, and the basic economic decisions of firms seeking to maximize profits—we will be able to construct a complete model of the economy in Chapter 11.

KEY QUESTIONS

1 What determines the level of output a firm will supply at any given price? In other words, how do we derive the firm's supply curve?

2 What determines whether or when a firm will enter or exit a market?

3 How do the answers to these questions enable us to analyze the market supply curve as to why it is upward-

sloping and why it may be more elastic than the supply curve of any single firm?

4 How do we reconcile economists' view that competition drives profits to zero with accountants' reports showing that most of the time most firms earn positive profits?

5 What determines firms' demand for inputs, such as labour or capital? Why is firms' demand curve for labour downward-sloping?

REVENUE

Consider the hypothetical example of the High Strung Violin Company, manufacturers of world-class violins. The company hires labour; it buys wood, utilities, and other materials; and it rents a building and machines. Its violins sell for $40,000 each. Last year the company sold seven of them, for a gross revenue of $280,000. Table 10.1 gives a snapshot of the firm's fi-

nancial health, its **profit-and-loss statement** for last year.

We see that High Strung's revenues were $280,000 and its costs were $180,000, so its profits were $100,000. If its costs had been $400,000 instead of $180,000, its profits would have been −$120,000. The firm would have made a negative profit, or a **loss.**

The relationship between revenue and output is shown by the **revenue curve** in Figure 10.1A. The horizontal axis measures the firm's output, and the vertical axis measures the revenues. Revenues are simply price times quantity sold (pQ). When the price of a violin is $40,000 and the firm sells nine violins its revenue is $360,000; when it sells ten, revenue rises to $400,000.

The revenue the firm receives per unit of output is its **average revenue.** It is revenue divided by output. Since revenue is price times quantity sold (pQ), average revenue is the price (pQ/Q). The extra revenue that a firm receives from selling an extra unit is called its **marginal revenue.** Thus, $40,000 is the extra (or marginal) revenue from selling the tenth violin. It is no accident that the marginal revenue, like average revenue, equals the price of the violin. A fundamental feature of competitive markets is that firms receive the same market price for each unit they sell. Thus, the extra revenue that firms in competitive markets receive from selling one more unit—the marginal revenue—is the same as the price of the unit. The average and marginal revenue curve is shown in Figure 10.1B. It is simply a horizontal line at the given price.

Table 10.1 PROFIT-AND-LOSS STATEMENT FOR THE HIGH STRUNG VIOLIN COMPANY

Gross revenues		$280,000
Costs		$180,000
Wages (including fringe benefits)	$150,000	
Purchases of wood and other materials	$ 20,000	
Utilities	$ 1,000	
Rent of building	$ 5,000	
Rent of machinery	$ 2,000	
Miscellaneous expenses	$ 2,000	
Profits		$100,000

Figure 10.1 THE REVENUE CURVE

The revenue curve in panel A shows a firm's revenues at each level of output. For the firm in a competitive industry, price does not change as more is produced, so the revenue curve is a straight line with a constant slope. Both average and marginal revenue equal the price. In this example, the average and marginal revenue of each additional violin is always $40,000 (panel B).

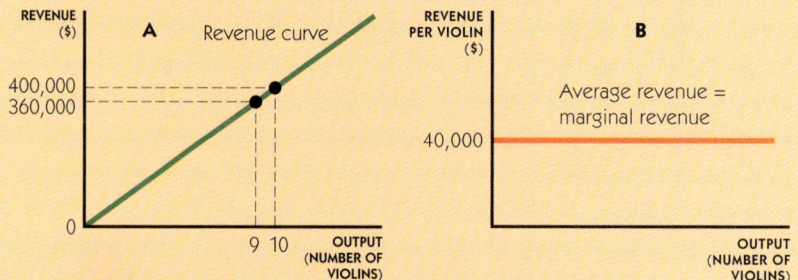

COSTS

High Strung incurs costs corresponding to each level of output. Total costs are given in column 1 of Table 10.2 and depicted diagrammatically in Figure 10.2A. Panel B shows the corresponding average and marginal costs. High Strung's average cost curve exhibits the typical U-shape that we associate with manufacturing firms.

Even before it builds its first violin, the company must spend $90,000. Space must be rented. Some employees will have to be hired. Equipment must be purchased. No matter how many or how few violins High Strung produces, its fixed costs will remain $90,000.

The *extra* cost of producing an additional violin, the marginal cost, is shown in column 3. Marginal cost is always associated with the additional cost of producing a *particular* unit of output. The marginal cost of increasing production from one to two violins, for example, is $10,000. Each additional violin costs $10,000 more until production reaches six violins. The extra (or marginal) cost of producing the seventh violin is $30,000. The marginal cost of producing the eighth violin is $40,000.

The High Strung Violin Company's average costs initially decline as its production increases, since the fixed costs can be divided among more units of production. But between six and seven violins average costs begin to increase, as the effect of the increasing average variable costs dominates the effect of the fixed costs.

BASIC CONDITIONS OF COMPETITIVE SUPPLY

In choosing how much to produce, a profit-maximizing firm will focus its decision at the margin. Having incurred the fixed cost of getting into this market, the decision is generally not the stark one of whether or not to produce, but whether to produce one more unit of a good or one less. For a profit-maximizing firm, the answer to this problem is relatively simple: the company simply compares the marginal revenue it will receive by producing an extra unit—which in the case of a price-taking (competitive) firm is just the price of the good—with the extra cost of producing that unit, the marginal cost. As long as the marginal revenue exceeds the marginal cost, the firm will make additional profit by producing more. If marginal revenue is less than marginal cost, then producing an extra unit will cut profits, and the firm will reduce production. In short, the firm will produce to the point where the

Table 10.2 HIGH STRUNG VIOLIN COMPANY'S COSTS OF PRODUCTION (in thousands of dollars)

Output	(1) Total cost	(2) Average cost	(3) Marginal cost	(4) Total variable cost	(5) Average variable cost
0	90				
			10		
1	100	100		10	10
			10		
2	110	55		20	10
			10		
3	120	40		30	10
			10		
4	130	32.5		40	10
			10		
5	140	28		50	10
			10		
6	150	25		60	10
			30		
7	180	25.72		90	12.72
			40		
8	220	27.5		130	16.25
			50		
9	270	30		180	20
			130		
10	400	40		310	31

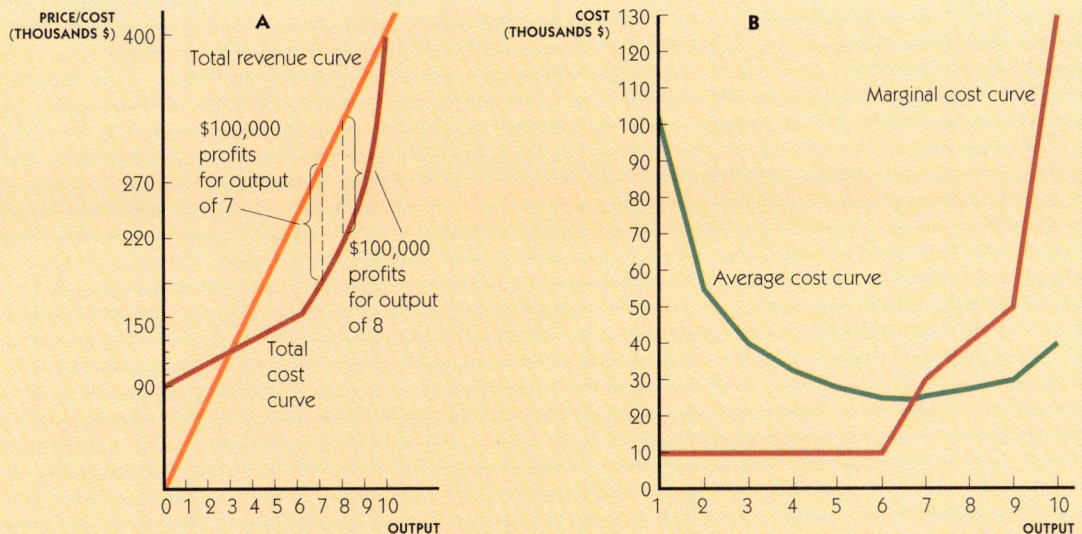

Figure 10.2 RELATING REVENUES AND COSTS

The firm's revenue and total cost curves can be drawn on the same graph, as in panel A. When total revenue exceeds total costs, the firm is making profits at that level of output. Profits, the difference between revenues and costs, are measured by the distance between the two curves; in this case, the highest level of profit is being made at a production level of 7 or 8. When total costs exceed total revenue, the firm is making losses at that level of output. When the two lines cross, the firm is making zero profits. The marginal and average cost curves for this company have their expected shape in panel B. Marginal costs are constant until a production level of 6, and then they begin to increase. The average cost curve is U-shaped.

marginal cost equals marginal revenue, which in a competitive market is equal to price.

The profit-maximizing level of output, where price equals marginal cost, can be seen in panel A of Figure 10.3, which shows the marginal cost curve for a firm facing increasing marginal costs. The firm produces up to the point where price (which equals marginal revenue) equals marginal cost. If it produces more than that, the extra cost will be more than the revenue received. The figure shows how much output the firm will produce at each price. At the price p_1, it will produce the output Q_1. At the price p_2, it will produce the output Q_2. With an upward-sloping marginal cost curve, it is clear that the firm will produce more as price increases.

The marginal cost curve is upward-sloping, just as the supply curves in Chapter 4 were upward-sloping. This too is no accident: a firm's marginal cost curve is actually the same as its supply curve. The marginal cost curve shows the additional cost of producing one more unit at different levels of output. A competitive firm chooses to produce at the level of output where the cost of producing an additional unit (the marginal cost) is equal to the market price. We can thus read from the marginal cost curve what the firm's supply will be at any price: it will be the quantity of output at which marginal cost equals that price. Figure 10.2A shows total revenues as well as total costs. We can see that profits—the gap between revenues and costs—are maximized at an output of either seven or eight. If the price were just slightly lower than $40,000, profits would be maximized at seven, and if the price were just slightly higher than $40,000, profits would be maximized at eight.

The profit-maximizing level of output can also be seen in panel B of Figure 10.3, which shows the total revenue and total cost curves. Profits are the difference between revenues and costs. In panel B, profits are the distance between the revenue curve and the cost curve. The profit-maximizing firm will choose the output where that distance is greatest. This occurs at Q_1. Below Q_1, price (the slope of the revenue curve) exceeds marginal costs (the slope of the total cost curve) so profits increase as output increases; above Q_1 price is less than marginal cost, so profits decrease as output increases.

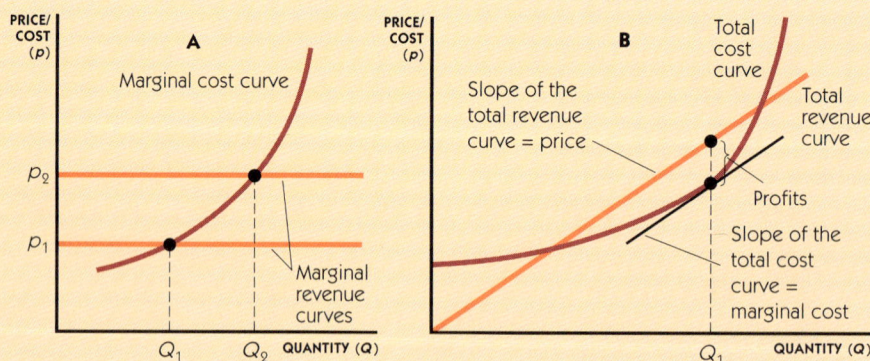

Figure 10.3 **THE PROFIT-MAXIMIZING LEVEL OF OUTPUT**

A competitive firm maximizes profits by setting output at the point where price (marginal revenue) equals marginal cost. In panel A, at the price of p_1, this quantity is Q_1. Panel B shows total revenue and total costs. Profits are maximized when the distance between the two curves is maximized, which is the point where the two lines are parallel (and thus have the same slope).

EQUILIBRIUM OUTPUT FOR COMPETITIVE FIRMS

In competitive markets, firms produce at the level where price equals marginal cost. A competitive firm's marginal cost curve is its supply curve.

ENTRY, EXIT, AND MARKET SUPPLY

We are now in a position to tackle the market supply curve. To do so, we need to know a little more about each firm's decision to produce. First let's consider a firm that is currently not producing. Under what circumstances should it incur the fixed costs of entering the industry? This is a relatively easy problem: the company simply looks at the average cost curve and the price. *If price exceeds minimum average costs, it pays the firm to enter.* This is because if it enters, it can sell the goods for more than the cost of producing them, thus making a profit.

Figure 10.4A shows the U-shaped average cost curve. Minimum average cost is c_{min}. If the price is less than c_{min}, then there is no level of output at which the firm could produce and make a profit. If the price is above c_{min}, then the firm will produce at the level of output at which price (p) equals marginal cost, Q^*. At Q^*, marginal cost exceeds average costs. (This is always true at output levels greater than that at which average costs are minimum.) Profit per unit is the difference between price and average costs. Total profits are the product of profit per unit and the level of output; the shaded area in the figure.

Different companies may have different average cost curves. Some will have better management. Some will have a better location. Accordingly, firms will differ in their minimum average cost. As prices rise, additional firms will find it attractive to enter the market. Figure 10.4B shows the U-shaped average cost curves for three different firms. Firm 1's minimum average cost is AC_1, Firm 2's minimum average cost is AC_2, and Firm 3's minimum average cost is AC_3. Thus, Firm 1 enters at the price p_1, Firm 2 at the price p_2, and Firm 3 at the price p_3.

Figure 10.4 COST CURVES, PROFITS, AND ENTRY

Panel A shows that if price is above the minimum of the average cost curve, profits will exist. Profits are measured by the area formed by the shaded rectangle, the profit per unit (price minus average cost, corresponding to the distance AB) times the output, Q^*. Panel B shows average cost curves for three different firms. At price p_1, only one firm will enter the market. As price rises to p_2 and then to p_3, first the firm whose cost curve is AC_2 and then the firm whose cost curve is AC_3 will enter the market.

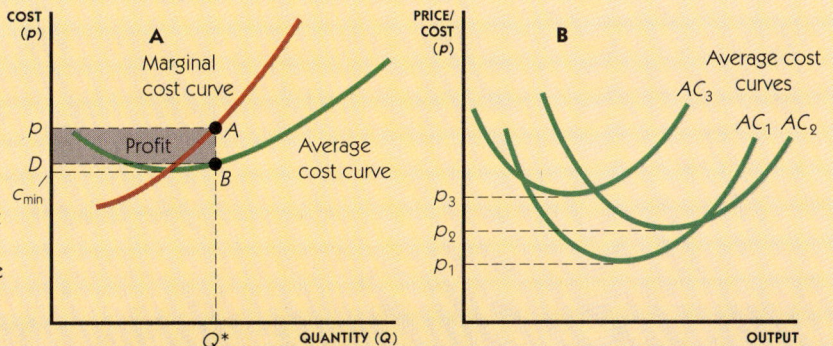

USING ECONOMICS: ENTERING THE PAINTING BUSINESS

Housepainting is a summer business, for days that are hot and long, and with available low-skilled labour on vacation from high school and university. As a way of picking up some cash, Michael decided to start Presto Painters during the summer after taking introductory economics.

Just getting started involves some substantial fixed costs. Michael ran the business out of his parents' home so he had no costs for office space. His fixed costs ended up looking like this:

Fixed costs	
Used van	$5,000
Paint and supplies	$2,000
Flyers and signs	$1,200
Business cards and estimate sheets	$ 500
Phone line and answering machine	$ 300
Total	$9,000

Michael went to work drumming up business. He took calls from potential customers and knocked on doors, made estimates of what he thought it would cost to paint someone's home, and then offered them a price. Of course, he was in direct competition with many other painters and had to meet the competition's price to get a job.

Michael found that the going rate for labour was $10 per hour. In the real world, labour is not the only variable input required for housepainting. There are also costs from buying additional paint and brushes, but for the sake of simplicity, let's assume that he started off the summer with all the paint he needed. Thus, his variable costs were related to the labour he needed to hire.

Variable costs are also related to the amount of time it takes to paint a house, which varies depending on the quality of the labour you can find. The variable costs for Presto Painters were as follows:

Houses painted	Hours of labour hired	Payroll cost
5	100	$ 1,000
10	300	$ 3,000
15	600	$ 6,000
20	1,000	$10,000
25	1,500	$15,000
30	2,100	$21,000

Given this information, Michael could calculate cost curves for Presto Painters (see table on next page).

On the basis of his marginal and average cost curves, Michael figured that if market conditions allowed him to charge $1,000 or more for a typical house, then he could make a profit by painting at least 25 houses. Roughly speaking, that is how his summer worked out: painting 25 houses for $1,000 apiece. Thus, he earned $1,000 in profits.

Or so he thought. Nowhere in this list of costs did Michael consider the opportunity cost of his time. He was not getting paid $10 an hour for painting houses; he was out there stirring up business, hiring and organizing workers, taking calls from customers, dealing with complaints.

Imagine that Michael had an alternate job possibility waiting on tables. He could earn $6 per hour (including tips) and work 40-hour weeks during a 12-week summer vacation. Thus, he could have earned $2,880 during the summer with little stress or risk. If this opportunity cost is added to the fixed costs of running the business, then his apparent profit turns into a loss. Since Presto Painters did not cover Michael's op-portunity cost and compensate him for the risk and aggravation of running his own business, he would have been financially better off sticking to the business of filling people's stomachs rather than painting their houses.

Number of homes	Total cost	Average cost	Marginal cost (per house)
0	$ 9,000		
			$2,000
5	$10,000	$2,000	
			$ 400
10	$12,000	$1,200	
			$ 600
15	$15,000	$1,000	
			$ 800
20	$19,000	$ 950	
			$1,000
25	$24,000	$ 960	
			$1,200
30	$30,000	$1,000	

SUNK COSTS AND EXIT

The converse of the decision of a firm to enter the market is the decision of a firm already producing to exit the market. However, the entry and exit decisions may not be symmetric because of the possibility that some of the firm's costs may be sunk. **Sunk costs** are costs that are not recoverable, even if a firm goes out of business. For example, the High Strung Violin Company may have had an extensive television advertising campaign. The cost of this campaign is a sunk cost. There is no way this expenditure can be recouped if production ceases. If there were no sunk costs the decision to enter and the decision to exit would be mirror images of each other. Firms would exit the market when their average costs rose above the price. But if some costs remain even if a firm stops producing, the question facing that firm is whether it can recover some of these costs by continuing to produce.

Let us assume for simplicity that fixed costs are always sunk costs. A firm with no fixed costs has an average cost curve that is the same as its average vari-able cost curve. It will shut down as soon as the price falls below minimum average costs—the cost at the bottom of its U-shaped cost curve. But a firm *with* fixed costs has a different decision to make. Figure 10.5A depicts both the average variable cost curve and the average cost curve for such a case. As in the case with no sunk costs, the firm shuts down when price is below minimum average *variable* costs (costs that vary with the level of output), p_1. But if the price is *between* average variable costs and average costs, the firm will continue to produce, even though it will show a loss. It continues to produce because it would show an even bigger loss if it ceased operating. Since price exceeds average variable costs, the revenues it obtains exceed the additional costs it incurs from producing. (Later in the chapter we will discuss the case when fixed costs are not necessarily all sunk costs.)

Different firms in an industry will have different average variable costs, and so will find it desirable to exit the market at different prices. Figure 10.5B shows the average variable cost curves for three different firms. Their cost curves differ; for instance, some

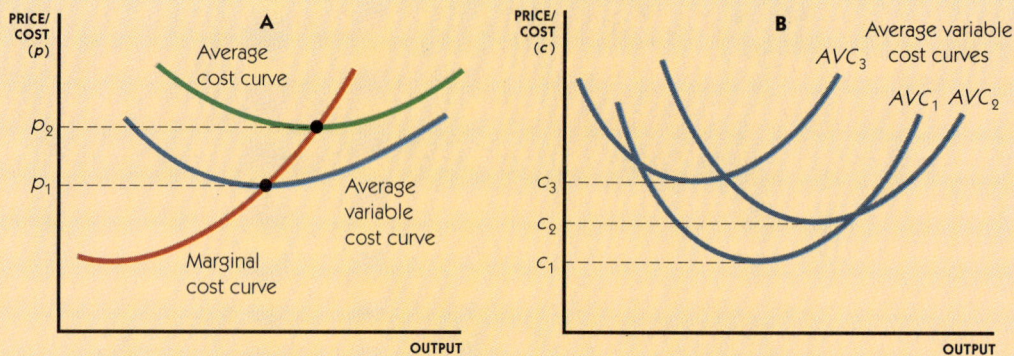

Figure 10.5 AVERAGE VARIABLE COSTS AND THE DECISION TO PRODUCE

Panel A illustrates that in the short run, firms will produce as long as price exceeds average variable costs. Panel B shows that firms with different average variable cost curves will decide to shut down at different price levels. As price falls below c_3, the minimum average variable cost for Firm 3, Firm 3 shuts down; as price falls still lower, below c_2, Firm 2 shuts down. Finally, when price falls below c_1, Firm 1 shuts down.

may have newer equipment than others. As the price falls, the firm with the highest minimum average variable costs finds it is no longer able to make money at the going price, and decides not to operate. Thus, Firm 3 (represented by the curve AVC_3) shuts down as soon as the price falls below c_3, Firm 2 shuts down as soon as the price falls below c_2, and Firm 1 shuts down as soon as the price falls below c_1.

THE FIRM'S SUPPLY CURVE

We can now draw the firm's supply curve. As Figure 10.6A shows, for a firm contemplating entering the market, supply is zero up to a critical price, equal to the minimum average cost. Thus, for prices below $p = c_{\min}$, the firm produces zero output. For prices greater than $c_{\min}$, the firm produces up to the point where price equals marginal cost, so the firm's supply curve coincides with the marginal cost curve. For a firm that has incurred sunk costs of entering the market (panel B), the supply curve coincides with the marginal cost curve so long as price exceeds the minimum value of average *variable* costs; when price is

below the minimum value of average variable costs, the firm exits, so supply is again zero.

THE MARKET SUPPLY CURVE

With this information about the cost curves of individual firms, we can derive the overall market supply curve. Back in Chapter 4, the market supply curve was defined as the sum of the amounts that each firm was willing to supply at any given price. Figure 10.7 provides a graphical description of the supply curve for a market with two firms. If the price rises, the firms already in the market (Firms 1 and 2) will find it profitable to increase their output and new firms (with higher average variable cost curves) will find it profitable to enter the market. Because higher prices induce more firms to enter a competitive market, the market supply response to an increase in price is greater than if the number of firms were fixed. In the same way, as price falls there are two market responses. The firms that still find it profitable to produce at the lower price will produce less, and the higher cost firms will exit the market.

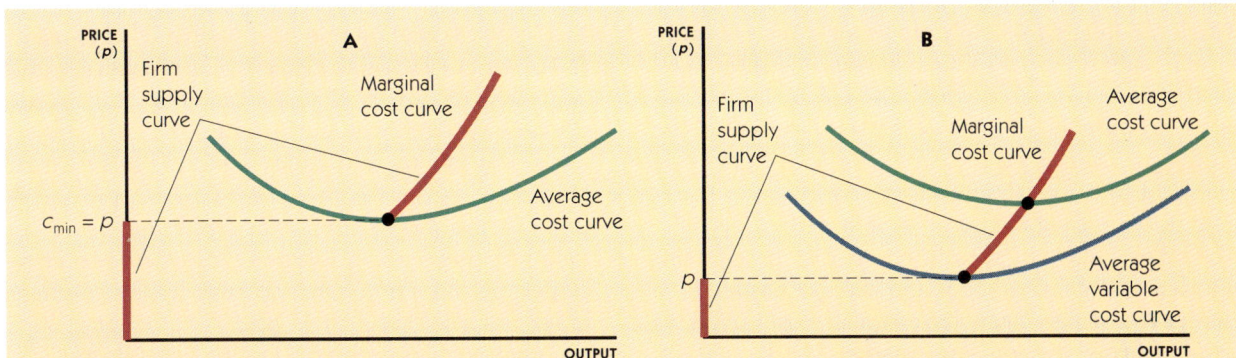

Figure 10.6 **THE SUPPLY CURVE FOR A FIRM**

Panel A shows that for a firm contemplating entering the market, supply is zero up to a critical price, equal to the firm's minimum average cost, after which the firm's supply curve coincides with the marginal cost curve. Panel B shows a firm that has already entered the market, incurring positive sunk, fixed costs; this firm will produce as long as price exceeds the minimum of the average variable cost curve.

Figure 10.7 **THE MARKET SUPPLY CURVE**

The market supply curve is derived by horizontally adding up the supply curves for each of the firms. As price rises, each firm produces more and new firms enter the market.

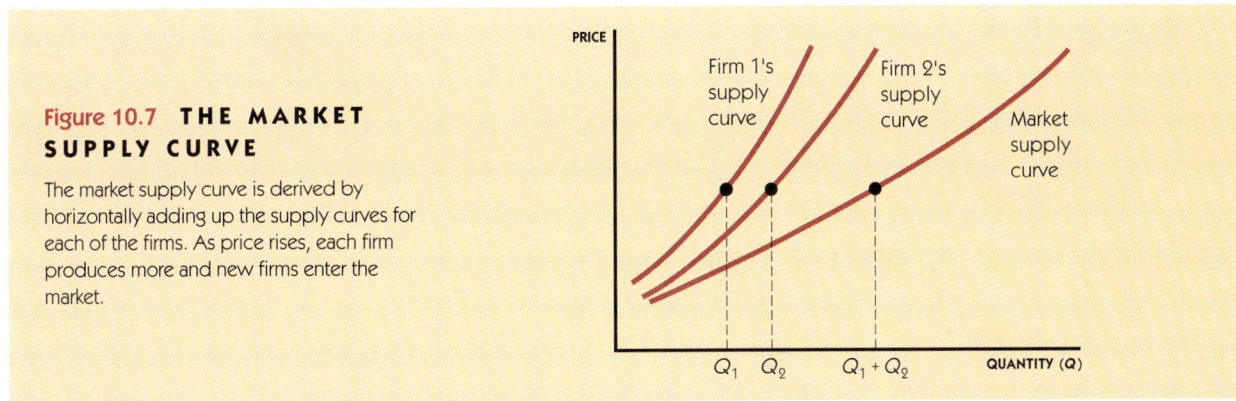

LONG-RUN VERSUS SHORT-RUN SUPPLY

As we saw in Chapter 9, in the short run the typical firm will have a U-shaped average cost curve, and a sharply rising marginal cost curve at output levels above the lowest point of the U. But its long-run average costs, and therefore marginal costs, are flatter. This is because adjustments to changes in market conditions take time, and some adjustments take longer than others. In the short run you can add workers, work more shifts, run the machines harder (or reduce the rate at which these things are done), but you are probably stuck with your existing plant and equipment. In the long run you can acquire more buildings and more machines (or sell them). Thus, the long-run supply curve for a firm is more elastic (flatter) than the short-run supply curve.

The same is true, only more so, for the industry— again because the number of firms is not fixed in the long run. Even if each firm can operate only one plant, the industry's output can be increased by 5 percent by increasing the number of firms by 5 percent. The extra costs of increasing output by 5 percent are approximately the same as the average costs of the new firms. If new firms have similar cost curves as existing firms, the long-run market supply curve is approximately horizontal. Under these conditions, even if the demand curve for the product shifts drastically, the market will supply much more of the product at pretty much the same price, as additional plants are constructed and additional firms enter the market. Of course, if new firms have higher average costs than existing firms, the long-run industry supply curve will slope upwards, though not as steeply as individual firms' supply curves.

Thus, the market supply curve is much more elas-tic in the long run than in the short run. Indeed, in the very short run, a firm may find it impossible to hire more skilled labour or to increase its capacity. Its supply curve, and the market supply curve, would be nearly vertical. In what was called the short run in Chapter 9, machines and the number of firms are fixed, but labour and other inputs can be varied. Figure 10.8A shows the short-run supply curve. Contrast the short-run market supply curve with the long-run market supply curve. The short-run curve slopes up much more sharply. A shift in the demand curve has a larger effect on price and a smaller effect on quantity than it does in the long run. In the long run, the market supply curve may be horizontal. In this case, shifts in the demand curve have an effect *only* on quantity, as in panel B. Price remains at the level of minimum average costs; competition leads to entry to the point where there are zero profits for all firms.

Again, it is worth asking, "How long is the long run?" That depends on the industry. For an electric power company to change its capacity takes years. For most other firms, buildings and equipment can

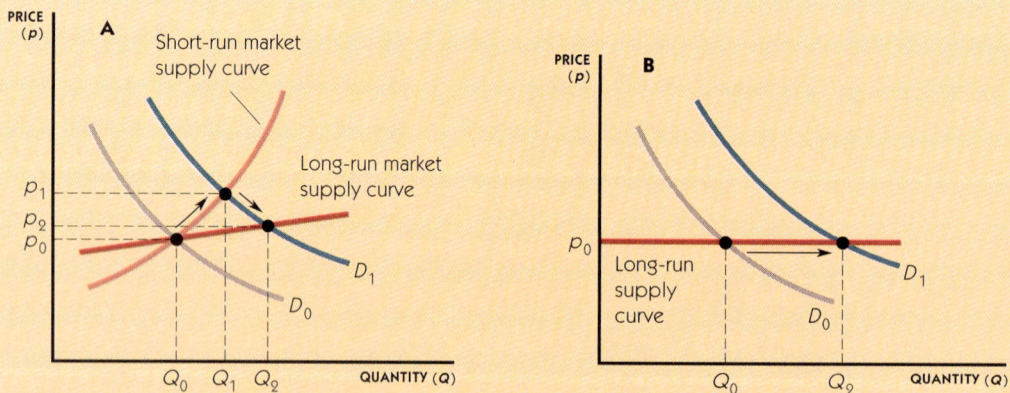

Figure 10.8 MARKET EQUILIBRIUM IN THE SHORT RUN AND LONG RUN

In panel A, the market equilibrium is originally at a price p_0 and an output Q_0. In the short run, a shift in the demand curve from D_0 to D_1 raises the price to p_1 and quantity to Q_1. In the long run, the supply elasticity is greater, so the increase in price is smaller—price is only p_2—and quantity is greater, Q_2. If supply is perfectly elastic in the long run, as shown in panel B, shifts in demand will only change the quantity produced in the long run, not the market price.

ADJUSTMENTS IN THE SHORT RUN AND THE LONG RUN

In the very short run, firms may be unable to adjust production at all; only the price changes.

In the short run, firms may be able to hire more labour and adjust other variable inputs.

In the long run, firms may be able to buy more machines, and firms may decide to enter or to exit.

The times required for these adjustments may vary from industry to industry.

be added, if not within months, certainly within a year or two. Recent improvements in technology, like computer-aided design and manufacturing, have made it possible for many companies to change what they are producing more rapidly, and thus have reduced the length of the long run and made supply curves more elastic than in the past.

EQUILIBRIUM IN THE COMPETITIVE INDUSTRY

For a competitive industry to be in equilibrium, we require that each firm be in equilibrium and that the industry as a whole be in equilibrium. The latter requires not only that demand equal supply but also that the market price be such that no firms will want

to enter or exit the industry. Figure 10.9 depicts a competitive industry in full equilibrium. Panel A shows the marginal firm. At the industry equilibrium price p^*, the marginal firm produces an output of Q_m and just earns zero profits. It produces where price equals marginal cost at the minimum point on its average cost curve. Panel B shows the equilibrium price being determined by the equating of supply and demand at the industry output level Q^*. (Note that the two panels use a different scale for measuring output; in fact, Q_m is much smaller than Q^*.) The demand curve is, of course, the market demand curve. The supply curve is the sum of the supply curves of all firms in the industry, as in Figure 10.8. The industry supply curve is shown as sloping upwards, indicating that whereas the marginal firm produces output at an average cost of p^*, the infra-marginal firms are willing to produce output at

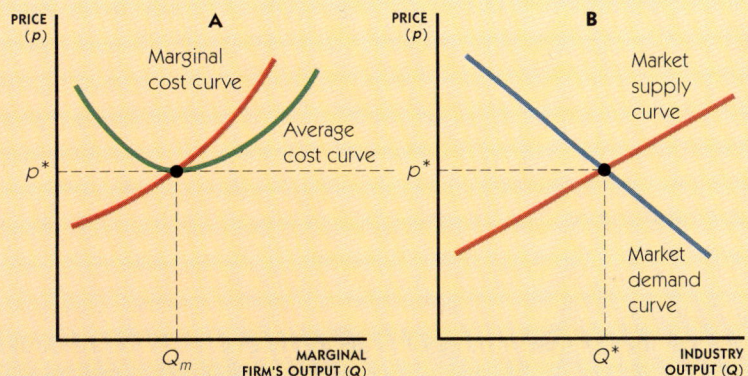

Figure 10.9 EQUILIBRIUM IN THE COMPETITIVE INDUSTRY

In industry equilibrium, the marginal firm will be making zero profits as shown in panel A. The industry price p^* will be determined by the equating of industry demand and supply as in panel B.

lower costs. Thus, in the industry equilibrium these firms will earn a profit. If all firms faced the same cost conditions, the industry supply curve would be horizontal at a price equal to the minimum point on the common average cost curve. That is, industry supply would be infinitely elastic.

Some features of market supply in a competitive industry are worth noting. The first is that whatever the output produced, it will be produced by the most efficient (least cost firms). That is because for any given market price, higher cost firms will not enter the market. Another is that since all firms face the same price, all will be producing at the same marginal cost. This implies that the industry as a whole is producing at least cost, since total industry costs cannot be reduced by reallocating production from one firm to another. To put it another way, if the marginal cost of production differed across firms in an industry, the total cost of producing the same output could be reduced by increasing the output of the firm with a lower marginal cost and reducing that of a firm with a higher marginal cost. Competition automatically ensures that this happens.

Finally, with free entry into an industry, firms will tend to enter until the profit of the last firm to enter is zero. The lowest cost, or inframarginal, firms will all be making positive profits reflecting their cost advantage.

LOOKING BEYOND THE BASIC MODEL: SUNK COSTS, ENTRY, AND COMPETITION

The degree of competition envisioned in the basic competitive model requires a large number of firms that vie with one another to sell a product. Competition among these firms drives the market price down to a level where there are no profits for the entering firms.

Even without a large number of firms in the market, the predictions of the basic competitive model may still hold. Here is where the distinction between *fixed* and *sunk* costs becomes important. Fixed costs are costs that are incurred regardless of the scale of production of the firm. A building is a fixed cost in this sense. But if a company ceases to operate, it can resell the building and might well recover its cost. The cost of the building in this case, though fixed, is not sunk. Now take the case of a company that not only bought a building but spent a lot of money commissioning a logo, which it then mounted conspicuously on its building. If this firm went out of business it could recover the cost of its building but *not* its logo. Who wants the secondhand logo of a bankrupt company? Advertising expenditures are typically sunk costs. Expenditures on assets that can readily be put to other uses—buildings and cars—are for the most part not sunk.

The theory of **contestable markets** predicts that even in a market with only one firm, that firm will make zero profits, just as in a market with many firms, *if* sunk costs are low. The threat that other firms will enter is sufficient to deter the single firm from raising its price beyond average cost. This result holds even in the presence of high fixed costs, so long as those fixed costs consist of buildings, cars, airplanes, and other assets that can easily be sold. A firm entering the industry has little to lose, since it can always reverse its decision and recover its investment.

But when the assets include major ones with no alternative use—such as a nuclear power plant—then the fixed costs become sunk costs, and the threat of competition diminishes. The firm that would otherwise have entered the market might now worry that if it enters, competition will get fierce. And the firm would be right to worry, as high sunk costs will make all firms reluctant to exit. If competition is fierce enough, the price might even drop below average costs, and still the firm's rivals may not leave. With prices below average costs, the new firm will not be able to get a return on its investment. Until it enters the market, the firm has an advantage: it has not taken on the sunk costs. Given the scenario just described, it may very well avert its gaze from the lure of the higher market prices, knowing they are like a mirage. The profits will disappear if the new firm tries to grab them by entering the market, but will remain for the limited number of firms already in the market if they can keep the would-be newcomer out. Thus, markets with high sunk costs may be able to sustain high profits without much fear of entry—a clear departure from the basic competitive model.

When large firms are in danger of failing, invariably there are calls for government to bail them out in order to protect jobs. Governments have often heeded this call. Perhaps the most famous example occurred in the early 1980s when the United States government made low-interest loans to Chrysler in order to prevent it from being forced to file for bankruptcy. A recent Canadian example involved the Nova Scotia steel producer Sydney Steel Corporation (Sysco). Sysco had for several years been functionally bankrupt. It continued to operate only because it received an estimated $2 billion in subsidies from the federal and provincial governments. By 1994, now owned by the provincial government, Sysco had shrunk from employing thousands of workers in the late 1960s to employing fewer than 500. Then a deal was struck to sell the firm to a Chinese government–led consortium, Minmetals. This episode was hailed by the Nova Scotia government as a successful example of a government bailout that saved jobs by preventing the complete failure of Sysco.

But one must ask what would have happened if Sysco had been left on its own. In fact, many firms go bankrupt, but the plants of these bankrupt firms often do not shut down. Instead, either they are taken over by other owners and kept in business, or creditors find a way to ease the financial burden on existing owners so that the firm can stay in business. Why is it that firms in difficulty often manage either to renegotiate their debt payments with creditors or find a willing buyer for their capital assets? If the firm could not make a profit, why are creditors so willing to give them a second chance—or, alternatively, why are the new owners so sure they can make a go of it?

This seeming paradox is really nothing of the kind. The answers to the above questions lie in understanding the difference between bankruptcy, a condition in which the revenue a firm receives for its output does not cover all of its costs (including sunk costs like the repayment of previously incurred debt), and the shutdown point for a firm, a situation in which the price is such that the firm cannot cover its ongoing (variable) costs. Many firms in difficulty can cover their variable costs but cannot cover, say, debt obligations that were accumulated in the past. Such firms should not shut down, even though they are facing long-run bankruptcy. Provided the output price is such that the firm is beyond the shutdown point, if the original firm can reschedule its debt so as to lower its per-period capital costs, or if a new owner can purchase the capital at a price below the old firm's book value, then a firm may again be viable. Creditors may be willing to take a lower return than agreed to originally, because the alternative is to scrap the capital for next to nothing. And a potential new owner may see long-run profit opportunities, given that he can purchase the capital at a discount.

Let's return to the case of the Sysco bailout. The government subsidized the company for many years while it was reorganized and downsized. Ultimately Minmetals was able to purchase the capital assets of the company for $30 million plus the repayment of the $15 million for capital improvements, considerably less than the original book value. The deal allowed the new owner not only to cover the short-run variable costs but the reduced capital costs as well, probably rendering the plant viable again in the long run. Most likely this would have happened had the government not intervened. The only difference is that because the government paid the subsidies and assumed the old debts , taxpayers bore the loss in value of the capital assets instead of the original owners and debt holders.

Sources: "How Ottawa's Millions Fail Cape Breton," *The Globe and Mail,* August 19, 1995, pp. A1 and A6; "'Privatized Sysco Will Likely Turn Profit,' says Boudreau," *The Halifax Chronicle-Herald,* August 19, 1995, p. A1.

ACCOUNTING PROFITS AND ECONOMIC PROFITS

We have learned in previous chapters that firms maximize profits, but now it appears that with competition, for entering firms profits are driven to zero. If all firms in an industry have similar cost curves, as might reasonably be the case in many manufacturing and service industries, all firms in the industry would have zero profits. To most people this seems like a contradiction: if profits were truly zero, why would firms ever produce? How do we reconcile the conclusion that competition drives profits to zero with the fact that, throughout the economy, firms regularly report making profits?

The answer is that accountants think about profits differently than economists do. To an accountant, the profits of a firm represent the return that the firm generates for the owners or shareholders of the firm. It provides useful information to the shareholders to allow them to determine how well the resources that they put into the firm are being used. To an economist, the profits of a firm represent the amount by which the revenues of the firm exceed the full opportunity costs of all resources used in the firm, including those of the firm's owners. The opportunity costs include more than just the costs incurred by the owners in using inputs that have been purchased from others.

To begin to see how opportunity costs affect the economist's view of profits, consider a small firm in which the owner has invested $100,000. Assume the owner receives a small salary and devotes sixty hours a week to running the enterprise. An economist would argue that the owner ought to calculate his full opportunity costs in relation to his investment of time and money in the business. The first is the best wage available to him if he worked sixty hours a week at an alternate job. His second opportunity cost is the return that the $100,000 invested in this enterprise would produce in another investment. These are the true costs of the owner's time and capital investment. To calculate profits of the firm as the economist sees them, these opportunity costs have to be subtracted out.

The accountant will not include as costs either the forgone return on the $100,000 that the owner has put into the firm (the forgone return on the equity capital of the firm) or the full opportunity cost of the owner's time. Thus, accounting costs will be lower than economic costs and therefore accounting profits will be higher. Indeed, accounting profits can be interpreted as the reward that the owner gets for the time and money she puts into the firm. Because she pays it to herself out of profits, it is not considered to be a cost on the accountant's books.

One can easily imagine a business whose accountant reports a profit equal to 3 percent of the capital investment. An economist would note that if the investment capital had been put in a bank account, it would have earned at least 5 percent. Thus, the economist would say the business is making a loss. Failure to take into account opportunity costs means that reported profits often overstate true economic profits.

Taking opportunity costs into account is not always a simple matter even for purchased inputs because they include alternative uses of a firm's resources. For example, managerial time spent in expanding the firm in one direction might have been spent in controlling costs or expanding the firm in another direction. Land that is used for a golf course for the firm's employees might have been used for some other purpose that could have saved more than enough money to buy golf club memberships for all who want them.

In taking decisions about resources like these, firms must constantly ask what price the resources might fetch in other uses.

Sometimes market data can provide appropriate prices for calculating opportunity costs. For example, the opportunity cost of giving huge offices to top executives can be gauged by the money those offices would bring if they were rented to some other company. But often the calculation is more difficult: for example, how can a company measure the opportunity cost of the vice president who cannot be fired and will not retire for five years?

What about the costs associated with an expenditure already made on, say, a building that is no longer really needed by the firm? The relevant opportunity cost of this building is not the original purchase or lease price but, instead, the value of the building in alternate uses, such as the rent that could be earned if the building were rented to other firms.

The fundamental point is that you cannot use past expenditures to calculate opportunity costs. Consider an automaker that has purchased a parcel of land for $1 million per hectare. It turns out, however, that the company made a mistake and the land is worth only $100,000 per hectare. The firm now must choose between two different plants for producing new cars, one of which uses much more land than the other. In figuring opportunity costs, should the land be valued at the purchase price of $1 million per hectare, or what it could be sold for—$100,000 per hectare? The answer can make a difference between whether or not the firm chooses to conserve on land. From an economics viewpoint, the answer to this valuation problem should be obvious: the firm should evaluate costs according to the *current* opportunity costs. The fact that the company made a mistake in purchasing the land should be irrelevant for the current decision.

Individuals and firms frequently do compound their economic errors, however, by continuing to focus on past expenditures. Business executives who were originally responsible for taking a bad decision may be particularly reluctant to let bygones be bygones. To do so, for example by publicly announcing that the correct market price of land would have been $100,000 per hectare, would be equivalent to announcing that a mistake had been made. Acknowledging such a mistake could jeopardize a business executive's future with the firm.

ECONOMIC RENT

We saw earlier that a firm is willing to produce at a price equal to its minimum average cost. Some firms might be more efficient than others, so their average cost curves are lower. Consider a market in which all firms except one have the same average cost curve, and the market price corresponds to the minimum average cost of these firms. The remaining firm is superefficient, so its average costs are far below those of the other firms. The company would have been willing to produce at a lower price, at its minimum average cost. What it receives in excess of what is required to induce it to enter the market is an **economic rent**—returns on its superior capabilities.

In some industries, including many manufacturing and service industries, rents are likely to be quite small. Most firms should have access to similar techniques of production. In other industries, rents can be quite large. The most obvious examples are in the resource industries, like agriculture, mining, and petroleum. In these industries, one of the inputs into production is a natural resource (land, minerals, oil and gas). Different firms will have access to differing qualities of natural resources. Those with higher-

---

ACCOUNTANTS' VERSUS ECONOMISTS' PROFITS

Accounting profits: Revenues minus expenditures

Economic profits: Revenue minus economic costs (including all opportunity costs of labour and capital)

quality natural resources will have lower costs of production. Their cost advantages are a reflection of the different rents of their resources.

Although economic rent has far broader applications than its historic use to refer to payments made by farmers to their landlords for the use of their land, the example of rent for land use is still instructive. The critical characteristic of land in this regard is that its supply is inelastic. Higher payments for land (higher rents) will not elicit a greater supply. Even if landlords received virtually nothing for their land, the same land would be available. Many other factors of production have the same inelastic character. Even if you doubled his salary, Wayne Gretzky would not "produce" more goals for the New York Rangers. The extra payments for this kind of rare talent fall into the economist's definition of rent. Anyone who is in the position to receive economic rents is fortunate indeed, because these "rents" are unrelated to effort. They are payments determined entirely by demand.

In some cases supplies of inputs are inelastic in the short run but elastic in the long run. An example is payment for the use of a building. In the short run the supply of buildings does not depend on the return, and hence payments for the use of a building are rents, in the economist's sense. But in the long run the supply of buildings does depend on the return—investors will not construct new buildings unless they receive a return equal to what they could obtain elsewhere. So the "rent" received by the building's owner is not really a rent, in the sense in which economists use the term.[1]

Natural resources have always played an important part in the development of the Canadian economy, and the rents accruing to them have been the source of many policy initiatives as well as political disputes. Rents on natural resources are defined in the same way as rents on any other factor that is inelasticly supplied: they are the value of the resources over and above the effort needed to exploit them. In other words, they are nature's gift to the economy. Natural resources are typically costly to use, and one must be careful when defining natural resource rents

to deduct from the value of the resource in use the full costs of using them.

It is useful to distinguish between two sorts of resources, nonrenewable and renewable. **Nonrenewable resources** are those that are ultimately fixed in supply and include such things as oil, natural gas, and minerals. The costs of making nonrenewable resources usable include the costs of finding them (exploration costs), extracting them (drilling and mining), and purifying and processing them. The rent from a given deposit will be the value of the usable resource less all of the above costs. Different deposits will have different rents, since they will have different costs of recovery. Deep mines with relatively impure ore deposits located long distances from markets will be more costly than those that are shallower, purer, and closer by. Indeed, if the mining industry is competitive, the marginal mine (i.e., the one that is the least profitable) will have no rents. It will be the inframarginal mines that earn the rents. Because nonrenewable resources are ultimately fixed in supply, one might expect that aggregate rents would fall over time as the better deposits are used up. As the resource becomes scarcer and more expensive, lower-quality mines become profitable to operate. In addition to having higher operating costs, these mines might be more dangerous to operate. Witness the Westray coal mine in Nova Scotia in which mine gases exploded in 1992, causing the death of 35 miners. As well, recycling becomes a more viable option.

Renewable resources are those that have a capacity to regenerate themselves as they are used, typically through a natural or biological growth process. Examples of these types of resources include marine fisheries, forests, and water. The regeneration process is often a relatively complicated and delicate one in which the ability to regenerate depends upon stock of resource maintained. Thus, the growth of fish stocks will depend upon the stock of fish in a given fishery. The lower the stock, the less fish will grow to replace those that die off or are taken out for commercial reasons. There will likely be a minimum stock below which the fishery is unable to generate enough replacement fish to maintain the given stocks. In this case, continued fishing could lead to complete extinction of the stock.

The rent on nonrenewable resources is again defined to be the value of the resources net of the costs of obtaining them. In the case of the fishery these

---

[1] Economists sometimes use the term "quasi-rents" to describe payments for the use of buildings or other factors that are inelastically supplied in the short run, but elastically supplied in the long run.

costs includes not only the labour, capital, and material costs incurred by the persons doing the fishing, but also the opportunity costs imposed on the fishery itself of reducing the stock; each additional fish taken makes it a bit more difficult for others to extract fish.

Similar principles apply to other renewable resources. The costs of logging include both the costs incurred directly in cutting the trees and the opportunity cost involved in reducing the stock of trees. There may also be significant environmental costs of logging to be taken into account. The same applies to the use of water, whether for consumption or for commercial use, such as irrigation or hydroelectricity. The size of rents obtained from renewable resources depends upon how intensively they are used. As the level of fishing increases, revenues rise, but the fish stocks fall, so fewer are regenerated, making it more costly to catch fish. There will be an optimal size of catch at which the difference between revenues and costs are maximized. If overfishing occurs, rents will fall. If there is enough overfishing, the stock itself may be in danger of disappearing altogether.

FACTOR DEMAND

In the process of deciding how much of each good to supply and what is the lowest cost method of producing those goods, firms also decide how much of various inputs they will use. This is called **factor demand.** It is sometimes called a derived demand, because it flows from other decisions the profit-maximizing firm takes. In Chapter 9 the analysis of cost was broken up into two cases, one in which there was a single variable input, or factor of production, and one in which there were several. We proceed along similar lines here. Labour is used as our main example of an input. The same principles apply to any factor of production.

FACTOR DEMAND WITH ONE VARIABLE FACTOR

When there is only a single factor of production, say, labour, then the decision about how much to produce is the same as the decision about how much labour to hire. As soon as we know the price of the good, we can calculate the supply (output) from the marginal cost curve; and as soon as we know the output the firm plans to produce, we know the labour required, simply by looking at the production function, which gives the output for any level of input of labour or, equivalently, the labour required for any level of output. Thus, in Figure 10.10 at the price p_1, the output is Q_1 (panel A), and the labour required to produce that output (factor demand) is L_1 (panel B).

There is another way of deriving the demand for a factor. If a firm hires one more worker, the extra cost is the wage, w. The extra revenue generated by the worker is the price of the good times the extra output. As we saw in Chapter 9, the extra output corresponding to the extra worker is the marginal prod-

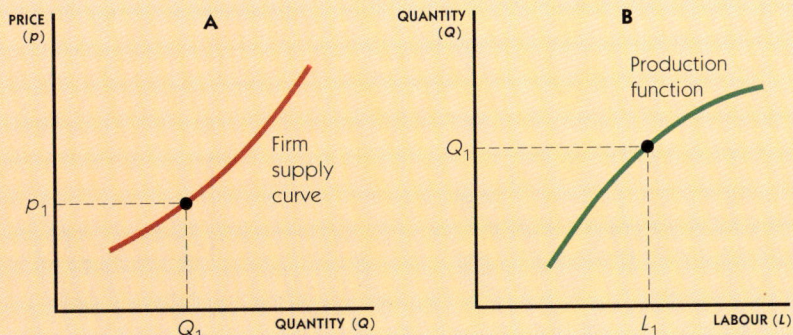

Figure 10.10 THE DEMAND FOR LABOUR

The demand for labour can be calculated from the firm's supply curve and the production function. Panel A shows how the firm, given a market price p_1, chooses a level of output Q_1 from its supply curve. Panel B shows how the firm, given the level of output Q_1 it has chosen, then chooses a level of labour L_1 to demand from its production function.

FACTOR DEMAND

A factor of production will be demanded up to the point where the value of the marginal product of that factor equals the price.

uct of labour. The price of the good thus produced times the marginal product of labour is referred to as the **value of the marginal product of labour.** If the value of the marginal product of labour exceeds the wage, hiring one more worker would increase the firm's revenues more than it would increase its costs; the firm would want to hire. Conversely, if the wage exceeds the value of the marginal product of labour, the firm would increase its profits by reducing its labour force. The firm will hire labour just to the point where the wage rate equals the value of the marginal product of labour.

Using p for the price of the good, MPL for the marginal product of labour, and w for the wage of the worker, we can write this equilibrium condition as

value of marginal product of labour $= p \times MPL = w =$ wage.

From this equilibrium condition we can derive the demand curve for labour. Figure 10.11 plots the value of the marginal product of labour for each level of labour. Since the marginal product of labour decreases as labour increases, the value of the marginal product of labour decreases. When the wage is w_1, the value of the marginal product of labour equals the wage with a level of labour at L_1. This is the demand for labour at a wage w_1. When the wage is w_2, the value of the marginal product of labour equals the wage with a level of labour at L_2. This is the demand for labour at a wage w_2. Thus, the curve giving the value of the marginal product of labour at each wage *is* the demand curve for labour.

It is easy to use this diagram to see the effect of an increase in the price of the good or service the firm produces. In Figure 10.12, the higher price increases the value of the marginal product of labour at each level of employment, and it immediately follows that at each wage, the demand for labour increases; the demand curve for labour shifts to the right. Thus, the demand for labour depends on both the wage and the price the firm receives for the goods it sells.

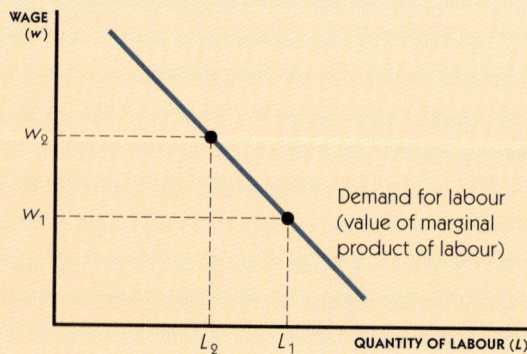

Figure 10.11 THE DEMAND CURVE FOR LABOUR

The value of the marginal product of labour declines with the level of employment. Since labour is hired up to the point where the wage equals the value of the marginal product, at wage w_1, employment is L_1, and at wage w_2, employment is L_2. The demand curve for labour thus traces out the values of the marginal product of labour at different levels of employment.

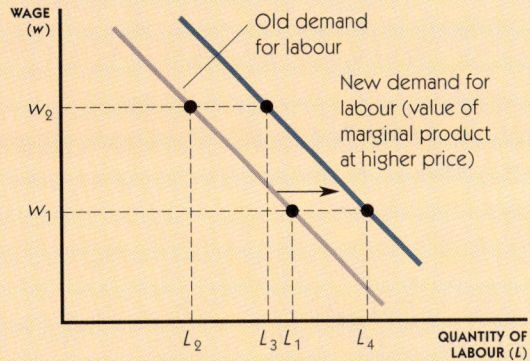

Figure 10.12 EFFECT OF PRICE CHANGE ON THE DEMAND CURVE FOR LABOUR

An increase in the price received by a firm shifts the value of the marginal product of labour curve up, so that at each wage, the demand for labour is increased. At wage w_1, employment rises from L_1, to L_4; at wage w_2, employment rises from L_2 to L_3.

FROM THE FIRM'S FACTOR DEMAND TO THE MARKET'S FACTOR DEMAND

Once we have derived the firm's demand curve for labour, we can derive the total market demand for labour. At a given set of prices, we simply add up the demand for labour by each firm at any particular wage rate. The total is the market demand at that wage rate. Since each firm reduces the amount of labour that it demands as the wage increases, the market demand curve is downward-sloping. Figure 10.13 shows how we add up diagrammatically the demand curves for labour for two firms, the High Strung Violin Company and Max's Fine Tunes Violin Company. At a wage of w_1, High Strung demands 30 workers and Max's Fine Tunes demands 30 workers, for a total demand of 60 workers. At a wage of w_2, High Strung demands 20 workers and Max's demands 10 workers, for a total demand of 30 workers.

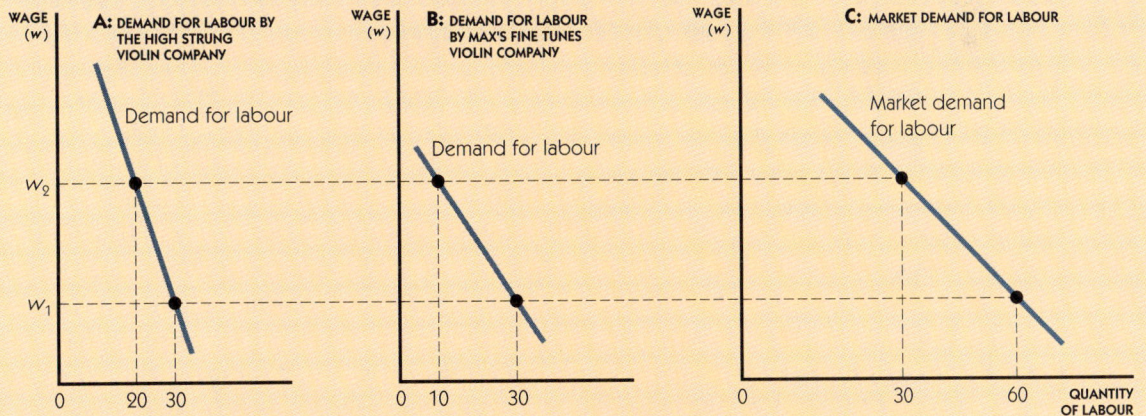

Figure 10.13 THE MARKET DEMAND CURVE FOR LABOUR

The market demand curve for labour at each wage is obtained by horizontally adding up the demand curves for labour of each individual firm. As the wage rises, at a fixed price of output, less labour is demanded.

CLOSE-UP: FACTOR ELASTICITIES ON THE FARM

In agriculture as in other industries, production depends not only on the price of farm products but also on the prices of basic inputs like durable equipment, real estate, hired labour, and materials such as energy and grains. The impact of an increase in the price of an input on its use depends both on the importance of the input and on the ability to reduce the amount needed by substituting other inputs for it. Some inputs may be harder to conserve on than others. For example, when the price of labour rises, it may be possible to reduce costs by adopting more capital-intensive means of production. On the other hand, some inputs such as fuel or veterinary services, may be essential and difficult to economize on.

Theodore Horbulyk of the University of Calgary has recently studied how activity on cattle farms in western Canada responds to changes in the prices of outputs (cattle and crops) and some key inputs, including farm machinery, supplies and services (hired labour, maintenance, utilities) and animal services (purchased feed, veterinary supplies, replacement animals). Changes in these input prices might have very different effects on cattle output. For example, one would not expect an increase in costs for supplies and services to affect the production of cattle as much as the same increase in the price of large, expensive capital equipment.

The accompanying table presents the elasticity relationships among outputs and inputs in the western Canadian cattle industry. The first column shows how cattle sales are affected by changes in the price of cattle, the expected price of cattle (the value of cattle held as inventory), crop prices, machinery prices, supplies and services prices, and animal services prices. For example, a 10 percent increase in the price

of supplies and services leads to a 2.15 percent decrease in cattle sales, as production in the industry declines.

The diagonal elements in the table are the *own price elasticities* of supply and demand: the proportionate change in output supply or input demand as the output's or input's own price increases. Notice that the percentage change in cattle sold is almost twice the percentage change in its own price. On the other hand, an increase in machinery prices causes a large drop in machinery purchased and used.

The off-diagonal elements in the table are cross-price elasticities of demand or supply. They show the proportionate change in the demand for one input as the price of another input or output rises. The table shows that cattle and crops are complements: a higher price of cattle causes cattle farmers to grow more crops and a higher price of crops causes farmers to produce more cattle. This is to be expected, given that some of the crops are used to feed the farmer's own animals.

If two inputs are substitutes, their cross-price elasticity is positive, so that a rise in the price of one will lead to increased usage of the other. For instance, a rise in the price of animal services causes an increase in grains crops. This might reflect that a higher price for purchased feed induces farmers to substitute away from this and grow their own cattle feed. More common in the table are inputs with negative cross-price elasticities; an increase in the price of an input leads to declines in the use of complementary inputs. When the price of machinery rises, total cattle production falls, so grain crops, machinery and supplies and services requirements are all lowered.

Some of the elasticity measures provide valuable economic intuition about cattle farming. Notice the two very high elasticities in the second column of the table. The value −25.789 reflects the fact that inventories of cattle on the farm are greatly reduced when cattle prices are high.

Younger cattle that would have been sold next year are sold early because of high prices. The value 30.725 suggests that farmers are willing to hold back sales of cattle this year and build up inventory if next year's prices are expected to be high.

ELASTICITY WITH RESPECT TO INPUT AND OUTPUT PRICES

| | Outputs | | | Inputs | | |
	Cattle sales	Inventory change	Crops	Machinery	Supplies & services	Animal services
P1	1.998	−25.789	.106	4.012	1.017	−2.758
P2	−2.268	30.725	.106	.202	.201	.089
P3	.086	.987	.151	1.074	.831	−.096
P4	−1.299	−.744	−.425	−17.504	−.546	3.81
P5	−.215	−.483	−.215	−.357	4.305	−.215
P6	.646	−.238	.028	2.756	−.238	−1.784

Source: T. M. Horbulyk, "Short-Run Output Response in the Western Canadian Cattle Industry," *Canadian Journal of Agricultural Economics* 38 (1990): 943–52.

FACTOR DEMANDS WITH TWO OR MORE FACTORS

It is now time to relax our assumption that firms require only one factor of production. With more than one factor, when the price of any input falls, the demand for that input will increase for two reasons. First, the firm (and the industry as a whole) substitutes the cheaper input for other inputs, so that for each unit of output produced, more of the cheaper input is employed. This is simply the principle of substitution referred to in Chapter 9. Second, the lower price of the input lowers the marginal cost of production at each level of output, and this leads to an increase in the level of production. Since

total demand for an input = demand for input per unit output × output,

and since both factor demand per unit of output and

output have been increased, total demand for the input has increased.

When we draw the demand curve for labour, which shows the quantity of labour demanded at each wage, in the background we are keeping the price of output and the price of other inputs fixed. When any of these prices change, the demand curve for labour shifts. For instance, as we have seen, if the price of output increases, the value of the marginal product of labour increases and the demand curve shifts to the right.

THE THEORY OF THE COMPETITIVE FIRM

We have now completed our description of the theory of the competitive firm. The firm takes the prices it receives for the goods it sells as given, and it takes the prices it pays for the inputs it uses, including the wages it pays workers and the costs of capital goods, as given. The firm chooses its outputs and inputs in order to maximize its profits.

We have seen where the supply curves for output and the demand curves for labour and capital that were used in Part One came from, and why they have the shapes they do. As prices increase, output increases; firms produce more, and more firms produce. Thus, supply curves are upward-sloping.

As wages increase, with the price of other in-puts fixed, firms' marginal cost curves shift up. This causes them to produce less at each price of their output. The higher *relative* price of labour induces firms to substitute other inputs for labour; they use less labour to produce each unit of output. Therefore, the demand curve for labour (and other inputs) is downward-sloping.

In the next chapter we will use these results, together with the analysis of the household's behaviour in Chapters 6–8, to form a model of the entire economy.

REVIEW AND PRACTICE

SUMMARY

1 A revenue curve shows the relationship between a firm's total output and its revenue. For a competitive firm, the marginal revenue it receives from selling an additional unit of output is the price of that unit.

2 A firm in a competitive market will choose the output where the market price—the marginal revenue it receives from producing an extra unit—equals the marginal cost.

3 If the market price for a good exceeds minimum average costs, more firms will enter the market, since they can make a profit by selling the good for more than it costs to produce the good.

4 If the market price is below minimum average costs and a firm has no sunk costs, the firm will exit the market immediately. If the market price is below minimum average costs and a firm has sunk costs, it will continue to produce in the short run as long as it can at least cover its variable costs.

5 For a firm contemplating entering a market, its supply is zero up to the point where price equals minimum average costs. Above that price, the supply curve is the same as the marginal cost curve.

6 The market supply curve is constructed by adding up the supply curves of all firms in an industry. As prices rise, more firms are willing to produce, and each firm is willing to produce more, so that the market supply curve is normally upward-sloping.

7 The economist's and the accountant's concepts of profits differ in how they treat opportunity costs.

8 A firm's demand for factors of production is derived from its decision about how much to produce. Inputs will be demanded up to the point where the value of the marginal product of the input equals its price.

9 The demand curve for factors of production is downward-sloping for two reasons. Output is reduced as the price of the factor increases, and at each level of output, the firm substitutes away from the factor whose price has increased.

KEY TERMS

revenue curve

average revenue

marginal revenue

sunk costs

economic rents

nonrenewable and renewable resources

factor demand

value of the marginal product of labour

REVIEW QUESTIONS

1 In a competitive market, what rule determines the profit-maximizing level of output? What is the relationship between a firm's supply curve and its marginal cost curve?

2 What determines firms' decisions to enter a market? to exit a market?

3 What is the relationship between the way accountants use the concept of profits and the way economists use that term?

4 How do firms decide how much of an input to demand? Why is the demand curve for inputs (like labour) downward-sloping?

5 Explain when and how the average variable cost curve determines whether firms will enter or exit the market.

PROBLEMS

1 The market price for painting a house in Centreville is $10,000. The Total Cover-up Housepainting Company has fixed costs of $4,000 for ladders, brushes, and so on, and the company's variable costs for housepainting follow this pattern:

Output (houses painted)	Variable cost (in thousands of dollars)
2	26
3	32
4	36
5	42
6	50
7	60
8	72
9	86
10	102

Calculate the company's total costs, and graph the revenue curve and the total cost curve. Do the curves have the shape you expect? Over what range of production is the company making profits?

2 Calculate and graph the marginal cost, the average costs, and the average variable costs for the Total Cover-up Housepainting Company. Given the market price, at what level of output will this firm maximize profits? What profit or loss is it making at that level? At what price will the firm no longer make a profit? Assume its fixed costs are sunk; there is no market for used ladders, brushes, etc. At what price will the company shut down?

3 Draw a U-shaped average cost curve. On your diagram, designate at what price levels you would expect entry and at what price levels you would expect exit if all the fixed costs are sunk. What if only half the fixed costs are sunk? Explain your reasoning.

4 José is a skilled electrician at a local company, a job that pays $50,000 per year, but he is considering quitting to start his own business. He talks it over with an accountant, who helps him to draw up this chart with their best predictions about costs and revenues.

	Predicted annual costs	Predicted annual revenues
Basic wage	$20,000	$75,000
Rent of space	12,000	
Rent of equipment	18,000	
Utilities	2,000	
Miscellaneous	5,000	

The basic wage does seem a bit low, the accountant admits, but she tells José to remember that as owner of the business, José will get to keep any profits as well. From an economist's point of view, is the accountant's list of costs complete? From an economist's point of view, what are José's expected profits?

We have now seen two different ways for determining the demand for labour. One uses the condition for equilibrium output—that price equals marginal cost—to determine the equilibrium level of output and then determine the required labour. The second is derived directly from the profit-maximizing condition for the demand for labour: the value of the marginal product of labour is set equal to the wage. This appendix shows how these conditions are, in fact, alternative ways of writing the same condition.

With a single factor of production, labour, the extra cost of producing an extra unit of output is just the extra labour required times the wage. The extra labour required is $1/MPL$, 1 divided by the marginal product of labour. If one extra worker produces two violins a year, it takes half of a worker to produce an extra violin. Hence, the competitive equilibrium condition, price equals marginal cost, can be rewritten as

$$p = w/MPL.$$

If we multiply both sides of this equation by MPL, we obtain

$$p \times MPL = w,$$

the familiar condition that the value of the marginal product ($p \times MPL$) equals the wage. These conditions are in fact alternative ways of writing the same equation.

Two important consequences follow from these conditions. First, note that if we divide both sides of the equation by p, we obtain $MPL = w/p$. This shows that the demand for labour depends only on the real product wage, that is, the wage divided by the price of the good produced. If wages and prices both double, then the demand for labour and the supply of output are unaffected.

Second, an increase in the wage, keeping prices fixed, reduces the demand for labour. This effect can be seen in two different ways. For the condition "the value of the marginal product of labour equals the wage" to be satisfied, the marginal product of labour must increase. But the principle of diminishing returns says that to increase the marginal product of labour, the input of labour must be reduced.

Alternatively, an increase in the wage can be seen as increasing the marginal cost of hiring an additional unit of labour, while with a fixed price the marginal benefit remains the same. Thus, at the old level of employment the marginal benefit of the last worker hired is less than the marginal cost, and it pays firms to lower their level of production. At a high enough wage, the average variable costs of production may exceed the price, and the firm will shut down.

CHAPTER 11

COMPETITIVE
EQUILIBRIUM

N ow that we have considered each aspect of the basic competitive model separately—the consumption decision, the work decision, the savings and investment decisions, and the production decision—it is time to put the pieces together. In doing so, we will come to understand how markets answer the basic economic questions posed in Chapter 1: what is to be produced and in what quantities, how these goods are to be produced, for whom they are to be produced, and, most fundamental, how these resource allocation decisions are to be made.

This chapter also provides a first glance at the interconnectedness of a modern economy. In the giant web of transactions that is the Canadian economy, pressure on any one part will affect all the rest. In 1982, for example, the sharp fall in the price of oil reduced oil-drilling activity in western Canada. This led to lower economic activity in oil-drilling provinces, most notably Alberta, which resulted in lower real estate prices. Many real estate developers were unable to pay off the money they had borrowed to build new homes, and defaulted. Since most of these loans were made through

KEY QUESTIONS

1 What is meant by the competitive equilibrium of the economy? Why is it that in competitive equilibrium, a disturbance to one part of the economy may have reverberations in others?

2 What implications does the interconnectedness of the economy have for policy issues such as the corporate income tax?

3 What is the circular flow diagram, and how does it show the many links between the different parts of the economy?

4 Why do so many economists believe that, by and large, reliance on private markets is desirable? How do competitive markets result in economic efficiency?

5 If markets result in distributions of income that society views as unacceptable, should the market be abandoned, or can the government intervene in a more limited to combine efficient outcomes with acceptable distributions?

banks, some banks went bankrupt, obliging the federal government deposit insurance corporation that guaranteed these deposits to partially pay off their depositors, many of whom lived outside Alberta. Furthermore, the reduced oil and gas activity in Alberta reduced the demand for manufactured inputs used in the industry, often fabricated in Ontario. And, the lower income levels attained in Alberta reduced the need for the federal government to make equalizing transfers of revenues to the poorer provinces, primarily in the East. Thus, a shiver in one part of the economic web sent a chill through many other parts.

Finally, this chapter explains why economists believe that, by and large, the market answers the fundamental questions efficiently.

GENERAL EQUILIBRIUM ANALYSIS

When we introduced the idea of a market equilibrium in Chapter 4, we focused on one market at a time. The price of a good was determined when the demand for that good equalled its supply. The wage rate was determined when the demand for labour equalled its supply. The interest rate was determined when the demand for savings equalled its supply. This kind of analysis is called **partial equilibrium**

analysis. In analyzing what is going on in one market, we ignore what is going on in other markets.

Interdependencies in the economy make partial equilibrium analysis overly simple because demand and supply in one market depend on prices determined in other markets. For instance, the demand for skis is influenced by the price of ski tickets, ski boots, and possibly even airline tickets. Thus, the equilibrium price of skis will depend on the price of ski tickets, ski boots, and airline tickets. But by the same token, the demand for ski tickets and ski boots will depend on the price of skis. Accordingly, the equilibrium price of ski tickets and ski boots will depend on the price of skis. **General equilibrium analysis** broadens the perspective, taking into account interactions and interdependencies within the various parts of the economy.

EXAMPLE I: THE CORPORATE INCOME TAX

Ascertaining the effect of the corporate income tax— the tax the federal and provincial governments impose on the net income of corporations—provides an example of why general equilibrium analysis is often essential. A partial equilibrium analysis of this tax is provided in Figure 11.1, where we have drawn the demand and supply curves for capital in the corporate sector. The corporate income tax is shown as a tax on capital because much of a corporation's in-

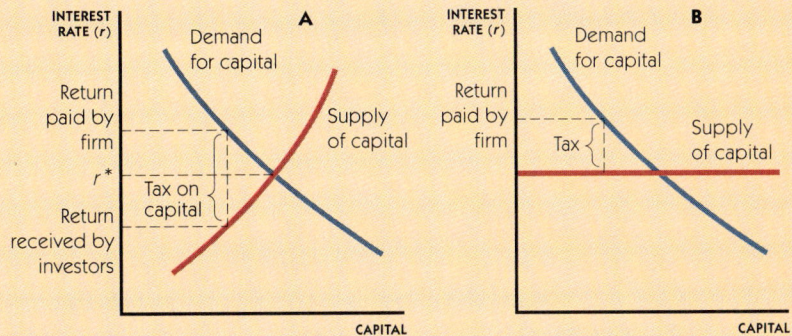

Figure 11.1 PARTIAL EQUI-LIBRIUM ANALYSIS OF THE CORPORATE INCOME TAX

In panel A, the tax, viewed as a tax on the return to capital in the corporate sector, leads to a lower return to investors and a higher cost of capital to firms. In panel B, the tax simply results in a higher cost of capital to firms.

come is in fact a return on the capital invested in it. As can be seen, this tax drives a wedge between the price of capital paid by the firm and the return received by investors.

Who bears the burden of the tax? The partial equilibrium analysis shown in panel A of Figure 11.1 makes it clear that investors bear only a part of the burden. Their after-tax return is lowered, but not by the full amount of the tax. Indeed, panel B of the figure shows a case in which investors bear none of the burden, when the supply of capital is horizontal (infinitely elastic).

If investors do not bear the burden of the tax, who does? Because the interest rate that firms pay increases, firms' costs have gone up, and this will be reflected in higher equilibrium prices. Thus, consumers bear some of the costs. If sales decrease as a result, the demand for labour may decrease, and thus wages may fall, in which case workers will bear some of the burden. But other factors need to be taken into account as well. The higher cost of capital may induce firms to substitute labour for machines, in which case the demand for labour will actually increase. At higher prices to consumers, however, the return to working is reduced. In this case, workers might supply less labour.

Account must also be taken of the interactions between capital in the corporate and unincorporated sectors of the economy. Because over 80 percent of nonfarm business takes place in the corporate sec-

tor, activities in that sector have major ramifications for the rest of the economy. If investors find it less attractive to invest in the corporate sector, they will shift their savings into the unincorporated sector. As capital flows into the unincorporated sector, the return to capital in that sector will be reduced to the point that it equals the rate of return in the corporate sector. A full general equilibrium analysis needs to take all these factors into account.

General equilibrium analysis focuses on the fact that in equilibrium, the returns to all investments throughout the economy must provide the same rate of return per dollar invested (adjusting for risk). An analysis of the corporate income tax that failed to take into account the responses in the unincorporated sector would be incomplete at best, and could be seriously misleading. Most economists agree that, in the long run, most of the burden of the corporate income tax rests on workers and consumers, and relatively little on corporations, their shareholders, or others who have lent money—contrary to popular belief.

EXAMPLE 11: TARIFF PROTECTION

Historically, Canadian governments have relied on the tariff as an instrument for industrial policy. The idea was that in order to build up a capacity for

Petroleum-based products permeate virtually every sector of the economy. Any major changes in their prices inevitably have general equilibrium consequences. One significant such change occurred in the mid-1970s when the Organization of Petroleum Exporting Countries (OPEC) cartel caused world oil prices to soar by restricting the rates of production of its members. Since Canada is a net oil exporter, producing more oil than we consume, the OPEC price rise might have been expected to have a positive effect, benefiting Canadian producers more than it cost Canadian consumers. But most of the producers of oil are concentrated in Alberta, while the users are spread across the country, so the gains would have been concentrated in Alberta.

In response to the oil crisis, the federal government introduced the National Energy Program (N.E.P.) in 1980 in an effort to shield users from the higher prices and to spread the benefits around the country. The NEP restricted the price of oil within Canada to well below the world price. This was partly accomplished by a tax imposed on exports sold from western Canada to foreigners, and by a subsidy paid on imports coming into eastern Canada. The federal government also imposed a tax on the production of oil, effectively reducing the ability of the Alberta government to do so. Finally, tax incentives were offered to encourage production by Canadian-owned firms in the oil industry.

To the extent that the NEP was successful both at keeping domestic oil prices lower than they would otherwise have been and at spreading the revenues from the sale of Canadian oil

abroad at the higher world price across the country, certain general equilibrium consequences could be avoided. For one thing, if the windfall profits from the OPEC oil price rise had been allowed to accrue to Alberta firms and the Alberta treasury, that province could offer fiscal benefits such as lower taxes and better services that would attract labour and capital out of neighbouring provinces. The NEP was partly intended to reduce this so-called "fiscally induced migration" by sharing the revenues from the oil price increase across the country as well as reducing the size of the price increase.

Quite apart from that were the ramifications that a large oil price rise would have had for industries in other parts of the country. A major study conducted for Transport Canada in 1982 found that the N.E.P. could be important for the survival of Maritime provinces producers who export to central Canada and the United States. For some Maritime goods the energy cost of transportation is a large component of the product price. In the case of New Brunswick green lumber, the cost of diesel fuel for trucking accounted for 4.8 percent of the product price in 1982. This cost was not nearly as high for the competing firms in Ontario, Quebec, and the northern states in the United States, where the Maritime products were sold. More generally, it was estimated that rising energy prices could have a "significant negative impact on the competitive position" of Maritime producers of canned fruits and vegetables as well as lumber. The canned and frozen fish industries were less sensitive to energy prices, since oil inputs make up a much smaller proportion of their costs. In a general equilibrium sense, then, by keeping energy prices low the NEP was seen to benefit Maritime sectors not directly involved in energy issues.

Of course, in attempting to address the unequal regional impact of the rise in oil prices by keeping them artificially low, the government prevented market economic forces from taking their natural course. As is often the case, objectives of fairness can be accomplished only at a cost of some economic inefficiency.

Sources: Edward A. Carmichael and J. K. Stewart, *Lessons from the National Energy Program,* (Toronto: C. D. Howe Institute, 1983); E. H. M. Jagoe and A. D. Fiander, *Assessment of the Impact of the NEP on the Long-Haul Freight Movements from the Maritime Provinces* (Ottawa: Transport Canada Strategic Planning, Group Project No. 59–86, June 1982).

manufacturing activity, Canada's small and young manufacturing industries had to be protected from foreign competition. Thus, tariffs—taxes applied selectively on imported products—were imposed.

A partial equilibrium analysis of the effects of tariffs on the protected manufacturing industry might conclude that workers in the industry would be better off. After all, industry output would increase as a result of the tariff as domestic production replaced foreign imports, and this would increase the demand for factor inputs in manufacturing, one of which is labour. Thus, wages should be bid up and manufacturing workers should be made better off by the tariff. Not surprisingly, union leaders in the manufacturing sector were among the strongest opponents to the dismantling of tariffs under the North American Free Trade Agreement.

However, this partial equilibrium view of the effects of tariffs is misleading. It neglects the fact that an important general equilibrium effect of tariffs is to cause a reallocation of factors of production from unprotected to protected sectors. It may well be that the protected sectors are much more capital-intensive—they may use relatively larger amounts of capital per worker—than the unprotected sectors. In this case, compared with capital proportionately more labour is released from the unprotected sectors as a result of tariff protection than is required by the manufacturing sectors. Thus, capital will become scarcer (in higher demand), while labour will become less scarce. Wage rates will fall. In this case, contrary to the results of the partial equilibrium analysis, labour will actually be made worse off by protection.

WHEN PARTIAL EQUILIBRIUM ANALYSIS SUFFICES

In the example of tariff protection just given, general equilibrium analysis is clearly important. But can we ever focus on what goes on in a single market without worrying about the reverberations in the rest of the economy? Are there circumstances in which partial equilibrium analysis will provide a fairly accurate answer to the effect of, say, a change in a tax? Fortunately, the answer is yes.

For example, partial equilibrium analysis is adequate when the reverberations from the initial imposition of a tax are so dispersed that they can be ignored without distorting the analysis. Such is the case when individuals shift their demand away from the taxed good toward many, many other goods. The prices of those goods change only a very little, and the total demand for factors of production like capital and labour changes only negligibly, so that the prices of different factors are virtually unchanged. Moreover, the slight changes in the prices of different goods and inputs have only a slight effect on the demand and supply curves of the industry upon which the analysis is focusing. In these circumstances, partial equilibrium analysis will provide a good approximation to what will actually happen.

EXAMPLE: A TAX ON CIGARETTES

The effect of a tax on cigarettes is an example where partial equilibrium analysis works quite well.

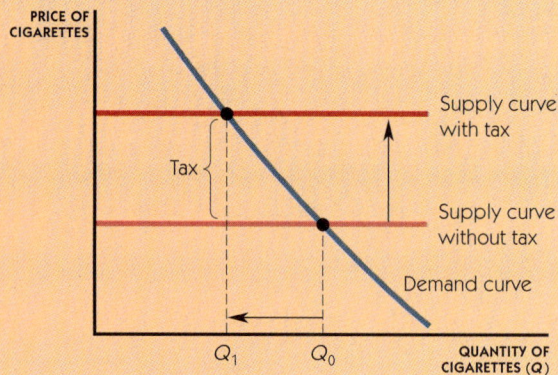

Figure 11.2 PARTIAL EQUILIBRIUM ANALYSIS OF THE EFFECT OF A TAX ON CIGARETTES

A tax on cigarettes raises the price of cigarettes and reduces consumption slightly. The second-round reverberations of this tax are sufficiently slight that they can be ignored.

Cigarettes are subject to a special tax (called an **excise tax**) at both the federal and the provincial levels of government. The combined rates of tax have increased dramatically in the past two decades, partly in response to demands by the public that cigarette consumption be discouraged and partly simply to raise revenues for the two levels of government. The rate of federal taxation rose from about 1.2 cents per cigarette in 1975 to 8.1 cents per cigarette in 1992, much more rapid than the rate at which cigarette prices have risen. As well, over the same period, provincial taxes rose by an average of less than one cent per pack to almost five cents per cigarette. What predictions could be made about the effects of this dramatic increase in the taxation of cigarettes?

Figure 11.2 shows the tax as shifting the supply curve of cigarettes up by the amount of the tax. Demand is reduced from Q_0 to Q_1. Since expenditures on cigarettes are a small proportion of anyone's income, a 15 percent increase in their price will have only a small effect on overall consumption patterns. While the reduced quantity demanded of cigarettes (and the indirect changed demand for other goods) will have a slight effect on the total demand for labour, this effect is so small that it will lead to no noticeable change in the wage rate. Similarly, the tax will have virtually no effect on the return to capital.

Under these circumstances, where more distant general equilibrium effects are likely to be so faint as to be indiscernible, a partial equilibrium analysis of a tax on cigarettes is appropriate.

THE BASIC COMPETITIVE EQUILIBRIUM MODEL

General equilibrium analysis requires a model of the entire economy. To analyze the effects of imposing a tax or tariff or of the immigration of labour or any other change, one "solves" for the full equilibrium before and after the change, and looks at how each of the variables—wages, prices, interest rates, outputs, employment, and so forth—has changed.

To see how this is done, we focus on a simplified version of the full competitive equilibrium model.

In this simplified model, we assume all workers have identical skills. Ignoring differences in skill level enables us to talk about the labour market as if all workers received the same wage. Similarly, we ignore all aspects of risk in our analysis of the capital market. This allows us to use a single interest rate. Finally, we assume that all firms produce the same good—in other words, the product market consists of only one good. We now have an economy made up of three markets—the labour market, the capital market, and the product market—and can use general equilibrium analysis to trace through how they depend on one another.

In Chapter 7, we saw how households determine the amount of labour they wish to supply. Households supply labour because they want to buy goods. Hence, their labour supply depends on both wages and prices. It also depends on other sources of income. If we assume, for simplicity, that households' only other source of income is the return to their investments (their return to capital, or the interest on their investments), then we can see that the labour supply is connected to all three markets. It depends on the wage, the price of the single good, and the return to capital. Similarly, in Chapter 7, we saw that the demand for labour depends on the wage, on the interest rate, and on the price at which the firm sells its product.

Equilibrium in the labour market requires that the demand for labour equal the supply. Normally, when we draw the demand curve for labour, we simply assume that p, the price of the goods being produced, and the interest rate (here, r) are kept fixed. We focus our attention solely on the wage rate, the price of labour. *Given p and r*, we look for the wage at which the demand and supply for labour are equal. This is a partial equilibrium analysis of the labour market.

The labour market is only one of the three markets, even in our highly simplified economy. There is also the market for capital to consider. In Chapter 8, we saw how households determine their savings, which in turn determine the available supply of capital. The supply of capital is affected, in general, by the return it yields (the interest rate, r) plus the income individuals have from other sources, in particular from wages. Since the amount individuals are willing to save may depend on how well off they feel, and how well off they feel depends on the wage rate relative to prices, we can think of the supply of capital too as depending on wages, interest rates, and prices. In Chapter 10, we learned how to derive firms' demand for capital. This too will depend on the interest rate they must pay, the price at which goods can be sold, and the cost of other inputs.

Equilibrium in the capital market occurs at the point where the demand and supply for capital are equal. Again, partial equilibrium analysis of the capi-

tal market focuses on the return to capital, r, at which the demand and supply of capital are equal, but both the demand and the supply depend on the wage and the price of goods as well.

Finally, there is the market for goods. Chapters 6 and 8 showed how to derive households' demand for goods. We can think of the household as first deciding on how much to spend (Chapter 8), and then deciding how to allocate what it spends over different goods (Chapter 6). Of course, with a single consumption good, the latter problem no longer exists. In our simplified model, then, we can think of the demand for goods as being determined by household income, which in turn depends on the wage, the interest rate, and the price of goods.

Similarly, in Chapter 10, we analyzed how firms determine how much to produce: they set price equal to marginal cost, where marginal cost depends on wages and the interest rate. Equilibrium in the goods market requires that the demand for goods equal the supply of goods. Again, while in the simple partial equilibrium analysis we focus on how the demand and supply of goods depend on price, p, we know that the demand and supply of goods also depend on both the wage rate and the return to capital.

The labour market is said to be in equilibrium when the demand for labour equals the supply. The product market is in equilibrium when the demand for goods equals the supply. The capital market is in equilibrium when the demand for capital equals the supply. The economy as a whole is in equilibrium only when all markets clear simultaneously—when demand equals supply in all markets. The general equilibrium for our simple economy occurs at a common wage rate, w, price, p, and interest rate, r, at which all three markets are also in equilibrium.

In the basic equilibrium model, there is only a single good, but it is easy to extend the analysis to the more realistic case where there are many goods. The same web of interconnections exists between different goods and between different goods and different inputs. Recall from Chapter 4 that the demand curve depicts the quantity of a good—for instance, beer—demanded at each price; the supply curve shows the quantity of a good that firms supply at each price. But the demand curve for beer depends on the prices of other goods and the income levels of

---

EQUILIBRIUM IN THE BASIC COMPETITIVE MODEL

The labour market–equilibrium condition: The demand for labour must equal the supply.

The capital market–equilibrium condition: The demand for capital must equal the supply.

The goods market–equilibrium condition: The demand for goods must equal the supply.

---

different consumers; similarly, the supply curve for beer depends on the prices of inputs, including the wage rate, the interest rate, and the price of hops and other ingredients. Those prices in turn depend on supply and demand in their respective markets. The general equilibrium of the economy requires finding the prices for each good and for each input such that the demand for each good equals the supply, and the demand for each input equals the supply.

THE CIRCULAR FLOW OF FUNDS

General equilibrium analysis is not the only way to think about the interrelations of the various parts of the economy. Another way is to consider the flow of funds through the economy. Households buy goods

and services from firms. Households supply labour and capital to firms. The income individuals receive, whether in the form of wages or the return on their savings, is spent to buy the goods that firms produce. All these transactions constitute what is called the **circular flow.**

The circular flow for a simplified economy—in which there are only households and firms, households do not save, and firms do not invest—is shown in Figure 11.3. This circular flow diagram serves two purposes. First, it shows how funds flow through the economy. We can see this by starting at point A and following the circular flow around to the right. The top arrow shows that households pay money to firms to buy goods for their consumption. The lower arrow (point B) shows that firms use the money to pay household members in the form of wages (for labour), rent (to the owners of land), and profit (to the owners of firms). The second purpose of the circular flow diagram is to focus on certain balance conditions in the economy that must always be satis-

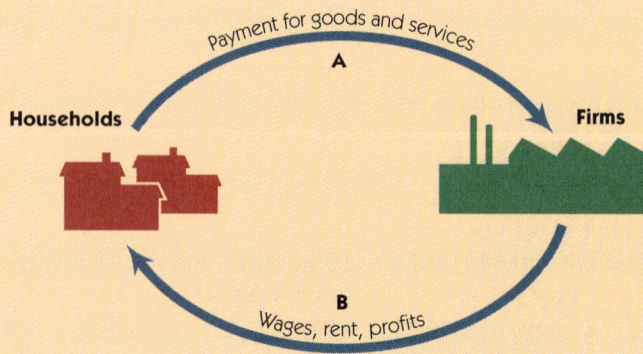

Figure 11.3 A SIMPLE CIRCULAR FLOW DIAGRAM

In this simple circular flow diagram, only labour and product markets and only the household and firm sectors are represented. It can be analyzed from any starting point. For example, funds flow from households to firms in the form of purchases of goods and services. Funds flow from firms to households in the form of payments for the labour of workers and profits paid to owners.

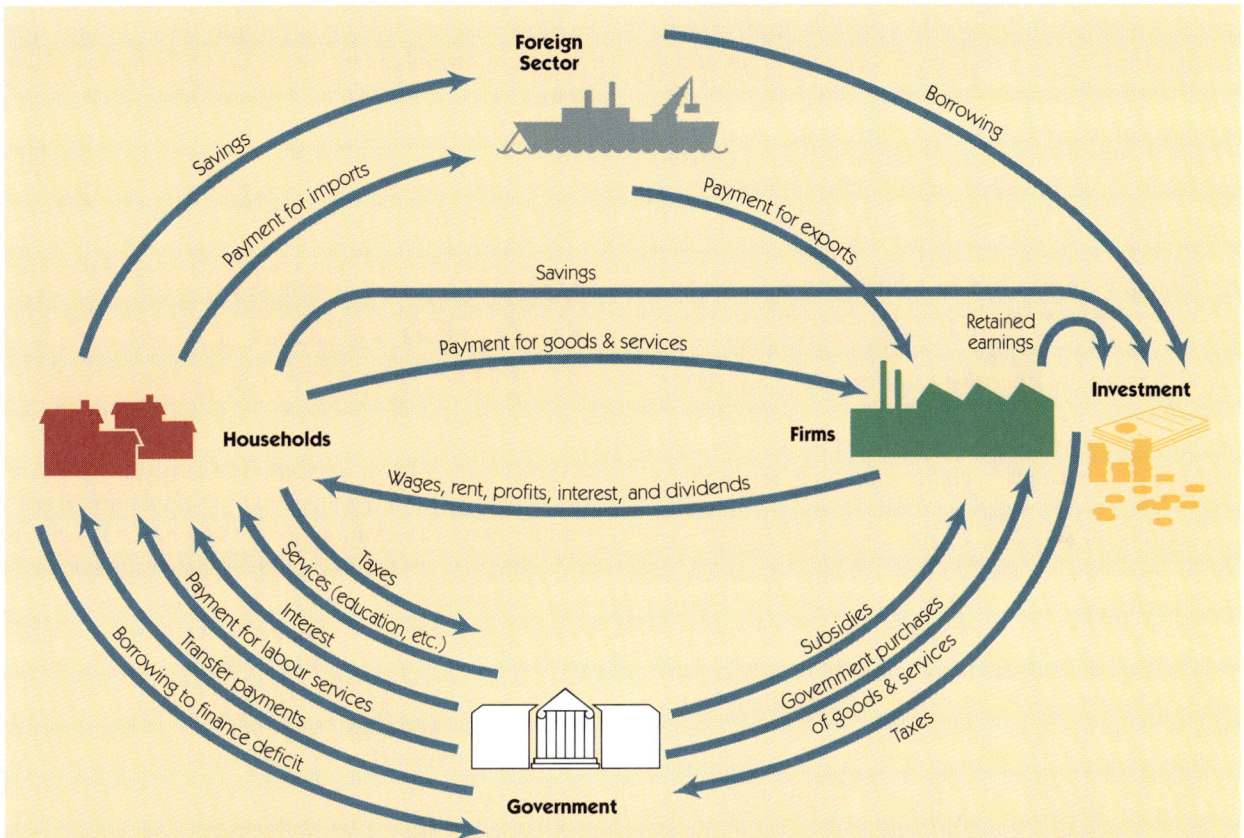

Figure 11.4 CIRCULAR FLOW WITH GOVERNMENT AND FOREIGN SECTOR ADDED

This expanded circular flow diagram shows the labour, capital, and product markets along with households, firms, government, and foreign countries; it too can be analyzed from any starting point. The flow of funds into each sector must balance the flow of funds out of each sector.

fied. In the case of the simple flow in Figure 11.3, there is one balance condition. The income of households (the flow of funds from firms, lower arrow) must equal the expenditures of households (the flow of funds to firms, upper arrow).

Figure 11.4 expands the circular flow in three ways. First, savings and capital are included. Thus, the funds that flow from the firm to the household now include a return on capital (interest on loans, dividends on equities). The funds that flow from the household to the firm now include savings, which go

to purchase machines and buildings. And firms now retain some of their earnings to finance investment.

Second, the circular flow now includes funds flowing into and out of the government. Thus, some households receive transfer payments from the government such as benefits like Old Age Security and welfare payments. Some sell their labour services to the government rather than private firms. Some receive interest on loans to the government (government bonds). And there is now an important additional outflow from households: income that goes to the government in the form of taxes. Similarly, firms have additional sources of inflow in the sales of goods and services they make to the government and in government subsidies to firms, and an additional outflow in the taxes they must pay to the government.

Just as the flow of funds into and out of households and firms must balance, the flow of funds into the government must balance the flow of funds out.[1] When there is a deficit—that is, when the government spends more than it collects in taxes, as has been the case in recent years—funds go into the government as borrowings. The government finances the difference by borrowing (in our diagram, from households).

Figure 11.4 adds a third factor, the flow to and from foreign countries. Firms sell goods to foreigners (exports) and borrow funds from foreigners. Households buy goods from foreigners (imports) and invest funds in foreign firms. Again, there must be a balance in the flow of funds into and out of the country. Canada's exports plus the amount it borrows from abroad (the flow of funds from abroad) must equal its imports plus what it lends abroad (the flow of funds to other countries).[2]

The interconnections and balance conditions making up circular flow analysis are the same as those that arise in the competitive general equilibrium model discussed earlier in the chapter. Even if the economy were not competitive, however, (i.e., if some firms were large enough to influence selling prices or if workers could influence their wage rate through unions) the interrelationships and balance conditions of the circular flow diagram would still be true. Thus, the circular flow diagram is a useful reminder that change in one element of the economy *must* be balanced by change in another element, whether or not the economy is competitive.

Let's put the circular flow diagram to work. Consider the case of a reduction in the personal in-

come tax, such as occurred in 1988. The flow of funds into the government was reduced. The circular flow diagram reminds us that flows in and out must remain balanced: either some other tax must be increased, government borrowing must increase, or government expenditures must decrease.

COMPETITIVE GENERAL EQUILIBRIUM AND ECONOMIC EFFICIENCY

The first part of this chapter introduced the basic model of competitive general equilibrium. Competitive general equilibrium entails prices, wages, and returns to capital such that all markets—for goods, labour, capital and other factors of production—clear. A change in economic conditions, such as the imposition of a tax, the immigration of labour, or a sudden decline in supply of some good, results in a new equilibrium to the economy. We have seen how the effects of such changes can be traced out.

But economists are interested not only in describing the market equilibrium, but also in evaluating it. Do competitive markets do a "good" job in allocating resources? One of the most important achievements of modern economic theory has been to establish in what sense and under what conditions the market is efficient.

PARETO EFFICIENCY

To economists, the concept of efficiency is related to concern with the well-being of those in the economy. When no one can be made better off without making someone else worse off the allocation of resources is called **Pareto-efficient,** after the great Italian economist and sociologist Vilfredo Pareto (1848–1923). Generally, when economists refer to efficiency Pareto efficiency is what they mean. Saying that a market is efficient is a positive evaluation. In the same way that an efficient machine uses its in-

[1] We ignore here the possibility that the government can simply pay for what it obtains by printing money. In Canada governments always finance any shortfall in revenue by borrowing.

[2] This condition can be put another way. The difference between Canadian imports and exports must equal the net flow of funds from abroad (the difference between what the country borrows from abroad and what it lends).

puts as productively as possible, an efficient market is one in which there is no way of increasing output with the same level of inputs. The only way one participant in the market can be made better off is by taking resources away from another, thereby making the second participant worse off.

It is easy to see how a resource allocation might not be Pareto-efficient. Assume the government is given the job of distributing chocolate and vanilla ice cream and pays no attention to people's preferences. Assume, moreover, that some individuals love chocolate and hate vanilla, while others love vanilla and hate chocolate. Some chocolate lovers will get vanilla ice cream, and some vanilla lovers will get chocolate ice cream. Clearly, this is Pareto-inefficient. Allowing people to trade resources makes both groups better off.

To some, *all* economic changes represent nothing more than redistributions. Gains to one only subtract from another. Rent control is one example. In this view, the only effect of rent control is redistribution—landlords receive less, and are worse off, by the same amount that their tenants' rents are reduced and the tenants are better off. In some countries, unions have expressed similar views, viewing wage increases as having no further consequences than redistributing income to workers from those who own or manage firms. This view is mistaken, because in each of these instances, there are consequences beyond the redistribution. Rent control that keeps rents below the level that clears the rental housing market and minimum wages above those that clear the labour market both result in inefficiencies. For those concerned about renters who cannot afford the going rate or workers earning too little to support a family, there are better approaches that make the renters or workers as well as the landlords or employers better off than under rent control or minimum wage.

CONDITIONS FOR THE PARETO EFFICIENCY OF THE MARKET ECONOMY

For the economy to be Pareto-efficient, it must meet the conditions of exchange efficiency, production ef-

ficiency, and product-mix efficiency. Considering each of these conditions separately shows us why the basic competitive model attains Pareto efficiency. (Recall the basic ingredients of that model: rational, perfectly informed households interacting with rational, profit-maximizing firms in competitive markets.)

EXCHANGE EFFICIENCY

Exchange efficiency requires that whatever the economy produces must be distributed among individuals in an efficient way. If I like chocolate ice cream and you like vanilla ice cream, exchange efficiency requires that I get the chocolate and you get the vanilla.

When there is exchange efficiency, there is no scope for further trade among individuals. Chapter 3 discussed the advantages of free exchange among individuals and nations. Any prohibition or restriction on trade results in exchange inefficiency. For instance, in war times, governments often ration scarce goods, like sugar. People are given coupons that allow them to buy, say, a kilogram of sugar a month. If sugar carries a price of $1 a kilogram, having $1 is not enough; you must also have the coupon. There is often considerable controversy about whether people should be allowed to sell their coupons, or trade their sugar coupons for, say, a butter coupon. If the government prohibits the sale or trading of coupons, then the economy will not be exchange-efficient—it will not be Pareto-efficient.

The price system ensures that exchange efficiency is attained. In deciding how much of a good to buy, people balance the marginal benefit they receive by buying an extra unit with the cost of that extra unit, its price. Hence, price can be thought of as a rough measure of the *marginal* benefit an individual receives from a good—that is, the benefit a person receives from one more unit of the good. If all individuals face the same prices, their *marginal* benefits will be the same at the quantities they actually consume. For those who like chocolate ice cream a great deal and vanilla ice cream very little, this will entail consuming many more chocolate ice cream cones than vanilla. Notice that no single individual or agency needs to know who is a chocolate and who is a vanilla lover for the goods to get to the right person. Not even the ice cream stores have to know

CLOSE-UP: PARETO IMPROVEMENT IN THE SKIES

Airlines want their planes to fly as full as possible. They also know that a certain percentage of people who purchased a ticket for any given flight are not going to show up. This gives the airlines an incentive to overbook flights: they sell more tickets than there are seats in the reasonable expectation that there will be room to take everyone who actually shows up. But sometimes everyone does show up, and a decision must be made about who will be bumped from the flight. Several methods of making this choice are possible.

In the 1960s, the airlines simply bumped whoever showed up last and gave those people tickets for a later flight. Bumped passengers had no recourse. This sort of policy causes high blood pressure.

To avoid imposing these costs on frustrated passengers, a second policy might be for the government to forbid airlines to overbook flights. But in this case, some planes will be forced to fly with empty seats that some people would have been willing to buy. Airlines would lose revenues, prices would have to rise to offset the lost revenue, and travellers who could have flown in the empty seat but could not get reservations under the no-overbooking rule would all be losers.

There is an alternative solution that is a Pareto improvement both over the practice of bumping and over rules forbidding overbooking. Today airlines offer a free ticket on a future flight or other bonus as compensation to anyone willing to wait. People willing to accept such a deal are clearly better off in their own estimation. The airlines benefit because they are allowed to continue their practice of overbooking and thus keeping their flights as full as possible. In fact, since the person who receives a free ticket will often occupy a seat that would have been vacant anyway, the marginal cost of offering the free ticket for the airline is very close to zero. This is a real-world Pareto improvement. Everyone involved is at least no worse off and many are better off.

Source: Julian L. Simon, "An Almost Practical Solution to Airline Overbooking," *Journal of Transport Economics and Policy* (May 1968): 201–202.

individual preferences. Each consumer, by his own action, ensures that exchange efficiency is attained.

Notice too that if different individuals face *different* prices, then the economy will not in general be exchange-efficient. This is because the marginal benefit of the good to the person who has to pay a high price will be far greater than to the person who pays a low price. If manufacturers charge some customers (say, those who buy in bulk) a lower price than others, then the economy will not be exchange-efficient. If airlines charge different customers different prices, then the economy will also not be exchange-efficient.

PRODUCTION EFFICIENCY

For an economy to be Pareto-efficient, it must also be **productively efficient:** it must not be possible to produce more of some goods without producing less of other goods. In other words, Pareto efficiency requires that the economy operate along the production possibilities curve first introduced in Chapter 2.

Figure 11.5 THE PRODUC-TION POSSIBILITIES CURVE

The production possibilities curve shows the maximum level of output of one good given the level of output of other goods. Production efficiency requires that the economy be on its production possibilities curve. Along the curve, the only way to increase production of one good (here, apples) is to decrease the production of other goods (oranges).

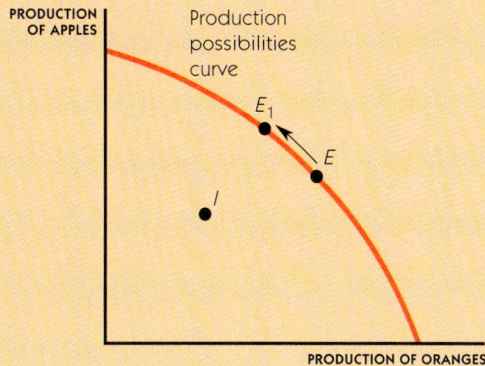

Figure 11.5 shows the production possibilities curve for a simple economy that produces only two goods, apples and oranges. If the economy is at point I, inside the production possibilities curve, it cannot be Pareto-efficient. Society could produce more of both apples and oranges, and by distributing them to different individuals, it could make people better off. Prices signal to firms the scarcity of each of the inputs they use. When all firms face the same prices of labour, capital goods, and other inputs, they will take the appropriate actions to economize on each of these inputs, ensuring that the economy operates along its production possibilities curve. Firms may face differing prices for labour if, for example, labour unions succeed in obtaining higher wages in some industries than in others for the same type of worker. They may face differing prices for capital if the government taxes capital incomes in one sector (e.g., the corporate sector) at a higher rate than in another. In both cases, society will be operating inside its production possibilities curve.

PRODUCT-MIX EFFICIENCY

The third condition for Pareto efficiency is **product-mix efficiency.** That is, the mix of goods produced by the economy must reflect the preferences of those in the economy. The economy must produce along the production possibilities curve at a point that reflects the preferences of consumers. The price system again ensures that this condition will be satisfied. Assume that the economy is initially producing at a point along the production possibilities curve, E in Figure 11.5. Consumers decide that they like apples more and oranges less. The increased demand for apples will result in the price of apples increasing, and this will lead to an increased output of apples; at the same time, the decreased demand for oranges will result in the price of oranges falling, and this in turn will lead to a decreased output of oranges. The economy will move from E to a point such as E_1, where there are more apples and fewer oranges produced; the mix of goods produced in the economy will have changed to reflect the changed preferences of consumers.

COMPETITIVE MARKETS AND PARETO EFFICIENCY

We now know what economists mean when they say that market economies are efficient, or that the price system results in economic efficiency. What they mean is that the economy is Pareto-efficient: no one can be made better off without making someone else worse off. We have also learned why competitive markets ensure that all three of the basic conditions for Pareto efficiency are attained: exchange efficiency, production efficiency, and product-mix efficiency.

The argument that competitive markets ensure Pareto efficiency can be put somewhat loosely in another way: a rearrangement of resources can only benefit people who voluntarily agree to it. But in competitive equilibrium, people have already agreed to all the exchanges they are willing to make; no one wishes to produce more or less or to demand more or less, given the prices he faces. If no one desires to change, then no one can benefit except at the expense of someone else.

Pareto efficiency does *not* say that there are no ways to make one or many individuals better off. Obviously, resources could be taken from some and given to others, and the recipients would be better off. We have seen how, for instance, government interventions with the market, such as rent control, do benefit some individuals—those who are lucky enough to get the rent-controlled apartments. But in the process, someone is made worse off. Indeed, in each of the cases where government interferes with competitive markets, some people are worse off.

COMPETITIVE MARKETS AND INCOME DISTRIBUTION

Efficiency is better than inefficiency, but it is not everything. In the competitive equilibrium, some individuals might be very rich, while others live in dire poverty. One person might have skills that are highly valued, while another does not. Competition may result in an efficient economy with a very unequal distribution of resources.

The law of supply and demand in a competitive economy determines how the available income will be divided up. The result will be economically efficient, but it may also produce distributions of income that seem, at least to some, morally repugnant. An economy where some individuals live in mansions while others barely eke out a living may be efficient, but that still hardly makes the situation desirable. Left to themselves, competitive markets may provide an answer to the question "For whom are goods produced?" that seems unacceptable.

This unacceptable response does not mean that the competitive market mechanism should be abandoned, at least not under the conditions assumed in our basic model, with perfectly informed, rational consumers and firms interacting in perfectly competitive markets. Even if society as a whole wishes to redistribute income, it should not dispense with competitive markets. Instead, all that is needed is to redistribute the wealth that people possess, and then leave the rest to the workings of a competitive market. Under some conditions, every point on the utility possibilities curve can be attained by such a redistribution of wealth.

Frequently government interferences with the market are justified on the grounds that they increase equality. These government policies are often based on the widely held but mistaken (as we have already seen) view that all redistributions are just that; some individuals get more, others get less, but there are no further repercussions. We now know that changing relative prices to achieve redistribution—such as imposing minimum wage laws or subsidizing some good—has effects in addition to redistributing income. Such changes interfere with the economy's efficiency. To put it another way, the

EFFICIENCY

An economy in competitive equilibrium is Pareto-efficient.

Any Pareto-efficient resource allocation that society desires can be obtained through the market mechanism.

economy will be operating below its utility possibilities curve. One consequence of lower rents for apartments, for example, is that the return on capital invested in rental housing will fall, and as a result the economy will invest too little in rental housing. Because of this underinvestment, the economy is not efficient.

Thus, interventions in the economy justified on the grounds that they increase equality need to be treated with caution. To attain an efficient allocation of resources with the desired distribution of income, if the assumptions of the competitive model are satisfied by the economy, the *sole* role of the government is to redistribute initial wealth. Not only can one rely on the market mechanism thereafter, but interfering with the market will actually put the economy below its utility possibilities curve.

LOOKING BEYOND THE BASIC MODEL: MARKET FAILURES AND THE ROLE OF GOVERNMENT

This chapter brings together the pieces of the basic competitive model. It shows how the competitive equilibrium in an ideal economy is achieved. To the extent that conditions in the real world match the approximations of the basic competitive model, there will be economic efficiency. Government will have little role in the economy beyond establishing a legal framework within which to enforce market transactions.

One group of economists, referred to as **free-market economists** for their strong faith in unfettered markets as the path to economic efficiency, believe that the competitive model provides a good description of most markets most of the time. These economists believe that there is a very limited role for government in economic affairs. In their view, government intervention should be restricted mainly to changing unacceptable distributions of income, and even in this area government should operate with restraint.

Another group of economists, called **imperfect-market economists,** see significant discrepancies between the basic competitive model and the conditions they observe when they study actual consumers, firms, and markets. Such discrepancies lead them to ask whether private markets, left to operate on their own, will produce economically efficient outcomes.

Imperfect-market economists would not, however, discard the model. For them it is an important baseline for investigation. For example, many economists who specialize in the study of the economy's industrial structure argue that competition is limited, and explain why this is so. If the cigarette market is not competitive, the competitive model will yield incorrect predictions concerning, for instance, the consequences of an increase in the tax on cigarettes.

Other imperfect-market economists contend that firms do not have perfect information about the quality of their workers and investors do not have perfect information about the returns to different investment opportunities. This imperfect information, they argue, has the result that capital and labour markets function in ways quite different from those described by the basic competitive model.

Still other imperfect-market economists argue that the model is generally appropriate but that there are important instances where markets cannot be relied upon without government intervention. They are concerned about pollution of the environment and about unemployment. They believe that

TWO VIEWS OF THE BASIC COMPETITIVE MODEL

Free-market view: The competitive model provides a good description of the economy, and government intervention is not required.

Imperfect-market view: In many markets, the competitive model does not provide a good description—for in-

stance, because competition is limited and information is imperfect. There are important market failures, evidenced by unemployment and environmental pollution, requiring at least selective government intervention.

these are instances where one or more of the assumptions of the basic competitive model are violated and that there is, therefore, scope for government intervention to increase economic efficiency.

What are the consequences when the underlying assumptions are not valid? Which of the assumptions are most suspect? What evidence do we have with which we can assess either the validity of the model's underlying assumptions or its implications? The next part of this book is devoted to these questions, and to the role of government that emerges from the answers.

A warning is in order before we embark on our study of market imperfections. That markets do not work perfectly—suggesting a possible role for government—does not necessarily mean that government intervention will improve matters.

Free-market and imperfect-market economists continue to debate the extent to which the basic

competitive model provides a good description of the economy. However, these disagreements should not mask the large and growing areas of consensus about the efficiency of competitive markets. This provides our sixth point of consensus.

6   The Efficiency of Competitive Markets

At the center of the modern economy are competitive markets. Through the profit motive and the price system, competitive markets lead to economic efficiency. However, there are situations where markets fail to produce efficient outcomes and where markets consequently may not be competitive. For instance, markets produce too much of goods with negative externalities, like pollution, and not enough of goods with positive externalities, like basic research.

REVIEW AND PRACTICE

SUMMARY

1 When an economic change affects many markets at once, general equilibrium analysis is used to study the interactions among various parts of the economy. But when the secondary repercussions of a change are small, partial equilibrium analysis, focusing on only one or a few markets, is sufficient.

2 General equilibrium in the basic competitive model occurs when wages, interest rates, and prices

are such that demand is equal to supply in all labour markets, in all capital markets, and in all product markets. All markets clear.

3 Circular flow of funds diagrams show capital, labour, and product market interrelationships among households, firms, government, and the foreign sector. The flow of funds in and out of each sector must balance.

4 Under the conditions of the basic competitive model, the economy's resource allocation is Pareto-efficient—no one can be made better off without making someone else worse off.

5 The distribution of income that emerges from competitive markets may possibly be very unequal. However, under the conditions of the basic competitive model, a redistribution of wealth can move the economy to a more equal allocation that is also Pareto-efficient. No further government intervention is required.

6 Some economists hold that the basic competitive model provides an essentially accurate view of most of the economy; markets ensure economic efficiency, and there is only a limited role for government. Others maintain that many markets are quite imperfect, the basic competitive model provides no more than a starting point for analysis, and government intervention is required to deal with some of society's problems.

KEY TERMS

partial equilibrium analysis

general equilibrium analysis

circular flow

Pareto-efficient allocations

exchange efficiency

production efficiency

product-mix efficiency

REVIEW QUESTIONS

1 What is the difference between partial and general equilibrium analysis? When is each one especially appropriate?

2 List the principal flows into and out of firms, households, government, and the foreign sector.

3 How does the economy in general equilibrium answer the four basic economic questions: What is produced, and in what quantities? How are these goods produced? For whom are they produced? Who decides how resources are allocated?

4 What is meant by Pareto efficiency? What is required for the economy to be Pareto-efficient? If the conditions of the basic competitive model are satisfied, is the economy Pareto-efficient?

5 If the distribution of income in the economy is quite unequal, is it necessary to impose price controls or otherwise change prices in the competitive marketplace to make it more equal?

PROBLEMS

1 Decide whether partial equilibrium analysis would suffice in each of these cases, or whether it would be wise to undertake a general equilibrium analysis:
   (a) a tax on alcohol
   (b) an increase in the personal income tax
   (c) a drought that affects farm production in the Prairie provinces
   (d) a rise in the price of crude oil
   (e) a major airline going out of business
Explain your answers.

2 Use the extended circular flow diagram, with the foreign sector included, to trace out the possible consequences of the following:
   (a) a law requiring that businesses raise the wages of their employees
   (b) a decision by consumers to import more and save less
   (c) an increase in government expenditure financed by a corporate income tax
   (d) an increase in government expenditure without an accompanying increase in taxes

3 Explain how each of the following might interfere with exchange efficiency:

(a) airlines that limit the number of seats they sell at a discount price

(b) dentists who charge poor patients less than rich patients

(c) firms that give volume discounts

In each case, what additional trades might be possible?

4 Assume that in the steel industry, given current production levels and technology, one machine costing $10,000 can replace one worker. Given current production levels and technology in the automobile industry, one machine costing $10,000 can replace two workers. Is this economy Pareto-efficient? Is it on its production possibilities curve? If not, explain how total output of both goods can be increased by shifting machines and labour between industries.

5 Consider three ways of helping poor people to buy food, clothing, and shelter. The first way is to pass laws setting price ceilings to keep these basic goods affordable. The second is to have the government distribute coupons that give poor people a discount when they buy these necessities. The third is for the government to distribute income to poor people. Which programme is more likely to have a Pareto-efficient outcome? Describe why the other programmes are not likely to be Pareto-efficient.

APPENDIX: PARETO EFFICIENCY AND COMPETITIVE MARKETS

The concept of the marginal rate of substitution, introduced in the appendix to Chapter 6, can be used to see more clearly why competitive markets are Pareto-efficient.

EXCHANGE EFFICIENCY

Exchange efficiency can be achieved only when all individuals have the same marginal rate of substitution, the amount of one good a person is willing to give up to get one unit of another. In competitive markets, individuals choose a mix of goods for which the marginal rate of substitution is equal to relative prices. Since all individuals face the same relative prices, they all have identical marginal rates of substitution, ensuring the exchange efficiency of the economy.

To see why exchange efficiency requires that all people have the same marginal rate of substitution, let's look at a simple example of Robinson Crusoe and Friday and their island economy. Assume that Crusoe's marginal rate of substitution between ap-ples and oranges is 2; that is, he is willing to give up two apples for one extra orange. Friday's marginal rate of substitution between apples and oranges is 1; he is willing to give up one apple for one orange. Since their marginal rates of substitution are not equal, we can make one of them better off without making the other worse off (or we can make both of them better off). The allocation is not Pareto-efficient.

To see how this is done, suppose we take one orange away from Friday and give it to Crusoe. Crusoe would then be willing to give up two apples, and be just as well off as before. If he gave up only 1½ apples to Friday, Friday would also be better off. Friday would have given up one orange in return for 1½ apples; he would have been willing to make the trade if he had received just one apple in return.

It is easy to see that Crusoe and Friday will continue to trade until their marginal rates of substitution are equal. As Friday gives up oranges for apples, his marginal rate of substitution increases; he insists on getting more and more apples for each orange he gives up. Similarly, as Crusoe gives up apples and gets more oranges, his marginal rate of substitution decreases; he is willing to give up fewer apples for each extra orange he gets. Eventually, the two will have identical marginal rates of substitution, at which point trade will stop. Thus, the basic condition for exchange efficiency is that the marginal rates of substitution of all individuals must be the same.

PRODUCTION EFFICIENCY

The condition of production efficiency—when the economy is on its production possibilities curve—is very similar to the condition of exchange efficiency. An economy can only be productively efficient if the marginal rate of technical substitution between any two inputs in any two firms is the same. The marginal rate of technical substitution is the amount that one input can be reduced if another input is increased by one unit, while total output remains constant (see appendix to Chapter 9).

Profit-maximizing firms in a competitive economy choose a mix of inputs such that the marginal rate of technical substitution of different inputs is equal to the relative prices of those inputs. If all firms face the same relative prices of inputs, their marginal rates of technical substitution will all be the same, and production efficiency will result.

For example, consider a case involving the steel and auto industries. Assume that in steel, the marginal rate of substitution between capital expenditures and labour is $2,000: if a company uses one more worker, it can save $2,000 on equipment—or equivalently, two $1,000 machines substitute for one worker. In the auto industry, the marginal rate of substitution is $1,000; one $1,000 machine substitutes for one worker. The marginal rates of substitution between inputs are not equal, which means that the economy is not productively efficient.

Consider a worker moving from the auto to the steel industry. Assume that in the auto industry one $1,000 machine substitutes for one worker. If the steel industry keeps its output at the same level, the additional worker in that industry frees up two machines. One of those machines can be transferred to the auto industry, and production in that industry would stay at the same level. But one machine is left over. It can be used in the steel industry, the auto industry, or both to increase production.

As we increase the number of workers in steel, the marginal productivity of labour in that industry will diminish, and as we reduce workers in the automobile industry, the marginal productivity of labour in that industry will increase; the converse is true for machines. As a result, the marginal rates of technical substitution will shift in the two industries, until they come closer. Spurred on by the profit motive of the individual companies in competitive markets, labour and capital will tend to move between companies until marginal rates of technical substitution are equated, and production efficiency is reached. Thus, production efficiency, which means that the economy is on its production possibilities curve, requires that the marginal rate of technical substitution between any two inputs be the same in all uses.

PRODUCT-MIX EFFICIENCY

The third condition of Pareto efficiency requires that the economy operate at the point along the production possibilities curve that reflects consumers' preferences. Look at a particular point on the production possibilities curve in Figure 11.5, say point E. The **marginal rate of transformation** tells us how many extra units of one good the economy can get if it gives up one unit of another good—how many extra cases of beer the economy can produce if it reduces production of potato chips by a tonne, or how many extra cars the economy can get if it gives up one tank. The slope of the production possibilities curve is equal to the marginal rate of transformation. The slope tells us how much one good, measured along the vertical axis, can be increased if the economy gives up one unit of the good along the horizontal axis.

Product-mix efficiency requires that consumers' marginal rate of substitution equal the marginal rate of transformation. To see why this is so, and how competitive economies ensure product-mix efficiency, consider an economy producing two fruits, apples and oranges. Assume that the marginal rate of substitution between apples and oranges is 2—that is, individuals are willing to give up two apples for an additional orange; while the marginal rate of transformation is 1—they only have to give up one apple to get an additional orange. Clearly, it pays firms to increase orange production and reduce apple production.

The competitive price system ensures that the economy satisfies the condition for product-mix efficiency. We know that consumers set the marginal rate of substitution equal to the relative price. In a similar way, profit-maximizing firms have an incentive to produce more of some goods and less of others according to the prices they can sell them for, until their marginal rate of transformation is equal to the relative price. If consumers and producers both face the same relative prices, the marginal rate of substitution will equal the marginal rate of transformation. Thus, product-mix efficiency comes about when both consumers and firms face the same prices.

To see more clearly why competitive firms will set the marginal rate of transformation equal to relative prices, consider a firm that produces both apples and oranges. If the company reallocates labour from apples to oranges, apple production is reduced and orange production is increased. Assume apple production goes down by two cases and orange production goes up by one case. The marginal rate of transformation is 2. If a case of apples sells for $4 and a case of oranges sells for $10, the firm loses $8 on apple sales but gains $10 on orange sales. It is clearly profitable for the firm to make the switch. The firm will continue to switch resources from apples to oranges until the marginal rate of transformation

equals the relative price. The same result will occur even if oranges and apples are produced by different firms.[3]

Thus, the basic condition for product-mix efficiency, that the marginal rate of substitution must equal the marginal rate of transformation, will be satisfied in competitive economies because firms set the marginal rate of transformation equal to relative prices, and consumers set their marginal rate of substitution equal to relative prices.

---

[3] The concept of product-mix efficiency can be illustrated by superimposing a family of indifference curves (Chapter 6, appendix) in the same diagram with the production possibilities curve. Assume, for simplicity, that all individuals are the same. The highest level of welfare that one representative individual can attain is represented by the tangency of her indifference curve with the production possibilities curve. The slopes of two curves that are tangent to each other are equal at the point of tangency. The slope of the indifference curve is the consumer's marginal rate of substitution; the slope of the production possibilities curve is the marginal rate of transformation. Thus, the tangency —and Pareto efficiency—requires that the marginal rate of substitution equal the marginal rate of transformation.

PART THREE

IMPERFECT MARKETS

n Part Two, the basic model of perfectly competitive markets was developed. If the circumstances of the real world matched the assumptions made in this model, then markets could be given free rein. They would generate efficient outcomes. If an outcome seemed inequitable, society would simply redistribute initial wealth and let markets take care of the rest.

In the two centuries since Adam Smith enunciated the view that markets ensure economic efficiency, economists have investigated the model with great care. Nothing they have discovered has shaken their belief that markets are, by and large, the most efficient way to coordinate an economy. However, they have found significant departures between modern economies and the competitive model. Still, the insights of this model are powerful, so most economists use the basic competitive model as the starting point for building a richer, more complete model. In Part Three, and later, in Part Four, we explore the ways in which the real world deviates from the competitive model. We can enumerate the basic differences here.

1 Most markets are not as competitive as those envisioned by the basic model. For evidence, one need look only as far as the nearest brand name. When we think of beer, we think of Labatts, Molson, and Moosehead (among domestic beers). Automobiles bring to mind Chevrolets, Fords, Chryslers, and Toyotas. The examples go on; in fact, it is hard to think of a consumer product without attaching a brand name to it. The basic competitive model focuses on products, like wheat or pig iron, for which the products produced by different firms are essentially identical and are perfect substitutes for one another: there is no room for brand names. If a firm raises its price slightly above that of its rivals, it loses all of its customers. In the real world, a firm that raises its price slightly above that of its rivals loses some, but far from all, of its customers. A Labatts enthusiast would probably pay 10 cents more for a six-pack of Blue than for one of Molson's Ex. In the basic competitive model, when firms contemplate how much to produce, they take the market price as given and do not need to consider how their rivals will react. In the real world, many firms spend enormous amounts of energy trying to anticipate the actions and reactions of rivals. In Chapters 12–14, we will take up failures of competition in product markets and governmental responses to them.

2 The basic model simply ignores technological change. It tells us about the striving for efficiency that occurs as consumers and firms meet in competitive markets, but it assumes that all firms operate with a given technology; competition in the basic model is over price. Yet in the real world, the primary focus of competition is the development of new and better products and the improvements in production, transportation, and marketing that allow products to be brought to customers at lower costs and thus at a lower price. This competition takes place not between the multitude of small producers envisaged in the basic competitive model but often between industrial giants like Du Pont and Dow Chemical and between the industrial giants and upstarts, like IBM and the slew of small computer firms that eventually took away a major share of the computer market. Chapter 15 will enrich the model to help us understand better this more general view of competition, and to enable us to see how technological change can be encouraged.

3 The individuals and firms envisioned in the basic model have easy and inexpensive access to the information they need in order to operate in any market they enter. Buyers know what they are buying, whether it is stocks or bonds, a house, a car, or a refrigerator. Firms know perfectly the productivity of each worker they hire, and when a worker goes to work for a firm, he knows precisely what is expected of him in return for his promised pay. In actuality imperfections of information arise in all markets—product, labour, and capital—and in each they take on different forms as discussed in Chapter 16. Consider, for instance, the product market. Consumers cannot ascertain all the characteristics of a product before they buy it; they rely in part on the seller's reputation. They may worry that, if the price is too low, the product is likely to be shoddy; they use price in part to *judge* quality—a quite different role from that upon which Part Two focused, with important consequences.

Or consider the labour market. In the basic model, employers know precisely the qualifications and productivity of their workers and pay each accordingly. In the real world, employers cannot be certain which potential employee will be the most productive. But workers can *signal* their competence to firms by the amount of education they invest in or by exhibiting behaviour that shows, for instance, that they are likely to be dedicated and hardworking employees.

Information problems also arise in the capital market. When a lender provides funds to a borrower to finance an investment project, there is always some risk that the project will fail. Because they have better information, borrowers may be in a better position to assess that risk than are lenders. Not only may they know the inherent probability of success or failure, they may also have some influence over the risk of failure by virtue of their own actions. In these circumstances, capital markets will not necessarily ensure that savings are efficiently allocated among lenders.

The basic model fails to answer other important questions because in that model the answer is either trivial or unimportant. For instance, *who* takes economic decisions makes no difference, when the outcome of that decision-making process would be the same whoever sat in the manager's chair. Whether one firm takes over another would make no difference because the profit-maximizing decisions—what and how much should be produced and how it should be produced—would be the same in either case. But in actuality the decision about who manages a firm *is* important, and the takeover of one firm by another *can* have important consequences. Chapter 17 discusses some of the key issues concerning controlling and managing firms.

While beyond the scope of Part Three, the following points are noted here to complete our comparison of the competitive model and the real world.

4 The competitive model assumes that the costs of bringing a good to market accrue fully and completely to the seller and that the benefits of consuming a good go fully and completely to the buyer. In the real world, however, we encounter the possibility of *externalities*, extra costs or benefits that do not figure in the market calculation. There may be both positive externalities (such as national defence) and negative externalities (such as pollution). We will discuss externalities in Part Four.

5 The basic model answers the question "What goods will be produced, and in what quantities?" by assuming that all desired goods that *can* be brought to market *will* be brought to market. Trees that bloom in gold coins and tablets that guarantee an eternal youth are out of the question. But if customers want to buy green hair colouring, cancer-causing tobacco products, or life insurance policies overladen with extras, then producers can be expected to supply such goods. However, there are many cases where markets have not provided goods or services that could be provided at a cost consumers would be willing to pay. Some of the most obvious examples are in insurance markets, where government has intervened with such programmes as unemployment insurance, public pensions, and medical insurance. We will return to the problem of missing markets in Part Four.

6 In the basic model, all markets clear—supply meets demand at the market price. Decades of evidence, however, suggest, in fact, that labour markets often do not clear. The result is involuntary unemployment, sometimes on a massive scale. During the Great Depression, for instance, one out of five workers was out of a job. While beyond our scope in Part Three, the recurrence of involuntary unemployment in the economy is an important deviation from the competitive model of Part Two.

7 Even if markets are efficient, the way they allocate resources may appear to be socially unacceptable. We address this issue in Part Four, in the discussion of how government may redistribute income when the distribution produced by the market is deemed socially unacceptable.

8 In the competitive model, there is no role for government, because markets ensure economic efficiency. The foregoing discussion highlights several reasons why there may be dissatisfaction with markets—why they may not in fact ensure efficiency or why, even if markets were efficient, the outcomes may not be acceptable. In each of these instances, government may be called upon to intervene. In each of the ensuing chapters, we will not only explore the limitations of the markets, but also describe and assess the roles government has undertaken to address those limitations.

THE BASIC MODEL VERSUS THE REAL WORLD

THE BASIC MODEL	THE REAL WORLD
1 All markets are competitive.	1 Most markets are *not* characterized by the degree of competition envisioned in the basic model.
2 Technological know-how is fixed and cannot change.	2 Technological change is a central part of competition in modern industrial economies.
3 Firms, consumers, and any other market participants have easy access to information that is relevant to the markets in which they participate.	3 Good information may be impossible to come by and in most cases is costly to obtain. In many markets, buyers of products know less than the sellers.
4 Sellers bear the full and complete costs of bringing goods to market, and buyers reap the full benefit.	4 Externalities mean that market transactions may not accurately account for costs and benefits.
5 All desired markets exist.	5 Some markets may not exist, even though goods or services in that market might be provided at a cost consumers would be willing to pay.
6 There is no involuntary unemployment.	6 There is involuntary unemployment.
7 Competitive markets provide an efficient allocation of resources.	7 Efficiency is not enough. The income distribution generated by the market may be socially unacceptable.
8 There is no role for government.	8 Government plays an important role in the economy, correcting market failures, redistributing income, and providing social insurance.

CHAPTER 12

MONOPOLIES AND IMPERFECT COMPETITION

In the competitive model discussed in Part Two, markets have so many buyers and sellers that no individual household or firm believes its actions will affect the market equilibrium price. The buyer or seller takes the price as given, and then decides how much to buy or sell. At the "market" price, the seller can sell as much as she wants. But any effort to outfox the market has dramatic consequences. If, for instance, she raises her price above that of her competitors, her sales will be zero.

Not all markets are that competitive, however. For years, Bell Canada was the only long-distance telephone carrier in central Canada. Inco controlled the market for nickel, and Alcan the market for aluminum. Some firms so dominated a product that their brand name became synonymous with the product, as with Kleenex and Skidoos.

In some industries, such as soft drinks, a handful of firms (Coca-Cola, Pepsi, Canada Dry) dominate a market, producing similar but not identical products. When one such firm raises its price a little—say, by 2 or 3 percent—it loses some customers but far from all. If it lowers its price by 2 or 3 per-

KEY QUESTIONS

1 If there is only one firm in a market—a monopoly—how does it set its price and output? In what sense is the monopoly price too high?

2 Why do firms with no competition or imperfect competition face downward-sloping demand curves?

3 What are the barriers to entry that limit the number of firms in a market?

4 What does equilibrium look like in a market with imperfect competition, where barriers to entry are small enough so that profits are driven to zero, yet in which there are few enough firms so that each faces a downward-sloping curve?

cent, it gains additional customers, but not the entire market. As a result, these companies do not simply "take" the price as dictated to them by the market. They "make" the price. They are the **price makers.** Markets in which competition is limited are the subject of this chapter and the next.

MARKET STRUCTURES

One way to simplify an economy is to break it up into its constituent markets. One market in Canada is the passenger car market, in which Ford, General Motors, Chrysler, Toyota, and various other firms are the suppliers.

When economists look at markets, they look first at the **market structure,** that is, at how that market is organized. The market structure that forms the basis of the competitive model of Part Two is called perfect competition. An example of perfect competition would be when there are so many wheat farmers (producers) that no individual wheat farmer can realistically hope to move the price of wheat from that produced by the law of supply and demand.

Frequently, however, competition is not "perfect." Rather, it is limited. Economists group markets in which competition is limited into three broad categories. In the most extreme, there is no competition. A single firm supplies the entire market. This is called **monopoly.** Your local electric company prob-

ably has a monopoly in supplying electricity in your area. Since one would expect the profits of a monopolist to attract entry into that market, for a firm to maintain its monopoly position there must be some barrier to entry by other firms. Below, we learn what these barriers are.

In the second structure, several firms supply the market, so there is *some* competition. This is called **oligopoly.** The automobile industry is an example, with three main producers in Canada. The defining characteristic of oligopolies is that the small number of firms forces each to be concerned with how its rivals will react to any action it undertakes. If General Motors offers low-interest-rate financing, for instance, the other companies may feel compelled to match the offer; consequently, GM will have to take this into account before making any such offer. By contrast, a monopolist has no rivals and thus considers only whether special offers help or hurt itself. And a firm facing perfect competition can sell as much as it wants at the market price without having recourse to any special offers.

In the third type of market, there are more firms than in an oligopoly, but not enough for perfect competition. This is called **monopolistic competition.** An example is the market for moderately priced clothing as represented by Mark's Work Wearhouse, Zeller's, Kmart, and other such chains of stores. Each chain has its own make of clothing, which no other chain sells. But the clothing in each chain is similar enough to that supplied by other chains so that there is considerable competition.

ALTERNATIVE MARKET STRUCTURES

Perfect competition: Many, many firms, each believing that nothing it does will have any effect on the market price.

Monopoly: One firm.

Imperfect competition: Several firms, each aware that its sales depend on the price it charges and possibly other actions it takes, such as advertising. There are two special cases, oligopoly and monopolistic competition.

Types of Imperfect Competition:

Oligopoly: Few enough firms so that each worries about how rivals will respond to any action it undertakes.

Monopolistic competition: Enough firms so that each believes that its rivals will not change the price they charge should it lower its own price.

Even so, the clothing supplied by the different chains is different enough to make competition limited, so that the chain is not a price taker. The degree of competition under monopolistic competition is greater than that of oligopoly. This is because monopolistic competition involves a sufficiently large number of firms so that each firm can ignore the reactions of any rival. If one company lowers its price, it may garner for itself a large number of customers. But the number of customers it takes away from any single rival is so small that none of the rivals is motivated to retaliate.

With both oligopolies and monopolistic competition, there is some competition, but it is more limited than under perfect competition. These in-between market structures are referred to as **imperfect competition.**

This chapter focuses on monopoly and monopolistic competition. Oligopolies are left for Chapter 13. We begin with an analysis of how a monopolist sets its price and quantity, and how monopoly outcomes compare with competitive outcomes. We then switch to imperfect competition, a more common structure, and analyze the principal determinants of competition within any market. We follow this with an analysis of the barriers to entry that enable imperfectly competitive firms to sustain higher than normal profits for long periods of time. The final section looks at the case where barriers to entry are weak enough so that profits are driven to zero, but competition is still sufficiently limited so that each firm can change its prices without losing all its customers.

MONOPOLY OUTPUT

Economists' concerns about monopolies and other forms of restricted competition stem mainly from the observation that the output, or supply, of firms within these market structures is less than would be the case if the firms were faced with perfect competition. To address these concerns, we consider a monopolist that charges the same price to all its customers and show how it determines its level of output.

A monopolist and a competitive firm are similar in some ways. Both try to maximize profits. In determining output, they compare the extra (or marginal) revenue they would receive from producing an extra unit of output with the extra (or marginal) cost of producing that extra unit. If marginal revenue exceeds marginal cost, it pays to expand output. Conversely if marginal revenue is less than marginal cost, it pays to reduce output. Thus, the basic principle for output determination for both a competitive firm and a monopolist is the same. Each produces at the output level at which marginal revenue equals marginal cost.

The essential difference between a monopolist and a competitive firm is that a competitive firm takes the price set by market forces. When such a firm increases production by one unit, its marginal revenue is just the price. For instance, the marginal revenue a wheat farmer receives from producing one more bushel of wheat is the price of a bushel of wheat. But the only way a monopolist can sell more is to lower the price it charges, so marginal revenue is *not* equal to the present market price.

The difference can be put another way. The demand curve facing a competitive firm is perfectly horizontal, as illustrated in Figure 12.1A. The price, p^*, is the "market price." The firm can sell as much as it wants at that price, and nothing at any higher price. In an industry such as wheat farming, if there are 100,000 wheat farmers, each farmer on average accounts for one thousandth of 1 percent (.001 percent) of the market. If a single average farmer even doubled his production, the total production would increase by a factor of .00001—a truly negligible amount that could be absorbed by the market with no perceptible change in price.

By contrast, the demand curve facing a monopolist is downward-sloping, as illustrated in Figure 12.1B. By definition the monopolist controls the entire industry, so that a doubling of *its* output is a doubling of industry output, which will have a significant effect on price. If Inco had increased its production by 1 percent in the days when it had a virtual monopoly on nickel, the total supply of nickel would have increased by 1 percent. Market prices would have fallen observably in response to a change in supply of even that magnitude.

The marginal revenue a monopolist receives from producing one more unit can be broken into two separate components. First, the firm receives revenue from selling the additional output. This additional revenue is just the market price. But to sell more, the firm must reduce its price. It must do so to sell the extra output. Marginal revenue is the price it receives from the sale of the one additional unit *minus* the loss in revenues from the price reduction on all other units. Thus, for a monopolist, the marginal revenue for producing one extra unit is always less than the price received for that extra unit. (Only at the "first" unit produced are marginal revenue and price the same.)

This can be represented by a simple equation:

marginal revenue =
net increase in revenue from selling one more unit =
price + $\Delta p \times Q$

where Δp represents the change in price and Q rep-

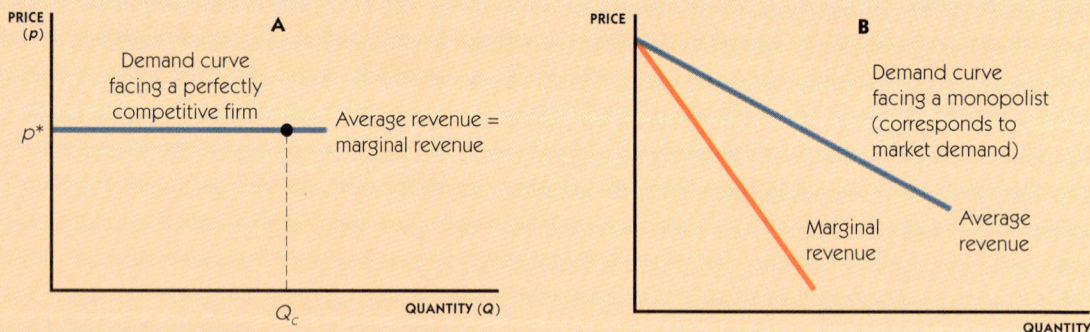

Figure 12.1 THE DEMAND CURVES FACING A PERFECTLY COMPETITIVE FIRM AND A MONOPOLIST

A perfectly competitive firm can sell any quantity it wishes at the market price, but cannot raise the price at all without losing all its business. It faces the horizontal demand curve, which is also its average revenue and marginal revenue curve, shown in panel A. A monopolist provides all the output in a market, so an increased output can only be sold at a reduced price. Panel B shows the downward-sloping demand curve—the market demand curve—faced by the monopolist. The demand curve is also the average revenue curve, and lies above the marginal revenue curve.

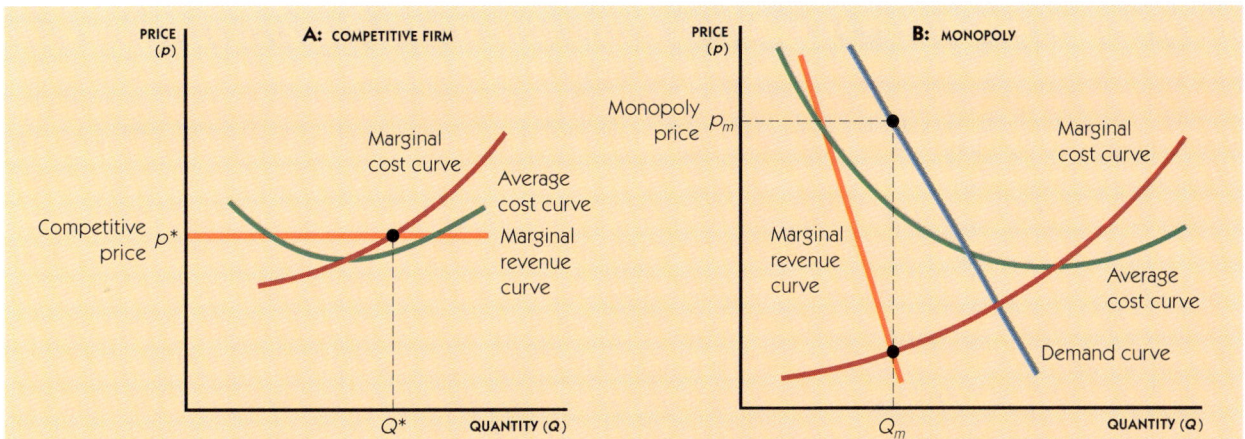

Figure 12.2 MARGINAL REVENUE EQUALS MARGINAL COST

A perfectly competitive firm gains or loses exactly the market price (p^*) when it changes the quantity produced. To maximize profits, the firm produces the quantity where marginal cost equals marginal revenue, which in the competitive case also equals price. Panel B shows the

downward-sloping marginal revenue curve for a monopolist. A monopolist also chooses the level of quantity where marginal cost equals marginal revenue. In the monopolistic case, however, marginal revenue is lower than price.

resents the initial quantity sold.[1] For a competitive firm, $\Delta p = 0$, so marginal revenue equals price. For a monopolist, Δp is negative, so marginal revenue is less than the price.

The price a firm receives for each unit of output it sells is simply its average revenue. Thus, we see that for a monopolist, marginal revenue is less than average revenue. Represented as a diagram, the average revenue curve facing a monopolist is simply the market demand curve; it shows the price or average revenue that would be obtained from selling various quantities of output. The marginal revenue curve lies below the average revenue curve because average revenue exceeds marginal revenue by the amount $\Delta p \times Q$. Figure 12.1B depicts the relationship between the average revenue curve and the marginal revenue curve for a monopolist.

Figure 12.2A shows the output decision of a competitive firm. Marginal revenue is just equal to the market price, p^*. Panel B shows the output decision

of a monopolist. Marginal revenue is always less than price. Note that with a monopoly, since marginal revenue is less than price and marginal revenue equals marginal cost, marginal cost is less than price. The price is what individuals are willing to pay for an extra unit of the product; it measures the marginal benefit to the consumer of an extra unit. Thus, the marginal benefit of an extra unit exceeds the marginal cost. This is the fundamental reason that monopolies reduce economic efficiency.[2]

The extent to which output is curtailed below the efficient level depends on the magnitude of the difference between marginal revenue and price. This in turn depends on the shape of the demand curve. When demand curves are very elastic (relatively flat), prices do not fall much when output increases. As shown in Figure 12.3A, marginal revenue is not much less than price. The firm produces at Q_m, where marginal revenue equals marginal cost. Q_m is slightly less than the efficient output, Q_c, where price

[1]More specifically, marginal revenue equals $\Delta(p \times Q) = p \times \Delta Q + \Delta p \times Q = p + \Delta p \times Q$ for a change in output of one unit ($\Delta Q = 1$).

[2]Chapter 14 will describe more precisely how the magnitudes of the losses associated with monopoly can be quantified.

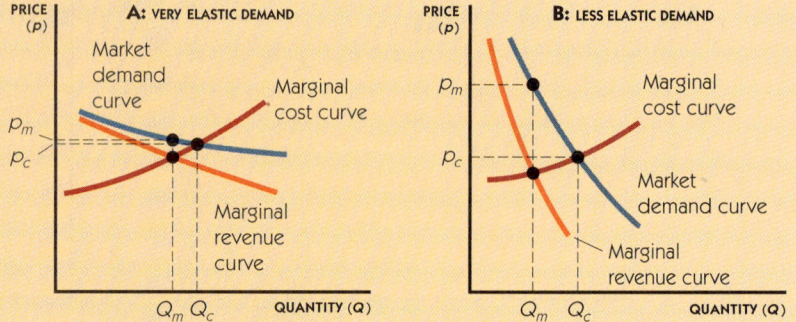

Figure 12.3 MONOPOLY AND THE ELASTICITY OF DEMAND

In panel A, a monopoly faces a very elastic market demand, so prices do not fall much as output increases, and marginal cost is not much less than price. In panel B, a monopoly faces a less elastic market demand, so prices fall quite a lot as output increases, and price is substantially above marginal cost.

equals marginal cost. When demand curves are less elastic, as in panel B, prices may fall a considerable amount when output increases, and then the extra revenue the firm receives from producing an extra unit of output will be much less than the price received from selling that unit.

The larger the elasticity of demand, the smaller the discrepancy between marginal revenue and price. This can be seen simply by using the definitions of the elasticity of demand and marginal revenue:

elasticity of demand =

$$-\frac{\text{change in market quantity}}{\text{market quantity}} \bigg/ \frac{\text{change in price}}{\text{price}} =$$

$$-\frac{\Delta Q}{Q} \bigg/ \frac{\Delta p}{p}.$$

If we consider a change in quantity by 1 (as we do when we calculate marginal revenue), so that $\Delta Q = 1$,

$$\text{elasticity of demand} = -\frac{1}{Q} \bigg/ \frac{\Delta p}{p} = -\frac{p}{Q\Delta p}$$

and

marginal revenue = price + change in price × quantity sold =

$$p + Q\Delta p =$$

$$p \left(1 + \frac{Q\Delta p}{p}\right) =$$

$$p \, (1 - 1/\text{elasticity of demand}).$$

Hence, if the elasticity of demand is 2, marginal revenue is ½ of price. If the elasticity of demand is 10, marginal revenue is 9/10 of price.

THE FIRM'S SUPPLY DECISION

All firms maximize profits at the point where marginal revenue (the revenue from selling an extra unit of the product) equals marginal cost.

For a competitive firm, marginal revenue equals price (average revenue).

For a monopoly, marginal revenue is less than price (average revenue).

Table 12.1 DEMAND CURVE FACING ABC-MENT COMPANY

Cubic metres (thousands)	Price	Total revenues	Marginal revenues	Total costs	Marginal costs
1	$10,000	$10,000		$15,000	
			$8,000		$2,000
2	$ 9,000	$18,000		$17,000	
			$6,000		$3,000
3	$ 8,000	$24,000		$20,000	
			$4,000		$4,000
4	$ 7,000	$28,000		$24,000	
			$2,000		$5,000
5	$ 6,000	$30,000		$29,000	
			0		$6,000
6	$ 5,000	$30,000		$35,000	

AN EXAMPLE: THE ABC-MENT COMPANY

Table 12.1 gives the demand curve facing the ABC-ment Company, which has a monopoly on the production of cement in its area. There is a particular price at which it can sell each level of output. As it lowers its price, it can sell more cement. Local builders will, for instance, use more cement and less wood and other materials in constructing a house.

At a price of $10,000 per unit of 1,000 cubic me-

tres, the firm sells one unit; at a price of $9,000, it sells two units; and at a price of $8,000, three units. The third column of the table shows the total revenues at each of these levels of production. The total revenues are just price × quantity. The marginal revenue from producing an extra unit of 1,000 cubic metres is just the difference between, say, the revenues received at three units and two units or two units and one unit. Notice that in each case, the marginal revenue is less than the price.

Figure 12.4 shows the demand and marginal revenues curves, using data from Table 12.1. At each

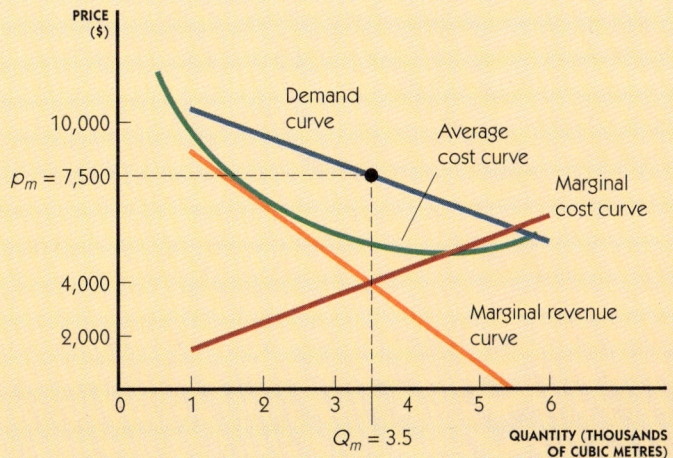

Figure 12.4 DEMAND AND MARGINAL REVENUE

At each level of output, the marginal revenue curve lies below the demand curve.

level of output, the marginal revenue curve lies below the demand curve. As can be seen from the table, not only does price decrease as output increases, but so does marginal revenue.

The output at which marginal revenues equal marginal costs—the output chosen by the profit-maximizing monopolist—is denoted by Q_m. In our example, $Q_m = 3,500$ cubic metres. When the number of cubic metres increases from 3,000 to 4,000, the marginal revenue is $4,000, and so is the marginal cost. We set the output corresponding to this marginal revenue at 3,500, midway between 3,000 and 4,000 cubic metres. At this level of output, the price is p_m, $7,500 per 1,000 cubic metres, which is considerably in excess of marginal costs, $4,000. Total revenues, $26,250 ($7,500 × 3.5), are also in excess of total costs, $22,000.

MONOPOLY PROFITS

Monopolists maximize their profits by setting marginal revenue equal to marginal cost. The total level of monopoly profits can be seen in two ways, as shown in Figure 12.5. Panel A shows total revenues and total costs (from Table 12.1) for each level of output of the ABC-ment Company. The difference between revenues and costs is profits—the vertical distance between the two curves. This distance is maximized at the output $Q_m = 3,500$ cubic metres. We can see that at this level of output, profits are $4,250 ($26,250 − $22,000). Panel B calculates profits using the average cost diagram. Total profits are equal to the profit per unit multiplied by the number of units produced. The profit per unit is the difference between the unit price and the average cost, and total monopoly profits is the shaded area ABCD. Again, the sum is $4,250: ($7,500 − $6,286) × 3.5.

In Chapter 10, we saw that competition drives profits to zero. This means price is equal to the minimum average cost of the least efficient firm in the industry. The difference between what the least efficient firm gets in net revenue and what more efficient, lower-cost firms receive—as we also saw in Chapter 10—is rent to an economist. Competitive firms can receive rent, for instance, because a firm

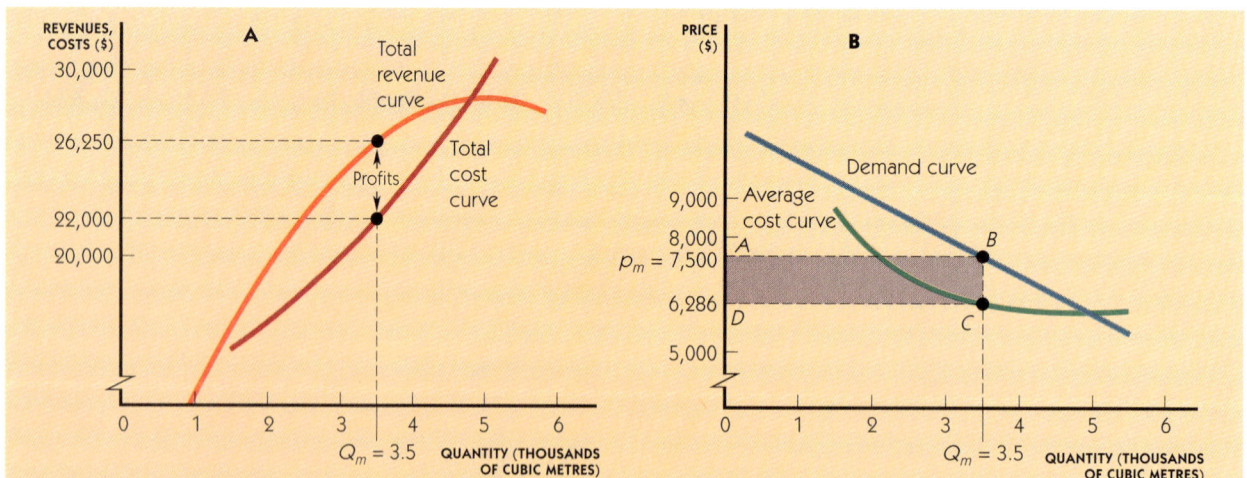

Figure 12.5 PRICE EXCEEDING AVERAGE COST MEANS PROFIT

Panel A shows profits to be the distance between the total revenue and total cost curves, maximized at the output $Q_m = 3,500$ cubic metres. Profits occur when the market price is above average cost, as in panel B, so that the company is (on average) making a profit on each unit it sells. Monopoly profits are the area ABCD, which is average profit per unit times the number of units sold.

USING ECONOMICS: DEMAND AND MARGINAL REVENUE

The relationship between marginal and average revenue curves can be seen readily for the case in which the demand curve is a straight line. For a linear demand curve the relationship between price (p) and quantity (Q) can be expressed algebraically by the standard expression for a straight line,

$$p = a - bQ,$$

where a is the intercept and $-b$ is the slope of the demand curve. This is depicted in the figure below. For a monopolist the demand curve shows the price, or average revenue (AR), at which any given quantity supplied could be sold. Increasing quantity sold by one unit causes the price to fall by b. The total revenue from selling an output Q is just price times quantity, or total revenue = pQ.

For small changes in output, the change in total revenue can be expressed as

$$\Delta(pQ) = p\Delta Q + Q\Delta p,$$

where Δ means "change in." Marginal revenue (MR) is just the change in total revenue from selling an additional unit of output. Setting $\Delta Q = 1$ in the previous expression and using the fact that a unit change in output causes the price to fall by b (so $\Delta p = -b$), marginal revenue is therefore

$$MR = p - bQ.$$

Finally, since $p = a - bQ$ from above, marginal revenue can be rewritten as

$$MR = a - bQ - bQ = a - 2bQ.$$

As with the demand or average revenue curve, this is just a straight line with the intercept a as the average revenue curve, but twice the slope $-2b$. The marginal revenue curve is also shown on the diagram. As can be seen, it is twice as steep as the average revenue curve and intersects the horizontal axis midway between the origin and the point where the demand curve intersects the horizontal axis.

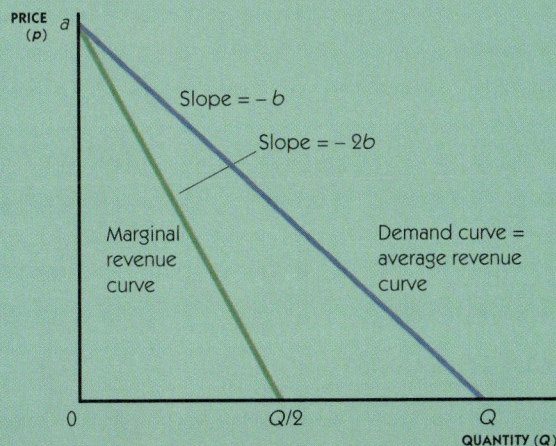

PRICE (p)

Slope = $-b$

Slope = $-2b$

Marginal revenue curve

Demand curve = average revenue curve

0   Q/2   Q

QUANTITY (Q)

has more knowledge than its competitors or some special advantage or fixed factor of production, and thus lower costs, yet faces the same market price as all other firms.

Rents are present in competitive markets as well as in monopolies. But for monopolists there is a different kind of return that cannot be traced to rents on technological capabilities. Even after taking these factors into account, a monopolist enjoys an extra return because it has been able to reduce its output and increase its price from the level that would have prevailed under competition. This return is called a **pure profit.** Because these payments are not required to elicit greater effort or production on the part of the monopolist (in fact, they derive from the monopolist's *reducing* the output from what it would be under competition), they are also called **monopoly rents.**

PRICE DISCRIMINATION

The basic objective of monopolists is to maximize profits, and they accomplish this by setting marginal revenue equal to marginal cost, so price exceeds marginal cost. Monopolists can also engage in a variety of other practices to increase their profits.

Among the most important is **price discrimination,** which means charging different prices to different customers or in different markets.

Figure 12.6 shows an international monopolist setting marginal revenue equal to marginal cost in the United States and Canada. For simplicity, marginal costs are assumed to be constant for the firm. The demand curves the firm faces in the two countries are different. Therefore, though marginal costs are the same, the firm will charge different prices for the same good in the two countries. In particular, the higher price will be charged in the country with the less elastic demand curve. (By contrast, in competitive markets, price equals marginal cost, so that regardless of the shape of the demand curves, price will be the same in the two markets, except for the different costs of delivering the good to each market.) With prices in the two countries differing, middleman firms will enter the market, buying the product in the country with the low price and selling it in the other country. Many companies attempt to thwart the middlemen by, for instance, having distinct labels on the two products and refusing to provide service or honour any guarantees outside the country in which the good is originally delivered.

Within a country, a monopolist can also price discriminate *if* resale is difficult and *if* it can distin-

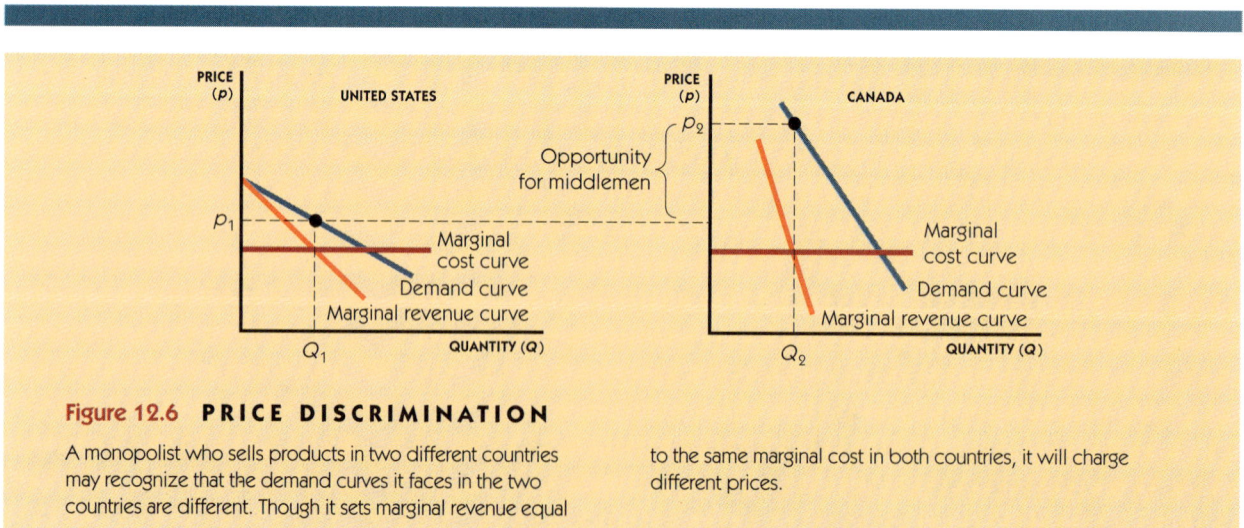

Figure 12.6 **PRICE DISCRIMINATION**

A monopolist who sells products in two different countries may recognize that the demand curves it faces in the two countries are different. Though it sets marginal revenue equal to the same marginal cost in both countries, it will charge different prices.

The term "price discrimination" conjures up notions of unfairness: Why should different customers be charged different prices for the same product produced at exactly the same cost? Canadian law seems to acknowledge that this is unfair by making the practice illegal. But the law against price discrimination is rarely enforced. There have been only three convictions since 1935 and all cases involved sales not to consumers but to retail firms that then compete with each other in the same market.

Yet price discrimination involving sales to consumers is not uncommon. Perhaps the most obvious example is the preferential prices offered to senior citizens and children: age-related discounts are offered by public transit companies, cinemas, hair stylists, theme parks, and many other services. One might argue that seniors and children are justified in getting a break, because they often use things like public transit and cinemas at off-peak times, so that cost differences could account for the discounted prices. But this is not convincing: it would be more fair if transit operators and cinema owners charged different prices in peak versus off-peak hours, regardless of the user.

Should the law against the common practice of price discrimination be enforced? The most compelling reason for allowing these pricing practices is that they may well offer an improvement in the efficiency of market outcomes over a "single-price" solution. As long as the movie theatre is not full to capacity, then it is difficult to see who is made worse off by the offering of the discount tickets. The children and seniors are clearly better off. The theatre owners are presumably better off—no one is forcing them to offer the discounts. And aside from those who are jealous of their younger and older fellow customers, the adults are left in essentially the same position they would be otherwise. Thus price discrimination which induces greater use of a facility with excess capacity is "efficiency-enhancing," and society would be worse off by banning the practice.

Even in cases where the buyers are firms in competition with one another, price discrimination is not necessarily inefficient. By segmenting a market and offering a lower price in the segment with the more elastic demand, total output is almost certain to rise. Thus, one of the sources of inefficiency in monopoly situations is countered.

What the law appears to be concerned with are situations in which the monopolist discriminates between buyers not only to increase its output and enhance its own profits, but also to expand its market power and keep out any potential competitors. Most complaints involving price discrimination are dealt with under other parts of the law dealing with competition, such as the prohibition of firms from monopolizing markets or abusing a dominant position. Perhaps it is not so surprising that the law against price discrimination is hardly ever enforced.

guish between buyers with high and low elasticities of demand. An electricity company can make its charge for each kilowatt hour depend on how much electricity the customer uses, because of restrictions on the retransmission of electricity. If the company worries that large customers faced with the same high prices that it charges small customers might install their own electric generators, or switch to some other energy source, it may charge them a lower price. An airline with a monopoly on a particular route might charge business customers a higher fare than vacationers. They do so knowing that business customers have no choice but to make the trip, while vacationers have many alternatives. They can travel elsewhere, on another day, or by car or train, so their demand is more elastic. Such business practices enable the monopolist to increase its profits relative to what they would be if it charged a single price in the market. Firms facing imperfect competition also engage in these practices, as we shall see. Airlines again provide a telling example. Canada's anti-combines legislation, the Competition Act of 1986, makes it illegal to engage in price discrimination that restricts competition. In particular, products cannot be sold at different prices to competing buyers for reasons unrelated to cost. But this provision has rarely been enforced. Other elements of Canada's competition policy will be discussed more fully in Chapter 14.

One form of price discrimination applying to international trade that most countries attempt to prevent is called **dumping.** The term dumping is meant to refer to the sale of a product abroad at a price lower than the cost of production. If an exporter faces a less elastic demand for its product abroad than at home, profit maximization would induce it to charge a lower price to foreigners. An economist might view such a practice as being beneficial to the importing country since it would be able to buy the good more cheaply. But, policy makers rarely see matters that way. Dumping by foreign firms is seen as unfair by domestic producers and as an attempt to inflict damage on the domestic industry by reducing its market artificially. Most countries, including Canada, impose anti-dumping duties on imports that are sold at a price below that prevailing in the home country, regardless of the cost conditions abroad. Thus anti-dumping duties have become one of the main ways of protecting domestic industry against imports. They have also become a source of some trade friction between Canada and the United States. In 1992 alone, major anti-dumping duties were imposed by the United States on imports of beef, softwood lumber, steel, Honda cars, and magnesium from Canada.

IMPERFECT COMPETITION

In most markets, there is more than a single firm. In the perfectly competitive model of Part Two, firms compete against one another while believing they cannot affect the price—that if they raise their price, they will lose all their business. But in industries other than agriculture, imperfect competition is more typical. Firms compete, often vigorously, against one another. But each believes that if it lowers its price, it can capture some but not all sales from other firms, and if it raises its price it will lose some but not all of its customers.

One way to assess the competitiveness of a particular market is to consider what will happen if a firm in that market raises its price. What percentage of its sales will it lose—in other words, what is its elasticity of demand? Firms in a perfectly competitive market face horizontal demand curves. The elasticity of demand for their output is infinite. By the same token, they are price takers. If they raise their price at all, they lose all their customers. They have no **market power,** a term meant to suggest the ability of a firm to throw its weight around the way a monopoly can. As imperfect competition sets in, the demand curve facing a firm in the industry begins to slope downwards. The more downward-sloping the demand curve, the more market power the firm has.

Two factors affect the elasticity of the demand curve facing a firm and, therefore, its market power. The first is the number of firms in the industry—more generally, how concentrated production is within a few firms. The second is the difference in the goods that are produced by the various firms in the industry.

Table 12.2 DEGREE OF COMPETITION IN VARIOUS INDUSTRIES, 1985

	Top 4 firms' percentage of sales
Petroleum refining	64
Motor vehicles and car bodies	95
Fish products	47
Breweries	98
Sawmills	17
Pharmaceuticals and medicines	27
Fruit and vegetable canners	41

Source: C. Green, *Canadian Industrial Organization and Policy* (Toronto: McGraw-Hill/Ryerson, 1990), p. 80.

NUMBER OF FIRMS IN THE INDUSTRY

Competition is likely to be greater when there are many firms in an industry (textiles, shoes) than when a few companies dominate (home refrigerators and freezers, greeting cards, soft drinks). Table 12.2 gives the percentage of output that is produced by the top four firms in a variety of industries ranging from fish products to petroleum refining. The percentage of output produced by the top four firms in an industry is called the **four-firm concentration ratio**, one of several measures used to study industry concentration. When the four-firm percentage is high, as in the automobile or brewing industries, companies have considerable market power. This is true even when they produce similar or identical products, as in the case of petroleum refining. When it is low, as in the case of sawmills or pharmaceuticals, market power is low; each firm faces a practically horizontal demand curve.[3]

[3]In both theory and practice, a critical issue in evaluating the extent of competition is defining the relevant market, an issue taken up in Chapter 14.

PRODUCT DIFFERENTIATION

In addition to the number of firms in a market—and how concentrated production is—the amount of competition depends on how similar the goods are that are produced by different firms. In some industries, the goods produced are essentially identical—nickel produced by Falconbridge is essentially identical to that produced by Inco. More typically, the firms in an industry with imperfect competition produce goods that are **imperfect substitutes**—goods sufficiently similar so that they can be used for many of the same purposes, but different enough so that one may be somewhat better than another, at least for some purposes or in some people's minds. Kellogg's Corn Flakes and the store brand may look alike, but more people purchase the Kellogg's version, even though it is more expensive.

The fact that similar products nonetheless differ from one another is referred to as **product differentiation.** Firms in imperfect markets spend considerable effort to produce goods that are slightly different from those of their competitors.

SOURCES OF PRODUCT DIFFERENTIATION

Many of the differences between products can be seen, heard, or tasted by consumers. But location can also provide the basis for product differentiation. People are willing to pay more for service at a neighbourhood garage, rather than drive fifty kilometres to a discount garage. They are willing to pay more for milk at the neighbourhood grocery store than at the supermarket out on the main road.

In cases where consumers find it difficult to assess the quality of a product before they purchase it, they rely heavily on firm reputations. They may buy Bayer aspirin even though it is more expensive than the store brand, because they believe it is of a higher quality. (In fact, aspirin itself is just acetylsalicylic acid, nothing more nor less. Still, the binding agents that hold the pill together may differ, so the effects may differ.) Consumers are often willing to pay more for goods with a trademark than for generic brands.

Ignorance and the costs of obtaining information often make the products of one firm an imperfect substitute for another. A consumer sees a dress for $45. She might know or suspect that some other store is selling the same dress for $35, but she does not know where, she is not sure it is in stock there, it will cost her money to drive around looking for it, and so she buys the dress at $45 anyway. If the store had raised its price to $55, she probably would have made the effort to search. If a store raises its prices, more customers decide to search out the bargains, and sales go down.

HOW PRODUCT DIFFERENTIATION IMPLIES IMPERFECT COMPETITION

When goods are perfect substitutes, individuals will choose whichever is cheapest. In an imaginary world where all brands of cornflakes really are perfect substitutes for all consumers, they would all sell at the same price. If one brand lowered its price slightly, all consumers (assuming they knew this) would switch to it. If it raised its price slightly, all consumers would switch to the rival brand. That is why the demand curve facing the manufacturer of a perfectly substitutable good is horizontal, as illustrated in Figure 12.7A.

By contrast, if most consumers view the different brands as imperfect substitutes, the demand curve facing each firm will be downward-sloping, as in panel B. This, we have already learned, implies a departure from perfect competition. Some individuals may prefer sogginess and be willing to pay more for cornflakes that rapidly become soggy. Others may prefer crispness and be willing to pay more for cereal that does not become soggy. Assume that Kellogg's Corn Flakes become soggy more slowly than the store brand. As the price for Kellogg's increases above that of the store brand, individuals

Figure 12.7 DEMAND CURVES WITH PERFECT AND IMPERFECT COMPETITION

Panel A shows the demand curve for a perfectly competitive firm: if it raises its price, all its customers will find substitutes. The marginal revenue curve for the firm is the same as its demand curve. Panel B shows the demand curve and marginal revenue curve facing a firm with only imperfect substitutes for its products.

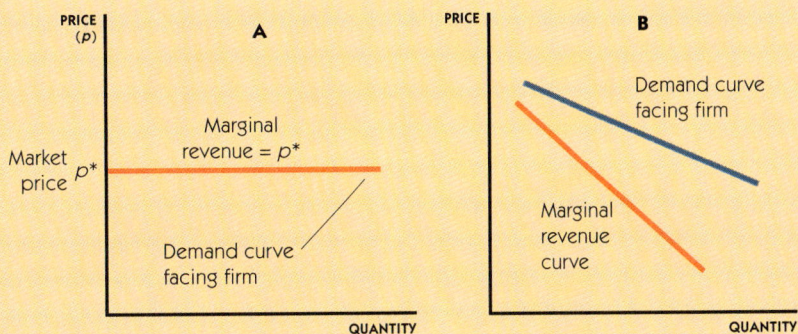

A

PRICE (p)

Market price p^*

Marginal revenue = p^*

Demand curve facing firm

QUANTITY

B

PRICE

Demand curve facing firm

Marginal revenue curve

QUANTITY

who care less about crispness will switch to the store brand. They are not willing to pay the price differential. But some are willing to pay a lot more for crisp flakes. Hence, Kellogg's does not lose all its customers, even if it charges considerably more than the store brand. By the same token, when Kellogg's lowers its price below that of the store brand, it does not steal all the customers. Those who love sogginess will pay more for the store brand.

It matters little whether the differences between the brands are true or simply perceived differences. The store brand and Kellogg's Corn Flakes could be identical, but if Kellogg's advertisements have convinced some consumers that there is a difference, they will not switch even if the price of Kellogg's is higher. Numerous studies attest to the fact that consumers often see differences where none exist. One study put the same soap into two kinds of packages, one marked Brand A, the other marked Brand B. Homemakers were asked to judge which brand

cleaned their clothes more effectively. Half saw no difference, but the other half claimed to see significant differences. Another study put the same beer into three kinds of bottles, one labelled premium, the second labelled standard, the third labelled discount. After drinking the differently bottled beers over an extended period of time, consumers were asked which they preferred. The "premium" beer was chosen consistently.

BARRIERS TO ENTRY: WHY IS COMPETITION LIMITED?

Normally, profits attract other firms to enter the market. For a monopoly to persist, some factors must prevent competition from springing up.

BASES OF PRODUCT DIFFERENTIATION

1 Differences in characteristics of products produced by different firms

2 Differences in location of different firms

3 Perceived differences, often induced by advertising

Similarly, when there are profits with imperfect competition, some factors must prevent other firms' entering and eroding those profits. Such factors are called **barriers to entry.** They take a variety of forms, ranging from government rules that prohibit or limit competition, for good or bad reasons, to technological reasons that naturally limit the number of firms in a market, to market strategies that keep potential competitors at bay.

When there are few barriers to entry, a monopoly can only be temporary—the profits of the monopolist will attract entry, and the firm's monopoly position will be lost. When there are many barriers, even if they only serve to delay entry, there is cause for concern, particularly when firms themselves take actions to create the barriers.

GOVERNMENT POLICIES

Many early monopolies were established by governments. In the seventeenth century, the British government gave a monopoly to the East India Company for trade with India and, later, to the Hudson's Bay Company for trade with British North America. The state salt monopoly in eighteenth-century France had the exclusive right to sell salt. Even today, governments grant certain monopoly franchises, for example, for electric and telephone service within a locality and for first-class mail delivery by Canada Post.

But the most important monopolies granted by government today are patents. As we learned in Chapter 1, a patent gives inventors the exclusive right to produce or to licence others to produce their discoveries for a limited period of time, currently twenty years. The argument for patents is that without them, copycat firms would spring up with every new invention, inventors would make little money from their discoveries, and there would be no economic incentive to invent. Patents are so important that the constitution of Canada, the British North America Act of 1867, explicitly included a provision—Section 91(22)—enabling the newly created federal government to grant patents.

Occasionally governments set policies that restrict entry, allowing some, but only limited, competition. Licensing requirements in many of the professions (law, accounting, medicine), whose ostensible purpose is to protect consumers against incompetent practitioners, may at the same time limit the number of qualified practitioners, and thus limit competition.

SINGLE OWNERSHIP OF AN ESSENTIAL INPUT

Another barrier to entry and source of monopoly power is a firm's exclusive ownership of something that is not producible. For example, an aluminum company might attempt to become a monopolist in aluminum by buying all the sources of bauxite, the essential ingredient. A single South African company, De Beers, has come close to monopolizing the world's supply of diamonds. There are relatively few instances of such monopolies.

INFORMATION

Information does not pass through the economy in the full and complete way envisioned in the basic competitive model of Part Two. In considering barriers to market entry, we encounter two of the many ways that information—and the lack thereof—affects market outcomes. First, firms engage in research to give them a technological advantage over competitors. Even if they do not get a patent, it will take time before what they learn disseminates to rivals. The fact that firms outside the industry do not know the trade secrets of the industry provides an important barrier to entry. Coca-Cola and Kentucky Fried Chicken guard their recipes with the greatest care.

Second, consumers have imperfect information concerning the products being sold by different firms. As a new firm, you must not only let potential buyers know about your product, you must convince them that the product is a better value than that of your rivals. When goods differ markedly in qualities that cannot easily be detected, it may not suffice simply to sell at a lower price. Customers may interpret the lower price as signalling lower quality. Thus, to get customers to try your product, you may have to advertise heavily and give away free samples. Entry costs like these constitute another significant barrier to entry.

ECONOMIES OF SCALE AND NATURAL MONOPOLIES

The technology needed to produce a good can sometimes result in a market with only one or very few firms. For example, it would be inefficient to have two firms construct power lines on each street in a city, with one company delivering electricity to one house and another company to the house next door. Likewise, in most locales, there is only one gravel pit or concrete plant. These situations are called **natural monopolies.**

A natural monopoly occurs whenever the average costs of production for a single firm are declining up to levels of output beyond those likely to emerge in the market. When the average costs of production fall as the scale of production increases, we say there are economies of scale, a concept first introduced in Chapter 9. In Figure 12.8, the demand curve facing a monopoly intersects the average cost curve at an output level at which average costs are still declining, Q_r. At large enough outputs, average costs might start to increase, but that level of output is irrelevant to the actual market equilibrium. For instance, firms in the cement industry have U-shaped average cost curves, and the level of output at which costs are minimized is quite high. Accordingly, in smaller, isolated communities, there is a natural monopoly in cement.

A natural monopolist is protected by the knowledge that it can undercut its rivals should they enter. Since entrants typically are smaller and average costs decline with size, their average costs are higher. Therefore the monopolist feels relatively immune from the threat of entry. So long as it does not have to worry about entry, it acts like any other monopolist, setting marginal revenue equal to marginal cost, as in Figure 12.8, where it produces at the output Q_m and charges p_m.

Whether a particular industry is a natural monopoly depends on the size of the output at which average costs are minimized relative to the size of the market. With high enough demand, the monopolist will be operating along the rising part of the average cost curve. At this point, the monopolist can be undercut by an entrant, since a new firm that enters at the output at which average costs are minimized has costs that are lower. Thus, with high enough demand, the industry is no longer a natural monopoly. In medium-sized cities, there may be several producers of cement, so that instead of a monopoly, there is an oligopoly.

Among the most important determinants of market size are transportation costs. Among the most important determinants of the quantity of output at which average costs are minimized is the size of the fixed costs. The larger the expenditures of the firm just to begin production, the larger the scale of production at which average costs are minimized.

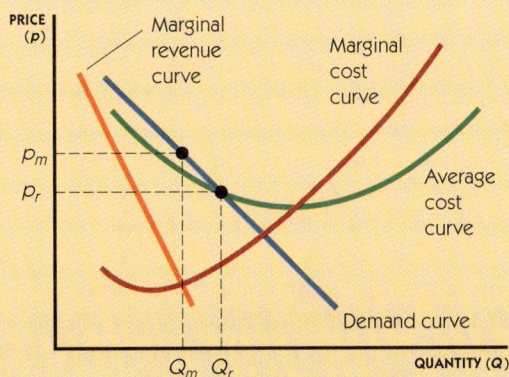

Figure 12.8 NATURAL MONOPOLY

In a natural monopoly, market demand intersects average cost in the downward-sloping portion of the average cost curve, at quantity Q_r and price p_r. Any firm that attempts to enter the market and produce less than Q_r will have higher average costs than the natural monopoly. Any firm that tries to enter the market and produce more than Q_r will find that it cannot sell all its output at a price that will cover its average costs.

ECONOMIES OF SCALE AND IMPERFECT COMPETITION

Fixed costs also help explain why only a limited number of firms produce each variety of a good, and why the variety of goods is limited. Setting up dyes to make a slight variant of an existing car, for example, may be very expensive. Automobile companies tend to produce cars in only a limited range of colours. Some individuals might prefer a car that is bright orange but most car manufacturers do not offer this option. Presumably this is because they realize that additional costs to paint some cars bright orange would exceed the marginal revenue they would receive from providing this option.

Because both technology and transportation costs may change over time, the number of firms in a market may change. Long-distance telephone service used to be a natural monopoly. Telephone messages were transmitted over wires, and it would have been inefficient to duplicate wires. As the demand for telephone services increased, and as alternative technologies like satellites developed, long-distance service ceased to be a natural monopoly. Several major firms now compete to provide long-distance services.

MARKET STRATEGIES

Some monopolies and oligopolies cannot be explained by any of the factors discussed so far. They are not the result of government policies and are not natural monopolies, nor can information problems explain the lack of entry. Many firms whose original monopoly position may have been based on some technological innovation or patent manage to maintain their dominant positions even after their patents expire, at least for a time. IBM, Kodak, and Polaroid are three examples. These firms maintained their dominant positions by the pursuit of market strategies that deterred other firms from entering the market.

When a company thinks about entering an industry dominated by a single firm, it must assess not only the current level of profits being earned by that firm but also what profits will be like after it has entered. If a potential entrant believes that the incumbent firm is likely to respond to entry by lowering its price and fighting a fierce competitive battle, then the potential newcomer may come to believe that while prices and profits look high now, they are likely to drop precipitously if it actually does enter the market.

Established firms would thus like to pursue a strategy to convince potential entrants that even though they are currently making high levels of profit, these profits will disappear should the new firm enter the market. There are three major ways to create this belief, collectively called **entry-deterring practices:** predatory pricing, excess capacity, and limit pricing.

Predatory Pricing If prices have fallen drastically in a certain market every time there has been entry in the past, then new firms may be reluctant to enter. This is because an incumbent firm may deliberately lower its price below the new entrant's cost of production, in order to drive the new arrival out and discourage future entry. The incumbent may lose money in the process, but it hopes to recoup the losses when the entrant leaves and it is free to raise prices to the monopoly level. This practice is called **predatory pricing** and is an illegal trade practice. However, shifting technologies and shifting demand often make it difficult to ascertain whether a firm has actually engaged in predatory pricing or simply lowered its price to meet the competition. Firms that lower their prices always claim that they were "forced" to do so by their competitors.

Excess Capacity Another action firms can take to convince potential rivals that prices are likely to fall if they enter the market is to build up production facilities in excess of those currently needed. By building extra plants and equipment, even if they are rarely used, a firm poses an extra threat to potential entrants. A newcomer will look at this **excess capacity** and realize that the incumbent firm can increase production a great deal with minimal effort. The excess capacity serves as a signal that the incumbent is willing and able to engage in fierce price competition.

Limit Pricing Other strategies for deterring entry involve clever patterns of pricing. A potential entrant may know what price is charged on the market and may have a good idea of its own costs of production. But it is not likely to know precisely the cost curve of

BARRIERS TO ENTRY

Government policies: These include grants of monopoly (patents) and restrictions on entry (licensing).

Single ownership of an essential input: When a single firm owns the entire supply of a nonproducible input, entry is by definition precluded.

Information: Lack of technical information by potential competitors inhibits their entry; lack of information by consumers concerning the quality of a new entrant's product discourages consumers from switching to the

new product, and thus inhibits entry.

Economies of scale: With a natural monopoly, economies of scale are so strong that it is efficient to have only one firm in an industry.

Market strategies: These include policies (such as predatory pricing, excess capacity, and limit pricing) aimed at convincing potential entrants that entry would be met with resistance, and thus would be unprofitable.

---

the incumbent firm. The established firm can try to persuade potential entrants that its marginal costs are low, and that it could easily reduce its price if threatened with a new entrant to the market.

Suppose a potential entrant knows that a monopolist firm's marginal revenue is 70 percent of price. If the monopolist charges a price of $10, then the marginal revenue (the extra revenue from selling one more unit) is $7. Reasoning that the monopolist is setting marginal revenue equal to marginal cost, the potential entrant might use a $7 marginal cost figure in deciding whether it pays to enter.

The monopolist is aware that such a calculation is probably going on. Thus, it has an incentive to make its costs look lower than they are—and hence to make entry look less attractive than it really is. It can do this by setting its price below its marginal cost. If it can persuade the potential entrant that marginal costs have to be below $6 (rather than $7) for entry to be profitable, it has protected its monopoly position that much better. This is an example of a broader practice known as **limit pricing,** in which firms charge less than the ordinary monopoly price and produce at a level beyond that at which marginal revenue equals marginal cost because they are afraid that at higher prices, entry will be encouraged. This may happen simply because a firm realizes that high profits attract attention. The greater the attention focused on a market, the more likely it is that some entrepreneur will believe that entry is profitable.

Some entry-deterring devices, such as maintaining excess capacity, may be socially wasteful. Others,

such as limit pricing, will benefit consumers, at least in the short run, though the long-run deleterious effects of monopoly or limited competition remain.

EQUILIBRIUM WITH MONOPOLISTIC COMPETITION

Barriers to entry are sufficiently weak in some markets that firms enter up to the point where profits are driven to zero. But even then competition is imperfect, if products are differentiated. With each firm producing a slightly different product, each faces a downward-sloping demand curve. In this section, we analyze the case where fixed costs are sufficiently large to ensure that each firm faces a downward-sloping demand curve but where there are *enough* firms so that each firm can ignore the consequences of its actions on others. This is the case of monopolistic competition, which combines elements of monopoly (price-making) with those of competition (free entry, zero profits).

Figure 12.9 illustrates a representative firm in a market in which there is monopolistic competition. Assume initially that all firms are charging the same price, say p_1. If one firm were to charge a slightly lower price, it would steal some customers away from other stores. If there were twenty firms in the market, this price-cutting firm would attract more than one twentieth of the total market demand. But if it should raise its price above that of its rivals, it

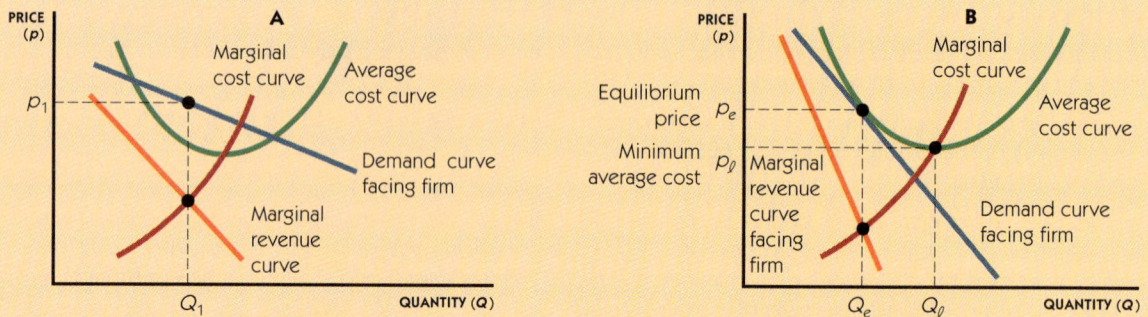

Figure 12.9 PROFIT MAXIMIZING FOR A MONOPOLISTIC COMPETITOR

A monopolistic competitor chooses the quantity it will produce by setting marginal revenue equal to marginal cost (Q_1), and then selling that quantity for the price given on its demand curve (p_1). In panel A, the price charged is above average cost, and the monopolistic competitor is making a profit. If a monopolistic competitor is earning profits, other firms will enter the market. As firms enter, the share of the market demand of each firm is reduced, and the demand curve facing each firm shifts to the left. Entry continues until the demand curve just touches the average cost curve (panel B). When the firm produces Q_e, it just breaks even. If it produces at any other level, it makes a loss (since average costs lie above price). Thus, Q_e maximizes profits. Since profits are zero, there is no incentive either for entry or exit.

would lose customers to them. Each firm assumes that the prices charged by other firms will remain unchanged as it changes its price or the quantity it produces. The demand curve facing each firm is thus the one shown in the figure.

In deciding how much to produce, the firm sets marginal revenue equal to marginal cost. The market equilibrium is (p_1, Q_1) in panel A, with marginal revenue equalling marginal cost. In the equilibrium depicted in the figure, price exceeds average costs. One can think of this situation as a sort of minimonopoly, where each firm has a monopoly on its own brand name or its own store location.

But if existing firms are earning monopoly profits, there is an incentive for new competitors to enter the market until profits are driven to zero, as in the perfectly competitive model. *This is the vital distinction between monopolies and monopolistic competition.* In both cases, firms face downward-sloping demand curves. In both cases, they set marginal revenue equal to marginal cost. But in monopolistic competition, there is entry. Entry continues so long as profits are positive. As firms enter, the share of the

industry demand of each firm is reduced. The demand curve facing each firm thus shifts to the left, as depicted in panel B. This process continues until the demand curve just touches the average cost curve, at point (p_e, Q_e). At that point, profits are zero.

The figure also shows the firm's marginal revenue and marginal cost curves. As we have said, the firm sets its marginal revenue equal to its marginal cost. This occurs at exactly the level of output at which the demand curve is tangent to the average cost curve. This is because at any other point, average costs exceed price, so profits are negative. Only at this point are profits zero. Accordingly, this is the profit-maximizing output.

The monopolistic competition equilibrium has some interesting characteristics. Notice that in equilibrium, price and average costs exceed the minimum average costs at which the goods could be produced. *Less is produced at a higher price.* But there is a trade-off here. Whereas in the perfectly competitive market every product was a perfect substitute for every other one, in the world of monopolistic competition there is variety in the products available. People value variety, and are willing to pay a higher price to obtain it. Thus, the fact that goods are sold at a price above the minimum average cost does not necessarily mean that the economy is inefficient.

Whether the market results in too little or too much product variety remains a contested subject. Either can occur. The important point to realize here is that there is a trade-off. Greater variety can only be obtained at greater cost.

SCHUMPETERIAN COMPETITION

The famous Austrian economist Joseph Schumpeter envisaged a rather different form of monopolistic competition. He saw different markets as being dominated at different times by one or two firms, depending on which had technological superiority.

The dominant firms were constantly subjected to competition for supremacy as new innovations supplanted old. Even when the lead firm is not supplanted by another, the threat of entry keeps it on its toes. While each company dominates the market, it acts like a monopolist: it sets marginal revenue equal to marginal cost, producing less than would be produced under perfect competition. But if it wishes to maintain its position, the firm must reinvest profits in further expenditures to make new products and to develop new, cheaper ways of producing. In Schumpeter's view, the disadvantage of the monopoly aspects of imperfect markets—the reduction in output—was more than offset by the advantages of the greater research the extra profits funded. Chapter 16 will take a closer look at these questions.

REVIEW AND PRACTICE

SUMMARY

1 Economists isolate four broad categories of market structure: perfect competition, monopoly, oligopoly, and monopolistic competition. The last two are referred to collectively as imperfect competition.

2 A perfectly competitive firm faces a horizontal demand curve; it is a price taker. In markets in which there is imperfect or no competition, each firm faces a downward-sloping demand curve and is a price maker.

3 Both monopolists and firms facing perfect competition maximize profit by producing at the quantity where marginal revenue is equal to marginal cost. However, marginal revenue for a perfect competitor is the same as the market price of an extra unit, while marginal revenue for a monopolist is less than the market price.

4 Since in a monopoly price exceeds marginal revenue, buyers pay more for the product than the marginal cost to produce it; there is less production in a monopoly than there would be if price were set equal to marginal cost.

5 Imperfect competition occurs when a relatively small number of firms dominate the market and/or when firms produce goods that are differentiated by their characteristics, by the location of the firms, or in the perceptions of consumers.

6 Monopolies and imperfect competition may be sustained by either natural or manmade barriers to entry.

7 With monopolistic competition, barriers to entry are sufficiently weak that entry occurs until profits are driven to zero; there are few enough firms that each faces a downward-sloping demand curve, but a sufficiently large number of firms that each ignores rivals' reactions to what it does.

KEY TERMS

monopoly

oligopoly

monopolistic competition

imperfect competition

pure profit or monopoly rents

price discrimination

product differentiation

barriers to entry

natural monopoly

predatory pricing

excess capacity

limit pricing

REVIEW QUESTIONS

1 What is the difference between perfect and imperfect competition? between oligopoly and monopolistic competition?

2 Why is price equal to marginal revenue for a perfectly competitive firm, but not for a monopolist with imperfect competition?

3 How should a monopoly choose its quantity of production to maximize profits? Explain why producing either less or more than the level of output at which marginal revenue equals marginal cost will reduce profits. Since a monopolist need not fear competition, what prevents it from raising its price as high as it wishes to make higher profits?

4 What are the primary sources of product differentiation?

5 What are barriers to entry? Describe the principal ones.

6 What is a natural monopoly?

7 Describe market equilibrium under monopolistic competition. Why does the price charged by the typical firm exceed the minimum average cost, even though there is entry?

PROBLEMS

1 Explain how it is possible that at a high enough level of output, if a monopoly produced and sold more, its revenues would actually decline.

2 Assume there is a single firm producing cigarettes, and the marginal cost of producing cigarettes is a constant. Suppose the government imposes a 10-cent tax on each pack of cigarettes. If the demand curve for cigarettes is linear, will the price rise by more or less than the tax?

3 Describe possible strategies a furniture firm might use to differentiate its products.

4 Suppose a gas station at a busy intersection is surrounded by many competitors, all of whom sell identical gas. Draw the demand curve the gas station faces, and draw its marginal and average cost curves. Explain the rule for maximizing profit in this situation. Now imagine that the gas station offers a new gasoline additive called zoomine, and begins an advertising campaign that says: "Get zoomine in your gasoline." No other station offers zoomine. Draw the demand curve faced by the station after this advertising campaign. Explain the rule for maximizing profit in this situation, and illustrate it with an appropriate diagram.

5 Explain how consumers may benefit from predatory pricing and limit pricing in the short run, but not in the long run.

6 Why might it make sense for a monopolist to choose a point on the demand curve where the price is somewhat lower than the price at which marginal revenue equals marginal costs?

APPENDIX A: MONOPSONY

In any market, imperfections of competition can arise on either the buyer or seller side. In this chapter, we have focused on imperfect competition among the sellers of goods. When there is a single buyer in a market, the buyer is called a **monopsonist.** Though monopsonies are relatively rare, they do exist. The government is a monopsonist in the market for a variety of high-technology defence systems.

In some labour markets, a single firm may be close to being a monopsonist. In many markets, an employer may face an upward-sloping supply curve

Figure 12.10 MONOPSONY

A monopsony wants to choose the most profitable point on the market supply curve. It knows the value of the marginal product of additional units of an input. As a monopsonist buys more of an input, it must pay not only a higher price for the marginal unit but a higher price for all the units it buys; thus, the marginal cost of buying an input will exceed the price. The monopsonist will set the marginal cost of the input equal to the value of its marginal product at employment level L^*, and set the wage at w_m. The firm hiring in a competitive labour market would hire up to the point where the value of its marginal product equals the wage; that is, up to point L_c, at wage w_c. Thus, a monopsonist hires less labour at a lower wage than competitive firms would.

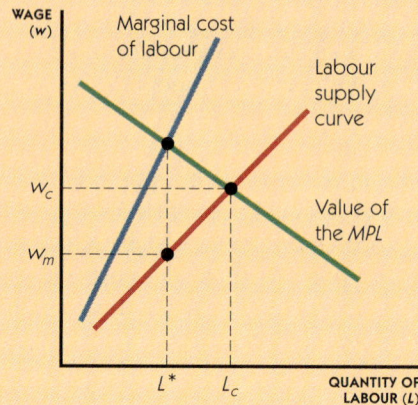

for labour, or at least labour with particular skills. Firms in one-company towns—like Thomson in Manitoba, Sydney in Nova Scotia, or Kitimat in British Columbia—particularly when they are geographically isolated, are most likely to face such upward-sloping supply curves for labour.

The consequences of monopsony are similar to those for monopoly. The basic rule remains: produce at the point where marginal revenue equals marginal cost. The buyer firm is aware, however, that if it buys more units, it will have to pay a higher price. Then if the firm cannot price discriminate, the marginal cost of buying one more unit is not only what the company has to pay for the last unit, but also the higher price it must pay for all previously purchased units.

In the case of a labour market, Figure 12.10 illustrates the consequence. Chapter 10 showed that in competitive markets, firms hire labour up to the point where the value of the marginal product of labour (MPL) equals the wage, the marginal cost of hiring an additional worker. The figure shows the curve that represents the value of the marginal product of labour; it declines as the number of workers hired increases. The figure also shows the labour

supply curve, which is upward-sloping. From this the firm can calculate the marginal cost of hiring an additional worker, the wage *plus* the increase in wage payments to all previously hired workers. Clearly, the marginal cost curve lies above the labour supply curve. The firm hires workers up to the point L^*, where the value of the marginal product of labour is equal to the marginal cost. Employment is lower than it would have been had the firm ignored the fact that as it hires more labour, the wage it pays increases.

APPENDIX B: DEMAND FOR INPUTS UNDER MONOPOLY AND IMPERFECT COMPETITION

In Chapter 10, we saw that competitive firms hire labour up to the point where the value of the marginal product (the value of what an extra hour of

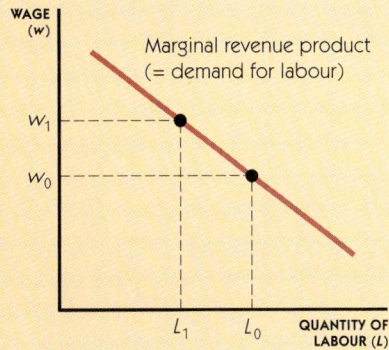

Figure 12.11 MARGINAL REVENUE PRODUCT CURVE

Firms hire labour up to the point where the marginal revenue product of an extra worker equals the marginal cost. In a competitive labour market, the marginal cost of labour is just the wage.

labour would produce) is equal to the wage. Similarly, any other factor of production is demanded up to the point where the value of its marginal product is equal to its price. From this we could derive the demand curve for labour or any other input.

A quite similar analysis applies with imperfect competition. A monopolist hires labour up to the point where the extra revenue it produces—what economists call the marginal revenue product—is equal to the wage. In competitive markets, the value of the marginal product is just equal to the price of the output times the marginal physical product, the extra quantity that is produced. In a monopoly, the marginal revenue product *(MRP)* is equal to the marginal revenue yielded by producing one more unit

(MR) times the marginal physical product *(MPP)*: $MRP = MR \times MPP$.

The quantity of labour that will be hired is illustrated in Figure 12.11, which shows the marginal revenue product curve. It is downward-sloping, for two reasons: the more that is produced, the smaller the marginal physical product (this is just the law of diminishing returns), and the more that is produced, the smaller the marginal revenue. The firm hires labour up to the point where the marginal revenue product equals the wage, point L_0. If the wage increases from w_0 to w_1, the amount of labour hired will fall, from L_0 to L_1. Thus, the demand curve for labour is downward-sloping with imperfect competition, just as it is with perfect competition.

OLIGOPOLIES

In industries characterized by monopolistic competition, there are enough firms so that each assumes its actions have no effect on the actions of its competitors. But in many industries, called oligopolies, there are so few firms that each worries about how its rivals will react to anything it does. This is true of the airline, cigarette, aluminum, automobile, and a host of other industries. For instance, airlines that offer frequent flier bonuses can expect their competitors to respond with similar offers.

If an oligopolist lowers its price, it worries that rivals will do the same and thus it will gain no competitive advantage. Worse still, a competitor may react to a price cut by engaging in a price war and cutting the price still further. Different oligopolies behave in quite different ways. The oligopolist is always torn between its desire to outwit competitors and the knowledge that by cooperating with other oligopolists to reduce output, it will earn a portion of the higher industry profits.

This chapter examines the key question facing an oligopolistic firm—whether it will earn higher profits colluding with rivals to restrict output or

1 Under what conditions will the firms in an industry collude in order to charge high prices? What are the incentives to collude?

2 What practices do firms in an oligopoly engage in to restrict the force of competition and hence increase their profits?

3 What are the main forms that competition among oligopolists takes? How do they compare in terms of the level of prices and output and of the nature of the market's response to changes in economic conditions?

competing with rivals by charging lower prices. The analysis of oligopoly behaviour is divided into three sections. The first discusses collusion, or cooperation, and the problems firms confront in colluding. The second shows how firms may restrict competition even when they do not formally collude. The third describes what happens if firms in an oligopoly compete.

COLLUSION

In some cases oligopolists try to **collude** to maximize their profits. In effect, they act jointly as if they were a monopoly and split up the resulting profits. The prevalence of collusion was long ago noted by Adam Smith, the founder of modern economics: "People of the same trade seldom meet together, even for merriment and diversion, but the conversation ends in a conspiracy against the public, or in some contrivance to raise prices."[1] A group of companies that formally operate in collusion is called a **cartel.** The Organization of Petroleum Exporting Countries (OPEC) is a cartel: it acts collusively to restrict the output of oil and to raise oil prices, and hence the profits of member countries.

Like monopolies, cartels try to maximize joint industry profits. However, since there is more than one participant, they also need to split the production and profits among themselves. The combina-

tion of maximizing the size of the pie and allocating it among members gives rise to a tension that does not exist in pure monopoly situations. On the one hand, it is in the interests of members of cartels to behave cooperatively so as to make the pie as large as possible. On the other, there is a temptation for each member to behave selfishly so as to increase its share of the pie at the expense of others. How this tension works its way out in any individual case determines the extent to which the cartel is able to exploit its market power. To see the nature of the tension, it is useful to begin with an analysis of how cartels act to maximize their joint profits. We then turn to three sorts of problems facing cartels that indicate why it is hard for them to maintain the cooperative behaviour required.

COLLUSIVE BEHAVIOUR BY A CARTEL

Cartels seek to maximize profits by restricting their joint output to raise the price above marginal costs. However, since there is more than one firm, the cartel must determine both its aggregate output and how its production and profits are to be shared among member firms. The principle of joint profit maximization is a straightforward extension of profit maximization of a monopolist. Aggregate output is set at the level at which marginal revenue equals marginal cost. Because there is more than one producer, marginal revenue must be set equal to the marginal cost of each and every producer. This will ensure that joint profits are maximized and that the cartel as a whole is producing at minimum cost. For if the marginal cost for one producer exceeded that of another, total costs could be lowered by increas-

[1]Adam Smith, *Wealth of Nations* (1776), Book 1, Part 2, Chapter 10.

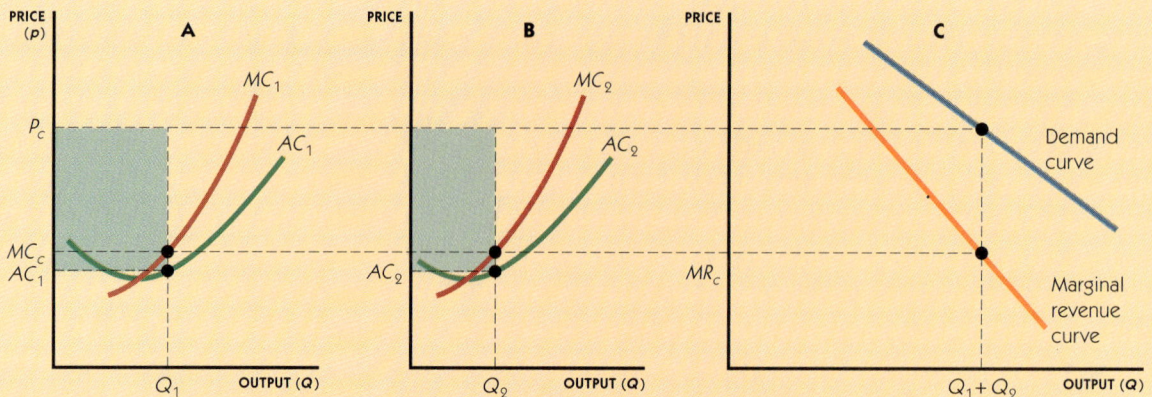

Figure 13.1 JOINT PROFIT MAXIMIZATION BY A CARTEL

In a two-firm cartel, output per firm will be chosen such that the common marginal cost in each firm (MC_c) equals the marginal revenue for the market as a whole (MR_c). The cartel price (p_c) is determined by the market demand curve in panel C. In panel A, Firm 1 produces an output Q_1 at an average cost of AC_1, sells it at the cartel price p_c, and earns a profit given by the shaded area. Similarly, in panel B, Firm 2 produces an output Q_2 at an average cost of AC_2, sells it at the cartel price p_c, and earns a profit given by the shaded area.

ing the output of the latter and reducing the output of the former.

Joint profit maximization is illustrated for the simple case of a two-firm cartel in Figure 13.1. Panels A and B show the average and marginal cost curves for Firms 1 and 2. Panel C shows the demand (average revenue) curve and the marginal revenue curve for the cartel as a whole. When joint profits are being maximized, marginal revenue equals the marginal cost of production at each firm. Moreover the sum of the outputs that the two firms produce must generate an industry output such that marginal revenue is in fact equal to the firms' marginal costs. This is the case in Figure 13.1 when the firms are producing Q_1 and Q_2 at a common marginal cost MC_c. At total output $Q_1 + Q_2$ in panel C, the marginal revenue is equal to the common marginal cost.

The selling price from the demand curve is p_c, which in turn generates profits shown by the shaded areas for the two firms. In principle, the total profits (the sum of the two shaded areas) could be allocated to the two members in any of a number of ways. In practice, a likely procedure might be simply to allocate them to the firm in which they are earned.

The same principles apply when there are more than two firms in the cartel. Joint profit maximization requires that the common marginal revenue be set equal to the marginal cost of each and every member firm. This joint profit maximization outcome requires that the members of the cartel determine cooperatively the outputs to be produced by each member. To be successful, such cooperative behaviour must be maintained. Unfortunately for the cartel, there are various factors that tend to induce noncooperative behaviour.

THE PROBLEM OF SELF-ENFORCEMENT

The central difficulty facing cartels is that it pays any single member of the cartel to cheat. That is, if all other members of the cartel restrict output, so that price exceeds marginal cost, it pays the last member of the cartel to increase its output and take advantage of the higher price. This firm is said to be free-riding on the cartel—the other firms pay the price of collusion by restricting their output, while the free-rider gets the higher price without giving up any sales. But if too many members of a cartel cheat by increasing their output beyond the agreed-upon levels, the cartel breaks down. This happened to the OPEC oil cartel during the 1980s. All the producers except for Saudi Arabia systematically increased production beyond their allotted quotas.

The incentive for members of the cartel to cheat arises from the fact that the marginal revenue for any one firm in a cartel is not the same as the marginal revenue for the cartel as a whole. In fact, the marginal revenue for the firm is greater than that for the cartel as a whole. To see this, recall from Chapter 12 that the marginal revenue is the price from selling the last unit less the reduction in revenue that occurs from the price reduction on all other units sold. For the cartel as a whole, the reduction in revenues from a fall in price is that borne by all members. From the point of view of a single member, however, the part of the reduction in revenues that is suffered by all other firms is not relevant. Therefore, the marginal revenue for a single firm is greater than that for the cartel as a whole.

This implies that at the joint profit maximization outcome of Figure 13.1, marginal revenue is greater than marginal cost from the point of view of each individual firm in the cartel. Any firm thinks it can cheat on the cartel and get away with it. If it shaves its price just lower than p_c and increases its production, it makes an additional profit of almost p_c minus MC_c on that additional unit. With a large gap between price and marginal cost, the incentives to cheat are strong.

Thus, the first major problem facing cartels is how to enforce their collusive arrangement on their members. This self-enforcement is a particular problem in Canada because the federal government has passed **anti-combines laws** prohibiting collusive behaviour. This makes it impossible for firms to get together and sign legally binding contracts that would require each firm to keep output low and prices high.

THE PROBLEM OF COORDINATION

In countries where explicit collusion is illegal, members of an oligopoly who wish to take advantage of their market power must rely on **tacit collusion.** Tacit collusion is an implicit understanding that the oligopoly's interests are best served if its members do not compete too vigourously and particularly if they avoid price cutting. However, the interests of particular firms may not coincide exactly. And an implicit agreement by its very nature makes it diffi-

cult to specify what each firm should do in every situation. When cost or demand curves shift, perhaps because of changes in technology or changes in tastes, the members of a cartel need to get together to agree upon the appropriate changes in output and prices. A new technology or development may benefit one firm more than another, and that firm will wish to increase output more than the others. If the oligopolists could bargain together openly, they might be able to cut a deal. But since the law prohibits them from such a straightforward solution, inventive oligopolists have developed a number of ways to circumvent this coordination problem.

One approach is for a particular firm to become the **price leader.** That firm, often the second- or third-largest member of the industry, sets the price and others follow. Price leaders have been alleged to exist in various industries at various times. Canadian Cement Ltd. was a price leader in the market for cement in the late 1940s. Canadian General Electric was said to have acted as a price leader in electric light bulbs in the 1950s. In the United States, U.S. Steel was a price leader for many years, and according to some economists, American Airlines was a price leader in its industry until the 1980s.

It is hard to prove that collusion through price leadership has occurred—the firms simply claim that they are responding to similar market forces. But sometimes such proof is available. The U.S. Justice Department caught firms in the airline industry communicating through the airline reservation system. Using fare codes for fares that were not actually being offered, the airlines devised a way to communicate how they would respond to a proposed change in the fare in a particular market.[2]

Yet another approach is to develop **facilitating practices** that serve to make collusion easier. One example is the "meeting-the-competition clause," in which at least some members of the oligopoly commit themselves, often in advertisements, to charging no more than any competitor. Electronics shops often make such claims. To the consumer, this looks like a great deal. To see why this practice may actually lead to higher prices, think about it from the perspective of rival firms. Assume that the electronics

[2]Not surprisingly, the airlines denied the charge. But in 1993 they signed an agreement to cease engaging in the practice.

LIMITS TO COLLUSION

Self-enforcement; incentives for each firm to cheat

Coordination problems in responding to changed economic circumstances

Entry

store is selling for $100 an item that costs the store $90; its selling costs are $5, so it is making a $5 profit on the sale. Consider another store that would like to steal some customers away. It would be willing to sell the item for $95, undercutting the first store. But then it reasons that if it cuts its price, it will not gain any customers, since the first store has already guaranteed to match the lower price. Further, the second store knows that it will make less money on each sale to its current customers. Price cutting simply does not pay so the second firm will resist cutting its price. It thus appears that a practice that seemingly is highly competitive in fact may facilitate collusion.

In many cases, oligopolists create a variety of cooperative arrangements that involve sharing inventories, research findings, or other information. In electronics and other high-technology industries, exchanging research information is particularly important. In retail and wholesale markets, helping one another out in the case of inventory shortages is important. Any firm that cheats on the collusive price arrangement will find itself cut out of these cooperative arrangements.

THE PROBLEM OF ENTRY

The third major problem cartels face is similar to the problem faced by a monopolist. High profits enjoyed by the members of the cartel attract entry from other firms or cause nonmembers of the cartel to expand production. This was one of the fates that befell OPEC. When its members raised the price of oil, noncartel countries like Britain, Canada, and Mexico increased their production of oil.

Some economists have argued that in some markets just the threat of entry is strong enough to keep prices low, even if one firm controls over 90 percent of the market. If prices were ever so slightly above costs of production, there would be rapid entry, forcing prices down. In these cases, **potential competition,** the possibility of entry, is sufficient to keep prices low. The costs of entry and exit have to be relatively small, however, for potential competition to be effective. Otherwise, firms will not enter, even when they see high prices, unless they have reason to believe that prices will remain high after entry.

Markets such as these, in which potential competition suffices to ensure competitive prices, are called **contestable.** At one time, advocates of the theory of contestable markets used airlines as the basic example of a contestable entry. An airline could easily enter a market in which price exceeded costs, for example, the Toronto–Montreal market, and thus potential competition would ensure low prices, even when there were only one or two airlines flying a particular route. But by the end of the 1980s, as airline prices skyrocketed on many routes on which competition was limited, potential competition did not seem strong enough to keep prices down. Potential entrants recognized that there were significant costs to entering a market—customers had to be informed, they had to be persuaded to switch from the usual carrier, airline offices had to be opened, and so forth—and experience had taught them that once they entered, prices would fall, making it impossible for them to recover these costs.

GAME THEORY: THE PRISONER'S DILEMMA

In recent years, economists have used a branch of mathematics called game theory to study collusion among oligopolists. The participants in a game are allowed to make certain moves, defined by the rules of the game. The outcomes of the game—what each participant receives—are referred to as its payoffs, and depend on what each player does. Each participant in the game chooses a strategy and decides what moves to make. In games in which there is more than one round, or period, and thus each player has the chance to make more than one move, moves can depend on what has happened in previous periods. Game theory begins with the assumption that each player in the game is rational and knows that his rival is rational. Each is trying to maximize his own payoff. The theory then tries to predict what each player will do. The answer depends on the rules of the game and the payoffs.

One example of such a game is called the **Prisoner's Dilemma.** Two prisoners, A and B, alleged to be conspirators in a crime, are put into separate rooms. A police officer goes into each room and makes a little speech: "Now here's the situation. If your partner confesses and you remain silent, you'll get five years in prison. But if your partner confesses and you confess also, you'll only get three years. On the other hand, perhaps your partner remains silent. If you're quiet also, we can only send you to prison for one year. But if your partner remains silent and you confess, we'll let you out in three months. So if your partner confesses, you are better off confessing, and if your partner doesn't confess, you are better off confessing. Why not confess?" This deal is offered to both prisoners.

The diagram below shows the results of this deal. The upper-left-hand box, for example, shows the result if both A and B confess. The upper-right-hand box shows the result if prisoner A confesses but prisoner B remains silent. And so on.

	Prisoner B	
	Confesses	Remains silent
Confesses	A gets 3 years B gets 3 years	A gets 3 months B gets 5 years
Remains silent	A gets 5 years B gets 3 months	A gets 1 year B gets 1 year

Prisoner A (labels: Confesses / Remains silent on left side)

From the combined standpoint of the two prisoners, the best option is clearly that they both remain silent and each serve their one year. But the self-interest of each individual prisoner says that confession is best, whether his partner confesses or not. However, if they both follow their self-interest and confess, they both end up worse off, each serving three years. The Prisoner's Dilemma is a simple game in which both parties are made worse off by independently following their own self-interest. Both would be better off if they could get together to agree on a story, and to threaten the other if he deviated from the story.

The Prisoner's Dilemma comes up in a variety of contexts. In each case, there is a joint gain to all parties from behaving cooperatively. At the same time, there is an incentive for each to behave noncooperatively in order to obtain a higher share of the gain, but at the expense of a reduced aggregate gain. Some examples are as follows.

Duopoly The game can be applied directly to collusion in an oligopoly consisting of two firms, referred to as a **duopoly.** Assume that both firms agree to cut back their production, so they obtain higher prices and higher profits. But each oligopolist reasons the following way. Whether my rival cheats or not, it pays for me to expand production. If my rival cheats, then he gets all the advantages of my restricting output but pays none of the price. And if he does not cheat and keeps production low, it pays for me to cheat. As both firms reason that way, production expands and prices fall to a level below that at which their joint profits are maximized.

The Cold War During the years of the Cold War, the arms race between the United States and the former U.S.S.R. was described in terms of the Prisoner's Dilemma. Each party reasoned that if the other side built weapons, it needed to match the buildup. And if the other side did not build, it could acquire an advantage by building. Even though both sides might have been better off by agreeing not to build, their incentives pushed them towards a solution where both continued to do so.

Global Pollution It is widely agreed that high emissions of greenhouse gases can cause global warming with all its associated costs. If all the nations of the world were to reduce their emissions, all

Close-up: Gas Price Wars in Vancouver

The Prisoner's Dilemma predicts that firms will not behave cooperatively in their pricing or engage in tacit, or hidden, collusion. This result holds not only for a one-shot game but also if the pricing game is repeated a known, finite number of times. But, if the number of repetitions is uncertain and if there is some variability in the demand conditions facing an industry, it has been shown that one possible outcome is collusive pricing punctuated by periodic price wars designed to punish those firms who may have defected from the unwritten agreement and to induce them to return to the collusive outcome.

Margaret Slade of the University of British Columbia collected price, cost, and sales volume data at 13 service stations in the Kingsway region of Vancouver during a three-month price war in the summer of 1983 and for an extended period of price stability that followed. Her aim in studying such a situation was to determine not only what strategies firms might actually have followed during the price war, but also whether or not these price wars were used to enforce a collusive outcome. Gasoline pricing is a good test of game theory predictions, since the goods sold are essentially identical and the prices are posted for all to see.

Many punishment strategies that can be used during a price war have been proposed by game theorists. One of the most obvious of these is the "grim" punishment, which involves a move to the low-price noncooperative outcome of the Prisoner's Dilemma game for a period of time until firms are induced to return to the cooperative outcome. Both this and various other proposed strategies were rejected in Slade's study, since the actual responses contained more "punishment" than the strategies would predict. A price reduction by a firm was followed by rival firms' prices falling well below the noncooperative outcome. Similarly, price increases by a firm during the price war were followed by larger than predicted increases in rivals' prices. Thus, firms seemed to react strongly to their rivals' previous price changes. Price wars were thus characterized by widely fluctuating prices. However, as the accompanying table shows, average prices during the price war actually equalled the noncooperative outcome. The table distinguishes between the two types of gas stations, independents and outlets of the major chains.

Does this complicated pattern of punishment during a price war tend to induce the firms to price at the collusive level in the absence of price wars? It seems not. As the table indicates, the observed stable outcome involved prices and profits well below those that would obtain with fully collusive (cartel) behaviour. It seems not only that actual responses during a price war are much more complex than predicted by game theorists but that this behaviour is being used to get only part way to the cartel outcome.

	Independent Price (cents/litre)	Major Price (cents/litre)	Industry Profit ($)
Model			
Noncooperative	44.6	45.1	277,628
Collusion	55.1	64.9	1,032,010
Observed			
Price War Average	44.7	45.2	282,369
Stable Outcome	50.0	50.0	428,678

Source: Margaret E. Slade, "Interfirm Rivalry in a Repeated Game: An Empirical Test of Tacit Collusion," *The Journal of Industrial Economics* 35 (June 1987): 499–516.

would be better off, despite the fact that some costs would be incurred by each. However, each country acting individually would be tempted to free-ride on the others by not cutting back on greenhouse gas emissions, thereby saving the costs. All countries face the same incentives, and if all cheat, everyone is worse off.

Conservation of Fish Stocks The size of the annual catch that a fishing ground in international waters can sustain depends upon the total stock of fish. The more fish are taken out, the lower the stock, and the less there is available for fishing in the future. The total value of the annual catch could be maximized if fishing nations could agree to restrict their catch each year to the maximum sustainable level. However, there is also a strong incentive for each nation individually to cheat on such a cooperative arrangement by overfishing, since part of the cost of overfishing will be borne by other fishing nations. Given these calculations, it is easy to see why species like the northern cod have virtually disappeared, and why levels of Pacific salmon stocks have become dangerously low.

Highway Congestion A final example involves rush-hour congestion on a stretch of highway, such as the 401 near Toronto. It has been documented that the faster drivers try to go during periods of heavy traffic, the slower is the flow of traffic. This occurs because faster driving makes the flow less even and increases the incidence of jams. If all drivers would cooperate and drive at 80 kilometres per hour during such periods, the rate of flow would be higher for all. Unfortunately, an incentive exists for any individual driver to drive faster than that. If others are driving at 80 kph, any one driver can move through the traffic faster by increasing her speed. All will be tempted to do the same and, in the end, the flow of traffic breaks down.

In all these examples of the Prisoner's Dilemma, the cooperative outcome breaks down and the noncooperative outcome prevails. Whether or not society is better or worse off depends on the example. In the case of an oligopoly, society is actually better off under the noncooperative outcome, since industry outputs are closer to competitive levels. In the other examples, however, the cooperative outcome is so-

cially preferred. Indeed, it is the failure of the cooperative outcome that results in a call for government action.

In the examples of the Prisoner's Dilemma presented so far, each party makes only one decision. But if firms (or countries) interact over time, then they have additional ways to try to enforce their agreement. For example, suppose each oligopolist announces that it will refrain from cutting prices as long as its rival does. But if the rival cheats on the collusive agreement, then the first oligopolist will respond by increasing production and lowering prices. Won't this threat ensure that the two firms cooperate?

Consider what happens if the two firms expect to compete in the same market over the next ten years, after which time a new product is expected to come along and shift the entire configuration of the industry. It will pay each firm to cheat in the tenth year, when there is no possibility of retaliation, because the industry will be completely altered in the next year. Now consider what happens in the ninth year. Both firms can figure out that it will not pay either one of them to cooperate in the tenth year. But if they are not going to cooperate in the tenth year anyway, then the *threat* of not cooperating in the future is completely ineffective. Hence in the ninth year, each firm will reason that it pays to cheat on the collusive agreement by producing more than the agreed-upon amount. Collusion breaks down in the ninth year. Reasoning backward through time, this logic will lead collusion to break down almost immediately.

Economists have tried to set up laboratory experiments, much like those used by other sciences, to test how individuals actually behave in these different games. The advantage of this sort of **experimental economics** is that the researcher can change one aspect of what is going on at a time, to try to determine what are the crucial determinants of behaviour. One set of experiments has looked at how individuals cooperate with one another in situations like the Prisoner's Dilemma. These experiments have a tendency to show that participants often evolve simple strategies that, although they may appear irrational in the short run, can be effective in inducing cooperation (collusion) as the game is repeated a number of times. One common strategy is "tit for

Many industries that are best thought of as oligopolies—where there is competition among a few large firms—are also characterized by the firms' offering products of different types and qualities. We already encountered product differentiation in the context of monopolistic competition in Chapter 12, where small firms each with a slightly different product were free to enter the industry. To see why product differentiation can also occur in oligopoly markets where firms take account of the actions of their rivals, consider the following example.

Suppose two oligopolists are each considering launching an addition to their product line that can be produced in either a luxury or an economy model, and each firm can launch only one new model each year. Assume that the payoffs for the various choices, given the choice of the other firm, are those given in the table below. (These figures can be thought of as millions of dollars.)

Consider the decision of Firm 1. If Firm 2 produces the luxury model, then Firm 1 is better off producing the economy model rather than its own luxury model: it will have profits of 15 versus profits of 12. If Firm 2 produces the economy model, then Firm 1 is better off producing the luxury model, with profits of 25 versus profits of 10. Firm 1 is always better off producing the "other" model, given the choice of Firm 2. This is also the case for Firm 2: it is always better off producing the "other" model than that chosen by Firm 1. Work this out carefully for yourself. There are thus two possible outcomes in this scenario: (1) Firm 1 produces the luxury model and Firm 2 the economy model, and (2) Firm 1 produces the economy model and Firm 2 the luxury model. While we cannot predict which of these combinations will occur (and which firm will get the higher profits from the luxury model), we can be reasonably sure that the market will see the introduction of both a luxury model and an economy model.

		Firm 2	
		Luxury	Economy
	Luxury	$\pi_1 = 12$ $\pi_2 = 12$	$\pi_1 = 25$ $\pi_2 = 15$
Firm 1			
	Economy	$\pi_1 = 15$ $\pi_2 = 25$	$\pi_1 = 10$ $\pi_2 = 10$

tat." If you increase your output, I will do the same, even if doing so does not maximize my profits. If the rival firm believes this threat, especially after it has been carried out a few times, the rival may decide that it is more profitable to cooperate and keep production low rather than to cheat. In the real world, such simple strategies may play an important role in ensuring that firms do not compete too vigourously in those markets where there are only three or four dominant firms.

RESTRICTIVE PRACTICES

If members of an oligopoly could easily get together and collude, they would. Their joint profits would thereby be increased. They would have a problem of how to divide the profits, but each of the members of the oligopoly could be better off than it would be if they competed. We have seen, however, that there are significant impediments to collusion. If the members of an industry cannot collude to stop competition and cannot prevent entry, at least they can act to reduce competition and deter entry.

Chapter 12 described some of the ways firms act to deter entry. Here, we look at practices firms engage in that *may* serve to restrict competition, called **restrictive practices.** While these practices may not be quite as successful at increasing profits for the firms as the collusive arrangements discussed above, they do have the effect of raising prices and making consumers worse off. Generally, these practices are considered illegal under the Competition Act of 1986, as discussed further in Chapter 14.

When one firm buys or sells another firm's products, the two companies are said to have a "vertical" relationship. Many restrictive practices are aimed at these wholesalers and retailers, and such restrictive practices are called **vertical restraints.** Arrangements among producers or wholesalers in a local market are referred to as **horizontal restraints.** Collusive price fixing is a horizontal price restraint, while **resale price maintenance,** where a producer requires a retailer to sell a good at a prescribed "list" price, is a vertical price restraint.

Both vertical and horizontal restraints may or may not involve prices. An example of a horizontal nonprice restraint might be the allocation of a market among competing firms. Examples of vertical nonprice restraints abound. Consider first the practice of **market restrictions,** also referred to as **exclusive territories,** where a producer gives a wholesaler or retailer the exclusive right to sell a good within a certain region. Soft-drink producers and fast-food chains typically give their local distributors exclusive territories. Coca-Cola manufactures its own syrup, which it then sells to bottlers who add the soda water. Coca-Cola gives these bottlers exclusive territories, so the supermarkets in a particular area can buy Coke in only one place. A store in New Brunswick cannot buy the soft drink from Coca-Cola bottlers in Quebec, even if the price there is lower. Similar arrangements apply with fast-food franchises. Exclusive territorial arrangements ensure that there is no "intrabrand" competition, only interbrand competition. The arrangements limit competition, enabling the local distributors to raise prices above competitive levels.

Another type of vertical nonprice restraint is **exclusive dealing,** in which a producer insists that any firm selling its products not sell those of its rivals. When you go into an Esso gas station you can be sure you are buying gas refined by the Esso Corporation, not PETRO Canada or Shell. Like most brand refiners, Esso insists that stations that want to sell Esso sell only its brand of gasoline.

A third type of vertical nonprice restraint is **tied selling,** also known as **tie-ins,** in which a customer who buys one product must buy another. Nintendo designs its console for electronic games so that it can only be used with Nintendo games. In effect, it forces a tie-in sale between the console and the computer game. Tied selling is also common in the fast-food and soft-drink bottling industries. Fast-food franchisors often require that franchisees purchase

FORMS OF RESTRICTIVE PRACTICES

Resale price maintenance

Market restrictions (exclusive territories)

Exclusive dealing

Tie-ins (tied selling)

Collusion among firms in the same industry can be damaging to the efficiency of the market economy by reducing competition and causing prices to be much higher than costs of production. It can effectively turn a reasonably competitive industry into one that operates as a monopoly. Virtually all industrialized economies have laws that make it illegal to engage in forms of collusive behaviour that restrict competition, and Canada is no exception. As discussed in the next chapter, the Competition Act of 1986 forbids firms from colluding to restrict competition.

An example of such legislation in action is found in the industry that supplies billboards for outdoor advertising. In the early 1970s, various companies involved in the production, maintenance, and transportation of these outdoor advertising structures entered into several interlocking agreements intended to increase their collective profitability. The companies divided the nation into territories such that each company controlled the outdoor advertising in that region. For example, the Mediacom organization was granted the sole right to solicit sales from national advertisers located in Ontario, Quebec, Manitoba, Saskatchewan, Nova Scotia, and New Brunswick. This implied that Mediacom would not attempt to solicit sales in the other remaining regions, which were left to the other firms involved in the agreement—the Hoal organization

was responsible for Alberta, and Seabord controlled British Columbia. Similar territorial agreements were written and agreed to by the participating firms with respect to the provision and operation of outdoor poster and panel spaces. There was also an agreement to manipulate the prices of outdoor advertising services through industrywide price discounts.

Several of the companies involved were accused of conspiring to restrict competition, which at the time was a criminal offense under the so-called Combines Investigations Act, the precursor of the Competition Act. In 1985, all of the above activities were found by the Supreme Court of Ontario to undermine competition. The indicted companies all pleaded guilty as charged. Mediacom was fined $400,000, the highest fine imposed on one company for one count, and the other firms were fined a total of $300,000. In addition, a prohibition order was issued that prohibited the companies named in the original indictment from engaging in any further anti-competitive behaviour. It required them to terminate all the regional and national sales agreements in question.

Source: Annual Report of the Director of Investigations and Research, Combines Investigations Act (Ottawa: Consumer and Corporate Affairs, 1981–1983).

certain ingredients of the food from them. Thus, McDonald's outlets are supplied with most of the food they cook and sell. As mentioned, Coca-Cola retains the right to supply its syrup to local bottlers. In fact, the Competition Act contains a provision, often referred to as the "Coca-Cola exemption," that specif-

ically allows franchisors in the fast-food and soft-drink bottling businesses to impose market restrictions as long as the franchisor supplies to the franchisee an ingredient of food or drink that is sold under licenced trademark. This exemption, which was apparently inserted into the Act after representation by soft-drink bottlers, provides an incentive for franchisors to use tie-in arrangements as a way of obtaining exemption from market restriction provisions.[3]

CONSEQUENCES OF RESTRICTIVE PRACTICES

Firms engaging in restrictive practices *claim* they are doing so not because they wish to restrict competition but because they want to enhance economic efficiency. They argue that market restrictions provide companies with a better incentive to "cultivate" their territory and that exclusive dealing contracts provide incentives for firms to focus their attention on one producer's goods.

Regardless of these claims, restrictive practices often reduce economic efficiency. For example, market restrictions for beer have limited the ability of very large firms that have stores in many different territories to set up a central warehouse and distribute beer to their stores in a more efficient manner. Whether or not they enhance or hurt efficiency, restrictive practices may lead to higher prices by limiting competitive pressures.

Some restrictive practices work by increasing the costs of or otherwise impeding one's rivals. In the 1980s several major airlines developed computer reservation systems that they sold at very attractive prices to travel agents. If the primary goal of these systems had been to serve consumers, they would have been designed to display all the departures near the time the passenger desired. Instead, each airline's system displayed only its own flights, although with additional work, the travel agent could find out about the flights of other airlines. Airlines benefited from these computer systems not because they best met the needs of the consumer but because they put competitors at a disadvantage and thereby reduced the effectiveness of competition.

[3]See R. J. Roberts, *Competition/Antitrust: Canada and the United States*, 2nd ed. (Markham, Ont.: Butterworths, 1992), Chapter 10.

An exclusive dealing contract between a producer and a distributor is another example of how a firm may benefit from hurting its rivals. The contract may force a rival producer to set up its own distribution system, at great cost. The already-existing distributor might have been able to undertake the distribution of the second product at relatively low incremental cost. The exclusive dealing contract increases total resources spent on distribution.

Because these practices may both serve valid business objectives, such as providing enhanced incentives to distributors, and reduce competition, in many cases it is not clear whether they should be judged to be against the public interest. Typically, Canadian firms have been allowed to engage in these practices.

THE MANY DIMENSIONS OF COMPETITION AMONG OLIGOPOLISTS

In the perfectly competitive markets described in Part Two, competitive behaviour is clear and simple. Firms work to lower their costs of production. They can sell as much as they want at the going market price. They don't have to worry about clever marketing strategies, new products, or advertising. In reality, these and a host of other decisions are the battlefields on which competition among oligopolists occurs. This competition is fierce, as firms constantly try to outwit rivals and anticipate their responses. It is like a game, but one in which not all the rules are clear, let alone written down. Air Canada might have thought it was getting a leg up on its rivals when it introduced its frequent flier programme, and Canadian Airlines might have thought it was doing likewise when it offered triple mileage. But some of the rival airlines had more empty seats than either Air Canada or Canadian. Since giving away free tickets may have been less costly for them, they could respond by offering even more attractive programmes. So were Air Canada and Canadian really better off?

PRICE AND OUTPUT COMPETITION

Even in the limited domain on which we have focused so far, that of determining prices and output, the life of an oligopolist is complicated. At one level of analysis, the oligopolist firm is just like a firm facing monopolistic competition. The oligopolist faces a demand curve specifying how much output it believes it can sell at each price it charges, or what the firm believes it will receive if it tries to sell a particular quantity. The oligopolist chooses the point along that demand curve at which its profits are maximized. In other words, it sets marginal revenue equal to marginal cost. But this statement, although valid as far as it goes, hides all the real difficulties in an analysis of oligopoly. What an oligopolist will sell at any particular price, or what the market price will be if it produces a particular level of output, depends on what its rivals do.

Economists have investigated the behaviour of oligopolies under different assumptions concerning what each firm believes about what its rival will do.

COURNOT COMPETITION

An oligopolist firm may believe that its rivals are committed to producing a given quantity and selling it on the market, and that they will keep this quantity fixed no matter what level of output the firm chooses to produce. If the firm considers producing more, it expects that its rivals will cut their prices until they sell the production level to which they are committed. Competition where an oligopolist firm assumes its rivals' output levels are fixed is called **Cournot competition,** after Augustin Cournot, the French economist and engineer who first studied it in 1838. Industries where Cournot competition is considered to prevail are those such as aluminum or steel, where the major part of the cost of production is the cost of machinery, and where variable costs are relatively unimportant once capital goods are in place. Adding new machinery would be expensive, and not using machinery to its capacity would save the firm relatively little money. Under these circumstances,

output is determined, at least in the short run, by the production capacity of the firm's capital goods.

To illustrate how output and price are determined under Cournot competition, we focus on the case of duopoly, a market in which there are only two firms, as illustrated in Figure 13.2. Since each firm assumes its rival's output is constant, a duopolist's demand curve in this case is simply the market demand curve shifted over to the left by the amount of output the rival is committed to producing. Given this demand curve, we can draw the marginal revenue curve, and the firm produces at the point where marginal revenue equals marginal cost.

Normally, the equilibrium output with Cournot competition is less than with perfect competition but greater than with monopoly. With a monopoly, firms can be thought of as setting marginal revenue equal to marginal cost. With perfect competition, marginal revenue is simply price. With a monopoly, marginal revenue is lower than price. It is price minus what the firm loses on its earlier sales, that is, the reduction in price from producing one more unit. This is also the case with Cournot competition. Thus, output is lower than it is with perfect competition. But if there are two identical firms, each is producing only half the total output. Hence, what each firm loses in profits on earlier sales is smaller than under monopoly. Part of the lost revenue from lower prices is borne by the rival firm, which under the Cournot assumption is expected to maintain its output. Marginal revenue is closer to price. At any level of output the marginal revenue is higher with Cournot competition than with monopoly, so equilibrium output is also higher.

To describe the market equilibrium, we need to see how the firms interact. The central tool in this analysis is the **reaction function,** which specifies the level of output of each firm, given the level of output of the other firm. In other words, it shows the reaction of one firm to the actions of the other. Consider the nickel industry in the period after World War II, when the two largest firms were Inco and Falconbridge. The reaction function for Inco is plotted in Figure 13.3A. It is downward-sloping.

To see why this is so, we need to recall how each Cournot oligopolist decides how much to produce. It sets marginal revenue equal to marginal cost, as in panel B. If Falconbridge increases production, the

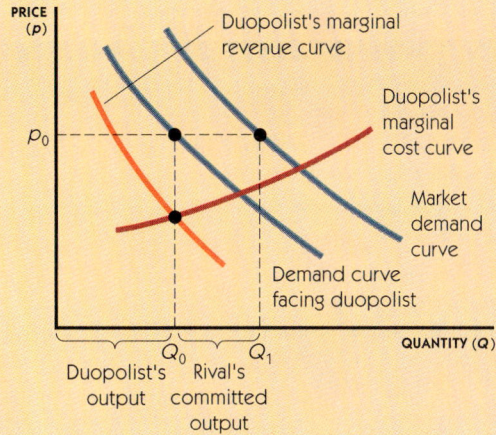

Figure 13.2 COURNOT COMPETITION IN A DUOPOLY

For a duopolist in a situation of Cournot competition, the firm's demand curve and the market demand curve are parallel, separated by the amount that the rival firm is committed to producing. Given the demand curve, the duopolist maximizes profit in the usual way, by setting its marginal revenue equal to marginal cost.

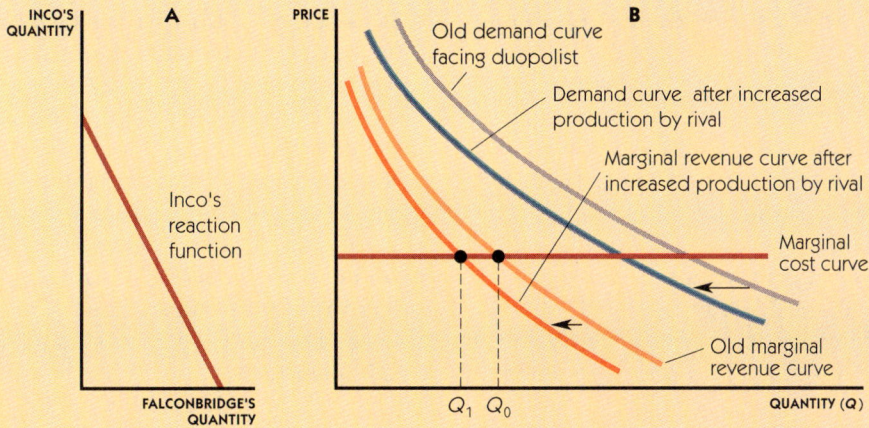

Figure 13.3 THE REACTION FUNCTION

The reaction function in panel A shows how much Inco will choose to produce for every level of output by Falconbridge. Note that Inco's output declines as Falconbridge's increases. Panel B shows why this is so. An increase in the rival's output shifts the demand curve facing the firm to the left. Similarly, the marginal revenue curve shifts to the left, and as a result, output is reduced.

demand facing Inco at any given price is reduced. Equivalently, if Inco wants to sell the same amount as before, it must lower its price. The figure shows the new demand and marginal revenue curves; they are to the left of the corresponding curves when Falconbridge produced less. Accordingly, the optimal level of output is lower: as Falconbridge increases production, Inco decreases production.

We can apply the same analysis to Falconbridge, in Figure 13.4. The reaction curve shows its level of

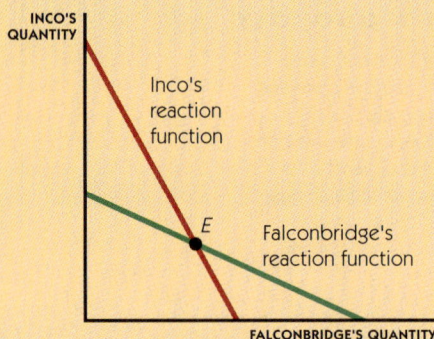

INCO'S QUANTITY

Figure 13.4 MARKET EQUI-LIBRIUM WITH COURNOT COMPETITION

Equilibrium will be at the intersection of the two reaction functions, where each firm is maximizing its profits given its belief that the output of the other firm is fixed. At that point, there is no pressure for either firm to change output.

Inco's reaction function

E

Falconbridge's reaction function

FALCONBRIDGE'S QUANTITY

output along the horizontal axis, given Inco's output along the vertical axis. The market equilibrium is the intersection of the reaction functions, point *E*. This point depicts the equilibrium output of Inco given the output of Falconbridge, and it depicts the output of Falconbridge given the output of Inco. The intersection of the reaction functions is an equilibrium because, given each firm's beliefs about the behaviour of its rival, neither firm wishes to change what it does. There are, in short, no pressures to change. Each firm is maximizing its profits, given its belief that the rival is committed to producing its current level of output.

BERTRAND COMPETITION

In Cournot competition, each firm maximizes profits by choosing what it will produce. In making its calculations it assumes the level of output of its rivals is fixed. As we have seen, this assumption is plausible for industries in which it takes time to change production capacity and in which capital goods represent the bulk of all production costs. But in many industries it is easy to expand capacity. A taxicab company in a large city can easily buy a new car and hire new drivers. While increasing the total number of planes in service may take some time, an airline that wishes to increase the number of planes flying the Toronto–Vancouver route can do so quickly.

Firms in these industries can be thought of as choosing a price to charge and adjusting their output to meet whatever demand arises at that price. They choose the price so as to maximize their profits, given their beliefs about the behaviour of their rivals. One commonly made assumption is that rivals' prices are fixed. Oligopolies in which each firm chooses its price to maximize its profits on the assumption that rivals' prices are fixed are said to have **Bertrand competition,** after the French economist Joseph Bertrand, who first studied this form of competition in 1883.

If rivals keep their prices unchanged, then the oligopolist may steal many of its rivals' customers when it lowers its price. But as long as the goods produced by two rivals are imperfect substitutes (for any of the reasons discussed in Chapter 12), when one firm lowers its price below that of its rivals, it does not capture *all* the customers.

This is the case depicted in Figure 13.5, which uses reaction functions to describe the market equilibrium of a Bertrand duopoly. This duopoly consists of two mattress companies, Supersleepers and Heavenlyrest, which produce imperfect substitutes. The reaction function in this case gives the price charged by one firm, given the price charged by its rival. As Supersleepers increases its price, Heavenlyrest finds it advantageous to increase its own price. That is why the reaction function is positively sloped. The equilibrium is at *E*.

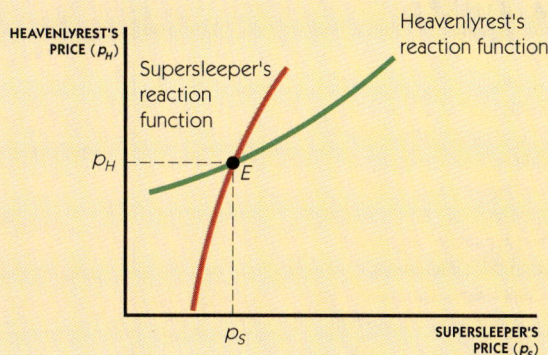

Figure 13.5 MARKET EQUILIBRIUM WITH BERTRAND COMPETITION

The intersection of the two reaction functions gives the equilibrium price (*E*).

With price-setting (Bertrand) competition, firms believe that they face more elastic demand curves than they do with quantity-setting (Cournot) competition. This can easily be seen when we consider the extreme case where the two goods produced by two different firms are perfect substitutes. Then if one firm charges slightly less than its rival, it garners for itself the entire market; if it charges slightly more, it loses all of its sales. Each firm faces a horizontal demand curve. Thus, even when there are only two firms, the market outcome is competitive if each believes the other has fixed its price and will not change the price in response to changes in prices it charges, and if the two firms produce *perfect* substitutes.

We can see this process of competition as follows. Assume both firms have constant marginal and average costs of production. Since each company believes its rival will not budge its price so long as price exceeds marginal costs, each one will find that it pays to shave its price by a small amount. By doing so it steals the whole market. But the rival firm, thinking the same way, then undercuts still further. The process continues until the price is bid down to the point where there are zero profits. It does not pay to cut prices any further.

In general, the products produced by two duopolists are not perfect substitutes but differ somewhat, so that each firm faces a downward-sloping demand curve. In equilibrium, price exceeds marginal costs.

Output is less than it would be with perfect competition, but more than it would be with Cournot competition.

KINKED DEMAND CURVES

A third hypothesis about how oligopolistic rivals may respond says that rivals match price cuts but do not respond to price increases. In this scenario, an oligopolist believes that it will not gain much in sales if it lowers its price, because rivals will match the price cut, but it will lose considerably if it raises its price, since it will be undersold by rivals who do not change their prices. The demand curve facing such an oligopolist appears kinked, as in Figure 13.6. The curve is very steep below the current price, p_1, reflecting the fact that few sales are gained as price is lowered. But it is relatively flat above p_1, indicating that the firm loses many customers to its rivals, who refuse to match the price increases.

The figure also presents the marginal revenue curve, which has a sharp drop at the output level corresponding to the kink. Why does the marginal revenue curve have this shape, and what are the consequences? The drop in the marginal revenue curve follows from the fact that the increase in the price from a reduction in sales by a unit is much smaller than the fall in the price if the firm wants to

Figure 13.6 A KINKED DEMAND CURVE

The demand curve facing a firm is relatively flat at price levels above the current level (p_1), showing that an oligopolist will lose a large amount of sales if it increases its price and rivals do not. However, the demand curve is relatively steep at prices below the current level, showing that the oligopolist will not gain much in sales if it lowers its price, since rivals will follow. The sharp drop in marginal revenue means that a firm may not change its level of price or output, even if marginal costs shift.

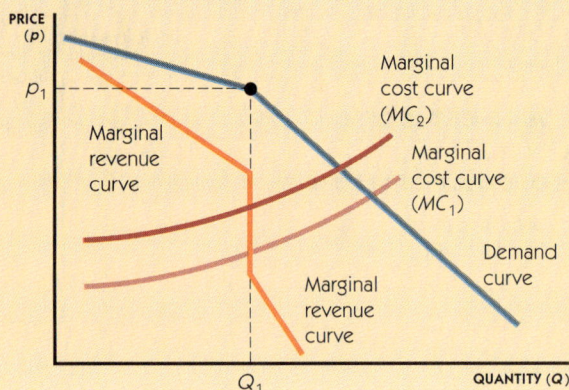

increase sales by a unit. Increases in output beyond Q_1 raise relatively little additional revenue, since to sell the increased output, price must fall by a considerable amount; any price cut by a firm is matched by its rivals, so relatively few customers are gained. But at levels of output less than those at the kink, marginal revenue is quite high, because, as we have seen, the demand curve is relatively flat to the left of Q_1. With a flat demand curve, price and marginal revenue are close together.

The drop in the marginal revenue curve means that at the output at which the drop occurs, Q_1, the extra revenue lost from cutting back production is much greater than the extra revenue gained from increasing production. This has one important implication. Small changes in marginal cost, from MC_1 to MC_2, have no effect on output or price. Thus, firms that believe they face a kinked demand curve have good reason to hesitate before changing their prices.

THE IMPORTANCE OF IMPERFECTIONS IN COMPETITION

Many of the features of the modern economy—from frequent flier mileage awards to offers to match prices of competitors, from brand names to the billions spent every year on advertising—not only cannot be explained by the basic competitive model, but are inconsistent with it. They reflect the imperfections of competition that characterize so many parts of the economy. Most economists agree that the extreme cases of monopoly (no competition) and perfect competition (where each firm has *no* effect on market prices) are rare, and that most markets are characterized by some, but imperfect, competition. However, there is disagreement about the accuracy

COMPETITION AMONG OLIGOPOLISTS

Cournot competition: Each firm believes its rivals will leave their output unchanged in response to changes in the firm's output.

Bertrand competition: Each firm sets its price believing its rivals will leave their own price unchanged in response to changes in the firm's price.

Kinked demand curves: Each firm believes its rivals will match price cuts but not price increases.

of the predictions of the perfectly competitive model whose advocates claim that in many if not most situations it provides a good approximation of reality. Even so, there is broad consensus among economists that various phenomena and markets can only be understood in terms of limitations of competition. Imperfect competition is the subject of our seventh consensus point.

7 IMPERFECT COMPETITION

There is limited competition in many markets. In imperfectly competitive markets, firms are aware that how much they sell, or other actions they take, may affect the price they receive. In many cases, firms must think strategically, considering how their rivals may react to their actions.

REVIEW AND PRACTICE

SUMMARY

1 Oligopolists must choose whether to seek higher profits by colluding with rival firms or by competing. They must decide what their rivals will do in response to any action they take.

2 A group of firms that have an explicit and open agreement to collude is known as a cartel. Although cartels are illegal in Canada, firms have tried to find tacit ways of facilitating collusion—for example, by using price leaders and "meeting the competition" pricing policies.

3 If the threat of potential entry is sufficient to cause firms to set price and output at competitive levels, the industry is said to be contestable.

4 Even when they do not collude, firms attempt to restrict competition with practices like exclusive dealing, tie-ins, market restrictions, and resale price maintenance. In some cases, a firm's profits may be increased by raising its rival's costs and making the rival a less effective competitor.

5 In Cournot competition, an oligopolist chooses its output under the assumption that its rivals' output levels are fixed.

6 In Bertrand competition, each firm chooses the price of its product on the assumption that its rivals' prices are fixed.

7 If the rivals to an oligopolist match all price cuts but do not match any price increases, then the oligopolist faces a kinked demand curve. A kinked demand curve will lead to a marginal revenue curve with a vertical segment, which implies that the firm will often not change its level of output or its price in response to small changes in costs.

KEY TERMS

collusion	contestable markets	vertical restraints	reaction function
cartel	Prisoner's Dilemma	horizontal restraints	Bertrand competition
anti-combines laws	duopoly	Cournot competition	kinked demand curve
price leader	restrictive practices		

REVIEW QUESTIONS

1 Why is the analysis of oligopoly more complicated than that of monopoly, perfect competition, or monopolistic competition?

2 Name some ways that firms might use tacit collusion, if explicit collusion is illegal.

3 What is a contestable market?

4 Name and define three restrictive practices.

5 Explain why Cournot competitors may produce more and charge a lower price than monopolists, but produce less and charge a higher price than perfect competitors.

PROBLEMS

1 Explain why every member of a cartel has an incentive to cheat on its agreement. How does this fact strengthen the effectiveness of anti-combines laws that outlaw explicit collusion?

2 How might cooperative agreements between firms —to share research information, share the costs of cleaning up pollution, or help avoid shortfalls of supplies—end up helping firms to collude in reducing quantity and raising price?

3 Explain how market restrictions, exclusive dealing, tie-ins, and resale price maintenance might help an oligopolist to make higher profits. How might a firm make the case that these practices add to efficiency?

4 Consider two oligopolists, with each choosing between a "high" and a "low" level of production. Given

6 What expectations must an oligopolist have about the behaviour of its rivals if it believes that it faces a kinked demand curve?

7 Why might a firm that faces a kinked demand curve not change its price even when its costs change?

their choices of how much to produce, their profits will be:

		Firm A	
		High production	Low production
Firm B	High production	A gets $2 million profit B gets $2 million profit	A gets $1 million profit B gets $5 million profit
	Low production	A gets $5 million profit B gets $1 million profit	A gets $4 million profit B gets $4 million profit

Explain how Firm B will reason that it makes sense to produce the high amount, regardless of what Firm A chooses. Then explain how Firm A will reason that it makes sense to produce the high amount, regardless of what Firm B chooses. How might collusion assist the two firms in this case?

GOVERNMENT
POLICIES
TOWARDS
COMPETITION

I n the minds of most Canadians, monopolies are not a good thing. They smell of income inequities and undemocratic concentrations of political power. To economists, however, the concern is economic efficiency. Motivated by both political and economic concerns, governments have taken an active role in promoting competition and in limiting the abuses of market power. In this chapter we review the economic effects of limited competition and look at government policies to reduce its negative effects.

KEY QUESTIONS

1 Why is government concerned about monopolies and imperfect competition? In what sense do markets with monopolies and imperfect competition result in inefficiency?

2 How have governments attempted to address the problem posed by a natural monopoly?

3 How have governments used anti-combines policies to break up monopolies, to impede the ability of any single firm to attain a dominant position in a market, and to outlaw practices designed to restrict competition?

THE DRAWBACKS OF MONOPOLIES AND LIMITED COMPETITION

Four major sources of economic inefficiency result from monopolies and other imperfectly competitive industries: restricted output, managerial slack, insufficient attention to research and development, and dissipation of profits through rent-seeking behaviour. The problems can be seen most clearly in the context of monopolies, which are our focus here, but they also arise in imperfectly competitive markets.

RESTRICTED OUTPUT

Monopolists, like competitive firms, are in business to make profits by producing the kinds of goods and services customers want. But monopolists can make profits in ways not available to competitive firms. One way is to drive up the price of a good by restricting output, as discussed in Chapter 12. They can, to use the popular term, gouge their customers. Consumers, by *choosing* to buy the monopolist's good, are revealing that they are better off than they would be without the product. But they are paying more than they would if the industry were competitive.

A monopolist who sets marginal revenue equal to marginal cost produces at a lower level of output than a corresponding competitive industry—an industry with the same demand curve and costs but in which there are many producers rather than one—where price equals marginal cost. Figure 14.1 shows that the monopoly output, Q_m, is much smaller than the competitive output, Q_c, where price (p_c) equals marginal cost. The price under monopoly, p_m, is thus much higher.

By definition, the price of a good measures how much an individual is willing to pay for an extra unit of a good. In other words, it measures the marginal benefit of the good to the purchaser. With perfect competition, price equals marginal cost, so that in equilibrium the marginal benefit of an extra unit of a good to the individual (the price) is just equal to the marginal cost to the firm of producing it. At the monopolist's lower level of output, the marginal benefit of producing an extra unit—the price individuals are willing to pay for an extra unit—exceeds marginal cost.

By comparing the monopolist's production decision to the collective output decisions of firms in a competitive market, we can estimate the value of the loss to society when there is a monopoly. To simplify the analysis, in Figure 14.2 marginal cost is assumed to be constant, the horizontal line labelled *MC*. The marginal cost is also the supply curve under competition, so the competitive output would be Q_c with a price p_c. The monopolist produces an output of Q_m, at the point where marginal revenue equals marginal cost, and finds that it can charge p_m, the price on the demand curve corresponding to the output Q_m.

Two kinds of loss result, both related to the concept of consumer surplus introduced in Chapter 6. There we learned that the downward-sloping demand curve implies a bounty to most consumers. At

Figure 14.1 WHY MONOPOLY OUTPUT IS INEFFICIENT

A perfect competitor will set price equal to marginal cost, and produce at quantity Q_c and price p_c. A monopolist will set marginal revenue equal to marginal cost, and produce at quantity Q_m and price p_m, where the market price exceeds marginal cost.

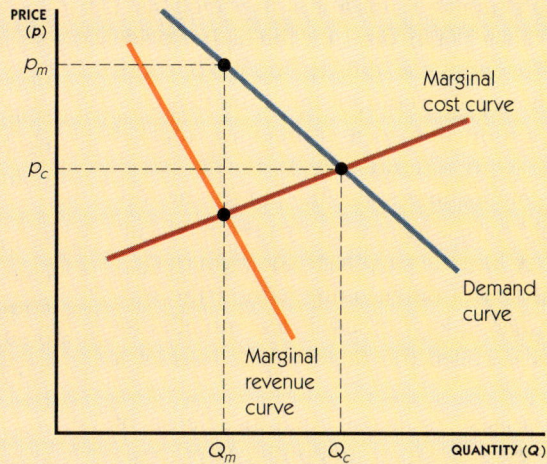

Figure 14.2 MEASURING THE SOCIAL COST OF MONOPOLY

The higher, monopoly price removes some of the consumer surplus. Part of this loss (the rectangle $ABCD$) is simply a transfer of income from consumers to the monopolist; the remainder (the triangle ABG) is known as the deadweight loss of monopoly.

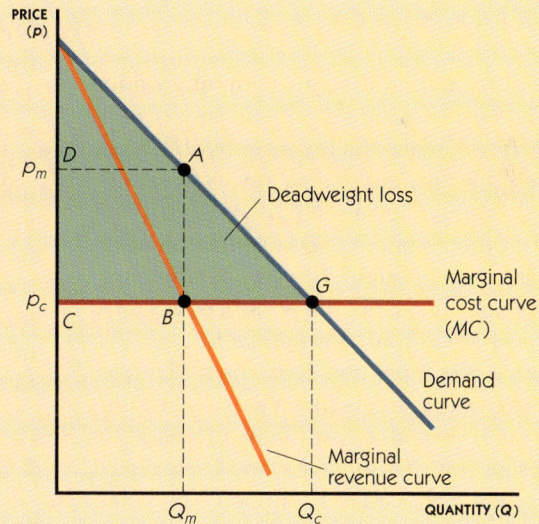

points to the left of the intersection of the price line and demand curve people are willing to pay more for the good than they have to. With competition, the consumer surplus in Figure 14.2 is the entire shaded area between the demand curve and the line at p_c.

The monopolist cuts into this surplus in two ways. First, it charges a higher price, p_m, than would be obtained in a competitive situation. Consumers who purchase from the monopolist end up paying extra for the amount they purchase, Q_m. The loss to them is measured by the rectangle *ABCD,* the extra price times the quantity actually produced and consumed. This loss to consumers is not a loss to society as a whole. It is a transfer of income, for the higher price winds up as revenues for the monopoly. Second, however, a monopoly reduces the quantity produced. While production in a competitive market would be Q_c, with a monopoly it is the lower amount, Q_m, so consumers lose the consumer surplus they would have obtained on this reduced output. That is, they lose the surplus to the right of Q_m, denoted by *ABG,* with no resulting gain to the monopolist. This second kind of loss is a complete loss to society, and is called the **deadweight loss** of a monopoly.

Some economists have argued that these costs of monopoly are relatively small, amounting to perhaps 3 percent of the monopolist's output value. Others believe the losses from restricting output are higher. Whichever argument is right, output restriction is only one source of the inefficiencies monopolies introduce into the economy.

MANAGERIAL SLACK

In Chapter 9 it was argued that any company wants to minimize its cost of production, and any profit-maximizing firm will make the highest possible level of profits when it keeps its costs as low as possible. But in practice, companies already making a lot of money without much competition lack the incentive to hold costs as low as possible. The lack of efficiency when firms are insulated from the pressures of competition is referred to as **managerial slack.**

In the absence of competition, it can be difficult to tell whether managers are being efficient. For instance, how much should it cost for Bell Canada to put a call through from Thunder Bay to Sherbrooke. Up to 1992, when Bell had a monopoly on long-distance telephone service in Ontario and Quebec, it might have claimed that its costs were already as low as possible, but not even trained engineers could really tell whether this was true. When competition developed for intercity telephone calls, shareholders in Bell could compare its costs with those of Unitel, Sprint, and other competitors, and competition provided each company with an incentive to be as efficient as possible.

REDUCED RESEARCH AND DEVELOPMENT

Competition motivates firms to develop new products and less expensive ways of producing goods. A monopoly, by contrast, may be content to let the profits roll in without aggressively encouraging technological progress.

The North American automobile and electronics industries are often blamed for falling behind foreign competition because of their technological complacence. By the end of World War II, these industries had attained a dominant position in the world. After enjoying high profits for many years, they were overtaken by foreign, especially Japanese, firms. The foreign firms were able to undersell their North American counterparts during the 1980s, not only because they paid lower wages but also because their technological advances had made production processes more efficient.

It should be noted that some economists argue that too much competition can actually be detrimental to research and development. The incentive for undertaking research is the reward that is obtained from the new products and processes developed. The more competition there is, the more these rewards will be lost to competitors who are able to imitate the new technologies created. Thus, competition can be a mixed blessing. Governments recognize this by instituting policies, such as patent protection, to ensure that firms reap at least some of the rewards of their research and development expenditures. A fine line must be drawn between protecting the monopoly profits of firms and encouraging them to be innovative.

RENT SEEKING

The final source of economic inefficiency under monopoly is the temptation for monopolists to spend their extra profits in economically unproductive ways. A major example is devoting resources to obtaining or maintaining their monopoly position by deterring entry. Since the profits a monopolist receives are called monopoly rents, the attempt to acquire or maintain already existing rents by acquiring or maintaining a monopoly position in some industry is referred to as **rent seeking.** The resources devoted to rent-seeking activities represent an additional loss from monopoly over and above the deadweight loss arising from the reduction in output per se.

Sometimes a firm's monopoly position is at least partly the result of government protection. Many less developed countries grant a company within their country a monopoly to produce a good, and they bar imports of that good from abroad. In these circumstances, firms give money to lobbyists and politicians to maintain regulations that restrict competition so that they can keep their profits high. Such activities are socially wasteful. Real resources (including labour time) are used to win favourable rules, not to produce goods and services. There is thus legitimate concern that the willingness of governments to restrict competition will encourage firms to spend money on rent-seeking activities rather than on making a better product.

How much would a firm be willing to spend to gain a monopoly position? The firm would be willing

to spend up to the amount it would obtain as monopoly profits. The waste from this rent-seeking activity can thus be much larger than the loss from the reduced output.

FURTHER DRAWBACKS OF LIMITED COMPETITION

We saw in Chapters 12 and 13 that markets in which a few firms dominated were more prevalent than monopolies. Relative to monopolies, some of the inefficiencies discussed above are smaller under limited competition. For example, output is lower than under perfect competition, but higher than under monopoly. And competition to produce new products (research and development) is often intense, as we shall see in the next chapter. But other inefficiencies are worse in markets with limited competition than in monopoly markets. For example, firms under imperfect competition expend major resources on practices designed to deter entry, to reduce the force of competition, and to raise prices. Such expenditures may increase profits but they waste resources and make consumers worse off. Under imperfect competition firms may also maintain excess capacity, again to deter entry. A firm may gain a competitive advantage over its rivals not by lowering its own costs but by raising its rival's—for instance, by depriving it of the use of existing distribution facilities. Finally, rivals may also spend money on uninformative advertising.

POLICIES TOWARDS NATURAL MONOPOLIES

If imperfect competition is as disadvantageous as the previous analysis has suggested, why not simply require that competition be perfect? To answer this question, we need to recall the reasons, discussed in Chapter 12, why competition is imperfect.

One reason is government-granted patents. Monopoly profits provide the return to inventors and innovators that is necessary to stimulate activities vital to a capitalist economy. We will discuss these issues more extensively in Chapter 15.

A second reason is that the cost of production may be lower if there is a single firm in the industry. This is the case with natural monopoly. Natural monopolies present a difficult policy problem. Like any other firm, a natural monopolist will produce at the level where marginal revenue equals marginal cost, at Q_m in Figure 14.3. At this level, it will charge a price of p_m, which is higher than the marginal cost at that point. Thus, it will produce less and charge more than it would if price were equal to marginal cost, as would be the case with perfect competition (the output level Q_c and the price p_c in the figure).

But in the case of natural monopoly, the very nature of the decreasing cost of technology precludes perfect competition. Indeed, consider what would happen if price were set equal to marginal cost. With a natural monopoly, average costs are declining, and marginal costs are below average costs. Hence, if price were equal to marginal cost, it would be less than average costs, and the firm would be losing money. Profits would be negative, as shown by the shaded area in the figure. If the government wanted a natural monopoly to produce at the point where marginal cost equalled price, it would have to subsidize the company to offset these losses. Taxes would have to be raised to generate the money for the subsidies, which imposes other economic costs. Moreover, the government would likely have a diffi-

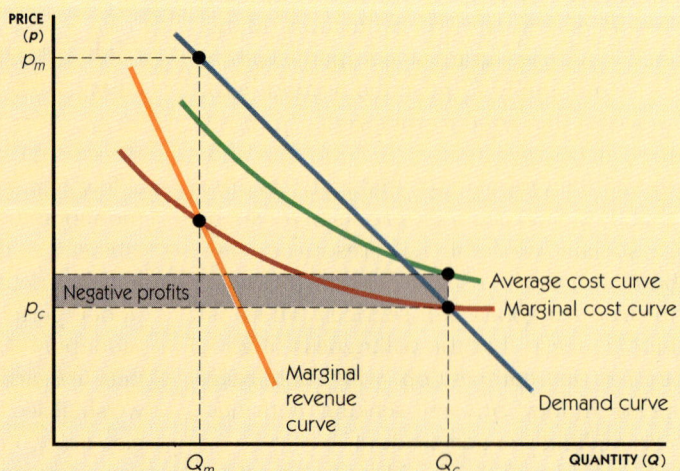

Figure 14.3 A PROBLEM WITH REGULATING NATURAL MONOPOLY

A natural monopoly will set marginal revenue equal to marginal cost, and produce at quantity Q_m and price p_m. In perfect competition, price would be equal to marginal cost, at Q_c and p_c. However, the perfectly competitive outcome is not possible in this case, since it would force the natural monopoly to produce at below its average cost, and thus to be making losses.

cult time ascertaining the magnitude of the subsidy actually required. Managers and workers in such a firm have a way of exaggerating their estimates of the high wages they "need" to produce the required output.

Following are three different solutions government has found to the problem of natural monopolies.

PUBLIC OWNERSHIP

In Canada and many European countries, in contrast with the United States, the government has often assumed ownership of a monopoly industry, or nationalized it. Federally owned firms in Canada, referred to as federal **Crown corporations,** have included Canada Post, Atomic Energy of Canada Limited, Canadian Broadcasting Corporation, PETRO Canada, Canadian National Railways, and Air Canada. Many provincial Crown corporations exist as well in sectors such as hydroelectricity (Manitoba Hydro, Ontario Hydro, Hydro Quebec), telecommunications (B.C. Tel, Sask Tel), broadcasting (TV Ontario), insurance (Saskatchewan Government Insurance), and other public utilities such as gas and water companies. There are problems with this approach, however, the primary one being that governments are not particularly efficient as producers.

Managers often lack adequate incentives to cut costs and modernize vigorously, particularly given the fact that government is frequently willing to subsidize the industry when it loses money. In addition, public ownership brings with it a number of political pressures. Political pressure may affect where public utilities locate their plants—politicians like to see jobs created in their home ridings —and whether they prune their labour forces to increase efficiency. Publicly run firms may also be under pressure to provide some services at prices below marginal cost and make up the deficit from revenues from other services, a practice referred to as **cross subsidization.** Thus, business customers of utilities are sometimes charged more, relative to the costs of serving them, than are households. There is in effect a hidden tax and a hidden subsidy; businesses are taxed to subsidize households. The same phenomenon can be seen in Canada Post. It charges the same price for delivering mail to small rural communities as it does to major cities, in spite of the large differences in costs. Small communities have their mail services subsidized by larger ones.

How much less efficient the government is as a producer than the private sector is difficult to determine. Efficiency comparisons between government-run telephone companies in Europe and American private firms provided much of the motivation for the **privatization** movement—the movement to convert government enterprises into private firms. Britain sold its telephone services and some other utilities, Japan its telephones and railroads, France its banks and many other enterprises. Privatization in Canada has been extensive, beginning with several smaller Crown corporations such as Canadian Arsenals and VIA Rail, and recently moving on to some major ones, including PETRO Canada, Air Canada, and Canadian National Railways.

Not all publicly run enterprises are less efficient than their private counterparts, however. When Canadian National Railways was a fully public enterprise, it differed little from Canadian Pacific Railways in the efficiency with which it was run. This may be because competition between the two forced the government railroad to be as efficient as the private. Many of the publicly owned enterprises in France seem to run as efficiently as private firms. This may be because of the high prestige afforded to those who work in the French civil service, which allows them to recruit from among the most talented people in their country. There may also be less difference between government enterprises and large corporations—particularly when both are subjected to some market pressure and competition—than popular conceptions of inefficient government would suggest.

REGULATION

An alternative to operating a natural monopoly as a Crown corporation is to leave the industry in the private sector and regulate the prices it charges. This has typically been the approach in the United States. In Canada, both practices have been followed, depending upon the industry. Thus, in some provinces telephone services are provided by privately owned monopolies and their prices are regulated by the federal government, and electricity companies are privately owned in some provinces and their prices regulated provincially. The same is true for many municipal utilities. Of course, regulation and nationalization may not be mutually exclusive alternatives. Crown corporations themselves may be subject to price regulation. For example, provincial Crown corporations in utilities and telecommunications may be regulated both by a provincial agency and by federal regulators in their business with out-of-province customers.

The aim of regulation is to keep the price as low as possible, commensurate with the monopolist's need to obtain an adequate return on its investment. In other words, regulators try to keep price equal to average costs, where average costs include a "normal return" on what the firm's owners have invested in the firm. If the regulators are successful, the natural monopoly will earn no monopoly profits. Such a regulated output and price are shown in Figure 14.4 as Q_r and p_r.

Two criticisms have been levelled against regulation as a solution to the natural monopoly problem. The first is that regulation often takes an inefficient form. The sources of inefficiency are several. The intent is to set prices so that firms obtain a "fair" return on their capital. But to make the highest level of profit, firms respond by increasing their amount of capital as much as possible, which can lead to too much investment. In addition, the structure of prices may be set so that some groups, often businesses, may be charged extra-high prices to make it possible to subsidize other groups. This problem of cross subsidies is no less a problem for natural monopolies if they are privately owned and regulated than if they are owned and operated by the government. Further, firms' incentives to innovate are weakened every time they lower costs. Recently regulators have recognized that unless they reward innovation, it will not happen. They have agreed to allow the utilities to retain much of the increased profits they obtain from improved efficiency, at least for a few years.

The second criticism is that the regulators lose track of the public interest. The theory of **regulatory capture** argues that regulators are pulled frequently into the camps of those they regulate. This could happen through bribery and corruption, but the much likelier way is just that over time, employees of a regulated industry develop personal friendships with the regulators, who in turn come to rely on those employees' expertise and judgment. Worse, regulatory agencies of necessity tend to hire from among those in the regulated industry. By the same

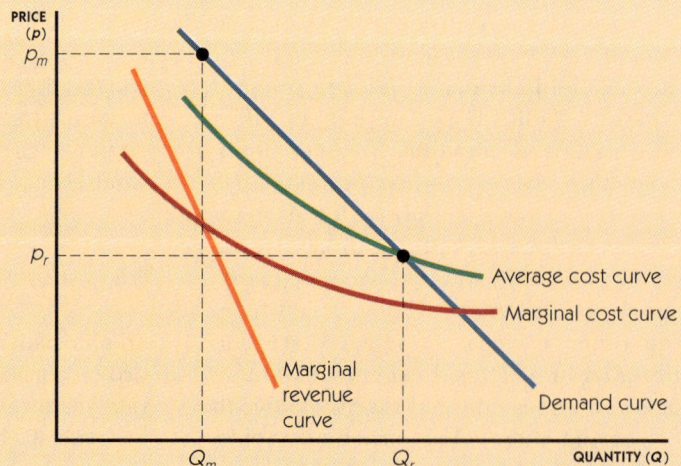

Figure 14.4 REGULATING NATURAL MONOPOLY

Government regulators will often seek to choose the point on the market demand curve where the firm provides the greatest quantity at the lowest price consistent with the firm's covering its costs. The point is the quantity Q_r and price p_r, where the demand curve intersects the average cost curve.

token, regulators who demonstrate an "understanding" of the industry may be rewarded with good jobs in that industry after they leave government service.

ENCOURAGING COMPETITION

The final way government deals with the hard choices posed by natural monopolies is to encourage competition, even if imperfect. To understand this strategy, let us first review why competition may not be viable when average costs are declining over the relevant range of output.

If two firms divide the market between them, each faces higher average costs than if either firm grabbed the whole market. As illustrated in Figure 14.5, Q_d denotes the output of each firm in the initial duopoly and AC_d its average costs. By undercutting its rival, a firm would be able to capture the entire market *and* have its average costs reduced. By the same token, a natural monopolist knows that it can charge a price slightly above its average cost, AC_m, without worrying about entry. Rivals that might enter, trying to capture some of the profits, know that the natural monopolist has lower costs because

of its larger scale of production, and so can always undercut them.

Even under these conditions, some economists have argued (as noted in Chapter 13) that a monopolist would not in fact charge higher than average costs, because a rival could enter any time and grab the whole market. (This zero-profit equilibrium is shown in the figure at output Q_1 and price $AC_1 = p_1$.) On this argument, all that is required to keep prices low is potential competition.

Most economists are not so sanguine about the effectiveness of potential, as opposed to actual, competition. Airline behaviour provides the most convincing demonstration of the importance of having more than one firm in the market. Routes between many cities are natural monopolies. These markets have experienced wild price fluctuations. The cycle starts with the natural monopolist charging higher than average cost. Another carrier (or carriers) enters the market. Prices fall dramatically as they try to force each other out. One carrier leaves. Prices rise again, and so on.

In the late 1970s and 1980s, as many governments became convinced that competition, however imperfect, might be better than regulation, there began a process of deregulation. Deregulation focused

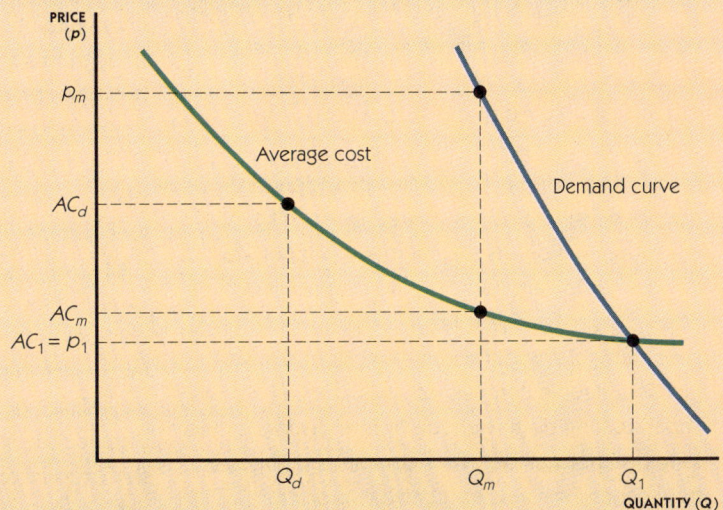

Figure 14.5 WHY COMPETITION MAY NOT BE VIABLE WITH DECREASING AVERAGE COSTS

If two firms share a market, each producing Q_d, one firm could double its output to Q_m, lower its cost, and undercut its rival. The larger firm has a cost advantage over the smaller competitor.

CLOSE-UP: DEREGULATING THE LONG-DISTANCE TELEPHONE SERVICE—LESSONS FROM THE UNITED STATES

Canadians talk on the telephone more than anyone else in the world and are naturally apprehensive about policy changes that might adversely affect their continued ability to do so. Until 1992, long-distance services were restricted to a single system: the Bell Canada network. Although different companies operated in different provinces, all had to tap into a single regulated system for inter-provincial calls. Technological improvements in telecommunications have made it possible to set up competing systems, and in 1992 the Canadian Radio-television and Telecommunications Commission (C.R.T.C.) decided that new entrants could be admitted into the long-distance telephone industry. Unitel was the first to enter and was followed by several others. What will be the consequence for the Canadian consumer who had become used to reliable telephone service? The experience of the United States, where one of the most celebrated instances of deregulation occurred in the telecommunications industry in 1984, may be of some relevance in predicting what will happen in Canada.

Before deregulation, American Telephone and Telegraph (AT&T) provided local and long-distance service essentially to everyone. After deregulation, a regional phone company (sometimes called a "Baby Bell") provided local telephone service as a regulated monopoly, while the long-distance market was opened up to competition among AT&T, MCI, Sprint, and others. From the public reaction, you would have thought it was the end of modern communication. People complained about dialing a separate long-distance code before dialing a long-distance number. They complained about how confusing it was to receive two phone bills, one for local service and one for long-distance. They complained about how phone service declined.

Well, fair is fair. The results are now starting to come in on how phone deregulation has worked, and they are reasonably positive. It is time to give the deregulation decision a little credit.

In the five years following deregulation, the cost of leasing a phone fell by half. New phone services like call waiting, phone mail, three-way calling, automatic redialing, and call forwarding have become popular. Phone cards are nearly as common as credit cards. Fax machines are now in almost every office. Of course, many of these technological changes would have happened over time with or without phone deregulation. Indeed, all of them have subsequently happened in Canada as well. But the increased competitive pressure helped speed them up.

The price story, however, is a little more ambiguous. The price of long-distance service fell as much as 40 percent in these five years. However, local phone bills increased substantially; not enough to absorb all of the 40 percent fall, but enough to absorb most of it. Much of this change had been predicted by economists. Before deregulation, AT&T used to charge long-distance callers more heavily in order to subsidize local phone service. With deregulation, both local and long-distance service are now closer to paying their own way. Overall phone service (combining local and long-distance) was slowly getting cheaper before deregulation; it has continued to fall in price gradually. The C.R.T.C. clearly hopes for a similar outcome in Canada, where long-distance users, especially businesses, have effectively subsidized local service. Whether the market is large enough to support more than one firm, however, remains to be seen.

APPROACHES TO NATURAL MONOPOLY
Public ownership

Regulation

Competition

on industries such as airlines, railroads, and trucking, where competition had a chance—there were, at most, limited increasing returns to scale. Government also sought to distinguish parts of an industry where competition might work from parts where competition was unlikely to be effective. In the telephone industry, for example, there were few economies of scale in the production of telephones. Accordingly, regulation of this part of the industry was reduced.

The virtues of competition have been borne out for the most part. Trucking—where the arguments for government regulation seemed most suspect— was perhaps the most unambiguous success story, with prices falling significantly as a result of deregulation. Railroads appear more financially sound than they did under regulation. But Prairie farmers, who rely on railroads to ship their grain, complain that railroads have used their monopoly power to charge much higher tariffs under deregulation.

Deregulation of Canada's airlines has proved to be controversial, especially in light of the experience in the United States. In the United States, initially the entry of new firms was accompanied by lower fares and more extensive routings. But as time went by, price competition led to a rash of bankruptcies, the development of regional domination by some airlines, and extensive price discrimination in the form of much higher fares for business travelers than for vacationers, who can plan their travel weeks in advance. In Canada the pros and cons of deregulating the airlines was hotly debated. Those in favour argued that regulation impeded competition and efficiency, especially since it resulted in the subsidization of routes to less densely populated areas via higher prices on other potentially more profitable routes. It also resulted in domestic fares being considerably higher than fares to international destina-

tions that were the same distance away. Those opposed to deregulation argued that, because of the small size of the Canadian market and the distances involved, deregulation would ultimately lead to the dominance of a small number of large firms who would be able to exercise monopoly pricing power and who would concentrate their efforts on the larger markets.

In the end, deregulation of Canadian airlines was achieved in 1987 with the passage of the National Transportation Act. Both the supporters and detractors of deregulation seem to have been partly right. Price competition ensued along with some rationalization of routes. And the dominance of the two major carriers, Air Canada and Canadian Airlines, increased with a series of mergers and takeovers. However, the two major airlines themselves were put in a precarious financial position by the price competition that resulted. It became apparent that deregulation of the domestic market in itself was not enough to ensure the health of the industry. As a result, both major Canadian airlines have sought to combine forces with partner firms in the United States to expand the size of their potential market and avoid bankruptcy.

ANTI-COMBINES POLICY

While some of the failures of competition in our economy arise from natural monopolies, other imperfections are the result of sharp business practices. Firms that are not natural monopolies may develop market power by means of strategies designed to deter the entry of competitors and to promote collusive behaviour among the firms in the industry.

The term "combines" is used to encompass all the various types of restrictive practices in which firms may engage to restrict competition. Forming a combine can consist of becoming a monopoly, or near monopoly, by takeover or merger; engaging in collusive behaviour with other firms in an industry to reduce competition or raise prices; or engaging in practices that restrict the terms of supply to firms further down in the production process, such as retailers. Legislation in Canada to promote competition has been referred to as "anti-combines" legislation. It has been as much concerned with controlling restrictive practices and collusive behaviour as with outlawing the domination of the market by a single firm through monopolization and merger. This general perspective has continued with the more recent practice of referring to anti-combines policy as simply competition policy and the act of Parliament enforcing it as the Competition Act.

ANTI-COMBINES LEGISLATION

In the years following Confederation, a preoccupation of the federal government was to protect and foster Canadian industry. The main policy instruments for doing so were the protective tariff, significant public-sector intervention in the provision of infrastructure such as the railways and the waterways, and an immigration policy designed to populate the West. The single most important milestone of economic policy was the legislation of 1879 by the Conservative government under Sir John A. Macdonald, the so-called National Policy, which relied on the tariff to protect central Canada's manufacturing industry. The National Policy effectively insulated the small Canadian market for domestic manufacturers from foreign competition. But such a small market could not efficiently support the large number of firms needed to ensure competition. The result of this was not only inefficiency in the size and productivity of Canadian industry but also an incentive for the small number of firms to form combines to restrict competition and to allow for larger firms to control the markets.

Concern in Parliament over the growing frequency of restrictive practices led to the passage of the first anti-combines legislation in 1889, one year before the first antitrust laws were passed in the United States. The legislation formed part of the Criminal Code of Canada and was therefore enforced through the criminal courts. The original legislation emphasized a "conspiracy in restraint of trade" as being an illegal act to the extent that it "unduly" lessened competition. No explicit mention was made of mergers and monopolies. As the practice of mergers grew, however, this became an obvious shortcoming of the law. In 1910 the legislation was amended to include reference to trusts, monopolies, and mergers. Nonetheless, the courts found it hard to preclude the formation of monopolies and mergers. Under the legislation no case of a merger was ever prevented by the law, and very few cases of monopolies were successfully prosecuted. The reason had to do with the fact that the anti-combines legislation was enacted as part of the criminal law rather than the civil law. Criminal law cases must be tried by the courts and must satisfy the strict requirements of proof of guilt beyond a reasonable doubt. It turned out to be difficult to make the case that monopolies and mergers restricted competition "to the public detriment." Almost all of the convictions obtained under the law were for restrictive practices, a subject to which we will return.

Subsequently the law underwent some further amendments. For example, one of the shortcomings of the original act was the absence of a body charged with investigating conspiratorial activities. This was remedied in 1919 with the institution of a board of investigation. Subsequent amendments in 1923, 1935, 1952, and 1960 specified additional forms of illegal practices, such as resale price maintenance and misleading advertising, and further developed the investigative machinery by forming the Restrictive Trade Practices Commission headed by a director of investigations who could initiate actions.

The enforcement of the act continued to be hampered by its criminal law nature, especially in the areas of merger and monopoly. For example, the criminal designation precluded the use of administrative tribunals that could determine the extent of harm done by certain practices. In 1976 this problem was partly remedied when some parts of the act were turned into civil law components. The Restrictive Trade Practices Commission was empowered to issue prohibition orders to major suppliers who engaged in some types of restrictive practices. The enforcement of laws against monopolies and mergers, however, remained part of the criminal law and thus was ineffective. Almost all convictions continued to be for restrictive practices, especially misleading advertising and collusive price agreements.

In 1986, the legislation was changed significantly after considerable study and public debate and discussion. The Combines Investigations Act, as it had by then come to be called, was replaced by the Competition Act. Under this act, several types of offences were transferred to the civil law and enforced by a quasi-judicial body called the Competition Tribunal. This tribunal was responsible for overseeing those parts of the Competition Act dealing with monopoly and merger as well as restrictive practices. The tribunal can issue prohibition orders precluding certain types of activities, or it can order other types of remedies. Most important, the civil rather than criminal nature of the law means that the tribunal is not restricted to applying the strict rules of proof that courts require for criminal procedures but can exercise discretion and weigh the benefits and costs in deciding on a remedy.

Companies considering mergers involving combined assets or revenues in excess of $400 million and assets or revenues of the acquiring firm in excess of $35 million must notify the director of investigations about the proposed merger. The director has up to three weeks to inform the parties whether he intends to proceed against the proposed merger. His decision is based not solely on market share or a measure of concentration but also on whether or not the proposed merger is likely to lessen or prevent competition substantially and whether the reduction in competition is more than compensated for by an improvement in efficiency. He is specifically asked to take into consideration whether the efficiency gains will result in increased exports or import substitutes. Obviously, the director has considerable discretionary power.

The Competition Act of 1986 sets out seven factors that the director and the Competition Tribunal may consider in determining the effect of a merger on competition: (1) the extent of foreign competition, (2) whether one of the firms is a failing one, (3) the availability of close substitutes, (4) the existence of barriers to entry, (5) the extent of remaining postmerger competition, (6) the likelihood of the merger's removing a strong competitor, and (7) the nature and extent of innovation in the relevant market. The merging parties then have the opportunity to defend their case in front of the tribunal, or to restructure their merger proposals in light of the objections of the director.

The sections of the Competition Act of 1986 dealing with mergers are among the most important of the changes put in place by the act. As mentioned earlier, prior to 1986 not a single merger case was prosecuted under the previous criminal law legislation. Since then, the director and the tribunal have been very active in overseeing potential mergers. In the first three years alone, some 369 mergers were investigated. Of these, the director objected to 19. Seven were abandoned by the parties and eight were restructured to satisfy the director. Four cases went to the tribunal.[1] In one of these, the computer reservation systems used by Air Canada and Canadian Airlines were allowed to merge to form Gemini, a single system serving most of the Canadian airline industry. The contract tying Canadian Airlines to the Gemini system subsequently turned out to be a temporary stumbling block to the acquisition of Canadian Airlines by American Airlines, which uses a different reservation system. Of course, the effectiveness of the new merger provisions cannot be deduced by looking solely at the record of cases brought to the attention of the director. There may have been many other potential mergers that were simply not proceeded with at all, given the possibility of being denied permission.

As with mergers, anti-combines legislation has not been very active at curbing monopolies. Before the amendments of 1986, only two cases had been

[1] These data are reported in Christopher Green, *Canadian Industrial Organization and Policy*, 3rd ed. (Toronto: McGraw Hill/Ryerson, 1990), p. 373. This book presents a detailed account of the history and application of competition policy in Canada.

Policy makers have always regarded competition in the newspaper business as especially important. Competition is valuable for the usual reasons of keeping prices low and quality high for consumers. But newspapers also fulfill a unique role in disseminating information, forming public opinion, and keeping elected officials honest, and competition ensures that more than one point of view is heard. As newspapers struggle with magazines for readership, as scarce advertising dollars get spread across more types of media, and as local newspapers get taken over by large chains that enjoy cost advantages, maintaining competition in local newspaper markets becomes more and more difficult. But relying on the courts to enforce competition laws has turned out not to be so easy.

The late K. C. Irving, long a household name in New Brunswick, owned a substantial portion of the transportation, forestry, and oil-refining and distribution industries in the province. In the early 1970s, the government attempted to prevent Mr. Irving from acquiring control of all of the English-language newspapers in New Brunswick. Under the Combines Investigations Act, the director of investigations and research first began the inquiry into Irving's acquisition of controlling interest in University Press of New Brunswick Ltd., which published the **Fredericton Gleaner** newspaper. The director believed that the acquisition not only substantially limited competition in the market, but also that K. C. Irving Ltd. was about to operate a monopoly, since the company apparently had control of all five English-language newspapers in New Brunswick. The director alleged that the only independently controlled newspaper in New Brunswick was the French-language newspaper **L'Evangeline**. On

December 8, 1971, four counts were laid under the Combines Investigations Act by the attorney general and the trial began on October 17, 1972.

In the trial, the Crown argued that this acquisition by K. C. Irving interfered with "free competition" in the supply of English-language daily newspapers in New Brunswick. On January 24, 1974, K. C. Irving Ltd., New Brunswick Publishing Company Ltd., Moncton Publishing Co. Ltd., and University Press of New Brunswick Ltd. were found guilty of being parties to a monopoly between August 10, 1960, and November 30, 1971. The fines to all companies totalled $150,000. An order was also issued under the Combines Investigations Act that dissolved the merger and thus the (apparent) monopoly that K. C. Irving had. However, the accused filed an appeal against the decision.

The Supreme Court of New Brunswick allowed Irving's appeal by reasoning that "it [could] not be concluded that acquisition of controlling interest in the five daily newspapers implies there is a detriment to the public or there was a lessening of competition which would have been detrimental to the public." It further reasoned that "because the newspapers had limited distribution without any material overlap, it cannot be said that there has been any lessening of competition among them through the merging of ownership because there has never been any competition among them to begin with." It concluded that so long as the management aspects of each paper—advertising rates, editorials, etc.—were independent, there was no apparent detrimental effect on the public. The Crown

successfully prosecuted. Some notable cases were
acquitted: in 1960 Canadian Breweries, which controlled half the market for beer sales in Canada, was
acquitted; in 1975 in the Atlantic Sugar Refineries
case, three companies controlling 95 percent of the
sugar market were acquitted of conspiring to maintain market shares by merger; and in 1976 the K. C.
Irving Company, which had succeeded in gaining
control of all English-language daily newspapers in
New Brunswick, was acquitted on appeal.

The Competition Act of 1986 also changed how
the problem of monopolies was addressed. The notion of a monopoly as defined in previous legislation
was replaced with a completely new concept called
"abuse of a dominant position." Like the merger law,
it was made part of the civil law and was enforced by
the director of investigations and the Competition
Tribunal. The act defined a number of "anticompeti-
tive acts" that constituted abuse of a dominant position. They included such things as using "fighting
brands" (offering one of the firm's many brands at a
discount) to eliminate competitors, withholding
from the market resources required by competitors,
adopting product specifications that have the effect
of eliminating other firms from the market, and selling below cost to eliminate a competitor. At the re-
quest of the director, the tribunal may issue a prohibition order to firms that substantially control a
business in some area of Canada and that engage in
anti-competitive acts that have the effect of lessening
competition. The tribunal is obliged to consider
whether the practice in question is anti-competitive

or the result of superior competitive performance.
Thus, monopolization as such is not an offence. It is
only an offence to the extent that it gives rise to anti-
competitive practices. Though it is still too early to
say whether this section of the act will be effective,
some observers feel that, given the requirements, it
will not be easy for the tribunal to find against firms.

PREVENTING MARKET DOMINATION

There is concern about the size of a firm, and one of
the purposes of anti-combines policies is to ensure
that no firm or combination of firms has too much
economic power. In practice, the question of
whether a firm is too big is usually phrased, "What is
its size relative to the market?" and thus the debate
centers on the question of what is the relevant market. The Competition Act defines the relevant market
as consisting of those firms that are the sources of
current and potential competition. To make this
more precise, we need to consider the factors that
affect the extent of competition in a market.

Market Share   One way to measure the amount of
competition in an industry is by the use of **concentration ratios,** defined as the proportion of sales accounted for by the largest four or eight firms. Measured this way, the degree of competition varies
considerably across industries. Table 14.1 shows
both the four- and eight-firm concentration ratios

Table 14.1 DEGREE OF CONCENTRATION IN VARIOUS CANADIAN INDUSTRIES, 1988

Industry	Percentage of Revenue Represented by	
	The top four firms	The top eight firms
Tobacco Products	98.9	100.0
Petroleum and Coal Products	74.5	90.8
Beverages	59.2	77.6
Primary Metals	63.3	76.6
Communications	64.8	76.4
Transport Equipment	68.4	74.4
Public Utilities	58.4	73.9
Metal Mining	58.9	73.0
Paper and Allied Industries	38.9	52.6
Transportation	36.4	43.3
Textile Mills	32.5	40.9
Chemicals and Chemical Products	25.5	35.4
Finance	16.4	28.9
Food	19.6	28.7
Wood Industries	17.8	25.2
Machinery	11.3	18.6
Retail Trade	9.7	14.8
Furniture Industries	7.6	13.4
Wholesale Trade	7.4	12.5
Services	4.5	6.9
Agriculture, Forestry, Fishing	2.6	4.4
Construction	2.2	3.5

Source: Statistics Canada, Annual Report (1988) of the Minister of Industry, Science and Technology under the Corporations and Labour Unions Return Act, Part 1 (Ottawa, 1991), Table 5.4, p. 94.

for all the broad industry groups in Canada. As can be seen, concentration tends to be highest in the resource sector and in some tertiary industries such as transportation, utilities, and communications. By and large, manufacturing industries are somewhat less concentrated. The least-concentrated industries are the service and trade sectors, as well as construction and the primary industries of agriculture, forestry, and fishing. These are averages for broad industry groups. Within these groups, some more specific industries can have much higher concentration ratios. For example, the four-firm concentration ratios in motor vehicles and breweries are both well over 90 percent.

However, market share alone cannot reflect the degree of competitiveness of an industry. We have learned that the extent to which a firm's demand curve is downward-sloping, so that it can raise prices without losing all its consumers, is related both to the number of firms in the industry and to the extent of product differentiation. Concentration ratios in Canadian industry do not fully capture either of these, both because they are based on the domestic market alone and because they do not reflect product differentiation.

Market Bounds   During the last quarter century, international trade has become ever more important to Canada and the world economy. This change has affected all aspects of economic analysis, including the extent of competition in many markets. Today, imports exceed 25 percent of national output —in some key industries the growth of imports has been especially rapid.

While the degree of concentration among domestic producers of automobiles has increased—three firms are responsible for more than 90 percent of all Canadian auto production—the industry has become more competitive in the 1980s and 1990s, as foreign competition has increased and as foreign companies such as Toyota, Hyundai, and Honda have established plants in North America. It used to be that North American firms could increase their price without worrying about their consumers' switching to Japanese or European imports, but no longer. Today, the degree of competition in a market must be assessed from a global viewpoint rather than by looking simply at how many firms produce a good in Canada. This is especially true in light of recent developments in liberalizing trade between Canada and other nations, such as the signing of the Canada-U.S. Free Trade Agreement in 1988, its expansion to the North American Free Trade Agreement with the inclusion of Mexico in 1992, and the formation of the World Trade Organization in 1995 to oversee the liberalization of global trade that was agreed to in the so-called Uruguay Round of GATT negotiations.

Product Differentiation   While all firms that produce the same good and sell in the same location are clearly in the same market, when the goods produced by different firms are imperfect substitutes, the definitional problem is more ambiguous.

What is the market for beer? Those in the industry might claim that premium beers and discount beers are really two different markets, with relatively few customers crossing over from one to the other.

In the early 1950s, Du Pont's cellophane had a virtual monopoly on the U.S. market for clear wrapping paper. In 1956 the company managed to fight off charges of monopoly by claiming that this market was part of a larger one for "wrapping materials." It claimed that brown paper was a good, though not perfect, substitute for cellophane, and in this broader market, Du Pont did not have a particularly large share (roughly 18 percent).

CURBING RESTRICTIVE PRACTICES

By far the most frequently used parts of anti-combines policy have been those applying to restrictive practices. The Competition Act makes it a criminal offence to engage in collusion, price discrimination, predatory pricing, misleading advertising, and resale price maintenance. The act made monopolies and mergers, as well as certain restrictive practices that are prohibited if they do economic harm, civil offences adjudicated by the Competition Tribunal. In particular, practices of exclusive dealing and tied selling were so treated.

Restrictive practices can be classified as being of two types—horizontal agreements and vertical agreements (see Chapter 13). Horizontal agreements, which include both price fixing and other collusive practices among competing firms, have been the object of the most frequently used parts of anti-combines legislation. The main form of horizontal agreement is that envisaged in the original act of 1889—a conspiracy, combination, or agreement to lessen competition. According to the 1986 Competition Act, such collusion can be inferred by circumstantial evidence, but it is necessary to prove that the parties *intended* to enter a collusive arrangement. That such agreements unduly restrict competition has been difficult to prove. Horizontal agreements have been especially difficult to prosecute in cases in which the collusion is not explicit but simply shows up as not unusual forms of behaviour, referred to as "conscious parallelism." For instance, competing firms may adopt a common schedule of prices for their products, not because of any explicit agreements but because of a tacit understanding or because one of the firms is accepted to be the price leader. An exception to the difficulty in prosecuting horizontal agreements is the practice of bid rigging, making agreements to submit prearranged bids for contracts; this practice is illegal per se, and there is no requirement to show that competition is unduly restricted by the practice.

Because horizontal agreements are so difficult to prosecute, recent enforcement emphasis has tended to be on vertical agreements. These involve the relations between a firm and its distributors or suppliers and can take a variety of forms, some of them mentioned already. The practice of resale price maintenance has been successfully prosecuted in recent years, despite the fact that it is a criminal offence. That is partly because the illegality of the practice is not contingent on competition being restricted. It is illegal per se. Another section prohibits various forms of contracts that restrict the freedom of a distributor to obtain goods from other suppliers. Under this section the tribunal can prohibit tied selling and exclusive dealing. Two other forms of pricing practices that are prohibited in certain circumstances are price discrimination and predatory pricing. They are illegal only to the extent that they substantially lessen competition; they have been prevented relatively rarely in Canada.

CURRENT ANTI-COMBINES CONTROVERSIES

Exactly how and when anti-combines laws should be enforced remains one of the most controversial subjects of economic policy. In recent years, controversy has focused on two major issues.

First, how stringent should the standards be for allowing mergers of competing firms? In 1986, with the introduction of the Competition Act, the government adopted a new approach to dealing with mergers, essentially requiring large ones to be vetted by the director of investigation. Previously, merger activity was regulated according to criminal law standards and many critics saw that as too strict a procedure.

Those who favour more lax anti-combines rules argue that in today's international markets, competition is almost always sufficiently keen to ensure low prices and economic efficiency. Any firm that tries to exercise monopoly power by charging too high a price or that is slack in keeping costs down would be faced with an onslaught of competition. At most, the firm could enjoy a monopoly position for only a short time. For example, Canon, followed by a host of other firms, unseated Xerox's monopoly position in copiers, and Fuji is now challenging Kodak's dominant position in film. Moreover, these advocates argue, attempts to restrict size penalize the more successful firms and inhibit their ability to take advantage of economies of scale and scope. Since foreign governments do not put similar restrictions on their own firms, Canadian companies find themselves at a disadvantage. Size is particularly important for financing large-scale research endeavours, necessary if Canada is to compete globally.

Critics of this view contend that international competition cannot be relied upon to ensure low prices—though admittedly, markets are more competitive with than without international competition. Furthermore, they question the importance of the economies of scale and scope. Many of Canada's leading exporters are relatively small companies. And the competition enhanced by strict anti-combines laws at home not only makes consumers better off through lower prices, but also sharpens the edge of businesses, making the more successful firms better able to compete not only at home but also abroad.

The second major controversial issue concerns what governmental policies should be toward restrictive practices—in particular, the contractual arrangements between firms and their suppliers and customers, such as exclusive dealing, tied selling, and market restrictions. Those who believe that by and large competition is effective think there should be a presumption that such practices are legal. Others believe that, frequently, competition is limited by the presence of such contractual arrangements. A review of the alleged "efficiency" gains of such practices suggests to these observers that the typical motive is to restrict competition further. If a change is needed from the current rule of reason, they argue, the presumption should be that these practices are restrictive. The burden would then be on any firm engaging in restrictive practices to show that the efficiency gains outweigh the losses from reduced competition.

REVIEW AND PRACTICE

SUMMARY

1 Economists have identified four major problems resulting from monopolies and imperfect competition: restricted output and excessive profits; managerial slack; lack of incentives for technological progress; and a tendency toward wasteful rent-seeking expenditures.

2 For a natural monopoly, average costs decline over the range of market demand, and consequently a large firm can undercut its rivals. Since marginal cost for a natural monopoly lies below average cost, an attempt by regulators to require it to set a price equal to marginal cost (as in the case of perfect competition) will force the firm to make losses.

3 Taking ownership of a natural monopoly allows the government to set price and quantity directly. But it also subjects an industry to political pressures and the potential inefficiencies of government operation.

4 In Canada, some natural monopolies are regulated. Government regulators seek to keep prices as low and quantity as high as is consistent with the natural monopolist's covering its costs. However, regulators must also face problems of cross subsidies and the possibility of being "captured" by the industry they are regulating.

5 In some cases, competition may be as effective as public ownership or government regulation at keeping prices low.

6 Anti-combines policy is concerned with promoting competition, both by prohibiting any firm from dominating a market and by eliminating practices that interfere with competition.

7 When accused by the Competition Tribunal of anti-competitive practices, companies may seek to defend themselves by claiming that the practices lead to greater efficiency. In such cases, the tribunal must often decide whether the potential efficiency of restrictive practices outweighs their potential anti-competitive effects.

KEY TERMS

deadweight loss	rent seeking	cross subsidization	concentration ratios
managerial slack	Crown corporations	regulatory capture	

REVIEW QUESTIONS

1 What does it mean when an economist says that monopoly output is "too little" or a monopoly price is "too high"? By what standard? Compared with what?

2 Why might a monopoly lack incentives to hold costs as low as possible?

3 Why might a monopoly lack incentives to pursue research and development opportunities aggressively?

4 What might an economist regard as a socially wasteful way of spending monopoly profits?

5 Explain why the marginal cost curve of a natural monopoly lies below its average cost curve. What are the consequences of this?

6 If government regulators of a natural monopoly set price equal to marginal cost, what problem will inevitably arise? How might public ownership or regulation address this problem?

7 What is the regulatory capture hypothesis?

8 Explain the difference between a horizontal and a vertical agreement.

PROBLEMS

1 Before deregulation of the telephone industry in 1992, Bell Canada provided both local and long-distance telephone service in Ontario and Quebec. A number of firms argued that they could provide long-distance service between major cities more cheaply than Bell, but Bell argued against allowing firms to enter only the long-distance market. If those other firms could actually have offered long-distance service more cheaply, what does that imply about cross subsidies in Bell's pricing of local and long-distance service? What would have happened if Bell Canada had been required to continue offering local service at the same price, but competition had been allowed in the long-distance market?

2 "The stories of enormous subsidies paid to VIA Rail and Canada Post prove that the private sector is more efficient than the public sector." Comment.

3 Explain the incentive problem involved if regulators assure that a natural monopoly will be able to cover its average costs.

4 Explain how some competition, even if not perfect, may be an improvement for consumers over an unregulated natural monopoly. Explain why such competition will not be as good for consumers as an extremely sophisticated regulator, and why it may be better than many real-world regulators.

5 Should greater efficiency be a defence against an accusation of an anti-combines violation?

15

TECHNOLOGICAL CHANGE

Ever since the Industrial Revolution, economic progress has been tied to the discovery and application of new technologies. In the nineteenth century, the railroad and newly invented radio and telegraph opened up continents to trade and settlement, and increased the ability of businesses to communicate worldwide. Soon after that, the discovery of the automobile led to a massive transformation of the manufacturing sector of industrialized economies. New methods of agriculture led to rapidly increased productivity in the production of foodstuffs and caused agricultural workers to shift to urban employment. Later, the commercialization of the airplane and the development of various electrical devices caused a further shift in economic activity. More recently, the discovery and application of computers and laser technology brought on the information revolution and increased the importance of the service sector of the economy. Ongoing discoveries in areas such as biotechnology and metals will undoubtedly make themselves felt in the years to come. The innovations leading to these new technologies have

KEY QUESTIONS

1 In what ways is the production of knowledge—including the knowledge of how to make new products and how to produce things more cheaply—different from the production of ordinary goods like shoes and wheat?

2 Why is the patent system important in providing incentives to engage in research and development?

3 As essential as patents are for encouraging competition in research, how may patents at the same time reduce some aspects of competition?

4 How can government encourage technological progress?

typically emanated from the private sector, and the market economy has always adapted to them.

The great strength of the market economy has been its ability to increase productivity, raise living standards, and innovate. Yet, the basic competitive model upon which we focused in Part Two simply *assumed* the state of technology as given. If we are to understand what determines the pace of innovation, we must go beyond the standard competitive model.

First, industries in which technological change is important are almost necessarily imperfectly competitive. Second, the basic competitive model presented in Part Two assumes that individuals and firms receive all the benefits and pay all the costs of their actions. This assumption takes no account of the external benefits conferred by technological change on individuals and firms not directly involved in innovating and inventing. There is little doubt that we have all benefited from the multitude of inventions that have occurred in the last century. Just imagine what life would be like without the radio, television, cars, airplanes, washing machines, dishwashers—the list is endless. Alexander Graham Bell, Henry Ford, the Wright brothers were all rewarded for their inventions, some richly so. But the creation of these new products confers benefits beyond what consumers have to pay for them. Inventions possess characteristics of what economists refer to as public goods.

This chapter shows why technological change is inevitably linked to imperfect competition. It then discusses the public good aspects of technological change and alternative ways to promote it.

LINKS BETWEEN TECHNOLOGICAL CHANGE AND IMPERFECT COMPETITION

In modern industrialized economies, much competition takes the form of trying to develop both new products and new ways of making old products. Firms devote a considerable amount of their resources to R & D: research—discovering new ideas, products, and processes—and development—for instance, perfecting a new product to the point where it is brought to the market. In industries such as computers and drugs in which technological change and therefore R & D is important, firms strive to earn profits by introducing goods that are new and better—at least in the eyes of consumers—or less costly methods of production. Only through such profits can the investment in R & D pay.

Technological change and imperfect competition are inevitably linked for three major reasons. First, in order to make R & D expenditure pay, and therefore stimulate innovation, inventions are protected from competition by patents. Patents are specifically designed to limit competition. Second, industries where technological change is important typically have high fixed costs—costs that do not change as output increases. This characteristic implies decreasing average costs over a wide range of output, another characteristic of imperfect competition. Finally, industries characterized by rapid technolog-

CLOSE-UP: WHOM HAVE CANADIAN INVENTIONS BENEFITED?

Patents exist to encourage innovative effort by allowing inventors to reap at least some of the rewards of their inventions. But the extent to which they do so varies from invention to invention. Some discoveries, such as finding a new chemical element, are simply not patentable even though they ultimately lead to socially useful products. Furthermore, obtaining a patent does not necessarily guarantee that the inventor will appropriate anywhere near the full economic value of the invention. For one thing, others may "infringe" on the patent—that is, use the idea without paying for it—in which case the inventor will have to engage in costly litigation. For another, the invention may result in others producing a substitute, though not identical, product to take advantage of the general idea discovered. Finally, the invention may be one that is so important to day-to-day living that most of its benefits accrue long into the future. Unlike a copyright for a work of art, patent protection expires after a fixed amount of time.

Canada has had its share of inventions with lasting benefits, some of which have reaped large rewards for the inventors, and some of which have not. Probably most Canadians know that Alexander Graham Bell invented the telephone in Brantford, Ontario, and that Banting and Best discovered insulin. Less well known is the fact that several major industries besides the telephone industry have relied heavily on Canadian inventions. Examples of such inventions include the AM radio, the making of paper from wood

pulp, kerosene, the variable-pitch propeller, the snowblower, the snowmobile, the McIntosh apple, frozen fish, Marquis wheat, and the combine harvester. In the sporting world, Canada can take credit for inventing hockey, basketball, and five-pin bowling. Arguably the most widely used Canadian invention is the simple zipper. Another common item invented in Canada is the paint roller. Obviously, the benefits of all these things, some of which had patents and some of which did not, have gone far beyond the original inventor.

More recently, some Canadian inventors have struck it rich by discovering products with immediate commercial value. Self-entertainment was revolutionized by Trivial Pursuit, which, in addition to appearing in several variants of its own, has spawned a whole industry of competing board games. Another Canadian invention, table hockey, has become a staple among youngsters and has inspired table games of other sports. Many inventions' commercial brand names have gone on to become commonly used generic names for the product itself. Some Canadian examples include the Skidoo, the Laser sailboat, the Jolly Jumper for babies, and the Abdomenizer exerciser.

Inventive activity continues to thrive in Canada; the Canadian Patent Office receives about 35,000 applications per year. Undoubtedly some of them will eventually become household names.

ical change are also industries where the benefits of increasing experience in a new production technique can lead to rapidly decreasing costs. All these make entry difficult, and reduce competition in the sense defined by the basic competitive model.

PATENTS

The writers of the Canadian Constitution recognized the importance of a **patent** as a device to stimulate invention. Section 91 of the British North America

Act of 1867 outlined the powers of Parliament, giving it the explicit right to legislate on the subject of "Patents of Invention and Discovery" (item 22). If inventors are to have an incentive to innovate, they must be able to reap or, as economists say, *appropriate* for themselves some of the fruits of their activities. Parliament has used this power to enact the Patent Act, whose purpose is to insure that inventors of new and useful inventions have exclusive rights over the use of their invention within Canada for a stipulated period of time. That period is currently twenty years. During this period, other producers are precluded from producing the same good, or even making use of the invention in a product of their own, without the permission of the patent holder. Patent holders can sell to others the right to use their product, or **licence** it, in exchange for a payment called a royalty.

THE TRADE-OFF BETWEEN SHORT-RUN EFFICIENCY AND INNOVATION

The patent system grants the inventor a temporary monopoly, allowing her to appropriate some part of the returns on her inventive activity. In Chapter 14 we learned that relative to competitive markets, monopolies result in lower output and higher prices. In spite of this, and in spite of the anti-combines policies discussed there, why does government sanction these monopolies?

In Chapter 11, where we explained why competitive markets, with price equal to marginal cost, ensure economic efficiency, we assumed that the technology was a given. We refer to the kind of economic efficiency that ignores concerns about innovation and invention as **short-run efficiency.**

But the overall efficiency of the economy requires balancing these short-run concerns with the long-run objectives of stimulating research and innovation. Innovation requires firms to reap a return on their investment, and that in turn requires some degree of monopoly power. An economy in which the balancing of short- and long-run concerns is appropriately managed is said to be **dynamically efficient.**

A key provision of the patent law for the trade-off

between short-run efficiency and the innovation necessary for dynamic efficiency is the **life of the patent.** If the life of a patent is short, firms can appropriate the returns from their innovation for only a short time. There is less incentive to innovate than if the patent protection and thus the monopoly lasted longer, but the economy has greater short-run efficiency. If the life of a patent is long, then there are large incentives to innovate, but the social benefits of the innovation are limited. In particular, consumers must wait a long time before prices fall. The twenty-year patent period is intended to strike a balance between the benefits to consumers and the return to investments in R & D.

AN EXAMPLE: THE SWEET MELON COMPANY

Figure 15.1 illustrates the effect of a patent owned by the Sweet Melon Company on a new, cheaper process for producing frozen watermelon juice. To make the example simple, the marginal cost of production is constant. Before the innovation, all producers face the same marginal cost of c_0. Sweet Melon's innovation reduces the marginal costs of production to c_1. Imagine that this industry is perfectly competitive before the innovation, so that price equals marginal cost, c_0. But now Sweet Melon is able to undercut its rivals. With patent protection, the firm sells the good for slightly less than p_0. Its rivals drop out of the market because at the new, lower price, they cannot break even. Sweet Melon now has the whole market. The company sells the quantity Q_1 at the price p_1, making a profit of AB on each sale. Total profits are shaded area $ABCD$ in the figure. The innovation pays off if the profits received exceed the cost of the research.

What happens when the patent expires? Other firms enter the industry, using the less expensive technology. Competition forces the price down to the now lower marginal costs, c_1, and output expands to Q_2. The new equilibrium is at E. Consumers are clearly better off. Short-run economic efficiency is enhanced, because price is now equal to marginal cost. But Sweet Melon reaps no further return from its expenditures on research and development.

If no patent were available, competitors would immediately copy the new juice-making process, and the price would drop to c_1 as soon as the innovation became available. Sweet Melon would receive

Figure 15.1 ECONOMIC EFFECT OF PATENTS

Here, an innovation has reduced the marginal cost of production from c_0 to c_1. Before the innovation, the equilibrium price is p_0, which equals c_0. However, an innovator with a patent will drop the price to p_1, just below p_0, and sell the quantity Q_1. Total profits are the shaded area $ABCD$. When the patent expires, competitors reenter the market, price falls to p_2, which equals c_1, and profits drop to zero.

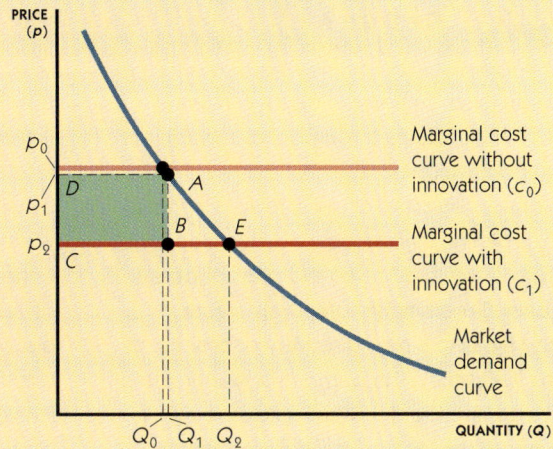

absolutely no returns. (In practice, of course, imitation takes time, during which the company would be able to obtain *some* returns from the innovation.) If the patent were made permanent, consumers would benefit only a small amount from the innovation, since other companies could not compete. Output would remain at Q_1, slightly greater than the original output, and the price would remain high.

BREADTH OF PATENT PROTECTION

How broad a patent's coverage should be is as important as its duration. If an inventor comes up with a product quite similar to one that has already been patented yet slightly different, can this inventor also get a patent for his variant? Or does the original patent cover "minor" variants? Chapter 1 discussed the patent claim of George Baldwin Selden, who argued that his patent covered all self-propelled, gasoline-powered vehicles. He tried to force Henry Ford and the other pioneers of the automobile industry to pay royalties to him, but Ford successfully challenged the patent claim. Recently controversies over patents have surrounded genetic engineering and superconductivity. Should a firm that decodes a fraction of a gene and establishes a use for that information get a patent? If so, does the patent cover the fraction in question or the whole gene?

The original innovators have every incentive to claim broad patent coverage of their own product and those that are in any way related. Later entrants argue for narrow coverage, so that they will be allowed to produce variants and applications without paying royalties. As usual in economics, there is a trade-off. Broad coverage ensures that the inventor reaps more of the returns of her innovation. But excessively broad coverage inhibits innovation, as others see their returns to further developing the idea squeezed by the royalties they must pay to the original inventor.

In practice, there are limits to the use of the patent system. For one thing, not every idea is patentable. To grant a patent, the Canadian Patent Office must be convinced that the invention satisfies three criteria: it must be truly novel, it must serve a useful function, and it must display an innovation that would not be obvious to someone working in the field. Only inventions are patentable, not theoretical ideas such as the theory of gravity or Einstein's theory of relativity. Marketing ideas, like Ray Kroc's idea for selling hamburgers through his McDonald's restaurant chain, are also generally not patentable. Many of the most important developments in modern manufacturing, such as the use of conveyor belts and assembly lines, were not patented.

Innovation takes the form of discovering new products or processes through investment in research and development. Unlike the rewards to other forms of investment, the property rights to the ideas behind innovations and inventions are inherently difficult to "own" and prevent others from using. Governments effectively create property rights to a new discovery or process by granting it a patent. The purpose of granting the patent is to give the discoverer exclusive rights to use or sell the idea or process for a limited period of time. In this way, the effort and expense of finding the discovery can be rewarded, and future inventors will have an incentive to engage in creative activity.

Patents are especially relevant in the pharmaceutical industry, where the process of developing new drugs is very costly and uncertain. In the absence of patents, companies would have little incentive to engage in research, since any discoveries would be available to other firms and the costs of the research could not be recovered from future drug sales. On the other hand, the granting of a monopoly through a patent is not without its disadvantages. When a pharmaceutical company introduces a new drug that will cure some disease, the patent would put the company in a monopolist position so that it would be able to charge such a high price that only the well-off Canadians would be able to afford the drug. Because of this, the federal government has acted to maintain some degree of control over the prices charged for patented medicines without unduly blunting the incentive to undertake research and development.

An amendment to the Patent Act in 1987 included several measures intended to accomplish this. For one thing, the Patented Medicine Prices Review Board (PMPRB) was created. Its main role is to regulate the prices of patented brand-name pharmaceutical products such as Novolin, which is a kind of insulin produced by Connaught Labs for the treatment of diabetes, or Ventolin, which is a widely used inhalator produced by Glaxo. The purpose of this regulation is to ensure that prices are not excessive. The PMPRB is also charged with monitoring both the prices of pharmaceuticals that are not patented, such as generic copies of brand-name pharmaceuticals, and the research and development expenditures made by pharmaceutical manufacturers of patented medicines.

Merely regulating these prices is not likely to be a complete solution. How does one determine the appropriate price for a patented drug? The drug manufacturer will argue that it has spent millions of dollars in research and development of the new drug, whereas the government would retort by suggesting that much of the millions of dollars were simply advertising and marketing expenditures made towards the end of the product-development cycle, or research expenditures incurred simultaneously on a variety of products. The danger is that price regulation by an agency like the PMPRB will reduce research expenditures excessively.

To address this concern, the amendment to the Patent Act also extended the patent life of new drugs from 10 years to 17 years, subsequently extended to 20 years by the federal government in 1993. The manufacturers had argued that the extended patent protection would assist in their efforts to retain talented Canadian researchers who are free to go elsewhere in the world with their expertise. In exchange for this increased patent protection, the pharmaceutical manufacturers have agreed to increase their levels of spending on research and development. Specifically, the pharmaceutical manufacturers agreed to increase the percentage of sales spent on research and development to 8 percent by 1991 and 10 percent by 1996. The table at right shows how this percentage changed from 1985 to 1994. The companies have obviously more than kept their promise. Whether this increased patent life combined with a promise to increase the ratio of research and development expenditures to sales is sufficient to overcome the disincentive effects of the regulation of drug prices remains to be seen.

Pharmaceutical Companies' Research and Development Expenditures as a Percentage of Sales	
1985	3.1
1986	3.5
1987	3.2
1988	6.1
1989	8.2
1990	9.3
1991	9.7
1992	9.9
1993	10.6
1994	11.3

Source: Patented Medicine Prices Review Board, Annual Reports for 1985–94 (Ottawa: Supply and Services Canada).

Government legislation may also restrict the ability of companies to obtain patent protection on inventions. An example of this is the case of prescription drugs, most of which are discovered by corporations whose head office is outside Canada and who initially obtain a patent in the country of origin. In 1969, the Trudeau government restricted the ability of these companies to receive the full benefits of patents for prescription drugs sold in Canada. Other companies were allowed to copy the drugs provided they paid a set royalty to the holders of the patent. This allowed the so-called generic drug companies to produce the drugs in Canada and sell them at a much reduced price, essentially using the fruits of the R & D done by the multinational firm without providing full compensation. This lasted until 1992, when legislation was introduced to provide full patent coverage to prescription drugs, essentially to abide by intellectual property rights provisions contained in NAFTA.

TRADE SECRETS

If patents protect the profits of innovation, why do many firms not bother to seek patent protection for their new products and processes? A major reason is that a firm cannot get a patent without disclosing the details of the new product or process—information that may be extremely helpful to its rivals in furthering their own R & D programmes.

To prevent such disclosure, companies sometimes prefer to keep their own innovations a **trade secret.** A trade secret is simply an innovation or knowledge of a production process that a firm does not disclose to others. The formula for Coca-Cola, for example, is not protected by a patent. It is a trade secret. Trade secrets play an important role in metallurgy, where new alloys are usually not patented. Trade secrets have one major disadvantage over patents. If a rival firm *independently* discovers the same new process, say for making an alloy, it can use the process without paying royalties, even though it was second on the scene.

Some of the returns to an invention come simply from being first in the market. Typically, the firm that first introduces a new product has a decided advantage over rivals, as it builds up customer loyalty and a reputation. Latecomers often have a hard time breaking in, even if there is no patent or trade secret protection.

R & D AS A FIXED COST

Patents and trade secrets are not the only reason that industries in which technological change is important are generally not perfectly competitive. A

Figure 15.2 COSTS OF RE-SEARCH AND DEVELOPMENT

R & D costs are fixed costs—they do not vary with the scale of production. In industries that are R & D–intensive, average costs will be declining over a wide range of outputs. Firms with low levels of output (Q_1) have higher average costs than those with higher output (Q_2).

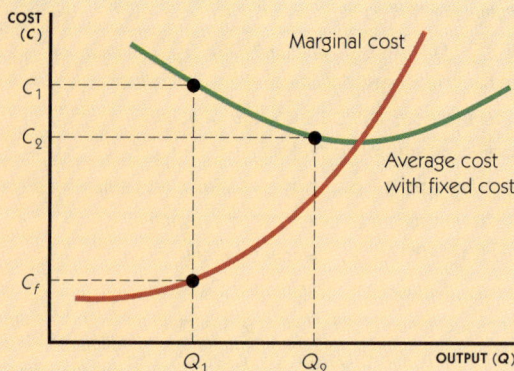

second explanation is that R & D expenditures are fixed costs. That is, the cost of inventing something does not change according to how many times the idea is used in production.[1] The size of fixed costs helps determine how competitive an industry is. The larger the fixed costs the more likely it is that there will be few firms and limited competition.

Because expenditures on research and development are fixed costs, industries with large R & D expenditures face declining average cost curves up to relatively high levels of output. We saw in Chapter 9 that firms typically have U-shaped average cost curves. The presence of fixed costs means that average costs initially decline as firms produce more, but for all the reasons discussed in Chapter 9, beyond some level of output average costs increase. When there are high fixed costs, large firms will have lower average costs than small firms and enjoy a competitive advantage (see Figure 15.2). Industries with large fixed costs thus tend to have relatively few firms and limited competition. It is not surprising, therefore, that the chemical industry—where R & D is tremendously important—is highly concentrated.

Increased size also provides firms with greater incentives to undertake research. Suppose a small firm produces 1 million pens a year. If it discovers a better production technology that reduces its costs by $1 per pen, it saves $1 million a year. A large firm that makes the same discovery and produces 10 million pens a year will save $10 million a year. Thus, large firms have more incentive to engage in research and development, and as they do, they grow more than their smaller rivals do.

But while a large firm's research and development department may help the firm win a competitive advantage, it may also create managerial problems. Bright innovators can feel stifled in the bureaucratic environment of a large corporation, and they may also feel that they are inadequately compensated for their research efforts. In the computer industry, for example, many capable people have left the larger firms to start up new companies of their own.

Thus, size has both its advantages and disadvantages when it comes to innovation. Important inventions and innovations, such as nylon, transistors, and the laser have been produced by major corporations; on the other hand, small enterprises and individual inventors have produced Skidoo snowmobiles, Apple computers, and Kodak film, all of which became major corporations as a result of their success. One objective of anti-combines policies is to maintain an economic environment in which small, innovative firms can compete effectively against established giants.

[1] R & D expenditures can themselves be varied. Differences in the expenditure level will affect when new products will be brought to market and whether a firm will beat its rivals in the competition for new products.

CLOSE-UP: CASHING IN ON AN IDEA—TRIVIAL PURSUIT

At some time in your life you have probably played or heard of the party game called Trivial Pursuit. The success of this board game has been compared to such household favourites as Monopoly and Scrabble, and has set off a spate of others based on the same question-and-answer format.

The game itself was born in a Montreal bar in 1982. Chris Haney, a photo editor with the *Montreal Gazette,* and Scott Abbott, a sportswriter for the *Canadian Press*, were enjoying a few beers when they hit upon the idea for this game based on six thousand trivia questions in six different categories ranging from Arts and Leisure to Sports. After these two budding entrepreneurs decided to create Trivial Pursuit, several other investors placed their money on the game. These were not multinational companies or millionaires, but simple, everyday Canadians who believed they had found a marketable idea.

The success of Trivial Pursuit is well documented. One hundred thousand units were sold in its first year on the market, and 2.4 million in the second year. In 1984, the game was expected to sell about 20 million units in the United States through the licensing agreements that were negotiated for the international production of Trivial Pursuit. The initial version has been supplemented by several specialty versions such as Genus II, Silver Screen, and Baby Boomer.

As with any successful product based on a general idea, however, copies and "takeoffs" have been produced. Two years after the introduction of Trivial Pursuit, the market was flooded by competing trivia games, each representing a slightly different variant. Nonetheless, Trivial Pursuit was able to maintain a strong market presence partly by reinventing the original game and partly by granting licences in other countries such as Germany, Spain, and Greenland. By 1986, Trivial Pursuit was being sold in 20 different countries, each country except the United States and Great Britain having Trivial Pursuit versions in its own language.

Today, several years later, Trivial Pursuit has lost some of its novel appeal, but it still maintains a dominant position in the games market. It has made some unassuming Canadians millionaires many times over and has provided millions of people around the world with hours of enjoyment. At the same time, part of the rewards from the invention of Trivial Pursuit have been spread around to the many other substitute games that have sprung up in the meantime. For while it was possible to patent the particular game of Trivial Pursuit itself, it was not possible to patent the general idea for a board game based on questions and answers. The patent was not strong enough to prevent other trivia-type games from flooding the market.

Sources: "Trivial Pursuit Game in Pursuit of Global Market," *The Globe and Mail*, May 9, 1984, p. B8; "Born to Win," *Canadian Business*, July 1984, pp. 87–90.

LEARNING BY DOING

Some increases in productivity occur not as a result of explicit expenditures on R & D but as a by-product of actual production. As firms gain experience from production, their costs fall. This kind of technological change is called **learning by doing.** This systematic relationship between cumulative production experience and costs—often called the **learning curve**—was first discovered in the airplane industry, where the costs of production fell dramatically as more planes of a given type were produced.

This is the third reason why technological change and imperfect competition go together—because the marginal cost falls as the scale of production and the experience accumulated increases. The first firm to enter an industry has a particular advantage over other firms. Even if some of what the first company has learned spills over into other firms, not all of it does. Because of the knowledge the first firm has gained, its costs will be below those of potential rivals, and thus it can always undercut them. Since potential entrants know this, they are reluctant to enter industries where learning by doing has a significant impact on costs. By the same token, companies realize that if they can find a product that provides significant benefits from learning by doing, the profits they earn will be relatively secure. Hence, just as firms race to be the first to obtain a patent, so too they race to be the first to enter a product market in which there is a steep learning curve. This behaviour is commonly seen in the computer chip industry.

When learning by doing is important, firms will produce beyond the point where marginal revenue equals *current* marginal costs, because producing more today has an extra benefit. It reduces future costs of production. How much extra a firm produces depends on the steepness of the learning curve.

ACCESS TO CAPITAL MARKETS

Banks are generally unwilling to lend funds to finance R & D expenditures because they are often very risky and these risks cannot be insured. When a bank makes a loan for a building, if the borrower defaults the bank winds up with the building. If the bank lends for R & D and the research project fails, or a rival beats the firm to the patent office, the bank may wind up with nothing. Investors also often have a hard time judging the prospects of an R & D endeavour—inventors are always optimistic about their ideas. This difficulty is compounded by an inventor's possible reluctance to disclose all the information about his idea, either to banks or potential investors, lest some among them steal his idea and beat him either to the market or the patent office.

HOW COMPETITION AFFECTS TECHNOLOGICAL CHANGE

Competition spurs R & D

A new innovation enables firms to enjoy profits (profits are driven to zero in standard markets).

Unless firms innovate, they will not survive.

Competition impedes R & D

Competitors may imitate, thus eroding returns from innovation.

Competition erodes the profits required to finance R & D.

HOW TECHNOLOGICAL CHANGE AFFECTS COMPETITION

R & D spurs competition

R & D provides an alternative to prices as a way for firms to compete; it is one of the most important arenas for competition in modern economies.

R & D impedes competition

Patents give a single firm a protected position for a number of years.

The fixed costs of R & D give large firms an advantage, and mean that industries in which R & D is important may have few firms.

Learning by doing gives a decided advantage to the first entrant into a market.

Limited access to capital markets for financing R & D is a disadvantage to new and small firms.

For established firms in industries with limited competition and growing demand, financing their research expenditures presents no serious problem. They can pay for R & D out of their profits. That is why when one looks at the economy as a whole, most R & D occurs in such firms. For new and small firms and for firms in industries where intense competition limits the profits that any one company can earn, raising capital is a problem. Thus, a firm's dominant position in an industry may be self-perpetuating. Its greater output means that it has more to gain from innovations that reduce the cost of production. Its greater profits give it more resources to expend on R & D.

Today, much of the R & D in new and small companies is financed by venture-capital firms. These firms raise capital, mainly from pension funds, insurance companies, and wealthy individuals, which they then invest in the most promising R & D ventures. Venture-capital firms often demand as compensation for their risk taking a significant share of the new enterprise, and they usually keep close tabs on how their money is spent. They also sometimes specialize in particular areas, such as computer technology or biotechnology. In less glamourous industries, it is often difficult to find financing for research and development.

BASIC RESEARCH AS A PUBLIC GOOD

R & D expenditures on inventions or innovations almost always give rise to **externalities.** Externalities arise whenever one individual's or firm's action produces costs or benefits to others that are not reimbursed within, are "external to," the price system. As we shall see in Chapters 18 and 19, the presence of externalities constitutes one of the main reasons for government intervention in a market economy. The total benefits produced by an R & D expenditure for both the party undertaking the expenditure and for other benefiting parties are referred to as its **social benefit.** Even with patents, inventors appropriate only a fraction of the social benefit of an invention. A firm that discovers a cheaper way of producing is

likely to lower its price during the life of the patent to steal customers away from its rivals. This benefits consumers. After the patent expires, consumers benefit even more as rivals beat the price down further. And the benefits of an invention in one area spill over to other areas. The transistor, which revolutionized electronics, was invented at American Telephone and Telegraph's (AT&T) Bell Laboratories. AT&T reaped the benefits from its direct application to telephone equipment. But the benefits in better radios, television sets, and other products accrued to others.

From society's viewpoint, a particularly valuable kind of R & D is **basic research.** Basic research is the kind of fundamental inquiry that produces a wide range of applications. For example, basic research in physics led to the ideas behind so many of the things we take for granted today—the laser, the transistor, atomic energy. The returns to firms from any basic research they might undertake—which in the absence of government intervention would dictate the amount of R & D spent on basic research—are negligible in comparison to its social benefits. Indeed, the externalities flowing from basic research are so extreme that it can be considered a **public good.**

The public good is defined by two properties. First, it is difficult to exclude anyone from the benefits of a public good. Basic research involves the discovery of underlying scientific principles or facts of nature. Such facts—like superconductivity, or even the fact that there exist certain materials that exhibit superconductivity at temperatures considerably above absolute zero—cannot be patented.

Second, the marginal cost of an additional individual's enjoying a public good is zero. We say that consumption is nonrivalrous. An additional person's being informed of a basic discovery does not detract from the knowledge that the original discoverer has, though it may, of course, reduce the profits the original discoverer can make out of the discovery. But sharing the fruits of basic research as soon as they are available can yield enormous public benefits, as other researchers use this knowledge in their quest for innovation.

As with all public goods, private markets yield an undersupply of basic research. Accordingly, the federal government undertakes basic research through

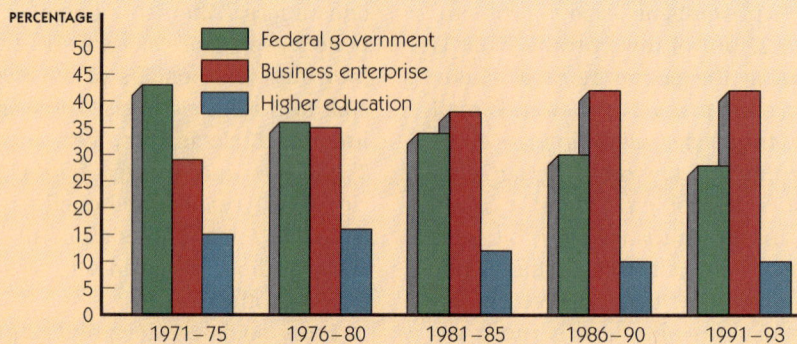

Figure 15.3 PERCENTAGES OF GROSS DOMESTIC EXPENDITURES ON RESEARCH AND DEVELOPMENT (GERD) FUNDED BY CERTAIN SECTORS, 1971–1993

The federal government's importance in the funding of R & D has declined over the last 25 years. It has been surpassed by business enterprise as the largest source of funding. *Source*: Statistics Canada, *Federal Scientific Activities*, 1994–95, Table 1.2.

the National Research Council and other federal agencies and provides financial support for research through the Natural Sciences and Engineering Research Council, the Medical Research Council, the Social Sciences and Humanities Research Council, and the Canada Council. Some of the expenditures of National Defence Canada, Agriculture Canada, and Environment Canada on R & D also go into basic research. There is increasing concern among economists that expenditures on basic research are inadequate.

Figure 15.3 shows how federal expenditure on R & D has declined in importance over the past three decades. There has been a steady rise in the percentage of R & D funding by business enterprise, now the largest contributor of funds. In the period 1995–96, the largest federal government expenditures on R & D are projected to be in the Canadian Space Agency, Natural Resources Canada, and Agriculture Canada. Only about 8 percent has been projected for defence, in contrast with the U.S. case, where over half of government expenditures on R & D are on defence.

It is of interest to know how total expenditures on R & D, not just those by the government, vary across countries. As shown in Figure 15.4, Canada's share of GDP devoted to R & D expenditures is just over 1 percent, which is considerably lower than some of our main competitors, especially the United States, Germany, the United Kingdom, and Japan. The U.S. case is somewhat special owing to the fact that 55 percent of U.S. government support for R & D goes to defence. Thus, the share spent in developing new products and processes to make industry more competitive is comparable to that of the Canadian case, and well below that of other major industrialized countries. This may explain why non-residents are getting almost one out of every two patents granted by the U.S. Patent Office, up from one in five during the 1960s. (Inventors have the right to obtain a patent from a foreign country as well as their own.) In Canada, over 90 percent of the patents granted by the Canadian Patent Office went to nonresidents, and that has been the case for three decades. At the same time, in terms of absolute numbers, the number of patents received by Canadian residents actually fell by 20 percent between 1969 and 1991. Thus, there is some evidence that innovative effort in Canada is lagging behind that in the rest of the world.

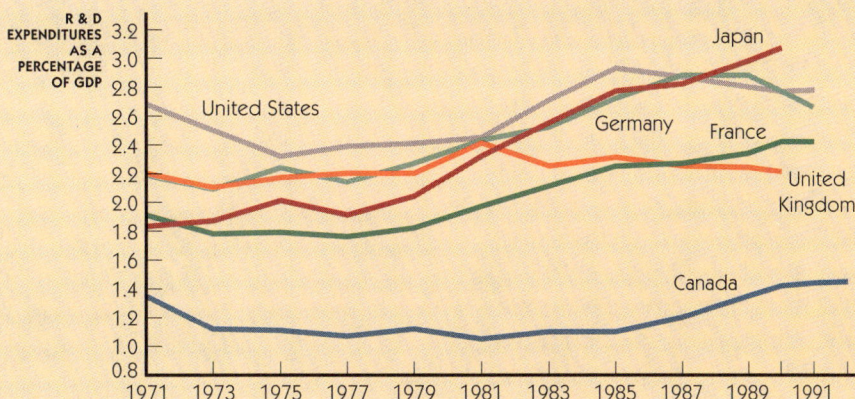

Figure 15.4 **COMPARISON OF R & D EXPENDITURES ACROSS COUNTRIES**

The share of Canadian GDP devoted to R & D is only about half that of other major industrialized countries. *Sources*: Statistics Canada, *Canada Year Book* 1994; National Science Foundation, *International Science and Technology Data Update*, Special Report NSF 91-309 (Washington, D.C., 1991); *OECD Jobs Study: Investment, Productivity and Employment* (Paris: Organization for Economic Cooperation and Development), 1995, Chapter 2.

GOVERNMENT PROMOTION OF TECHNOLOGICAL PROGRESS

While there is widespread agreement that government should encourage innovative activity through the protection of intellectual property rights and through support of basic R & D, other ways by which the government promotes R & D have been far more controversial.

SUBSIDIES

Government support for applied research has been attacked by critics. Among the reasons given is that the government has a bad record in picking what to subsidize. Many advocates of this view still support broad-based subsidies such as R & D tax credits (discussed below), which do not depend on government selection of particular projects.

But there are still supporters of more active involvement of government in R & D; they claim that there are large positive externalities associated with applied research, implying that the private sector underinvests in applied research. Policies aimed to support particular sectors of the economy are called **industrial policies.**

Advocates of public support of applied R & D admit that government has not always picked winners. But they claim R & D is by its very nature risky, and a record of complete success cannot be expected. They also claim that, in fact, government's success record has been impressive. They point, for example, to the over 100 percent increase in the productivity of agriculture over the past century. This has resulted from research undertaken both by government itself and by government-supported institutions such as universities and agricultural colleges.

One rationale behind government R & D expenditures in agriculture extends to other parts of the economy as well. The argument is that an industry made up of many firms will fall further below the socially efficient level of R & D expenditure than industries in which a few firms dominate and can, therefore, reap for themselves most of the benefits of their R & D investment.

INTERNATIONAL COMPLICATIONS

Subsidies have, however, raised the spectre of unfair competition in the international arena. Countries facing competition from foreign firms with government subsidies impose countervailing duties: taxes levied on imports are intended to offset the benefits of these subsidies. The concern is that if, for instance, Canada and the United States become engaged in a contest to support some industry, the industry will indeed benefit, but at the expense of the taxpayers in both countries. Thus, international agreements have tried to reduce the extent of subsidization. Broad-based R & D subsidies such as

through the tax system are still permitted, but more narrowly focused subsidies are either prohibited or put into the category of questionable practices.

TAX CREDITS

Since firms view R & D expenditures as a form of investment, such spending will be affected by some of the same factors that affect other forms of investment. In particular, tax changes that reduce a firm's profits will also be reflected in lower levels of R & D. Because of its concern that the level of R & D expenditures would otherwise be too low, the government provides tax incentives to encourage R & D in the form of a **tax credit.** Specifically, firms that undertake R & D expenditures are able to deduct from their tax bill 20 percent of the full cost of such expenditures. The amount of the tax credit rises to as much as 35 percent in special circumstances, such as for expenditures in the depressed region of Atlantic Canada. This is a relatively generous tax incentive compared with other countries'. For example, in the United States, firms are able to claim a tax credit of 25 percent on *increases* in the level of R & D expenditures, which is typically much lower than total expenditures.

PROTECTION

Firms in less developed countries often argue that they need to be insulated from competition from abroad in order to develop the knowledge base required to compete effectively in world markets. This is the **infant industry argument for protection.** Most economists are skeptical. They see this argument mainly as an attempt at rent seeking by firms

who will use any excuse to insulate themselves from competition so they can raise prices and increase profits. The best way to learn to compete is to compete, not to be isolated from competition. If some help is needed to enable firms to catch up, it should be provided in the form of subsidies, the costs of which are explicit and obvious, unlike the hidden costs of higher prices that result from protection.

RELAXING ANTI-COMBINES POLICIES

The anti-combines policies explored in Chapter 14 were founded on the belief that government should push markets towards the model of perfect competition. But an increasing awareness of the importance of R & D in modern industrial economies has led some to argue for a reassessment of anti-combines legislation.

One argument for changing the law is that a firm that makes a major innovation may not be able to exploit it fully, lest it be subject to anti-combines

TECHNOLOGICAL CHANGE AND THE BASIC COMPETITIVE MODEL

Basic Competitive Model	Industries in Which Technological Change is Important
Assumes fixed technology.	The central question is what determines the pace of technological change. Related issues include what determines expenditure on R & D and how learning by doing affects the level of production.
Assumes perfect competition, with many firms in industry.	Competition is not perfect; industries where technological change is important tend to have relatively few firms.
Assumes perfect capital markets.	Firms find it difficult to borrow to finance R & D expenditures.
Assumes no externalities.	R & D confers benefits on others besides the inventor; even with patents, the inventor appropriates only a fraction of the social benefits of an invention.
Assumes no public goods.	Basic research is a public good: the marginal cost of an additional person making use of a new idea is zero (nonrivalrous consumption), and it is often difficult to exclude others from enjoying the benefits of basic research.

prosecution. Knowing that it cannot take full advantage of major discoveries that enable it to, say, produce a product at much lower costs than its competitors and put them out of business, the firm has less incentive to spend as much on R & D than it otherwise would.

The anti-combines laws might also inhibit firms from engaging in **joint ventures** in which several firms undertake projects together—whether to share research ideas and the risks and costs of their R & D expenditures or to produce a new product. The government has traditionally feared that cooperative R & D efforts might easily turn into collusion on pricing and production and might lead to a violation of the anti-combines laws. But cooperative ventures in R & D are not outlawed as such. Indeed, they have long been permitted under the Patent Act, where specific provision is made for joint applications.

The arguments in *favour* of joint ventures have to do with the externalities of R & D. Any single firm knows that if it makes a new invention, other firms in the industry are likely to benefit either directly from imitation, or indirectly from some of the knowledge acquired in the process of making the discovery. Society as a whole would like those benefits, but no individual firm has a sufficient incentive to pursue them. It would be in the firms' interest to group together for R & D efforts and thereby "internalize" part of the resulting benefits.

Arguments earlier in the chapter suggested that perfect competition is not an ideal to strive for, because markets that are highly competitive may undertake less R & D than their less competitive counterparts. On the other hand, if markets are not competitive enough, R & D may be limited by the lack of spur that competition provides. Thus, the economy must strive to strike a balance between enough competition to provide a spur to innovation and efficiency, and limited enough competition so that firms can appropriate sufficient returns to their innovative activity to give them both the incentive and the resources to undertake R & D.

TECHNOLOGICAL CHANGE AND ECONOMIC GROWTH

Living standards in Canada are far higher today than they were a hundred years ago. The reason is that productivity—output per hour—has increased enormously. Underlying this increase is technological change. Many discoveries occurred almost by accident, such as Fleming's discovery of penicillin, but in the modern economy most advances are a result of the deliberate allocation of resources to research and development. The importance—and consequences—of technological change constitutes our eighth major point of consensus among economists.

8 Innovation

Modern economies are based on innovation. Imperfect competition is widespread in the sectors of the economy in which innovation is most important. Government plays a crucial role in innovation, in protecting intellectual property through patents and copyrights and also in supporting basic research.

REVIEW AND PRACTICE

SUMMARY

1 Industries in which technological change is important are almost necessarily imperfectly competitive. Patents are one way the government makes it difficult and costly for firms to copy the technological innovations of others. A firm with a patent will have a government-enforced monopoly. The expenditures on R & D are fixed costs; when they are large, there are likely to be few firms in the industry, and price competition is more likely to be limited.

2 Long-lived and broad patents discourage competition (at least in the short run), but provide greater incentives to innovate. Short-lived and narrow patents reduce the incentive to innovate, but encourage competition.

3 Learning by doing, in which companies (or countries) that begin making a product first enjoy an advantage over all later entrants, may be a source of technological advantage.

4 Research and development generally provides positive externalities to consumers and other firms. But since the innovating firm cannot capture all the social benefits from its invention, it will tend to invest less than a socially optimal amount.

5 Basic research has both the central properties of a public good: it is difficult to exclude others from the benefits of the research, and the marginal cost of an additional person making use of the new idea is zero.

6 A number of governmental policies encourage technological advance: patents; direct spending on research; subsidies and tax incentives to encourage corporate R & D; temporary protection from technologically advanced foreign competitors; and relaxing anti-combines laws to allow potential competitors to work together on research projects.

KEY TERMS

patent	learning by doing	public good	infant industry argument
license	learning curve	industrial policy	
trade secret	externalities	tax credit	joint ventures

REVIEW QUESTIONS

1 In what ways do industries in which technological change is important not satisfy the assumptions of the standard competitive model?

2 Why are industries in which technological change is important not likely to be competitive?

3 Why do governments grant patents, thereby conferring temporary monopoly rights? Explain the trade-off society faces in choosing whether to offer long-lived or short-lived patents, and whether to offer broad or narrow patents.

4 How does the existence of learning by doing provide an advantage to incumbent firms over prospective entrants?

5 Why might it be harder to raise capital for R & D than for other projects? How can established firms

deal with this problem? What about start-up firms?

6 How do positive externalities arise from R & D? Why do externalities imply that there may be too little expenditure on research by private firms?

7 Explain how basic research can be thought of as a public good. Why is society likely to underinvest in basic research? What is the economist's reason for supporting government subsidies in areas that help produce new technology?

8 What are industrial policies? What are the arguments for and against government support of research in particular industries?

9 What possible trade-off does society face when it considers loosening its anti-combines laws to encourage joint research and development ventures?

PROBLEMS

1 Imagine that Parliament is considering a bill to reduce the current twenty-year life of patents to eight years. What negative effects might this change have on the rate of innovation? What positive effect might it have for the economy?

2 Suppose that many years ago, one inventor received a patent for orange juice, and then another inventor came forward and requested a patent for lemonade. The first inventor maintained that the orange juice patent should be interpreted to cover all fruit juices, while the second inventor argued that the original patent included only one particular method of making one kind of juice. What trade-offs does society face in setting rules for deciding cases like these?

3 Although a patent assures a monopoly on that particular invention for some time, it also requires that the inventor disclose the details of the invention. Given this requirement, under what conditions might a company like Coca-Cola prefer to use trade secret law rather than patents to protect its formulas?

4 Why might a company invest in research and development even if it does not believe it will be able to patent its discovery?

5 Learning by doing seems to be important in the semiconductor industry, where the United States and Japan are the main producers. Explain why U.S. and Japanese firms may race to try to bring out new generations of semiconductors. If learning by doing is important in the semiconductor industry, why might other nations try to use an infant industry strategy to develop their own semiconductor industry?

IMPERFECT INFORMATION

It was never any secret to economists that the real world did not match the model of perfect competition. Theories of monopoly and imperfect competition such as those covered in Chapters 12–14 have been propounded from Adam Smith's time to the present.

Another limitation of the model of perfect competition has recently come to the fore: its assumption of **perfect information**—that market participants have full information about the goods and services being bought and sold. By incorporating **imperfect information** into their models, economists have come a long way in closing the gap between the real world and the world depicted by the perfect competition, perfect information model of Part Two.

This chapter provides a broad overview of the major information problems of the product, capital, and labour markets, the ways in which market economies deal with them, and how the basic model of Part Two has to be modified as a result.

KEY QUESTIONS

1 Why is information different from other goods, such as hats and cameras? In particular, why do markets for information often not work well?

2 When does the market price affect the quality of what is being sold? How does the fact that consumers believe price affects quality influence how firms behave?

3 When customers have trouble differentiating good from shoddy merchandise, what are the incentives firms have to produce good merchandise? What role does reputation play?

4 How does advertising affect firm demand curves and profits? Why may the firms in an industry be better off if they collectively agree not to advertise?

5 How do people mitigate the risks they face? Why are there many risks for which insurance is not available?

6 How do firms acquire information to help determine how productive various candidates for jobs will be? How do the workers themselves signal their suitability for a job?

THE INFORMATION PROBLEM

The basic competitive model assumes that households and firms are well informed. This means that they know their opportunity set, or what is available. More striking, they know every characteristic of every good, including how long it will last. Were these assumptions true, shopping would hardly be a chore.

The model also assumes that consumers know their preferences, what they like. They know not only how many oranges they can trade for an apple, but also how many oranges they are willing to trade. In the case of apples and oranges this may make sense. But how do students know how much they are going to enjoy, or even benefit from, a university education before they have experienced it? How does an individual know whether she would like to be a doctor or a lawyer? She gets some idea about what different professions are like by observing those who practice them, but her information is at best imperfect.

According to the basic model, firms too are perfectly well-informed. They all know the best available technology. They know the productivity of each applicant for a job. They know the prices at which inputs can be purchased from every possible supplier

(and all of the inputs' characteristics). And they know the prices at which they can sell the goods, not only today, but in every possible circumstance in the future.

HOW BIG A PROBLEM?

That individuals and firms are not perfectly well informed is by itself not necessarily a telling criticism of the competitive model, just as the criticism that markets are not perfectly competitive does not cause us to discard the model. The relevant questions have to do with the danger that the competitive model will mislead us. Are there important economic phenomena that can be explained only by taking into account imperfect information? Are there important predictions of the model that are incorrect as a result of the assumptions concerning well-informed consumers and firms?

Increasingly over the past two decades, economists have come to believe that the answer to these questions is yes. We have already seen evidence of this. Chapter 7, for instance, pointed out that university graduates may receive a higher income than high school graduates not only because they have learned things in university that make them more productive, but because their university degree helps them through a sorting process. Employers cannot determine from an interview which applicants for a job will be productive workers. They therefore use a university degree to help them identify those who are better at learning. University graduates *are*, on average, more productive workers. But it is wrong to conclude from this that university has necessarily *increased* their productivity. It may simply have enabled firms to sort out more easily the more productive from the less productive.

Similarly, Chapter 8 discussed the problem of the investor choosing among alternative stocks. The basic maxim for success in investing is simple. Buy when the price is low, and sell when the price is high. The problem is how to know when the price of a stock is low or high.

HOW PRICES CONVEY INFORMATION

The price system provides brilliant solutions for some information problems. We have seen how prices play an important role in coordinating production and communicating information about economic scarcity. Firms do not have to know what John or Julia likes, what their trade-offs are. The price tells the producer the marginal benefit of producing an extra unit of the good, and that is all he needs to know. Similarly, a firm does not need to know how much natural gas is left in Alberta, the cost of extracting and transmitting the gas, or a thousand other details. All it needs to know is the price of natural gas. This tells the company how scarce the resource is, how much effort it should expend in conserving. Prices and markets provide the basis of the economy's incentive system. But there are some information problems that markets do not handle, or do not handle well. And imperfect information sometimes inhibits the ability of markets to perform the tasks it performs so well when information is good.

MARKETS FOR INFORMATION

Information has value; people are willing to pay for it. In this sense, we can consider information just as we do any other good. There is a market for information, with its price—just as there is a market for labour and a market for capital. Indeed, our economy is sometimes referred to as an information economy. Every year, investors spend millions of dollars on newsletters that give them information. Magazines sell specialized information about hundreds of goods.

However, the markets for information are far from perfect, and for good reasons. The most conspicuous one is that information is *not* just like any other good. When you buy a chair, the furniture dealer is happy to let you look at it, feel it, sit on it, and decide whether you like it. When you buy information, you cannot do the same. The seller can either say, "Trust me. I'll tell you what you need to know," or show you the information and say, "Here's what I know. If this is what you wanted to know, please pay me." You would rightfully be skeptical in the first scenario, and might be unwilling to pay in the second. After you were given the information, what incentive would you have to pay?

In some cases, there is a basic credibility problem. You might think, if a stock tipster *really* knows that a stock is going to go up in price, why should he tell me, even if I pay him for the information? Why doesn't he go out and make his fortune with the information? Or is it that he really is not sure, and would just as soon have me risk my money rather than risk his?

Most important, even after the firm or consumer buys all the information he thinks is worth paying for, his information is still far from perfect. Let's look now at some of the consequences of imperfect information.

THE MARKET FOR LEMONS AND ADVERSE SELECTION

Have you ever wondered why a three-month-old used car sells for so much less—often 20 percent less—than a new car? Surely cars do not deteriorate that fast. The pleasure of owning a new car may be worth something, but in three months, even the car you buy new will be "used." A couple thousand dollars or more is a steep price to pay for this short-lived pleasure.

A simple explanation for this is based on imperfect information. Some cars are worse than others. They have hidden defects that become apparent to the owner only after she has owned the car for a while. Such defective cars are called lemons. One thing after another goes wrong with them. While warranties may reduce the financial cost of having a lemon, they do not eliminate the bother—the time it takes to bring the car into the shop, the anxiety of knowing there is a good chance of a breakdown. Of course, the owners know they have a lemon and would like to pass it along to someone else. Those with the worst lemons are going to be the most willing to sell their car, whatever the price. But at a high used-car price, they will be joined by owners of better-quality cars. As the price drops, more of the good cars will be withdrawn from the market as the owners decide to keep them. And the average quality of the used cars for sale will *drop*. We say there is an **adverse selection** effect. The mix of those who elect to sell changes adversely as price falls.

Figure 16.1 shows the consequences of imperfect information for market equilibrium in the used-car market. Panel A depicts, for each price (measured along the horizontal axis), the average quality of used cars being sold in the market. As price increases, quality increases. Panel B shows the supply curve of used cars. As price increases, the number of cars being sold in the market increases, for all the usual

reasons. The demand curve is also shown. This curve has a peculiar shape: upward- as well as downward-sloping. The reason is that as price increases, the average quality increases. Demand depends not just on price but on quality—on the "value" being offered on the market. If, as price falls, quality deteriorates rapidly, then quantity demanded will actually *fall* as price falls—consumers are getting less for their dollars. The equilibrium is depicted in panel B.

This particular example is often referred to as one with **asymmetric information.** That is, the seller of the used car has more information about the product than the buyer. Many markets are characterized by asymmetric information. One of the consequences of asymmetric information is that there may be relatively few buyers and sellers, far fewer than there would be with perfect information. Economists use the term **thin** to describe markets in which there are relatively few buyers and sellers. In some situations, a market may be so thin as to be essentially nonexistent. Economists say the economy has an **incomplete** set of markets. The used-car market, for example, is a thin one. Buyers may know that there are some legitimate sellers, those who for one reason or another always want to drive a new car. But mixed in with these are people who are trying to dump their lemons. The buyers cannot tell the lemons apart from the good cars. Rather than risk it,

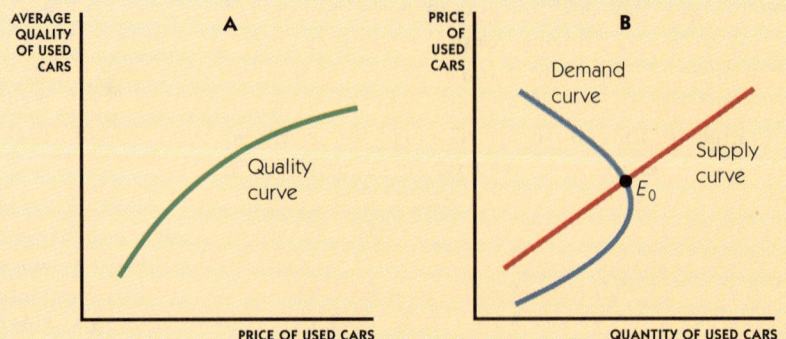

Figure 16.1 A MARKET FOR LEMONS

Panel A shows the average quality of a used car increasing as the price increases. Panel B shows a typical upward-sloping supply curve, but a backward-bending demand curve. Demand bends back because buyers know that quality is lower at lower prices, and they thus choose to buy less as the price falls. Panel B shows the market equilibrium is at point E_0.

they simply do not buy. (Of course, the fact that demand is low drives down the price, increasing the proportion of lemons. It is a vicious cycle.)

SIGNALLING

If you have a good car and you want to sell it, you would like to persuade potential buyers that it is good. You could tell them that it is not a lemon, but why should they believe you? There is a simple principle: *actions speak louder than words.* What actions can you take that will convince buyers of the quality of your car?

The fact that Chrysler is willing to provide a five-year, fifty-thousand-mile warranty on its cars says something about the confidence Chrysler has in its products. The warranty is valuable, not only because it reduces the risks of having to spend a mint to repair the car, but also because the buyer believes that Chrysler would not have provided the warranty unless the chances of defects were low. Actions such as this are said to "signal" higher quality. A signal is effective if it differentiates—here between high-quality cars and low-quality cars. The cost to the producer of a five-year guarantee is much higher for a car that is likely to fall apart within five years than for a car that is unlikely to break down. Customers know this, and thus can infer that a firm willing to provide this warranty is selling high-quality cars.

Automobile manufacturers like Chrysler may not be the only firms willing to signal the quality of their cars by warranty. Used-car dealers frequently do so as well. They can do so if they have been able to acquire information about the cars on their lots by means such as mechanical inspection or even knowledge of the previous owners.

When you go to a car dealer, you want to know that it will still be around if you have trouble. Some firms signal that they are not fly-by-nights by spending a great deal of money on their showroom. This indicates that it would be costly for them to just pack up and leave. (There are, of course, other reasons why they may spend money on a fancy showroom.)

Actions such as providing a better guarantee or a larger showroom are taken not just for the direct benefit that the consumer receives from them, but because those actions make consumers believe that the product is a better product or the firm is a better firm to deal with. In a sense, the desire to convey information "distorts" the decisions taken relative to what they would have been in a perfect-information world.

JUDGING QUALITY BY PRICE

There is still another clue that buyers use to judge the quality of what they are about to purchase. This is price. Consumers make inferences about the quality of goods on the basis of the price charged. Generally, if the price of a used car is low, consumers know that the chance of getting a lemon is higher. Firms know that consumers know this.

In markets with imperfect information, firms *set* their prices. And in setting their prices, they take into account what customers will think about the quality of the good being sold. Concerns about consumers correctly or incorrectly making inferences about quality impede the effectiveness of price competition. In the used-car example, we saw that, as price rose, the average quality of cars on the market increased. But if firms think customers believe that cars being sold at a lower price are lower quality— that the quality deteriorates more than the price declines—they will not lower the price because they will think lower prices *lose* them their customers. Under such circumstances, even if the firms cannot sell all they would like at the going price, they will still not cut prices.

A situation can be sustained in which there is a seeming excess supply of goods. Imperfect information means that equilibrium will be achieved away from the intersection of supply and demand curves. This is a profound result, one that recurs in many of the chapters that follow.

Information problems fascinate economists because they turn the basic competitive model upside down. Prices convey critical information in a market economy. Sellers will manipulate prices when they can to control the information conveyed. Buyers, for their part, see through these manipulations. And their concern that the seller is trying to pass off a lemon discourages trade. When information problems like these are severe, markets are thin or even nonexistent. Alternatively, price competition may be

SOLUTIONS TO ADVERSE SELECTION PROBLEMS IN MARKET ECONOMIES

Signalling

Judging quality by price

limited. Even when there is an excess supply of goods, firms may not cut their prices and the market may not clear.

THE INCENTIVE PROBLEM

We have seen throughout this book that providing incentives that motivate individuals to do the efficient thing, to make the most efficient choices, is one of the central economic problems. The central problem of incentives, in turn, is that individuals do not bear the full consequences of their actions. The collapse in 1985 of the Alberta-based banks Northlands and Canadian Commercial was largely attributable to incorrect incentives. Because deposits were guaranteed by the Canadian Deposit Insurance Corporation, the banks had an incentive to take high risks: if they were successful they kept the gain, whereas if they failed the government picked up the loss. Similarly, the fact that laid-off workers can claim unemployment insurance benefits provides an incentive for firms to lay workers off temporarily in times of low demand rather than reducing hours of work or building up inventories. The government rather than the firm or its workers effectively bears the cost of the layoffs.

In the basic competitive model of Part Two, private property and prices provide incentives. Individuals are rewarded for performing particular tasks. The problem arises when an individual is not rewarded for what he does, or when he does not have to pay the full costs of what he does. In our economy, incentive problems are pervasive.

In product markets, firms must be given the in-centive to produce quality products. Again, the incentive problem is an information problem. If customers could always tell the quality of the product they were getting, firms that produced higher-quality products would always be able to charge a higher price, and no company could get away with producing shoddy goods. Most of us have had the experience of going to a newly established restaurant, having a good meal, and then returning a few months later to find that the quality had deteriorated. Evidently something went wrong with incentives.

MARKET SOLUTIONS

In simple transactions, incentive problems can be solved with schemes of penalties and rewards. You would like a document typed. You sign a contract with someone to pay him $25 to deliver the typed document by tomorrow at five P.M. The contract stipulates that $.50 will be deducted for each typographical error, and $1.00 for every hour the paper is late. The contract has built-in incentives for the paper to be delivered on time and without errors.

But most transactions, even simple ones, are more complicated than this one. The more complicated the transaction, the more difficult it is to solve the incentive problem. You want your grass mowed, and your neighbour's twelve-year-old son wants to mow it. You want him to take care of your power mower. When he sees a rock in the mower's path, he should pick it up. But what incentive does he have to take care of the mower? If you plan to charge him for repairs if the mower does hit a rock, how can you tell whether the rock was hidden by the grass? If he owned his own mower, he would have the appropriate incentives. That is why private property combined with the price system provides such an effective solution to the incentive problem. But your

CLOSE-UP: AUTOMOBILE BROKERS AND IMPERFECT INFORMATION

A broker is someone who arranges contracts between two parties. In earlier times, marriage brokers brought together prospective couples. Stockbrokers bring together buyers and sellers of stocks. Car brokers bring together buyers and sellers of cars.

In every case a broker is someone whose job exists only because of imperfect information. After all, why can't a person just go out and choose a spouse or a stock or a car? The obvious problem is that many different varieties are available, and it costs time and energy and money to collect the information to take an informed decision. A good broker is out there in the market all the time, keeping track of what is going on. Having a relatively small number of people keeping track of buyers and sellers is certainly more efficient than having all buyers and sellers duplicating one another's efforts.

Consider how car brokers work. You call up a broker (usually they are listed in the Yellow Pages of the phone book) and describe what sort of car you want—make, model, year, accessories. The broker then finds you the best deal.

Working as a broker may seem like a funny way to make a living. How can someone get paid for shopping for cars? The answer is that shopping for a car involves time and the energy of confronting dealers and haggling over price. Even if the buyer spends several days or weeks shopping, it is not clear she will find the best deal. Paying a knowledgeable broker will certainly save time and energy, and might result in a cheaper price too. A good broker will know the sales representative's typical commission or the "preparation fee" that dealers receive for getting a car ready to sell. By taking factors like this into account, the broker can often negotiate a better price.

Not everyone will need or want an automobile broker. But for those who feel their information about the car market is extremely imperfect, a broker may be a wise choice.

Source: "A Better Way to Buy a Car?" *Consumer Reports,* September 1989, pp. 593–95.

---

neighbour's son probably does not have the money to buy his own power mower. Then an incentive problem is inevitable. Either you let him use your lawn mower and bear the risk of his mistreating it, or you lend him money to buy his own, in which case you bear the risk of his not paying you back.

Many private companies must hire people to run machinery worth hundreds or thousands of times more than a lawn mower. Every company would like its workers to exert effort and care, to communicate clearly with one another and take responsibility. Beyond private property and prices, the market economy has other partial solutions to these incentive problems, loosely categorized as contract solutions and reputation solutions.

CONTRACT SOLUTIONS

When one party (firm) agrees to do something for another, it typically signs a contract, which specifies the conditions of the transaction. For example, a firm will agree to deliver a product of a particular quality at a certain time and place. There will normally be "escape" clauses: if there is a strike, if the weather is bad, and so on, the delivery can be postponed. These **contingency clauses** may also make the payment dependent on the circumstances and manner in which the service is performed.

Contracts attempt to deal with incentive problems by specifying what each of the parties is to do in each situation. But no one can think of every contingency.

And even if they could, it would take them a prohibitively long time to write down all the possibilities.

There are times when it would be extremely expensive for the supplier to comply with all the terms of the contract. He could make the promised delivery on time, but only at a very great cost; if the buyer would only accept a one-day delay, there would be great savings. To provide suppliers with the incentive to violate the terms only when it is really economically worthwhile, most contracts allow delivery delays, but with a penalty attached. The penalty is what gives the supplier the incentive to deliver in a timely way.

Sometimes the supplier may think it simply is not worth complying with the contract. If he violates the agreement, he is said to be in **breach** of the contract. When a contract has been breached, the parties usually wind up in court, and the legal system stipulates what damages the party breaking the contract must pay to the other side. By stipulating what parties are supposed to do in a variety of circumstances, contracts help resolve incentive problems. But no matter how complicated the contract, there will still be ambiguities and disputes. Contracts are incomplete and enforcement is costly, and thus they provide only a partial resolution of the incentive problem.

REPUTATION SOLUTIONS

Reputations play an extremely important role in providing incentives in market economies. A reputation is a form of guarantee. Even though you may know that you cannot collect from this guarantee yourself—it is not a "money-back" guarantee—you know that the reputation of the person or company will suffer if it does not perform well. The incentive to maintain a reputation is what provides firms with an incentive to produce high-quality goods. It provides the contractor with an incentive to complete a house on or near the promised date.

For reputation to be an effective incentive mechanism, firms must lose something if their reputation suffers. The "something" is, of course, profits. For reputations to provide incentives, there must be profits to lose.

Thus, we see another way that markets with imperfect information differ from markets with perfect information. In competitive markets with perfect information, competition drives price down to marginal cost. In markets in which quality is maintained as the result of a reputation mechanism, whether competitive or not, price must remain above marginal cost.

Why, in markets where reputation is important, doesn't competition lead to price cutting? If price is "too low," firms do not have an incentive to maintain their reputation. Consumers, knowing this, come to expect low-quality goods. This is another reason that cutting prices will not necessarily bring firms more customers. Most consumers have at one time or another encountered companies that tried to live off their reputation. Take the example of Head skis, the high-quality skis in the early 1970s. At high prices, of course demand was limited. When the company lowered its price, sales increased. Consumers, knowing about the high quality, bought the skis thinking they were getting a bargain. But the incentive to continue to provide high-quality skis at bargain prices was short-lived. At the lower prices, profits were lower and Head had little incentive to maintain its reputation for selling high-quality skis over the longer run.

Reputation as a Barrier to Entry Competition is frequently very imperfect in markets where reputa-

---

SOLUTIONS TO INCENTIVE PROBLEMS IN MARKET ECONOMIES

Private property and prices   Reputations

Contracts

tion is important. The necessity of establishing a reputation acts as an important barrier to entry and limits the degree of competition in these industries. Given a choice between purchasing the product of an established firm with a good reputation and the product of a newcomer with no reputation at the same price, consumers will normally choose the established firm's good. Why try an unknown brand of television set when you know the high quality of a Sony or Panasonic? The newcomer must offer a sufficiently low price, often accompanied with strong guarantees. In some cases, newcomers practically must give away their product in order to establish themselves. Entering a market thus becomes extremely expensive.

ADVERTISING

Customers have an incentive to find out where the best buys are. Firms have a corresponding incentive to tell customers about the great deals they are providing. Companies may spend great sums on advertising to bring information about their products, prices, and locations to potential customers.

In the classic joke about advertising, an executive says, "We know half the money we spend on advertising is wasted, but we don't know which half." That joke says a lot about the economics of advertising. Many firms spend 2 percent, 3 percent, or more of their total revenues on advertising. Today, total expenditures on advertising are over $3 billion per year, with slightly more than half spent on national advertising campaigns. To add some perspective, these expenditures are roughly what the federal government spends on foreign aid.

Advertising can serve the important economic function of providing information about what choices are available. When a new airline enters a market, it must convey that information to potential customers. When a new product is developed, that fact has to be made known. When a business is having a sale, it must let people know. A firm cannot just lower its price, sit on its haunches, and wait, if it wants to be successful. Companies need to recruit new customers and convey information in an active way.

Take the typical beer or car advertisement. It conveys no information about the product, but seeks to convey an image, one with which potential buyers will identify. That these advertisements succeed in persuading individuals either to try a product or to stick with that product and not try another is a reminder that consumer behaviour is much more complicated than the simple theories of competitive markets suggest. Few people decide to go out and buy a car or a new suit solely because they saw a TV ad. But decisions about what kinds of clothes to wear, what beer to drink, what car to drive, are affected by a variety of considerations, including how peers view them or how they see themselves. These views can in turn be affected by advertising.

To emphasize the different roles played by advertising, economists distinguish between **informative advertising** and **persuasive advertising.** The intent of the former is to provide consumers with information about the price of a good, where it may be acquired, or what its characteristics are. The intent of persuasive advertising is to make consumers feel good about the product. This can even take the form of providing "disinformation" aimed at confusing consumers into thinking there is a difference among goods when there really is not.

ADVERTISING AND COMPETITION

Advertising is both a cause and a consequence of imperfect competition. In a perfectly competitive industry, where many producers make identical goods, it would not pay any single producer to advertise the merits of a good. You do not see advertisements for wheat or corn. If such advertising were successful, it would simply shift the demand curve for the product out. The total demand for wheat might increase, but this would have a negligible effect on the wheat grower who paid for the advertisement. If all wheat farmers could get together, it might pay them to advertise as a group. In recent years, associations representing producers of milk, eggs, cheese, raisins, and pork have done just that.

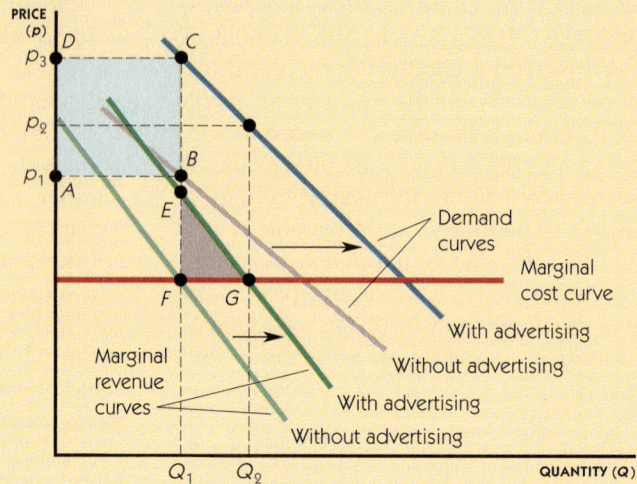

Figure 16.2 HOW ADVERTISING CAN SHIFT THE DEMAND CURVE

Successful advertising shifts the demand curve facing a firm. When the imperfect competitor equates its new marginal revenue with its old marginal cost, it will be able to raise both its price and its output.

ADVERTISING AND PROFITS

The objective of advertising is to shift the demand curve. The increase in advertising by one firm may divert customers away from rivals, or it may divert customers away from other products. Advertising a particular brand of cigarettes may be successful in inducing some smokers to switch brands and in inducing some nonsmokers to smoke.

When a firm is already in an imperfectly competitive situation, advertising shifts the demand curve for its product out, as in Figure 16.2. The increase in profits consists of two parts. First, the firm can sell the same quantity it sold before but at a higher price—p_3, rather than p_1. Profits then increase by the original quantity (Q_1) times the change in price ($p_3 - p_1$), the rectangle $ABCD$ in the figure. Second, by adjusting the quantity it sells it can increase profits still further. This is because the advertising has shifted the firm's marginal revenue curve up. As usual, the imperfectly competitive firm sets marginal revenue equal to marginal cost, so it increases output from Q_1 to Q_2. The additional profits thus generated are measured by the area between the marginal revenue and marginal cost curves between Q_1 and Q_2. Marginal cost remains the same, so the second source of extra profits is the shaded area EFG. The net increase in profits is the area $ABCD$ plus the area EFG minus the cost of advertising.

So far, in studying the effect of an increase in ad-

CONSEQUENCES OF IMPERFECT INFORMATION

Adverse selection problems

    Thin or nonexistent markets

    Signalling

    Possibility that markets may not clear

Incentive problems

Desirability of designing incentive schemes

    Increased importance of contracts and reputations

Advertising

    Provides information to consumers

    Diverts consumers from one firm to another

vertising on one firm's profits, we have assumed that other firms keep their level of advertising constant. The effect of advertising on both industry and firm profits is more problematical once the reactions of other firms in the industry are taken into account. To the extent that advertising diverts sales from one firm in an industry to another, advertising may, in equilibrium, have little effect on demand. We have here another example of a Prisoner's Dilemma. If the firms could cooperate and agree not to advertise, they would both be better off. But without such co-operation, it pays each to advertise, regardless of what the rival does.

IMPERFECT INFORMATION IN CAPITAL MARKETS

Imperfect information is a particularly important feature of capital markets. As we have seen in Chapter 8, capital markets (markets for loanable funds) are markets in which present dollars are traded for future dollars. Savings constitutes the supply side of the market; households are willing to supply savings to the capital market in return for an expected rate of return in the future. Investment makes up the demand side; firms are willing to pay a return in the future to acquire funds today. With most future-oriented economic activity, there is some uncertainty about what the exact outcome will be, though we will know the various possibilities and the chances of each occurring. Economists say there is some **risk** associated with intertemporal trades.

Most of us would prefer certainty to risk. We might spend a few dollars on some lottery tickets or playing the horses at the local racetrack, but for the most part we try to avoid or minimize serious risks. Psychologists who have studied this "risk-avoidance behaviour" focus on the anxiety to which uncertainty gives rise. Economists refer to risk-avoidance behaviour by saying that individuals are **risk-averse.**

THE MARKET FOR RISK

Even though most individuals are risk-averse, our economy needs to encourage risk taking. New ven-tures are risky, but they are the engine of economic growth. Out economy has developed a number of ways by which risks are transferred, transformed, and shared. The institutions and arrangements by which this is done are known collectively as the **market for risk.**

AVOIDING AND MITIGATING RISKS

The simplest way to respond to risk is to avoid it: don't gamble. But if everyone avoided all risks, eco-nomic activity would come to a standstill. No invest-ments would be made. Firms wouldn't even hire workers: there is always the chance that an em-ployee won't work out.

So risks cannot be avoided. But there is much in-dividuals and firms can do to reduce the degree of risk and soften its impact. Thorough research—ob-taining as complete information as possible—before undertaking an investment project reduces the risk. Preventive action may also be taken; for example, firms invest in fire detection and suppression equip-ment to reduce the damage from a fire.

MAINTAINING OPTIONS

A second way to respond to risk is to keep one's op-tions open. Many uncertainties get resolved over time. At the beginning of the week Tim doesn't know whether it will rain on Saturday. By Friday, the weather forecasters will have provided him with much better information—a better estimate of the probability of rain. By Saturday morning, he will have a still better estimate. Tim would like to go to the football game Saturday afternoon, provided it does not rain. If it rains, he would rather go to the movies. But by Friday all the football tickets will be sold out. He has to take his decision earlier. He may decide to buy the ticket on Monday, knowing that there is a chance that he will not use it if it rains. Buying the ticket on Monday maintains his options. Failing to buy the ticket forecloses the option of going to the football game. On Saturday morning it does rain. Tim recognizes that the expenditure on the football ticket is a sunk cost. Even though he spent the money, he prefers spending an extra $5 and going to the movies to getting cold and drenched at the football game. It was worth spend-ing the money to keep his options open.

Businesses often spend considerable amounts to maintain options. For example, they may enter a market knowing they will lose money for a year or two. But they hope to learn a lot from the experience, and they know that if they fail to enter the market now, it will be much harder (costlier) to enter later. It is worth losing money for a while to keep their options open.

DIVERSIFYING

A third response to risk is: don't put all of your eggs in the same basket. Firms may enter several lines of business to reduce risk. Farmers may grow several different crops. If things go badly in one area, there is a chance they will go better in some other area, thereby cancelling out the chances of a large loss.

POOLING RISKS

A fourth response is to **pool risks** with other persons in similar circumstances. Suppose the chances

of my having a fire are 1 in 100 (.01), and the damages I would incur are $10,000 if I were unlucky. I am obviously in a risky situation because I stand to lose that amount, albeit with a small probability. However, suppose I am just one of one million people facing the same risk. Given that the chances are .01 that each of us may have a fire, we can be reasonably certain that in the aggregate there will be $.01 \times 1,000,000 = 10,000$ fires, and the total damage done would be $10,000 \times \$10,000 = \$100,000,000$. We just do not know which 10,000 of us will be unlucky. In these circumstances, if each of us contributed $100 to a fund, $100,000,000 would be raised, exactly enough to pay the losses of the unlucky ones. Such a scheme would result in full risk pooling and would completely eliminate the risk of loss for everyone.

This is precisely the principle used by insurance companies. They charge premiums to customers, accumulate the premiums paid in a fund, and pay for the damages to those who suffer losses. In the above example, each person buys $10,000 worth of insurance at a premium of $100, and in the process all risk is eliminated by pooling. It is no accident that the premium is a proportion .01 of the loss. This is just the probability of the accident occurring.

TRANSFERRING RISK

Some risks cannot be pooled but must be borne by someone. In these circumstances response to risk might be to transfer it to someone else who is more willing to take it on. Different persons may be more or less adverse to risk, and one of the important functions of capital markets is to trade risks from those less willing or able to bear them to those more able. When an individual entrepreneur starts or expands her firm, she may well worry about risking all her savings in the venture. She will typically go to the capital market and try to either borrow money or acquire new shareholders. In either case, the persons putting money into the firm recognize the risk they are taking on. They will only do so if they are compensated for that risk. That compensation consists of a rate of return that is expected to be high enough above the rate of return that could be obtained on a "safe" investment to compensate for taking the risk. This excess return is called the **risk premium.** Higher-risk firms will have to pay their creditors higher risk premiums than lower-risk firms to compensate for the fact that the firm may go bust.

LIMITS ON INSURANCE AS PROTECTION AGAINST RISK

Insurance firms are the institutions in our economy that specialize in absorbing risks. The earliest insurance firms—collectively known as Lloyd's of London—did nothing more than pull together a group of investors willing to absorb large risks, such as those associated with shipwrecks. Today, insurance firms absorb risk directly.

Even though insurance companies specialize in absorbing risks, individuals and firms cannot buy insurance to protect themselves against all types of risk. A business cannot buy insurance that protects it against the risk that the demand for its product will fall, or the risk that a competitor will develop a better

product that will drive the company into bankruptcy. Economists have identified two inherent problems that limit the use of insurance as a mechanism for handling risk: adverse selection and moral hazard. Although the following discussion focuses on these problems in the context of insurance, they apply more generally to other methods of sharing risk, including stocks and bonds.

Adverse Selection The probability that an individual will have an accident depends on characteristics of that individual's life and behaviour that an insurance firm cannot perfectly observe. If the accident probabilities of different individuals could be accurately estimated, then in a competitive insurance market, premiums would accurately reflect those accident probabilities. For example, "hot dog" skiers would pay higher medical insurance rates than people with safer pastimes, because of their higher average medical expenses.

But insurance firms do not know everything about each individual's risks. Insurance rates can only be based on observable factors; auto insurance rates, for example, depend on the record of past accidents, age of driver, and type of vehicle. The same rate is charged to all people with identical observable traits. Those who are higher risk will face premiums that are lower than what would reflect their probability of making a claim and will be encouraged to buy large amounts of insurance. Those who are lower-risk would not buy as much as they would if the premium reflected their chances of a claim. Thus, insurance markets would not function to pool risks fully. Moreover, problems can arise for the insurance companies. When an insurance company perceives that the premiums it is charging for a particular group of individuals are too low for the risks of the group, it raises the premiums. This is when the problem of adverse selection can appear.

The **adverse selection** problem arises when insurance companies try to raise their premiums and the best risks stop buying insurance. The best risks may decide either to **self-insure** (not buy insurance from any company) or to switch to another company. The worst risks—those who know that they really need insurance because they are unhealthy and so will not self-insure, or those who cannot get insurance elsewhere—stick with the firm. As the best

CLOSE-UP: ADVERSE SELECTION AND DISCRIMINATION IN THE AUTO INSURANCE MARKET

Private automobile insurers do not have complete information about the risk level of their clients, but they know that, as a group, young single males demonstrate the highest claim frequency. Insurers would like to segment their market by charging higher premiums to high-risk individuals. But they cannot monitor the driving of automobile insurance buyers to see who drives too fast or who drives when tired or when drinking. The problem of adverse selection arises because the insurers cannot identify the individuals who are high risk. Pricing based on gender discrimination partially solves this problem.

In 1983, at the time when some provincial courts were addressing the issue of gender discrimination in auto insurance, Beverly Dahlby of the University of Alberta conducted a study evaluating the relative riskiness of male versus female drivers. He used Canadian auto insurance statistics for 1975–1978. These show that the claim frequency on collision insurance was as follows:

    .142 for single males aged 21–22
    .123 for single males aged 23–24
    .109 for married males aged 21–24
    .0998 for females aged 21–24

Interestingly enough, of single males ages 21–22, the riskiest group, only 47.9 percent purchased collision insurance, as opposed to 74.7 percent of females aged 21–24. This was presumably due to the fact that insurance companies charged them much higher premiums in light of their collective accident record.

The policy of discriminating by gender is bound to be an imperfect way to overcome the adverse selection problem. There will undoubtedly be some young males who are cautious drivers but who have to pay high premiums because of the accident record of others of their gender and age group. In 1978 the Alberta Board of Industry responded to the complaints of gender discrimination made by numerous male drivers. The board ruled that the premiums policies of insurance companies in the province contravened the Individual's Rights and Protection Act, which prohibits discrimination on the basis of race, religion, colour, gender, ancestry, or place of origin.

In the case of collision insurance, Dahlby demonstrates that the equalization of premiums between males and females causes young females to face much higher premiums. The effect is largest for single females aged 21–22, whose premiums would increase by 61 percent. Approximately 10 percent of females in this category would be expected to stop purchasing collision coverage.

The end result is that young females are less insured than they would like to be, because of high prices. Is this the most efficient economic outcome, or can it be argued that this is an instance where gender discrimination is more fair?

Source: B. G. Dahlby, "Adverse Selection and Statistical Discrimination: An Analysis of Canadian Automobile Insurance," *Journal of Public Economics* 20 (1983): 121–30.

risks leave, the *average* riskiness of the insured risks worsens. It may deteriorate so much that average profits actually fall—the increased average riskiness more than offsets the increased premiums.

For many kinds of insurance, such as fire insurance, adverse selection problems may not be too bad. The critical information (determining the likelihood of a fire) can easily enough be observed—for instance, by building inspectors. But for many of the kinds of risks against which individuals would like to buy insurance, adverse selection effects are important. With health or automobile insurance, for instance, an insurance firm is likely to find it difficult to determine any particular individual's risk. Even worse, consider the problem of measuring the risk that a firm's new product will fail to meet expectations. It would be nearly impossible for an insurance company to decide precisely what the prospects for the product are. The business firm itself is certainly more likely to be better informed than the insurance company about the markets in which it is trying to sell the product. Not surprisingly, then, because of their disadvantage in obtaining crucial information, insurance firms do not supply insurance against such business risks.

Moral Hazard   A second problem faced by insurance companies is an incentive problem: insurance affects people's incentives to avoid whatever contingencies they are insured against. A person who has no fire insurance on a house may choose to limit the risk of fire by buying smoke alarms and home fire extinguishers and being especially cautious. But if that same person had fire insurance, he might not be so careful.

This general feature of insurance, that it reduces the individual's incentives to avoid the insured-against accident, is called **moral hazard.** Of course, from an economist's point of view, what is at issue is not a question of morality, but only a question of incentives. If a person bears only a portion, or none, of the consequences of his actions—as he does when he has purchased insurance—his incentives are altered.

Moral hazard concerns may not be important for many kinds of insurance; an individual who buys a large life insurance policy and thus knows that her children will be well cared for in the event of her demise is hardly likely to take much bigger risks with her life. (There was, however, a grisly case in California some years ago in which a person cut off one foot with an axe to try to collect on disability insurance.) But for many kinds of risks against which a firm's managers would *like* to buy insurance, moral hazard concerns are important. For example, if a company could buy insurance to guarantee a minimum level of profit, managers would have less incentive to exert effort.

When moral hazard problems are strong, insurance firms will offer limited—or even no—insurance. The limitations often take one of two forms: deductibility provisions and co-insurance. Insurance policies may pay damages only above some initial amount, referred to as a **deductible.** For example, your car insurance policy may require you to pay the first $500 of damages before insurance benefits kick in. This reduces the moral hazard problem associated with small claims; drivers might be much more vigilant about avoiding minor accidents than major ones. Alternatively, insurance policies may pay only some specified proportion of damages. This is referred to as **co-insurance.** It forces those who are insured to bear some cost of any accident and so to behave with greater care.

The use of co-insurance reflects the fact that there is a risk-incentive trade-off. The more the individual divests himself of risk, the weaker his incentives to avoid "bad results" and to foster "good results." This principle applies in many contexts other than simple insurance markets. A store manager whose salary is guaranteed faces little risk, but also has little incentive. If his pay depends on the store's sales, he has stronger incentives, but faces greater risk. In spite of his best efforts, sales may be low—perhaps because of an economic downturn, perhaps because buyers have simply turned away from his products; in either case, his income will be low.

Similarly, a firm that borrows money for a project is generally required to invest some of its own funds in the project, or to supply the lender with collateral—provide the lender with an asset that the firm forfeits if it fails to repay the loan. Lenders know that with more of their own money at stake, borrowers will have better incentives to use the funds wisely.

Canada spends about 20 percent more per person on health care than Sweden, 35 percent more than Germany, 60 percent more than Japan, and a whopping 100 percent more than the United Kingdom. Only the United States spends more. Almost 10 percent of Canadian GDP is devoted to health expenditures, slightly above the average for the Organization for Economic Cooperation and Development (OECD) countries, but much lower than the 13.5 percent found in the United States. Moreover, health care expenditures are the most rapidly growing component of government expenditures in Canada. In 1994, health care expenditures by governments in Canada (mainly provincial governments) were almost twice as high as they were ten years earlier. The containment of health care expenditures has become one of the policy priorities of the decade.

Why have health costs increased so rapidly? Economists have offered several explanations, many of which focus on the incentives that exist in the system for using and financing health care, the absence of competitive pressures for economizing, and the role of imperfect information in the provision of health care.

Sick people do not usually act as cautious self-interested consumers, carefully shopping around for different medical-care providers and balancing the marginal benefits of various treatments. Most people have incomplete information about what is wrong with them, what treatment might help, and what medical actions are really needed. Moreover, under our system of publicly provided health care, a patient has little reason to care about costs. Her attitude might be that if a trip to the doctor might help, it is worth a try.

Unlike with the markets for other goods and services, prices are not used as a rationing device for consumers.

Uncertain information about what health care is truly necessary presents another problem, this one to do with health care professionals. Under our fee-for-service system, doctors are paid for the amount of care they provide, the number of tests they run, and the number of procedures they perform. When patients have both full insurance and incomplete information, they are unlikely to question whether another test or procedure is really necessary. Health care professionals are trained to look after a patient's health. So they face strong economic and professional pressures to try everything, rather than weighing costs of treatment with potential benefits.

If adverse incentives are the problem, it is natural to look for ways in which the system can be changed so as to correct them. Several suggestions have been made. One is simply to institute user fees on patients for the use of health services. Detractors argue that this may have little deterrent effect since it is really the doctor rather than the patient that determines how many services are used. Furthermore, user fees will make health care less accessible to those least able to afford it. Another suggestion is to put doctors on salaries instead of paying them fees for each service performed. After all, other health-care workers, such as nurses, are salaried, not to mention other public-sector professionals such as professors and judges. But while this would reduce the incentive for doctors to overuse health services, it might also reduce their incentive to take on additional patients and to perform time-consuming procedures.

A more wide-ranging reform would involve changing not only the compensation scheme for doctors but also the organization through which doctors deliver their services. Today many doctors operate their own practices individually. The proposal is that groups of doctors would join together in health maintenance organizations (HMOs) and provide a wide range of medical services to their patients. Patients would be free to join the HMO of their choice, and the HMO would be obliged to accept all patients who have selected it. The HMO would receive a specific sum of money per patient (referred to as a "capitation fee") and would be responsible for providing comprehensive health care to each patient. The HMO would pay the health-care professionals in their own organization in a manner of their choice. This could be by salary or fee-for-service or some combination of the two.

The use of the HMO for delivering health care is intended to introduce into the system incentives for cost effectiveness as well as competitive pressures. Since patients would be free to shop around, HMOs would effectively compete with each other for patients and would be induced to offer the best mix of services they could. The fact that the payment per patient in the HMO is fixed implies that the HMO has an incentive to economize on the use of health services. And since each HMO would have to compete for health care professionals, each would be induced to offer good working environments with adequate facilities.

The HMO concept is not without difficulties, however. Since the HMO would be obliged to provide services to all patients who choose to join it, there is obviously an advantage to attracting those patients who are less likely to have serious health problems. The HMO might try to do this by putting more effort into providing the sorts of services that attract the healthier elements of the population. It might be difficult for the government to preclude this "cream skimming" through regulation.

These and other options will undoubtedly be considered as governments try to contain rising health costs.

IMPERFECT INFORMATION IN THE LABOUR MARKET

Information problems have an even more significant impact on the labour market than on product and capital markets. This is partly because workers are not like lumps of coal. They have to be motivated to work hard. And they are concerned with work conditions and how their pay compares with others'. Firms are aware of the importance of these considerations in attracting and keeping workers, and design employment and compensation policies that take them into account.

SIGNALLING IN THE LABOUR MARKET

We have seen that buyers of goods often do not have full information about the quality of goods that they wish to purchase, and that this leads sellers to engage in expenditures that signal product quality. Similar issues arise in the labour market. When employers hire workers, they do not know all the pertinent characteristics of potential employees. They know that some candidates will be far more productive than others, but they simply cannot tell which candidates these will be. To take their hiring decisions, they have to use whatever information is available. One obvious source of information is the level of educational attainment of each candidate.

Education helps employers identify whom they should hire. In some jobs what is important is brains, the ability to think quickly. Students who have done well in university taking difficult courses have demonstrated that they have the kinds of minds these employers want. From this perspective, what education does is not so much *increase* productivity but identify which people are more productive or have certain scarce abilities. Economists say that universities **screen** individuals, and that level of education **signals** their abilities. Those who graduate from university get higher pay; the higher pay reflects their higher productivity; but the higher productivity is not acquired in university. Universities simply identify talent.

Of course, what students learn at university does increase their productivity. University is not *just* a screening device. But there are some striking pieces of evidence suggesting just how important the screening and signalling role is. Examination of the year-by-year returns to education in the United States, suggests that the final year of high school or college produces much higher returns than any other year. This seems a bit odd; one would expect that learning is a continuous and gradual process, implying a smoothly increasing relationship between years of education and earnings. Nevertheless, the evidence is well documented. What it seems to demonstrate is that there are definite increasing returns to *completing* high school and college. Studies in the United States have shown that the return (percentage increase in wage) to the final year of high school is three times that of the preceding (eleventh) year, and to the final year of college is two and a half times that of finishing only one to three years of college.[1] Unfortunately, there is no comparable evidence for Canada. But the systems of education are similar enough that one might expect to observe a similar phenomenon here.

There is another, related puzzle: if individuals who go to school receive higher wages because they

have learned more, why does it seem to make so little difference what they study? Art history and music appreciation may enhance the quality of your life, but do they really contribute significantly to your productivity in the purchasing department or sales department of a company? Yet those who major in art history or other liberal arts subjects experience an increase in their wages just as do those who major in subjects more directly related to their future careers, such as engineering, nursing, or business.

This can also be explained by the fact that education performs a screening and signalling role for employers. On average, those individuals who complete four years of university are better bets for, say, managerial jobs than those who drop out after three. Thus, employers look for a high school or a university degree not just because of the skills that job candidates acquire in their senior year, but because the completed degree is a signal that that person may be more productive. Completing four years of university shows a kind of perseverance that is highly valued in the business community. Brighter students find it easier to do university work, and hence have less incentive to drop out. Students who know that they will not be able to make the grade may quit, figuring it is better not to waste another year; among those who drop out, there are likely to be some who would not have graduated even if they had tried.

Such signals are important because it is costly to give a worker a try; the employer must advertise, search, interview, hire, and train each employee. Hiring a dud means wasted training expenses and having to go through the hiring procedure again. Hence, the employer is going to give a chance to the person she thinks has the greatest chance of succeeding, the worker with the "best" signal or credential.

Naturally, students know that employers interpret the completion of a university education in this way. They are therefore induced to stay in school longer than they might otherwise; they may stay in school not so much to acquire productive skills as to convince potential employers that they are among the more productive members of society, deserving of high wages. Get that diploma! Get that degree! This trend gives rise to what has been called the **credentials competition.** The more able individuals have an incentive to try to distinguish themselves, to per-

[1] A. Weiss, "High School Graduation, Performance, and Wages," *Journal of Political Economy* 96 (1988): 785–820; K. Murphy and F. Welch, "Wage Premiums for College Graduates," *Educational Researcher* 18 (May 1989): 17–26.

suade potential employers that they are truly among the gifted. To signal their higher ability, they stay in school still longer, acquiring still more advanced degrees. The increased qualifications required for many jobs over the past several decades may reflect this credentials competition as much as it reflects the increased knowledge required for performing these jobs.

There are many other ways that workers can signal their competence besides by investing in education. For example, in a world of perfect information, there might be no good reason why young lawyers typically would work sixty to ninety hours per week. It is not that they are learning much during those extra hours, or that they enjoy their work that much. Instead, they may be trying to prove to their employers that they are extremely able individuals in love with and dedicated to their profession. In an interview, all workers may claim the same for themselves. But those who are really able and in love with their work will find it less onerous to work that eighty-fifth hour a week. By working long hours they can distinguish themselves from the others.

MARKET RESPONSES TO IMPERFECT INFORMATION

Participants in all three major markets—product, capital, and labour—are often imperfectly informed about the items being bought and sold. The quality of goods and services may not be known to con-sumers. Firms will have an incentive to provide information to households, through such things as advertising, warranties, or price signals. Uncertainty about the future is a major source of imperfect information in capital and insurance markets. Some of this uncertainty can be resolved by risk pooling. But moral hazard and adverse selection may arise because purchasers of insurance have better information about their riskiness than insurers do. Insurance prices adjust to take account of this asymmetric availability of information. And, in labour markets firms often know less about the productivity of individual workers than the workers themselves. The market will establish various signals to convey information to firms about the ability of workers.

That imperfections of information fundamentally alter the behaviour of individuals and markets constitutes an important area of consensus among economists, and forms the basis for our ninth consensus point.

9 Imperfect Information

The fact that individuals and firms typically take decisions based on imperfect information affects the behaviour of the three main markets in various ways. Firms and individuals compensate for the scarcity of information. In many markets where problems of adverse selection and moral hazard arise, firms adjust prices to convey information about quality. Individuals and firms may attempt to signal information about their characteristics and work to establish reputation.

REVIEW AND PRACTICE

SUMMARY

1 The model of perfect competition assumes that participants in the market have perfect information about the goods being bought and sold and their prices. But this is not the case in the real world, and economists have thus incorporated imperfect information into their models of the economy.

2 A problem of adverse selection may arise when consumers cannot judge the true quality of a product. As the price of the good falls, the quality mix changes adversely, and the quantity demanded at a lower price may actually be lower than at a higher price.

3 Producers of high-quality products may attempt to signal that their product is better than those of competitors, for instance, by providing better guarantees.

4 When consumers judge quality by price, there may be some price that offers the best value. Firms will have no incentive to cut price below this "best value" price, even when, at this price the amount they would be willing to supply exceeds demand. As a result, the market can settle in an equilibrium with an excess supply of goods.

5 When there is perfect information, private property and prices can provide correct incentives to all market participants. When information is imperfect, there are two methods of helping to provide correct incentives: contracts with contingency clauses, and reputations.

6 Advertising attempts to change consumers' buying behaviour, either by providing relevant information about prices or characteristics, by persuasion, or both.

7 Problems of imperfect information are inherent to capital markets since they involve intertemporal trading, and the future is typically not known with certainty. Risk can be mitigated by maintaining options, by pooling risks, or by transferring risks to others.

8 Insurance is one way people attempt to reduce the risks they face. Insurance companies face two problems. The first is called adverse selection: people who buy insurance tend to be those most at risk, and yet charging higher prices for insurance will discourage those less at risk from buying insurance at all. The second problem is called moral hazard: insurance reduces the incentives people have to avoid whatever they are insured against.

9 Firms typically do not know the true productivity of candidates for a job. They rely on signals to help screen workers. Education level may serve a screening and signalling function, identifying those workers who are in some sense likely to be more productive.

KEY TERMS

imperfect information	thin or incomplete markets	market for risk	moral hazard
adverse selection	contingency clauses	risk pooling	signalling
asymmetric information	reputations	risk premium	credentials competition

REVIEW QUESTIONS

1 Why are markets for information not likely to work well?

2 Why would "lemons" not be a problem for consumers in a world of perfect information? Why do they lead to a backward-bending demand curve in a world of imperfect information?

3 Why is signalling unnecessary in a world of perfect information? What does it accomplish in a world of imperfect information?

4 Explain why, if consumers think that quality increases with price, there will be cases where firms will have no incentive to cut prices in an attempt to attract more business.

5 How do contingency clauses in contracts help provide appropriate incentives? What are some of the problems in writing contracts that provide for all the relevant contingencies?

6 What role does reputation have in maintaining incentives? What is required if firms are to have an incentive to maintain their reputations? How might the good reputation of existing firms serve as a barrier to the entry of new firms?

7 Describe how advertising might affect the demand curve facing a firm. How do these changes affect prices? profits?

8 What is meant by risk aversion? What are the consequences of the fact that some people are risk-averse?

9 Why do people pay insurance premiums if they hope and expect that nothing bad is going to happen to them?

10 Describe the signalling function of education.

11 What is credentials competition and why does it arise?

PROBLEMS

1 The We Pick 'Em Company collects information about horse races, and sells a newsletter predicting the winners. Why might you possibly be predisposed to distrust the accuracy of the We Pick 'Em newsletter?

2 When you apply for a job, possible employers have imperfect information about your abilities. How might you try to signal that you would be a good employee?

3 Explain how the incentives of someone to look after a car she is renting may not suit the company that is renting the car. How might a contingent contract help to solve this problem? Is it likely to solve the problem completely?

4 L. L. Bean, a U.S. mail-order company, has a long-standing policy that it will take back anything it has sold, at any time, for any reason. Why might it be worthwhile for a profit-maximizing firm to enact such a policy?

5 You hire a student to paint your house. Since it is a large job, you agree to pay the student by the hour. What moral hazard problem must you consider? Explain the trade-off between risk and incentives in this situation.

6 Suppose a worker holding a job that pays $15 per hour applies for a job with another company that pays $18 per hour. Why might the second company be suspicious about whether the worker is really worth $18 per hour? How might the worker attempt to overcome those fears?

7 Imagine that a company knows that if it cuts wages 10 percent, then 10 percent of its employees will leave. How might adverse selection cause the amount of work done by the company to fall by more than 10 percent?

8 To help build loyalty among its staff, a company extends its prescription drug plan to cover more items. It finds that both the number of sick days taken and its expense for prescription drugs rise sharply. Explain why this might happen.

17

FINANCING, CONTROLLING, AND MANAGING THE FIRM

Who controls a company? The simple answer is: the executives. Presidents, vice presidents, chief executive officers—these are the people who take decisions, and they deserve a major share of the responsibility for a company's actions. But executives of most corporations are not entirely autonomous. There is an old saying "He who pays the piper calls the tune." In the context of corporate behaviour, investors who provide money to a firm certainly have some control over the executives who manage it.

In Chapter 8 we looked at equity and debt from the perspective of the household investing its funds. Here we use the perspective of the corporation that issues securities and receives the money. The branch of economics concerned with how firms raise capital and the consequences of various methods is called **corporate finance.** We next turn to the question of who controls the firm. The firm's owners? Its executives? The banks and other institutions that help finance its operations? Or some combination of these groups? Finally, we look at the major issues facing managers of firms at all levels. Today's firms are complicated institutions. The organization of the

KEY QUESTIONS

1 What difference does it make whether a firm raises capital through debt or through equity? How do concerns about taxes, bankruptcy, and managerial incentives affect firms' choices of financial structure?

2 Why is credit frequently rationed? And why, in spite of the advantages in risk sharing, is so little new capital raised in the form of equity?

3 What is the relationship between financial structure and control of the firm?

4 What role do takeovers play in enhancing the efficiency of the economy? Why is there such criticism of takeovers?

5 What are the central problems facing organizations in which the manager is not the sole owner?

6 How do firms motivate their workers to ensure that they put out effort commensurate with their pay?

7 What difference does it make whether decision taking is centralized or decentralized? What are the pros and cons of each?

8 What determines what a firm produces itself as opposed to what it purchases from other companies? What determines, in other words, the boundaries of the firm?

firm and the way in which decisions are shared among managers at various levels helps determine how efficiently the firm operates and how effectively employees are motivated to serve the interests of the firm.

Curiously enough, none of the issues we will be concerned with here arises in the basic competitive model of Part Two. There, firms all have a single objective, to maximize their profits or market value. That is also what most investors want firms they invest in to do. And because there is unanimity about what firms should do, the issue of "control" never arises. Indeed, even the issue of how the firm should raise its capital—through debt or equity financing—turns out to make no difference in the basic competitive model. In the real world, issues of finance and control not only grab headlines but also absorb the attention of Bay Street and firm managers. And for good reason, as we will see.

THE FIRM'S LEGAL FORM

Business firms in Canada take one of three legal forms: proprietorship, partnership, or corporation. A **proprietorship** is the simplest form. The firm has a single owner. If you went into business selling class notes to other students, your business would be listed as a proprietorship by Revenue Canada. Because of the advantages of incorporation (which we will see below), only the smallest firms remain proprietorships.

When two or more individuals decide to go into business together, they typically form a **partnership.** As with proprietorships, most partnerships are small—Sally and Sue's Delicatessen, or Bob and Andy's Laundromat. However, some partnerships are huge. Many of the major national accounting firms are organized as partnerships, with hundreds of partners. Likewise, many law firms with one hundred or more lawyers are organized as partnerships.

The final form of organization is the **corporation.** Corporations divide ownership into shares, also known as the stock of a company. The purchase of a corporation's stock entitles the purchaser to a corresponding share of ownership in the firm. The key feature of the corporation and the one that has made possible the huge firms we know today—like Bell Canada, Inco, and Canadian Pacific—is **limited liability.**

With proprietorships and partnerships, there is no limit to the liability of the owner(s). Consider Joe Smith, who decides to open up a restaurant and has not yet hired a lawyer to advise him of the advantages of the corporate form of business. He invests

$50,000 of his savings and borrows $200,000 to buy furniture for the restaurant, to decorate it, and to pay for a five-year lease. Unfortunately, he has limited talents both as a chef and as a businessman and fails to attract customers. After trying it for a year, he closes his business. But he is still responsible for the debts of the firm. Not only has he lost the $50,000 he took out of his savings, but he may be forced to sell his home to repay the $200,000 in loans because he is fully liable for them.

In a partnership, each partner is fully liable for all the debts of the firm. Now, when Joe Smith and his partner, Alfred Jones, go into business together, they each put up $25,000 and together borrow $200,000. If Alfred has no house or other form of wealth and thus cannot help to pay off the debt when the restaurant goes bankrupt, Joe will again find himself fully liable for the $200,000 debt.

By choosing the corporate form, owners avoid full liability. If Joe Smith sets his restaurant up as a corporation he can invite Alfred Jones and any others to purchase shares and join him as owners of the company. He can put his $50,000 into the corporation and have the corporation borrow the $200,000. The corporation is liable for all the debts it incurs, and in the case of bankruptcy, its assets will be sold. The money recouped in this way will go first to those who have lent the firm money (banks, bondholders) and then, if any is left over, to Joe and his fellow shareholders. In the event of bankruptcy, the shareholders are likely to lose all the money they invested in the corporation, but *they will not lose any more.* When Campeau Development declared bankruptcy in 1989, none of the developer's shareholders had to worry about selling her house to help pay off the billions of dollars of debts incurred.

Limited liability provides larger corporations with another important advantage over other forms of organization: it facilitates public trading of the company's shares. Buying such a share always involves the risk that the investor will lose all the money invested, as we have seen. Yet this risk may be tiny compared with the risk faced by the investor in a partnership. In the latter, each partner is liable for all the partnership's bills, if his fellow partners cannot pay their share. Therefore, an investor purchasing a partnership share needs to know something about the wealth of each of the other partners in

order to know how much risk he faces. Such information is unnecessary to the investor in a corporation, which means the potential pool of investors in corporations is much, much larger. The limited liability feature of corporations is attractive enough so that today most businesses small and large are set up as corporations. Even the single proprietor, if he has a good lawyer, is likely to set his business up as a corporation to protect his family's assets. In fact, not all large corporations take advantage of public share trading, of becoming **public corporations.** Many prefer to remain **private corporations** and thereby to maintain full control. Some of Canada's biggest corporations are private, including Irving, Olympia & York, and Eaton's. As the example of Olympia & York indicates, private corporations are certainly not immune to bankruptcy.

There is another important distinction among the three legal forms. When there is a single proprietor, there is no question about who takes the final decisions. When there are many owners, whether they are partners or shareholders, there are potential disagreements. There must be a set of rules concerning how these disagreements are to be resolved. Take, for instance, the question of who hires the firm's managers. Shareholders elect directors, who choose managers. If a majority of shareholders do not like what their board of directors is doing, they can elect new directors—though this seldom happens.

CORPORATE FINANCE

Corporations can finance their investments in many ways. We focus on three of them. (1) A corporation can borrow funds, either from a bank or directly from investors by issuing bonds. (2) It can issue new shares of stock, the buyers of which become entitled to a share of whatever profits the firm distributes to its owners in dividends. Or, if its profits are high enough, (3) the corporation can finance its investment with its own earnings, rather than paying them out in dividends.

Figure 17.1 provides a schematic representation of a corporation's cash flow. The corporation re-

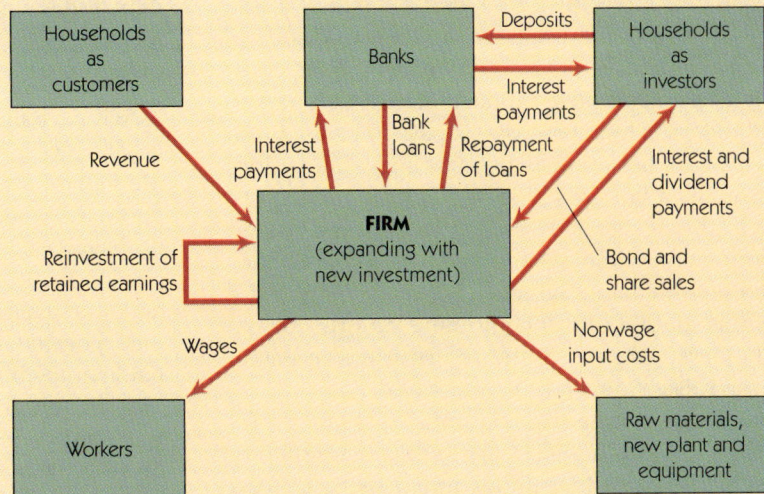

Figure 17.1 CORPORATE CASH FLOW

Money flows into a corporation from customers, bank loans, and investors who buy the company's bonds or new issues of stock. Money flows out to pay workers, purchase materials and equipment, repay lenders, and distribute dividends to shareholders.

ceives cash in three forms: income from the sale of its products, borrowed funds from banks and bond sales, and funds from sales of new shares. The corporation uses its cash to pay its expenses—wages, raw materials, and other costs of production. It also pays back outstanding loans. Any cash left over after expenses and debt payments may be distributed to the shareholders as dividends. Or some cash—called **retained earnings**—may be kept by the firm for the corporation to use for further investments or as a cash reserve.

In Chapter 8 we learned the attributes of investments: average return, risk, tax treatment, and liquidity. There we took the perspective of the investor. Bonds yielded a lower average return and had lower risks than stocks. Stocks yielded returns in the form of both dividends and capital gains. And capital gains had major tax advantages.

Here we take the corporation's perspective. A corporation's management wants to raise capital in a way that best serves the interests of its shareholders. In particular, managers want to maximize the value of the firm's shares. According to traditional theory a firm's treasurer focuses on two issues when deciding between debt and equity financing. First is the cost of capital, what the firm must pay to *new* in-

vestors in return for using their funds—the "average return" to investors. The average return paid to those who supply debt capital is lower than the average return paid to those who supply equity capital. Thus, debt is less attractive from the viewpoint of new investors but more attractive from the viewpoint of the firm.

The second issue is risk, particularly the risk of bankruptcy. While firms do not have to pay their shareholders on any fixed schedule, they do have fixed obligations to pay certain amounts at certain times to bondholders and other lenders. Debt therefore imposes greater risks on the firm. If it does not have the cash to meet those obligations, and cannot get the cash by borrowing from someone else, then the company goes into bankruptcy. The more the firm borrows, the greater become these fixed obligations and the chance that it will not be able to meet them. Thus, although to the investor debt appears safer, to the firm debt is riskier. On this account equity is preferable to the firm.

The traditional analysis of corporate finance sees the firm as facing a risk-return trade-off. In general, the greater the debt, the lower the costs (lower average payments to those who provided the capital), but the higher the risk, in terms of the likelihood of bankruptcy. The problem of the corporate treasurer in this scenario is to choose the appropriate balance between risk and return.

The nature of the trade-off between risk and return is complicated. Assume the firm only cares about its *average* cost of capital. Since what it pays to bondholders is less than what it pays to equity holders, it might be tempted to issue more and more debt. But as it borrows more—that is, as it becomes more **highly leveraged**—the equity becomes riskier. The return on equity is simply what is left over after paying debtholders. The more it borrows, the more likely it is that there will be nothing left over for equity holders. As a result, the return it has to pay in order to raise equity must be increased.

In 1958, two American economists, Franco Modigliani and Merton Miller, proved a remarkable result. They showed that under much more general conditions than the traditional analysis, how the firms raised funds still made no difference, because as more debt is issued the increasing cost of equity just offsets the savings from the reduced cost of capital raised from debt.

We can liken the firm in the Modigliani-Miller perspective to a pie. Bondholders and shareholders get different pieces of the pie. But the size of the pie—the real value of the firm—is not affected at all by how it is sliced. The corporation's financial structure affects *who* gets the dollars earned by the corporation—how the profits pie is divided and who bears the risk of the firm—but that is all.

WHY CORPORATIONS CARE ABOUT FINANCIAL STRUCTURE

The Modigliani-Miller theorem is like the simple model of profit-maximizing firms in perfectly competitive markets. It provides a useful starting point and organizing framework for thinking about the central issues. Describing when the corporate finance decision does not matter helps focus attention on what is truly important about corporate financial structure. The sections that follow examine the confounding factors of bankruptcy, taxation, management incentives, the market perception of a firm's value, and corporate control. Each provides an explanation of why in particular cases a firm may care a great deal about its financial structure, its blend of debt and equity.

CONSEQUENCES OF BANKRUPTCY

As we have already seen, increased debt imposes a greater risk of bankruptcy on a corporation. Modigliani and Miller's analysis ignored any direct costs associated with bankruptcy. And there are thousands of bankruptcies a year. But bankruptcy has high direct costs—to shareholders, creditors, and managers. While 13,000 new businesses were incorporated in 1994, there were 11,000 filings of bankruptcy in that year. These statistics are typical. They include major firms like International Harvester, once one of the world's largest manufacturers of agricultural machinery, Nationair, Northlands Bank, Wardair, and Atlantic Stereo. Were it not for the fact that lenders limit the amounts they are willing to lend and monitor closely the firms to which they have lent money, bankruptcy rates might be substantially higher.

Concerns about bankruptcy thus provide an important limit on the use of debt. Banks are likely to limit the amount they are willing to lend. And even if they were willing to lend more at high enough interest rates to compensate them for the risk of default, borrowers would limit the amount they borrow, recognizing that borrowing more exposes them to an excessively high risk of bankruptcy.

TAX CONSEQUENCES

Taxes affect a firm's choice of financial structure because interest payments are tax deductible, but payments to shareholders (dividends) are not. Consequently the firm would rather pay interest than dividends, if these are its options. Of course, the firm also should take into account the taxes that its investors have to pay on their individual incomes. The tax law treats capital gains, dividends, and interest differently. Under the current tax law, capital gains and dividends receive slightly favoured treatment. Since the return to stocks takes the form of capital gains plus dividends, this aspect of the income tax system gives shares an advantage over debt to individuals. Overall, it appears that the tax system gives some advantage to corporate borrowing.

Thousands of companies of all sizes declare bankruptcy every year. They represent billions of dollars of assets and thousands of jobs. Once-healthy companies that have declared bankruptcy in recent years include Nationair, Northlands Bank, Wardair, and Atlantic Stereo. Obviously, when a firm declares bankruptcy, many parties are damaged: the owners of the firm, the managers and workers who must find other jobs, the investors who stand to lose part of their investment, the suppliers to whom the firm may owe money, and society at large, which must foot the bill for unemployment insurance and possibly forgo some tax revenues. Bankruptcy laws are in place to protect the various persons involved, not only the person or organization declaring bankruptcy, but also the creditors to whom money is owed.

Bankruptcy in Canada is governed by the Bankruptcy Act, which was enacted in 1949, and amended in 1966 and again in 1992. Under the act, after declaring bankruptcy or being forced to do so by one or more of its creditors, insolvent firms have two options: reorganization or liquidation. The 1992 amendments were designed to fulfill two objectives: (1) to increase the protection for those who are owed wages by the firm, and (2) to tilt the balance in favour of reorganization over liquidation.

If a firm chooses to reorganize, its debts are frozen and it is given time to negotiate new payment schedules with its creditors. Usually these new payment schedules will allow the firm longer repayment periods. The changes to the act allow the firm to choose to include the secured creditors (those with liens on certain assets) as well as the unsecured creditors in this negotiation phase. Prior to 1992, secured creditors, usually banks, could seize assets at any time. For the plan to be accepted, it must be approved by a majority (in number) of the creditors, and they must represent two thirds of the total value of the claims, down from three quarters before 1992. Once a plan has been accepted, the agreement goes to the court for approval. Approval will now be granted only if the plan calls for the immediate and complete payment of any wages and salaries owed, and within six months any federal income tax owed, a change from immediate payment under the old act. Rejection by the creditors or the court implies automatic bankruptcy of the debtor. The possibility of court-protected reorganization may help to keep in business a firm that is viable in the long run, but that may have otherwise been forced into bankruptcy by a small number of the creditors to whom it owes money. Olympia & York is one recent noteworthy example of a firm that went through this reorganization process.

If the firm chooses, or if its reorganization plan is rejected, the firm is liquidated. A trustee appointed by the creditors sells the assets of the bankrupt firm and distributes the proceeds according to the following outline. Secured creditors have first claim; unsecured creditors have their claims against the firm frozen until the secured creditors are paid. Preferred creditors are then paid. These include, in the order in which they are paid: the administrators of the bankruptcy, those owed wages and salaries to a maximum of $2,000 for work done and $1,000 in expenses for the previous six months (up from $500, $300, and three months prior to 1992), municipal governments owed taxes, and federal and provincial governments owed income taxes. Finally, all other unsecured creditors, including small suppliers not yet paid for goods delivered, are paid on a pro rata basis.

Jocelyn Martel of the Université de Montréal has studied a random sample of bankruptcies for the period 1977–87. Some salient facts emerge from this study. Firms that go bankrupt are overwhelmingly very small firms with average assets of just $74,000. They are typically in very bad shape, with a ratio of liabilities to assets for most firms exceeding 8:1. Administrative costs of bankruptcy proceedings are large, 56 percent of the market value of the average bankrupt firm, reflecting the small size of many of the firms involved. Average wage claims are above the old limit of $500 but well below the new limit of $2,000. And payout rates are low. Preferred creditors receive on average about 23 percent of the value of their claims while other unse-cured creditors receive only 2.5 percent.

The 1992 amendment to the Bankruptcy Act seems to have accomplished both its goals. The increased protection for workers who are owed wages seems sufficient, both in the event of a reorganization or a liquidation. The change in the voting procedure and the ability of debtors to force secured creditors to be part of any ne-gotiated plan is likely to increase the incidence of successful reorganization as opposed to liqui-dation. However, the evidence makes one won-der whether an efficiency cost will be incurred by ensuring that more small, deeply troubled firms will continue to operate rather than be liq-uidated.

Sources: Timothy Fisher and Jocelyn Martel, "Will the Bankruptcy Reforms Work? An Empirical Appraisal of Financial Reorganization in Canada," *Canadian Public Policy* 20 (September 1994): 265–77; Jocelyn Martel, "Commercial Bankruptcy in Canada," *Canadian Business Economics* 3 (Summer 1995): 53–64.

MANAGERIAL INCENTIVES

Another reason a firm cares about how it is financed is that debt and equity provide managers with different incentives. A backs-to-the-wall theory of corporate finance holds that firms should be encouraged to borrow, so that managers are forced to work hard to avoid bankruptcy. According to this theory, if a firm is financed by equity and is making at least some money, managers have little incentive to push for greater efficiency.

In the 1970s, the sharp increase in the price of oil yielded enormous profits to oil companies. Flush with profits, the firms invested poorly, which resulted in a rash of takeovers financed largely with debt. There is evidence that under the pressure of the increased debt, the management of these firms did become more effective.

But the higher chance of bankruptcy that accompanies high debt loads can also cause a problem. All the managers' efforts may be directed at keeping the firm alive, not at making the sound investments necessary for long-run prosperity. Firms near the threshold of bankruptcy also undertake excessive risks. They gamble—knowing that if they fail they are likely to have gone down anyway, but if the gamble pays off they may be able to get themselves out of their hole. Thus, finding the right financial structure represents a real challenge. Too little debt and the firm's resources may be inefficiently used; too much debt and the bankruptcy threat will distort the incentives to invest wisely for the longer term.

CONSEQUENCES FOR MARKET PERCEPTION OF VALUE

A firm's financial structure may also affect the market's beliefs about the firm's prospects. Most investors believe that a firm's managers are in a better position to judge the company's prospects than they are. If the managers believe there is little risk, they will be willing to issue more debt, because they can do so without incurring a risk of bankruptcy. Their willingness to issue debt thus conveys in a forceful and concrete way management's confidence in the firm—a far more convincing display of confidence than a glossy and glowing report on the firm's future. Because debt both leads managers to work hard and convinces prospective shareholders about the value of the firm's prospects, issuing debt reduces the overall cost of capital to the firm and increases the company's market value.

We have seen that three of the factors discussed so far—tax considerations, managerial incentives, and market perceptions of value—tend to steer firms in the direction of debt financing, when they can obtain it. Established firms finance most of their investments in excess of retained earnings by borrowing from banks or issuing bonds.

CONTROL

There is a final, important respect in which debt and equity financing differ, and it relates to who controls the firm.

Previous chapters treated the "firm" as a monolithic entity. The firm decided what to produce, how to produce it, and how much to produce in order to maximize its profits or its market value. In practice, however, individuals within the firm take these decisions, and their interests and beliefs differ. Furthermore, the interests of individuals within the firm may not be perfectly aligned with the objectives of profit maximization. And even if they are aligned, it may not be obvious what actions the firm should take to accomplish those goals. In the world of perfect information of Part Two, it was easy to answer the basic questions of what to produce, how to produce it, and how much to produce. But in practice, even the simplest question is fraught with uncertainties. In the 1980s the question arose for GM whether it should invest more in robotics. GM took a gamble of heavy investment in robotics, which at least in the short run did not pay off. Can machines really replace men? Should we wait until the technology improves? Or should we invest now to get ahead of our competitors?

Because different individuals might answer the basic questions of what the firm should do differently, it matters who takes these decisions. Who controls the firm and how it is controlled are key issues.

FINANCE AND CONTROL

How firms raise capital has implications for control. An entrepreneur needing additional cash often is reluctant to issue equity, since shareholders have the right to elect the board of directors—which nominally controls the firm by appointing the officers who run it. Every entrepreneur is familiar with the story of Steven Jobs, who co-founded Apple Computer but was pushed out of the company a few years later when Apple faced financial problems. Perhaps the most celebrated Canadian case of a chief executive losing power as a result of issuing equity to raise capital is that of Robert Campeau. His corporation engineered the largest takeovers in Canadian history, acquiring first the largest U.S. retailer, Federated Department Stores, for U.S.$6.6 billion and then the third-largest, Allied, for U.S.$4.9 billion. As a consequence, Campeau's share of ownership fell to 43 percent, and he eventually lost control of Campeau Corporation and was ousted from control of both Federated and Allied. By contrast, bondholders and banks have no formal role in the management of the corporation, except when there is a bankruptcy.

In reality, however, shareholders may have less control over a firm's decisions than banks and other lenders. This is because shareholders' control is weakened by information and incentive factors. They have to rely on managers for information, and they will tell them what they want them to hear to the extent possible. Also, shareholders have little incentive to invest the effort and resources required to become really well informed about management quality, because they typically own such a small proportion of the shares. In most large firms, no shareholder has more than a few percent of the outstanding shares.

WHY FINANCIAL POLICY MATTERS

The amount of debt affects the likelihood of bankruptcy.

Debt and equity receive different tax treatment.

The amount of debt affects managerial incentives.

The firm's choice of financial structure may affect the market's perception of the firm's value and risk.

Bonds, bank finance, and new equities have different implications for the question of who controls the firm.

This is a classic public goods problem. All shareholders would benefit from better management, but none has the full incentive to learn how to judge the managers.

Banks and other lenders are in a more powerful position, because most firms are critically dependent on them for funds—at least from time to time—and lenders at any time can withdraw the credit they have extended. Accordingly, corporation managers pay close attention to their bankers' views.

The safest course for an entrepreneur who worries about the loss of control is to finance her investments with retained earnings. But if her retained earnings are small, as is typically the case with new firms, and if she believes that the return to additional investment is high enough, she will be tempted to turn to outside sources for funds. In this case, she believes the expected return is worth risking loss of control.

LIMITED FINANCIAL OPTIONS

The consequences of raising funds by alternative means help explain the choices that individual firms make in financing new investments, but choices are limited. In many circumstances, firms may not be able to borrow or issue new equities, except at very disadvantageous terms. A company may then be forced to limit its investment to retained earnings.

CREDIT RATIONING

When individuals or firms are willing to pay the current interest rate but simply cannot obtain funds at that rate, they are said to be **credit rationed.** To understand credit rationing, picture a medium-sized corporation, Checkout Systems, that produces software. When used with retailers' checkout registers, this software handles inventory and all other accounting functions as well. The software has been popular, but Checkout Systems realizes that it would be much more successful if it also sold the hardware—computer systems, terminals, and cash register drawers—that stores must have in order to use the software. Checkout can get the hardware from a computer manufacturer, but it needs $2 million for warehouse and inventory. The company is fully confident that the $2 million expansion will produce a steady return of at least 30 percent. However, it has no retained earnings with which to pay for the expansion.

This is only the beginning of Checkout's problems. Assume that the going interest rate for loans to small firms is 14 percent. The company has a $400,000 line of credit at a local bank, but its banker refuses to make a further loan. Checkout executives offer to pay a higher price—16 percent interest for the $2 million. The bank turns the company down. Is there any interest rate at which the bank would be willing to lend, the Checkout executives ask? The bank says no.

The bank knows that some borrowers are more likely to default than others, but it has no way of knowing which ones are most likely to do so. Thus, it faces an adverse selection problem. As it raises interest rates to accommodate firms like Checkout, its average returns may actually decrease. The reason for this is that at higher interest rates, the "best" borrowers—those with the lowest likelihood of default—decide not to borrow.

Figure 17.2 shows the return to a lender being maximized at the interest rate r_0. The bank will not

Figure 17.2 HIGHER INTER-EST RATES, LOWER RETURN

As the interest rate increases, safe borrowers tend to drop out of the market, and only risky borrowers remain. Beyond some point, rises in the interest rate increase defaults on loans by enough to reduce the expected return to a lender. At higher interest rates, borrowers may also undertake greater risks, again lowering lenders' expected returns.

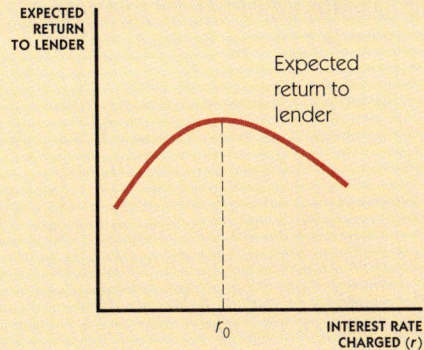

EXPECTED RETURN TO LENDER

Expected return to lender

r_0

INTEREST RATE CHARGED (r)

raise its interest rates beyond this level, even though at this rate the demand for funds may exceed the supply.

Let's look now at the market for funds for a particular category of loan, say, small mortgages under $100,000 for owner-occupied houses. The supply curve for funds for loans differs from the supply curve depicted in the basic model. Figure 17.3, which is based on the information in Figure 17.2, shows the supply curve for funds as backward-bending. This shape reflects the reasonable assumption that as the average return to loans (which differs from the interest rate charged for these loans because some of the borrowers default) increases, the

Figure 17.3 SUPPLY AND DEMAND FOR CAPITAL CREDIT WITH RATIONING

The supply of funds depends on the expected return. If that return begins to fall when the interest rate charged gets high, the supply of funds will be backward-bending. Even if demand for funds exceeds supply at interest rate r_0, the lender will not raise his interest rate, since that would reduce expected returns. As a result, an excess demand for funds can exist in equilibrium.

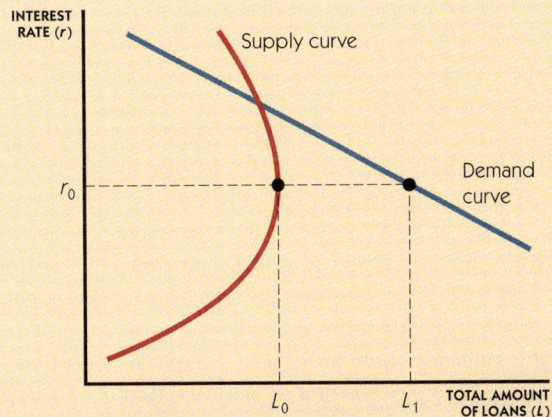

INTEREST RATE (r)

Supply curve

r_0

Demand curve

L_0 L_1

TOTAL AMOUNT OF LOANS (L)

supply of funds increases. The supply curve thus bends backwards beyond r_0. As the interest rate charged rises to this point, average returns increase and so does the supply of funds; but at interest rates beyond this point, average returns decline and so does the supply of funds.

Credit rationing takes three forms. Some borrowers get funds, but less than they would like. Some loan applicants are denied credit, even though similar applicants receive credit. And some whole categories of applicants are simply denied credit. A bank may, for instance, refuse to give loans for vacations or to finance a university education or to buy a house in a particular part of the town. In each of these cases, those who have their credit denied or limited will not be any more successful if they offer to pay a higher interest rate.

If lenders had perfect information, there would be no rationing. They would charge higher interest rates to reflect differences in the likelihood of default, but all applicants willing to pay the appropriate rate would get loans. Thus, underlying credit rationing is lack of information. No matter how many forms are filled out, references requested, or interviews held, lenders know there is a residual amount of missing information. They therefore develop rules of thumb for loans: yes to well-run, small businesses; no to loans for university students or to new high-tech computer software firms, both of whom typically have high rates of default.

Of course, the lower the interest rate charged, the greater the demand for funds. As the demand curve is drawn in Figure 17.3, average returns are maximized at interest rate r_0, but the supply of funds is less than the demand at this point. There is credit rationing; L_0 loans are actually made, while total demand is L_1. Many qualified borrowers would like to take out loans at the going interest rate but cannot. The magnitude of the credit rationing is measured by the gap between the demand, L_1, and the supply, L_0.

In addition to adverse selection, there is a second reason for credit rationing. Let's return to the example of Checkout Systems. The bank knows that Checkout's executives can engage in excessively risky behaviour, some of which the bank will find impossible to monitor. It may worry that the higher

the interest rate charged, the more likely that such risk-taking behaviour will occur. The greater the risk taking, the higher the probability of bankruptcy, the lower the possibility that the lender will be able to recoup his funds, and thus the lower the expected return to the loan. As we saw in Figure 17.2, expected returns to the bank may actually decrease as the interest rate charged increases, because of this induced risk taking, or moral hazard, effect.

EQUITY RATIONING

We might suppose that firms that are unable to borrow would raise money by issuing more stock. In fact, established firms seldom raise capital in this way. In recent years, less than a tenth of new financing has occurred through the sale of equity. The reason is not hard to see: when firms issue new equity, the price of existing shares tends to decline, and by more than the amount one would expect, given the dilution of the ownership of existing shareholders. Say that a firm worth $1 million issues $100,000 worth of new shares, and the price of the stock falls by 5 percent. The firm's existing shareholders have to give up $50,000 to raise $100,000 in funds from new investors. This is clearly an unattractive deal.

There are several reasons why issuing more equity frequently has such an adverse effect on the price of shares. First, issuing equity reduces the market's perception of a firm's value. Investors reason that the firm's original owners and its managers will be most anxious to sell shares when these well-informed individuals think the market is overvaluing the shares currently outstanding. These concerns are compounded by the fact that the market is well aware that firms normally turn first to banks to raise funds. Investors wonder, "Is the firm trying to issue new shares because banks will not lend to it, or at least not on very favourable terms, or at least not as much as the firm wants? If banks are reluctant to lend, why should I turn over my money?" Reasoning this way, they will only invest in the firm if they believe they are getting a good enough deal, that is, if the price of the shares is low enough.

Also, as we saw earlier, debt has a positive incentive effect on managers. By the same token, giving the firm more money to play with without any fixed commitment to repay—which is exactly what new issues of equity do—has an adverse effect on incentives.

For these and other reasons, the issue of new shares generally depresses the share value. Accordingly, only infrequently do established firms raise new capital by issuing shares.

OVERVIEW: THE LIFE CYCLE OF A FIRM

We have now identified various considerations affecting the relative attractiveness of different ways of raising capital. In the life cycle of a firm these considerations play out in different ways. In its early days, a firm typically finds it impossible to issue shares and has difficulty borrowing. Owners must rely on their own savings and investments of friends and relatives. In some high-technology areas they may turn to providers of venture capital (see Chapter 8). Such businesses provide not only capital but also managerial help, in return for a substantial share in the firm. As the young firm gets more established, it will find access to borrowing easier, and eventually it may issue an initial public offering on the stock market. Throughout the remainder of its life it will finance much of its investment through retained earnings. In its later years it may even turn to buying back its shares.

TAKEOVERS, CONTROL OF FIRMS, AND THE MARKET FOR MANAGERS

If you are a small shareholder and you think management is not using the company's assets in ways that maximize profits, there is little you can do other than sell your shares. But if you are rich—or if you have access to others' capital—you can attempt to buy enough of the shares to gain control of the firm. This need not be a majority of the shares. You may be able to persuade other shareholders to vote their shares in support of you. You may even be able to

persuade the existing management to leave quietly (by providing them with generous pensions) and to support the change in control. When one management team (one firm) takes over the control of another, it is called a **takeover.** When the second firm resists, it is called a **hostile takeover.** Sometimes takeovers occur through mergers: the two firms combine, with shareholders in the new firm getting shares in the new combined firm in exchange for their shares in the original firm. Sometimes takeovers occur through acquisitions, when one firm buys another outright.

Takeovers increased sharply in the 1980s and then began to decline after 1988, for a variety of reasons. Many of the mergers and acquisitions had been financed by **junk bonds** carrying interest rates of 15 percent or higher. Even these seemingly high interest rates failed to reflect the true risk of default. Company after company found itself unable to meet its debt obligations, particularly as the economy went into recession in 1991.

The takeover movement also got a bad reputation because of unsavoury practices like insider trading. To ensure that the markets are viewed as a "level playing field," the government does not allow managers of firms who have access to inside information about their firms to trade on their information (as noted in Chapter 8). Thus, if you are president of an oil company and you know that your firm has just made a major oil discovery, you cannot go out and buy more shares of the firm's stock. Nor can you tell your wife and family to do the same. The courts have extended this basic "insider" principle to those involved in buying and selling companies. If you know that your firm is about to make an offer to acquire another firm, which will send that firm's share prices soaring, you cannot use that information for private gain.

Another unsavoury practice was **greenmail,** so called because of its similarity to blackmail. Takeover artists would buy shares in a firm and then threaten a takeover. Their intent was not actually to buy the company but to get a "bribe" to go away—to get the company to buy back their shares at a premium to ward off a takeover.

Opposition to takeovers came not only from the management that was displaced but also from

THE TEN HIGHEST PUBLICLY REPORTED EXECUTIVE SALARIES IN CANADA IN 1995

Name	Company	Total compensation in 1995[†]
1. Gerald Pencer	Cott Corp.	13,005,559
2. John Doddridge	Magna International	10,853,543
3. David Walsh	Bre-X Minerals	10,008,000
4. Paul Desmarais	Power Corp.	5,654,258
5. Stephen Hudson	Newcourt Credit Group	4,221,471
6. Brent Ballantyne	Maple Leaf Foods	3,588,306
7. Clayton Woitas	Renaissance Energy	3,483,600
8. Richard Thomson	Toronto Dominion Bank	3,372,804
9. Bernard Isautier	Canadian Occidental Petroleum	3,303,120
10. Lawrence Bloomberg	First Marathon Inc.	3,252,000

[†]Total compensation includes salary, bonuses, housing and other allowances, benefits from incentive and retirement schemes, and the exercise of stock options.

Source: "Best-Paid CEOs," *Report on Business* magazine, July 1996.

As the table above shows, some top executives earn mind-bending sums of money, sometimes millions of dollars a year. Defenders of these high salaries point out that top executives take life-or-death decisions for their companies and that they deserve to be compensated for taking those decisions wisely. Much of top executive pay comes in the form of stock options. Their high pay is therefore due in part to the fact that the company's stock did well, which offers an incentive for top management to look out for the interests of shareholders.

In the past few years, however, critics of high executive salaries have become considerably more vocal. Here are some of their main arguments:

1 Pay for top executives has grown disproportionately. In 1974 the typical chief executive officer (CEO) received pay that was 30 times that of the average manufacturing worker. In the early 1990s, the typical CEO earned about 75 times the pay of an average manufacturing worker.

2 Pay for Canadian top executives is out of line with what non-American foreign companies pay. In Japan, the average CEO earns 20 times the pay of the average worker; in the United Kingdom, he or she earns 35 times the pay of the average worker. Yet Japanese managers seem to be every bit as productive as Canadian managers—not to mention those in the United States who earn 120 times the pay of the average worker.

3 Pay for top executives does not offer a true incentive, because it often rises even when the company does badly. During the recession of the early 1990s, for example, corporate profits fell by close to 10 percent, while executive salaries rose by over 5 percent. This holds true even when one looks at a good year for corporate profits, like 1995. The accompanying table shows that not only does pay as a percentage of profits vary widely, but changes in pay seem not to be closely related to changes in profits.

Critics of high executive pay point out that compensation levels are often set by a board of directors chosen by the top executive, with the help of an outside consultant who is also cho-

sen by the top executive. These critics argue that, although a well-designed plan of linking the top executives' pay to the long-term price of the company's stock can provide useful incentives, too many stock plans have become a way to funnel money to the top executive without limit or control.

Sources: "Best-Paid CEOs," *The Globe and Mail, Report on Business Magazine,* July 1996, page 83; "Payday at the Top: What Some Bosses Earn," *The Globe and Mail,* April 4, 1992, p. B4.

workers in the affected firms. Often, following a takeover, firms faced with heavy debt tightened their belts, laying off workers and even shutting down whole plants. Of course, some of these changes were exactly the reason for the takeover: previous management had not been effective in minimizing costs.

TAKEOVERS: PROS AND CONS

The debate about takeovers is often a debate about how well markets work—in this case the markets for managers and for financial assets.

The central argument in favour of takeovers is that they represent a successful way to replace ineffective managers. Under existing management, a firm may be worth $1 million, with 100,000 shares that trade at $10. An alternative management team may be able to use the firm's resources better, raising its value to $2 million ($20 per share). Even if the acquiring firm (the firm making the takeover) pays a 10 percent premium for the shares—that is, pays $1.1 million for the firm—it makes a profit of $900,000 on the deal. From this perspective, takeover battles are like auctions. The firm is sold to the bidder willing to pay the highest price, the one that thinks it can most effectively utilize the firm's resources.

Having won the auction, the highest bidder must

get the company to earn enough money to justify its bid. If the post-takeover managers can indeed do a better job, the takeover firm realizes a profit. From this perspective, then, takeovers reflect the competition to be managers. They are evidence that the market for managers works. Much of the takeover activity of the 1980s in the oil industry was an attempt by various investors to redirect Canada's oil companies toward more profitable activities.

Thus, takeovers provide an important source of discipline even for managers not threatened with one. Managers know that if they do not work hard, they may be threatened with a hostile takeover. They also know that a well-managed firm is unlikely to be taken over, because outsiders will recognize the quality of the management and know they are unlikely to raise the firm's profits. Even though the typical small shareholder does not look over the shoulder of the existing management team, an army of corporate raiders is always on the lookout for a mismanaged firm that could be renovated under new management.

Takeovers are particularly important, because the other methods of controlling managers of large corporations are relatively ineffective. We saw earlier that most shareholders have neither the information, the incentives, nor the tools to exercise much control over management. The one way they have of exercising control is voting to elect members of the board of directors. Most investors, if they become dissatisfied with how the firm is being run, just sell their shares. In addition, supporters of takeovers (and of free markets) tend to believe that since shareholders are the real owners of a company, they should have a chance to sell what they own to the highest bidder when they desire to do so.

TAKING DECISIONS

In Chapter 1 we listed four basic questions: What and how much is to be produced, how it is to be produced, for whom it is produced, and *who takes these decisions.* Most of this book focuses on the first three questions. The question of who controls the firm goes to the heart of the final question: Who takes these decisions? The rest of this chapter addresses how the organization of the firm and of the economy determines who takes the decisions and how they take them.

DELEGATION AND THE PRINCIPAL-AGENT PROBLEM

Even if the firm were owned by a single individual, there would be a problem of control, because the owner cannot take all the decisions himself. He must *delegate* some to subordinates, who in turn must engage in further delegation. The central problem is how to ensure that these managers act in the same way that the owner would have acted. This is an example of a broad class of incentive problems.

In Chapter 16 it was noted that incentive problems arise whenever an individual does not bear, or receive, the full consequences of her actions. If the manager takes a good decision, the firm prospers and the shareholders benefit. If she takes a bad decision, they suffer. Thus, shareholders would like to motivate the manager to act in a way that maximizes the value of their shares. In this form, the incentive problem is referred to as the **principal-agent problem.** The principal (here, the owner) would like to

motivate the agent (here, the manager) to act in the principal's interests. But both parties know the owner cannot judge whether the manager has taken the appropriate action simply by the observable results.

The interests of managers and owners frequently differ. The manager going on a business trip may choose to buy a ticket on a more expensive airline because he is trying to accumulate frequent flier points for himself on that airline, rather than use a cheaper alternative. The sales representative for a computer firm may give some account especially close attention, not because of the prospects of increased sales but because he is trying to land a new job.

There are two important aspects of the principal-agent problem: how hard the agent works, and what risks the agent takes. If a manager works especially hard, the owners of the firm (often the shareholders) will receive some of the reward. But because the manager does not receive all the reward, she may have insufficient incentives for exerting maximum effort.

The manager's taste for risk will rarely match the owner's interests. On the one hand, managers may act in a more risk-averse (cautious) manner than the owners of the firm might like. After all, the managers know that they may lose their jobs should projects under their supervision fail. On the other hand, managers may be willing to take risks when the owners would not be willing to do so. They are gambling with someone else's money. If the project is a flop, the firm loses money; if it is successful, the manager will receive credit. The consensus among economists is that under most circumstances, managers act in a way that is *more* risk-averse than the owners would like.

Ownership as a Solution The most obvious solution to the principal-agent problem would be for the owner of the firm to sell each manager a portion of the firm. As the owner, the manager would have all the right incentives. If he worked harder, he would reap the rewards. If he took more risks, he would receive the gains and bear the losses. In general, however, the manager does not have the requisite capital to buy part of the firm, and even if he did, he might not be willing to buy it. An owner's income is a lot

When executive salaries are made public, they include the current value of any stock options that are typically part of the executive's total compensation package. These are often a large part of the pay that is reported. The inclusion of stock options as part of a manager's compensation gives him an incentive to take decisions that will increase the price of the company's stock. To see how this works consider a simple example.

Suppose that a CEO's current pay package includes "call" options that entitle the executive to buy 1 million shares of the company's stock two years hence for the present share price of $20 (this is called the "strike price" of the option). If two-year $20 call options are currently trading at $2 each, then the CEO's reported pay will include the value of the options, $2 million. But unlike the options that the public buys and sells through the stock market, these options are vested, meaning that they cannot be sold, but must be held for the full two years.

Of course, these options are not the same as $2 million cash. In two years when the CEO is allowed to exercise the options, they will only be worth something if the share price is above the strike price of $20. If the share price is $25 the total value of the options is $5 million, if the share price is $27 the value of the options is $7 million. However, if the share price is $20 or below the value of the options is zero.

Thus by paying the CEO with options rather than cash, shareholders ensure that the executive has an incentive to increase the share price. The CEO's objective is now in line with that of the shareholders, which is to make the share price as high as possible.

---

more variable than a pay-cheque, depending not only on his own efforts but also on the vagaries of the market. A manager may not be willing to take that risk.

In any case, most modern corporations cannot be split into the right parts to make each manager an owner and still operate efficiently. We can sometimes divide a large corporation into several parts, each run separately. But within each of these parts, there remain large principal-agent problems.

Incentive Pay as a Solution A second-best solution to the principal-agent problem is to include in the agent's compensation package incentives that reflect the principal's interest. Thus, sales representatives earn commissions, and many workers can qualify for performance bonuses if they or their department exceeds production quotas. One form of incentive programme for top managers is the **stock option** bonus, related to how well their firms per-

form. Suppose stock in a particular company is currently selling for $30. The stock option allows the manager to purchase a specified number of shares at $30 for a specified period of time. For instance, the manager may be given the option to buy 100,000 shares at $30 at any time during the next three years. If the firm's shares rise in value to $40, the manager can purchase the shares for $3 million and then immediately resell them for $4 million, receiving a bonus—presumably as a reward for her contribution in increasing the value of the firm—of $1 million. It is common for firms to provide their top managers with stock option bonuses valued in the millions of dollars.

Monitoring as a Solution Appropriately designed compensation schemes help align the interests of the agent with that of the principal. But they do not fully resolve the problem. Principals further reduce

DELEGATION

The principal-agent problem

    Work effort of agent

    Risk taking of agent

Solutions

    Ownership

    Incentive pay

    Monitoring

the scope for agents to take actions that are not in their interests by monitoring and obtaining information not only about what the agent *is* doing, but also about what she *should* be doing.

It is not easy for top management to know what is going on in a large corporation. They can, of course, easily tell whether the factories are producing, but are they really doing what it takes to maximize profits? An essential aid in gathering requisite information are the accounting systems that all modern corporations employ. They are intended to provide top management with essential information concerning, for instance, the relative profitability of each of its parts.

Still, monitoring is imperfect. Long-term relationships between most principals and agents improve the effectiveness of even imperfect monitoring because both sides see the gains from continuing the relationship. A manager will not take advantage of every opportunity to gain at the expense of the firm. She knows that even if the firm does not detect self-serving behaviour every time, it is likely to observe it some of the time, and that even if the firm does not fire her, her behaviour might affect her prospects for promotion.

MOTIVATING WORKERS

Workers have a price—the wage—analogous to the price of machines. But even to the most profit-hungry and coldhearted employer, people are different from machines. They bring adaptability and a multitude of skills and experiences to a job. Most machines can only do one task, and even robots can only do what they are programmed to do. However, machines have one advantage over humans. Except when they break down, they do what they are told.

Workers have to be motivated if they are to work hard and to exercise good judgment.

This can be viewed as an information problem. In the basic competitive model of Part Two, workers were paid to perform particular tasks. The employer knew perfectly well whether the worker performed the agreed-upon task in the agreed-upon manner. If the worker failed to do so, he did not get paid. The pay was the only form of motivation required. But in reality, workers frequently have considerable discretion. Employers have limited information about what a worker is doing at each moment. So they have to motivate their work force to exercise their abilities to the fullest.

To motivate workers, employers use both the carrot and the stick. They may reward workers for performing well by making pay and promotion depend on performance, and they may punish workers for shirking by firing them. Sometimes a worker is given considerable discretion and autonomy; sometimes he is monitored closely. The mix of carrots and sticks, autonomy and direct supervision, varies from job to job and industry to industry. It depends partly on how easy it is to supervise workers directly and how easy it is to compensate workers on the basis of performance.

PIECE RATES AND INCENTIVES

When workers can be paid for exactly what they produce, with their pay increasing for higher productivity and falling for lower productivity, they will have appropriate incentives to work hard. The system of payment in which a worker is paid for each item produced or each task performed is called a **piece-rate system.** But relatively few Canadians are paid largely, let alone exclusively, on a piece-rate system. Typically, even workers within a piece-rate system get a base pay *plus* additional pay, which increases the more they produce.

Why don't more employers enact a piece-rate system, if it would improve incentives? One major reason is that piece rates leave workers bearing considerable risk. A worker may have a bad week because of bad luck. For example, sales clerks, who are often paid commissions on the basis of productivity—a form of piece rate—may simply find the demand for their products lacking.

By providing a certain amount of guaranteed pay, a firm gives the worker a steady income and reduces the risk she must bear. But with lower piece-rate compensation, the worker has less incentive to work hard. There is thus a trade-off between risk and incentives. Thus, compensation schemes must find some balance between offering security and offering incentives linked to worker performance. In many jobs, employers or managers achieve this balance by offering both a guaranteed minimum compensation (including fringe benefits) and bonuses that depend on performance.

A second reason more employers do not use piece-rate systems is a concern for quality. For workers on an assembly line, the quantity produced may be easily measured, but quality cannot. If the workers' pay just depends on the number of items produced, the worker has an incentive to emphasize quantity over quality. The result may be less profitable for the firm than a lower level of higher-quality output.

In any case, most workers are engaged in a variety of tasks, only some of which can easily be defined and rewarded by means of a piece-rate system. For example, although employers would like experienced workers to train new workers, employees who are paid on a piece-rate system have little incentive to do this, or to help their co-workers in other ways. Similarly, when salesmen are paid on the basis of commissions, they have little incentive to provide information and service to potential customers whom they perceive as not likely to be immediate buyers. Even if providing information enhances the likelihood that a customer will return to the store to buy the good, there is a fair chance that some other salesperson will get the commission. To see this effect at work, visit a car dealer's showroom, make it clear that you are not going to buy a car that day, and see what kind of service you get.

EFFICIENCY WAGES

When output is easily measured, the carrot of basing pay at least partially on performance makes sense. And when effort is easily monitored, using the stick of being fired for failure to exert adequate effort makes sense. But monitoring effort continuously is often expensive. An alternative is to monitor less frequently, and impose a big penalty if the worker is caught shirking. One way of imposing a big penalty is to pay above-market wages. Then, if a worker is fired, he suffers a big income loss. The higher the wage, the greater the penalty from being fired. Similarly, rewarding workers with higher pay who are observed to be working hard whenever they are monitored provides incentives for workers to continue to work hard.

These are examples where higher wages help motivate workers and lead to increased productivity. There are additional reasons why it may pay a firm to pay high wages. High wages reduce labour turnover, lead to more loyalty and higher-quality work by employees, and enable the firm to attract more productive workers. This two-way link is captured by **efficiency wage theory.** This theory says that not only do higher productivities result in higher wages, but also that higher wages result in higher productivity. When wages increase with productivity, you cannot tell what is causing what.

Efficiency wage theory provides an explanation for some wage differentials. In jobs where it is very costly to monitor workers on a day-to-day basis or where the damage a worker can do is very great (say, where the worker can destroy a machine punching one wrong button), employers are more likely to rely on high wages to ensure that workers perform well.

These "wages of trust" may explain why wages in more capital-intensive industries, those requiring massive investments, are higher for workers with otherwise comparable skills than wages in industries using less capital. They may also explain why workers entrusted with the care of much cash which they could abscond with are paid higher wages than are other workers of comparable skills. It is not so much that they receive high wages because they are trustworthy, but that they become more trustworthy because they receive high wages—and the threat of losing those high wages encourages moral behaviour.

OTHER INCENTIVES

After paying piece rates, bonuses, and higher-than-market wages, among the most important incentives to increase job performance are enhanced promotion possibilities for those who perform well (where pay rises with promotions) and contests among workers. Contests are particularly useful when it is hard to determine the difficulty of the task a worker is performing. Consider a firm that is trying to figure out how much to pay its sales force when it is promoting a new product. If a salesperson is successful, does that represent good salesmanship, or is the new product able to "sell itself"? All sales representatives are in roughly the same position, so their performance can be compared. The representative who sells the most gets a bonus—and wins the contest.

In recent years, firms have explored the consequences of alternative ways of encouraging worker motivation and hence worker productivity. Some use teams. When pay depends on team performance, members of a team have an incentive to monitor and help one another. The automaker Volvo believes that such team arrangements have increased the productivity of its own work force. Some firms have encouraged worker participation in decision taking. Such participation may help both sides see that there is more to be gained by cooperation than by conflict. For instance, new ways of producing goods can make both the firm and the workers better off; if the company sells more goods, all share in the benefits.

At least in the long run, wages and labour costs reflect the attitudes of workers. If workers find that a certain firm provides an attractive workplace, the wages it must pay to recruit people may be lower than other firms' wages, and the people that it re-cruits will work harder and stay longer. If workers as a whole become concerned about having more autonomy, more say in decision taking, or any other attribute of the workplace, it will pay firms to respond to their concerns.

CENTRALIZATION AND DECENTRALIZATION

The most basic issue in a firm's decision-taking structure is the extent to which decision taking is **centralized** or **decentralized.** A firm in which the president or chief executive officer (CEO) takes all decisions is highly centralized, just as an economy where all decisions are taken by a central Ministry of Economics is highly centralized. However, all large organizations involve some degree of decentralization. The president of a corporation simply does not have the time, much less the information, with which to take all the day-to-day decisions.

The consequence of decentralization is that the firm's subunits have considerable autonomy—freedom to take their own decisions. Should the copper division of Noranda Inc. be allowed to take its own decisions concerning what mining properties to develop, or should the corporation's CEO be consulted? Which decisions are of sufficient importance that the CEO needs to be involved? Which decisions should the CEO actually take? These fundamental decisions are faced by every economic organization.

There are trade-offs to differing degrees of centralization and decentralization. Centralized decision taking usually involves a hierarchical structure. A project must pass through a set of well-defined approval layers, like a fine sieve. This reduces the likeli-

WAYS OF MOTIVATING WORKERS

Piece rates, or pay based on measured output.

Efficiency wages, or higher wages to workers who work harder. These introduce an extra cost to those dismissed for unsatisfactory performance.

Relative performance: promotions, contests.

Team rewards, pay based on team performance.

hood that bad projects are approved, but the sifting process also leads to good projects being rejected. Decentralized decision taking provides fewer checks on any project. Some bad projects are more likely to get adopted, but by the same token, fewer good projects are rejected.

ADVANTAGES OF CENTRALIZATION

Hierarchical decision taking may allow for better co-ordination across the divisions of a large corporation, which may be important in instances where activities in one part of the firm, such as research, may be of benefit to another. Thus, in developing a new communications system, it might pay the different divisions of Northern Telecom to coordinate their research and development efforts. Even if in the end the different units decide to produce different systems, they will still find it profitable to coordinate their research programmes.

Another argument in favour of centralized decision taking is that it avoids the duplication that results from operating autonomous corporate divisions, where personnel from several units are often engaged in quite similar activities. Thus, advocates of centralization claim that it is inefficient for each division of a firm to have its own legal staff or its own marketing department.

ADVANTAGES OF DECENTRALIZATION

Some of the arguments used by advocates of greater centralization can be turned on their head and used as arguments for decentralization. For example, supporters of decentralization point out that having different units within an organization doing similar things may have decided advantages: the resulting competition not only provides a strong motivation for members of the different production units, but also provides a basis for judging whether one unit is doing better than another, and hence for taking decisions about who is performing well and who should receive more funds.

Decentralized decision taking also enables a production unit to adapt decisions to its own particular circumstances, so that they reflect the diversity of attitudes and skills among workers. As hard as they may try, centralized authorities have difficulty in obtaining the requisite information from those who are actually engaged in the production process. Decentralization also allows a range of experimentation greater than that found under more centralized regimes and enables projects to be approved more quickly.

The advantages of decentralization are great enough so that many firms have decentralized considerably. Large corporations like General Motors are separated into divisions, each of which may have considerable autonomy, at least over some functions (such as marketing). While there may be centralization in certain issues, like the design of a new motor or body frame, there is great decentralization in others. Pontiac and Buick see their markets as slightly different, and even if they have the same basic engineering, each division believes it can adapt the car—with its own interior design, for example—and adopt a marketing strategy aimed at its part of the market far better than central headquarters could do. The space technology company Spar Aerospace divides itself into a large number of units, each of which has the authority to undertake research projects.

CENTRALIZED VERSUS DECENTRALIZED DECISION TAKING

Centralized	Decentralized
Fewer bad projects are accepted.	More good projects are accepted.
There is greater coordination; externalities are taken into account.	Comparison between competing units provides (a) incentives and (b) bases of selection.
Duplication is avoided.	There is greater diversity and experimentation.

THE BOUNDARIES OF THE FIRM

Many firms sell "clones" of IBM's personal computer. Most of these firms are "assemblers": they buy circuit boards, cases, monitors, and keyboards in bulk, assemble the parts into personal computers, and sell them. Why don't they expand, and make their own circuit boards, cases, monitors, and keyboards? To turn the question around, why don't those who make these parts assemble them? After all, firms always want more profits, and these expansions seem to be prime areas for growth.

Economists are interested in the conditions that cause a firm to limit itself in size or in the number of products it manufactures. What determines the boundaries of firms? To put the same question a different way, when does a company find it easier to deal with another company through the market, rather than produce what it needs itself? What are the advantages and disadvantages of markets? In modern economies, the degree of centralization and decentralization is closely related to the issue of what is produced within the firm, and what each firm purchases from other firms.

In the case of the personal computer market, there is a great deal of decentralization. Companies make extensive use of the market. The circuit board manufacturers have a much larger market than just personal computers, so they can achieve economies of scale they would not enjoy if they restricted their output to the personal computer level. The same is true for those who make the other parts—they fear the loss of flexibility entailed in putting all their eggs in the personal computer market "basket." This pattern of specialization, however, leaves a profit opportunity for the assemblers, who can buy the parts from outside and still wind up with a computer they can sell at a good profit.

But the degree of decentralization within the personal computer market is unusual. Much economic activity occurs within firms rather than between firms. That is, companies produce intermediate products that are used as inputs for the goods the company eventually sells, and firms may even produce the inputs that are used in these intermediate products. Such activity is known as **vertical integration.** (By contrast, **horizontal integration** involves bringing together firms producing the same goods.) The Irving Corporation based in New Brunswick owns its own trucking company to transport the timber from its own forest operations to its own paper mills to produce paper for sale to its own newspaper companies. It also owns its own fleet of ships to carry imported oil to its own refineries in eastern Canada. Indeed, it even builds some of its own ships. Similarly, McCain's Foods has acquired its own farms to produce some of the foodstuffs it uses in its food-processing operations.

A number of factors go into the decisions about whether to vertically integrate—whether to produce the inputs used to produce a firm's goods—or whether to use the market. One important factor is **transactions costs,** the extra costs (beyond the price of the purchase) of conducting a transaction, whether those costs are money, time, or inconvenience. The American economist Ronald Coase was awarded the Nobel Prize in 1991 partly for his work in identifying the role of transactions costs in determining the "boundaries" of the firm: what activities occur within a firm and what activities occur between firms.

Consider the problem of a large manufacturing company that offers dental insurance to its employees. The company could continue to pay premiums to an outside insurance company that would then be liable for any claims. Because of its large work force, however, the option of paying its employees' dental bills directly has become economically viable. The company could set up a division to run its dental insurance, but then it will face all the managerial problems discussed in this chapter. Although this company is good at manufacturing, it has no comparative advantage at running a dental insurance company, and its managerial talent is scarce. Accordingly, the firm may find it cheaper, once these transactions costs are taken into account, to continue with the outside dental insurance company. It is more efficient to make use of the market in obtaining dental insurance services.

In other cases, transactions costs may be lower if the firm vertically integrates. Consider a chemical firm eager for new products to sell. It could hire an outside laboratory to try to develop a new drug and use outside sales representatives to sell existing ones. But how can the company make sure that the outside laboratory really tries to make a breakthrough discovery? How can the company make sure that the outside sales firm makes a sincere effort to sell its products?

Transactions costs are at least as important as the costs of production. Indeed, as innovations in manufacturing (such as the invention of the assembly line)

have reduced production costs, transactions costs have taken on increasing importance. Many of the innovations of the past two decades have in turn reduced transactions costs. For example, computers have enhanced our ability to keep track of records and process other information required for engaging in transactions.

Finding a balance between centralization and decentralization and between what the firm produces and what it purchases are thus two of the central problems facing managers of all large enterprises.

REVIEW AND PRACTICE

SUMMARY

1 The three main forms of business ownership are proprietorships, partnerships, and corporations. Only corporate ownership has the advantage of limited liability, which means that investors will not be liable for debts incurred by the company.

2 The Modigliani-Miller theorem says that under a simplified set of conditions, the manner in which a firm finances itself is a matter of indifference. Nevertheless, issues of bankruptcy, taxation, management incentives, and corporate control mean that firms care about their financial structure.

3 Shareholders have nominal control of corporations, but when share ownership is widely distributed, shareholders may not exercise effective control. While lenders like banks have nominal control over a corporation only if it declares bankruptcy, their ability to control the immediate flow of capital to the firm may actually give them a fair amount of say in what the firm does.

4 Credit rationing occurs when a borrower cannot find a source of funds even when he is willing to pay a higher-than-market interest rate. Lenders fear their average return may *decrease* (the chance of default is greater) as the nominal interest rate increases.

5 Firms will not be willing to issue new equity if doing so results in large decreases in the market value of outstanding shares.

6 The argument for takeovers is that they provide a means by which less efficient management teams can be replaced by more efficient teams. The argument against takeovers is that they often are more matters of power or ego rather than efficiency and that the threat of takeovers diverts companies from focusing on their actual business.

7 The problem owners of firms have in motivating the managers to work hard and take decisions about risk in the general interests of the firm, rather than in their own personal interest, is known as the principal-agent problem.

8 Employers try to motivate workers and induce high levels of effort through a combination of direct supervision, incentives for doing well, and penalties for doing badly. They pay wages higher than workers could get elsewhere (efficiency wages), give promotions and bonuses, base pay on relative performance (contests), and grant team rewards.

9 Centralized decision taking reduces the likelihood that unproductive projects will be approved, improves coordination, and avoids duplication, but also tends to weed out good projects. Decentralized decision taking reduces the likelihood that good projects will be rejected and provides a basis for experimentation and comparison, but also tends to allow a greater number of unproductive projects to go forward.

10 Every firm must decide whether to make a product or provide a service inside the firm or buy it in the marketplace. The choice depends on transactions costs.

KEY TERMS

corporate finance	limited liability	takeover	efficiency wages
proprietorship	retained earnings	principal-agent problem	centralization
partnership	Modigliani-Miller theorem	stock option	decentralization
corporation	credit rationing	piece rates	transactions costs

REVIEW QUESTIONS

1 Explain the difference between a proprietorship, a partnership, and a corporation.

2 Explain how the risk of bankruptcy and the tax treatment of dividends and interest payments affect the attractiveness of equity to a business. How does debt provide incentives for management to work harder?

3 Why might the market interpret the issue of new equity as a negative signal concerning the value of a company?

4 Do banks or small shareholders have greater effective control over a corporation? Is your answer the same for large shareholders?

5 What is credit rationing? Why does it occur?

6 What are the arguments for and against takeovers?

7 What is a principal-agent problem? How might ownership and incentive pay address this problem?

8 How do piece rates provide incentives to work hard? Why isn't there greater reliance on piece-rate systems?

9 What is efficiency wage theory?

10 What are the advantages and disadvantages of centralized and decentralized decision taking within a firm?

11 When will a firm try to do a job itself, and when will it try to hire someone to do it in the market?

PROBLEMS

1 Consider a firm that needs $350,000 in capital to get started. First, think about this firm organized as a proprietorship, where you put up $50,000 and borrow the rest from a bank. Second, think about this firm organized as a partnership, where you and nine friends each put up $5,000 and borrow the rest from a bank. Third, think about the firm organized as a corporation, where you and nine friends each buy $5,000 worth of stock and then borrow the rest from a bank. If the firm goes broke without earning any money, how large are your potential losses in each case?

2 Suppose that bankruptcy laws were changed to make it easier and less costly for a firm to declare bankruptcy. Would you expect these new laws to lead to more partnerships or to more corporations? Why?

3 Speak Software, a small firm attempting to design new computer software, applies for a bank loan to purchase some new computer hardware. The bank turns the company down for the loan. When Speak Software offers to pay a higher interest rate, the bank still turns it down. Explain why the bank might practice this form of credit rationing, using a diagram that compares the interest rate charged with the bank's expected return.

4 The Kitbits Company, which makes cat treats, has a stock price of $40 per share. A raider is trying to take over the company and is offering $50 per share. Shareholders must decide whether to sell their stock to the raider and take a $10 per share gain, or to hold on to the stock. Consider the effect of future management of the company. When might it make sense to hold on to the stock?

5 How might a firm harm itself in attempting to avoid a takeover? How might it strengthen itself in attempting to avoid a takeover?

6 Think up an incentive scheme that would encourage managers to take more risks.

7 Advances in computer technology have allowed some firms to monitor their typists by a system that counts the number of keystrokes they make in a given workday. Telephone operators are sometimes monitored according to how many calls they take, and how long they spend on an average call. Would you expect these changes to increase productivity? Why or why not?

8 Explain why a profit-maximizing firm might find that a department was making losses when costs of overhead are included, but might still decide to keep that department open.

9 A company is considering setting up two new divisions. One division would be a corporate fleet of cars, as an alternative to renting cars from existing firms. The other division would be an R & D laboratory, as an alternative to contracting out projects to labs. Consider issues of transactions costs and comparative advantage, and analyze the pros and cons of setting up these functions inside the company or bringing them from outside.

10 In several European countries there have been strong movements for worker participation in management, entailing, for instance, unions sending representatives to sit on the board of directors. Discuss the problem of getting worker representatives to act in the interests of the workers in terms of the principal-agent problem.

PART FOUR

The Public Sector

T he basic competitive model presented in Part Two focused on the private sector—firms and households. Yet government plays a central role in our modern economy. Over two fifths of the economy's output passes through the hands of the government (at the local, provincial, or federal level). Government programmes touch our lives—and our economy—in a myriad of ways. In Part Three we saw how government seeks to encourage competition and promote technological change. But we have yet to discuss some of the most important activities of the government—both what the government does and why.

Chapter 18 presents an overview of the role of government. Markets are generally very good at allocating goods and services, but there are some instances in which they fail to produce efficient outcomes. In some cases, referred to as *public goods,* markets cannot work because the goods can be used simultaneously by several individuals and because individuals cannot easily be excluded (so they cannot be forced to pay a price for the privilege of consuming). In other cases, externalities exist where some of the benefits or costs of production and use are not fully reflected in the price, so market outcomes are not efficient. Market inefficiencies may also occur because some of society's resources are unemployed. Markets may be inefficient because of imperfect information or limited competition. In each of these cases, the government may intervene to improve the efficiency of the allocation of resources. But, unlike the private sector, the government lacks the guidance and discipline of the profit motive. In a democratic society, different individuals have different preferences. Some would like the government to spend more money on education; others, more on parks; and still others, more on purchasing fighter aircraft. Government decision making may be influenced by lobbyists and pressure groups as well as by the self-interest of government bureaucrats. Chapter 18 discusses some of the problems facing collective decision making. While we have seen that markets often fail to allocate resources efficiently, government interventions are also subject to failure. Chapter 18 analyzes some of the systematic reasons for these public-sector failures.

In Chapter 19 we return to the subject of externalities, considering the impact of negative externalities upon the environment. In the last twenty-five years, governmental efforts to limit environmental degradation have enjoyed great success. We will explore the market failures that give rise to pollution and review the alternative ways in which governments have attempted to remedy those failures. We will also examine the depletion of natural resources, a growing concern in recent years: Do markets provide adequate incentives to conserve natural resources such as oil and mineral deposits? Finally, Chapter 19 discusses an important category of circumstances in which the consumption of certain products is mandated (as in compulsory education) or prohibited (as in illegal narcotics) by government. Here, government intervention is not only based on economic efficiency, but also on moral grounds.

Even when markets are efficient, how they allocate resources among individuals may appear to be socially unacceptable, leading to poverty, homelessness, and limited access to health care to name but a few examples. The distribution of income is a major concern of modern societies and their governments. What individuals have to spend depends not only on how much they earn, but also on how much they receive in transfers and pay in taxes. In Canada, governments actively redistribute income from the better off to the less well off by a combination of transfers to the poor and progressive income taxes. Chapter 20 provides a description of the Canadian tax system and evaluates it in terms of certain criteria. It also outlines the various types of transfers in place to assist the poor.

A related subject involves governmental social insurance programmes, also discussed in Chapter 20. Markets often fail to provide insurance against some of the most important risks that individuals face, including the loss of a job through unemployment or disability and the coverage of health expenses. Chapter 20 looks at these social insurance programmes and the problems they face today, as well as the broader role of government in redistribution.

18

GOVERNMENT AND PUBLIC DECISION MAKING

Most Canadians have great faith in our economic system, with its primary reliance on private markets. Yet despite this basic faith, we have a public, or governmental, sector that reaches out into all spheres of economic activity. How do economists explain the role of government in the economy?

In earlier chapters we saw how the profit system provides firms with the incentive to produce the goods consumers want. Prices give firms the incentive to economize on scarce resources. Prices also coordinate economic activity and signal changes in economic conditions. Private property provides incentives for individuals to invest in and to maintain buildings, machines, land, cars, and other possessions. Chapter 3 explained the incentives that motivate individuals and countries to engage in mutually advantageous trades and to specialize in areas of comparative advantage. Chapter 11 showed that free and competitive markets result in gains from the fullest exploitation of trade, leading to an efficient allocation of resources.

If this private-market system works so well, what role do economists see for the government? Economists recognize that the government must set

KEY QUESTIONS

1 What distinguishes the private from the public sector?

2 What explains the economic roles the government has undertaken?

3 What are externalities and public goods, and why do they imply that markets may not work well?

4 How has the role of government changed in recent decades? And how does the role of government in Canada compare with its role in other industrial countries?

5 How are public-sector decisions taken in a democracy? Does majority voting provide a unique and reasonable answer to policy issues?

6 What is the role of bureaucrats and interest groups in decision making in a democracy?

7 What are some of the current controversies concerning the role of government? Do the failures of the market system necessarily imply that government action is desirable?

8 What should be the relationship between federal and provincial governments? What activities should be undertaken by each?

and enforce the basic laws of society, including the protection of private property rights without which a market economy could not function, and provide a framework within which firms can compete fairly against one another. Beyond this, however, economists' understanding of the market's ability to answer the basic economic questions leads them to look hard at any additional function the government serves: Why are private markets not serving that function? This chapter will explore the roles the government has undertaken, and how, why, and how well it carries out those roles.

THE CHANGING ROLES OF GOVERNMENT

The appropriate balance between the public and private sectors is a subject of constant debate; different countries answer the question differently. In Hong Hong the public sector is small and government activities are severely limited. In China, the government tries to control virtually all aspects of economic activity. Between these extremes lies a wide spectrum. Canada falls roughly in the middle, somewhere between the United States and Western Europe. Like the United States, we rely largely on the private sector for the provision of goods and ser-

vices, but in the transportation, telecommunications, utilities, and broadcasting industries there is a mixture of public and private enterprises. And, as in Western Europe, governments in Canada plays a relatively active role in the provision of services such as health and postsecondary education.

The balance between government and the private sector seems to swing over time. From 1930 to 1970, in most countries governments took on an increasingly important role. In this period, many private industries were **nationalized,** taken over and run by the government. The provision of social programmes in health, welfare, and pensions expanded rapidly, especially in the postwar period. The 1980s and 1990s have been a time for retrenchment of the public sector and a reevaluation of its role, both in formerly communist countries like the former Soviet Union and most Eastern European countries and in Western industrialized countries. Some of these countries have been selling off their government enterprises to the private sector, referred to as **privatization.** In Canada, many Crown corporations have been privatized, though they have frequently been smaller ones which did not monopolize entire industries. There are still over fifty federal Crown corporations, ranging from the Bank of Canada to the Canadian Broadcasting Corporation to the Canadian Wheat Board. The provinces also have their own provincial Crown corporations. At the same time, government regulations that were in force in many industries, such as airlines, railroads, and trucking, have been reduced or eliminated, a process called **deregulation.**

THE PICTURE IN STATISTICS

Changes in the size and role of government can be seen clearly in government statistics measuring the share of the total output of the economy (gross domestic product, or GDP) devoted to government expenditures. In Canada today, expenditures by all levels of government are over 48 percent of GDP. This compares with about 20 percent in 1939, immediately before World War II. The figure for the United States is 36 percent, and in the industrialized countries overall it is 40 percent. Some of these expenditures include pure transfers of money rather than expenditures on goods and services. In Canada, government expenditures on goods and services are about 20 percent of GDP; in other words about one fifth of the output of the economy is used by the government.

Canada has a **federal structure of government,**

which means that government activities take place at several levels—federal, provincial, territorial, and local or municipal. The federal government is responsible for defence and foreign affairs, money and banking, international trade and investment, communications, pensions, and unemployment insurance. The provinces and territories and their municipalities are responsible for health, education, welfare, and natural resources within their boundaries, for the regulation of labour markets and non-bank financial institutions, and for the provision of services of a local nature. Joint federal-provincial responsibility has been exercised in the areas of agriculture, housing, and environmental protection. Through the use of grants to the provinces and territories, the federal government has been able to influence the provision of basic services by the provinces, especially in the areas of health, welfare, and transportation. Expenditures at all levels of government increased as a percentage of GDP until the early 1990s. They have declined somewhat in recent years as governments have imposed austerity measures designed to deal with budget deficit problems.

Figure 18.1, which shows the relative importance

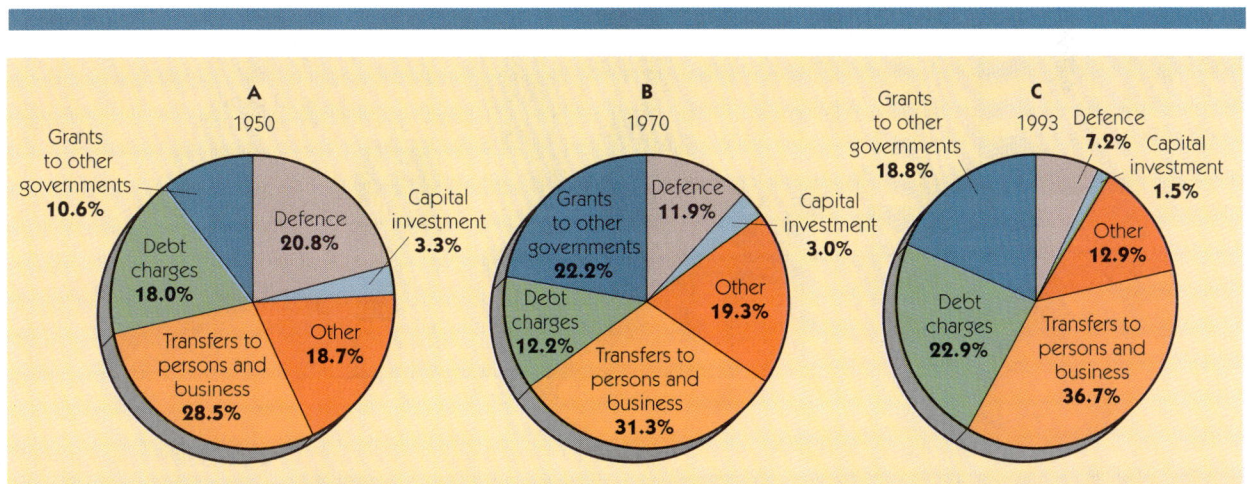

Figure 18.1 THE CHANGING PATTERN OF FEDERAL EXPENDITURES

The period 1950–93 has seen a marked decrease in the share of defence expenditures. Grants to other governments rose from 1950 to 1970 but then fell, while interest payments declined and then rose. *Source:* Canadian Tax Foundation, *The National Finances,* 1994 (Toronto: Canadian Tax Foundation, 1994), Table 3.7, p. 3.8.

The increase in government expenditures during the twentieth century has been dramatic, but major differences exist in the relative importance of such expenditures across countries. Expenditures in Japan and the United States are still among the smallest of the major industrial countries as a fraction of the economy: about one third. At the other end of the spectrum, about half of the GDPs of France and Germany are government expenditures. Canada falls between these two extremes: about two out of every five dollars of GDP go to government expenditures (this amount includes only government spending on programmes and not on interest on the public debt).

The composition of spending also varies considerably across countries. The United States spends a much higher proportion on defence; its nondefence expenditures are about 30 percent of GDP, roughly the same as Japan's. Nondefence expenditures in Canada are 38 percent, considerably larger than in the United States, but smaller than the 45 percent in France and Germany. A key difference is in social security and welfare programmes. They are close to 20 percent of GDP in Germany and France and about 16 percent of GDP in Canada. In the United States and Japan, these expenditures account for only about 8 percent of GDP.

These foreign comparisons mean different things to different people. Opponents of more government spending argue that Japan is a better model to emulate. Advocates of more government spending argue that the United States is an example of a country that is out of step.

PERCENTAGE OF GDP

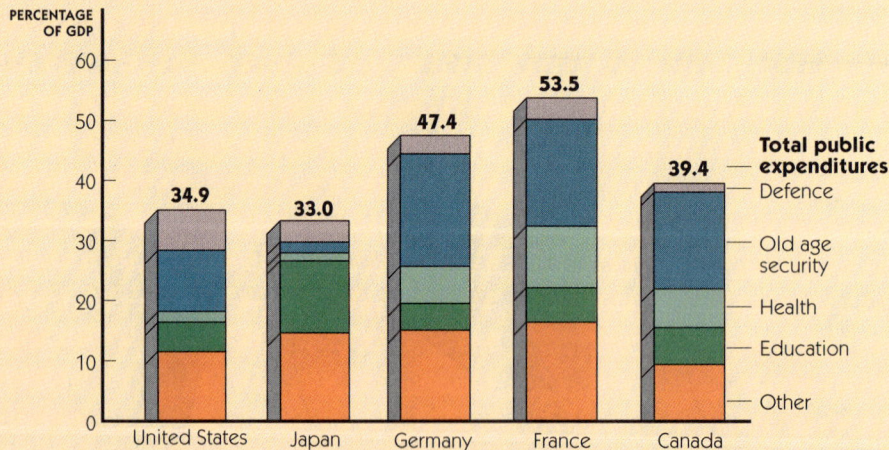

of different categories of federal expenditures in 1950, 1970, and 1993, helps us to see what accounts for this increase at the federal level. None of it is due to expenditures on goods and services; these have actually fallen as a percentage of GDP, largely owing to a decline in the importance of defence expenditures. Transfers to persons have increased rapidly, reflecting especially the growing importance of two categories of transfers, unemployment insurance and payments to the elderly. Grants to other levels of government have also increased significantly. In the 1960s, the federal government instituted some significant shared-cost programmes with the provinces in the areas of health and welfare. The Equalization scheme, whereby the federal government transfers funds to the less well off provinces, also increased in importance, especially in the 1970s, when resource revenues of the western provinces increased dramatically. More recently the growth of transfers to the provinces has declined relative to GDP as the federal government has reformed the major programmes to make them less costly.

Another factor contributing to the growth in federal government expenditures in the last decade has been the interest the government must pay on the huge debt it has been accumulating. During the 1970s and 1980s the government spent more than it took in in taxes and had to borrow to finance the difference and consequently must pay interest on that debt. These interest payments grew significantly during the 1980s, and they now account for over one quarter of the federal budget.

The expenditures of the provinces and their municipalities have grown more rapidly than those of the federal government. By 1994 they had risen to over 27 percent of GDP, a much larger percentage than that of the federal government. This increase reflects the rapid growth of provincial expenditures in the areas of health, welfare, and education as the provincial governments took more and more responsibility for providing these services on a comprehensive and accessible basis.

WHAT DISTINGUISHES THE PRIVATE AND PUBLIC SECTORS?

In a democracy, two important features distinguish private from public institutions. First, the people responsible for running public institutions are elected or appointed by someone who is elected. The legitimacy of the person holding the position is derived directly or indirectly from the electoral process. Second, any government has certain rights of compulsion. For instance, the Canadian government has the right to force its citizens to pay taxes; if they fail to do so, it can confiscate their property and even imprison them. The government has the right to force its young people to attend school and, in times of war, to serve in the armed forces. The government also has the right of **eminent domain,** which is the right to seize private property for public use, provided it compensates the owner fairly.

The government's ability to use compulsion means that it can do things private institutions cannot do. Once a decision has been taken to build a public road, for instance, a local government can make sure that everyone in town helps to pay for it. Sometimes governments create rules to bind their own hands, so that they cannot do *anything* they wish. For instance, the government has established elaborate hiring procedures for government organizations that private firms generally do not find worthwhile. The owner of a private firm can decide whom she wants to hire. If she hires someone incompetent, she and her firm suffer, but if the

---

THE CHANGING ROLE OF GOVERNMENT

Sources of expenditure growth in the early postwar period

    Increased provision of public service (health, education)

    Increases in transfer payments (unemployment insurance, pensions, welfare)

    Public enterprises

Retrenchment of government in the 1980s and 1990s

    Privatization

    Deregulation

    Fiscal restraint to reduce government debt

Characteristics of the public sector relative to the private

    Accountability to the electorate

    Right of compulsion (levy of taxes, eminent domain)

    Constitutional constraints

    Absence of profit motive

manager of a public enterprise hires someone incompetent, the public pays. The government's strict hiring procedures help avoid bad hiring, but they may also result in rigidities that make if difficult for government enterprises to compete against private firms for the most talented individuals.

In no sphere does the government of the day have absolute power. It is constrained to act according to the rules set out in the Constitution. For example, the government cannot discriminate on the basis of race, religion, or gender. Nor can it interfere with the rights of individuals to live where they choose. The ultimate constraint on government, of course, comes from the threat of being voted out of office at the next election.

These and other constraints imposed on the public sector—as well as the absence of the profit motive, which provides the private sector with strong incentives to be efficient, reduce costs, and produce what consumers want—put the public sector at a general disadvantage relative to the private sector in markets that work well. It is the job of economists concerned with the most efficient solutions to economic problems to ask: When do markets work well? When do they fail? And, when they fail, when might government improve matters?

ADAM SMITH'S "INVISIBLE HAND" AND THE CENTRAL ROLE OF MARKETS

The modern economic faith in private markets can be traced back to Adam Smith's 1776 masterpiece *The Wealth of Nations*. Smith argued that workers and producers, interested only in helping themselves and their families, were the root of economic production. The public interest would best be promoted by individuals pursuing their own self-interest. As Smith put it:

Man has almost constant occasion for the help of his brethren, and it is in vain for him to expect it from their benevolence only. He will be more likely to prevail if he can interest their self-love in his favor, and show them that it is for their own advantage to do for him what he requires of them. . . . It is not from the benevolence of the butcher, the brewer, or the baker, that we expect our dinner, but from their regard to their own interest. We . . . never talk to them of our own necessities but of their advantages.[1]

Smith's insight was that individuals work hardest to help the overall economic production of society when their efforts help themselves. He argued that an "obvious and simple system of liberty" provided the greatest opportunities for people to help themselves and thus, by extension, to create the greatest wealth for a society.

Smith used the metaphor of the **"invisible hand"** to describe how self-interest led to social good: "He intends only his own gain, and he is in this as in many other cases led by an invisible hand to promote an end which was no part of his intention. . . . By pursuing his own interest he frequently promotes that of the society more effectually than when he really intends to promote it."

Economics has progressed since Adam Smith, but his fundamental argument still has great appeal. Greater liberty for individuals in country after country has indeed led to huge increases in production that have benefited if not everyone, almost everyone. Nevertheless, it is not difficult to find discontent with the market. There is concern that markets produce too much of some things, like air and water pollution, and too little of other things, such as support for the arts or child care facilities. Generally, concern with market outcomes can be placed into two broad categories: those having to do with redistribution of income, and those having to do with genuine failures of private markets.

GOVERNMENT AND INEQUALITY

Market economies may be productive and efficient at producing wealth, but they may also cause some people to get very rich and others to starve. Someone who has a rare and valuable skill will, by the laws of supply and demand, receive a high in-

[1] Book 1, Chapter 2.

come. Someone else who has few skills, and common ones at that, will find his wage low—perhaps even too low for survival. This situation describes an economy with a very unequal distribution of income.

Most economists see an important role for the government in addressing income inequalities. In their view, society need not accept whatever distribution of income results from the workings of private markets. There are three ways that governments undertake that role. The first is by income redistribution policies that involve taking income from those who have more and giving it to those who have less. High income taxes on the rich and welfare programmes for the poor are part of the government's role in promoting equality.

The second is by providing security against misfortunes that can befall individuals in society and that cannot be insured against privately. This includes our system of universal health insurance to care for persons who fall ill, unemployment insurance for those who are temporarily unemployed, workers' compensation for those injured on the job, and disability pensions for those who are forced to retire early because of impairment. These programmes are referred to as **social insurance programmes,** and together they form the **social safety net.**

The third way governments address income inequality is by implementing programmes that equalize opportunities to earn incomes. The most important of these is the system of universal primary and secondary education that is available to all children.

Concern for greater economic equality is a generally accepted role for government, but there is still much disagreement about the benefits and costs of programmes aimed at reducing inequality. And even if government reaches agreement on the degree to which income inequality should be reduced, economists will disagree as to what is the best method because income redistribution affects incentive.

Questions of redistribution are often posed as, How should the economy's pie be divided? What size slice should each person get? The poorest 20 percent of the population get a relatively small slice—only 3.2 percent of the economy's income—while the richest 20 percent of the population get a relatively large slice, 46.6 percent of the economy's income. Often redistribution is viewed as simply cut-

ting the pie differently, giving the poor somewhat larger slices and the rich somewhat smaller. But if the process of redistributing income weakens economic incentives and makes the economy less productive, the size of the whole pie will shrink. Then the poor get a larger share of a smaller pie. The rich are much worse off now—they get a smaller share of a smaller pie. If the size of the pie has shrunk enough, even the poor may be worse off. By designing governments redistribution programmes appropriately, it may be possible to limit the size of these effects on productivity.

GOVERNMENT AND MARKET FAILURES

The second category of discontent with private markets concerns areas where the market does indeed fail in its role of producing economic efficiency. Economists refer to these problems as **market failures,** and have studied them closely. When there is a market failure, government may be able to correct the market failure and enhance the economy's efficiency.

STABILIZATION OF THE ECONOMY

The most dramatic example of market failures is the periodic episodes of high unemployment that have plagued capitalist economies. It is hard to tout the virtues of an efficient market when a fifth of the industrial labour force and capital stock sits idle, as it did in the Great Depression of the 1930s. Although many economists believe there are forces that eventually restore the economy to full employment, the costs of waiting for the economy to correct itself—in terms of both forgone output and human misery—are enormous, and virtually all governments today take it as their responsibility to try to avoid extreme fluctuations in economic activity—both the downturns (when much of the economy's resources, its workers and machines, remain idle) and the booms (which may result in high inflation). The causes of these fluctuations, and how and whether the government can succeed in significantly reducing them, are topics in macroeconomics.

Even when the economy is at full employment, resources will not be efficiently allocated if (1) competition is limited, (2) there are externalities, (3) public goods are involved, and (4) information is limited.

LACK OF COMPETITION

Competition is essential for a market to function efficiently. Competition is what forces firms to look for more efficient ways of producing goods and to meet the desires of consumers more effectively. Without competition, prices will be higher and production lower than with competition. But life for the firms themselves is easier without competition, and profits are higher. Thus, firms try to reduce the extent of competition. As we saw in Chapter 14, governments have passed anti-combines laws in an attempt to enhance competition in the market economy.

EXTERNALITIES

But even when there is competition, the market may supply too much of some goods and too little of others. One of the reasons for this is the presence of **externalities.** Externalities are present whenever an individual or firm can take an action that directly affects others but for which it neither pays nor is paid compensation. It therefore does not bear all the consequences of its action. The effect of the action is "external" to the individual or firm; it is not reflected in any prices or costs associated with the action. Externalities are pervasive. A hiker who litters, a driver whose car emits pollution, a child who leaves a mess behind after he finishes playing, a person who smokes a cigarette in a crowded room—all create externalities. In each case, the actor is not the only one who must suffer the consequences of his action; others suffer them too. Externalities can be thought of as instances when the price system works imperfectly. The hiker is not "charged" for the litter she creates, nor does the car owner pay for the pollution his car makes.

Externalities can also be positive. A common example of a positive externality is a new invention, as we learned in Chapter 15. When someone makes a new discovery that leads to greater economic productivity, other people or companies benefit. The inventor receives, through the prices he charges, only a fraction of the total gains to society from the invention. Other firms will copy it and learn from it. Inventions like the laser and the transistor have benefited consumers, both by providing new products and allowing other products to be made less expensively. The individual researcher bears the costs of making a discovery, but society receives positive external benefits. If everyone who benefited from an invention had to pay money to the inventor, there would be far higher incentives for research and development. And indeed, patents and other government laws enable the inventors to get a larger return than they otherwise would.

When externalities are present, the market's allocation of goods will be inefficient. When the production of a good such as steel entails a negative externality—like smoke and its effect on the air—the market level of production is too high. This is because the producer fails to take into account the "social costs" in deciding how much to produce. To put it another way, the price of steel determined in competitive markets by the law of supply and demand only reflects *private costs*, the costs actually faced by firms. If firms do not have to pay *all* of the costs (including the costs of pollution), equilibrium prices will be lower and output higher than they would be if firms took social costs into account.

The government can offset this effect in several ways. For instance, it might impose a tax. Panel A of Figure 18.2 shows the demand and supply curves for steel, and depicts the market equilibrium at the intersection of the two curves, Q_0. The supply curve for steel before tax reflects the private costs of production to steel producers for supplying varying amounts. At the equilibrium quantity Q_0, the price p_0 is the marginal benefit to demanders of the last unit produced, and also the marginal private cost to firms of producing the last unit, c_0. The externality is not taken into account. The role of the tax is to increase the costs faced by the producers. If the government imposes a tax on the production of steel,

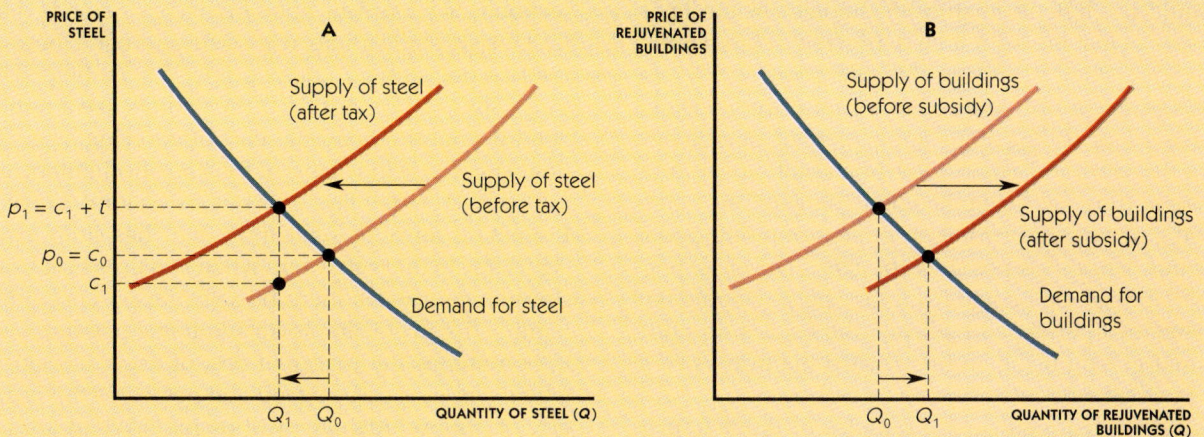

Figure 18.2 SUPPLY, DEMAND, AND EXTERNALITIES

The steel industry produces a negative externality of pollution. In panel A, a tax on steel production shifts the supply curve to the left, reducing both steel production and pollution. In panel B, a subsidy for rejuvenated buildings, which create the positive externality of neighbourhood beautification, shifts the supply curve to the right, causing more buildings and neighbourhoods to be renovated.

the supply curve will shift to the left, and the equilibrium level of production will be less, Q_1. If the government could set the tax equal to the value of the externality emitted by the firm, the market price including the tax would reflect the full social cost of production and the efficient amount would be produced. In panel A, at the new equilibrium, the private cost is c_1. If the tax t is set equal to the external cost, the price faced by consumers, p_1, will equal the private cost plus the external cost, or the social cost, of production.

Similarly, when the production of a good involves positive externalities, the market level of production is too low, and the government can try to enlarge the supply. The rejuvenation of an apartment building in a decaying part of a city is an example of a positive externality; it will probably enhance the value of buildings around it. Panel B of Figure 18.2 shows the demand and supply curves for rejuvenated buildings. A government subsidy for rejuvenation shifts the supply curve to the right, increasing the number of rejuvenated buildings from Q_0 to Q_1.

PUBLIC GOODS

A particular category of goods, called **public goods,** is an extreme case of positive externalities. Public goods are goods that it costs nothing extra for an additional individual to enjoy (their consumption is **nonrivalrous**), and that it costs a great deal to exclude any individual from enjoying (they are **nonexcludable**). The standard example of a public good is defence. Once Canada is protected from attack, it costs nothing extra to protect each new citizen from foreign invasion. Furthermore, it would be virtually impossible to exclude a new citizen from the benefits of this protection.

Public parks along the sides of a highway are another example. Anyone driving along the highway enjoys the view. The fact that one person is enjoying the view does not exclude others from enjoying it; and it would in fact be expensive to stop anyone who is driving along the highway from benefiting from the view. A lighthouse to guide ships around dangerous shoals or rocks is still another example of a public good. No additional costs are incurred as an additional ship navigates near the lighthouse, and it would be difficult to shut off the light in the lighthouse at just the right time to prevent a ship passing by from taking advantage of the lighthouse.

A **pure public good** is one where the marginal costs of providing it to an additional person are strictly zero and where it is impossible to exclude people from receiving the good. Many public goods that government provides are not *pure* public goods in this sense. It is possible, though relatively expensive, to exclude people from (or charge people for) using an uncrowded highway; the cost of an additional person using an uncrowded highway is very, very small, but not zero.

Figure 18.3 compares examples of publicly provided goods against the strict definition of a pure public good. It shows the ease of exclusion along the horizontal axis and the (marginal) cost of an additional individual using the good along the vertical axis. The lower left-hand corner represents a pure public good. Of the major public expenditures, only national defence is close to a pure public good. Completely uncongested highways, to the extent that they exist, are another example. The upper right-hand corner represents a pure private good (health services or education), where the cost of exclusion is low and the marginal cost of an additional individual using the good is high.

Many goods are not pure public goods but have one or the other property to some degree. Fire protection is like a private good in that exclusion is relatively easy—individuals who refuse to contribute to the fire department could simply not be helped in the event of a fire. But fire protection is like a public good in that the marginal cost of covering an additional person is low. Most of the time, firefighters are not engaged in fighting fires but are waiting for calls. Protecting an additional individual has little extra cost. Only in that rare event when two fires break out simultaneously will there be a significant cost to extending fire protection to an additional person.

Sometimes the marginal cost of using a good to which access is easy (a good that possesses the property of nonexcludability) will be high. When an uncongested highway turns congested, the costs of using it rise dramatically, not in terms of wear and tear on the road but in terms of the time lost by drivers using the road. It is costly to exclude by charging for road use—as a practical matter, this can only be done on toll roads, and, ironically, the tollbooths often contribute to the congestion.

Many of the goods that are publicly provided, such as education and health services, have high costs associated with providing the service to additional individuals. For most of these goods, exclusion is also relatively easy. In fact, many of these goods and services are provided privately in some coun-

Figure 18.3 PUBLICLY PROVIDED GOODS

Pure public goods are characterized by nonrivalrous consumption (the marginal cost of an additional individual enjoying the good is zero) and nonexcludability (the cost of excluding an individual from enjoying the good is prohibitively high). Goods provided by the public sector differ in the extent to which they have these two properties.

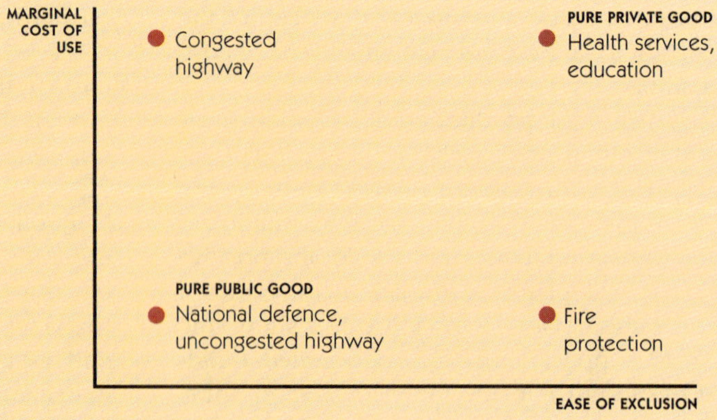

tries, or provided both publicly and privately. Though they are publicly provided in this country, they are not *pure* public goods, in the technical sense in which the term is defined.

Private markets undersupply public goods. If a single shipowner used the port near which a lighthouse is constructed, he could weigh the costs and benefits of the lighthouse. But if there were one large shipowner and many smaller owners, it would not pay any one of the small owners to build the lighthouse, and the large shipowner, in deciding whether to construct the lighthouse, would only take into account the benefits he would receive, not the benefits to the small shipowners. If the costs of construction exceeded the benefits that he alone would receive, he would not build the lighthouse. But if the benefits accruing to *all* the shipowners, large and small, were taken into account, those benefits would exceed the costs; it would then be desirable to build the lighthouse.

One can imagine a voluntary association of shipowners getting together to construct a lighthouse in this situation. But what happens if some small shipowner refuses to contribute, thinking that even if he does not contribute, the lighthouse will be built anyway? This is the **free-rider** aspect of public goods; because it is difficult to preclude anyone from using them, those who benefit from the goods have an incentive to avoid paying for them. Every shipowner has an incentive to free-ride on the efforts of others. When too many decide to do this, the lighthouse will not be built.

Governments bring an important advantage to bear on the problem of public goods. They have the power to coerce citizens to pay for them. There might be *some* level of purchase of public goods—lighthouses, highway parks, even police or fire ser-vices—in the absence of government intervention. But society would be better off if the level of production were increased, and citizens were forced to pay for the increased level of public services through taxes.

INFORMATION AND KNOWLEDGE

The efficiency with which it handles information is one of the great strengths of the market economy. Producers do not have to know what each consumer likes; and consumers do not have to know the details of production of any of the products which they consume. Prices convey information about scarcity. Working through the law of supply and demand, prices convey information from consumers to producers about how consumers value different goods, and from producers to consumers about the resources required (at the margin) to produce different goods.

But some kinds of information, like information about the weather, are public goods: the marginal cost of an additional individual benefiting from the information is negligible, and the cost of excluding individuals from this information may be considerable. This kind of information can also be important for efficient functioning of the economy, but markets do not produce efficient amounts of it. Thus, weather information is supplied by Environment Canada, a department of the federal government.

Earlier, we saw how innovations typically give rise to externalities. Research can be thought of as the process of acquiring information, and innovation as the process of translating ideas, information, into new products. We discussed in Chapter 15 the array of government actions and programmes whose

ECONOMIC ROLES FOR THE GOVERNMENT

Addressing inequality

Correcting major market failures

    Episodes of high unemployment

    Lack of competition

Externalities

Public goods

Information and knowledge (including innovation)

purpose is to ensure not only that the level of resources allocated to knowledge acquisition is appropriate, but that they are directed in the right way.

BEYOND MARKET FAILURES

Government actions are of course not limited to issues of economics. Governments try to discourage robbery, rape, and murder. By and large, however, so long as individuals' actions do not directly affect another person, they are left to do what they please. I may think it strange that someone prefers vanilla to chocolate ice cream, or cherry to blueberry pie, but why should I impose my preferences? The principle that individuals are the best judges of what is in their own interests and that their preferences should be respected is called the **principle of consumer sovereignty.** There are, however, instances when government violates this principle. Smoking marijuana may not cause anyone else harm, yet smoking marijuana is a criminal offence. Until recently there were various localities in Canada that were "dry," that is, where the sale of alcohol was prohibited, so that individuals' preferences to purchase alcohol were overridden by a local government prohibition. Often, other rationales (such as externalities) for such actions are put forward, yet the underlying basis for government action remains inconsistent with the principle of consumer sovereignty. One of the reasons for prohibiting the sale of alcohol was the ill effects of drinking on others, such as alcohol-related accidents, yet the view that drinking was *morally* wrong was what provided the fervour to the prohibition movement.

Government intervenes not only to discourage or prohibit certain actions but to encourage or force others—for instance, it requires parents to send their children to school. Goods the government encourages because it believes there is some "public interest" in their consumption that is not an externality (although it goes beyond the private interests of those consuming the goods) are called **merit goods.** In addition to education for children, other examples of merit goods are the broadcasting of Canadian news, the support of Canadian culture in areas of music, art, and literature, and the encouragement of charitable and nonprofit organizations.

GOVERNMENT'S OPTIONS

Once society has decided that government should do something, there is a second question: How can government accomplish society's ends most efficiently? The government has four choices. It can do something directly, it can provide incentives for the private sector to do something, it can mandate the private sector to do something, or it can take some combination of these.

TAKING DIRECT ACTION

One option is for the government simply to take charge itself. If it believes there is a market failure in the provision of education it can provide educational services itself, as is done in all provinces and territories in Canada. If it believes there is market failure in the provision of housing for the poor, it can build government housing projects.

Direct action does not, however, require the government to produce the good itself. It can also purchase it from the private sector. Thus, the military purchases virtually all of the equipment it uses from the private sector. Although the government operates a comprehensive medical insurance system, the hospitals are not run by the government, nor are doctors members of the public service. Those provinces that operate public automobile insurance schemes use the services of independent firms to administer them.

PROVIDING INCENTIVES TO THE PRIVATE SECTOR

The government can also choose to operate at a distance, providing incentives to alter the workings of private markets in desirable ways. It can provide such incentives directly through subsidies, as it does for agriculture, or indirectly through the tax system, as is more commonly done in Canada. The government has used energy tax credits to encourage energy conservation. It has also used an investment tax credit, which gives firms a tax break for investing in

GOVERNMENT'S OPTIONS

Taking direct action

    Production of a good or service

    Purchase of a good or service

Providing incentives to the private sector

    Subsidies

    Taxes

Mandating private-sector action

---

new machines, to encourage investment. And special provisions of the income tax encourage employers to provide disability insurance and pensions for their employees by reducing the cost of these benefits to the firm.

Subsidies and taxes put the government in the position of manipulating the price system to achieve its ends. If the government is worried about the supply of adequate housing for the poor, it can provide builders with direct payments or it can grant tax reductions for those who make investments in slum areas. Both lower the price to the builder of building housing. If the government wants to encourage oil conservation, it can impose a tax on oil or gasoline, which will encourage conservation by raising the price of oil. It can also tax cars that are not energy-efficient, raising their price.

MANDATING ACTION IN THE PRIVATE SECTOR

Concern about the effectiveness of incentives in achieving the desired result or about their cost, in tax forgiveness or outright payments, may lead government to mandate the desired action. A mandate is simply a requirement backed up by the threat of legal punishment. The government may mandate that private firms provide a safe work environment for their employees. The government may mandate that automobile manufacturers produce fuel-efficient cars, specifying particular standards for kilometres per litre of gas. Real estate developers who want to get a permit for a large housing project may be required to provide a certain number of units for low-income individuals, or to help improve a local road or build a local school. In all these cases, the government re-

quirement does not show up as a cost on the government's budget. Mandates do have costs, however. These costs are borne indirectly by workers, firms, and consumers, and can be very high.

GOVERNMENT FAILURES

Whenever there is a market failure, there is a *potential* role for government. Government needs to consider each of the alternatives discussed in the previous section, and assess the likelihood that one or the other alternative will succeed. Such an assessment may conclude that it is better not to intervene after all. Recent decades have provided numerous examples of government programmes that either have not succeeded to the extent their sponsors had hoped or have failed altogether. Regional development programmes meant to generate private-sector economic activity in depressed regions and to make them more self-sufficient often ended up making some of those regions more rather than less dependent on government assistance. Welfare programmes, intended to provide a safety net for the poor, are thought by some to have helped perpetuate the cycle of poverty. Out of the failures and limited successes of government programmes has emerged a better understanding of the causes of government failure.

IMPERFECT INFORMATION

Imperfect information poses a problem in the public as well as the private sector. The government would like to make sure, for instance, that welfare assistance goes only to those who really need it. But it is costly to sort out the truly deserving from those who are not. Spending more on screening applicants lets fewer of the undeserving through the application process. But spending more on administration leaves less to spend on benefits. As always, there are trade-offs.

INCENTIVES AND THE EFFICIENCY OF GOVERNMENT

Problems of incentives can be worse in the public than in the private sector. In the private sector, homeowners have an incentive to maintain their property, not only because an attractive house is more enjoyable to live in, but also because when they sell, an attractive house will yield a higher price. Similarly, owners of a private apartment building have incentives to maintain the building. And tenants in private apartments have an incentive not to abuse the property: they can be evicted or fail to have their lease renewed. Tenants in public housing have no such incentives. From their perspective, the quality of their apartment building is like a public good; each individual has too little incentive to maintain public amenities. Managers of public housing have no incentives comparable to private landlords, since they typically have limited discretion in evicting tenants or even in refusing to renew leases. The problem of incentives is made worse in the public sector because public officials work under a set of civil service rules about salary levels and job tenure that can make it difficult to hire first-rate workers or to reward workers for efficient performance. The rules make it difficult to pay good public officials a salary comparable to what similarly qualified and hardworking people receive in the private sector, or to offer them opportunities for rapid promotion. It is even more difficult to fire or demote incompetent and lazy workers.

Incentives in the public sector can actually lead to perverse decisions that are against broad social welfare. Legislators' concern about votes leads to discretionary public spending whose primary value is to create jobs or improve amenities in a legislator's home riding. Presumably, most such projects would not be undertaken if those who lived in the riding had to pay for it themselves, but the projects sound good if the rest of the country is footing the bill. For example, it is widely believed that a large number of unneeded military bases have been kept open because of political pressure.

Moreover, elected officials need funds to run their campaigns, and this makes them particularly attentive to those who can assist with campaign finances. The influence of the farm lobby in obtaining support far out of proportion to the number of voters whose livelihoods depend on agriculture is frequently attributed to this sort of special-interest lobbying. Businesses and their associations have traditionally provided financial support to the major political parties, especially the Liberals and Conservatives. Unions, on the other hand, have supported the New Democratic Party. Naturally, lobbyists for these special-interest groups claim that they are not buying politicians, simply providing them with information needed to make an informed judgment.

WASTE IN GOVERNMENT

Whether for these or other reasons, many Canadians view government as *necessarily* less efficient than private firms. These views have been supported by some statistical studies that show systematically higher costs associated with municipalities that operate their own utilities and local services as opposed to contracting them out to private firms. While there are numerous instances of government inefficiency, when one views all the evidence, it casts doubt on the view that the public sector is inevitably less efficient than the private sector. For instance, when government enterprises are subjected to competition—as in the case of the Canadian National Railways (a government enterprise), which competes vigorously against the Canadian Pacific Railways—the discipline of competition forces them to be equally efficient. The administrative costs of many private insurance companies, amounting to up to 30 percent or more of the premiums, are considerably higher than the administrative expenses of public social insurance such as Medicare. France's state-run electricity company is reputedly as efficient as any private firm.

There are also theoretical reasons to question the conclusion that public enterprises are doomed to be less efficient. This is because *some* of the problems

POLICY PERSPECTIVE: THE TAXPAYER AS CUSTOMER

As both the federal and provincial levels of government in Canada deal with debt and deficit problems, Canadians are certain to be paying more in taxes than they receive in services for years to come, the balance going to service and/or reduce the debt. This has led governments to search for new ways to deliver services at lower cost and to make these services more effective at achieving programme objectives.

One new approach has been tried recently in New Brunswick. Called "Service New Brunswick," it applies the principles of one of the latest management strategies, Total Quality Management (T.Q.M.), to the provision of government services. The principal ideas behind T.Q.M. are focusing on the customer (here, the taxpayer), rethinking inefficient processes, and encouraging employee input. The result is a new form of government office in which a staff trained in many areas is able to provide up to 60 services at a single location. Driver's licence renewals, income assistance inquiries and applications, and the payment of provincial government–owned utility bills are some of the services available at these "one-stop shopping" locations. In addition, the province is taking advantage of new technology by installing computer kiosks in smaller centres that cannot support large service centres. These kiosks can be used by taxpayers to obtain access to provincial government services.

Combined with the new approach to the delivery of services is a renewed attention to measuring the performance of the public sector, a notoriously difficult matter owing to the nature of the "product" produced by many government programmes. But valid measurement is seen as being important to the ability of the government to set clear goals and to assess progress towards these goals.

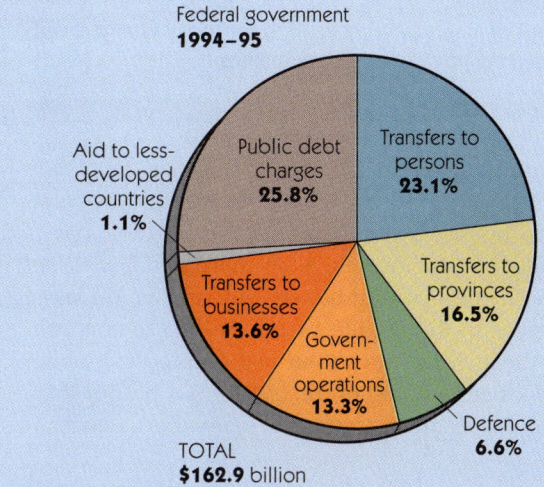

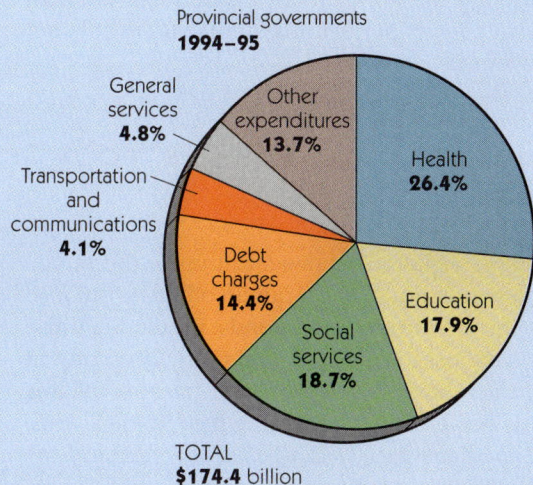

**Federal government
1994–95**

Aid to less-developed countries **1.1%**

Public debt charges **25.8%**

Transfers to persons **23.1%**

Transfers to provinces **16.5%**

Transfers to businesses **13.6%**

Government operations **13.3%**

Defence **6.6%**

TOTAL **$162.9** billion

**Provincial governments
1994–95**

General services **4.8%**

Other expenditures **13.7%**

Health **26.4%**

Transportation and communications **4.1%**

Debt charges **14.4%**

Education **17.9%**

Social services **18.7%**

TOTAL **$174.4** billion

No one can say for sure that the New Brunswick approach will be widely emulated by other governments, or whether some other model will emerge in other jurisdictions. One thing is certain however: governments will continue to search for ways of dealing with increasing demands in a time of diminishing resources.

Source: "The Taxpayer as Customer," *Globe and Mail Report on Business* magazine, January 1995, pp. 86–90.

CAUSES OF FAILURES OF PUBLIC PROGRAMMES

Imperfect information

Problems of incentives, particularly for those charged with administering government programmes

Waste in government

Failure to assess the full consequences of government programmes, including responses of the private sector

generating inefficiencies in the public sector plague the private sector also. Public-sector employees typically do not receive any incentive pay—their pay is not linked to performance, so there are few *direct* returns to performing better; but neither do most employees in the private sector. And large corporations, those with more than 500 employees, which still produce one half of the economy's output, face the same types of bureaucratic problems as government.

A consensus is thus emerging among economists that although the government is *often* less efficient than private firms performing similar tasks, it is not necessarily so.

UNFORESEEN RESPONSES TO A PROGRAMME

The success or failure of programmes in the public sector depends not only on public officials, but also on how the private sector responds. Predicting those private responses is difficult, and many government programmes have faced problems because of this difficulty. For example, providing free medical care to all Canadians greatly increased the demand for medical services by the aged, leading to increases in costs well beyond those originally projected. Government student loan programmes neglected to take into account the incentives of those with large debts to declare bankruptcy after completing their education when they had almost no assets to lose.

Another example of an unforeseen private-sector response to a government programme occurred a few years ago, when the government waged an aggressive campaign against cigarette smoking. Among the measures taken was a significant increase in the excise tax on cigarettes. This caused the price of cigarettes in Canada to be much higher than in the United States. This price differential made it more attractive for persons to engage in smuggling cigarettes across the border for illegal resale in Canada at lower prices; smuggled cigarettes included Canadian cigarettes previously exported to the United States free of tax. It has been suggested that in some border areas at least one quarter of the cigarettes purchased by consumers were smuggled, thereby partly defeating the purpose of the excise tax on cigarettes, which was to discourage smoking by raising the price.

Often a problem arises not from the overall design of a government programme, but from a particular regulation. When the federal government introduced the Scientific Research Tax Credit (S.R.T.C.) in 1981, offering a refundable tax credit to encourage Canadian firms to engage in scientific research, many businesses claimed the credit without ever engaging in the research. The programme ended up costing the federal treasury several billions of dollars with very little scientific research to show for it. The problem was that the credit was paid out before any research was undertaken, and this enabled some persons to abuse the system.

AN APPRAISAL OF THE ROLE OF GOVERNMENT

The appropriate role of government is one of the most highly contested political issues. Consider the case of government's role in income redistribution. There are disagreements in assessing the trade-offs, such as the magnitude of the negative incentive effects arising from taxes upon the well-off to finance programmes for the poor. And even if there were agreement about the magnitude of the incentive effects, there may be disagreements about whether the costs—in terms of reduced efficiency and reduced welfare of those who are hurt by higher taxes—are worth the gains—in terms of the benefits to the poor who are helped. Also, there are disagreements about basic values, such as whether the higher income of the well-off is their "just reward" for greater effort. Nonetheless, while there is disagreement about what role the government ought to play in the economy, there is general consensus among economists over the important role the government currently does play. This is our tenth consensus point:

10 The Role of Government

> Government plays an important role in modern economies: it redresses market failures, redistributes income, and provides social insurance against risks such as unemployment, health care costs, disability, and retirement. Although the design and scope of government activity are often debated, there is broad agreement about the importance of the role of government in the economy.

DECISION MAKING IN A DEMOCRACY

In a democracy, the wishes of the majority are supposedly reflected in the actions government takes. Political scientists focus on the whole range of issues and actors that define the political process, including party policy formation, interest groups, and the media. Economists have a narrower focus, analyzing how rational individuals express their preferences

through the political process of voting, and how, in models of the political process, their votes are reflected in the public choices that mark collective decision making.

THE VOTING PARADOX

Governments are not always consistent in their actions. This may not be surprising, given that government choices do not reflect the preferences of a single individual. This is referred to as the **voting paradox.** More fundamentally, majority voting may not yield a determinate outcome even when only three people choose among only three alternatives, as was noted more than two hundred years ago by the French mathematician and political philosopher Marquis de Condorcet. Consider the simple example of three people who want to go to a movie together. They have narrowed their choices down to three movies, ranked as shown in the table below.

When they compare each of the movies, they find that *Young and Romantic* is preferred over *Third and Goal to Go* by a 2–1 margin and that *Third and Goal to Go* is also preferred to *Automatic Avengers* by a 2–1 margin. Taking this information alone, they might reason that—since *Young and Romantic* is preferred over *Third and Goal to Go* and *Third and Goal to Go* is preferred over *Automatic Avengers*—*Young and Romantic* is also preferred to *Automatic Avengers*. But when they put it to a vote, they find that *Automatic Avengers* is preferred to *Young and Romantic* by a 2–1 margin. There is no majority winner. Majority voting can rank any two of these choices, but is incapable of ranking all three of them.

The American economist and Nobel laureate Kenneth Arrow proved an even more remarkable

	Jessica's preferences	Ralph's preferences	Brutus's preferences
First choice	Young and Romantic	Third and Goal to Go	Automatic Avengers
Second choice	Third and Goal to Go	Automatic Avengers	Young and Romantic
Third choice	Automatic Avengers	Young and Romantic	Third and Goal to Go

result. All voting systems (two-thirds majority, weighted majority, or any other) yield the same lack of a clear outcome in certain circumstances. Inconsistencies are simply inherent in the decision-taking process of any democratic government. The only way around this problem, to ensure that consistent choices are made, is to entrust a single individual with all decisions. Such a system yields consistent choices, but is hardly democratic!

THE MEDIAN VOTER

Fortunately, inconsistencies in democratic decision taking are not inevitable. What happens if there is a vote over a simple issue like how much to spend on public schools? Some individuals want more to be spent, some less. Whose preferences dominate? The answer depends on the rules by which decisions are taken. The **median voter theory** provides a remarkably simple prediction of the outcome in the case of majority voting. It is the median voter—half of the population want more to be spent than this voter, and half want less—whose preferences dominate. For instance, assume the median voter wants $5,000 to be spent per pupil and there are 40,001 voters. Consider a vote between $5,000 per pupil and $3,000, and 20,000 voters favouring $5,100 or more and 20,000 favouring $3,000 or less. Since all of those who want $5,100 or more spent will vote for $5,000, $5,000 will win. It gets 20,001 votes. This is the choice the median voter would have made if the decision had been left to her. The same outcome would result if the vote was between $5,000 and a larger amount. The median voter would join those wanting even less than $5,000, ensuring that $5,000 wins.

Of course, voters do not decide most issues directly but elect politicians who vote on issues. Politicians, however, want to get elected. To increase the likelihood that they get elected, they take positions that will increase the number of votes they receive. If both parties take positions to maximize their votes, both will take positions reflecting the views of the median voter.

To understand this point, imagine that the amounts different individuals would like the government to spend are arranged from the smallest to the largest. Suppose there are two parties, and one party

takes the position reflecting the individual at the 40th percentile: 40 percent would like the government to spend less; 60 percent would like it to spend more. The other party will win simply by taking a position close to that of the voter representing the 41st percentile. That party would get 59 percent of the vote— a landslide. Of course, the first party knows this and tries to find a position such that the opposition cannot undercut it and win a majority. There are thus strong incentives for both parties to take positions closely reflecting the views of the median voter.

This theory explains why voters often feel that they do not have a choice: the two parties are both trying to find the middle position, so that they will not be defeated. It also gives us a way of forecasting government behaviour: government will approximate the interests of the median voter.

It is important to stress that the median voter theory does not resolve the voting paradox. As long as there is a single variable being voted upon—say the level of expenditure on education—and different individuals have a "most preferred" level and vote for outcomes closer to that level, then the median voter will determine the outcome. But when alternatives cannot be simply ranked in terms of "more" or "less" (as in the three-movie example given earlier), the voting paradox will arise and there is no clear theoretical prediction of the outcome of the electoral process.

INTEREST GROUPS AND RENT SEEKING

The median voter theory is neat, but frequently government action does not even remotely reflect the interests of the median voter but more nearly represents interests of particular groups.

One economic explanation for this has to do with the increasing needs of candidates for funds to run successfully for election, and the willingness of special-interest groups to provide those funds as long as their interests are served. In Canadian politics, these groups argue that it is in the general interest for their special interests to be served. Thus, the textile manufacturers want protection from "unfair" foreign competition; the dairy industry argues for maintenance of its marketing boards; the gas and oil industry argues for subsidies through the tax system, stressing the importance of energy for the Canadian economy.

Economists refer to these activities as **rent seeking.** Rents, as we learned in Chapter 10, are returns enjoyed by a factor of production that go beyond those required to elicit its supply. The term "rent *seeking*" is used when individuals or firms devote their energies to the procurement of rents or other special favours from the government. Government, through its power to tax, to set tariffs, to provide subsidies, and to intervene in other ways with private markets, can affect the profitability of various enterprises enormously. For example, the attempt by car producers to restrict foreign competition is referred to as rent seeking. As a result of protection from foreign competition, they find that they can get higher prices and make bigger profits.

As long as the government has the discretion to grant rents and other special favours, firms and individuals will find that it pays to engage in rent-seeking behaviour—to persuade government to grant them tariffs or other benefits—and the decisions of government accordingly get distorted. It makes little difference whether this behaviour comes in the form of direct bribes, as is frequently the case in less developed countries, or campaign contributions that serve to influence how politicians vote. Either way, a second aspect of government behaviour has emerged: governments respond to the rent-seeking behaviour of special-interest groups.

BUREAUCRACIES

The final aspect of government behaviour that we will take up is the theory of bureaucracy, which involves a principal-agent problem. The government consists not only of elected officials, but also of those appointed by elected officials and the civil service, whose job it is to administer government programmes. Just as in the private sector managers' interests may not perfectly coincide with those of shareholders, in the government sector public managers may not do what the electorate, or its elected representatives, would ideally like—or what is, in some broader sense, in the public interest.

Even if they are partly concerned with doing a good job, bureaucrats are also concerned with their own careers. For instance, concern about making mistakes may lead them to act in a risk-averse manner. Because it is so difficult to assess the "output" of administrators, performance may be judged more on the extent to which an individual has conformed to certain bureaucratic procedures, which partially accounts for the proliferation of red tape. Bureaucrats may have an interest in expanding their spheres of influence, just as any businessperson has an interest in the growth of her business. But while a businessperson expands her business by providing a good at a cheaper price, bureaucrats expand their influence by persuading the legislature either that they need more funds or personnel to do what has to be done, or that there should be more of whatever it is they do. This leads to competition among bureaucrats that may have deleterious effects.

DECENTRALIZATION AND THE FEDERAL ROLE

Canada was formed in 1867 by the joining together of four separate British colonies into a single federal nation; distinct responsibilities were assigned to the federal and provincial levels of government. Ever since that time, debate has raged not only about government's role generally, but also about the role of the federal government in contrast to that of the provinces and municipalities. This has been especially true of the post–World War II period, which has seen a dramatic rise in the share of economic activity passing through government and a growing sense in many provincial capitals that they would like to be more the masters of their own destiny.

In fact, Canada has gradually become more decentralized since the war. Much of the increase in government expenditures has occurred in areas that are the legislative responsibility of the provinces, such as education, health, and welfare. While the federal government initially contributed significantly to the costs of these programmes by a system of transfers to the provinces, the relative size of the transfers has been declining steadily. Thus, the provinces have become much more financially self-sufficient, with the result that they are responsible for a growing proportion of revenue raising through taxation. The share of government expenditures attributable to the provinces and municipalities rose from 42 percent in 1955 to 59 percent in 1994. Over the same period, the provincial and municipal share of tax revenues rose from 29 to 48 percent. This makes Canada one of the most decentralized federations in the world. There are those who think decentralization has gone too far and that the Canadian economic and social union is in danger of being fragmented. Others welcome decentralization as a way of improving the quality of public-service delivery. The fundamental debate is over the virtues of centralization versus decentralization in government decision taking.

Decentralization in this context refers both to the provision of government goods and services and transfers, and to the raising of revenues at the provincial or local levels. The alleged benefits of decentralizing fiscal responsibilities are many. Programmes that are decentralized are delivered at a level of government that is closer to the people being served, and this is said to result in public services that are more responsive to community needs and preferences. Provinces and municipalities have good incentives to be aware of and adapt to their communities' political, social, and economic conditions. Decentralization can give rise to healthy competition between jurisdictions; constituents can compare the types and qualities of services and the tax burdens being provided elsewhere and expect their governments to do at least as well. It is argued that this fiscal competition results in more efficient service provision and more accountability in government. Decentralization also allows different provinces to try out different solutions to common problems. In a sense, the provinces are like a set of laboratories, with the successful experiments providing examples for imitation elsewhere. This has allowed the provinces to experiment with different methods of cost control in areas such as health, education, and welfare. Decentralization of service provision can also reduce administrative costs by eliminating an upper level of bureaucracy and improving the management of public-service delivery systems. Finally, to the extent that decentralization of expenditure re-

sponsibility is accompanied by decentralization of responsibility for financing from community sources, fiscal responsibility is enhanced.

However, decentralization has its disadvantages as well. First, provincial or municipal programmes may result in benefits or costs to residents of neighbouring jurisdictions, forms of externalities analogous to those we have already encountered. Pollution in Quebec can lead to acid rain in Ontario. The poor from one province may migrate to another to collect welfare benefits. These are negative externalities. There are also positive externalities. Students from Saskatchewan may attend university in Alberta. Workers benefiting from labour-training programmes in Ontario may move to British Columbia and put their skills to use there. Individuals and businesses in Nova Scotia may use the roads in New Brunswick.

Second, although some goods, called **local public goods**—such as libraries and fire fighting—benefit only residents of a particular area, others benefit the whole nation. Defence protection against foreign aggression is a **national public good.** Efficiency requires that national public goods be provided at the federal level.

Third, just as we cannot count on markets to yield a socially acceptable distribution of income, we cannot rely on particular provinces to ensure an acceptable distribution of income. For example, by reducing benefits to the poor, each province can reduce its poor population, for the poor will feel forced to move elsewhere to survive. This has been called "a race to the bottom" of distributional fairness. By the same token, provinces may be discouraged from taxing the rich too much for fear that they may relocate elsewhere and perhaps take their businesses with them. When responsibility for the estate tax was turned over to the provinces in the tax reform of 1971, one by one almost all provinces eliminated the tax.

Fourth, while interjurisdictional competition can be healthy and lead to responsive and efficient provision of public services, it can also lead provinces to implement policies that are designed solely to attract business from other provinces. These policies, so-called "beggar-thy-neighbour" policies, include the provision of subsidies and special services as well as tax breaks to potential businesses. To the extent that several provinces engage in them, they can be self-defeating. The outcome will be generally beneficial treatment of business with relatively little new business being attracted to any one jurisdiction.

Fifth, provincial governments may engage in policies that are analogous to those that national governments use to protect their industries and workers from foreign competition. Procurement policies of provincial governments may favour local suppliers. Provincial licensing schemes for trades and professions may make it difficult for out-of-province workers to obtain employment in a given province. And provincial regulation of the sale of some commodities, such as alcohol and agricultural products, may discriminate against producers in other provinces. These practices, all of which have been a feature of Canadian life, cause inefficiencies in the Canadian economic union by restricting the flow of goods, services, labour, and capital among provinces.

Finally, the decentralization of tax responsibilities to the provinces can give rise to very different tax systems in different provinces. This can impose significant compliance costs on businesses operating in more than one jurisdiction, and can result in an inefficient allocation of economic activity across provinces.

So while there is no doubt that decentralization can bring very real advantages in terms of delivering public services more effectively, it can also give rise to inefficiencies and inequities in the federation. One might wonder how the advantages of decentralization might be achieved without the worst of its disadvantages. Various possibilities exist.

First, the assignment of responsibilities might be such that the worst excesses of decentralization are avoided. Thus, while the provision of public services is decentralized to the provinces, some of the major transfer programmes are not. In this way, the advantages of efficient service delivery are obtained without unduly compromising the goals of redistribution.

Second, a system of federal provincial-transfers might be maintained. These transfers fulfill two key functions. One, they serve to equalize fiscal capacities across provinces and thereby ensure that adequate levels of public services are available in different regions, a goal that is enunciated as a federal responsibility by the Constitution. Two, federal transfers to the provinces for particular programmes— health, welfare, and postsecondary education—can be made conditional on the provinces' abiding by certain national norms of efficiency and equity. Thus, federal support of health and welfare programmes has been conditional on provincial programmes' not discriminating against persons migrating from other provinces.

Finally, the worst excesses of interprovincial competition might be tempered by agreements negotiated among the provinces themselves, with or without the participation of the federal government. The interprovincial trade agreement negotiated in 1994, which included provisions involving procurement policies and removing barriers to trade in commodities across provinces, is an example of this. In principle, provinces could also agree among themselves on national standards to apply to their public services without the stick of federal transfers to enforce them.

The debate over the appropriate federal-provincial split of responsibilities has been going on since Confederation. It is unlikely to stop anytime soon, especially with the fiscal pressures the federal government is facing and the strength of the separatist movement in Quebec.

REVIEW AND PRACTICE

SUMMARY

1 Government plays a pervasive role in the economy. Government expenditures in Canada are approximately one half of national output—a much larger proportion than thirty years ago. A major reason for the increase has been increased expenditures on social programmes such as unemployment insurance at the federal level and health, education, and welfare at the provincial level, and on interest payments on government debt.

2 In a democracy, the public sector differs from the private in two main ways. Its legitimacy and authority are derived from the electoral process; it also has certain powers of compulsion, such as requiring households and firms to pay taxes and obey laws.

3 By and large, private markets allocate resources efficiently. But in a number of areas they do not, as is the case with externalities and public goods. Moreover, when the economy fails to use the available resources fully, there may be idle industrial capacity and unemployed workers. Even when the economy is efficient, there may be dissatisfaction with the distribution of income.

4 Individuals and firms produce too much of a good with a negative externality, such as air or water pollution, since they do not bear all the costs. They produce too little of a good with a positive externality, such as a new invention, since they cannot receive all the benefits.

5 Public goods are goods that it costs little or nothing for an additional individual to enjoy, but that it costs a great deal to exclude any individual from enjoying. National defence and lighthouses are two examples. Free markets underproduce public goods, since it is by definition difficult to prevent anyone from using them without paying for them.

6 Government has a variety of instruments it can use to change markets that are not functioning efficiently. It can take direct action, provide incentives to the private sector, or mandate action by the private sector.

7 While market failures provide a potential rationale for government action, government action may not provide an effective remedy. There are systematic reasons for "government failure" just as there are for "market failure."

8 Different voters have different views about what the government should do. In some cases majority voting may not yield a determinate outcome. In other cases the choices made in majority voting reflect the preferences of the median voter.

9 Government actions sometimes reflect the interests of particular groups, who seek special favours. The activities they engage in to get these special favours are called rent-seeking activities.

10 Sources of systemic public failure include imperfect information, weak or distorted incentives, and inability to foresee fully the consequences of government programmes, particularly changes in behaviour.

11 Centralized (federal) provision of public goods and services is preferred in the case of externalities and national public goods or when income distribution issues are involved. Decentralized (provincial and local) provision is preferred for local public goods and services, is more responsive to community preferences and needs, and facilitates experimentation in different ways to solve common problems.

KEY TERMS

nationalization	eminent domain	externalities	voting paradox
privatization	"invisible hand"	public goods	median voter theory
deregulation	social insurance	nonrivalrous	rent seeking
federal structure of government	social safety net	nonexcludable	
	market failures	free-rider problem	

REVIEW QUESTIONS

1 Name some of the ways government touches the lives of all citizens, both in and out of the economic sphere.

2 "Since democratic governments are elected by the consent of a majority of the people, they have no need for compulsion." Comment.

3 How can individual selfishness end up promoting social welfare?

4 Name areas in which market failure can occur.

5 Why do goods with negative externalities tend to be overproduced? Why do goods with positive externalities tend to be underproduced? Give an example for each.

6 What two characteristics define a public good? Give an example.

7 What three broad types of instruments does government have to try to achieve its goals?

8 Does the presence of a market failure necessarily mean that government action is desirable? If not, why not?

9 Describe some of the major economic roles of government.

10 What is the voting paradox?

11 What is the median voter? Why does the median voter matter so much in a system of majority rule?

12 What role do special-interest groups and bureaucrats play in determining what government does?

13 Describe the advantages and disadvantages of providing public goods and services at the local or provincial level versus the national level.

PROBLEMS

1 In each of the following areas, specify how the government is involved, either as a direct producer, a regulator, a purchaser of final goods and services distributed directly to individuals or used within government, or in some other role:
  (a) education
  (b) mail delivery
  (c) health care
  (d) air travel
  (e) national defence.
In each of these cases, can you think of ways that part of the public role could be provided by the private sector?

2 Can you explain why even a benevolent and well-meaning government may sometimes have to use the power of eminent domain? (Hint: Consider the incentives of one person who knows that her property is the last obstacle to building a highway.)

3 Explain why government redistribution programmes involve a trade-off between risk and incentives for *both* rich and poor.

4 Each of the situations below involves an externality. Tell whether it is a positive or negative externality, or both, and explain why free markets will overproduce or underproduce the good in question:

(a) a business performing research and development projects
(b) a business that discharges waste into a nearby river
(c) a concert given in the middle of a large city park
(d) an individual who smokes cigarettes in a meeting held in a small unventilated room

5 The prime minister is trying to decide which of three goals he should put at the top of his agenda—deficit reduction (*d*), a middle-class tax cut (*m*), and preserving the safety net for the poor (*p*). He puts the matter before his advisers in three separate meetings. Assume he has three advisers, and he takes a vote in each meeting. His political adviser's ranking is {*m*–*d*–*p*}, his economic adviser's ranking is {*d*–*p*–*m*}, and his health care adviser's ranking is {*p*–*m*–*d*}. What is the outcome?

6 While the medial voter theory predicts that the two political parties will converge towards the centre, in practice the two parties often seem far apart. Use median voter theory to predict the outcome of a two-stage election. In the first stage, voters within each party choose their candidate. If in the first stage voters do not vote strategically—if they vote for their preferred candidate, not for the candidate that they think will win—describe the outcome of the election. How might the fact that voters at the extremes of the political spectrum are more likely to vote affect the outcome?

7 In shared-cost programmes, the federal government pays half of all expenditures but leaves it to the provinces to decide how much will be spent. How might this cost-sharing arrangement affect the level of expenditure? How might the wealth of a province affect the extent to which it takes advantage of such programmes?

8 Evaluate the advantages and disadvantages of transferring responsibility to provinces for the following programmes: (a) unemployment insurance; (b) immigration; (c) environmental regulation; (d) cash assistance to the elderly; (e) job-training programmes.

EXTERNALITIES AND THE ENVIRONMENT

In this and the next chapter, we probe the economic role of government in more detail. Beyond providing a legal framework within which economic relations take place, government may have an economic role to play when markets fail to produce efficient and equitable outcomes. The possibility of inequitable outcomes gives rise to the redistributive role of government, which is taken up in the next chapter.

We have discovered several ways in which markets can fail to produce efficient outcomes. For example, competition may be less than that envisaged by the basic model, and less-than-perfect competition produces inefficient economic outcomes. Competitive markets may, for all the reasons set forth in Chapter 15, fail to produce the technological innovation needed by a thriving economy. Government has responded with patent laws and other legislative efforts to spur innovation. Markets may also fail in the face of information problems (see Chapter 16). For instance, producers tend to know more about their products than they reveal to customers. Government has responded with truth-in-advertising laws. And, as we saw in the last chapter, markets may fail because of the existence of public goods and externali-

KEY QUESTIONS

1 Why do externalities such as pollution result in a market failure? What alternatives can government employ to remedy this market failure?

2 What are the market forces that lead to an efficient use of society's natural resources? What may impede markets from using scarce natural resources efficiently?

ties. These arise because the provision of some goods and services simultaneously provides benefits or costs for several parties, and these are not fully reflected in market prices.

We discussed how governments might respond to these forms of market failure by providing public goods and by internalizing externalities by, for example, taxes or subsidies, depending on whether the externality was a negative or a positive one. In this chapter we focus in more detail on negative externalities and on the important policy issues they give rise to for the protection of the environment and the depletion of natural resources.

NEGATIVE EXTERNALITIES AND OVERSUPPLY

Perfect competition assumes that the costs of producing a good and the benefits of selling it all accrue to the seller and that the benefits of receiving the good and the costs of buying it all accrue to the buyer. This is often not the case. As was explained in Chapter 18, the extra costs and benefits not captured by the market transaction are called externalities.

Externalities can be either positive or negative, depending on whether individuals enjoy extra benefits they did not pay for or suffer extra costs they did not incur. Goods for which there are positive externalities, such as research and development, will be undersupplied in the market. In deciding how much of the good to purchase, each individual or firm thinks only about the benefits it receives, not the benefits conferred upon others. By the same token, goods for which there are negative externalities, such as air and water pollution, will be oversupplied in the market. The fact that the market might not fully capture the costs and benefits of a trade pro-

vides a classic example of a market failure and a possible role for the public sector.

Figure 19.1A shows the demand and supply curves for a good—say, paper. Market equilibrium is the intersection of the curves, the point labelled E, with output Q_p and price p_p. Chapter 11 explained why, in the absence of externalities, the equilibrium E is efficient. The price reflects the marginal benefit individuals receive from an extra unit of paper: it measures their marginal willingness to pay for an extra unit. The price also reflects the marginal cost to the firm of producing an extra unit. At E, marginal benefits equal marginal costs.

Consider what happens if, in the production of paper, there is an externality: producers are polluting the air and water without penalty. The **social marginal cost,** the marginal cost borne by all individuals in the economy, will now exceed the **private marginal cost,** the marginal cost borne by the producers alone. Note that in a competitive industry, the supply curve corresponds to the horizontal sum of all producers' *private* marginal cost curves. Panel B contrasts the two situations. It shows the social marginal cost curve for producing paper lying above the private marginal cost curve. Thus, with social marginal costs equated to social marginal benefits, the economically efficient level of production of paper will be lower, Q_s, than it would be if private costs were the only ones, Q_p.

Thus, the level of production of paper, which generates negative externalities, will be too high in a free market. We can also ask, what about the level of expenditure on pollution abatement? Such expenditures confer a positive externality on others—the benefits of the equipment, the cleaner air, accrue mainly to others. Figure 19.2 shows a firm's demand curve for pollution-abatement equipment in the absence of government regulation. It is quite low, reflecting the fact that the firm itself derives little benefit: the firm's marginal private benefit from ex-

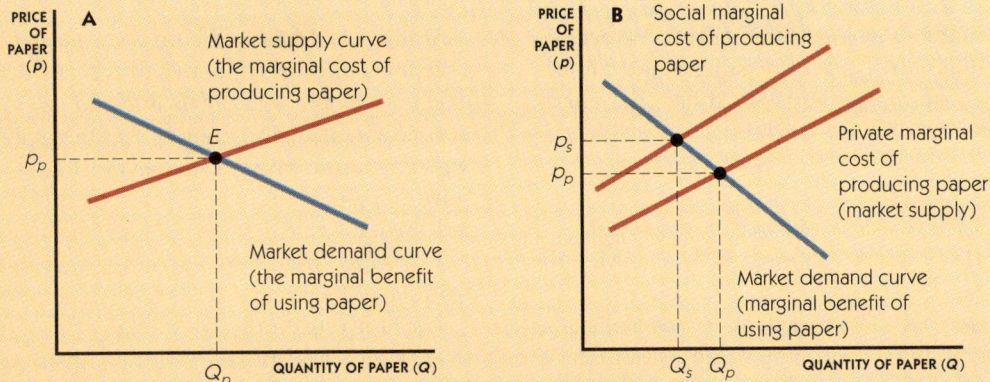

Figure 19.1 HOW NEGATIVE EXTERNALITIES CAUSE OVERSUPPLY

In a perfectly competitive market, the market supply curve is the (horizontal) sum of the marginal cost curves of all firms, while market demand reflects how much the marginal consumer is willing to pay. In panel A, the intersection or equilibrium, at quantity Q_p and price P_p, will be where marginal cost is equal to the marginal benefit for society as a whole.

The private marginal cost includes just the costs actually paid by the producing firm. If there are broader costs to society as a whole, like pollution, then the social costs will exceed the private costs. If the supplier is not required to take these additional costs into account (as in panel B), production will be at Q_p, greater than Q_s, where price equals social marginal cost, and the quantity will exceed the amount where marginal cost is equal to marginal benefit for society as a whole.

penditures on pollution-abatement equipment are small. The firm sets its marginal private benefit equal to the marginal cost of pollution abatement, which results in a level of expenditure on pollution abatement at E. The figure also depicts the marginal social benefit of pollution abatement, which is far greater than the marginal private benefit. Efficiency requires that the marginal social benefit equal the marginal cost, point E'. Thus, economic efficiency requires greater expenditures on pollution abatement than there would be in the free market.

One of government's major economic roles is to

Figure 19.2 HOW POSITIVE EXTERNALITIES CAUSE UNDERSUPPLY

The private marginal benefit includes just the benefits received by the firm, but since pollution-abatement equipment provides a positive externality, it will have a social marginal benefit that is higher. If the firm takes only its private benefit into account, it will operate at point E, using less equipment than at the point where marginal benefits are equal to marginal costs for society as a whole (E').

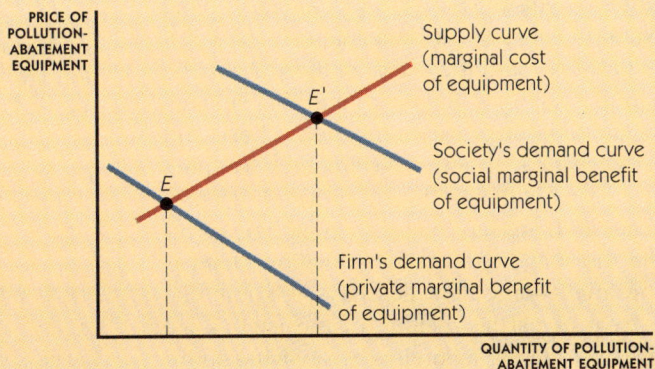

correct the inefficiencies resulting from externalities. Among the many types of negative externalities, perhaps the most conspicuous are those that harm the environment.

ENVIRONMENTAL PROTECTION AND CONSERVATION: EXAMPLES

Freon gas, used as the propellant in aerosol cans and as a coolant in air conditioners, appears to have destroyed some of the ozone layer of the atmosphere, with a resultant risk of major climatic changes and possible exposure of humans to radiation that may cause cancer and other injury. This is a worldwide externality. A major treaty among the nations of the world was signed in early 1990 that would eventually ban the use of this and related gases. The nature of the externality in this case was clear: the use of the freon anywhere could have disastrous effects on everyone.

Another major international treaty was signed in Rio de Janeiro in 1992. Since the beginning of the Industrial Revolution in the mid-1700s, enormous quantities of fossil fuels—coal, oil, and gas—have been burned. When they burn, they produce carbon dioxide (CO_2). Carbon dioxide is absorbed into the oceans and used by plants in photosynthesis. But the rate of emissions in recent decades has been far greater than the rate of absorption—so much so that the concentration of CO_2 in the atmosphere is 25 percent higher than it was at the beginning of the Industrial Revolution. Worse, in the next few decades, the percentage is projected to double, or more, unless decisive measures are taken. The United Nations convened an international panel of scientists to assess both the extent of these dramatic changes in the earth's atmosphere and their consequences. Their findings were alarming. These and other gases create a "greenhouse effect" by trapping radiation arriving at the earth, and preventing its reflection back into space; this leads to global warming. While the magnitude of the warming effect is likely to be small—only a few degrees—the potential harm is great: a partial melting of the earth's ice caps, a rise in sea levels, a flooding of low-lying countries such as Bangladesh, and an increase in the spread of deserts.

At Rio, the developed countries agreed to restrain their level of emissions and to return them to their 1990 level by the year 2000. Since emissions increase with energy use, and energy use normally increases with economic growth, achieving this goal will require both substantial increases in energy efficiency and switching from energy sources, such as coal, that produce high levels of emissions to those that produce little or none (such as hydroelectric power).

These are examples of global externalities. Most externalities are more local. Scientists say that the thousands of freshwater lakes in Ontario are dying because of an increase in the level of their acidity caused by acid rain. Rainfall containing high levels of acid occurs as a result of the emission into the atmosphere of sulfur dioxide and nitrous oxides from the fossil-fuel-burning smokestacks of industry in Ontario and the northern United States. In the absence of regulation or other policies, there is no financial incentive for the builder of a smelter for processing nickel ore to construct a costly smokestack that reduces sulfur dioxide emissions. The damage done by the emission of particles containing sulfur dioxide represents an external cost to the users of the lakes that is not taken into account in the production of nickel and materials in other heavy industries.

POLICY RESPONSES TO PROBLEMS IN THE ENVIRONMENT

As the negative externalities associated with pollution and other environmental issues are increasingly recognized, the alternative ways government can curtail their bad effects have received considerable attention from economists and others. This section evaluates several of the major options.

PROPERTY RIGHTS RESPONSES

Large-scale environmental degradation is a conspicuous form of negative externalities. Having identified them as market failures, what can the government

CLOSE-UP: THE MARKET FOR WHALES

The average Canadian eats thirty-five kilograms of beef, twenty-eight kilograms of pork, and twenty-three kilograms of chicken in a year, and one never hears concerns that this consumption will drive cows or pigs or chickens into extinction. Relatively few Canadians eat whale meat, yet in certain countries like Japan, whale meat is considered a delicacy. In 1986, fearing that whales were being hunted into extinction, an international convention passed a moratorium on all commercial whaling. Why does the market system work to assure plenty of cows and pigs and chickens, but threaten to exterminate certain breeds of whales?

Economists approach this question by analyzing the property rights in each case. The farmers who raise cows and pigs and chickens own them, and thus have an incentive to build up the supply of animals. But no country or individual owns the ocean or the whales in it. Thus, although there is an economic incentive to hunt whales and sell their meat, there is no individual or company with a direct economic incentive to help nurture and increase the overall number of whales.

This pattern has been called "the tragedy of the commons." When an area is owned in common, like the ocean, everyone has an economic in-centive to exploit it, but no one has an economic incentive to care for it. The result can be the disappearance of the whales in the ocean.

Of course, the problem of the commons is not limited to whales. The decimation of the buffalo on the commonly owned Canadian prairie is another example, as is the disappearance of the northern cod off the East Coast.

Soon after the moratorium on whaling for commercial purposes was passed in 1986, several countries felt a sudden need to hunt whales for scientific purposes. Japan, for example, announced in 1987 an urgent need to kill for research purposes nearly half the number of whales they had been catching for commercial purposes. Iceland announced that it would be shipping much of the whale meat from its "research whales" to Japan, where the meat would sell at premium prices. More recently, international agreements have placed tight limits on the number of whales that can be caught for research. As a result, the number of Minke whales quickly made a recovery, to the point where limited commercial whaling has begun once again.

Sources: Figures on meat consumption from Statistics Canada: *Canada Yearbook*, 1994, Table 15.10; information about whaling in 1986 and 1987 comes from Timothy Appel, "Japan Finds Loophole in Whaling Ban," *Christian Science Monitor*, April 15, 1987, p. 1.

do to improve matters? Some economists argue that government should simply rearrange property rights. The **Coase theorem,** named for the American Nobel laureate Ronald Coase, says that, with appropriately designed property rights, markets could take care of externalities without direct government intervention. Consider, for example, the case of a small lake in which anyone can fish without charge. Each fisherman ignores the fact that the more fish he takes out of the lake, the fewer fish there are for others to take out, and the more resources are required to catch a given amount of fish. If the government were to rearrange property rights and grant to a single individual the right to fish, then he would have every incentive to fish efficiently. There would be no externalities. He would take into account the long-run interests as well as the short-run. He would realize that if he fished too much this year, he would have fewer fish next year. If it were a large lake, he might let others do the fishing and charge them for each fish caught or regulate the amount of fish they could catch. But the prices he charged and the regulations he imposed would be designed to ensure that the lake was not overfished.

The point of this example is that the problem of overfishing is solved with only limited government intervention. All the government has to do is assign the property rights correctly.

This kind of problem arises repeatedly. The provincial government of British Columbia leases public land to forestry firms. Since the firms only lease the land, they often impose a negative externality on future potential users by not engaging in good reforestation practices, with the result that the forest does not regenerate itself properly for the next user. If the property rights were altered so that the land was sold to the forestry firms rather than leased, they would have reason to look after the forest rather than abusing it. In deciding how many trees to cut this year and how many resources to put into reforestation, they would take into account the effect on the productivity of the forest in the future, much like a farmer who looks after his land with the long term in mind rather than allowing its soil to erode through overuse. Even if the firm itself did not expect to be operating there for a long time, it would still have an incentive to take care of the forest because the forest's resale value to the next user would be affected by how well it had been managed.

To take another example, consider a factory that discharges chemicals into a river. Suppose the aggregate value of swimming in the river is $20,000 a year, and the property rights to the use of the river are assigned to the swimmers. The swimmers announce that the firm can pollute the river if it pays them $20,000 a year. If the cost of a filter to keep the chemicals out of the river is $15,000, then the firm chooses to install the filter; the result is efficient. If the cost of the filter is $25,000, then the firm pays the swimmers $20,000 instead and proceeds to pollute, assuming that the value of producing from the factory is worth at least that amount to the firm. If it is not, the factory does not produce; in either case, the outcome is still efficient. Exactly the same outcomes obtain if the property rights are assigned to the factory. If the filter

costs $15,000, the firm announces that it will stop polluting if the swimmers pay for the cost of the filter. Since the value of swimming is $20,000, the swimmers are willing to "bribe" the firm not to pollute. On the other hand, if the filter costs $25,000, they are not willing to bribe the firm, and the factory will pollute. Thus, no matter how the property rights are assigned, the outcome is efficient.

The appeal of Coase's theorem is that it assigns a minimal role to government. Government simply makes the property rights clear, and leaves the efficient outcome to private markets. Opportunities to apply the theorem are limited, however, because the costs of reaching an agreement may be high, particularly when large numbers of individuals are involved. Imagine the difficulties of assigning property rights to the atmosphere, and having all the individuals adversely affected by air pollution negotiating with all those contributing to it!

Today there is general agreement that while assigning property rights clearly may take care of some externality problems, most externalities, particularly those concerning the environment, require more active government intervention. Some forms this intervention might take include regulatory measures, financial penalties, subsidization of corrective measures, and creating a market for the externality.

REGULATION

The strongest response government can make to a negative externality is to outlaw it. In the case of environmental externalities, many governments impose regulatory measures that define permissible levels of pollution and penalize firms that exceed them. Any level of pollution that falls within the regulated levels is permitted.

In most cases, economists see better alternatives than the strict, all-or-nothing standards called for in regulatory measures. This is because economists do not see pollution as an all-or-nothing matter. The air can be cleaner, or it can be dirtier. Water can be more or less polluted. There are, of course, certain limits beyond which air is unbreathable or water is undrinkable. But up to these points, one can ask, what is the extra cost of having slightly cleaner air? Compare that cost with the extra benefit. Economists believe in marginal analysis in the area of the environment as much as they do in any other area. Regulatory measures often do not allow for an exploration to find the efficient level of pollution.

Further, regulatory measures probably require more involvement of government than it can reasonably be expected to provide efficiently. The regulatory approach is sometimes called the **command and control** approach because it requires so much direction from the government. In the case of pollution, the government must ascertain the level at which emissions become dangerous, and then set appropriate standards for every smokestack and waste pipe. In practice, the government cannot have separate standards for each factory. Typically, it applies a uniform standard, regardless of the marginal costs firms face; it may, for instance, order the same cutback in pollution from everyone, without regard for differences in the costs of abatement. This may seem fair, but it is inefficient. In addition, although businesses clearly have an economic incentive to avoid the fines or legal penalties that the government can impose, once they have met the standard, they have no real incentive to find innovative ways of reducing pollution further or exceeding the standard.

Indeed, one of the criticisms of the regulatory system is that firms seem to spend more energy fighting the regulations and working to have them altered than they do trying to improve their performance with respect to the environment. If businesses have a chance of being exempted from the regulations, perhaps by arguing that such restrictions will produce a loss of jobs or other hardships, it may be more cost effective to pay lawyers to lobby the government than to pay engineers to develop a less polluting technology.

TAXES AND SUBSIDIES

Most economists believe that taxes and subsidies provide a better way than regulation to encourage the behaviour society wants. Taxes are the stick, while subsidies are the carrot. Both have the aim of adjusting private costs to account for social costs. In Chapter 18, we analyzed how a tax on the output of a polluting industry could be used to offset the social costs of pollution.

In one respect, taxes on pollution are similar to fines for violating regulations: they both increase the cost of and thereby discourage pollution. But taxes differ from regulation in a fundamental way. Regulations are a clumsy weapon. They penalize firms for polluting over a specified level, but polluters who stay just below that level get off scot-free. Pollution taxes can be set so that they reduce aggregate pollution by the same amount as a regulator would under a command and control system. But the economic effects are very different. Taxes add the cost of pollution to the costs a company has to cover to remain in business. As a result, companies will have the incentive to reduce their pollution as far as possible and to find new, low-cost ways of reducing pollution, rather than keeping it just below the legal standard. This is "efficient pollution abatement," in which the producers who pollute less have their reward in lower costs.

Subsidies are an alternative way of providing incentives to reduce pollution, perhaps in the form of tax credits for pollution-abatement devices. Subsidies are economically inefficient. When firms get subsidies they are not paying the full costs of production; part of the costs are picked up by the government. This allows producers to sell and users to buy their product for less than its full cost of production. Plus, pollution remains above the socially efficient level. This, of course, is why firms prefer subsidies to taxes.

THE MARKETABLE PERMIT RESPONSE

Still another approach to curbing pollution is **marketable permits,** first advocated over three decades ago by the University of Toronto economist John Dales. Companies purchase or are granted a permit from the government that allows them to emit a certain amount of pollution. The government can issue the number of permits that allows the company to

USING ECONOMICS:
THE MARKET FOR POLLUTION PERMITS

One way for regulators to control the emissions of a pollutant is to create pollution permits and let them be freely bought and sold. As a pollution-control device, this has two advantages. First, it allows the regulators to control precisely the amount of pollution that can be legally emitted, according to their judgment of the marginal social benefits and costs of the polluting activity. Second, it ensures that the emission rights are acquired by those firms that value it most.

The figure below illustrates how the market for pollution permits works. The curve labelled *MB* (for "marginal benefit") represents the demand for emissions by firms in the economy. Like any other demand curve, it indicates the marginal value that the firms place on various quantities of emissions. If firms could costlessly emit pollutants, they would do so until the marginal benefit fell to zero, shown as 100,000 units of pollutant in the diagram. But suppose the regulator reck-

ons that each unit of pollutant causes $100 of damage to society. The curve *MSC* shows the marginal social cost associated with pollution. The regulator would like to allow an amount of pollution such that *MB = MSC*, shown as 80,000 units.

One way to ensure this outcome is to sell 80,000 units worth of permits to whoever wishes to buy them. Competition among polluting firms will result in a price of $100 being established on the market. At that price, the amount demanded will equal the amount supplied. In this case, the market price is simply $100. The total market value of the permits is $8 million, which is also the total social cost of the pollution. This is an efficient solution to the pollution-control problem, since the firms that acquire the right to pollute are those for whom the value of the polluting activity is at least $100 per unit. Any firm that values it less than that will not be willing to purchase a permit.

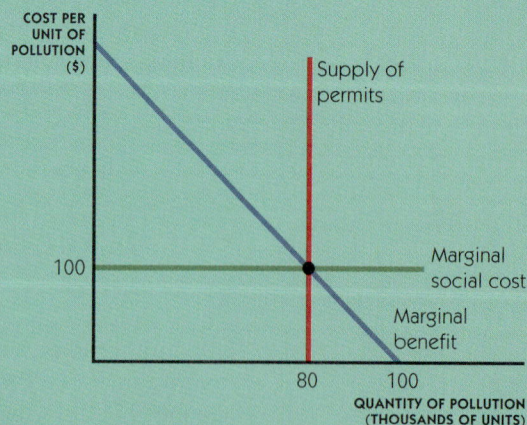

produce the same level of pollution that it would under the command and control approach. However, companies are allowed to sell their permits. Thus, if a company cuts its pollution in half, it could sell some of its permits to another company, say, one that wants to expand production and hence its emission of pollutants.

The incentive effects of marketable permits are very much like those of taxes. A market for pollution permits encourages development of the best possible antipollution devices, rather than giving an incentive for firms to maintain their emission of pollution just under a government-set limit. If the government wishes to reduce pollution over time, the permits can be designed to reduce the amount of pollution they allow by a set amount each year. Canadian regulators have yet to experiment with marketable permits to enforce pollution standards. However, experience in the United States suggests that this can be a workable solution to environmental externalities. The Environmental Protection Agency (EPA) used tradable permits to control the level of lead content in gasoline. Refineries were allowed to trade these permits, whose size was made to shrink to lower the amount of lead in gasoline. Trading in these permits was brisk. The EPA has also allowed trading in permits to control other types of air pollutants, such as sulfur dioxide.

WEIGHING THE ALTERNATIVE APPROACHES

Incentive programmes such as taxes or marketable permits have an important advantage over direct controls, like regulations. The issue of pollution is not whether it should be allowed—after all, it is virtually impossible to eliminate all pollution in an industrial economy. Nor would it be efficient; the costs of doing so would far exceed the benefits. The real issue is how sharply pollution should be limited. The *marginal* benefits have to be weighed against the marginal costs. This is not done under regulation. If government ascertains the marginal social cost of pollution and sets charges and permits accordingly, private firms will engage in pollution control up to the point at which the marginal cost of pollution control equals the marginal social return of pollution abatement (which is, of course, just the marginal cost of pollution). Each firm will have the correct marginal incentives.

Governments often prefer direct regulations because they believe that they can control the outcomes better. But such control can be illusory. If an unreachable standard is set, it is likely to be repealed. For example, as automobile companies have found the costs of various regulations to be prohibitive, they have repeatedly appealed for a delay in the enforcement of the regulations, often with considerable success.

It must also be kept in mind that choosing the socially efficient method of pollution abatement is the easy part of the policy problem. Figuring out the "right" level of pollution to aim for is much harder. Uncertainty about the consequences of pollution abounds and how to value certain options is an issue of hot debate. To what extent can environmental degradation be reversed? How much value should be placed on the extinction of a species like the spotted owl, or the preservation of the Arctic wilderness?

SOLVING THE PROBLEM OF EXTERNALITIES

Externalities, which occur when the extra costs and benefits of a transaction are not fully accounted for in the market price, give rise to market failure. Four main solutions have been proposed and used:

1 The assignment of property rights

2 Regulations that outlaw the negative externality

3 Tax and subsidy measures to encourage the behaviour society wants

4 Marketable permits

Think twice before you hit the print button. The paper in your printer is the result of a production process with numerous environmental impacts: it begins with the cutting of forest, and includes a chemical treatment that can harm waterways. Moreover, after the paper is used, its disposal may lead to further environmental degradation. The use of paper is just one of the activities undertaken by households and firms that can lead to environmental pollution. Many of the common functions of everyday life do so as well, such as heating the house, driving the car, refrigerating perishable food, and doing the laundry. Given the immensity of the problem, it is no wonder that governments have trouble eliminating the worst effects of pollution.

In Canada, environmental policy is shared among all levels of government. The federal government, through legislation such as the Canadian Environmental Protection Act, has assumed responsibility for pollution control in such areas as shipping (including oil spills) and the inland waterways, transportation and international trade involving dangerous goods, the use of toxic substances such as PCBs and CFCs, and wildlife preservation. It has also engaged in international initiatives, such as with the United States to clean up the Great Lakes. Furthermore, under the Environmental Assessment Act of 1990 the federal government is to conduct an environmental assessment of projects built in areas of federal jurisdiction, including such things as dams and pulp and paper mills on the nation's waterways.

The provinces and municipalities, on the other hand, tend to be more concerned with environmental matters within the limits of their jurisdictions. These include water and drainage systems, garbage disposal, and sewage treatment. The two levels of government share explicit responsibility in the areas of agriculture and fishing, but there is also considerable overlap in jurisdiction, partly because the responsibility for environmental control is not spelled out in the Constitution. Thus, the provinces through their own environmental control legislation attempt to control the discharge of contaminants into the air, water, and soil in their own provinces alongside similar controls placed by federal legislation.

Despite the views of economists that the market mechanism should be used for environmental regulation, virtually the universal tendency among the federal government and the provinces is to use regulatory methods: outright prohibitions, the issue of permits and licences, or the establishment of minimal standards. Moreover, control tends to be administered mainly by conciliation and negotiation between government and industry rather than through criminal or civil court proceedings.

No matter what approach is chosen to externalities and the environment, such questions will remain controversial.

NATURAL RESOURCES

A recurrent theme among environmentalists is that our society is squandering its natural resources too rapidly. We are using up oil and energy resources at an alarming rate, hardwood timber forests that took hundreds of years to grow are being cut down, and supplies of vital resources like phosphorus are dwindling. There are repeated calls for government intervention to enhance the conservation of our scarce natural resources. Those who believe in the infallibility of markets reply, nonsense! Prices give the same guidance to the use of natural resources that they give to any other resource, these people say. Prices measure scarcity, and send consumers and firms the right signals about how much effort to expend to conserve resources, so long as consumers and firms are well informed, and so long as there is not some other source of market failure.

There is, in fact, some truth in both positions. Prices, in general, do provide signals concerning the scarcity of resources, and *in the absence of market failures*, those signals lead to economic efficiency. We have seen some cases where a private market economy without government intervention will not be efficient—when there are negative externalities (pollution) or when a resource (like fish in the ocean) is not priced.

But what about a privately owned resource, like bauxite (from which aluminum is made) or copper? The owner of a bauxite mine has a clearly defined property right. Let's assume that he pays a tax appropriate to any pollution his mining operation causes. Thus, the price he charges will reflect both social and private costs. The question of resource depletion now boils down to the question of whether his bauxite is worth more to him in the market or in the ground. The answer depends on what bauxite will

be worth in the future, say thirty years from now. If it will be worth more thirty years from now, he will keep the bauxite in the ground even though he may not be alive. That way he maximizes the value of his property, and he can enjoy his wise decision by selling the mine when he retires. The price at which he sells it should reflect the present discounted value of the bauxite.

If this miner and all other bauxite producers choose to bring the bauxite to market today, depleting the world's supply of bauxite, there are two possible reasons. Either, this is the socially efficient outcome—society values bauxite more highly today than it will tomorrow. Or, the miners have miscalculated the value of bauxite thirty years from now and underestimated future prices, though they have every incentive to get as accurate a forecast as they can. If they have indeed miscalculated, we might view the result as a market failure; but there would be no reason to expect a government bureaucracy to do any better than the firms at guessing future prices.

However, from society's viewpoint there are two plausible reasons why private owners may undervalue future benefits of a natural resource. First, in countries where property rights are not secure, owners of a resource may feel that if they do not sell it soon, there is a reasonable chance that the resources will be taken away from them. There may be a revolution, for example, in which the government will take over the resource with no or only partial compensation to the owners. Even in countries like Canada, where owners are not worried about government confiscating their property, increased regulations might make it more expensive to extract the resource in the future, or higher taxes might make it less attractive to sell the resource in the future. Second, individuals and firms often face limited borrowing opportunities and very high interest rates. In these circumstances, capital markets discount future returns at a rate far higher than society or the government would discount them.

Higher interest rates induce a more rapid depletion of resources. Suppose an oil company is deciding whether to extract some oil today or to wait until next year. For simplicity, assume there are no extraction costs, so the net return to selling the oil is just its

CLOSE-UP: THE VALUE OF A LIFE

"If this policy saves even one life, it is worth the cost!" Such words often pass the lips of advocates of a particular policy. Though the rhetoric may be inspiring, economists have found the reasoning to be false. Life is extraordinarily precious, but a decision to save lives at any cost would mean, for example, that no one would be allowed to drive, because sooner or later driving would result in a death. Life cannot be lived in a cocoon.

In passing new regulations, the government must put some value on life, to determine when new regulations make economic sense. By how much should exposure to pesticides be reduced? Should air bags be required equipment in cars? What exposure to radiation is acceptable inside a nuclear plant, and outside it? What chemicals must be controlled in the workplace, and to what extent? Each of these regulations involves reducing the risk of death. How should this reduction be evaluated?

Economists argue that one way to evaluate the risk of death in order to take public-sector decisions is to use information on the amount that people must be compensated for exposure to the risk of death in other contexts. One source of such information is the premium that must be paid for working in jobs that involve some risk of death. Thus, if one knows the fatality rate for a given occupation, and one also knows the wage premium required to attract workers to that occupation compared with safe jobs, one can cal-

culate the total wage premium per death on the job. This is rather loosely referred to by economists as the "value of life." It is not meant to represent the worth of any one person's life, nor the value of a newborn baby to society. Instead, it is the amount of money that persons must be compensated in order to willingly accept the risk of loss of life. In the case of wage premiums paid to workers who accept jobs that involve a risk of death, it represents the total evaluation that the workers themselves put on the risk involved in losing one life.

Two Canadian economists, Ronald Meng and Douglas Smith, have used these methods to estimate that the value of a life in Canada was $5.2 million in 1983. This figure was arrived at by estimating that workers in jobs in which 1 worker in 1,000 is expected to die require on average $5,200 per year more in pay than those in jobs that are free of risk. Thus, 1,000 workers, of whom 1 is expected to die on the job, must be paid $5.2 million per year to compensate them for the possibility of dying. This is the estimated value of life that could be used to put a cost on the loss of life in public projects. Meng and Smith argue that this should be regarded as a lower bound for public-policy applications in Canada because individuals may accept risk in the workplace that they would not accept outside the workplace.

Source: Ronald A. Meng and Douglas A. Smith, "The Valuation of Risk of Death in Public Sector Decision-Making," *Canadian Public Policy* 15 (June 1990): 137–44.

price. If the price of a barrel of oil is the same today as a year from now, the firm's decision is simple. The firm will sell the oil today. But what if the price of oil is expected to go up 10 percent? Now the firm must compare the present discounted value of the oil sold a year from now with what it could receive

today. To calculate the present discounted value, we simply divide next year's price by 1 plus the interest rate. If the interest rate is 10 percent, then a dollar a year from now is worth 10 percent less than a dollar today. So if the interest rate is less than 10 percent, it pays the firm to wait; if the interest rate is more than

10 percent, it pays the firm to extract the oil today. At higher interest rates, firms have a greater incentive to extract oil earlier.

Government is not always blameless. In fact, it can aggravate the perceived waste of natural resources. In Canada, much of the timber grows on provincial Crown lands. Provincial governments have made the land available to timber companies and in so doing have paid less attention to concerns about economic efficiency than to the pleading of timber interest groups. Timber is not the only resource mismanaged by government. Government policies aimed at encouraging the production of oil

and natural gas, in some cases before it was socially efficient to do so, have accelerated the resources' depletion. The absence of proper pricing of water has led to excessive use in some locations, draining water from underwater basins built up over eons and lowering water tables. Similarly, the absence of pricing for garbage disposal has caused available landfill sites to be used up and has put immense pressures on municipalities to find other means of disposal. In each of these cases, private property rights and market outcomes would have supplied solutions that almost everyone in society would regard as better than what happened.

REVIEW AND PRACTICE

SUMMARY

1 Government may have a role in the economy when markets fail to produce an efficient outcome. When positive or negative externalities exist, markets will not provide an efficient outcome.

2 One way to deal with externalities is to assign clear-cut property rights.

3 Governments may deal with environmental externalities by imposing regulatory measures (the command and control approach), levying taxes and granting subsidies, or issuing marketable permits.

4 In a perfect market, natural resources are used up at an efficient rate. However, privately owned resources may be sold too soon, for two reasons. First, owners may fear that if they do not sell the resources soon, new government rules may prevent them from selling at all or lower the return from selling it in the future. Second, interest rates facing owners may be higher, so they may value future income less than society in general. High interest rates lead to a faster exploitation of natural resources.

KEY TERMS

social marginal cost	Coase theorem	command and control	marketable permits
private marginal cost			

REVIEW QUESTIONS

1 Name several market failures. Why do economists see the existence of these market failures as a justification for government action?

2 Why does a free market produce too much of goods that have negative externalities, like pollution?

Why does a free market produce too little of goods that have positive externalities, like pollution control?

3 What are the advantages and limitations of dealing with externalities by assigning property rights?

4 What are the advantages of marketable permits over command and control regulation? What are the advantages of using taxes for polluting rather than subsidies for pollution-abatement equipment?

PROBLEMS

1 Marple and Wolfe are two neighbouring dormitories. Wolfe is considering giving a party with a very loud band, which will have a negative externality, a sort of sound pollution, for Marple. Imagine that the school administration decides that any dormitory has the right to prevent another dorm from hiring a band. If the band provides a negative externality, how might the residents of Wolfe apply the lessons of Coase's theorem to hire the band they want?

Now imagine that the school administration decides that no dormitory can prevent another dorm from hiring a band, no matter how loud. If the band provides a negative externality, how might the residents of Marple apply the lessons of Coase's theorem to reduce the amount of time they have to listen to the band? How would your answer change if the band provided a positive externality?

2 The manufacture of trucks produces pollution of various kinds; for the purposes of this example, let's call it all "glop." Producing a truck creates one unit of glop, and glop has a cost to society of $3,000. Imagine that the supply of trucks is competitive, and market supply and demand are given by the following data:

Price (thousand $)	19	20	21	22	23	24	25
Quantity supplied	480	540	600	660	720	780	840
Quantity demanded	660	630	600	570	540	510	480

Graph the supply curve for the industry and the demand curve. What are equilibrium price and output? Now graph the social marginal cost curve. If the social cost of glop were taken into account, what would be the new equilibrium price and output?

If the government is concerned about the pollution emitted by truck plants, explain how it might deal with the externality through fines or taxes and through subsidies. Illustrate the effects of taxes and subsidies by drawing the appropriate supply and demand graphs. (Don't worry about the exact units.) Why are economists likely to prefer fines to subsidies?

3 Consider a small lake with a certain number of fish. The more fish one fisherman takes out, the fewer fish are available for others to take out. Use graphs depicting private and social costs and benefits to fishing to describe the equilibrium and the socially efficient level of fishing. Explain how a tax on fishing could achieve the efficient outcome. Explain how giving a single individual the property right to the fish in the lake might also be used to obtain an efficient outcome.

The more fish taken out this year, the less fish will be available next year. Explain why if the lake has one owner, the fish will be efficiently extracted from it. Assume that anyone who wants to fish can do so. Would you expect that too many fish would be taken out this year?

4 Consider a crowded room with an equal number of smokers and nonsmokers. Each smoker would be willing to pay $1.00 to have the right to smoke. Each nonsmoker would be willing to pay $.50 to have the room free from smoke. Assume there is a rule that says that no smoking is allowed. Could everyone be made better off if smoking were allowed? How? If property rights to clean air are assigned to the nonsmokers, how might the efficient outcome be obtained? What difference does it make to the outcome whether there is initially a rule that smoking is allowed or smoking is not allowed? What problems might you envision occurring if no smoking is allowed unless all the nonsmokers agree to allow smoking?

20

TAXATION, REDISTRIBUTION, AND SOCIAL INSURANCE

D uring this century, governments have become increasingly involved in reducing inequality in the distribution of income provided by the market. Without help, some segments of the population would have too little income to do more than barely survive. Children who have the bad fortune to be born into impoverished families face bleak prospects. Persons who suffer from ill health or whose earning power is low through no fault of their own may not be well served by the market economy. Governments of most industrialized countries have therefore sought to provide a safety net for the poor, and most have taken an even more active stance in promoting economic equality.

Governments undertake a wide variety of redistributive programmes; indeed, the bulk of government spending has a redistributive aspect to it. Broadly speaking, we can distinguish two types of redistribution. The first, **income redistribution,** operates mainly through the system of taxes and transfers. When most people think about redistribution, the tax system comes to mind; virtually every tax system in the world attempts to change the proportion of income enjoyed by different groups in society. The second type of redistributive policy referred to as **social insurance** is equally

KEY QUESTIONS

1 What are the characteristics of a good tax system, and how does Canada's current tax system fare under these criteria? What are the various ways government raises revenues?

2 What do economists mean when they talk about a fair or equitable tax system? What arguments are used to decide how the burden of taxation should be shared among various groups in the population?

3 What are the basic programmes designed to provide assistance for the poor? What are the trade-offs between equity and efficiency in the design of these programmes?

4 What is the rationale for social insurance programmes? What are some of the current public-policy controversies surrounding them?

important. Typically it is based on something other than low income, such as ill health, employment status, or age and operates through the expenditure side of the government budget. In this chapter these two types of redistribution are taken up in turn.

THE CASE FOR INCOME REDISTRIBUTION

Income redistribution policies are justified in ways different from other governmental economic policies. The roles of government developed in earlier chapters are based on the premise that public-sector intervention may be appropriate to ensure efficient outcomes when there are market failures—whether from lack of competition, imperfect information, or the presence of externalities. In such situations, markets fail to provide completely satisfactory answers to three of the basic economic questions: "What goods are produced?" "In what quantities?" "How are the goods produced?"

When it comes to the question "For whom are the goods produced?" to which this chapter is devoted, the rationale for public-sector intervention is different. Individuals' incomes determine who consumes the goods produced in a market economy. People with higher skills or more capital earn higher incomes and therefore get to consume more of the goods produced. Labour and capital markets may be efficient, in the sense that wages and returns to capital get the incentive structure right for the economy. But the market distribution may result in some indi-

viduals having billions of dollars and others being homeless with inadequate food and medical care. Thus, the case for income redistribution is not based on the pursuit of economic efficiency. It is based on overriding social values. There is a general consensus that when the market results in incomes so low that people cannot sustain a minimally decent standard of living, government should help out. *How* it helps out is crucial, however, because redistribution programmes often interfere with economic efficiency.

TAXES

In Canada, the federal government raises tax revenues from a variety of sources. There are direct taxes on the earnings of individuals and corporations, known as **individual income taxes** and **corporation income taxes.** There are also indirect taxes on purchases of goods and services. These include a general tax called the **Goods and Services Tax** (GST), which is collected on almost all purchases of consumer goods and services in Canada, with the major exception of food. There are also taxes on the purchase of specific goods and services, known as **excise taxes and duties.** The two heaviest excise taxes are on alcohol and tobacco; they are sometimes referred to as **sin taxes.** Customs duties, or **tariffs,** are levied by the federal government on the importation of certain types of goods and services from foreign sources. The purpose of tariffs is less to raise revenues than to provide protection for

Other taxes
1.9%

Nontax revenue
7.5%

Customs duties
2.5%

Excise taxes
and duties
4.8%

Payroll
taxes
14.2%

Federal
sales tax
14.0%

Personal
income tax
47.1%

TOTAL
$136,136
million

Corporation
income tax
8.1%

B: PROVINCIAL/MUNICIPAL RECEIPTS, 1993–94

Transfers
from the federal
government
14.6%

Personal
income tax
20.8%

TOTAL
$186,019
million

Corporation
income tax
2.6%

Other
revenue
19.2%

Property
taxes
17.1%

Other taxes
2.4%

Natural resource
revenues
3.0%

Excise taxes
4.6%

Health and
social insurance
levies
5.2%

Retail
sales tax
10.6%

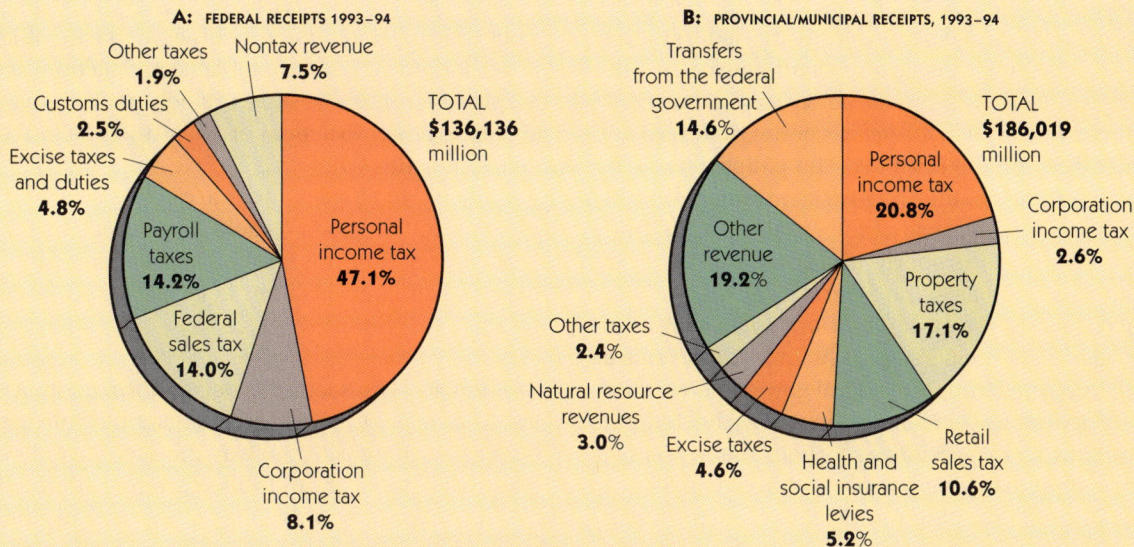

Figure 20.1 THE IMPORTANCE OF VARIOUS TAXES

At the federal level, the largest share of taxes comes from the individual income tax, followed by unemployment insurance contributions and the sales tax, as shown in panel A. Sources of revenue at the provincial and municipal levels include income, sales, and property taxes, as well as transfers received from the federal government. *Sources: Finances of the Nation 1995* (Toronto: Canadian Tax Foundation, 1995), Table 6.7; *Provincial and Municipal Finances 1991* (Toronto: Canadian Tax Foundation, 1992), Tables 2.4 and 17.1.

domestic producers—whose products are not liable to the tax—against foreign competition. Finally, the federal government also levies **payroll taxes,** which are taxes levied on the employment earnings of a person and paid either by the employer or deducted from the employee's pay-cheque, or some combination of both. Payroll taxes are earmarked for specific uses, in particular, to finance unemployment insurance and the Canada Pension Plan.

The provinces and territories levy many of the same taxes as the federal government. All impose both individual and corporation income taxes, usually quite similar in form to the corresponding federal taxes. All provinces except Alberta impose a general tax on purchases of goods and services, known as a **retail sales tax,** though typically a wide variety of items, such as food and most services, are exempted. The provinces also levy specific excise taxes, also often on the same items taxed by the federal government. Moreover, the provinces have been given jurisdiction for the taxation of natural resources, and they exercise the right extensively on the resources within their boundaries. The taxes used vary according to province and type of re-

source. Oil- and gas-producing provinces obtain revenues through **royalties** charged on production and through the **sale of leases** to operate on provincial Crown lands. All provinces have **mining taxes,** which are usually imposed on the profits of mining firms within the province. Those provinces with forests obtain revenues both from leasing Crown lands and from **stumpage fees** based on the number of trees cut. Some provinces use payroll taxes to finance specific expenditure programmes, such as health care; others impose **health care premiums.**

Municipalities also have their own sources of revenue. The most important of these is the **property tax,** which is levied annually on real estate—buildings and land—within the municipal borders. In some of the smaller provinces, the property tax is actually imposed at the provincial level and passed on at least in part to the municipalities. The municipalities also obtain revenues from licences (such as on businesses, pets, and bicycles) and from user fees on municipal services such as water and garbage.

As the list indicates, few transactions in our economy escape taxation. Figure 20.1 shows the relative importance of various types of taxes at the federal and provincial/municipal levels. At the federal level (panel A), the single most important source of revenue is the tax on individuals' personal income (contributing almost half of total revenue), followed by payroll taxes and the sales tax. The pattern is somewhat different at the provincial/municipal level (panel B), largely because of the reliance of the municipalities on the property tax. For the provinces, the pattern is similar to the federal level: the individual income tax is the most important, followed by the retail sales tax. Provinces also obtain a sizable share of their revenues from the federal government in the form of **transfers** (payments made by the federal government to the provinces to help them finance their expenditure programmes). Although it is not shown in the figure, the municipalities also receive large transfers from the provincial government.

CHARACTERISTICS OF A GOOD TAX SYSTEM

More than one out of every three dollars produced by the Canadian economy goes to the government. Not surprisingly, there is great concern about how the government raises its revenue. At one time, the art of taxation was likened to the problem of how to pluck a goose without making it squawk. The basic fact of life is that everyone enjoys government services but few enjoy paying taxes. Even so, there is substantial agreement about what constitutes a "good" tax system. It has four characteristics.

Fairness In most people's minds, the first criterion is fairness. But fairness, like beauty, is often in the eyes of the beholder. In trying to define fairness, economists focus on two principles: **horizontal equity**—individuals who are in identical or similar situations should pay identical or similar taxes; and **vertical equity**—people who are better off should pay more taxes.

Tax systems in which the rich pay a larger fraction of their income than the poor are said to be **progressive,** while those in which the poor pay a larger fraction of their income than the rich are called **regressive.** If rich people pay more taxes than the poor but not proportionately more, the tax system is still considered regressive.

The Canadian income tax is progressive, since the

rates that apply to higher incomes are larger than for lower incomes. Taxes on tobacco and alcohol are examples of regressive taxes, since poor individuals spend a larger fraction of their income on these goods. On the whole, sales taxes like the GST and provincial retail sales taxes are regressive, since in general not all goods—such as vacations in Europe—are taxed, and the fraction of income of the rich that thus escapes taxation is larger than that of the poor.

Efficiency The second criterion for a good tax system is efficiency. The tax system should interfere as little as possible with the way the economy allocates resources, and it should raise revenue with the least cost to taxpayers. Very high taxes may discourage work and savings, and therefore interfere with the efficiency of the economy. Taxes that select out particular goods to be taxed—such as excise taxes on perfume, boats, and airline tickets—discourage individuals from purchasing those goods, and therefore also interfere with efficiency.

The Canadian income tax has many provisions that have the effect of encouraging some types of economic activity and discouraging others. For instance, the income tax system allows child care expenses to be deducted against taxable income. The government thus subsidizes child care. Similarly, when individuals contribute to Registered Retirement Savings Plans (RRSPs), their taxable income is reduced accordingly. The government is encouraging saving for retirement.

Furthermore, when firms spend money on R & D, their expenditures may reduce the amount they have to pay in taxes. Such arrangements are called **tax subsidies.** These subsidies cost the government money just as if the government paid out money directly for child care, retirement saving, or research. Accordingly, the revenue lost from a tax subsidy is called a **tax expenditure.**

Administrative Simplicity The third criterion is administrative simplicity. It is costly—to the government and, therefore, to those who must pay taxes—to collect taxes and administer a tax system. Millions of hours are spent each year in filling out tax forms, hours that might be spent producing goods and services. Millions of dollars are spent on accountants and lawyers by taxpayers and by Revenue Canada in the annual ritual of preparing and processing tax forms. In addition, with a good tax system, it should be difficult to evade the taxes imposed.

Transparency   The fourth criterion is transparency. A good tax system is one in which it can be ascertained what each person is paying in taxes. The principle of transparency is analogous to the principle of "truth in advertising." Taxpayers are consumers of public services. They should know what they and others are paying for the services they are getting.

GRADING THE CANADIAN TAX SYSTEM

How well does the Canadian tax system match up to these four criteria? Equally important, have major changes in the tax laws—there have been several during the past decade—resulted in a better tax system?

Fairness   In Canada as in most countries, the income tax is intended to be progressive: the proportion of one's taxable income paid in tax increases with income. Progressivity is achieved by the combination of a graduated rate structure and a set of personal tax credits. The rate structure consists of three brackets. In 1996, for taxable incomes up to $29,590

the federal tax rate is 17 percent, and the combined federal and the average provincial tax rate is 26.35 percent. This means that for each extra $100 an individual earns, she must pay $26.35 in taxes; we thus speak of this tax rate as the **marginal tax rate** in the first tax bracket. In the second tax bracket, from $29,591 to $59,180, the federal marginal tax rate rises to 26 percent, and the combined federal and provincial rate to 40.3 percent. In the third bracket, beyond $59,181, the federal marginal rate is 29 percent. The combined federal and provincial is 44.96 percent. At incomes above $63,310 the combined rate is 46.4 percent. These are the actual tax rates legislated, but the tax law is complicated; other provisions affect the additional taxes a person might pay as her income rises. For example, high-income taxpayers have to pay back certain types of transfers they receive, such as their Old Age Security pensions.

The **average income tax rate** gives the ratio of taxes to taxable income. It indicates the degree of progressivity of the tax and reflects not just the rate structure but also various tax credits, including a basic personal credit and refundable tax credits that vary with the number of children and are reduced as one's family income rises. Figure 20.2 shows the average and marginal tax rates (federal and provincial combined) in 1995 for individuals with a non-working spouse and two dependent children. As the diagram shows, the marginal tax rate increases in

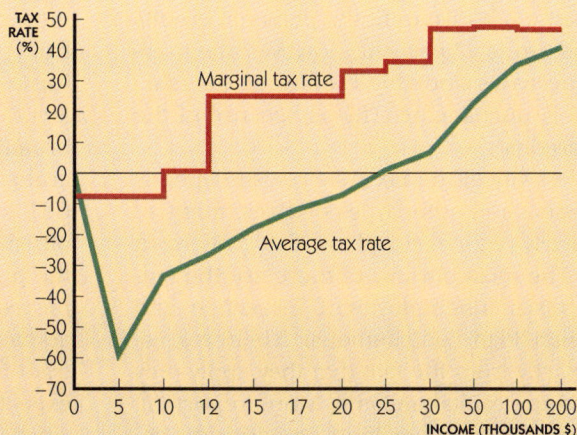

Figure 20.2 AVERAGE AND MARGINAL TAX RATES, 1995

Marginal tax rates tend to change by jumps. Average tax rates increase gradually, and are less than marginal ones. *Source: Finances of the Nation 1995* (Toronto: Canadian Tax Foundation, 1995), Table 3.15.

The proportion of your income you pay in taxes (your average tax rate) can vary a lot from the proportion of any additional income you earn that you pay in taxes (your marginal tax rate). Suppose you earn $50,000 in employment income in Ontario and that is your only source of income. Suppose also that you have a nonworking spouse and two dependent children. In 1995, your federal income tax would be calculated as follows. On the first $29,590 you would pay 17 percent, or $5,030.30. On the remaining $20,410 you would pay 26 percent, or $5,306.60. Thus, your basic federal tax liability is $10,336.90. But things do not end there. You are entitled to two tax credits, one for yourself of $1,097.52 and one for your spouse of $914.60, for a total of $2,012.12. Subtract this from your federal tax liability and you are left with basic federal taxes of $8,324.78. However, on top of this there is a federal "surtax," which was instituted as part of the government's deficit reduction strategy. It is 3 percent of federal taxes, or $249.74. Finally, you must pay taxes to your province of residence. In Ontario, income taxes are 58 percent of basic federal taxes, or $4,828.37.

Taking the sum of all these taxes, your total taxes are $13,402.89 ($8,324.78 + $249.74 + $4,828.37). Your average income tax rate is total taxes divided by income, or 26.8 percent ($13,402.89/$50,000 x 100 percent). Your marginal income tax rate is the amount of federal and provincial tax you must pay on the last dollar of income you earn. To determine the marginal tax rate, start with the federal marginal tax rate of 26 percent. Add to this the federal surtax of 3 percent of the federal tax rate, or .78 percent, and Ontario taxes of 58 percent of the federal tax rate, or 15.08 percent. Thus, your overall marginal tax rate is 41.86 percent (26 + .78 + 15.08). Not surprisingly, your marginal tax rate is higher than your average tax rate. This is a characteristic of a progressive tax system.

steps from being negative until the personal credits are exhausted, up to 47 percent. However, the average tax rate increases smoothly, even when the marginal tax rate is unchanging. This is because of the effect of the credits.

The progressivity of the tax system also depends upon the existence of other types of taxes, many of which are clearly regressive and are also growing in importance. The most obvious of these are the federal payroll taxes (unemployment insurance and Canada Pension Plan contributions). Their regressivity arises partly from the fact that they apply only to labour, and not capital, income. More important, they are subject to an upper limit on earnings, beyond which there is no additional tax payable. In fact, for persons above the limits, and that includes most full-time workers, the taxes are effectively a fixed total amount, what economists refer to as **lump-sum taxes.** We have already mentioned the fact that sales taxes tend to be regressive, especially broadly based ones like the federal GST. If the federal government begins to rely more heavily on the GST for its revenues, which has been the trend in other countries that have implemented such taxes, the progressivity of the tax system as a whole could be reduced. On the other hand, some taxes might add to the progressivity of the system rather than detract from it. Property taxes, for example, might be expected to apply more to higher-income persons, since housing values should rise rapidly with incomes.

For some taxes, the taxpayer who pays the tax may

not bear the actual burden of it; he may be able to shift the cost of the tax to someone else. For example, the owners of corporations must pay the corporation income tax, but they may be able to shift the burden to consumers through higher prices or to workers through lower wage payments. When tax shifting takes place, the **incidence** of the tax, that is, who ultimately bears the burden of the tax, may not be the person or entity who pays the tax.

It is clear that assessing the overall progressivity of the tax system is not an easy task. Not only must many different components of the tax system be taken into account, but also the incidence of some components of it are not readily determined. There have, however, been some attempts to estimate the overall incidence of the Canadian tax system by assigning total tax liabilities to different income classes. One well-known study was that of Irwin Gillespie of Carleton University.[1] He calculated that the overall tax system in Canada was actually regressive over the poorest two fifths of families, and mildly regressive over the top income classes. These results suggest that the tax system does not achieve as much redistribution as one might expect. But the results depend very much on how one attributes taxes to income class, and exactly which taxes one includes. For example, John Whalley of the University of Western Ontario found that the tax-transfer system could be made to appear mildly progressive if one simply included transfers, and could be made to look more progressive by adopting different assumptions about who bears the burden of each tax.[2]

One other important dimension of the fairness of the Canadian tax system involves comparing the tax rates that citizens of different provinces pay. This is important in Canada because the provinces raise almost as much tax revenues as the federal government. Economic resources are inherently unequally distributed across provinces. For example, Ontario has about 37 percent of the population and generates 42 percent of the income, while Newfoundland has over 2 percent of the population but accounts

for only 1.3 percent of the income. Despite the fact that provinces have very different resources and that fiscal responsibility is highly decentralized in the Canadian federation, actual differences in tax rates and in the provision of public services do not reflect these wide disparities in provincial incomes. That is because of the presence of a set of federal-provincial transfers whose purpose is to equalize the ability of the different provinces to provide public services. The main such transfers are the **equalization payments** that are made from the federal government to the so-called "have-not" provinces, provinces whose tax capacities are below the average of a representative group of provinces: Quebec, Ontario, Manitoba, Saskatchewan, and British Columbia. All the provinces except Alberta, British Columbia, and Ontario are have-nots. Equalization payments are made to the have-not provinces each year in the amount by which their ability to raise taxes falls short of the five-province average. This is on top of a system of equal per capita transfers from the federal government to all provinces. The importance of federal transfers to the poorest provinces can be seen from the fact that the Newfoundland and Prince Edward Island governments each obtained over 45 percent of their revenues from federal transfers in 1994–95, while Ontario only received 16 percent, Alberta about 15 percent, and British Columbia less than 14 percent. In the absence of equalization payments, otherwise identical persons in different provinces would face very different tax burdens.

Efficiency Between 1988 and 1991, the federal tax system underwent a major reform. The main intent of the reform was to make the system more efficient, fairer, and administratively simpler. That was done by broadening the income tax bases to eliminate some tax expenditures, by simplifying the rate structure of the individual income tax base and converting many of the deductions to credits, and by replacing the narrow-based Manufacturers Sales Tax (MST), which applied only to manufactured goods, with the much broader GST.

From an efficiency point of view, the most important objectives were to broaden the revenue base and reduce the rates of taxes. This was intended both to create a "level playing field" by not favouring one type of activity over another, and to reduce the disincentives in the tax system to work, save, invest,

[1] W. Irwin Gillespie, *The Redistribution of Income in Canada* (Ottawa: Gage Publishing Inc., 1980).

[2] John Whalley, "Regression or Progression: The Taxing Question of Incidence Analysis," *Canadian Journal of Economics* 17 (November 1984): 654–82.

Almost all industrialized countries have a national sales tax in place and rely on it to raise a significant proportion of tax revenues, the United States being the major exception. It is obviously important that such taxes be designed to be as efficient, as equitable, and as administratively simple as possible. One by one, countries have turned to *value-added taxes* as the chosen form.

Under a value-added tax system, taxes are applied to the sales made by all firms in the economy. The firms, in turn, remit to the tax authorities the taxes they collect on these sales less the taxes they paid on their purchases of inputs (materials and capital goods, but not labour) from other firms. Thus, they end up paying taxes only on the net value they add to inputs they have purchased elsewhere. As products work their way through the successive stages of production, they are taxed at each stage on the value added there. When they finally reach the consumer, the full value will have been taxed, making the valued-added tax equivalent to a tax levied on consumer sales directly at the retail level.

The multistage nature of the tax has a number of advantages. For one, there is no "cascading" of taxes. Under a retail sales tax, a firm that purchases inputs from retailers pays a tax that is not credited when its own product eventually gets sold and taxed at the retail level. Cascading is eliminated with a value-added tax, since all the taxes that have been applied on purchased inputs are credited, ensuring that the tax applies uniformly to all goods and services. For another, if goods are exported, the exporting firm is able to deduct all taxes that had been paid on inputs

used in producing the exported good. Being tax-free, exports are not put at a disadvantage in international markets. Similarly, imports coming into the country can be taxed at their full value, just as if they had been taxed in the various stages of production had they been produced in the domestic economy. They too are on a level playing field with domestically produced goods. Finally, tax compliance is potentially easier for the government to enforce since the system of crediting leaves a paper trail that can be used by tax auditors. Thus, a value-added tax has the potential to apply in a nondiscriminatory fashion to a very broad base.

For these reasons, in 1991 the Canadian government implemented the Goods and Services Tax (GST), which is just another name for a value-added tax. The tax, which replaced a tax on the sales of manufactured goods only, is applied at the uniform rate of 7 percent to virtually all goods and services sold to Canadian consumers, the main exceptions being food, which is tax-exempt, and new housing, which is taxed at a lower rate. At the same time, to address the adverse distributional effect that would otherwise result from a tax on consumption (given that lower-income persons consume a larger proportion of their incomes), the GST is accompanied by a GST Tax Credit to compensate low-income taxpayers for the increased tax liabilities that they are faced with.

Despite the considerable efficiency advantages of having a broad-based uniform sales tax alongside the other major taxes such as the income tax, there are still some concerns. Taxpayer discontent with the tax seems unusually high, even discounting the fact that no one likes to pay taxes. Part of this may be due to the fact that, unlike virtually all value-added taxes elsewhere, the GST is highly visible: the tax is typically not included in the list price of goods but is added at the cash register. The fact that the tax applies to such a broad base, including services like hairdressers, insurance, and movies, seems to be a further irritant. Firms, especially small ones, are unhappy with the tax since every one of them has to expend resources collecting it for the government. Many observers have suggested that tax avoidance has increased significantly because of displeasure with the GST. The displeasure is compounded by the fact that in all provinces except Alberta, there is a provincial retail sales tax, also highly visible at the retail level, but applying to a much smaller number of products.

and undertake innovative and perhaps risky activities. In the individual income tax, the top marginal tax rates were lowered from 51 percent to 44 percent, and the preferential tax treatment of capital gains and dividends was reduced. Other tax breaks, such as those on rental housing, were eliminated. Corporate tax rates were also lowered from 46 percent to 38 percent, and the base was broadened by eliminating such things as investment tax credits and accelerated writeoffs for depreciation of machinery and equipment.

The GST itself represented a substantial broadening of the federal sales tax base to include virtually all goods and services with the exception of food. The rate of GST was set at 7 percent, as compared with the previous 13.5 percent under the MST. The GST also avoided what were thought to be two major problems with the MST. First, though the MST was only intended to apply to manufactured consumer goods, it was practically impossible to prevent some manufactured goods used as capital and business inputs by firms from being taxed. For example, computers and automobiles are used as both consumer goods and capital goods. Second, the MST tended to favour foreign-produced goods over domestically produced goods. Imports were taxed at the border and did not include costs of transportation and distribution; domestically produced goods, however, were taxed at the point of sale by the manufacturer and did include these costs. Similarly, though exports were meant to be tax-exempt, in practice it proved impossible to purge a product's export price of taxes that had been paid at earlier stages of production. The GST avoided these problems because of its multistage nature. All firms pay the GST on their final sales, but are able to claim a GST credit on the input purchases; thus, they pay a tax only on the amount of value added at each stage. Such a system ensures that taxes on business inputs are all purged from the system, and when products are exported their value does not include any elements of tax paid at earlier stages of production.

These tax reforms accomplished a lot in terms of rationalizing the tax system and making it more efficient. Nonetheless, many inefficiencies remain. Within the income tax system, not all tax preferences were abolished. Manufacturing and processing industries still have preferential corporate tax rates, and the resource industries still tend to be treated generously in terms of the way in which their capital costs may be deducted. In the personal tax system, some forms of capital income (among them, capital gains, retirement savings, imputed rent on owner-occupied housing) are still treated favourably relative to others (interest). The sales tax systems do not apply to all goods and services. For example, the federal system excludes food, while the provinces typically tax very few services. Still, the reform achieved some improvement in efficiency and did so without adversely affecting the redistributive properties of the system through a system of tax credits to low-income taxpayers.

Administrative Simplicity Despite the apparent gain in efficiency, the whole tax collection machinery remains an administratively complex one, for both taxpayers and the government. This is probably inevitable, given the many objectives the system is intended to fulfill, the large number of taxpayers, the many different ways in which income can be earned, and the number of goods and services on which it can be spent. Undoubtedly, the broadening of the tax base and the lowering of the rate structure reduced some of the complexity of the tax system. For example, it made it less attractive for taxpayers to search for ways to find loopholes that enabled them to avoid paying taxes. The lowering of tax rates also reduced the incentive to engage in nonmarket activities to avoid or even to evade taxes.

At the same time, the introduction of the GST may well lead to a more costly tax system. The number of tax-paying firms has increased dramatically, from only manufacturers to virtually all firms in the economy. The complication is particularly burdensome for retailers, who are responsible for collecting both the GST and provincial retail sales taxes. The federal government had hoped that the provinces would be willing to harmonize their sales taxes with the GST by making their bases—the items to which the sales tax applies—more comparable. However, to date only Quebec, New Brunswick, Nova Scotia, and Newfoundland have chosen to do so. The remaining provinces have retained their own retail sales taxes, which apply on a much narrower range of products than the GST, exempting virtually all services, for example.

An important source of administrative simplicity in the Canadian tax system is the extent to which the income taxes collected by the federal and provincial governments are harmonized. All provinces and territories except Quebec have entered into **tax collection agreements** with the federal government whereby Revenue Canada collects individual income taxes on behalf of the provinces in return for which the provinces abide by the federal tax base and rate structure. Each province is allowed to choose a single provincial income tax rate to apply to federal taxes payable. As well, Revenue Canada administers provincial tax credits for provinces for a small fee, provided the credits are nondiscriminatory. Examples include credits for property and sales taxes paid, political contributions, and contributions to venture capital and stock savings funds. As a result, the federal progressive rate structure is preserved and taxpayers are required to fill in only one tax re-

turn. A similar arrangement applies for the corporate tax, though three provinces (Alberta, Ontario, and Quebec) choose not to participate. Nonetheless, their tax structures are very similar to that of the federal government and the other provinces.

Transparency Of all the parts of the tax system, the corporation income tax is perhaps the least transparent. Although corporations write the cheque to the Receiver General, most economists agree that much of the burden is shifted to individuals and households, through reduced wages and/or higher product prices. The GST ranks second lowest on the transparency scale. Politicians love the sales tax, because they know that many, perhaps most, individuals never figure out the total amount they are actually spending on government services.

TRANSFERS

In addition to tax policy, government affects income distribution through **transfer programmes.** Transfers are payments that households receive without having to engage in any current productive activity in return. Transfer payments can be private, such as company pensions or scholarships from private universities. Government engages in a wide range of transfer programmes. Two major groups of government transfer programmes concern us here: **income-tested transfers,** the direct purpose of which is to redistribute income from upper-income to lower-income Canadians, and **social insurance,** which protects individuals, irrespective of income, in times of need. We consider these in turn.

PROGRAMMES TO REDRESS INCOME INEQUALITY

Politicians frequently appeal to voters by expressing their concern for the poor. Compassion for others less fortunate is a fundamental human value. Government programmes to aid the poor reflect the belief that all citizens have a collective responsibility to take care of those among them who are in need. Though the extent to which responsibility should be borne by government or by voluntary charities is a matter of debate, governments in all the developed countries have assumed a major role in providing at least a safety net to protect the most disadvantaged.

Government programmes have been mostly aimed at reducing the extremes of inequality—in particular, preventing poverty and providing a safety net for the very poor. The poor include those who are not working and those with low wages. Those not working can be grouped into at least three categories: (1) people who cannot work because of either age (too young or too old) or disability; (2) people who cannot find work, perhaps because the economy is in recession and there is a shortage of jobs; and (3) people who choose not to work, usually because the wages they would receive are so low relative to what they can get from government transfer programmes that it does not pay them to work. Government has sought to reduce poverty by focusing on each of these groups. It has sought to reduce the number of unemployed, increase the incomes of those who are employed but earning low wages, and provide support to those who for one reason or another cannot work.

Unemployment Governments attempt to reduce unemployment and its costs by means of three measures:

1 Unemployment insurance provides income for those *temporarily* unemployed. It is also regarded as a social insurance programme and discussed further in the next subsections.

2 The government's commitment to keeping the economy at close to full employment serves to reduce the total number of persons who are involuntarily unemployed, especially in depressed regions. It does this both through macroeconomic policies discussed elsewhere and through preferential tax policies directed at depressed regions and industries.

3 Job-retraining programmes and employment placement centres help those who have lost a job to get another one.

There remain important gaps. The long-term unemployed and new entrants to the labour force do not receive unemployment compensation. Despite the government's commitment to maintaining a high level of employment, in recent years unemployment rates have varied between 9 and 12 percent, and in many regions of the country for much of the decade of the 1980s as many as one out of six workers was unable to find a job. Job-retraining programmes, while helping a little, have had only limited success. There is a marked difference between the skills required for the jobs that the economy is creating and those required for the jobs being destroyed.

Income of the Employed The government further addresses income inequality by attempting to raise the incomes of low-wage individuals who do work. There are two broad programmes for this purpose:

1 Minimum wage legislation is intended to raise the wages of those without skills.

2 Refundable tax credits are delivered to low-income persons through the income tax system. At the federal level, these include the GST tax credit and the child tax credit. Various provinces offer property tax credits and sales tax credits as well, which are available whether or not the person is employed.

The minimum wage legislation has been, at best, controversial. As discussed in Chapter 5, the higher wages have made it more difficult for unskilled workers to obtain a job. Thus, while wages of those working have risen slightly, the number of those who are poor because they cannot get a job may have increased.

Support for Unemployables The federal and provincial governments sponsor several programmes targeted at helping those who cannot participate, or participate fully, in the labour force:

1 Old Age Security (OAS) and the Guaranteed Income Supplement (which supplements OAS for the very poor aged) provide federal support for the aged and disabled; many provinces supplement this with their own programmes.

CLOSE-UP: ARE POVERTY LINES INFLATED?

In Canada, no official method of defining poverty exists. Nonetheless, Statistics Canada produces a set of measures called Low Income Cut-Offs (LICOs), which politicians, researchers, journalists, and social agencies use as if they were poverty lines.

LICOs are calculated periodically for seven different family sizes (one to six members, and seven and above), and for five different community-size categories (rural; less than 30,000; 30,000–99,999; 100,000–499,999; and 500,000 and over). For each of these thirty-five categories, a LICO is calculated statistically that measures the income level at which 58.5 percent of family income is spent on three basic necessities—food, shelter, and clothing. The figure 58.5 comes from the fact that in a base year (1978) the average family spent 38.5 percent of their income on these necessities. To this, 20 percent was arbitrarily added.

Though Statistics Canada's LICO is the most commonly cited measure of the extent of poverty, it is not the only one. For example, the Canadian Council on Social Development (CCSD), an independent, national, nonprofit organization, also has an unofficial poverty line. The CCSD line is simply half the average income of all the households of a given type. In 1988, 3.3 million Canadians were poor according to Statistics Canada's LICO, while 5 million were below the CCSD poverty line.

Both the LICO and CCSD poverty lines are relative measures, since they are defined in relation to average income. Rather than measuring poverty, they measure the extent of inequality. After all, if poverty is just a statement that some

people are relatively worse off, then poverty can never be reduced, because some people will always be closer to the bottom. Moreover, a relative concept of poverty might be seen to reduce the moral urgency of fighting poverty.

Some persons have advocated adopting a more absolute measure of poverty applicable worldwide, arguing that measures such as LICO overstate the actual extent of poverty. Applying the absolute approach involves measuring only the cost of acquiring essential goods and services. It is not without problems either, however. There is bound to be subjectivity in drawing up the list of basic necessities, and that list may differ from year to year, or country to country. For example, an indoor flush toilet may be viewed as a necessity in Canada, but may well not be a necessity in some developing countries. (In fact, 99 percent of 1989 LICO's poor had a flush toilet.)

In a recent study Christopher Sarlo has developed an alternative poverty line, one that is an absolute line. He follows Statistics Canada and the CCSD in using income as a poverty indicator. His set of poverty lines is based on the cost of necessities for seven family sizes (one to six, and seven and over), and for the ten provinces.

The construction of Sarlo's poverty lines is as follows: First, he calculates the cost of the basic necessities. These include the expenditures required to obtain a nutritious diet, shelter, clothing, personal hygiene, health care, and necessary transportation, but exclude social amenities such as alcohol, vacations, and piano lessons. Second, he adds up all these costs for each family type and location. The sum is the poverty line ($13,615 for a family of four in Thunder Bay).

COMPARATIVE POVERTY LINES AND POVERTY RATES, 1988 (FAMILY OF FOUR, COMMUNITY OF 100,000–499,999)

	LICO	CCSD	Sarlo
Poverty line ($ income)	$22,371	$26,941	$13,140
Poverty rate (% of population)	10.1%	15.4%	2.5%
Number of poor families	172,115	262,262	43,292

Using a weighted average for populations of metropolitan areas, the poverty lines of the metropolitan areas are converted into poverty lines for provinces. Finally, Statistics Canada information on family incomes is used to determine the number of poor.

The absolute poverty line calculated by Sarlo is considerably lower than that obtained by Statistics Canada or the CCSD. As the accompanying table shows, Sarlo's poverty line is roughly half that of the CCSD, and the rate of poverty is only one-sixth as large.

Source: Christopher Sarlo, *Poverty in Canada* (Vancouver: The Fraser Institute, 1992).

2 Welfare assistance programmes are operated by each of the provinces to provide support to all non-working low-income families who are not eligible for unemployment insurance. The funding of these provincial programmes is shared by the federal government through a set of federal-provincial transfers. Welfare programmes have special provisions for those like the disabled and children who are unable to work. In addition to cash payments, various services are provided such as housing, transportation, and prescription drugs and dental services.

There has been much concern about the adequacy of programmes to assist those who do not have their own means of support. There is a particular level of income (varying by family size) such that if a family's income falls below that level, or **poverty line,** the family is considered to be in poverty. The National Council of Welfare defines its poverty line as the income level at which the proportion of income spent on the essentials of life—food, shelter, clothing—is 20 percent above the proportion spent on the same essentials by the average Canadian family of the same size in the same province. This corresponds with Statistics Canada's definition of the low-income line. In 1994, the poverty line for a family of four in Ontario was $30,708. Over one in six persons in Canada were below the poverty line, and almost two thirds of children being raised by a single female parent were below it. The National Council of Welfare calculates that welfare assistance rates are well below the poverty line. For example, in Ontario, which has the most generous welfare rates, the incomes of welfare recipient families and unemployables is only about three quarters of the poverty line, while in Alberta it is closer to one half. Single employables fare much worse: in Ontario welfare income among this group is about half of the poverty line, while in Alberta it is about one third.

SOCIAL INSURANCE

Life is full of risks. The job a person has may disappear as the economy restructures in response to competition from abroad or technological change. A major illness may befall an individual or one of her family. Disability may occur because of accident, injury, or natural causes. The country might have to go to war and devote most of its human and physical resources temporarily to the war effort. We have seen in Chapter 16 that one of the roles of markets, especially capital markets, is to provide insurance against the risk that misfortunes may occur. Property insurance compensates a home owner in the event of a fire or theft; automobile insurance pays the costs of an accident; earthquake insurance covers the cost of earthquake damage; even uncertainty about how long we will live can be insured against by purchasing annuities from life insurance companies. However, private insurance companies may not be able to insure us adequately against some of the major risks that affect our livelihood, such as unemployment, large fluctuations in income, disability, major shocks like wars, and so on. This may be partly because of the problems of moral hazard or adverse selection that we encountered in Chapter 16. Or some persons may be uninsurable because of characteristics that they are born with. One of the major achievements of the postwar welfare state has been the provision of security against major adversities that might occur.

Government programmes that provide security against adversities such as unemployment, disability, and ill health are referred to as **social insurance programmes.** Whereas other transfer programmes are directed to those in need, the beneficiaries of social insurance programmes include a much broader group of people, including the middle class. Indeed, the support of the middle class has been critical in establishing and maintaining such programmes, given that they represent an enormous block of votes. We begin with a review of some of the major social insurance programmes.

UNEMPLOYMENT INSURANCE

The Unemployment Insurance (UI) programme, which the federal government began calling Employment Insurance in 1996, is the largest single expenditure item of the federal government, amounting to about $13 billion in 1995–96, roughly 12 percent of total federal programme expenditures. It

has grown at an average rate of 8 percent per year since 1984–85, largely because of a persistently high unemployment rate. Its purpose is to provide temporary payments to persons who lose their jobs through no fault of their own. To be eligible, workers must be employed and contribute to the programme for a minimal period of time, ranging from ten to twenty weeks depending upon the regional unemployment rate. Benefits may be claimed for up to 45 weeks, depending upon weeks worked and the regional unemployment rate. The amount of payment is related to wages while the employee contributed, with an upper bound. Benefits are also available for maternity leave and sickness, as well as in support of job-training and job-creation projects.

The UI system has come under considerable criticism in recent years not only because of its rapidly escalating costs, but also because of its alleged adverse effects on the economy. Critics have argued that rather than being an insurance programme, it has become part of the system of redistribution and regional development giving rise to adverse incentive effects that increase the costs of the system. For example, since premiums paid are at the same rate for all, there is no relationship between premiums and the probability of the event being insured against. Thus, jobs in industries that are high risk for layoffs and seasonal jobs are effectively favoured relative to low-risk ones. Since laid-off workers are eligible for UI benefits, there is an incentive for firms to hire workers temporarily as well as for employers to use temporary layoffs in response to slowdowns rather than other methods, such as reducing hours worked. It is also argued that workers themselves respond to the UI system by quitting jobs too frequently, staying unemployed too long, and joining the labour force for short stints simply to become eligible for UI benefits. Finally, far from addressing the issue of regional disparities, the system may well help to perpetuate them by encouraging workers to stay in depressed regions rather than seeking jobs elsewhere.

Various commissions, official and otherwise, have recommended reforming the UI system to make it more like a genuine insurance system. One way to do this would be to have contribution rates reflect the risk of unemployment. This can be done by relating the premiums paid by firms to their past histories of claiming benefits, referred to as **experience rating.** Purely redistributive elements of the programme would then be assumed by other programmes. Some have also suggested devoting a larger proportion of funds to retraining rather than pure income support. This approach is taken in the Scandinavian countries.

PAYMENTS TO THE ELDERLY

The system of payments to the elderly is another form of social insurance, essentially providing income support to those who need it in retirement. It has various components, including Old Age Security payments to all persons 65 and over; the Guaranteed Income Supplement, which provides additional amounts to those with lower incomes; and the Canada Pension Plan (Quebec Pension Plan in that province), which is a contributory pension for employees.

Several controversies have surrounded the public pension programme. The most important question is whether the benefits that the elderly receive today can be sustained—will the country be able to pay the same kind of benefits to those who are currently in their twenties, thirties, and forties? With private pensions, an individual's benefits are paid from monies he and others paid when they purchased insurance while they were working many years earlier. The public pension programme, on the other hand, is basically a pay-as-you-go system: current tax revenues are used to pay the benefits of today's retirees. The viability of a pay-as-you-go public pension system depends on the existence of a large number of workers to support those who are retired. As the old have come to live longer and retire earlier, the number of workers per public pension beneficiary has dropped dramatically, from 16.5 in 1950 to slightly more than 5 today. As the baby boomers, the large number of people born in the years immediately after World War II, reach retirement, this number is expected to drop still more.

Pay-as-you-go public pensions have a further disadvantage compared with private pensions. The latter use the funds accumulated for future pension payments as a source of money for capital investment in the economy. Since public pensions have no such fund, they do not contribute to investment and thus to the growth of the economy. Given the relatively low rate of saving and investment in the Canadian economy compared with some of the faster-growing economies elsewhere, this represents a significant drawback.

In recognition of these drawbacks of pay-as-you-go public pensions and of the continuing challenge of financing the federal budget deficit, the Canadian government has in recent years begun to institute measures to alleviate the worst of the problems. It has introduced tax incentives to assist Canadians in saving for their own retirement, thereby partly reducing the need for future taxpayers to support the growing number of pensioners. Alongside that, changes in the Old Age Security system have served both to reduce its cost and target it more to those who really need it. Thus, payments are now "clawed back" from high-income pensioners.

HEALTH INSURANCE

Perhaps the most cherished social insurance programme in Canada is health insurance, which covers the full costs of treating medical problems for all persons. Each province administers its own health insurance system. The systems are financed partly from a federal grant to the provinces and partly from the provinces' own revenue sources. Most provinces use either a payroll tax or a system of premiums, but some rely heavily on general tax revenues. Public health insurance is now treated as virtually an essential public service enabling persons to obtain health care regardless of their means and their "insurability."

However, health insurance suffers from burgeoning costs. Moreover, funds to meet escalating costs are ever scarcer—a fact that the large deficits in the public sector have brought home forcefully to governments. The federal government has substantially reduced the transfers that it makes to the provinces in support of health care, and there is widespread concern that the principle of free and universal coverage will be compromised.

The provincial governments have tried to contain health costs by designing programmes with better incentives and by limiting the size of reimbursements for medical procedures. These programmes have been partially successful, but there is a growing conviction that you can squeeze only so much water out of a stone. Cost reductions will become increasingly difficult, and attempts to reduce payments further may have marked effects on the quality of health care.

THE COSTS AND BENEFITS OF REDISTRIBUTION

Tax, welfare, and social insurance programmes in Canada all play an important role in answering one of the fundamental questions posed in Chapter 1: For whom are goods and services produced (who gets to enjoy the goods and services that are available)? Each group in society would like to pay as little in taxes as possible and receive as many benefits as possible, and complaints about fairness abound. But issues of what is fair may never be resolved. And economists worry that at least some attempts to make sure everyone has a fair slice may so reduce the size of the economic pie to be divided that almost everyone is worse off.

EQUITY/EFFICIENCY TRADE-OFFS

Economists enter the discussion of redistribution to clarify the costs and consequences of various programmes, including different tax systems. Systems that tax the rich heavily or provide support for the poor regardless of their employability are likely to have adverse effects on incentives. Economists try to calculate precisely how important these effects are.

All economists agree that as government redistributes more income to the poor, it has to raise taxes on the rich and middle-income individuals, which weakens their incentives to work. But economists disagree about the magnitudes of the trade-offs. Most economists agree that at high enough tax rates, incentives are greatly reduced. The high marginal tax rates of 80 percent or more that used to

prevail in the top income brackets probably had large negative effects on efficiency. But whether at current marginal tax rates, an increase in taxation would have a *large* effect on incentives is much more debatable.

We have seen how economists focus on the trade-offs—between equity (how the pie is divided) and efficiency (the size of the pie); and between reductions in the risks of life (through the provision of social insurance) and economic incentives. Beyond these trade-offs lie basic issues of social values, of what kind of society we want to have, *recognizing the economic constraints on the choices that we can make.* These values touch not only on issues of efficiency, equality, and risk protection, but also on individual rights and social responsibilities.

HOW WELL DO WE DO?

Taking all of the government programmes into account—the tax system, welfare, social insurance—does the government succeed in changing the answer to the question "Who gets the goods produced in the economy?" To answer this question, we need some way of measuring the distribution of income.

Economists often represent the degree of inequality in an economy by a diagram called the **Lorenz curve.** The Lorenz curve shows the cumulative fraction of the country's total income earned by the poorest 10 percent, the poorest 20 percent, the poorest 30 percent, and so on. Figure 20.3A shows Lorenz curves for Canada both before and after government tax and transfer programmes have had their effect. If there were complete equality, then 20 percent of the income would accrue to the lowest 20 percent of the population, 40 percent to the lowest 40 percent, and so on. The Lorenz curve would be a straight 45-degree line. If incomes were very concentrated, then the lowest 80 percent might receive almost nothing, and the top 5 percent might receive 80 percent of total income; in this case, the Lorenz curve would be very bowed. Twice the area between the 45-degree line and the Lorenz curve is a commonly employed measure of inequality, called the **Gini coefficient.**

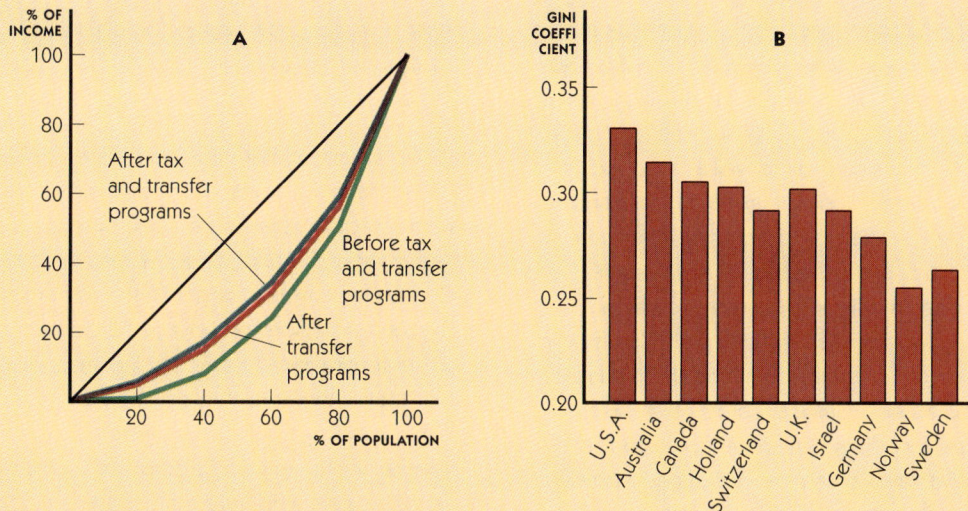

Figure 20.3 INEQUALITY MEASURES

Taxes and subsidies affect the distribution of income. Panel A shows three Lorenz curves for Canada in 1993, one for income before taxes have been levied and government transfers have been received, another after transfers but before taxes, and the other after both taxes and transfers. Clearly, some redistribution does take place through these mechanisms, as they move the Lorenz curve toward greater equality. Panel B shows how other developed countries rank relative to Canada on one standard measure of inequality, the Gini coefficient. Canada ranks third among the ten. *Sources:* Statistics Canada, *Income after Tax: Distributions by Size in Canada, 1993,* Catalogue No. 13-210; *Luxembourg Income Study Database,* 1989.

As can be seen, the 1993 after-transfer curve for Canada is decidedly inside the pre-tax and transfer curve, and the after-tax curve is yet further inside, indicating that both the transfer system and the tax system make incomes more equal than the market would have made them. But despite the many government programmes to improve the opportunities for the less well off, there is still considerable inequality in Canada. For example, from the diagram we can infer that the bottom 60 percent of the families in the income distribution obtain just under 35 percent of the economy's income (virtually unchanged from twenty years earlier).

Relative to other industrialized countries, our degree of inequality is quite high. Panel B in Figure 20.3 gives the measure of inequality for ten such countries. Canada ranks third, behind only the United States and Australia. The United States has by far the most unequal distribution of income.

THE ROLES OF GOVERNMENT: A REVIEW

Part Two, which set forth the basic competitive model, closed with a chapter that explained how the market system envisioned by that model will produce efficient economic outcomes. Beyond establishing a legal framework within which markets could operate, the only role seen for government in Part 2 was possibly to correct the unacceptable distributions of income that have also been the subject of this chapter.

In Part Three, we have learned of many instances in which markets in the real world can be expected to depart from the basic competitive model. Failures of competition were discussed in Chapters 12 and 13, and government responses to them formed the subject of Chapter 14. Chapter 15

Income inequality has been a major issue in most recent policy debates. Critics of the federal government's tax reform of the late 1980s, which included reducing the rates and broadening the base of the income tax as well as introducing the Goods and Services Tax (GST), have argued that it will worsen the distribution of income. Opponents of the Canada-U.S. and North American Free Trade agreements claim that workers will suffer as wages are bid down by increased competition and as social programmes are threatened. Groups representing lower-income Canadians demand a "social contract" as part of a new Canadian constitution to protect the disadvantaged in society. There is a general feeling that increasing competitiveness and globalization of the world economy is causing an increase in income inequality in Canada. Most recently, government attempts to deal with deficit problems have been criticized by those who feel that cuts in government spending will widen the gap between rich and poor.

The table below shows the proportions of income going to each quintile of income groups for selected postwar years. It shows that the Canadian distribution of annual income is remarkably stable. Looking at those figures, one can detect a 4-40 rule: the lowest fifth (20 percent of families and unattached individuals) of income earners obtain roughly 4 percent of the total income, while the highest fifth earn about 40 percent of total income in Canada. This rule has applied for almost the entire postwar period. The share for the bottom quintile fell slightly in the 1970s but has returned to comparable levels more recently, and has even improved slightly. The top quintile has improved its

share by about 2 percentage points. In 1994, the share of the top quintile was 43.6 percent, and of the bottom quintile was 4.7 percent.

Annual income distribution statistics do not tell the whole story, however. For one thing, they are misleading because the same person can appear in different quintiles of the distribution at various times over his or her lifetime. For example, retired persons or those just entering the labour force typically have low incomes, yet over their entire lives they may be no worse off than the average person. Because the extreme quintiles include a disproportionately large number of persons who have temporarily large or small incomes, annual income distribution statistics tend to exaggerate the extent of inequality. In a recent study, three Canadian economists, James Davies, France St.-Hilaire, and John Whalley, calculated the income distribution using incomes earned over the lifetime rather than annual income. They found that this dramatically reduced the degree of inequality. According to their calculations, about one half of annual income inequality disappears when lifetime income is used. On a lifetime income basis, the 4-40 rule becomes a 10-30 rule: the lowest fifth earns 10 percent of total lifetime income while the highest fifth earns 30 percent.

Another problem with annual income statistics is that they do not distinguish between those whose income comes mainly from working and earning wages and salaries, and those who obtain capital income from their wealth. Looking at wealth (the amount accumulated over time or inherited) rather than income (the amount received in a year) makes inequality look more extreme. A study done by Statistics Canada

DISTRIBUTION OF INCOME BY QUINTILES
(PERCENTAGE)

	Lowest fifth	Second fifth	Third fifth	Fourth fifth	Highest fifth
1965	4.4	11.8	18.0	24.5	41.4
1971	3.6	10.6	17.6	24.9	43.1
1975	4.0	10.6	17.6	25.1	42.6
1981	4.6	10.9	17.6	25.1	41.8
1986	4.7	10.4	17.0	24.9	43.1
1991	4.7	10.3	16.6	24.7	43.8
1994	4.7	10.2	16.7	24.8	43.6

showed that in 1984, the average wealth of Canadian households was $86,000 (total wealth divided by the number of households). Wealth includes the value of homes, vehicles, and investments of all sorts. At the same time, the median wealth of Canadian households was $41,200; that is, the number of households who had wealth above $41,200 equalled the number who had wealth below that number. This in itself indicates that the distribution of wealth is skewed towards the upper end: a small number of households have relatively large amounts of wealth, and a large number have relatively small amounts. The study found that the top 7 percent of families based on income has 24 percent of the wealth, and had an average wealth of $306,400. On the other hand, households in the bottom 28 percent of income earners had only 11 percent of the wealth and an average wealth of only $32,500,

roughly a tenth of the wealth controlled by the top 7 percent.

Problems inevitably arise with any statistical measure. Did the data correctly account for the value of government subsidies to the poor (housing, medical care, welfare services)? Should gains in the value of shares and other assets be included in income? But almost any way the statistics are sliced, they still show that despite the many redistributive policies implemented over the years, inequality remains a feature of the Canadian economy.

Sources: Raj K. Chawla, "The Distribution of Wealth in Canada and the United States," *Canadian Economic Observer*, April 1990, pp. 4.1–4.17; James Davies, France St.-Hilaire, and John Whalley, "Some Calculations of Lifetime Tax Incidence," *American Economic Review* 74 (September 1984): 633–49; and François Vaillancourt, ed., *Income Distribution and Economic Security in Canada* (Toronto: University of Toronto Press, 1986), pp. 1–86; Statistics Canada, *Income Distributions by Size in Canada*, Catalogue No. 13-207 various years.

pointed out the absence of any analysis of technological advance in the basic model, and discussed the patent system development as responses to this shortcoming.

The basic model assumes that parties to transactions are armed with all the information they need about the goods being traded. Chapter 16 pointed out why this might not be the case in the product,

labour, and capital markets. For instance, there may be an information imbalance between sellers and consumers: consumers may be ill informed because information is costly to obtain, so that they can't afford to become completely informed; sellers tend to have better information than buyers and may try to take advantage of this. Government has responded with truth-in-advertising laws designed to protect

THE MARKET FAILURE ROLES OF GOVERNMENT

Market failures	Examples of government responses
Markets not competitive	Anti-combines policies
Product markets (Chapters 12–14)	
Labour markets (Chapter 7)	
Public goods and externalities (Chapters 18, 19)	Regulation of pollution
	Provision of national defence
Basic research as a public good; externalities associated with R & D (Chapter 15)	Public support of basic research; patents
Imperfect information and thin (incomplete) markets (Chapter 16)	Consumer protection legislation (including securities regulations); government loan and insurance programmes
Redistribution (Chapter 20)	Welfare and social insurance programmes

consumers from this information imbalance. Similarly, the regulations surrounding securities trading were promulgated largely out of concern that buyers needed more information than they were given. In certain insurance and loan markets, where systematic information problems create a thin (incomplete) or nonexistent market, government has stepped in to supply the insurance or loans itself.

In this part we have focused directly on the public sector. Chapter 18 discussed market failures that arise from public goods and externalities. These provide a major justification for governments to take over from the private sector the provision of some goods and services. Public provision of goods and services is not perfect either, since the incentives and pressures facing governments differ from those facing private firms. Just as there can be market failure, so there can be public-sector failure. Chapter 19 dealt in more detail with a specific form of market failure, that caused by externalities. One of the major forms of externalities is environmental pollution and degradation. Public intervention is required to correct for the fact that market prices fail to account for environmental externalities. In the realm beyond market failures is income redistribution, the subject of this chapter. As has been pointed out earlier, markets generally produce economically efficient outcomes, but there is nothing to say that the income shares it produces will be socially acceptable.

REVIEW AND PRACTICE

SUMMARY

1 Even if markets are efficient, there may be dissatisfaction with the resulting distribution of income.

2 At the federal and provincial levels, the largest share of taxes comes from the individual income tax, followed by sales and payroll taxes. At the municipal level the main source of revenue is the property tax.

3 A tax system can be judged by four criteria: horizontal and vertical equity, efficiency, administrative simplicity, and transparency.

4 The government has enacted a variety of programmes to fight poverty, including welfare programmes, refundable tax credits, job retraining and placement, and minimum wage laws.

5 All public assistance programmes force society to balance the concerns of equity, which involve help-ing those in need, with the concerns of efficiency, which involve making sure that both poor people and taxpayers have good incentives to work.

6 Social insurance programmes, such as health insurance, public pensions, and unemployment insurance, are designed to reduce risks of income loss or misfortune that would otherwise be uninsurable. Unlike programmes to fight poverty, they provide protection to persons at all income levels.

KEY TERMS

income redistribution	excise taxes and duties	stumpage fees	tax expenditures
social insurance	tariffs	property tax	marginal and average tax rates
individual income taxes	payroll taxes	horizontal and vertical equity	
corporation income taxes	retail sales tax		equalization payments
Goods and Services Tax (GST)	royalties	progressive and regressive taxes	tax collection agreements
	mining taxes		Lorenz curve
			Gini coefficient

REVIEW QUESTIONS

1 Will an efficient market necessarily produce a fairly equal distribution of income? Discuss.

2 What is the main source of federal revenue? of provincial and municipal revenue?

3 What are the four characteristics of a good tax system? How well does the Canadian tax system measure up in terms of these criteria? What is the differ-ence between horizontal equity and vertical equity? What is the difference between a progressive and a regressive tax?

4 Define the difference between a social insurance programme and a redistribution programme, and give examples of each.

5 What is a Lorenz curve? What does it reveal?

PROBLEMS

1 Suppose the UI system is changed so that premiums paid by firms vary according to past layoff experience. What effect would this have on the number of days off in the future? What effect would it have on employment in seasonal industries? in industries that have steady employment patterns?

2 Suppose you have an income of $30,000. In the income tax system, incomes up to $20,000 are taxed at 20 percent, while those from $20,001 to $40,000 are taxed at 30 percent. There is a personal tax credit of $3,000 available to you as a single tax payer. What are your average and marginal tax rates? How would they change if the personal tax credit were changed to $2,000? if the tax rate in the first bracket were reduced to 15 percent? if the tax rate in the second bracket were increased to 40 percent?

3 Assume that a country has a simple tax structure in which all income over $10,000 is taxed at 20 percent. Evaluate a proposal to increase the progressivity of the tax structure by requiring all those with incomes over $100,000 to pay a tax of 80 percent on income in excess of $100,000. Draw a high-wage earner's budget constraint. How does the surtax affect his budget constraint? What happens to his incentives to work? Is it possible that imposing the tax actually will reduce the tax revenues the government receives from the rich?

4 Explain how the following changes might affect how welfare assistance influences the incentive for poor people to work:

(a) increasing the amount paid to welfare recipients.

(b) allowing welfare recipients to earn some income without losing all their welfare assistance.

(c) requiring welfare recipients to do some work in return for receiving welfare assistance.

5 Draw Lorenz curves for the following countries Which country has the greatest and least inequality?

| | Percentage of total income received by | | | | |
	Lowest fifth	Second fifth	Third fifth	Fourth fifth	Top fifth
United States	4.7	11.0	17.4	25.0	41.9
Japan	8.7	13.2	17.5	23.1	37.5
Germany	6.8	12.7	17.8	24.1	38.7

GLOSSARY

absolute advantage: the advantage one country has over another country in the production of a good it can produce more efficiently (with fewer inputs)

acquired endowments: the resources a country builds for itself, like a network of roads or an educated population

adverse selection: the principle that, for example, those who most want to buy insurance tend to be those most at risk, which leads to a high price for insurance (to cover those at high risk) and discourages those at less risk from buying insurance at all; similar phenomena occur in credit, labour, and product markets

aggregate demand curve: the curve relating the total demand for the economy's goods and services at each price level, given the level of wages

aggregate savings: the sum of savings of all individuals, firms, and governments in the economy

aggregate supply curve: the curve relating the total supply of the economy's goods and services at each price level, given the level of wages

anti-combines laws: laws that discourage monopoly and restrictive practices and encourage greater competition

arbitrage: the process by which assets with comparable risk, liquidity, and tax treatment are priced to yield comparable expected returns

arc elasticity: an elasticity calculated for large changes in price

asset: any item that is long-lived, purchased for the service it renders over its life and for what one will receive when one sells it

assistance in kind: public assistance that provides individuals with particular goods and services, like housing or medical care, rather than cash

asymmetric information: a situation in which the parties to a transaction have different information, as with the seller of a used car, who has more information about its quality than the buyer

average costs: total costs divided by total output

average fixed costs: fixed costs divided by output

average productivity: total quantity of output divided by total quantity of input

average revenue: revenue divided by quantity sold

average tax rate: the ratio of taxes payable to total income

average variable costs: total variable costs divided by total output

barriers to entry: factors that prevent firms from entering a market, such as government rules or patents

basic competitive model: the model of the economy that pulls together the assumptions of self-interested consumers, profit-maximizing firms, and perfectly competitive markets

basic research: fundamental research that can produce a variety of applications

benefits in kind: see assistance in kind

bequest savings motive: the impulse to save so that one can leave an inheritance to one's children

Bertrand competition: an oligopoly in which each firm believes that its rivals are committed to keeping their prices fixed and that customers can be lured away by offering lower prices

bilateral trade: trade between two parties

black market: the market for buying and selling illegally

breach of contract: the decision by a party to an agreement (such as a supplier of products to another firm) not to abide by the terms of the contract

budget constraints: opportunity sets whose constraints are imposed by money

budget deficit: the excess of government spending over taxes in a given year

capital gain: the difference in the value of an asset due to a rise in its price between the time it is purchased and the time it is sold

capital goods: the machines and buildings firms invest in with funds obtained in the capital market

capital loss: the difference in the value of an asset due to a fall in its price between the time it is purchased and the time it is sold

capital market: the market in which savings are made available to those who need additional funds, such as firms that wish to invest, and in which ownership claims on different assets and their associated risks are exchanged

cartel: a group of producers with an agreement to collude in setting prices and output

causation: the relationship that results when a change in one variable is not only correlated with but actually determines a change in another variable: the change in the second variable is a consequence of the change in the first variable, rather than both changes being a consequence of a change in a third variable

centralization: a situation in which decisions are taken at the top layer of an organization

certificate of deposit (CD): an account in which money is deposited for a set length of time and that yields a slightly higher return to compensate for this reduced liquidity

choices: decisions taken from among scarce alternatives

circular flow: the way in which funds move through the capital, labour, and product markets between households, firms, the government, and the foreign sector

Coase theorem: the assertion that if property rights are properly defined, then people will be forced to pay for any negative externalities they impose on others and market transactions will produce efficient outcomes

co-insurance: the requirement that an insured individual pay a share of the costs of an accident along with the insurance company

collusion: an agreement among oligopolists to maximize their joint profits

command and control: a government policy implemented by regulation of quantities rather than by using the price system

common property resource: a natural resource that is collectively owned rather than privately owned and that is treated as being freely accessible to the users

comparative advantage: the advantage one country has over another country if its *relative* efficiency in the production of a particular good is higher than the other country's

compensating wage differentials: differences in wages that can be traced to nonpecuniary attributes of a job, such as the degree of autonomy and risk

competitive equilibrium price: the price at which the quantity supplied and the quantity demanded are equal

complement: a good the demand for which decreases (at a given price), as the price of another good increases

compound interest: interest earned on interest previously earned and saved

concentration ratios: the proportion of output in an industry produced by the largest four or eight firms

constant returns to scale: production conditions such that output increases in proportion to increases in all inputs

constraints: factors that limit the options available

consumers: individuals who buy goods and services

consumer surplus: the difference between what a person would be willing to pay and what he actually has to pay for a certain amount of a good

contestable markets: markets in which the potential entry of competitors keeps prices near their competitive levels

contingency clauses: statements within a contract that make the level of payment or the work to be performed conditional upon various factors

corporate finance: the study of how firms raise financial capital

corporate income tax: a tax based on the income, or profit, earned by a corporation

corporation: a firm with limited liability that is owned by shareholders who elect a board of directors that chooses the top executives

correlation: the relationship between variables such that a change in one variable is consistently associated with a change in another variable

coupon rationing: rationing items by giving out coupons entitling the bearer to a certain number of the items in question

Cournot competition: an oligopoly in which each firm believes that its rivals are committed to a certain level of production and that rivals will reduce their prices as needed to sell that amount

credentials competition: the trend for prospective workers to acquire higher educational degrees, not so much because of anything they actually learn in the process but to convince potential employers to hire them by signalling that they will be more productive than those with lesser degrees

credit rationing: limiting the amount lenders are willing to extend to borrowers, even if the borrower is willing to pay more than other borrowers of comparable risk for more

cross subsidization: the practice of charging higher prices to one group of consumers to subsidize prices for another group

Crown corporations: firms that are owned by the federal or provincial governments

deadweight loss: the loss in consumer and producer surplus that results from a market price being interfered with

deductible: the fixed amount an insured person is required to pay of the costs of an accident before the insurance policy covers the rest

demand: the quantity of an item that households or firms offer to buy

demand curve: the relationship between the quantity demanded of a good and the price, whether for an individual or for the market (all individuals) as a whole

demographic effects: effects that arise from changes in characteristics of the population, such as age, birthrate, and location

deregulation: the lifting of government regulations to allow the market to function more freely

diminishing marginal rate of substitution: the principle that the less of one product a person has relative to another, the less that person will be willing to trade of the first product to get more of the second

diminishing marginal rate of technical substitution: the principle that the marginal rate of technical substitution for an input is smaller and smaller as the ratio of the other input to the first input increases

diminishing marginal utility: the principle that with each successive unit of a good consumed the consumer's utility, or enjoyment, increases less and less

diminishing returns: the principle that as one input increases, with other inputs fixed, increases in output get smaller and smaller

diminishing returns to scale: production conditions such that output increases less than in proportion to increases in all inputs

dissaving: borrowing, or saving a negative amount

distortion: something, such as a tax, that interferes with a market price settling freely to its competitive market equilibrium value

diversification: the reduction of risk by holding a variety of assets

dividends: that portion of corporate profits paid out to shareholders

division of labour: the dividing up of jobs among workers so that each one can specialize on fewer tasks

dumping: the sale of a product abroad at a price less than the cost of production

duopoly: an industry with only two firms

econometrics: the application of statistics to economics

economic rents: payments made to a factor of production that are in excess of what is required to elicit the supply of that factor

economics: the study of how choices made by individuals, firms, governments, and other organizations determine the way the society's resources are used

efficiency wage theory: the theory that paying higher wages (up to a point) lowers total production costs, for instance by leading to a more productive labour force

efficient market theory: the theory that all available information is reflected in the current price of an asset

elasticity of labour supply: the percentage change in labour supplied resulting from a 1 percent change in wages

elasticity of supply: see **price elasticity of supply**

eminent domain: the right to seize private property for public use with fair compensation

employment equity: the principle that all types of persons should have equal access to employment opportunities

entrepreneurs: individuals who create new businesses and introduce innovations in products and processes

entry-deterring practices: strategies pursued by firms to deter other firms from entering their industry

equalization payments: transfers paid by the federal government to the provinces whose tax capacities are below average, designed to equalize their ability to provide public service to their residents; currently paid to all provinces except Alberta, British Columbia, and Ontario

equilibrium price: see **competitive equilibrium price**

equilibrium quantity: the amount demanded and supplied when a market is in equilibrium

equity concerns: concerns about equality among individuals

equity, shares, stock: terms that indicate part ownership of a firm; the firm sells these in order to raise money, or capital

excess capacity: production capacity that is greater than that currently needed

excess demand: the situation in which the quantity demanded at a given price exceeds the quantity supplied

excess supply: the situation in which the quantity supplied at a given price exceeds the quantity demanded

exchange efficiency: the condition in which whatever the economy produces is distributed among people in such a way that there are no gains to further trade

excise tax or **duty:** a tax on a particular good or service

exclusive dealing: an arrangement such that firms selling a product do not sell its rivals'

exiting the market: ceasing to sell or buy in a given market

exogenous effects: sources of business cycle fluctuations that originate in events outside the economy, such as an oil price shock

expected return: the average return—a single number that combines the various possible returns per dollar invested with the chances that each of these returns will actually be paid

experience rating: setting premiums for unemployment insurance according to past layoff records

experimental economics: the analysis of economics in laboratory settings

exports: goods produced domestically but sold abroad

externality: a phenomenon that arises when an individual or firm takes an action but does not bear all the costs (negative externality) or receive all the benefits (positive externality)

facilitating practices: actions taken by oligopolists in the absence of an explicit agreement that increase their joint profits

factor demand: the amount of an input (factor of production) demanded by a firm, given the price of the input and the quantity of output being produced; in a competitive market, an input will be demanded up to the point where the value of the marginal product of that input equals the price of the input

factors of production: inputs, such as labour and capital, used by firms to produce output

federal governmental structure: a system in which governmental activity takes place at several levels—national, provincial, municipal

fixed or **overhead costs:** the costs resulting from fixed inputs

fixed or **overhead inputs:** (a) inputs that do not change regardless of the quantity of output; (b) sometimes, inputs that are fixed in the short run—that is, they do not depend on *current* output, but may depend on output in the long run

free-market economists: those who believe that unfettered markets are necessary for economic efficiency

free-rider problem: the problem that occurs when someone enjoys something without paying for it; free-rider problems arise in the provision of public goods

full capacity: the level at which a plant is producing its maximum output

funded pensions: pension schemes in which payments to retirees are from a fund accumulated on their behalf during their working lives

gains from trade: the benefits that each side enjoys from a trade

general equilibrium analysis: a simultaneous analysis of all capital, product, and labour markets throughout the economy; it shows, for instance, the impact of immigration or a change in taxes on all prices and quantities

Gini coefficient: a measure of inequality (equal to twice the area between the 45-degree line and the Lorenz curve)

Goods and Services Tax (GST): a tax levied by the federal government on the purchases of almost all goods and services in Canada

government regulation: rules imposed by government that affect the way the economy's resources are used

greenmail: the threat of a takeover in which shares in a firm are purchased with the understanding that the purchasers will be bribed to sell those shares later

health-care premiums: charges citizens pay to participate in government health-insurance programmes

highly leveraged: relying heavily on borrowed funds

horizontal equity: the principle that those who are in identical or similar circumstances should pay identical or similar amounts of taxes

horizontal merger or **integration:** a merger between two firms that produce the same goods

horizontal restraints or agreements: restrictive practices, such as price fixing or collusion, engaged in by two or more firms selling in a given market

hostile takeover: the takeover of one firm by another when the former resists

human capital: the accumulated skills and experience that make workers productive

imperfect competition: any market structure in which there is some competition but firms face downward-sloping demand curves

imperfect information: a situation in which market participants lack information (such as information about prices or characteristics of goods and services) important to their decision making

imperfect-market economists: those who question the efficiency of markets that are left to operate on their own

imperfect substitutes: goods sufficiently similar that they can be used for many of the same purposes

imports: goods produced abroad but bought domestically

incentive-equality trade-off: the fact that the greater the incentives given to individuals to produce, the more inequality there is

income effect: the reduced consumption of a good whose price has increased that is due to the reduction in a person's buying power, or "real" income; when a person's real income falls, she will normally consume less of all goods, including higher-priced goods

income elasticity of demand: the percentage change in quantity of a good demanded as the result of a 1 percent change in income (the percentage change in quantity demanded divided by the percentage change in income)

income redistribution: the reallocation of income from one group to another

income-tested transfers: transfers to low-income persons that depend upon the incomes of the recipients

incomplete markets: situations in which no market may exist for some good or for some risk, or in which some individuals cannot borrow for some purposes

increasing returns to scale: the situation in which increases in inputs by a certain proportion result in increases in output of a greater proportion; also called **economies of scale**

indexed funds: mutual funds that are made up of a representative mix of assets on the stock market, such as the Toronto Stock Exchange 35 Index

indifference curve: a curve showing combinations of goods the choice among which leaves an individual equally well off

individual income tax: a tax based on the income received by an individual or household

industrial policies: government policies aimed at fostering certain sectors of the economy

infant industry argument for protection: the argument that fledgling industries must be protected from foreign competition until they acquire the skills needed to compete

inferior good: a good the consumption of which falls as income rises

infinite elasticity of demand: the situation in which any amount of a good will be demanded at a particular price, but none will be demanded if the price increases by even a small amount

infinite elasticity of supply: the situation in which any amount of a good will be supplied at a particular price, but none will be supplied if the price declines by even a small amount

inflation rate: the percentage increase in the general level of prices

information-based wage differentials: wage differentials that exist because workers do not know about higher-paying jobs elsewhere

informative advertising: advertising that educates consumers about price or other characteristics of a product

inputs: resources used by firms to produce their products

interest: the return a saver receives in addition to the original amount deposited (loaned), and the amount a borrower must pay in addition to the original amount borrowed

intertemporal trades: the exchanging of something now for something in the future

investors: individuals who supply savings to the capital market

invisible hand: the expression coined by Adam Smith (1723–1790) to describe the way prices are determined in competitive markets

isocost curve: the curve describing the combination of a firm's inputs that cost the same amount

isoquant curve: the curve describing the combination of a firm's inputs that produce the same quantity

job discrimination: the limiting of access to better-paying jobs of disadvantaged groups

joint products: products produced together by a firm

joint ventures: projects undertaken jointly by more than one firm

junk bonds: bonds used to finance very risky enterprises

labour force participation decision: the decision of whether or not to seek employment

labour force participation rate: the fraction of the working-age population that is employed or seeking employment

labour market: the market in which labour services are bought and sold

law of supply and demand: the observation that actual prices tend to be equilibrium prices, the prices at which demand equals supply

learning by doing: the increase in productivity that occurs as a firm gains experience and that results in a decrease in the firm's production costs

learning curve: the curve describing the decline in costs of production as cumulative output increases over time

legal entitlement: a right to engage in some activity given by law

less-developed countries (LDCs): the poorest nations of the world, including much of Africa, Latin America, and Asia

licences and **user fees:** charges imposed by governments for specific types of activities, such as driving an automobile, hunting, fishing, etc.

life-cycle savings motive: the impulse to save during one's working life so that one can consume more during retirement

life of the patent: the length of time for which a firm can be granted a patent

limited liability: the fact that the owner of a corporation can lose all the money he invests in the shares of the corporation, but no more

limit pricing: the practice of charging a lower price than that at which marginal revenue equals marginal cost, as a way of deterring entry by persuading potential competitors that their profits from entering are likely to be limited

linear demand curve: a demand curve that is a straight line

liquidity: the ease with which an asset can be sold

local public goods: goods that serve a particular limited community

long run: the length of time required for a market to adjust fully to changes in demand or supply conditions

long-term bonds: bonds that mature in ten years or more

Lorenz curve: a curve that shows the cumulative proportion of income that goes to each cumulative proportion of the population, starting with the lowest income group

loss: a situation in which costs exceed revenues, so profits are negative

lotteries: the allocation of items by a random draw

lump-sum taxes: taxes that are fixed in amount for an individual and do not depend upon any actions taken by the individual

luxury goods: goods whose demand rises more than proportionately with a person's income

macroeconomics: the top-down view of the economy, focusing on aggregate characteristics

managerial slack: the lack of managerial efficiency (for instance, in cutting costs) that occurs when firms are insulated from competition

marginal benefits: benefits associated with an incremental change

marginal cost: the additional cost corresponding to an additional unit of output produced

marginal product: the amount output increases with the addition of one unit of an input

marginal rate of substitution: the rate at which a consumer is willing to substitute a bit more of one product for a bit less of another

marginal rate of technical substitution: the additional amount of one input that a firm needs to produce a given output when the first input is substituted for a little less of the other input

marginal rate of transformation: the additional amount of one product that can be produced by reducing production of another

marginal revenue: the extra revenue received by a firm for selling one additional unit of a good

marginal tax rate: the tax paid on the last increment of income obtained

marginal utility: the extra utility, or enjoyment, a person receives from the consumption of one additional unit of a good

market: the institution through which trades are made among buyers and sellers

market demand curve: total quantity of a good demanded by all individuals at each price

market economy: an economy that allocates resources primarily through the interaction of individuals (households) and private firms

market equilibrium: a situation in which the market price has settled at the point where market demand equals market supply

market failure: the situation in which a market economy fails to attain economic efficiency

market for risk: markets, like those for insurance and

capital, in which households or firms can transfer risk to others

market labour supply curve: the relationship between the wage paid and the amount of labour willingly supplied, found by adding up the labour supply curves of all the individuals in the economy

marketplace: the location where buyers and sellers meet

market power: the ability of a firm to affect the market price by changing its output

market restrictions or **exclusive territories:** exclusive rights to sell a product within a particular region given by a producer to wholesalers or retailers

market structure: the number of firms and the amount of competition there is in an industry

market supply curve: the total quantity of a good supplied by all firms at each price

marketable permits: permits for the right to emit a given quantity of pollutants, issued by the government and tradable among firms

maturity: the period remaining until a loan or bond must be repaid

median voter theory: the theory that the person with median preferences determines the outcome of a vote

merit goods and bads: goods that are determined by government to be good or bad for people, regardless of whether people desire them for themselves or not

microeconomics: the bottom-up view of the economy, focusing on individual households and firms

minimum wage: the lowest amount that can legally be paid to employed labour

mining taxes: taxes levied on mining firms

mixed economy: an economy that allocates resources through a mixture of public (governmental) and private decision making

model: a set of assumptions and data used by economists to study an aspect of the economy and make predictions about the future or about the consequences of various policy changes

monopolistic competition: imperfect competition in which the market has so few firms that each faces a downward-sloping demand curve, but enough so that each can ignore the reactions of rivals to what it does

monopoly: a market consisting of only one firm

monopsony: the situation in which there is only one buyer in a given market

moral hazard: the principle that those who purchase insurance have a reduced incentive to avoid what they are insured against

multilateral trade: trade among more than two parties

mutual fund: a fund that gathers money from different investors and purchases a range of assets; each investor owns a portion of the entire fund

nationalization: the process whereby a private industry is taken over by the government, whether by buying it or simply by seizing it

national public good: a public good the benefits of which are felt nationwide

natural endowments: a country's natural resources, such as a good climate, fertile land, or abundant minerals

natural monopoly: a monopoly that exists because average costs of production are declining below the level of output demanded in the market, thus making entry unprofitable and making it efficient for there to be only a single firm

necessity goods: goods the demand for which rises less than proportionately with a person's income

negatively sloped: the description of a curve whose value on the vertical axis falls as the value on the horizontal axis rises

nominal interest rate: the interest rate actually paid on a loan in dollar terms, uncorrected for inflation

nonexcludable: the property of a public good whereby it is difficult to exclude persons from using it who have not paid

nonpecuniary job attributes: the rewards of a job that are nonmonetary

nonrenewable resources: natural resources that are fixed in supply, such as oil, gas, and minerals

nonrivalrous: the property of a public good whereby benefits to additional users do not detract from those of existing users

normal good: a good the consumption of which rises as income rises

normative economics: economics in which judgments about the desirability of various policies are made; the conclusions rest on value judgments as well as facts and theories

oligopoly: the form of imperfect competition in which the market has several firms but so few that each must take into account the reactions of rivals to what it does

opportunity cost: the cost of a resource, measured by the value of the next-best alternative use of that resource

opportunity sets: a summary of the choices available to individuals as defined by budget constraints and time constraints

outputs: products produced by firms

overhead costs: the costs incurred by a firm to set the firm up and run its administrative services

Pareto-efficient allocations: resource allocations such that one person cannot be made better off without making someone else worse off

partial equilibrium analysis: an analysis that focuses on only one or a few markets at a time

partnership: a business owned by two or more individuals, who share the profits and are jointly liable for any losses

patent: a government decree giving an inventor the exclusive right to produce, use, or sell an invention

pay-as-you-go system: the system by which public pensions pay benefits by taxing the current working population rather than by drawing on a fund accumulated from past contributions

pay equity: the principle that comparable jobs should receive comparable pay no matter what type of person holds them

payroll tax: a tax based on payroll (wages) that is used to finance programs like Unemployment Insurance and the Canada Pension Plan

perfect competition: a situation in which each firm is a price taker—it cannot influence the market price; at the market price, the firm can sell as much as it wishes, but if it raises its price, it loses all sales

perfect information: a situation in which market participants have all the information important to their decision making

persuasive advertising: advertising aimed at making consumers feel good about a product

physical capital: a business's investment in plant and equipment

piece-rate system: a compensation system in which workers are paid according to the amount they produce

point elasticity: an elasticity calculated for small changes in price

pooled risk: the reduction of risk by combining assets with different risks in a single portfolio

portfolio: an investor's entire collection of assets and liabilities

positive economics: the branch of economics that describes how the economy behaves and predicts how it might change—for instance, in response to some policy change

positively sloped: the description of a curve whose value on the vertical axis rises as the value on the horizontal axis rises

potential competition: possible entrants into an industry

poverty line: the income level below which persons are deemed to be living in poverty, defined differently by different organizations

precautionary savings motive: the impulse to save so that one will be able to meet the costs of unexpected illnesses, accidents, or other emergencies

predatory pricing: the practice of cutting prices below the marginal cost of production to drive out a new firm (or to deter future entry), at which point prices can be raised again

present discounted value: the amount a sum of money to be received in the future is worth right now

price: the amount of money that is given in exchange for an item

price ceiling: a maximum price above which a market's price is not legally allowed to rise

price discrimination: a firm's practice of charging different prices to different customers or in different markets

price elasticity of demand: the percentage change in quantity of a good demanded as the result of a 1 percent change in price (the percentage change in quantity demanded divided by the percentage change in price)

price elasticity of supply: the percentage change in quantity of a good supplied as the result of a 1 percent change in price (the percentage change in quantity supplied divided by the percentage change in price)

price floor: a minimum price below which a market's price is not legally allowed to fall

price leader: the dominant firm in an industry, which sets prices for others to follow

price maker: an individual or firm that can influence the prices it faces by changing its behaviour

price system: the allocation of products and resources from sellers to buyers by using prices

price taker: an individual or firm that cannot influence the prices it faces

principal: the original amount a saver lends or a borrower borrows

principal-agent problem: any situation in which one party (the principal) needs to delegate actions to another party (the agent) and thus wishes to provide the agent with incentives to work hard and make decisions about risk that reflect the interests of the principal

principle of consumer sovereignty: the principle that each individual is the best judge of what makes him better off

principle of substitution: the principle that, as the price of one input rises, firms will substitute other inputs for it

prisoner's dilemma: a situation in which the noncooperative pursuit of self-interest by two parties makes them both worse off

private corporations: corporations whose shares are not traded publicly and that tend to be owned by a small number of persons

private marginal cost: the marginal cost of production borne by the producer of a good; when there is a negative externality, such as air pollution, private marginal cost is less than social marginal cost

private property: property that has an owner with a right to use or sell it

privatization: the process whereby functions that were formerly undertaken by government are delegated instead to the private sector

producer surplus: the difference between what a firm receives for selling a product and what the firm would be willing to sell that product for

product differentiation: the fact that similar products (like breakfast cereals or soft drinks) are perceived to differ from one another and thus are imperfect substitutes

product market: the market in which goods and services are bought and sold

product-mix efficiency: the condition in which the mix of goods produced by the economy reflects the preferences of consumers

production efficiency: the condition in which firms cannot produce more of some goods without producing less of other goods; output is at a point along the economy's production possibilities curve

production function: the relationship between the inputs used in production and the level of output

production possibilities curve: a curve that defines the opportunity set for a firm or an entire economy and gives the possible combinations of goods (outputs) that can be produced from a given level of inputs

productivity wage differentials: wage differences accounted for by differences in the productivity of workers

profit-and-loss statement: a table summarizing all the revenues and costs of a firm over the year

profits: total revenues minus total costs

progressive tax: a tax that requires the rich to pay a larger fraction of their income than is required of the poor

property rights: the rights of owners to use property as they see fit, including the right to sell or rent it

property tax: a tax based on the value of property

proprietorship: a business owned by a single person, usually a small business

protectionism: the policy of protecting domestic industries from the competition of foreign-made goods

public corporations: corporations whose shares are traded publicly

public good: a good, such as national defence, that costs little or nothing for an extra individual to enjoy and for which the costs of preventing any individual from enjoying them are high; public goods have the properties of nonrivalrous consumption and nonexcludability

pure profit or **monopoly rents:** the profit earned by a monopolist that results from its reducing output and increasing the price from the level at which price equals marginal cost

pure public good: a public good that is perfectly nonrivalrous

quotas: limits on the quantity of a product that producers can sell

random walk: a phrase used to describe the way the prices of stocks move: the next movement cannot be predicted from previous movements

rational expectations: the expectations of individuals that are formed by using all available information

rational choice: decisions taken by weighing the costs and benefits of all options

rationing systems: ways of distributing goods that do not rely on prices, such as queues, lotteries, or coupons

reaction function: the output chosen by a duopolist for any given level of output produced by the other firm in the market

real rate of interest: the actual rate of interest less the rate of inflation

regressive tax: a tax that requires the poor to pay a larger fraction of their income than is required of the rich

regulatory capture: a phrase describing a situation in which regulators serve the interests of the regulated rather than the interests of consumers

relatively elastic demand: the demand for a quantity that increases more than in proportion to price reductions

relatively inelastic demand: the demand for a quantity that increases less than in proportion to price reductions

relative price: the ratio of the prices of two goods, reflecting how much of one must be given up to get more of the other

renewable resources: natural resources that have the capacity to regenerate themselves, such as forests and fisheries

rent: see **economic rent**

rent control: a law setting the maximum rent a landlord can charge

rent seeking: the name given to behaviour that seeks to encourage government decisions that will benefit the seeker, such as protection from foreign competition

reputation rents: returns earned on the basis of a firm's good reputation

resale price maintenance: a producer's demand that a retailer selling its product do so at a prescribed price

reservation wage: the minimum wage at which an individual will participate in the labour force

restrictive practices: practices by firms that serve to limit competition

retail sales tax: a tax levied by all provinces and territories (except Alberta) on the sale of most goods by retailers in their jurisdictions

retained earnings: the portion of a firm's income that is not paid as dividends but is kept for investment by the firm

revenue curve: the relationship between a firm's total output and its revenues

revenues: the amount a firm receives for selling its products, equal to the price received multiplied by the quantity sold; also called **total revenues**

risk: uncertainty about what future outcomes will be

risk averse, risk loving, risk neutral: characteristics of individuals who, given equal expected returns and different risks, will choose assets with lower risk, will choose assets with higher risk, or will not care about differences in risk, respectively

risk premium: the additional interest required by lenders as compensation for the risk that a borrower may default; more generally, the extra return required to compensate an investor for bearing risk

royalties: charges to firms who extract resources from Crown lands

sale of leases: the selling of the right to exploit Crown lands

savings account: a bank account that pays interest, that can be withdrawn from at any time, and against which cheques typically cannot be written

scarcity: the fact that there are not enough resources to satisfy all wants

screening: the process of differentiating among job candidates when the information needed to determine who will be the most productive is incomplete

sectoral free trade: free trade between countries in the products of a particular industry, such as automobiles

self-insure: take measures to reduce one's own risk

shortage: the situation in which people would like to buy something that is not available at the going price

short-run: the length of time required for a market to adjust partially but not fully to changes in demand or supply conditions

short-run efficiency: economic efficiency that ignores innovation and invention

short-term bonds: bonds that mature within a few years

signalling: conveying information to persuade an employer that a prospective employee has characteristics that will enhance his productivity—for example, a prospective worker's having earned a university degree

simple interest: interest that is paid on the principal but not on interest previously earned

sin taxes: taxes levied on alcohol and tobacco products

slope: the amount by which the value along the vertical axis increases as the result of a change in one unit along the horizontal axis; the slope is calculated by dividing the change in the vertical axis (the "rise") by the change in the horizontal axis (the "run")

social benefit: the benefit an entire society receives from an action

social insurance: programmes to protect citizens against unexpected economic adversity

social marginal cost: the marginal cost of production, including the cost of any negative externality (such as air pollution), borne by individuals in the economy other than the producer

social safety net: the set of government programmes designed to protect citizens against adversity

social science: the study of social interactions using scientific methods

statistical discrimination: discrimination among persons in employment and wages according to characteristics they have that, on average, reflect differing levels of productivity

sticky prices: prices that take some time to adjust to changes in demand or supply

stock options: the option offered to a firm's executives to purchase a specified number of shares at a specified price and open for a specified period of time

strike: withdrawal of labour by a union as a tool to bargain for better compensation

stumpage fees: fees charged to timber firms to cut trees

substitute: a good the demand for which increases when the price of another good increases

substitution effect: the reduced consumption of a good whose price has increased that is due to the changed trade-off—the fact that one has to give up more of other goods to get one more unit of the high-priced good; the substitution effect is associated with a change in the slope of the budget constraint

sunk cost: a cost that has been incurred and cannot be recovered

supply: the quantity of an item that households or firms offer to sell

supply curve: the relationship between the quantity of a good supplied and its price, whether for a single firm or for the market (all firms) as a whole

supply management: government control of agricultural prices by restricting the amount of a product that can be supplied by farmers

surplus, fiscal: tax revenues in excess of government expenditures in a given year

tacit collusion: an implicit understanding by firms not to compete too vigourously with each other and to avoid price cutting

takeover: the purchase of one firm by another

target savings motive: the impulse to save for a particular target, for example to make a down payment on a house or to pay for a future vacation

tariffs: charges levied by the federal government on the importation of certain goods and services from abroad

tax collection agreements: agreements that the federal government will collect income taxes on behalf of a province provided the province abides by the federal tax base and rate structure

tax credit: the ability of a firm to reduce its taxes payable by engaging in certain activities, such as research and development or investment

tax expenditures: tax revenues lost to the government as a result of special tax concessions or tax breaks given to encourage certain types of activities or to achieve certain social objectives

tax-favoured asset: an asset whose rate of return is taxed at a lower rate than that of other assets

tax subsidies: see **tax expenditures**

theory: a set of assumptions and the conclusions derived from those assumptions put forward as an explanation for some phenomenon

theory of revealed preference: the use of a change in a consumer's budget line in response to a price change to illustrate income and substitution effects

thin markets: markets with relatively few buyers and sellers

tie-ins or **tied selling:** the obligation of a firm to buy one product when it buys another

time constraints: opportunity sets whose restrictions are imposed by time

time value of money: the value attached to receiving a dollar now rather than some time in the future

total costs: the sum of all fixed costs and variable costs

total revenues: see **revenues**

trade secret: an innovation or knowledge of a production process that a firm does not disclose to others

trade-offs: the need to give up some of one item to get more of another

transaction costs: the extra costs (beyond the price of the purchase) of conducting a transaction, whether those costs are money, time, or inconvenience

transfer programmes: programmes directly concerned with redistribution, such as welfare assistance, that move money from one group in society to another

Treasury bills (T-bills): bills the government sells in return for a promise to pay a certain amount in a short period, usually less than 180 days

unit price elasticity: the fact that the quantity demanded increases in proportion to reductions in price

utility: the level of enjoyment an individual attains from choosing a certain combination of goods

value of marginal product of labour: the output price multiplied by the marginal product of labour

variable: any item that changes and can be measured

variable costs: the costs resulting from variable inputs

variable inputs: inputs that rise and fall with the quantity of output

velocity: the speed with which money circulates in the economy, defined as the ratio of income to the money supply

vertical equity: the principle that people who are better off should pay more tax

vertical merger or **integration:** a merger between two firms, one of which is a supplier or distributor for the other

vertical restraints or **agreements:** restrictions placed by a firm on the purchase or sale of its products by other firms; examples include market restrictions, resale price maintenance, and tie-ins

voting paradox: the fact that under some circumstances there may be no determinate outcome with majority voting: choice A wins a majority over B, B wins over C, and C wins over A

wage discrimination: the practice of paying lower

wages to certain identifiable groups, such as women or minorities

workers: individuals who sell their labour

zero price elasticity: the fact that the quantity demanded does not change in response to price changes